In Turns of Tempest

A Reading of Job

But ah, but O thou terrible, why wouldst thou rude on me
Thy wring-world right foot rock? lay a lionlimb against me? scan
With darksome devouring eyes my bruisèd bones? and fan,
O in turns of tempest, me heaped there; me frantic to avoid thee and flee?

—Gerard Manley Hopkins, "Carrion Comfort"

In Turns of Tempest

A Reading of Job

with a translation

Edwin M. Good

Stanford University Press
Stanford, California

Stanford University Press
Stanford, California

Printed in the United States of America

CIP data are at the end of the book

For Brian
with love

Preface

It is remarkable, and perhaps rare, for a person to recognize the circle of a career. This book seems to bring my career back to a starting point. It was during graduate study at Union Theological Seminary with Samuel L. Terrien, whose name appears a number of times later, that I did my first serious work on Job. I have never ceased to work on it since then, and my record of publications shows that I have constantly returned to Job as I have returned to nothing else. Never did I doubt that some day I would write a book on Job. Though that certainty must at first have stemmed from admiration and emulation of Samuel Terrien, it matured through the years to the realization that perhaps I would have something of my own to say about Job.

What I have written before also shows that I have changed my mind about Job several times, and this book is consistent with that pattern. Indeed, it is perhaps as much about changing one's mind as it is about anything else. I have come to think that, though one sometimes firmly states an opinion, sure perceptions of undoubtable truth are impossible and misleading when we are dealing with any work that possesses interesting depth, and especially with a work of such dense complexity as the Book of Job. We can be sure of truth only with works of numbing banality. That is a significant change of mind for a person whose image of himself when he left graduate study was as a biblical theologian. The stock in trade of theologians is truth and often Truth, and mine was too. A career spent in the company of Job (and of the faculty and students of Stanford University) has knocked that out of me, as has a long preoccupation with literary reading. I now read for the quite different kinds of truth presented by art, and I no longer answer when someone addresses me as a theologian.

Without doubt some readers, recognizing how thoroughly a deconstructive indeterminacy permeates this reading of Job, will think the book (and its author) irresponsible both to the religious traditions in which Job is principally read and to the duty of a scholar and expositor of texts. As to the traditions, there has been quite enough of scriptural dogmatism in them, and I see no reason to perpetuate an aspect of the Jewish and Christian heritages that I find repugnant. Utter certainty about the meaning of the Bible, in whole or in part, has caused and still causes among persons who are subjected to it misery incommensurate with its revelatory claims. It is time someone suggested that the meaning of the Bible is not as evident as we often shrilly claim out of our gropings and guesses. It is far more complex than our usually simpleminded proposals of "right" answers are willing to conceive; indeed it is often, perhaps usually, multiple and self-contradictory.

As for the scholar's duty to the text, I spell out my understanding in Chapter 1 below.

Some might think it ironic—I do not—that I find the Book of Job immensely more fascinating, more moving, more humanly true than ever I did when I thought my job was to jam a single truth down upon it. Then I was busily fitting Job to what I already thought and believed. Now I think I am free enough in myself to let the book fit itself to its own appropriate templates—or to no template at all. To watch so marvelously intricate a work play itself out with one's own mind is an experience rich beyond the telling. And there is no point in my trying to transfer my experience to the reader. She must have her own, which will be different from mine, and I hope that my book may assist it.

In order to be a believable assistant to readers' own reading, I must take my place in the continuing debate of scholars about the book. Many of them have taught me what I could not have learned without them. I name Robert Gordis, Norman Habel, Marvin Pope, and Samuel Terrien (and will name them again and again throughout the book, sometimes depending on their learning, sometimes disagreeing with their opinions) in order to say that I have traveled a longer distance with them than with some others and to salute them happily as intimate companions and friends as well as instructors. My disagreements with them, as I am sure they know, are signs of respect and honor. Others of my scholarly colleagues and predecessors have also helped me greatly, and failure to name them here indicates no lack of appreciation. They are named, quoted, and argued with below.

I am especially grateful to Frank M. Cross, Jr., Michael Coogan, and John Huehnergard for friendship and many courtesies during a happy sabbatical year as a Visiting Scholar in the Department of Near Eastern Literature and Civilizations at Harvard University, where I began to write the book. Were I to name everyone who had ever helped or encouraged me, space and memory would run out before the list of names did. But students in a Stanford seminar on Job kept me very alert indeed, and several graduate students, especially Chaplain Janet Y. Horton, USA, Louise Masri, and Jacqueline Bocian, gave me various kinds of aid in the project. M. Alexandra Eddy substantially aided the cause of clarity. With one remarkable paragraph and just in time, Helen Tartar, Humanities Editor of the Stanford University Press, showed me how to make my conception of translation coherent with my conception of reading. John R. Ziemer of the Press editorial staff made final improvements forthrightly and with extraordinary sensitivity. An anonymous reader for the Press demonstrated profound comprehension and friendly approbation of the book's direction and method, which greatly enhanced my sense of liberation.

Only I can accept responsibility for the many pages that follow. Yet that too is liberating, since I have abandoned the delusion that a teacher's business is to turn a student into the teacher's clone. As I take responsibility for what I have done, I enjoin the reader to be responsible for reading in freedom with and from the teacher. It's much more fun that way!

E.M.G.

Contents

Abbreviations

For full bibliographic information on the books in the following list, see the Bibliography, pp. 445–65.

ANET	James B. Pritchard, ed., *Ancient Near Eastern Texts Relating to the Old Testament*, 3rd ed.
Bib	*Biblica*
CBQ	*Catholic Biblical Quarterly*
GK	E. Kautzsch, *Gesenius' Hebrew Grammar*, 2nd English ed.
HUCA	*Hebrew Union College Annual*
IB	G. A. Buttrick et al., eds., *The Interpreter's Bible*, vol. 3
Irony	Edwin M. Good, *Irony in the Old Testament*, 2nd ed.
JBL	*Journal of Biblical Literature*
JPS	*Tanakh: A New Translation of the Holy Scriptures According to the Traditional Hebrew Text*
JSOT	*Journal for the Study of the Old Testament*
K-B	L. Koehler and W. Baumgartner, *Lexicon in Veteris Testamenti Libros*
KJV	*The Holy Bible*, Authorized (King James) Version
LXX	Septuagint (3rd century B.C.E. and later Greek translation of the Hebrew Bible)
MT	Masoretic Text
NEB	*The New English Bible*
RSV	*The Holy Bible*, Revised Standard Version
Sem	*Semeia*
UF	*Ugarit-Forschungen*
VT	*Vetus Testamentum*
ZAW	*Zeitschrift für die alttestamentliche Wissenschaft*

Biblical Books (listed in the order in JPS)

Gen	Genesis
Exod	Exodus
Lev	Leviticus
Num	Numbers
Deut	Deuteronomy
Josh	Joshua
Judg	Judges
Sam	Samuel
Ki	Kings
Isa	Isaiah
Jer	Jeremiah
Ezek	Ezekiel
Hos	Hosea
Joel	Joel
Amos	Amos
Obad	Obadiah
Jon	Jonah
Mic	Micah
Nah	Nahum
Hab	Habakkuk
Zeph	Zephaniah
Hag	Haggai
Zech	Zechariah
Ps	Psalms
Prov	Proverbs
Song of S	Song of Songs
Ruth	Ruth
Lam	Lamentations
Eccl	Qoheleth (Ecclesiastes)
Est	Esther
Dan	Daniel
Ezra	Ezra
Neh	Nehemiah
Chron	Chronicles

Apocrypha

Ecclus	Ecclesiasticus

In Turns of Tempest

A Reading of Job

A Dispensable Introduction

One shouldn't try to dance at two weddings.
—Jewish proverb

People who read interpretations of the Book of Job, or of any biblical book, often expect answers to certain questions. Who wrote the book? When was it written, and where? How did it achieve its present form? How is it related to other books in the biblical tradition and to similar books in other ancient traditions? Who were its first readers, and how would they have understood the book? What is its language, and how does it use that language?

Answers to such questions may reveal many important facts. Nevertheless, the heading to this introduction is intended to suggest that I feel a certain testiness about some of these questions. The reason is that in this book I am engaged in a particular undertaking: to investigate how the Book of Job goes about happening as a book, as a work of literary art. For that purpose, some of the questions above are not, in my judgment, very important. But because some readers may be curious about them, and because I do not wish to be high-handed about their curiosity, I will discuss them, with the proviso that I believe them to be irrelevant to what I wish to do in this book. Anyone who is satisfied to give me my way in deciding what questions are and are not important may skip to the Indispensable Introduction.

The curmudgeon now recedes somewhat into the background.

The Author of the Book

Some scholars believe that the book had one author, some that it had more than one. Some believe that one editor put the book into its present form, others that there were more editors. These are conjectures, for we possess no early texts that demonstrate the existence of separate books that were later combined. We will examine this question below in considering the book's composition and compilation.

Grant any or all of the following possibilities: (1) that more than one mind produced the Book of Job; (2) that more than one mind put it into its final form; (3) that the book underwent changes in the process of copying and, perhaps, of editing. Who did all that? There is absolutely no way of answering the question with names or places. The "author" or "authors" left no discernible traces of themselves in the book or anywhere else.

I believe that even if we could identify the author, we would learn nothing useful for understanding the book. Meaning in a literary work is in the work's text, and knowledge about its author's life and even the author's stated intentions about the book offer no unambiguous assistance in interpretation. It may even hinder our understanding of the book; authors may be mistaken about their own work. The view that the author's intention determines the meaning of a work is called, by those of my persuasion, the "intentional fallacy."[1] In any case, with the Book of Job we are delivered from such hindrance, for, though conjectures have been made, no one has the slightest idea who the author may have been.

The Language of the Book

The Book of Job comes to us, of course, in ancient Hebrew. I raise the question of language only because three admirable scholars answered it differently from most others. N. H. Tur-Sinai concluded that the present text of Job is a translation into Hebrew of a book originally written in Aramaic, a language similar to classical Hebrew in roughly the way Italian is similar to French. Alfred Guillaume proposed that the Hebrew of Job is shot through with Arabic, which belongs to the same linguistic family as Hebrew, and that it was written for Arabic readers of Hebrew. Frank H. Foster went further to argue that the book was originally written in Arabic.[2]

These views depend on detailed philological scholarship, and a case for or against them necessitates access to the languages involved. The proponents of the translation theory reason that, because certain statements in the text do not make sense, someone misunderstood the presumed original or translated it badly into Hebrew. By recourse to words in another language, the scholar perceives the "correct" meaning, however dimly, in a reconstructed original text behind the "garbled" translation.

I will not attempt to prove that the Book of Job was composed in Hebrew but will assume it. That the Hebrew text of the book was translated from Aramaic or Arabic is a scholarly conjecture. The conjecture cannot be knowledge, however, because no Aramaic or Arabic original of Job exists, though we have translations from Hebrew into both languages. Without a text other than one composed by the proposer of the theory (and neither Tur-Sinai nor Foster produced one), one cannot *know* what the original said. Conjecture, even by first-class scholars, produces nothing more than conjecture.

The reputation of the Book of Job as a literary classic is well deserved. It has acquired that reputation, moreover, as a work of *Hebrew* literature. Translations are seldom better literature than their originals. If this towering masterpiece is a somewhat botched translation, imagine the stature of the original and the magnitude of our loss. Given that the literary tradition has assimilated Job through the Hebrew language, the fact that the book is in Hebrew is by no means irrelevant, and we shall have to think about it.

The Location of the Book's Writing

For similar reasons, we cannot know where the book was written. Some have thought that, because Job 40–41 describes the hippopotamus and the crocodile, Job must have been written in Egypt, where these animals were to be found.[3] Like many other scholars, I do not think that the animals in those chapters are the hippopotamus and the crocodile,[4] and without that ground, the case for an Egyptian location pretty much dissolves.

If the book was written in Hebrew, it was probably written in Israelite territory, unless we can show that the text implies some other landscape or social setting. No credible argument has, in my opinion, been made. The language cannot be identified with any regional dialect; evidence for such dialects in classical Hebrew is too skimpy to allow conclusions in any case. It is interesting that the book's action does not take place in Israel. Its characters come from Edom, southeast of Israel, toward the Gulf of Aqaba in the Red Sea. But the setting is no more reason for thinking that Job was composed in Edom than the setting of *Hamlet* is reason to look for evidence that Shakespeare wrote the play in Denmark. Geographical location plays no part in the book's meaning, though some passages betray knowledge of desert travel, for example, and of various kinds of wild and domestic animals.

The Book's Date

Because the prophet Ezekiel referred to Job alongside Noah and Dan'el as an important and presumably ancient person,[5] Rabbinic tradition dated Job to the period of the patriarchs (Abba ben Kahana even thought that Job's wife was a daughter of Jacob[6]) and assumed that the book was therefore very ancient, or even that its author was Moses.[7] Modern scholarship, though more skeptical, has nevertheless proposed dates from the eleventh to the third centuries B.C.E.

The book itself is silent as to its own date, with never a reference or allusion to any historical event or topical subject, not a breath that we could take as relevant to anything contemporary with the book. To ascribe a date to an ancient book that gives no hint of its own date is very nearly impossible.

We might refer to external matters that might bear on the date, such as the supposed history of Hebrew literature, the relations between Job and other books of the Hebrew Bible or analogous books from other cultures, the supposed history of the Hebrew language, and the supposed history of Israelite religion. I repeat the adjective "supposed" deliberately, because all these histories are scholarly reconstructions of temporal relations among books of the Hebrew Bible, of phenomena in the language, and of changes in religious ideas and activities among the ancient Hebrews. Reasoning from such data to historical conclusions is full of pitfalls.

The ambiguities in the Book of Job so impress me that I doubt all the reconstructions and am unable to be certain about the date of the book. It can be argued that Job 3 resembles parts of the Book of Jeremiah, especially 20.7–18. Jeremiah lived before and early in the Babylonian Exile, which began in 587–586 B.C.E., but it seems to me impossible to date Jeremiah 20.7–18 precisely. Moreover, which work contributed to which? Did Jeremiah influence Job, or did Job influence Jeremiah?

It has been argued that the style of Job and its handling of the question of suffering are related to Isaiah 40–55, written during the Babylonian Exile by an unknown prophet.[8] I find little that persuades me of a stylistic relation, and I think the two books deal with the problem of suffering in markedly different ways. Moreover, I have the same problem as with Jeremiah 20; namely, how to decide, on the basis of what little material we have, which of the two works preceded—and therefore, presumably, influenced—the other.

Moreover, my annotation to Job 3.4 proposes that it parodies Genesis 1.3, and that to Job 12.7 indicates an allusion to the creation story in Genesis 1. Most scholars date that account of the creation rather late in Israel's history, usually after the Babylonian Exile of the sixth century B.C.E., though some scholars argue that pre-exilic material might have been incorporated into that strand of Pentateuchal literature.[9] I am persuaded that the author(s) of those two passages in Job knew the first chapter of Genesis, but being uncertain of the date of the creation story in Genesis 1, I cannot deduce the date of Job from it.

On the whole, I think that the Book of Job took its present form after the Babylonian Exile. I have no idea how long thereafter. The fact that the setting of the book is distant in time and place from its readers—entirely outside of Israel, in fact—makes it most useful to deal with the work as fiction. It is not usable as a historical work, nor does it help in historical reconstructions of other works.

Deciphering the history of religious ideas is difficult, even if materials for chronological ordering are at hand. In the case of ancient Israel, most reconstructions rest on circular arguments. In my opinion, Job's friends make statements about the meanings of suffering that apply to the individual a theory of divine retribution that in the prophets and the Book of Deuteronomy applies exclusively to collectivities such as Israel or other nations. Establishing that opinion solidly enough to make a historical claim for it is at best difficult, and it is an opinion, moreover, that makes no difference to the reading of the book. There can be no question that the retributive theory is applied to individuals in the Book of Job, and that application is not affected by speculation on the history of the idea.

One might like to know the date at which the Book of Job was written, if only to have the knowledge. Perhaps the book was written at several times and has no single date. In any case, in the absence of allusion to contemporary events, the date is irrelevant to the meaning of the book.

The Composition of the Book

By "composition" I mean the process through which the Book of Job achieved its final form. "Composition" implies either that an author "composed" the book over a period of time, long or short, or that the work is a "composite."

Today we are much more confident than the ancients were that we know what a book is. We are more accustomed to seeing them, having them, handling them from day to day. Ancient books were rare and precious things, and one didn't wander out to the bookstore or the drugstore and buy one.

Our assumptions about books include the supposition that books have authors, and that they are published at specific times. Modern scholars sometimes even use the term "published" about an ancient book. It is an anachronism. Books in the ancient world were circulated in hand-copied manuscripts. The author might or might not know anything about the copying, might or might not approve of its being done. There was no copyright, no right of an author to an exclusive claim on a book. There was no assurance that a copy had the same words as the original. A copyist could freely omit something from the original or insert something that was not there before. The owner of a copy of a book might very well have it recopied with his name attached as author. By the Middle Ages, Jews had come to care deeply about the accuracy of copies of the Bible. Earlier, evidence for that concern is meager at best.

Indeed, the ancient world's assumptions about the authorship, composition, and integrity of a book were so different from ours that all our habitual moves in thinking about books are wrong. Biblical scholars have wasted decades wrangling over the authorship of biblical books.[10] We cannot know, and there is no point in basing anything on guesses. Authors in the ancient world receded so far behind their texts that, even if we know the author of a given piece—Aeschylus, say, or Virgil—we cannot be certain that a text before us is what that "author" wrote. Several of Aristotle's works, for example, seem to have been compiled from his students' notes, not exactly the best assurance of high accuracy of quotation. In ancient as in modern times, the script of a play often changed radically between the playwright's composition and the opening performance. The exigencies of copying, moreover, might produce something quite different from what the original author wrote; a copyist oftentimes considered himself at least as important a thinker as the writer whose works he was copying.

If such was the treatment of written works by the Greeks, who highly valued knowledge, imagine how books would be dealt with in Israelite culture, where knowledge had much less value (though Job may provide some evidence to the contrary). We know even less about how literary works were produced, reproduced, and circulated in Israel than in Greece and Rome, and it is nearly impossible to claim anything as knowledge. The result has been that scholars have piled guess upon conjecture, using questionable criteria for decision.

Scrutiny of Job itself shows that it takes the following form:

1. The story of Job's misfortunes (chaps. 1–2)
2. A dialogue between Job and his friends, Eliphaz, Bildad, and Zophar (chaps. 3–31)
3. A series of speeches by a previously unmentioned friend, Elihu (chaps. 32–37)
4. A rather one-sided conversation between Yahweh, the deity, and Job (38.1–42.6)
5. The story of Job's restoration (42.7–17)

This structure can illuminate some problems about the book's composition. Its first and last elements are prose narrative, written in a rather simple style, somewhat like a folktale in their straightforward, sometimes formulaic manner. The middle three sections are poetry, though Elihu's entrance is introduced briefly in prose (32.1–5). In contrast to the prose, the poetry of the book is complex and difficult, full of unusual words and thoughts. The sophisticated modern scholar will ask. How could these different kinds of material have been produced by the same mind? Modern scholarship tends to assume that ancient intellectuals did their work as specialists, like modern intellectuals. A historian of Russia does not publish books on molecular biology, nor does an operations-research engineer write articles on music theory. Just so, the modern scholar will likely say, a writer of folktales does not write sophisticated, difficult poetry, and a sophisticated, learned poet does not write simple, naive stories. We are surprised and sometimes offended if a fine scholar of history or literature writes detective novels or romances.

Modern scholars sometimes think too quickly about how to explain a problem away. For example, Elihu turns up without prior mention in chap. 32, speaks nonstop through chap. 37, and then drops completely from sight. Where did he come from and why? That is not a dispensable question. What is dispensable is the answer rapidly given by those who are interested only in the process through which the book went: that Elihu's speeches were interpolated by some "author" in addition to the two "authors" so far perceived. Why was Elihu added to the book? Perhaps because he expresses a viewpoint some reader felt should be there.[11]

More complications yet. The dialogue between Job and his three friends (chaps. 3–31) twice follows a pattern (chaps. 3–11 and 12–20) in which Job speaks, then Eliphaz, Job, then Bildad, Job, then Zophar. In the third cycle, however, Job speaks in chap. 21, Eliphaz in chap. 22, Job in chaps. 23–24, Bildad briefly in chap. 25 (only ten lines of poetry), then Job nonstop in chaps. 26–31. Zophar has no speech at all in this third cycle. Moreover, chap. 28 interrupts a discussion of Job's problems about the deity with a disquisition on mining, metallurgy, and wisdom. Why is the symmetry of the dialogue's pattern broken in the third cycle, and what is the point of chap. 28 (often referred to as the "Hymn to Wisdom")?

Below I summarize a consensus on these problems. One or another scholar will disagree with some of these statements, but on the whole, biblical scholars explain the composition of the Book of Job as follows:

1. In the beginning was the prose tale, chaps. 1–2, 42.7–17, perhaps a folktale, which presents the ancient, heroic Job to whom Ezekiel refers and his successful passage through an ordeal of suffering and bereavement.[12]

2. Then a poet, realizing that the folktale was a fine setting for some ideas about suffering and retribution, inserted the dialogue between Job and the friends (chaps. 3–27, 29–31) and the conversation between Job and Yahweh (38.1–42.6) into the middle of it.[13]

3. The next stage was the garbling of the third cycle: the omission of Zophar's third speech and the truncation of Bildad's, and their displacement into Job's speeches in chaps. 23–24 and 26–27.[14] Interpolation of the "Hymn to Wisdom," whether at the same or another time, further complicated the third cycle.

4. Finally, the speeches of Elihu (chaps. 32–37) were inserted, and the book as we have it was complete.[15]

I will not offer to sell you the Golden Gate Bridge.

The conjectures represented by this view are based on careful, close scrutiny of the text of Job. They presume that incoherences within a text cannot be original to it because authors do not write texts with incoherences. Therefore, incoherences betray the presence of some mind other than that of the "author."[16] The phenomena of the text are taken as pointers to the external process through which the book went, as representing the archaeological strata of the Book of Job.[17] These investigations of the book's composition have been carried out with meticulous care and scrupulous accuracy. I criticize only the supposition that we have thereby gained knowledge. We have not.

Of course, the Book of Job may have undergone the process described. I refuse to pretend that I know. My opinion is that the Elihu speeches were probably interpolated, and the poet of the dialogue probably used a well-known folktale more or less intact.[18] If the third cycle was disarranged—and I doubt that it was—the job was very well done, because the third cycle in its present form carries Job to remarkable heights of poetic expression. If someone interpolated chap. 28, it was with great sensitivity to the course of the argument in the third cycle.

In short, I do not find the consensus view about the composition of Job helpful or necessary for reading and understanding what the book says and how it says it. Hence this subject's presence in the Dispensable Introduction. We can read and understand the Book of Job as we now have it, and we need not wait for certainty about the process of composition before embarking on reading. Indeed, that is what I propose to do in the second part of this book.

Relation to Other Literature

No book is an island. Indeed, some theorists of literature think that every book is a comment on other books.[19] Insofar as any work derives some element of its meaning from the ways in which it reflects, continues, and departs from its tradition or traditions, the relationship of Job to other works in the ancient world is a crucial aspect in the analysis of its literary quality. We must be interested in other works if they have influenced Job's handling of its themes, its linguistic or poetic style, or its formal characteristics.

I am less impressed by the evidence for such dependence than are some of my predecessors. The problem of undeserved suffering was an important issue throughout the history of Near Eastern literature, beginning from Sumerian literature in the second millennium B.C.E., and probably even earlier.[20] But the ways in which that problem was perceived and solved varied tremendously from one work to another. I cannot point to a single Mesopotamian, Canaanite, or Egyptian work that has clearly influenced the ways in which the Book of Job handles or closes upon suffering. It remains to be seen, indeed, whether undeserved suffering is the (or a) central issue in Job.

As to form and structure, one might argue influence in one of two ways. Job is unique in classical Hebrew literature in using formal dialogue as its mode of literary presentation.[21] Other works in the ancient Near Eastern world used that form, such as the "Babylonian Theodicy," the mordantly humorous Babylonian dialogue between master and slave sometimes titled "A Dialogue of Pessimism," and the Egyptian "Dialogue of a Man with His *Ba*," which deals with a man's wish for death.[22] Such dialogical works may stem from folkloristic argument texts, such as the Mesopotamian dispute of the Tamarisk and the Date Palm.[23] Job's relation to them, and what we would gain from the proposal that they are connected, remains unclear. The poignant, ambiguous Egyptian text depicts a gentle, not very sophisticated Weltschmerz. The "Babylonian Theodicy" raises sharp questions about suffering but turns into a disappointingly conventional praise of the Babylonian deity Marduk, and it offers no solution except the claim that Marduk removed the suffering. Except for the device of dialogue, nothing in these texts resembles Job. Even the dialogues are not so complex or extensive as that in Job, and complexity in this case seems to introduce a difference of more than degree.

The other frequently mentioned influence is "wisdom literature," both in the Hebrew Bible, where the Books of Proverbs and Qoheleth (Ecclesiastes) are the other exemplars, and in the other Near Eastern literatures. The term *wisdom literature* is modern, not ancient, and it emphasizes the high value placed on "wisdom" in the literature that scholars so classify.[24] Some texts reflect uncertainty that wisdom is the key to success; the term is used very ambiguously in Qoheleth, for example.[25]

Such literary classifications represent modern perceptions of the ancient literature and may not match categories used by ancient readers. Not that the original views of any matter close the conversation. Of course, we see things in ancient texts that their first readers probably did not, and they are often actually there.

The problem arises if we use the modern classification to determine our interpretation, and here I have some difficulties with identifying Job as wisdom literature.[26] What possible common cause could join Job and Proverbs? The latter is an anthology of brief, pithy sayings, mostly conventionally pious, frequently humorous, occasionally provocative. In Proverbs, wise people are righteous and good, and good people are righteous and wise, whereas fools are wicked and unsuccessful, and unsuccessful people are wicked and foolish. The book characteristically judges actions and attitudes by stereotypes. To be sure, various speakers in Job seem to quote proverbs or proverbial sayings.[27] But the stereotypical views appear in the speeches of the friends, and we will see in the second part how those attitudes are, if anything, portrayed as unproductive and false.

Perhaps we should not expect all works classified as wisdom literature to present a unified front. No one expects all English drama to agree in all respects, save in being formally dramatic. If wisdom literature is not a point of view but a literary genre, consisting of the use of formal devices like the proverb or the discourse, not of the ideas contained in them, I not only have no objection to calling Job wisdom literature but think the term may be positively useful.

But the interpreter's use of the devices themselves as the sole path to meaning may be equally misleading. If interpretation depends exclusively on the assumed generic context of a book or on formal usages, I think wisdom literature or any genre designation is a dispensable concept.[28] Such an interpretive procedure too easily degenerates into a way to avoid reading the work. Any formal conclusion that allows the reader to walk around the text or that requires the interpreter to produce another text is dangerous.

Many interpreters of Job have used insights from wisdom literature, and some of them are more subtle and perceptive than others.[29] I object only if some reader, seeing a term like wisdom literature and finding it linked to Proverbs and Qoheleth, supposes too quickly and simplemindedly that identifying Job as wisdom literature tells us immediately what the book means and how it goes about meaning. Just as there is no free lunch, there is no shortcut to the perception of meaning and method in a complex work like Job.

Let us move on now to the interesting and indispensable questions.

An Indispensable Introduction

> Once what is to be opened is open, it will open other things in its turn.
>
> —Edmond Jabès, "The Key"

The second part of this book presents a reading of the Book of Job; the first part presents the Book of Job that the second part reads. Because most English-speaking readers do not know Hebrew, the book must be presented in an English translation. Even good English translations, however, have serious flaws. To refer readers to them would necessitate constantly interjecting disagreements with this rendering or that one. So I present my own.

Does the world need another translation of Job? The question can be answered in the affirmative only on the grounds that (1) this translation is better than, or as good as, others; or (2) this translation is necessary to what follows it. I cannot make the first claim with a straight face, though I think mine is better in some respects than others. I can make the second claim. Only one translation always agrees with me: my own.[1] That is the only possible excuse for attempting it, and it may be my translation's sole virtue and major fault. Among other subjects covered in this introduction, I discuss and present issues involved in translating the Book of Job.

Overview and Structure

A summary of the Book of Job, somewhat more detailed than the synopsis in the previous introduction, is a useful starting point. The book begins with the story of a great man, Job, who as a result of discussions between the deity and another character loses his wealth and children and undergoes the indignities of a painful disease. He is invited and expected to curse the deity because of this experience, and he refuses to do so. Three friends come to comfort him, and they sit together in silence for seven days (chaps. 1–2).

Now follows a debate between Job and his friends (chaps. 3–31) in which they urge Job to admit his fault and return to good terms with the deity, while Job insists that he has always done what is right and does not deserve punishment. The debate ends with a long speech by Job setting forth how good his life used to be (chap. 29) and how painful it now is (chap. 30), and, with a series of curses upon himself, Job calls on the deity to respond to him (chap. 31).

A fourth friend steps forward, a young man named Elihu who is mentioned neither before nor after his intervention. He makes a long speech proposing that both Job and the friends are wrong about what Job's suffering means (chaps. 32–37).

At last, the deity speaks to Job "out of the whirlwind," asking difficult questions about the structure of the universe and the control of various powerful animals (chaps. 38–39), closing with a challenge to Job in 40.2. Job responds noncommittally in 40.4–5, and Yahweh insists that he answer, inviting him to control human evil in the world (40.7–14) and two monstrous creatures named Behemoth and Leviathan (40.15–41.26). Job answers conciliatingly (42.2–6).

We return at the end to narrative (42.7–17). The deity criticizes the three friends and reinstates them in his favor (vv. 7–9), Job's friends and relatives comfort him (v. 11), he receives twice his former wealth (v. 12) and a new family of sons and daughters (vv. 13–15). Finally Job's long life is brought to a satisfactory conclusion (vv. 16–17).

A broad structure is immediately perceptible.

I. Prose narrative (1.1–2.13)
II. Dialogue in poetry (3.1–42.6)
III. Prose narrative (42.7–17)[2]

The long poetic middle (Part II) has an asymmetrical structure.

A. Dialogue of Job and the three friends (chaps. 3–31)
B. Speeches of Elihu (chaps. 32–37)
C. Dialogue of Yahweh and Job (38.1–42.6)

The dialogue in Part A goes through three cycles, the first two of which follow a consistent pattern, and the third of which has a slightly different structure.

First Cycle (chaps. 3–11)[3]
Job (chap. 3)
Eliphaz (chaps. 4–5)
Job (chaps. 6–7)
Bildad (chap. 8)
Job (chaps. 9–10)
Zophar (chap. 11)
Second Cycle (chaps. 12–20)
Job (chaps. 12–14)
Eliphaz (chap. 15)
Job (chaps. 16–17)
Bildad (chap. 18)
Job (chap. 19)
Zophar (chap. 20)
Third Cycle (chaps. 21–31)
Job (chap. 21)
Eliphaz (chap. 22)
Job (chaps. 23–24)
Bildad (chap. 25)
Job (chaps. 26–31)

Elihu's intervention (Part B) is preceded by a short narrative (32.1–5), and introductory formulae divide his speech into sections: (1) 32.6–33.33; (2) 34.1–37; (3) 35.1–16; (4) 36.1–37.24. The fourfold division also appears in the dialogue between Yahweh and Job (Part C), which alternates two speeches by Yahweh (38.2–40.2; 40.7–41.26) with two by Job (40.4–5; 42.2–6).

Problems of Translating

Translation is, of course, impossible. We are sometimes uncertain about apparently clear sentences even in our own language. One often-paraded example is the proverb-like "Time flies like an arrow." No question what that says, right? Wrong. Instead of reading "flies" as the verb, take "time" as the verb, and notice the several totally different subjects that emerge, depending on the kinds of "flies" you think of. Or hyphenate "time flies" and take "like" as the verb.

The problems multiply when we work on texts in another language. First we must read any sentence in its own language as that language works, and then we must work at ways of reading it in English. The former involves all the analysis and consideration of alternatives that I illustrated with "Time flies like an arrow," leaving us with a beginning idea of the sentence's complexities and its range of alternative and multiple meanings. Now we face the question of an English sentence to represent what the original says.

There the real impossibilities arise, for two reasons. No two languages work in precisely the same ways, both because they are structured differently and because they reflect and embody entire cultural patterns and ways of thinking that are quite different. Moreover, the specific set of multiplicities and ambiguities in the English sentence differs from the set in the sentence in the other language. And those differences vary in scope and intensity from one culture to another.

A translation is very like a palimpsest, a manuscript in which one text has been erased in order that the parchment may be reused for another text. The earlier letters and words may be discernible beneath the later ones, but sometimes reading them requires infrared light and other image-enhancing technologies. Translations are more complex, for each layer of the text is more complicated than mere letters on a page. The English in itself is necessarily ambiguous and necessarily inaccurate as a representation of the other language.

Nevertheless a translation requires the illusion of accuracy.[4] From the many possible English sentences, the translator can select only one. That decisiveness is, of course, a smoke screen over the impossibility of the entire enterprise. Add to that, with specific reference to the Book of Job, the effects of two millennia and more of religious and theological traditions, to which the modern translation is heir, and the layers of the palimpsest simply multiply.

Can the translator cast all this aside and get back to the original? In simple fact, no. The Book of Job is surrounded by layers of interpretation. We may get some distance through them, may cut away part of the interpreted meaning that prevents our access to any "original." But we cannot get to the "original," because there is none to begin with; even if there were, it would be bewilderingly multiple, not "original" but "originals." Like any text, Job is both translatable and untranslatable. For example, as I show later, English *cannot* reflect the way the Hebrew verbal system works, because English verbs work completely differently. So Hebrew is untranslatable. But we can approach an approximation of Job, and Hebrew is *to some extent* translatable.

It is a paradox that if a text in one language were totally translatable into another, if the varying meanings and connotations of every word corresponded perfectly to the meanings and connotations of every word in the translation, then there would be no difference, and texts once translated would disappear, and their translations as translations would disappear, and it would not matter. On the other hand, if any work in any language is totally untranslatable, if there is no way even of approximating the work in another language, then there is no commonality across languages, and the text is written in a private language that is finally inaccessible to anyone except its author. So it will die.[5] Even in our own language, texts perdure only because they are both translatable and untranslatable.

So the translator must make decisions in the certainty that, if they are not wrong, they are certainly not right. It is worth exhibiting some examples of these decisions. The annotations to the translation show others. Along the way, I criticize some existing translations for their illusions of accuracy. Such criticisms cannot hide the fact that my own pretensions of accuracy are as illusory as anyone else's.

In 1.5, Job worries about his children: "Perhaps my children have sinned and blasphemed God in their thoughts" (JPS). The Hebrew sentence refers not to "thoughts," inner intellectual reflections, but to the "heart" (*lēbab*). To the ancient Israelite, the heart was the locus of thought, decision, intention, and will. Its function was similar to what we call the mind. We think of the mind as an interior function, even sometimes as an organ, though we locate it in the head, not in the chest. The text refers not to the activities carried on in the organ, however, but to the organ. The illusion of accuracy in the JPS translation is that "hearts" is a metonymy for what happens in the hearts. "Thoughts" in effect attempts to tell the reader what the original "author" would have said, we suppose, if that author had been a native speaker of American English.

The question is Is it better for the translation to mention the organ to which the Hebrew text refers or to give what the ancient writer might have said in twentieth-century English? On the whole, I decide for the former with "Perhaps my children have blessed Elohim sinfully in their hearts." My illusion of accuracy is that the bodily organ is central to the point.[6]

In my translation, I try to give metaphors where the Hebrew has metaphors, similes where it has similes. I try to exhibit its images with English images, as close as I can come to the original ones. I attempt to convey, though I cannot reproduce, its syntactic and grammatical confusions when I think it has them. And if, as happens in several places, I cannot make anything intelligible out of the Hebrew text, I indicate this with ellipses.

I am capable of inconsistency. In the JPS translation cited above occurs the word "blasphemed." The translators present an interesting interpretation of a sentence that says "Perhaps my sons [children generally?] have sinned and blessed Elohim in their hearts." The Hebrew verb *brk* is used a number of times in the first two chapters of Job, sometimes clearly with its usual meaning, "to bless," sometimes almost certainly with the opposite meaning (as a euphemism?), namely "to curse." One may guess that the JPS translators sought a word that means something like "curse" but sounds or looks like "bless"; "blaspheme" is a brilliant solution.

It is, however, an imprecise solution to the broader problem of presenting the sentence. The sentence does not refer to blasphemy. Curses are very important in Job, but curses differ from blasphemy. Blasphemy uses terms of divinity for trivial or unworthy ends, such as loudly blaming the deity when one has stumbled or calling perdition down on someone for misunderstanding a request. A curse, on the contrary, is a solemn statement of wish and expectation that if a specified event does or does not occur, a specified result will come upon the curser or the accursed. Job utters a number of curses in chap. 31, for example:

> If I have shaken my fist at the orphan
> because I saw my helpers in the gate,
> may my arm fall from my shoulder,
> my forearm be broken at the elbow. (31.21–22)

In 1.5, Job is worried not that his sons may have referred to God in unflattering or trivial ways but that they may have called down a catastrophe upon God.

Should the translator retain the usual sense of Hebrew *brk* or give the illusion that a different word is being used? Either is reasonable. I decided to take the rather odd conjunction of "sinned" and "blessed" and join them in an odd expression, "blessed sinfully." In those places where *brk* seems to mean "curse," I render it so with a note of explanation to the reader. The alternative is to translate "bless," with a note of explanation to the reader.

As this example shows, it is impossible to translate without interpreting. No amount of supposed literalness or rigid use of the same English word to translate every occurrence of a Hebrew word can overcome this. Words carry more than one sense and therefore can have more than one "equivalent" in another language. The sooner we reject the idea that any word in one language is the equivalent of a word in another, the more quickly we may begin to understand other languages.

Even an apparently ordinary, easily understood sentence may be loaded with traps and ambiguities. An unimportant instance is the second half of 1.3. JPS: "That man was wealthier than anyone in the East"; RSV: "so that this man was the greatest of all the people of the east"; NEB: "Thus Job was the greatest man in all the East"; Stephen Mitchell: "He was the richest man in the East." The translations are divided between an unspecified idea of "greatness" and "wealth." The Hebrew is *gadōl*; "wealthy" is not the primary meaning, though one would not exclude it. The main idea is "big," which can include personal "greatness." "Wealthy" seems too narrow, "great" too broad. Reference to power might approach the idea—"That man was the most powerful [or "one of the most powerful"; see the note to the translation] of the sons of the East."

And what to do with the very un-English phrase "sons of the East" (*bᵉnē-qedem*)? A literal translation looks silly, and none of the translations quoted above choose that route. "Sons" becomes "people" or some variant of it, or it is simply left out, a choice not made, we may be sure, in the interests of nonsexist language. "Sons" is most likely a metaphor—perhaps a dead one—in Hebrew. But metaphors are slippery, and here we are sliding around upon one in a seemingly inoffensive and straightforward sentence.

Another point about this sentence. JPS renders *ha'īš hahū'* as "that man," RSV has "this man." The demonstrative pronoun *hū'* ordinarily refers to what is over there, not over here (for "this," Hebrew would usually have *zeh*). The same words occur in the second half of 1.1, and the statement here verbally echoes the earlier one. JPS reflects the echo by translating the phrase as "that man" in both places; RSV prefers the English virtue of stylistic variety and says "that man" in verse 1 and "this man" in verse 3. NEB does not have "that man" in either place.

This lengthy attention to an insignificant statement (and at least one problem remains unmentioned) shows, first, that even apparently simple Hebrew statements are not the same as equally simple ones in English, and, second, that one needs to pay attention not merely to the sentence at hand but also to other sentences that may bear on it.

A rather more important instance is 40.8, where Yahweh asks if Job wants to annul (*tapēr*) Yahweh's *mišpaṭ*. *Mišpaṭ* is a critically important word in the Israelite tradition—and in the Book of Job—ordinarily translated in 40.8, as in many passages, "justice." The supposition is that Yahweh is asking Job whether he wishes to undermine Yahweh's moral governance of the universe. But there are many other possible ideas in the word. *Mišpaṭ* sometimes means something like custom, expected or habitual behavior, and sometimes refers to a legal trial or to the outcome of a trial, a decision or a judgment. It may refer to a negative decision or punishment, and it may refer to justice as the abstract idea of the proper conduct of or in human affairs. The word can also signify order, either in human society or in the cosmic realm. Consider how different are the following questions:

Would you even annul my justice?
" custom?
" litigation (trial procedure)?
" legal decision?
" judgmental punishment?
" governance?
" order?

Apart from other possible translations of Hebrew *tapēr*, which I have rendered "annul," *mišpaṭ* doubtless has more meanings.

We can read the tone of that question in several different ways. Consider the somewhat aggrieved tone of:

Will you even put me in the wrong? (RSV)
Wilt thou even disallow my right? (S. R. Driver and Gray, p. 349)

the aggressive tone of:

Do you dare to deny my judgment? (Mitchell, p. 84)
Dare you deny that I am just? (NEB)

the defensive tone of:

Would you impugn my justice? (JPS)
Will you deny my justice? (Gordis, *Book of Job*, p. 468)
Will you even frustrate my judgment? (Cox, p. 141)

Examples could be multiplied, but these seem the basic tones translators have perceived.

One might give the reader all the alternatives right in the text, printing something barbarous like

Would you really/even annul/frustrate/deny/impugn my justice/judgment/right/order?

That is to adopt the "reception theory" of literature with a vengeance, though in the context of that theory, the perpetrator of the sentence might be criticized for allowing so narrow a range of alternatives.[7]

The translation of the question in 40.8 (or half-question, since the second line continues the sentence) is a touchstone for interpretations of the book. Those who think that the divine majesty finally overwhelms Job tend to use aggressive or defensive tones; those who find a reconciliation between Job and the deity use gentler tones. That is not surprising, for there is no way a translation can avoid interpreting. My translation is no exception. It is all part of the making of decisions.

In any case, *literal* translation, whatever that might be, is unthinkable. No English word, let alone a sentence, is the exact equivalent in ranges of meanings and fields of connotation of its corresponding Hebrew word or sentence. Anything the translator says in English distorts the Hebrew, in terms both of the meanings of words and of the structures of the languages. For example, all English verb forms necessarily indicate the *time* of the action: "he said," "she was saying," "I will say," "we will have said," "they had said," and so on. English can draw precise, subtle distinctions of time, using nothing but verb forms. Classical Hebrew verb forms do not contain any time reference (the modern Hebrew forms have been modified under Indo-European influence). No matter how the translator renders Hebrew verbs, then, the very act of writing down the English words distorts the original. I cannot put it more bluntly. One does the best one can, muddles through, hopes the reader will not notice the inconsistencies, the illogicalities, the oddities of the verb renderings. I have made excessive use of the present tense in translating, for it seems to me temporally the least precise of the English tenses.

I have talked in the foregoing paragraphs as if the original of Job were somehow the template to which the translation had to and could not correspond. Certainly it cannot correspond to it without remainder. The question is Must it? And if so, in what ways must it correspond, and to what extent and degree? What is the bind that the translator enters? How much originality may inhere in the "translation"? Below I discuss certain types of originality that I have eschewed: the temptation to revise the text, rewrite the "original," and translate what was rewritten. That is a kind of tyranny exerted over the text by the translator. Equally, however, translators are bidden to exercise the most abject humility, effacing themselves before the "original" in order to pass on to the reader a version (itself an interesting word: a "turning") that will be recognized as the child of its father.[8] Is there an approach the translator can take that neither rapes the text nor submits to rape by it? I argue in Chapter 1 that there is a way of reading that succeeds in that. But I am not satisfied that I have yet discovered how to translate that way, and I suspect that I am too submissive to authority.

I now turn to some recurring problems that the translator faces and illustrate them with passages in Job. These do not by any means exhaust the possibilities.

Idiomatic Phrases

In Job 1.1 the narrator characterizes Job as *y^erē' ^elōhīm* in Hebrew, which we can translate as "one who fears Elohim [God]." Translators meet the problem of the idiomatic phrase in nearly every sentence. The question here is what to do with a phrase that does not mean precisely what it seems "literally" to say. Granted that the translator cannot avoid interpreting, ought the translation to suggest what the phrase meant in its original cultural context, how it felt to those who used it? Or must the reader figure that out alone?

The primary meaning conveyed to an ancient Israelite by the phrase "fear God" was not only "be afraid of God" but more like "fulfill one's duties to God." To be sure, a connotation of fright attached to the word. To "fulfill one's duties to God" included the thought that consequences might be dire if one did not. I use a word that is very general indeed, that contains in English a connotation of awe if not of fright and an implication of certain kinds of actions and obligations, which in ordinary parlance conveys the notion that these duties are *owed* to a deity: "religious." In some passages, of course, the verb *yr'* means quite clearly "to be afraid," and there I have used the conventional rendering.

Inadequate Vocabulary

In Job 4.10–11, the poet was showing off. In the JPS translation, the lines read:

> The lion may roar, the cub may howl,
> But the teeth of the king of beasts are broken.
> The lion perishes for lack of prey,
> And its whelps are scattered.

Those four lines of poetry use five different Hebrew words for "lion": *'aryēh* and *šaḥal* in the first line, *k^epīrīm* (a plural) in the second, *layiš* in the third, and *b^enē labī'* ("sons of the lion") in the fourth. By dint of one repetition and of hiding one of the words for "lion" in the possessive "its"—but at the price of implying that the "whelps" are those of the lion in line 3, which they are not—the JPS translators have produced something that deals with lions and their difficulties.

Such English as I control does not possess five words for "lion." One can use "lion" in the first line for the most common word, *'aryēh*; one can use "cub" with assurance that the context will show that a lion cub is meant, and *šaḥal* can plausibly be translated "cub." "King of beasts" is an English cliché; the Hebrew word in the second line is plural and denotes young (but not infant) animals. Ancient Israelites seem not to have thought of the lion as "king of beasts" (according to Genesis 1, the "king of beasts" was the human being).[9] We still have two words for "lion" to find. Maybe someone with a better vocabulary than mine can think of them. One thing to do, of course, is to move out to relatives of the lion, and I have done that with "cougar" at 4.11a. One might also try "catamount," "puma," or the like.

Expressions Without Equivalents

An issue quite crucial to the understanding of the Book of Job is to be found in the dialogue in chapter 1 between the deity and the somewhat difficult character known in some translations as "Satan." Part of the problem is that character himself. "Satan" is inaccurate, because the Hebrew word is not a proper name but a noun with the definite article. It is best understood as a title, and if we want to use "Satan," we ought at least to call him "the Satan." He turns up elsewhere in the Hebrew Bible, most notably in chap. 3 of Zechariah, where his function is very like what it is in Job 1–2, a kind of heavenly prosecuting attorney who roves the earth bringing malefactors to justice. That legal function explains why some versions translate the term as "the Adversary." But to identify "Satan" as the Devil, a principle of evil or, in a dualistic system, *the* principle of evil, is anachronistic. By the Common Era Satan had become one of the proper names of the Devil, but in Job the word is not a proper name. Nor is there the slightest hint that the person is evil. He attends upon Yahweh at the times when the "sons of Elohim" normally do so, and by every indication he belongs with that group. For that reason, I am uncomfortable with "the Adversary," especially if it be capitalized. "The Adversary" too easily becomes the opponent of the deity. I incline to "the Prosecutor." The main point is that he is not an evil figure, however unfriendly he may be, and therefore to use the word "Satan" for him cannot but wrap him in a misleading connotation.

As Yahweh and the Prosecutor converse, Yahweh calls attention to Job and uses, in a somewhat incautiously boastful way, the same language the narrator had used of Job in 1.1: “scrupulously moral, religious, a person who avoids evil.” The Prosecutor argues that Job is religious because Yahweh has made it hard for him not to be: “Haven’t you yourself hedged around him and his family and all he has, blessed anything his hands do, so that his possessions burst out over the earth?” (1.10) He suggests that the deity change his actions toward Job. As JPS has it: “But lay Your hand upon all that he has and he will surely blaspheme You to Your face” (1.11). Like all other translations, JPS makes the second clause an extremely confident, indicative prediction.

But in Hebrew that second clause is an incomplete sentence: *’im lō’ ‘al-paneyka y*^{e}*bar*^{e}*kekka*; somewhat literally, “if he does not bless you to your face.” Two facts about that sentence: “bless” (*brk*) is “bless/curse,” to which I referred above; the clause itself is not an indicative statement but a curse formula. It says “If he does not ‘curse’ you to your face—” and it implies but does not state a result clause, something on the order of “may my teeth rot from my gums.” Curse formulas stating the condition with “if” or “if not” but not stating the catastrophe called down on the curser are fairly common in classical Hebrew; indeed, they are much more common than curses with the result clause.[10]

The recognition that this sentence is a curse vitiates the classic interpretations of the transaction between Yahweh and the Prosecutor as a wager or as an experiment on Job to see how much the poor fellow can take. “If he does not curse you to your face” is not “Let’s see if he does,” or “I’ll bet you a ham sandwich that he does.” The sentence says, “May I be cursed if he does not.” (I say much more about this in Chapter 2.)

The problem is that English has no comparable expression. To be sure, “May I be cursed if he does not” approaches “He certainly will.” Yet no one could pretend that they are the same. In some ways, the omission of the result clause is more powerful than its inclusion would be. To supply the missing clause would be to rewrite the text, to make explicit what the text leaves implicit. I have decided to give the sentence as it is, “If he does not curse you to your face—” The dash implies that something is missing from the sentence, and the annotation supplies the necessary information.

Allusions to the Tradition

Several passages in Job allude to specific statements or texts in the Israelite tradition. The translator must bring out these allusions, which in Job are not direct quotations.

In chapter 3, at the beginning of the dialogue, Job refers to the day of his birth and the night of his conception (3.3) and goes on to say (3.4, JPS): "May that day be darkness." As the curse proceeds, the imagery of darkness triumphing over light is constant. It is not difficult to recognize an allusion to the creation story in Genesis 1. But this is more than allusion: we may justly call it parody. The Hebrew statement "May that day be darkness" is *hayyōm hahū' y^e^hī ḥōšek*. The phrase *y^e^hī ḥōšek* is a parody of *y^e^hī 'ōr*, "Let there be light," in Genesis 1.3. God goes on in verse 5 to name the light "Day." Job, on the contrary, wants to name his day (*hayyōm*) "Darkness." He not only curses his own coming into being but also, by alluding to Genesis 1, curses all coming into being, all of creation. The allusion to Genesis 1.3 seems to me worth making explicit, and I do so by translating Job's expression: "That day, let there be darkness." An annotation calls attention to the allusion.

Figures of Speech

Each language has its standard figures of speech, and some figures, such as metaphor, are found in every language. Too many biblical translations have ridden roughshod over metaphors in the text. One illustration may be enough: Job complains of physical pain in 30.27, but you would never know it from the RSV translation: "My heart is in turmoil, and is never still." It is a little clearer in the JPS version: "My bowels are in turmoil without respite." JPS is right to refer to the bowels, for that is the organ the Hebrew sentence mentions. RSV, recognizing that the ancient Hebrews located in the belly or the bowels the emotion we moderns locate in the heart, sounds like a psychological description. But JPS flattens out the second half of the line, whereas RSV only makes it a bit ambiguous. "Is never still" is better than "without respite" for *lō' dammū*, which is "is not silent." The two translations agree that the organ is "in turmoil," which is only a bit colorless. I prefer: "My bowels are boiled, they are not silent." If the Hebrew verb *rutt^e^ḥū* were not definitely a passive, I would have rendered "My bowels boil." In any case, the metaphor refers to a terribly upset and noisy belly.

Some literatures use figures of speech that are rare in other literatures, and there the translator has a problem. At the very beginning, Job is described in 1.1 as *tam w^e^yašar*, usually translated as "blameless and upright." Both Hebrew words have connotations of morality or of ritual purity. *Tam*, "blameless," is used frequently of an animal flawless enough to be sacrificed (such animals were required by the law to be unblemished), and, by extension, of a person who is ritually pure. But it can also indicate one who is complete (healthy is one connotation of that; unmarred is another), faultless. On the other hand, *yašar*, "upright," almost always refers to morality. The problem with the rendering "upright," however, is that *yašar* has no connotations of the vertical but, on the contrary, suggests the horizontal, something straight or flat or even. I have found no way to express that metaphor. *Yašar* is used in a general enough sense to allow the rather imprecise and very general term "moral." The problem is the combination of the two words: "faultless and moral" seems redundant, and it may not convey the element of ritual purity in *tam*.

What we seem to have here, however, is a figure of speech frequently used in Hebrew literature: hendiadys.[11] In a hendiadys, a pair of things emphatically states one thing: "A and B" is "very A" (or "very B"). A familiar hendiadys in English is the idiom "good and mad," meaning "very angry." *Tam wᵉyašar*, then, suggests "very moral," something like "completely or perfectly moral," somewhat excessive expressions. I take a suggestion made to me by my colleague Bruce Rosenstock, "scrupulously moral." Why not simply reproduce the pair of words? The main reason is that the hendiadys is not a figure of speech characteristic of English style, and English readers will not readily recognize a pair of words used in that way. The text of Job has many instances of hendiadys, and the annotations mention them as they occur.

Interpretation and Translation

Verse 42.6 poses an interesting problem in translation (and illustrates a problem in evaluating translations). JPS renders Job's final response to Yahweh's speeches "out of the whirlwind" as:

> Therefore, I recant and relent,
> Being but dust and ashes.

RSV reads:

> Therefore I despise myself,
> and repent in dust and ashes.

One could go on quoting mistranslations,[12] but it is not necessary. The Hebrew is *'al-kēn 'em'as wᵉniḥamtī 'al-'apar wa'ēper*. To be more or less literal: "Therefore I despise and I am sorry upon dust and ash."

Both JPS and RSV betray their interpretations. The JPS emphasizes Job's realization of smallness in the face of the cosmic power depicted in those astonishing visions of the universe in chaps. 38–39. The RSV emphasizes Job's realization of unworthiness in the face of this eminently worthy God. Both seriously distort the Hebrew.

JPS's "recant and relent" looks good on first glance, though its alliteration is not present in Hebrew. But "recant" is a weak stand-in for *'em'as*, which is a much more visceral notion of detesting than the rather intellectual abandonment of a prior opinion. And turning "upon dust and ashes" into "being but dust and ashes" is a dubious logical move. The preposition *'al*, "upon, over, above," can sometimes approach "because," and perhaps (I am guessing at the committee's thinking) the translators thought they could twist "because dust and ashes" into "because [I am] dust and ashes." It seems to me very stretched indeed.

The RSV is, if anything, worse. The reflexive sense "despise myself" is impossible for *'em'as*, which is an indicative, "I despise," needing an accusative. RSV did not find an accusative, but the presumption is even greater that the committee members, all but one being Christian, were affected by the long Christian tradition of contrition, which calls for the sinner's awareness of sinfulness. They were certainly affected by it in "repent in dust and ashes." To use dust and ashes as a symbol of mourning, grief, and repentance is not without precedent in Hebrew, though the dust and ashes were ordinarily put on oneself, sprinkled on the head, for example, not spread on the ground to sit on.

In 42.3 and 5, Job expresses some respects in which he has been ignorant and inexperienced, but the self-abnegations that JPS and RSV put into verse 6 are simply not there. The close examination of the expression *niḥam 'al* in Hebrew by Dale Patrick shows that the preposition *'al* in that expression never denotes the place of repentant activity but always refers to what one is repenting.[13] *Niḥamtī 'al-'apar wa'ēper*, then, is closer to "I repent of [or change my mind about] dust and ashes." The accusative of "despise" nearest to hand is that same dust and ashes.

> Therefore, I despise and repent
> of dust and ashes.

The syntactical and philological facts of the matter point to some such rendering (see Chapter 8 for further discussion of this passage).

The Problem of Poetry

An extremely important aspect of the Book of Job is that most of it is poetry.[14] Classical Hebrew poetry is unlike English poetry in several respects. Part of the tradition of English poetry involves the use of rhyme; Hebrew poetry never seems to use rhyme as a poetic device. I suspect that the occasional rhymes in classical Hebrew poems are inadvertent and that ancient readers might not even have noticed them.

English poetry often exhibits regular meter, where all lines of a poem have the same basic pattern of accented and unaccented syllables. Thus the *iambic* meter alternates unaccented and accented syllables, as in the word "todáy."[15] Iambic pentameter is the typical meter of Shakespeare's plays, as in these lines from *The Tempest* (I mark the accented syllables):

> Now dóes my próject gáther tó a héad.
> My chárms crack nót, my spírits obéy, and tíme
> Goes úpright wíth his cárriage. Hów's the dáy?[16]

In the English tradition, a poem does not usually shift meter from line to line, although, for example, an intervening refrain may have a meter different from that of surrounding stanzas.

A third aspect of English poetic conventions is the use of standardized forms. The English sonnet conventionally has fourteen lines in iambic pentameter, arranged either in three stanzas of four lines each (quatrains) followed by a concluding two-line stanza (couplet), or in two 4-line stanzas followed by two 3-line stanzas (tercets).[17]

This is not an essay on English poetry. I want only to convey that English poetry differs from classical Hebrew poetry. Not only does Hebrew poetry not use rhyme, it does not appear to fall into regular, conventional forms analogous to the sonnet, nor does its rhythm exhibit the regularity that English poems tend to have. It has rhythm, I think, and it also has certain kinds of formal characteristics, chief among them parallelism.

Rhythm

Efforts to scan classical Hebrew poetry metrically have not been very successful. The most common mode of scansion is to count accents in a line, ignoring the number of unaccented syllables between the accents.[18] Most lines have three accents, some have four or two, few have more. This method of analysis does not ask about the rhythm provided by unaccented syllables. The reason is clear enough, I think: this approach has not produced evidence of regular patterns of unaccented syllables, and therefore the assumption is that they do not count. Another reason is that all efforts to analyze classical Hebrew poetry are frustrated by our uncertainty about ancient pronunciation. We can be quite sure, on the analogy of every known language, that it was *not* pronounced as modern Hebrew is. No language ever maintains its pronunciation intact for long.

An example may help to show how this method works. Here are the first few verses of Job’s first speech, 3.3–6 (I mark the probable accented syllables):

3 *yó’bad yôm ’iwwâled bó*
w^{e}*hallây*^{e}*lah ’amár hórah gêber*
4 *hayyôm hahú’ y*^{e}*hí-ḥôšek*
’ál-yidr^{e}*šéhū ’*^{e}*lóah mimmá‘al*
w^{e}*’ál-tōpá‘ ‘alâyw n*^{e}*haráh*
5 *yig‘alúhū ḥôšek w*^{e}*ṣalmâwet*
tiškán-‘alâyw ‘^{a}*nanáh*
y^{e}*ba’*^{a}*túhū kimrīré yôm*
6 *hallây*^{e}*lah hahú’ yiqqaḥéhū ’ópel*
’ál-yiḥádd bīmé šanáh
b^{e}*mispár y*^{e}*raḥím ’al-yabó’.*

There are some problems with this analysis. For example, the word *gêber* in the second line may have been pronounced as a monosyllable (*gabr*), as might the word *ḥôšek* in the third and sixth lines (*ḥušk*), as well as *ṣalmâwet* in the sixth line (*ṣalmút*), and *’ópel* in the ninth (*’úpl*).[19] On the other hand, *‘alâyw* in the fifth and seventh lines may have had three syllables instead of two, perhaps *‘alêhū*. We do not know.[20]

Taking the text as given above and giving an accented syllable the sign / and an unaccented one –, we have the following scansion (the numbers after each line show the number of accents/number of syllables):

/ – / – / – /	(4/7)
– – / – – – / / – / –	(4/11)
– / – / – / / –	(4/8)
/ – – / – – / – / –	(4/10)
– / – / – / – – /	(4/9)
– – / – / – – – / –	(3/10)
– / – / – – /	(3/7)
– – – / – – – / /	(3/9)
– / – – – / – – / – / –	(4/12)
/ – / – / – /	(4/7)
– – / – – / – – /	(3/9)

Seven lines have four accents, and four lines have three. The number of syllables differs greatly from line to line. Only two combinations are repeated, 4/7 in lines 1 and 10 and 3/9 in lines 8 and 11.

If we adopt the alternative pronunciations mentioned above, we have something that looks a bit more regular, especially when we group the lines into sense units.

/ – / – / – /   (4/7)
– – / – – – / / – /   (4/10)

– / – / – / /   (4/7)
/ – – / – – / – / –   (4/10)
– / – / – / – – – /   (4/10)

– – / – / – – /   (3/8)
– / – / – – – /   (3/8)
– – – / – – – / /   (3/9)

– / – – – / – – / – /   (4/11)
/ – / – / – /   (4/7)
– – / – – / – – /   (3/9)

The last tercet exhibits the most variety. Perhaps some of these rhythmic combinations were conventional; for example, it may be that a tercet could have the same number of accents in each line but a different number of syllables in one of the three (like the tercets in lines 3–5 and 6–8 above)—a rhythmic subtlety that ancient readers might very well have noticed and enjoyed.

The problem of Hebrew meter has gone unsolved for many decades. I will not solve it here, and one short instance, which contains several asymmetries, does not prove any point. I suspect—though I do not have the statistics to prove it—that we would find that lines show a limited number of combinations of accented and unaccented syllables, suggesting a system of complex and mixed meters. For example, in 3.3–6, romanized above, two lines, verses 3a and 6b, can be scanned as trochaic tetrameters, both ending on a strong syllable, whereas verse 4a combines two iambic feet (_hayyóm hahû'_) with one bacchius foot (– / / : _y^{e}hî_ *_ḥûšk_[21]) in a tetrameter line. Verse 4c shows two iambic feet (_w^{e}'ál tōpâ'_) followed by an amphibrach (– / –: * _'aléhū_) and an anapest (– – / : _n^{e}haráh_), and verse 5b contains an iamb, an amphibrach, and an anapest. Some similarities in the combinations can be seen even in so brief a compass. One would need to establish the most common combinations of these rhythmic variations, both for single lines and for couplets. I suspect that conventional combinations of meters would recur in the short poetic units such as couplets, tercets, and quatrains.

Parallelism

Parallelism is the characteristic that provided the breakthrough to the modern perception that large parts of the Hebrew Bible are poetry. As

James Kugel has shown, the long interpretive tradition realized somewhat vaguely that there was poetry in the Hebrew Bible, and a few writers, such as Josephus, Origen, Jerome, and others were sometimes more specific about it.[22] Throughout its history, the tradition followed a complicated path in considering poetry, a story that Kugel has told with a wealth of detail and subtlety to which I need only refer.

If Bishop Robert Lowth did not discover parallelism, he was the one who, in his inaugural lectures as Professor of Poetry at Oxford in 1753,[23] set out to demonstrate that the poetry of the Hebrew Bible was every bit as good as anything in the whole Western tradition. Among other things, Lowth sought to disprove an old theory that, whatever else in the Hebrew Bible might be poetry, the prophets certainly were not. In his lectures and in a later book on Isaiah, he emphatically asserted the contrary, and on the whole his idea has carried the day. Lowth most influentially called to people's attention the characteristic of parallelism in Hebrew poetry (he called it in Latin *parallelismus membrorum*, parallelism of the members), which has dominated subsequent study.[24]

Parallelism is sometimes crudely defined as saying the same thing in a second line as in the first. Job 4.4 shows how inadequate that notion is.

> Your talk has raised the stumbler,
> you have braced up tottering knees.

Superficially, the two lines refer to Job's encouraging people who, metaphorically, have had a hard time walking. It is not clear whether the verb in the second line implies the subject of the first, "talk," or not. But there is more to this couplet than two statements of the same idea. The first line says that Job has restored to a walking position someone who has fallen, but in the second line, he is assisting someone who is walking. It is a much subtler, more complete picture of gracious kindness than the surface impression of repetition.

No serious student of parallelism now argues that repetition is the point. That view was derived from a misconstruction of Lowth's analytic categories of parallelism. He spoke of "synonymous" and "antithetical parallelism" as the two major types, and the notion of synonymity was corrupted into an idea of mere repetition. Perhaps the most elegant account of parallelism—elegant because at once simple and capable of unending flexibility—is Kugel's formulation of its principle as "seconding," or, in formulaic terms, "A is so, and *what's more*, B is so."[25] It is absolutely not that B is the same as A, but that it "seconds" A, adds to what A says something related to it.

It may be related in various ways. To take some instances from Job 3:

> Why was I not dead from the womb,
> come out of the belly and perish? (3.11)

Though both lines express Job's wish that he had died at birth, they are not synonymous. They refer to two different types of death at birth, stillbirth (line a) and death immediately after birth (line b). If I hadn't died before birth, Job asks, why couldn't I die just after it?

> Perish the day on which I was born,
> the night that said, "A man is conceived." (3.3)

Job knows that conception precedes birth, but his point is not the temporal sequence but precisely "A, and what's more, B." To paraphrase, "I wish that my birthday had been canceled," and what's more, "I wish that even the night of my conception had been canceled." Temporal sequence is reversed in emphasizing completeness. Notice, moreover, that the governing verb, "perish," occurs in the first line but not in the second. The absence of a verb in the second line underscores the connection between the two lines, the "what's more," as well as the difference between them.

Sometimes we have parallelisms among the three lines of a tercet:

> That day, let there be darkness,
> may Eloah not seek it from above
> or daylight beam over it. (3.4)

After the parody of Genesis 1.3 in "let there be darkness," thus eliminating Job's birthday from the creation, the creator's not "seeking" the day and the day's having no light—the definition of "day" in Genesis 1—carry along Job's wish to see a total distinction drawn between the first days of earth's coming to be and the day of his own coming to be.

Sometimes we may have what look less like parallel ideas than the kind of seconding that moves the thought forward:

> Why did knees receive me
> and breasts, so I could suckle? (3.12)

"Breasts" implies "why . . . receive me" from line a, and "so I could suckle" continues the thought to a new point about the continuation of life. The parallel of "breasts" in line b to "knees" in line a is enough to call up the entire association and to free the line to go on to the new thought.

There wicked people stop their turmoil,
there those weary in power have rest,
prisoners take their ease together,
not hearing the oppressor's voice. (3.17–18)

The two couplets have different subjects, but verse 18b harks back to the formerly active powerful ones. Just by putting the two subjects together the comparison between weak and powerful points on to verse 19:

Small and great alike are there,
and a slave is freed from his lord.

But the two lines of verse 17 are subtly different. In the first, the "turmoil" (*rōgez*) of "wicked people" ceases, whereas line b sounds like a sigh of relief from someone exhausted from the exertions of being powerful. A is paraphrasable as "Wicked people must stop their activity that troubles other people," and B as "What's more, powerful people get to have some rest." That brings us to verse 18, where "prisoners" also have some rest, because they need not leap to obey when the "oppressor" shouts. And even in verse 19, the seconding is not mere synonymity. Death is the leveler, as many cultures have said, but the slave is not merely present along with the lord. "What's more," he has a new relation to the lord, is "freed."

I need not give a complete account of parallelism. Others have done so and have ranged widely over the matter. One point may be emphasized, however. Some accounts of parallelism are most interested in the relations between the words in the member lines. When, as in 3.3, a word is missing from the second line, we have the phenomenon called "gapping."[26] A similar parallel is in verse 15:

or with princes who possessed gold,
filled their houses with silver.

"Princes" is gapped in line b, and the parallelism is most clearly visible between "gold" and "silver." The many conventions in parallelism include the conventional recurrence of specific pairs of words in parallel lines.[27] The presence of such pairs—and "gold" (*zahab*) and "silver" (*kesep*) is one—does not mean, however, that parallelism makes its effect merely by the formulaic pairing of words. Kugel's larger structure of "A, and what's more, B" covers both formulaic word pairing and more subtle connections.

Several scholars have sought to be more precise about parallelism. Adele Berlin ranges through various linguistic phenomena, pointing out that Kugel did not consider that aspect. It remains uncertain whether any concord is possible between the realm of linguistics, which tries to explain parallelism by grammar, lexicography, semantics, and phonology (Berlin's major interests), and the realm of poetic style, which is most interested in how parallelism works in the poem (Kugel's concern).[28]

The linguist, concerned with how and why a language works as it does, may tend to downplay distinctions a stylist may emphasize of how language is used in different sorts of discourse. The psycholinguistic perception of word pairs is by no means irrelevant to the subject of poetic parallelism. Yet the psycholinguist may neglect poetic conventions within genres of poetry, such as why lyric poems may exhibit one tendency in associating words while narrative or epic poems follow quite different tendencies. Poetry's conventions, I believe, differ from the conventions of ordinary talk, and poetry, which is much more self-conscious about language than is conversation, is formed not only by the workings of the psyche but also by the workings of poetic traditions in cultures.

I miss that dimension in Berlin's book. She, for her part, rightly misses the considerations of linguistics in Kugel. To be sure, Kugel doubts that the distinction between "poetry" and "prose" or some similar term is applicable to classical Hebrew literature, and he finds the "A, and what's more, B" formula in what is usually termed prose. For Kugel the density of what I take to be poetry differs only in degree from the more casual conventions of what I take to be prose, and he posits a continuum of styles without a definite distinction of genre. I believe that that is because he finds his shoes getting muddy when he steps into what he calls the "quagmire" of metrics and rhythmic analysis.[29]

If one is careful to recognize parallelism where it occurs, then the translation will exhibit parallelism where it is present. And it is not always present. Robert Lowth concocted what he called "synthetic parallelism," by which he meant something that does not look like parallelism, either synonymous or antonymous, but, because parallelism is supposed always to be there, must be called parallelism. It is long past time to drop "synthetic parallelism" into the garbage can as a residue of a more rule-bound world. A line like Job 4.8 is not in my judgment parallel at all:

> As I have seen, those who plow iniquity
> and sow toil harvest it too.

There is a certain superficial parallelism between "plow iniquity" and "sow toil," but the sentence that contains the two phrases does not fall in any way into two statements. That is quite all right. Eliphaz has another nonparallel couplet:

Is not their cord pulled out with them,
and they die? But not with wisdom. (4.21)

Again, one might argue that "they die" parallels line a, but syntactically the thought is more a sequence than a parallel. On the other hand, perhaps these are instances of failed parallelism, incompetent poetic technique. No classical Hebrew poet has to be faultless.

In my translation, I have often omitted typical Hebrew conjunctions. Nearly every second (and third) line in Hebrew poetry begins with "and" (*wᵉ*), a convention that did not bother the Hebrews in the slightest. It does bother us. Repeated "ands" in English flatten out the movement of the poetry. Take 4.3–4, reinstating the "ands" that I have omitted:

Think how you have corrected many
and strengthened weak hands.
Your talk has raised the stumbler,
and you have braced up tottering knees.

I believe that is weaker than my version without either "and." Rather than let them get in the way, I have omitted many "ands," except where they seem to me helpful to understanding. Sometimes the Hebrew even begins a new section or sentence with "and," as in 4.12, where I have omitted the conjunction at the beginning of both lines to avoid what seems to me mindless literalism:

And I received a stolen word,
and my ear took a whisper from it.

In a few cases, I have used "or" in its conjunctive sense:

That day, let there be darkness,
may Eloah not seek it from above
or [*wᵉ*] daylight beam over it. (3.4)

Because parallelism is more important to the style of the Joban poem than to translating it, I need say no more of it here. The careful reader may recognize the wonderful flexibility of the ways in which parallelism can be used.

Job and Northwest Semitic Languages

It seems necessary to clarify one respect in which I stand back from what some take as the plain facts of the Book of Job. A considerable amount of recent work has attempted to show that many misunderstandings of this and other biblical books can be rectified by applying Northwest Semitic philology. The discovery of Canaanite texts at Ras Shamra, ancient Ugarit, has shed a flood of light on the history of the Northwest Semitic languages, of which Hebrew was one. It has done more: it has illuminated the religious and literary culture of the indigenous Canaanites of Palestine, the religion of the fertility deity Baal, and a number of local mythologies to which the Hebrew Bible often refers.[30]

A series of publications, especially those of Mitchell Dahood and his students in Rome, has marshaled evidence to show how words and forms attested in Northwest Semitic texts permit a proper understanding of Job.[31] D. N. Freedman has used this evidence to propose a date for the Book of Job considerably earlier than the standard of recent decades.[32]

Given the difficulty of the poetry of Job, one must welcome any information that might ease solution of the problems. But those familiar with the work of Dahood and his students will quickly see in the translation and its annotations that I accept little from them. I cannot claim to have mastered the Ras Shamra texts, but neither have I seen a sufficiently clear statement of method by these scholars to allow me to assess their proposals. And their enthusiasm for this sizable body of evidence has led them to what may without exaggeration be called ridiculous lengths.

Take a couple of relatively minor points. In Hebrew and the other Northwest Semitic languages, a pronominal form affixed to a noun establishes a kind of genitive relationship. In Hebrew, "his house," *bētō*, is formed by adding the suffix *ō* (probably a contraction of *hū*, "he") to what grammarians call the "construct" form, *bēt*, of the noun "house" (*bayit*). "My house" is *bētī*, "their house" *bētam*, and so on. It has been noted that Phoenician not infrequently uses an *ī* suffix for a third-person masculine singular, though in Hebrew *ī* is first-person singular. One sometimes finds in the text of Job a noun or verb with a first-person singular suffix where one might prefer to find a third-person masculine pronoun. We need only to point to the parallel in Phoenician, and we can have our third-person masculine pronoun without having to change the Hebrew text to get it. There are even places where one might wish a third-person feminine pronoun that can be supplied in the same form.

The problem is that there is no discipline in this. We have a batch of more or less interchangeable forms, and at any point in the text it seems that we can call them anything we wish. Theoretically, in one line *bētī* can be "my house," two lines later it might be "his house," and six lines below that, it could even be "her house."

Biblical scholarship went through a long period in the latter part of the nineteenth and the first half or more of the twentieth centuries in which scholars felt at liberty to change what seemed to them "mistakes" in the Hebrew text. Where possible, they referred to ancient translations into Aramaic (the Targum), Syriac, Greek (the Septuagint), and Latin (the Vulgate), and translations made from them, that often contain readings preferable to those in the Masoretic Text. This allowed them to retranslate the expressions into Hebrew satisfactory to themselves. If no aid could be found in those quarters, scholars could easily discover copyists' errors and "restore" the wording to its presumed original. This long tradition of textual emendation can be seen in full panoply in the massive, important commentary on Job by Georg Fohrer, *Das Buch Hiob*. German scholars brought this method of dealing with the text to its highest development, but the infection spread far beyond that.[33]

The important monographs of Anton Blommerde and Anthony Ceresko and the articles by Dahood remind me of nothing so much as the older German commentaries. Where the latter lightheartedly rewrote the text by changing it, the former lightheartedly rewrite it without changing it, by pleading grammatical forms not necessarily typical of Hebrew and by arguing that words bear meanings otherwise not found in the Hebrew Bible but attested in Canaanite and Phoenician texts. In our ignorance of much of classical Hebrew, we ought not to put rigid barriers around it. But the general effect of this approach is not merely to rewrite the Book of Job to make it conform to "what it ought to mean" but also to transform ancient Hebrew into a language that is neither Hebrew nor Canaanite nor Phoenician but a rather whimsical amalgam of all three, a kind of "comparative Northwest Semitic." It is very like what we used to find when scholars variously mined the Septuagint, the Targum, the Vulgate, and the Sahidic Coptic for emendations. I do not mean that we ought to reject all help from the Northwest Semitic texts, or that I do reject it all. I have accepted it where I find it sensible.

One other frequently adduced Northwest Semitic phenomenon, of which I have accepted not a single instance, is the "enclitic *mem*." Especially in the Canaanite mythical texts from Ugarit, datable mostly to the early fourteenth century B.C.E., we sometimes find affixed to words an *m*, whose function is unclear. It is not a pronominal suffix or a plural form, but seems to be a vaguely emphatic affixed particle. There is no apparent consistency to its presence or absence, and it is untranslatable. To some scholars this enclitic looked like a solution to problems raised by questionable third-person masculine plural suffixes (*-am* in Hebrew) or masculine plural nouns (ending *-īm*). It was asserted (but not demonstrated) that this enclitic had once been common in Hebrew but as time went along had been dropped and forgotten; ancient copyists mistook it in the consonantal text for masculine plurals, for third-person masculine plural pronouns, or for the preposition *min*, "from," which is often prefixed to a word as *m*. What could be more useful than a floating *mem* that seems not to change the meaning at all and is substitutable for all sorts of "wrong" forms?

I have steadfastly refused to acknowledge the enclitic *mem* in Hebrew. Its proponents never show its proper use in its home territory, never explain what makes this affix idiomatically correct in one context in Ugaritic but incorrect in another, or what would make it idiomatically acceptable at one place in Hebrew but not in another. Some conventions, implicit or explicit, must have governed the enclitic in Ugaritic, but no one has spelled them out. We are given only proposals about specific passages in which an inconvenient masculine plural noun or third-person masculine plural pronoun or a preposition is corrected to an enclitic *mem*.[34] I object, and I will not buy.

In a few places, I have accepted meanings for words that are best attested in other Northwest Semitic languages. The problem of meaning is very intricate, and I am not always satisfied with proposals of denotations and connotations. The vocabulary of the Book of Job is very complex, with a larger proportion of words not found elsewhere in classical Hebrew than any other biblical book. In some places, I have been unable to arrive at a decision about possible meanings and have left words untranslated, with the conventional three-dot ellipsis marking each word. That seems to me better than sprinkling a text with question marks, or omitting question marks and giving a dishonest illusion of accuracy. Printing an ellipsis, moreover, prevents my even attempting to base an interpretation on a word whose meaning I say publicly I do not know.

The Hebrew Text of Job

That brings me to the text of Job. I have translated and read the Hebrew text of Job, that is, the received text of the Masoretic tradition.

That statement must be qualified. The Masoretic text contains three important aspects: the consonantal text, the vowel pointings, and the marginalia. The consonantal text reflects the long centuries of copying from the autographs down to the Middle Ages, when the textual tradition was fixed by the scholars the Jewish tradition calls Masoretes. Among other things, the Masoretes supplied the consonantal text with vowel signs, which, save for certain consonants that came in certain forms to designate vowels, it did not have. The vowels were added to the text, it seems, in a way that preserved the pronunciations used in contemporary synagogues and that presented the language in the morphology current at that time. It is more than probable that the morphology and pronunciation were not identical to what they had been some eight or nine centuries earlier when, we may suppose, the Book of Job was written.

We must, therefore, differentiate between the consonantal text and the "pointed" (i.e., voweled) text. I have made every effort not to introduce changes into the consonantal text, except where on infrequent occasions it seems to me copyists misdivided words, attaching consonants that belong on one word to an adjacent one. I have not been nearly so tender with the pointed text, feeling rather free to revise the reading the vowels imply on the supposition that pronunciation was fluid as centuries passed and perceptions of forms changed.

As for the marginalia, most of it is statistical, and I have paid little attention to it. But sometimes the Masoretes pointed out places where the vowels they put in the text implied consonants different from what were there. The word implied by the consonants alone is called *Ketīb*, Aramaic for "what is written," and the word given by the added vowels is called *Qerē*, Aramaic for "what is read." The latter was expected to be pronounced when the text was read aloud in the synagogue. The consonantal text, having been handed down, as the Masoretes and other pious Jews believed, under divine protection, could not be altered and was sacred—though being sacred did not necessarily keep it from being mistaken.[35] Many of these Ketib-Qere pairs are relatively unimportant, as in 21.20, where the Ketib has *'ynw* (= *'ēnō*), "his eye," but the Qere is *'ēnayw*, "his eyes."

Sometimes the problem is greater. At 21.13, Job is propounding the thesis that wicked people have it better in this life than do good people. According to the Ketib of the first line, he says, "They wear out [*yᵉballū*] their days with good," a vividly sarcastic way of describing the experience of wicked people. The Qere requires a different second consonant in the word, *yᵉkallū*, which gives a rather bland, uninteresting sentence: "They end their days with good." The Ketib is so much more colorful than the Qere that I cannot understand why anyone would adopt the latter.[36]

I adopted or rejected the Qere depending on what makes the best sense in the context. But if the Qere requires a modification of the consonantal text (sometimes it does not), I incline to reject it for that reason.

Sometimes the difference between the Ketib and the Qere is of real moment. Such an instance is the famous line in 13.15, which the KJV, reading the Qere, has "Behold, though he slay me, yet will I trust in him." The RSV, reading the Ketib, has "Behold, he will slay me; I have no hope." Two readings more opposed in meaning are hard to imagine. The consonantal text behind the KJV's "in him" and the RSV's "no" is *l'*, pronounced *lō*, and meaning "not." One can understand how pious Jews would not care for that sentiment and would cast around for something else. The Qere is a word pronounced the same as the Ketib, *lō*, but spelled *lw*, meaning "to him." It is not really satisfactory, because objects of the verb used do not take the preposition *l^e^* (nor does the verb even remotely mean "trust" as the KJV committee had it). In this case, syntax and grammar make the Ketib preferable. In addition, the KJV's reading makes little sense in the context.

I have not investigated all the variant readings implied in the ancient translations of Job. Their relevance is at best doubtful. The ancient translators were concerned not with meticulous accuracy in turning the original text into their own languages but with presenting truth for the edification of their religious communities. People translated the Bible not for literary reasons but for religious ones. Some studies of the Septuagint version of Job have perceived profound theological reasons behind its wording (not to mention that the Septuagint does not contain some sizable pieces of the Hebrew text).[37] In the same ways, religious bent informs the other ancient translations, as it does modern ones (mine included, let me admit). In the face of the predilections of translators to find in a text what they already know to be true, these translations are useless for correcting the Hebrew text of Job. We come no closer to the original text but simply land ourselves in a morass of the varying truths held by ancient groups, both Christian and Jewish. These groups had every right to read the Bible as they wished, and it is no surprise to find that the various translations reflect the ways in which cultures and subcultures around the Mediterranean read and understood the Bible.

Thus, even though we may suppose that an ancient translator was looking at a Hebrew word or phrase different from the one now in the Masoretic text, to identify the Hebrew word or words is an enterprise crammed with guesses. And guesses do not add up to knowledge.[38] We are left with a Hebrew text that itself has undergone some changes, that is frequently puzzling and sometimes unintelligible, and we must simply make do.

I have worked with the consonantal Hebrew text and assumed that the vowels are probably right unless they seem too far from what is reasonable. At three places I have changed the consonantal text, marking each in the translation with an asterisk: in 24.5, in the interests of sense, I changed "for him food" (*lō leḥem*) to "for food" (*laleḥem*); in 35.14 I changed a third-person masculine singular pronoun into a second-person masculine singular; and in 39.21 I changed a plural verb form into a third-person masculine singular. Otherwise, if I could not make satisfactory sense of a word, phrase, or sentence, I have marked it with an ellipsis. And I rest no interpretive weight on the three changes I have made. In a few places I have also interpolated words in square brackets. In each case, the annotation explains why the Hebrew expression seems elliptical.

I take the liberty of setting the poetry of Job on the page according to the conventions of English poetry. Analyzing the poetry into lines and groups of lines allows, I think, a sense of the movement of the work, and it exhibits the parallelism that is so crucial a characteristic of this poetry. I also organize groups of lines into larger stanzas or strophes, delimited in the translation by spaces like those between the stanzas of an English poem. This formation of stanzas rests not on any theory of formal structures in Hebrew poetry—I do not hold one—but on my perceptions of appropriate divisions of sense, which often show marks of structure. For instance, in Job's first speech, chap. 3, the first stanza, verse 3, seems to me to function as an exclamatory cry, opening Job's curse. The next stanza, verses 4–10, calls down curses on Job's birthday and night of conception. Both the other two stanzas, verses 11–19 and 20–26, begin with the same interrogative, "why," introducing sets of questions that differ from each other. The decisions about the stanzas reflect both sense divisions and indications of rhetorical structure. As with other such decisions, they could have been different.

I am by no means the first to display Hebrew poetry in this way, but the Israelites themselves did not do so. The biblical manuscripts that survive do not present poetry on the page any differently from prose, though most modern editions of the Hebrew Bible arrange what their editors take to be poetry in lines. The typographical decision is an interpretive decision, for which I take full responsibility. It is a way, I believe, to make the Book of Job more accessible to readers of English, and I hope it may assist their appreciation of the book's literary power.

The Annotations

I have annotated the translation with notes keyed to chapter and verse numbers and, in boldface, to words in the text. These rather telegraphic annotations have two functions: first, they explain changes I have made and in general account for the translation. Many of them are intended to show my scholarly colleagues the reasons behind my translation, my perception of a problem, how I solve it, and my view of other solutions. Second, the annotations point to alternative and additional possibilities, competing and acceptable versions. They are there to make some small gestures toward dispelling my illusions of accuracy. In a few cases, I have argued with other scholars' treatments, but more often I have not cited others' opinions. The central point of the annotations is to exhibit the problems and the multiple options we have. I have not hesitated to use rather technical terms and procedures, and the reader who cannot use Hebrew will find some notes incomprehensible.

To give such assistance to those readers as I can, I append a short essay on Hebrew. Anyone who knows any Hebrew will see how rudimentary that section is and can forthwith skip over it, but I hope that it may help some readers to understand something they may otherwise miss.

I avoid substantial interpretative questions in the annotations, leaving them for the second part. I hope that the translation takes its readers further into the book than others may have done. The point of a book on Job is, of course, that its readers be moved into Job to see for themselves. The second part pursues how the Book of Job can be read to mean.

A Little Hebrew for the Hebrewless

The annotations to the translation often refer to the Hebrew text of Job. This may be frustrating to readers who know no Hebrew, but it ought not to bar them from getting something out of the notes. You must take on faith (1) that I do not tell you lies about the Hebrew language and (2) that the facts about the Hebrew text of Job that I state in the annotations are actually facts.

Below is the transliteration scheme I am using, and, for readers with an aural bent, some idea of pronunciation of this language.

Transliteration	Hebrew letter		Pronunciation
'	א	Aleph	light glottal stop, a slight grunt
b	ב	Beth	b (when preceded by a vowel, v, unless doubled)

Transliteration	Hebrew letter		Pronunciation
g	ג	Gimel	g (as in "go")
d	ד	Daleth	d (when preceded by a vowel, th as in "that," unless doubled)
h	ה	He	h (usually silent at the end of a word)
w	ו	Waw	w (pronounced v in modern Hebrew)
z	ז	Zayin	z
ḥ	ח	Ḥeth	like German ch
ṭ	ט	Ṭeth	t (a t made with tongue on palate)
y	י	Yod	y (silent when preceded by i or e)
k	כ ך	Kaph	k (when preceded by a vowel, like heavy German ch, unless doubled)
l	ל	Lamed	l
m	מ ם	Mem	m
n	נ ן	Nun	n
s	ס	Samek	s
ʿ	ע	Ayin	heavy glottal stop, grunt in the throat
p	פ ף	Pe	p (when preceded by a vowel, f, unless doubled)
ṣ	צ ץ	Tsadhe	ts
q	ק	Qoph	throaty k, halfway between k and g
r	ר	Resh	r
ś	שׂ	Sin	s (just like Samek)
š	שׁ	Shin	sh
t	ת	Taw	t (when preceded by a vowel, th as in "thin," unless doubled)

Those are the consonants. The Hebrew alphabet is all consonants, though in later times *he*, *waw*, and *yod* (in some instances also *aleph*) stood for vowels. In the Middle Ages, vowel signs were added to the text, and the following are my transliterations of them:

Transliteration	Pronunciation
a	ah (this covers two Hebrew vowels, a grammatically short *a* and a grammatically long one; since no difference in pronunciation is known, I use one transliteration, with apologies to purists, who may want to know whether the sign is for the long vowel or the short one)
ē	ey in "grey"
e	e in "set"
ī	e in "evil"
i	i in "sit"
ō	o in "home"
o	o in "off"
ū	u in "rude"
u	u in "put"
^{e}	half-vowel, a in "affect"
^{a}	half-vowel, a in "about"
^{o}	half-vowel, o in "observe"

The last three are the type of vowel that linguists call a schwa after its Hebrew name, *shewa* (accent the final syllable).

On the whole, the accent falls on the final syllable of a word. Verb forms with some suffixes are accented on the next-to-last syllable, as are some nouns, especially those with the short vowel "e" in the last syllable (e.g., the noun *melek*, "king," is accented on *me-*, *ḥōšek*, "darkness," on *ḥō-*).

Hebrew words, both verbs and nouns, are constructed around roots, each of which consists of a group of (usually three) consonants. I will illustrate with the root *šmr* (you may pronounce it *šamar*), which has to do with guarding, keeping, watching over. The three root consonants, *shin*, *mem*, and *resh*, appear in every form, always in the same order (the few exceptions need not concern us). The verb occurs in all its forms; e.g., *šamartī* is something like "I watched," whereas *yišmōr* is "he watches," *šᵉmōr* is "watching," and *šōmēr* is "someone who (or something that) watches, a watcher." Nouns are derived from the same root; *šomrah* is a "guard or watch," *šᵉmūrah* an "eyelid" (what "guards" the eye), *šimmurīm* apparently a "night watch or vigil." Other forms have suffixes and/or affixes, such as *mišmar*, "custody or the custodian, a sentinel," and *mišmeret* (accent the next-to-last syllable), "something preserved, a duty or obligation." Certain consonants were weak enough that they tended to disappear in certain forms, so that roots with *yod*, *waw*, and *he* often sport rather confusing forms.

Nouns

There are two genders, masculine and feminine. Many, but not all, feminine singular nouns end in *-ah* (probably originally *-at*). There is no masculine singular ending. The masculine plural ending is *-īm*, and the feminine plural is *-ōt*. Sometimes those forms force other vowel changes in the word. For example, the plural of *melek*, "king," is *mᵉlakīm*.

The definite article, the syllable *ha-*, is prefixed to the noun and usually doubles the noun's initial consonant. Thus "a book" is *sēper*, "the book" *hassēper*. There are other ways of asserting a noun's definiteness, and it is sometimes implied in the translation when no Hebrew definite article is present.

Nouns and adjectives (which act very much like nouns) agree in number, gender, and definiteness, and the adjective usually follows the noun, as in French. "Large books" would be *sᵉparīm gᵉdōlīm*, whereas "the large books" is *hassᵉparīm haggᵉdōlīm*. Feminine adjectives have the usual *-ah* ending in the singular and *-ōt* in the plural.

Verbs

The mainstay of the Hebrew language is the verb, and the verbal system is by far the most complex element in the language. It is not necessary to set forth the entire system, but several comments are in order.

Tenses. The verb appears in two typical finite forms, for which the term *tenses* is somewhat misleading and both of which contain their pronominal subjects. (Thus the addition of an independent pronoun to a verbal form with a pronoun subject indicates a very emphatic meaning.) One form has its pronouns in suffixes, the other has them in prefixes (and, in some forms, also in suffixes). The suffixed form (e.g., *šamartī* above, often called the "perfect" tense) presents the action of the verb as complete, whereas the prefixed form (e.g., *yišmōr*, the "imperfect" tense) presents it as incomplete. But "complete" does not mean "past," nor does "incomplete" mean future. The Hebrew verb form, unlike the English one, does not contain a necessary time reference.[39] That makes translating Hebrew into English difficult, because, as I noted above, the moment the translator writes down an English verb, the damage of necessary time reference is already done. I remarked above that my translation probably has too much of the present tense, because the present is the English tense most ambiguous about the time of the action. "I go" may mean "I am now going," "I often go," "I regularly go about this time of day," or "I will go at some time not too far in the future."

Verbal nouns. Some grammarians argue that the participle is sometimes a true present tense, as in modern Hebrew. I have never seen an instance of it that persuaded me. The participle in Hebrew is the verbal noun of the actor, the person or thing doing the action (e.g., *šōmēr* above, "watcher"), and it may appear in either gender and in plurals. The infinitive is the verbal noun of the abstract action, and it does not change gender or number. The Hebrew infinitive is very close to the English gerund in meaning, e.g., *šᵉmōr*, "watching."

Stems. The two "tenses," the imperatives, the participle, and the infinitives appear in several patterns of forms ("stems"), some active, some passive, some approximately reflexive, some with more than one mood (e.g., the *Niph'al* can be reflexive or passive). Some stems are formed by doubling the second of the three root consonants, and some of these doubled stems suggest an intensification of the action. For example, the root *ntq* seems to mean to tear something away or draw someone away from something, whereas the active double-consonant stem (called the *Pi'el*; for some types of verb, it is called Polel or Pilpel) has to do with tearing up things, lacerating, pulling up roots, a somewhat intensified sense. The passive is *Pu'al* (or Polal for some classes of verbs); a reflexive or iterative *Hithpa'el* (or Hithpolel). Another stem is sometimes called "causative." For some verbs, like *sbb*, which means basically "to turn around, circle," the "causative" active stem (*Hiph'il*) often means "to make something do something circular," cause people to go in circles, build a wall around something, or the like. Sometimes the Hiph'il stem turns an intransitive verb into a transitive one (as does the Pi'el). The verb *npl*, "to fall" in the simple (*Qal*) stem, becomes in the Hiph'il "to fell (something like a tree)"—that is, "to cause it to fall." *Str*, which is "to be secret or hidden" in the Qal, is "to hide something" in Hiph'il. The passive of Hiph'il is *Hoph'al.*

In dealing with a language structured so differently from English, we must sometimes suspend our assumptions about how words go together to make thoughts. To be sure, in Job we are dealing mostly with poetry, and one characteristic of poetry in any language is a density of style, where words carry a heavy weight of connotation and allusion and much can be said in few words. Yet even prose may contain its hazards. I have translated the first half of Job 1.4 as:

His [Job's] sons used to have feasts, each one being host on his day.

The sentence, reproducing the Hebrew word order and hyphenating where one Hebrew word covers two or more English ones, would be:

And-they-walk his-sons and-they-make feast house (of)-man his-day.
Wᵉhalᵉkū banayw wᵉ'aśū mišteh bět 'īš yōmō.

The verb precedes the subject, though this sentence has a compound verbal predicate. In translating, I decided that "they walk" (*halᵉkū* —the *wᵉ* at the beginning is "and") is an idiom meaning to do something regularly or habitually (therefore "used to"), that to "make" (*'aśū*) a feast (*mišteh*) means to have one (the verb can mean "do," as in "do lunch"), that "house" (*bēt*) refers to the place where the "feast" was held, that "of [a] man" (*'īš*) means "each man," and that "his day" (*yōmō*) refers (1) to the time when the "feast" was held and (2) to the birthday of the one in whose house the feast was held. I also allow the "perfect" tenses in "walk" and "make" to refer to regular past actions. The language is mildly elliptical, even in Hebrew. We might have expected a preposition, such as "in," with "house" and even the same preposition with "his day." This sentence is not particularly difficult, yet to make something English of it takes some gyrations.

In the annotations, I ordinarily give the vowels of nouns, but I sometimes refer to verbs and their forms with only the consonants that are in the Hebrew text or with the root consonants. That is to some extent conventional in scholarly writing, but the convention can be flouted if it seems confusing.

The Book of Job

A Translation

For complete authors' names, titles, and publication data, see the Bibliography, pp. 445–65. For complete forms of abbreviations used here, see the List of Abbreviations, pp. xiii–xiv.

[1] **Scrupulously moral.** I take *tam w*^{e}*yašar*, "perfect and moral," as a hendiadys, a figure of speech in which two terms denote only one subject. The usual English translation of *yašar* is "upright," but the metaphor in the word seems not vertical but horizontal, what is straight, flat, or even.

religious. *Y*^{e}*rēʾ ʾ*^{e}*lōhīm*, "one who fears Elohim." In a number of passages in the Hebrew Bible, "to fear the deity" describes less an emotion than a disposition to fulfill one's duties to the deity. That disposition, basic to religion, doubtless includes a component of fright.

[3] **A great many slaves.** The Hebrew phrase, *ʿ*^{a}*buddah rabbah*, is an unusual abstraction for a group of slaves. We might say "a large slaveholding." In Gen 26.14, the same phrase describes Isaac's wealth as a "blessing" from Yahweh.

[4] **Day.** The expression might mean only that the sons held feasts in turn, but the fact that in 3.1 "day" must mean "birthday" may suggest a series of birthday parties. I know of no evidence that the ancient Israelites celebrated birthdays, but *hiqqīpū* in v. 5 (see **Cycle of feast days** below) implies that the feasts followed an annual cycle.

invite. Here and in v. 5 (see **sanctify them** below, v. 5), I take *šlḥ*, "send," as part of a hendiadys ("send and call" = invite). But in v. 11, I render the same kind of hendiadys in "send [put out] your hand and touch" literally in order to match the phrase "put your hand" in v. 12.

[5] **Cycle of feast days.** The verb *hiqqīpū* suggests the completion of a cycle, and

The Book of Job

1 [1]Once there was a man in the country of Uz named Job, a man scrupulously moral, religious, one who avoided evil. [2]Seven sons and three
daughters were born to him, [3]and he owned seven thousand sheep and
three thousand camels, five hundred span of oxen, five hundred female
asses, and a great many slaves. So that man was one of the greatest people
of the East.

[4]His sons used to have feasts, each one being host on his day, and they
would invite their three sisters to eat and drink with them. [5]When the
cycle of feast days was complete, Job would sanctify them, getting up
early in the morning and offering sacrifices for each one. For Job said,

---

therefore I take *y^{e}me hammišteh*, "days of the feast," collectively. "Every cycle of feast days," at the end of the verse, is *kol-hayyamīm*, "all the days." The phrase can be taken in its colloquial sense of "all the time," meaning that Job did it for every occasion. "Cycle" carries the thought that Job sacrificed on behalf of his children only once a year.

sanctify them. I take *yišlaḥ . . . way^{e}qadd^{e}šēm* ("he sent . . . and sanctified them") as a hendiadys. Jacob (p. 278) argues that *šlḥ wqdš* means that Job invited ("sent for," as in v. 4) his children to a religious observance after the cycle of their secular feasts. "Them" can refer either to the children or to the "days." For the verb *qdš* as making a religious occasion holy, see, e.g., Gen 2.3; Exod 20.11 (the Sabbath); 2 Ki 10.20 (an assembly, *'^{a}śarah*); and Joel 1.14; 2.15 (a fast, *ṣōm*).

sacrifices. *'ōlōt*, "burnt offerings," are aimed at expiation for sin.

blessed. *Brk*, "to bless," is used in these two chapters both positively, "to bless" (1.10, 21), and negatively, "to curse" (1.11; 2.5, 9). Most translators take the verb here as "curse." The problem is considered in Chap. 2 below. In "blessed Elohim sinfully," I again take the two verbs *ḥṭ'* and *brk* as a hendiadys: "Perhaps my children have sinned and blessed Elohim in their hearts."

Elohim. Rather than translate the various terms for the deity, I transliterate them. Elohim is the most common Hebrew word for the deity, odd mainly because, though plural in form (*Eloah*, which occurs often in Job, is its singular), it takes singular adjectival and verbal forms.

in their hearts. The heart in ancient psychology is the location of thinking, deciding, intending. From our standpoint, the faculty being used is the mind, but we place the mind in the brain, as the Hebrews did not. The Hebrew word here is singular, not plural (*l^{e}babam*, not *libbōtam*).

6 **Elohim's sons.** It is difficult to decide whether "sons" is used here in its ordinary generational sense, or whether it means a category of beings (e.g., "people of the East," v. 3, is in Hebrew "sons of East," Easterners). It denotes members of the divine court, and JPS's "divine beings" seems accurate.

Yahweh. The Israelite deity's proper name occurs often in the tale (chaps. 1–2; 42.7–17) and several times in the dialogue between Job and the deity (38.1; 40.1, 3, 6; 42.1), but only once in the dialogue between Job and the friends (12.9).

7 **the Prosecutor.** *Haśśaṭan* is often transliterated as Satan, the proper name of the principle of evil, an identification that occurred in Judaism long after Job was written. The definite article on the word makes it a title here and in Zech 3.1–2 (without the article in 1 Chron 21.1, it looks like a proper name, though it may be indefinite). The term can be used of an ordinary adversary or opponent (e.g., 1 Sam 29.4; 1 Ki 11.14) or of an extraordinary one (the "angel of Yahweh," Num 22.22). Both Zech 3 and our passage imply that in the divine court this character had the function of searching out malefactors and bringing them to trial as a kind of divine prosecuting attorney. See Terrien, *Job*, p. 55; Lacocque, p. 35; and Day.

8 **Given thought to.** Hebrew "set your heart on" reveals the function of the heart as the seat of thinking.

9 **Religious.** Hebrew uses a verb: "Does Job fear Elohim?" See annotation to 1.1.

10 **Burst out.** The verb *prṣ* ordinarily means to make a breach in something, as in troops bursting through a city wall (see 2 Ki 14.13). In 16.14, Job uses the verb with its nominal cognate to describe Yahweh's attack on him.

11 **If he doesn't curse you to your face—.** The verb is *brk*; see the note to v. 5. The Hebrew expression is an incomplete sentence. I argued in "Job and the Literary Task" (p. 475) that this is a formula of self-curse: "If A (or not A), then B," in which "B" is the result that the curser calls down; e.g., "If (A) I tell a lie, (B) may my nose grow longer." The result clause (B) is almost always omitted. See Blank, "Curse."

12 **All right.** The interjection *hinnēh* is usually rendered "Behold!" but no etymological evidence suggests that it refers to sight.

"Perhaps my children have blessed Elohim sinfully in their hearts." Job
did this for every cycle of feast days.

6 It was the day when Elohim's sons came to take their places by Yahweh, and the Prosecutor also came among them. 7 Yahweh said to the
Prosecutor, "Where have you come from?"

The Prosecutor answered Yahweh, "From roving around the earth and
going here and there."

8 Yahweh said to the Prosecutor, "Have you given thought to my servant Job? There's certainly no one like him on the earth, a scrupulously
moral man, religious, one who avoids evil."

9 The Prosecutor answered, "Is Job religious for nothing? 10 Haven't
you yourself hedged around him and his family and all he has, blessed
anything his hands do, so that his possessions burst out over the earth?
11 Then put out your hand and touch all he has. If he doesn't curse you to
your face—"

12 Yahweh said, "All right, all that he has is in your hand; but on
him don't put your hand." And the Prosecutor went out from Yahweh's
presence.

13 It was the day when Job's sons and daughters were eating and drink-
ing wine at the home of their eldest brother. 14 And a messenger came to
Job and said, "The oxen were plowing, the asses grazing nearby, 15 and
Sheba fell on them and took them, killing the servants with swords. And
I escaped all alone to tell you."

16 He was still speaking when another came and said, "Elohim's fire fell
from the sky and burned the flocks and the servants, burned them up.
And I escaped all alone to tell you."

17 He was still speaking when another came and said, "The Chaldeans
formed into three bands and dashed in on the camels and took them, killing the servants with swords. And I escaped all alone to tell you."

---

15 **Sheba.** Sheba was at the southern end of the Arabian Peninsula, where Yemen now is, but these Sabeans may be related north-Arabian groups. Unlike "Chaldeans," v. 17, the word is not gentilic in form.

17 **Chaldeans.** In the late seventh century B.C.E., after the Assyrian empire had crumbled, Chaldean tribes took control of Babylonia in southern Mesopotamia, and the Chaldean dynasty, which lasted until perhaps 540 B.C.E., was responsible for the Babylonian Exile of the Jews. Earlier, the Chaldeans were apparently seminomadic tribes, known in the Babylonian area only from the ninth century onward, and it is a bit strange to hear of them so far west as the Edomite territory implied by our story.

19 **Smashed.** The Prosecutor challenged Yahweh in v. 11 to "touch [*ga'*] all that he has"; here, in a grim understatement, which my translation masks, the wind "touched [*yigga'*] the four corners of the house."

youngsters. *N^e'arīm* is a puzzling word. Each of the other reports says that the "servants" (*n^e'arīm*) are killed. Here the house falls on the *n^e'arīm*, and Job's response makes it clear that he understands that his children are dead. Because *n^e'arīm* is an ordinary word for servants and for sons but not for daughters, some interpreters have argued that only Job's sons are killed.

20 **Tore his robe**, etc. The conventional response of mourning.

21 **Naked I came out**, etc. I have given this familiar quatrain a somewhat jiggy meter, because the verse feels to me rather conventionally pious.

4 **Skin up to skin**. The preposition *b^e'ad* means primarily "beyond" or "up to" (a boundary). I find no parallels to the frequently used idea of exchange. The expression is as puzzling in Hebrew as it is in English. I use "up to" to match the same preposition in "right up to his life."

the man. *Ha'īš*, referring to Job in particular, not to men in general.

7 **Sores.** Job's malady cannot be identified medically. The most recent attempt I have seen, Schoental's (pp. 119–20), diagnoses pellagra on the basis of dermatitis, diarrhea, and dementia (which he turns into depression). It depresses me when people assume that ancient fiction describes symptoms clinically enough to permit modern diagnosis of the hero's actual complaint. Schoental interprets *š^{e}ḥīn*, which seems to refer generally to skin inflammation, to mean itching but gives no evidence.

9 **You're still holding**, etc. The statement, modified to the second-person address, is identical to what Yahweh says to the Prosecutor in v. 3. The Hebrew has no interrogative marker, but most scholars think this statement has the feel of a question.

10 **Fool.** "You're talking as one of the [feminine plural] fools talk."

we receive good, etc. All translations render this as a question, though no interrogative particle or prefix requires it. Only Jacob (p. 281) among the accounts I know allows the possibility of an indicative. The decision between statement and question is an interpretive one, and the two forms propose quite different meanings.

11 **From Teman**, etc. Because the sentence emphasizes that each has come from "his own place," I have turned the Hebrew gentilics ("Temanite," "Shuchite," etc.), awkward in English, into their corresponding place-names.

18 He was still speaking when another came and said, "Your sons and
daughters were eating and drinking wine at the home of their eldest
brother, 19 and—Ah!—a huge wind came across the desert and smashed
into the four corners of the house, and it fell on the youngsters, and
they're dead. And I escaped all alone to tell you."
20 Job got up and tore his robe, shaved his head, and fell prostrate to
the ground. 21 He said,

Naked I came out at birth,
and naked I'll return.
Yahweh gave, and Yahweh took;
Yahweh's name be blest.

22 In all this, Job did not sin or accuse Elohim of anything unworthy.

2 1 It was the day when Elohim's sons came to take their places by Yahweh, and the Prosecutor also came among them, taking his place by Yahweh. 2 Yahweh said to the Prosecutor, "Where have you come from?"
The Prosecutor answered, "From roving around the earth and going
here and there."
3 Yahweh said, "Have you given thought to my servant Job? There's
certainly no one like him on earth, a scrupulously moral man, religious, a
person who avoids evil. He is still holding to his integrity, even though
you urged me against him to swallow him up for nothing."
4 The Prosecutor answered, "Skin up to skin! Everything the man has
he will give over, right up to his life. 5 Then put out your hand and touch
his bone and his flesh. If he doesn't curse you to your face—"
6 Yahweh said, "All right, he is in your hand; but protect his life." 7 And
the Prosecutor went out from Yahweh's presence.
He struck Job with dreadful sores from the sole of his foot to the top of
his head, 8 and he took a potsherd to scrape himself. There he was, sitting
in the middle of the ash heap.
9 His wife said to him, "You're still holding to your integrity? Curse
Elohim and die!"
10 He said, "You're talking like a fool! We receive good from Elohim
and do not receive evil." In all this Job did not sin with his lips.
11 Three of Job's friends heard about all the evil that had come upon
him, and each one came from his own place, Eliphaz from Teman, Bildad
from Shuach, and Zophar from Na'amah. They agreed together to come
and console and comfort him. 12 When they raised their eyes from a dis-

[1] **Started to speak.** "Opened his mouth."
day. From what follows it is clear that the word refers to Job's birthday.
[4] **Let there be darkness.** *Y^e^hī ḥōšek* alludes to Gen 1.3, *y^e^hī 'ōr*, "let there be light."
Eloah. This term for the deity, occurring 41 times in Job but rarely elsewhere, is the singular of Elohim.
[5] **Avenge.** A case can be made for "redeem" or "reclaim," darkness taking the light back. The only other occurrence of *g'l* in Job (19.25) has, I think, this sense of taking vengeance.
blackness of day. Reading *kamrīrē* for MT *kimrīrē*, "like bitternesses," though Grabbe (pp. 30–31) demonstrates how slim the evidence for *kmr* = "black" is. Gordis (*Book of Job*, p. 33) takes *kimrīrē yōm* as "demons of the day."
[6] **Rejoice.** The form, *yiḥadd*, suggests that the verb is *ḥdh*, "to rejoice," as in Exod 18.9. Repointing to *yēḥad*, from the verb *yḥd*, produces "to be counted, numbered," which also makes good sense. Blommerde (*Northwest Semitic Grammar*, p. 38), wanting synonymity of parallelism, takes that form as Niph'al of *ḥdh[y]* = *ḥzh[y]*, "to see," meaning "may it not appear." Gordis (*Book of Job*, p. 34) adduces the Rabbinic principle of *talḥīn* (simultaneous double meanings) to urge that both "rejoice" and "be counted" are meant. I cannot say what the author meant, but a double (or triple) meaning is always interesting.
[8] **Sea.** With most interpreters, I repoint *yōm*, "day," to *yam*. The two words would have been spelled identically, and "day" makes perfectly good sense in the context. I choose "Sea" as a slightly closer parallel with Leviathan. "Sea" is not a mere ocean but the divinity Yamm, well known from Canaanite mythic texts.
[10] **Or hide.** The negative in the first line also governs the verb in the second.
[12] **Why.** This "why," *maddūa'*, is not the same as *lammah* in vv. 11, 20.
[13] **Now . . . then.** The Hebrew expression is odd, and some interpreters, repairing it, assume that "then" (*'az*) means "now," and some suppose that "now" (*'attah*) means "then."

tance, they didn't recognize him, and they raised their voices, weeping. Each tore his robe, and they sprinkled dust on their heads toward the sky.
13 They sat with him on the ground for seven days and nights, and none spoke a word to him, because they could see that his pain was very great.

3 1 After that, Job started to speak and cursed his day, 2 and he spoke thus:

3 Perish the day on which I was born,
the night that said, "A man is conceived!"

4 That day, let there be darkness,
may Eloah not seek it from above
or daylight beam over it.
5 May darkness and thick gloom avenge it,
clouds settle down upon it,
blackness of day terrify it.
6 That night, may dusk take it,
may it not rejoice among the year's days,
not arrive among the months' number.
7 Ah, that night, may it be barren,
no cry of pleasure come in it.
8 May those who put spells on Sea curse it,
those skilled at rousing Leviathan.
9 May its evening stars be dark,
wait for light and see nothing,
no sight of dawn's eyelids,
10 because it did not close the belly's doors
or hide toil from my eyes.

11 Why was I not dead from the womb,
come out from the belly and perish?
12 Why did knees receive me
and breasts, so I could suckle?
13 For now I would have quietly lain down,
would be asleep; then I'll have rest
14 with kings and the country's counselors
who built themselves ruins,
15 or with princes who possessed gold,
filled their houses with silver.

[16] **I was not.** I think this sentence presumes the interrogative *lammah*, "why," in v. 11 (so, e.g., JPS).

[17] **Weary in power.** Gordis (*Book of Job*, p. 38) takes the phrase as an objective genitive, "exhausted by violence, hence victims of oppression." Influenced by "wicked" in the prior line, I read a subjective genitive with an opposite meaning, "those wearied by exerting power." Either seems to me all right.

[21] **More than for concealed treasure.** The comparative is one usage of the preposition *min*, but "among" is another. "Dig for him among the concealed things" (*maṭmōnīm*) echoes the "concealed [*ṭamūn*] miscarriage," v. 16a. I have intruded "treasure" anachronistically from our images of piracy.

[22] **Burial mound.** I repoint MT *gīl* to *gal*. The former produces the phrase "who rejoice to exultation," a seemingly redundant phrase that occurs in Hos 9.1.

[23] **Or for a man.** The sentence continues from v. 20, whose verb governs this clause.
hedged around. The expression, *yasek ʼ^{e}lōah baʻ^{a}dō*, is nearly identical to that in 1.10, where the verb is spelled with *sin*: *h^{a}lōʼ ʼatta śakta baʻ^{a}dō*.

[24] **Before my bread.** *Lipnēy* can mean temporal precedence or spatial presence "in front of," and I would accept either.
bellowing. The word denotes "roaring" as by a lion.

[2] **Up to it.** The word seems to signify "to be unable," a nice antonym to "be able" in the second line. It occurs again in v. 5, where I have translated it "falter."

[3] **Many.** Ceresko (*Job 29–31*, p. 157) suggests that *rabbīm* here means "the great" or "the aged."

[6] Many translations of the second line omit the "and" on "integrity." I take *yir'atka*, "your religion" ("your fear"; see 1.1), as the subject.

[7] **Moral people.** See the comment on *yašar* in 1.1.

16 Or, like a concealed miscarriage, I was not,
like infants who never see light.
17 There wicked people stop their turmoil,
there those weary in power have rest,
18 prisoners take their ease together,
not hearing the oppressor's voice.
19 Small and great alike are there,
and a slave is freed from his lord.

20 Why is there light for a toiler
and life for bitter souls
21 who long for Death, and he's not there,
dig for him more than for concealed treasure,
22 who rejoice over the burial mound,
gladly discover the grave;
23 or for a man whose way is hidden,
whom Eloah has hedged around?
24 For my groaning comes before my bread,
my bellowing pours forth like water.
25 For I was terrified of something, and it arrived,
what I feared comes to me.
26 I am neither tranquil nor quiet,
and I have no rest; turmoil comes.

4 1 Eliphaz the Temanite answered thus:
2 If someone tries a word to you, are you up to it?
And who can restrain talk?
3 Think how you have corrected many,
strengthened weak hands.
4 Your talk has raised the stumbler,
you have braced up tottering knees.
5 But now it comes to you, and you falter,
touches against you, and you've panicked.
6 Is not your religion your confidence,
your hope, and the integrity of your ways?
7 Think, who that was innocent has perished,
where have moral people been destroyed?
8 As I have seen, those who plow iniquity
and sow toil harvest it too.

10–11 Five different Hebrew words for "lion" occur in these four lines (see the "Indispensable Introduction"). English has a more limited leonine vocabulary than Hebrew.

roar. The noun is the same as that in 3.24b.

15 **Hair.** The line has given some trouble, partly, perhaps, because the Targum reads *s*^{e}*‘arah*, "storm" (the same word as in 38.1), instead of *śa*$^{‘a}$*rah*, "hair." Paul's article is persuasive.

17 **More righteous.** The verb *ṣdq*.

hero. I do not like this translation of *geber* but can find nothing better. The word sometimes means a male with more than ordinary capacities, yet it often has no necessary ingredient of the unusual.

18 **He.** The sentence begins with *hēn*, a form of the interjection *hinnēh*, often rendered "behold." I noted above that the word has no essential connection to sight, and I have not translated it here.

19 **Disintegrate.** I repoint and redivide *y*^{e}*dakk*^{e}*’ūm lipnē*, "they crush them before," to *y*^{e}*dukk*^{e}*’ū millifnē*.

21 **Cord.** Only here does *yeter*, usually a bowstring or an animal sinew, seem to mean "tent cord." The verb *niśśa‘* is a technical term for pulling up tent stakes and setting out on a journey.

wisdom. The quotation that forms the major part of Eliphaz's vision begins in v. 17, but there is no clear indication where it ends.

3 **Cursed.** Commentators are uncomfortable with the first-person verb, as am I, nor am I certain of the meaning of "suddenly." The verb *nqb* has to do with piercing, and the sense "curse" might suggest putting spells on people.

4–5 If these lines are the content of the curse in v. 3, the verbs should be translated in the subjunctive, "May X happen," as in JPS.

9 They perish by Eloah's breath,
are finished by his nostril's wind.
10 The roar of a lion, the voice of the cub,
the teeth of young lions are broken off;
11 the cougar perishes without prey,
and the lion's children are separated.

12 I received a stolen word,
my ear took a whisper from it
13 in disturbances from night visions,
when deep sleep falls upon men.
14 Terror confronted me, and trembling,
and many of my bones shook in terror.
15 A wind swept across my face,
made the hair on my body bristle;
16 it stopped, I saw no shape.
Something before my eyes—
silence—and I heard a voice:
17 "Is a man more righteous than Eloah,
or a hero purer than his maker?
18 He does not trust even his slaves
and ascribes error to his messengers.
19 What then of those who dwell in clay houses,
whose foundations are in dust,
who disintegrate before a moth?
20 From morning to evening they are crushed,
without setting anything permanent they perish.
21 Is not their cord pulled out with them,
and they die? But not with wisdom."

5 1 Cry out, then. Will anyone answer?
To whom among the holy will you turn?
2 For passion murders the fool,
and jealousy kills the gullible.
3 I myself have seen a fool taking root,
and I cursed his shanty suddenly.
4 His sons go far from safety,
are crushed in the gate, no rescuer near.

[5] **Fasts.** I am persuaded by Gordis's etymology (*Book of Job*, p. 54).

[7] **The race.** *'adam* may signify "human" generically or Adam, the person in Gen 2–3. I take the former sense.

is born to. Many commentators repoint the passive *yūlad* to the causative *yōlīd*, "breeds," a diametrically opposite meaning.

Reshef's sons. Reshef was a Syrian deity of fire and plague; his sons are usually interpreted as sparks or as the fever associated with pestilence.

[8] **If it were I.** *'ūlam 'anī* implies both a strong adversative, "on the other hand," and an emphasis on the pronoun.

[13] **Hasty counsel.** I take *nimharah* as a Niph'al feminine participle in apposition to "counsel." Others call it a finite verb form.

[16–18] **And injustice**, etc. Gordis (*Book of Job*, p. 57) asserts that this and the four lines following are "based on" other passages. It is true that v. 16b is almost identical to Ps 107.42b, that v. 17a is very like Ps 94.12a, that v. 17b is nearly the same as Prov 3.11a, that v. 18a and Hos 6.1b are comparable, and that v. 18b is similar to Deut 32.39d (a misprint in Gordis gives 32.34). I am not sure that the textual comparison demonstrates borrowing. On the other hand, if Eliphaz is quoting, his slight inaccuracies do not increase our confidence in him.

[17] **Shaddai.** A divine epithet, the meaning of which is disputed. English versions usually use "Almighty," which no scholar seriously proposes now as its meaning. Some think the word is related to Akkadian *shadu*, mountain, and refers to a mountain deity, and others connect the word to the root *šdd*, having to do with destruction. Cross (*Canaanite Myth*, pp. 52–56) comes down solidly for the mountain, though he calls Shaddai the "most enigmatic" of all the divine epithets (p. 52).

[21] **Destruction.** Pope (*Job*, p. 45) repoints *šōd* to *šēd*, "demon," with some rather persuasive arguments. Note the sound echo of Shaddai, whatever vowels one prefers.

[22] **Fear.** The form is the usual one for a negative imperative.

5 What he harvests the famished eats,
and he takes what he has from thorns
and one who fasts pants for their strength.
6 For iniquity does not spring from dust,
nor does toil sprout from the ground,
7 but the race is born to toil,
and Reshef's sons fly high.

8 If it were I, I would seek for El,
to Elohim commit my cause,
9 who does great things, inscrutable,
wonderful things, innumerable,
10 gives rain across the land,
sends water on the countryside,
11 sets what is low up high,
what is gloomy raises to safety,
12 frustrates the schemes of the shrewd
so that their hands contrive no success,
13 catches the wise in their shrewdness,
the hasty counsel of the devious.
14 By day they encounter darkness
and grope at noon as at night.
15 He rescues the poor from the sword,
from their maw, and from the hard hand.
16 And hope comes to the weak,
and injustice shuts its mouth.

17 Ah, happy the man whom Eloah corrects;
do not despise Shaddai's discipline.
18 For he wounds, and he binds up;
pierces, and his hands heal.
19 In six troubles he will rescue you,
in seven, evil will not touch you.
20 In famine he redeems you from Death,
in war, from the sword's hands.
21 When tongue scourges, you'll be hid,
you'll not fear destruction that comes.
22 At destruction and hunger you'll laugh,
fear nothing from wild beasts;
23 for with the stones of the field is your treaty,
and the beasts of the field make peace with you.

[24] **Fold.** *Naweh* is a general word for dwelling, used in v. 3b. I use it in parallel to "tent" as the place where, in the pastoral context presumed by much of the poem, one's possessions are.

[26] **Vigor.** *Kelaḥ* occurs only here and in 30.2, and its meaning is uncertain. I follow Pope (*Job*, pp. 46–47) in thinking that "vigor" fits both passages.

[2] **Passion.** The same word (*ka'aś*) that Eliphaz used in 5.2.

disaster. Reading Qere, *hawwatī*; Ketib is *hayyatī*, "my being." (For an explanation of Qere and Ketib, see the "Indispensable Introduction.")

[4] **Whose poison.** I find no information about the use of poisoned arrows in ancient Near Eastern warfare. Terrien (*Job*, p. 80) refers the image to hunting rather than warfare. The referent of plural "whose" is the arrows.

[6] **Egg white.** The meaning of *ḥallamūt* is unknown. We want an edible substance that is both slimy and disgusting.

[7] **Throat.** This is not the only place where *nepeš* seems to have primary reference to the throat rather than to the "soul"; see Isa 5.14; Jon 2.6 (Eng. 5); and Eccl 6.7, among a great many other passages.

they. The independent pronoun in Hebrew makes this emphatic. Its probable referent is the unpleasant foods in vv. 5–6.

[9] **Free.** *Yattēr* can be derived either from *ntr*, "to jump up" and in Hiph'il "go free," or from an identical root that may mean "to fall" (perhaps in Job 37.1) and in Hiph'il "drop" (transitively). To drop the hand is clear enough. The other verb would imply that Job wishes the deity to release his hand from disciplined constraint.

[10] . . . Post-biblical Hebrew *sld* means to jump back from danger (see Pope, *Job*, p. 52; Gordis, *Book of Job*, p. 72), and LXX's *hēllomēn*, "I jumped," suggests it. Other scholars give variations on "exult." All the possibilities are too far from certainty to enable a decision.

[13] The rhetorical question of the first line implies an affirmative answer, "yes, there is help," which seems out of place in the context, and the second line reverses it. Perhaps these are not rhetorical questions.

[14] **Melts.** *Mas* is Qal participle of *mss*, "to melt" (the form does not occur elsewhere), and the preposition *l*^{e} is emphatic. The propriety of the metaphor of melting shows up in the references to ice and snow in v. 16 and the floods resulting from them in v. 15.

[24]You'll know that your tent is at peace,
will visit your fold and not miss anything.
[25]You'll know you have many descendants,
issue like the grass of the land.
[26]You'll come in vigor to the grave
as a ripe shock comes up when it's time.

[27]Oh, we have explored all this, it's true.
Hear it, and know for yourself.

6 [1]Job answered thus:
[2]If only my passion could be weighed,
my disaster laid with it in scales;
[3]for now it's heavier than sea sand,
therefore my words are wild.
[4]For Shaddai's arrows are with me,
whose poison my spirit drinks;
Eloah's terrors are ranged against me.

[5]Does the wild ass bray over his grass,
the ox low over his mash?
[6]Does one eat what is flat without salt?
Does egg white have any taste?
[7]My throat refuses to touch them;
they remind me of my repulsive bread.

[8]Would that what I ask would come,
that Eloah would give me my hope,
[9]would make up his mind and crush me,
free his hand and cut me down.
[10]It might yet be my consolation,
and . . . with strength, not hold back;
for I have not concealed the Holy One's words.

[11]What strength have I that I should wait?
What end, that I extend my life?
[12]Is my strength the strength of rock
or my flesh bronze?
[13]Is there no help for me,
is all success banished from me?

[14]Who melts away his loyalty from his friend
departs the fear of Shaddai.

[16]**Torrents.** The word is not repeated from v. 15b in Hebrew, and I repeat it only to clarify the referent.

[17]**Quenched.** A very curious image. Everywhere else the verb *d'k* means to extinguish a lamp or fire. Here the "heat" appears to be the context, perhaps even the agent (in = by), of extinction, and the streams themselves seem to be the subject. I wish the verb meant "dried up," as K-B holds, but I cannot really believe it.

[19]**Tema.** A city in northern Arabia, lying on the caravan routes.

Sheba. See the annotation to 1.15.

[20]**Ashamed, abashed.** One might expect stronger terms from the images of death in vv. 17–18.

[21]**That way.** One group of MSS reads *l'*, "not," as the Ketib, with *lw*, "to him, to it," as Qere; another group reads simply *lw*. In the latter reading, the phrase *hᵉyītem lō* is, roughly, "you [plur.] have become it."

stare, scared. A fine pun in Hebrew, *tirᵉ'ū* and *tīrᵉ'ū*.

[26]**Blow.** I take *lrwḥ* as an infinitive parallel to *lhwkḥ* in the preceding line, though *rūaḥ* can be the substantive "wind." In either case, the verb in the first line governs the second. To take *lrwḥ* as a noun requires that *tḥšbw*, the verb in the first line, mean simultaneously "scheme" and "consider."

desperate man. "Man" is there not for the sake of a masculine generic, but to suggest a pun in *nō'aš* with *'ᵉnōš*, "man."

[29]**Come back.** The verb, *šwb*, suggests that the friends have turned away, insulted by Job's sarcasm. The second occurrence is Qere, Ketib being *šby*, a feminine imperative.

at stake. "My innocence is still in it," perhaps in the entire situation, of which the friends' presence is a part.

[1]**Conscripted.** *Ṣaba'* refers primarily to military service, though the rest of the statement refers to slavery and wage labor. The ancient world had no positive evaluation of wage labor; the laborer was, if anything, less secure than the slave.

[3]**They apportion.** The referent of "they" is "months." A whole system of inheritance and its disposition is implied here.

15 My brothers are treacherous, like a wadi,
like torrents in wadis they vanish away,
16 torrents murky from ice
on which the snow was hid.
17 Time comes they're scorched, wiped out,
in its heat they're quenched from their place.
18 Caravans wrench away from the road,
go up to the waste and perish.
19 Tema's caravans are eager,
Sheba's travelers expectant.
20 They're ashamed because they trusted;
come to the place, they're abashed.

21 But now you act that way:
you stare at ruin, and you're scared.
22 But have I said, "Make me a deal,
from your strength bribe for me,
23 rescue me from the enemy's hand,
from terrorizers' hand get me off"?

24 Instruct me, and I'll be quiet.
How have I erred? Make me understand.
25 How offensive are honest words!
And how your indictment indicts!
26 Are you scheming to indict talk,
to blow at a desperate man's words,
27 even throw dice over an orphan,
make a trade over your friend?
28 But now, make up your minds, face me.
Would I lie to your faces?
29 Come back, now, let no wrong be done!
Come back, my innocence is at stake!
30 Is any wrong upon my tongue?
Does not my palate understand a disaster?

7 1 Is not a man conscripted on earth,
his days like those of a laborer,
2 like a slave who gasps for shade,
a laborer who counts on his work?
3 So I am bequeathed empty months,
and they apportion me toilsome nights.

[4] **Is measured.** I repoint *middad*, an active, to *muddad*.
gorged. Job does mix his metaphors, and this metaphor of being stuffed with food is not very successful.

[7] From here to the end of the speech, Job addresses the deity in the second-person singular. He speaks to the friends in the plural.

[8] **I'll not be there.** *'ēnennī*, "and none of me." The same word is the last word of the speech, v. 21d.

[9] **Sheol.** The place of the dead in the underworld. Like the Greek Hades, Sheol has no connotation of a place of punishment.

[11] **Shortened breath.** *Rūaḥ* has basically to do with breath, though it is often translated "spirit," and the verb *ṣr* proposes a narrowing. The image, in parallel with mouth and throat (see note to 6.7), is one of constriction.

[12] **Sea monster.** *Tannīn* may be not a general term for sea monster but a specific, named mythic creature. Diewert (pp. 204–9) cites the Ugaritic evidence.

[15] **Bones.** The expression is odd. Many commentators emend *mē'aṣmōtay*, "from my bones," to *mē'aṣbōtay*, "from my pains." Gordis (*Book of Job*, p. 81) takes "bones" as synecdoche for "frame, entire person," hence something like "my present existence." Sarna ("Some Instances," p. 109) redivides *mwt m'ṣmwty* to *mwtm 'ṣmwty*, the *mem* on the end of *mwt* being enclitic, meaning "the death of my bones." If that were the sense, *nepeš* would mean not "throat," which accords nicely with "suffocation," but "soul, self." On the other hand, *mōt* may point to mythological Death, associated in the Canaanite texts with dryness, who overcomes fertility and life. See Job's question whether he is Sea (Yamm), v. 12a.

[16] **Refuse.** The basic meaning of *m's* is "despise."

[17–18] A sarcastic parody of Ps 8.5: *mah-'*^{e}*nōš kī-tizk*^{e}*rennū / ūben-'adam kī tipq*^{e}*dennū*.

[20] **To myself.** Nearly everyone emends *'alay* to *'aleka*, "to you," because the remark as it stands seems illogical. Some commentators argue, with no evidence I can find, that this is one of the *tiqqūnē sōferīm*, corrections that scribes made in Rabbinic times in order to avoid blasphemy or unworthy statements about God.

4 If I lie down and say, "When can I get up?"
the evening is measured off,
and I'm gorged with tossing till dark.
5 My flesh is clothed with maggots,
crusted with dust,
my skin hardens and dissolves again.
6 My days go faster than a shuttle
and are finished at the end of hope.

7 Consider that my life's a wind,
my eye will not again see good.
8 No eye that looks will spy me;
your eyes will be on me, but I'll not be there.
9 A cloud is finished and goes;
so one descends to Sheol, does not come up,
10 never returns to his house,
and his place never recognizes him again.

11 And I, I will not restrain my mouth,
I'll speak with shortened breath,
complain with bitter throat.
12 Am I Sea or a sea monster
that you station a guard over me?
13 When I say, "My bed will comfort me,
my couch will ease my complaint,"
14 then you terrify me in dreams
and startle me from visions.
15 My throat prefers suffocation,
Death, more than my bones.
16 I refuse! I won't live forever.
Leave me alone, my days are a puff.

17 What's a man, that you magnify him so,
set your mind on him,
18 visit him every morning,
test him every moment?
19 How long will you not turn your gaze away,
let me be till I swallow my spit?

20 I sin. What have I done to you,
you watcher of men?
Why have you set me up as your target,
so I've become a burden to myself.

[21] **Lift.** The verb is cognate to *maśśa'*, "burden," in the previous line. To "lift guilt" might be to "forgive" it, but I leave the metaphor.
search. The verb has a lexical connection to *šaḥar*, "dawn," and I have pondered rendering it "you will dawn on me."
I won't be there. See v. 8b.

[3] **Bend.** Some commentators are troubled by the repetition of the verb, which most translate as "pervert." *'wt* denotes bending or turning something, but the bending in English "pervert" is a dead metaphor, and I prefer to keep the metaphor alive.
[4] **If.** Granted the evident allusion to the tale, this sentence might be either conditional or emphatic. Pope (*Job*, p. 64) and Gordis (*Book of Job*, pp. 86, 88) take it as the latter; Guillaume (*Studies*, p. 26), S. R. Driver and Gray (Pt. I, p. 76), and Fohrer (*Das Buch Hiob*, p. 183) as the former. Though appreciating Gordis's argument against rigid uniformity of meaning when a word recurs nearby, I take the three occurrences of *'im*, "if," in vv. 4–6 as parallel in meaning as well as in syntax.
in custody. "In the hand of." In combination with the verb of sending (causative of *šlḥ*, used in 1.11; 2.5), I see an image of the "guilt" as a kind of arresting officer.
[5] **Make the search.** Job used the same verb in 7.21d of the deity's search, and Bildad turns the idea around.
[6] **Moral.** *Yašar*, the word used in 1.1, etc., of Job. See also v. 20.
though now. The interplay between what Bildad says here and what Job said in 7.21 is complex, and there is at least one other connection to the same verse in 8.22. I take the second and third lines as consecutive and contrastive, not parallel.
[9] **Our days' shadow.** Or "Our days are a shadow upon the earth."
[11] The verse is probably a proverb, and its plant image continues intermittently through v. 19.
Grow. The same word, *yiśgeh*, as "increase" in v. 7b.
[14] **. . . .** *Yqwṭ* is a notorious crux, and I cannot solve it. A demonstrated relation to Arabic *qaṭṭa*, "to cut," would be nice.
confidence. *Kesel*, cognate to Eliphaz's word in 4.6a.

[21] Why not lift my guilt,
carry away my iniquity?
For now I lie down in the dust;
you'll search for me, but I won't be there.

8 [1] Bildad the Shuchite answered thus:
[2] How long will you prattle like this,
your mouth's words a gusty wind?
[3] Does El bend justice,
Shaddai bend the right?
[4] If your sons have sinned against him,
he has sent them off in custody of their guilt.

[5] If you make the search for El,
ask mercy of Shaddai,
[6] if you are pure and moral,
though now he rouses up against you,
he will repay your innocent dwelling.
[7] Your past will turn out to be small,
and your future will greatly increase.

[8] Ask, then, a past generation,
adhere to what their fathers found!
[9] For we're but yesterday—we don't know.
Our days' shadow still lies across earth.
[10] Can they not teach you, talk to you,
bring forth words from their mind?

[11] Does papyrus come up without a swamp,
a reed grow without water?
[12] Still in blossom, not yet picked,
before all the plants it dries away.
[13] Such are the paths of all who forget El,
and the hope of the impious perishes.

[14] What . . . his confidence,
and what he trusts is a spider's house.
[15] He leans on his house, and it doesn't stand up,
strengthens it, and it doesn't last.

[16] He's well watered before the sun,
and his shoots spread across his garden.

17 **Pool.** *Gal* is often understood to be a heap of stones, and the image that of a root system that succeeds even in adverse conditions (see Gordis, *Book of Job*, p. 92). I incline to think of *gal* as a pool, as in Song of S 4.12. Roots twining about a pool are in a favorable environment, and a "house of stone" is a very prosperous dwelling.

18 **Swallowed up.** I reluctantly use the passive for what appears an impersonal verb ("if he [or it] swallow him up").

19 **Joy.** Even commentators who think this line is ironic are not confident of its meaning, and most prefer to emend it.

other dust. The sentence is puzzling in several ways, especially for the unexpected plural verb. Because *'aḥēr*, "another," looks like the subject of the verb, most commentators change the plural verb to a singular. With Gordis (*Book of Job*, p. 93), I take *'aḥēr* as an adjective to *'apar*. The implied plural subject of the verb is related to the roots in v. 17.

21 **Yet.** I repoint MT *'ad*, "until," to *'ōd*.

22 **Not be there.** The same word, with a third-person masculine suffix, as the one with which Job finished his previous speech, 7.21d.

2 **Innocent.** Job echoes what Eliphaz said in 4.17: "Is a man more righteous than Eloah?" (*ha'enōš mē'elōah yiṣdaq*) in somewhat different terms (*ūmah-yiṣdaq 'enōš 'im-'ēl*).

3 **Wished.** I take *ḥpṣ* in its usual sense of desire or taking pleasure in something. Pope (*Job*, p. 68) reads a different root, meaning "to bend down" (which he finds elsewhere only in 40.17), for "If he deigned to litigate with him," and he takes the deity as the subject of the sentence. The pronouns in the sentence are ambiguous, and either decision seems possible.

4 The first line refers to the deity, but only in the second is this clear.

5 **Whom.** Some interpreters are troubled by the appearance of the relative pronoun *'ašer* in poetry. It occurs 32 times in the poetry of Job and 8 times in the prose, and I see no reason ever to excise it. One can read the sentence without a caesura or with one after the first line, implying an accusative "it" to "they do not know." I accept the former.

7 **Sun.** An unusual word for the sun, perhaps chosen for its chiastic relation to the following verb: *ḥrs / zrḥ*.

9 The list of constellations in 38.31–32 has some of the same names. I have not attempted to correlate the constellations with ours; the ancient Israelites may not have seen the same configurations as we do or even as the Greeks did. LXX identifies "the Lion" (*'aš* [in 38.32, *'ayiš*]) as the Pleiades, "the Fool" (*kesīl*) as Venus, "the Herd" (*kīmah*) as Arcturus. Most modern scholars equate the Lion with the Bear (Ursa Major, or the Big Dipper), the Fool with Orion, occasionally with Canopus, and the Herd with the Pleiades, sometimes with Draco, though G. R. Driver ("Two Astronomical Passages," p. 1) accepts Schiaparelli's argument that the Lion

[17] His roots twine about the pool,
he gazes on a house of stone.

[18] If he's swallowed up from his place,
it denies him: "I've never seen you."
[19] Oh! that's the joy of his way,
and from other dust they will sprout.

[20] Oh! El does not refuse a perfect person
or strengthen the hand of evil ones.
[21] He will yet fill your mouth with laughter,
your lips with festal shout.
[22] Those who hate you will be dressed in shame,
and the tent of the wicked will not be there.

9 [1] Job answered thus:
[2] Surely I know that it's true:
how can a man be innocent with El?
[3] If one wished to enter a case against him,
he couldn't answer him once in a thousand.
[4] Wise of mind and powerfully strong,
whoever is stubborn to him, and safe?

[5] He who removes mountains, and they don't know
whom he's overturning in his anger;
[6] who shakes earth from its place,
and its pillars shudder;
[7] who speaks to the sun and it does not rise,
and puts a seal on the stars;
[8] who stretches out the sky all by himself
and treads on the back of Sea;
[9] who made the Lion, the Fool,
the Herd, and the Southern Chambers;

---

is Aldebaran (but on p. 10 he calls it the Hyades—see note to 38.31–32, below). Pope (*Job*, p. 71) thinks that *tēman* is "south wind," and the Southern Chambers is not a constellation. Though recognizing a Hebrew tendency to asymmetry, I see no reason to doubt that these are the names of four constellations.

[10] A repetition, with one word added (the preposition *'ad*, v. 10a), of Eliphaz's remark in 5.9. The added word produces an idiom stylistically superior to Eliphaz's.

[11] **Passes me by.** Is this a parody on Moses? Cf. Exod 33.22–23; 34.6. Exod 34.10 is also related to v. 10.

sweeps on. Another allusion in *yaḥlōp* to the same form in Eliphaz's vision, 4.15a.

[12] **Seizes.** A hapax legomenon; Gordis (*Book of Job*, p. 105) suggests the more brutal meaning "rob," which is supported by the noun *ḥetep*, apparently with that meaning in Prov 23.28. See also Terrien (*Job*, p. 95), who uses the term (in French) "gangster."

[13] **Rahab.** 26.12 also refers to this sea monster, apparently a West Semitic variation of the Babylonian Tiamat in a combat-type creation myth (cf. Ps 89.11 [Eng. 10]; Isa 51.9), which has not survived in narrative form. The sarcastic references to Egypt as Rahab in Ps 87.4 and Isa 30.7 may have the same referent. "Rahab the harlot," who aided the conquest of Jericho (Josh 2; 6.22–25), is unrelated.

[15] The Hebrew sentence has no interrogative marker.

[17] **Whirlwind.** *Ś*^{e}*'arah*, used with the spelling *s*^{e}*'arah* in 38.1.

[19] **A case of strength.** I translated the same words, in reverse order, as "powerfully strong" in v. 4a.

Oh! The exclamatory *hinnēh*. It sounds like an inarticulate outcry of frustrated fury.

docket my suit. "Set the time for me" (*yō'īdēnī*).

[20] **Perfect.** The word is also used in v. 21a. Job implicitly (and in the next verse explicitly) claims what the narrator and the deity attributed to him in chaps. 1–2 (*tam*). The conditional particle *'im* in the first line also governs the second.

do me fraud. "He'll twist me, be crooked to me." The verb can be either transitive or intransitive.

[21] **I don't know myself.** Perhaps another ejaculatory outcry (I like Gordis's "I am beside myself").

[23] **Flash flood.** The etymology of *šōṭ* suggests a sudden onslaught of water.

melt away. Commentators take *massat n*^{e}*qīyyīm* variously as "trial, despair, plea, of the innocent." I derive the hapax legomenon *massah* from the root *mss*, "to melt, become liquid, be dissolved," an image that beautifully fits the flash flood. See also 6.14.

[24] **Covers.** A somewhat odd phrase. Our familiar figure of blindfolded justice is reminiscent of the Hebrew expression for illicit judicial favoritism, "to recognize faces" as in Deut 16.19. But this context seems to show that covering judges' faces meant injustice.

[25] **Runner.** Cf. 7.6.

[26] **Vulture.** Or "eagle." *Nešer* is a carrion bird, which fits both the eagle and the vulture. The bird described in 39.27–30 is a *nešer*.

[27] **I say.** I take *'omrī* to be the same as *'amartī*.

stop looking sad. "Abandon my face."

[28] The second-person masculine singular in the second line makes vv. 27–31 an address to the deity. At v. 32, Job reverts to the third-person form.

10 who does great things, even inscrutable,
wonderful things innumerable;
11 Ah, he passes me by, and I don't see him,
sweeps on, and I don't discern him.
12 Ah, he seizes, who can turn him back?
Who can say to him, "What are you doing?"

13 Eloah will not turn back his anger.
Rahab's helpers bowed beneath him.
14 So I'm supposed to answer him,
choose my words against him,
15 I who, though innocent, couldn't answer
must beg my opponent for mercy?
16 If I summoned and he answered me,
I wouldn't believe he was hearing my voice,
17 he who tramples me down with a whirlwind,
enlarges my wounds for no reason.
18 He won't even let me catch my breath
but gorges me with bitter things.

19 If it's a case of strength, Oh!—
and if of justice, who'll docket my suit?
20 If I'm innocent, my own mouth condemns me;
if I'm perfect, he'll do me fraud.
21 I am perfect—
I don't know myself—
I despise my life.
22 It's all the same. Therefore I say,
he finishes off both perfect and wicked.
23 If a flash flood suddenly kills,
he scoffs as the guiltless melt away.
24 Earth is given over to a wicked hand;
he covers its judges' faces—
if not, then who is it?

25 My days go faster than a runner,
they flee, see nothing good,
26 sweep by on skiffs of reed
like a vulture swooping on a meal.

27 If I say, "I think I'll forget my complaint,
stop looking sad, and cheer up,"
28 I'm afraid of all my pains,
knowing that you won't hold me guiltless.

29 **With the breeze.** *Hebel*, usually translated "in vain," has the basic sense of a puff of wind.

30 **Snow water.** I read Qere, *b*^{e}*mēy šeleg*. Ketib is *b*^{e}*mō šeleg*, "with snow," and several scholars connect *šeleg* with later Hebrew words for various cleansing agents such as soapwort (Pope, *Job*, p. 75) or niter (Gordis, *Book of Job*, p. 109). Perhaps special cleansing properties were attributed to snow because it came from the sky.

31 **Muck.** *Šaḥat* often refers to the underworld, and it could be rendered "Pit." See Pope's exhaustive but unsuccessful search for its etymology in "The Word *šaḥat*."
make me disgusting. For this sense of the Pi'el of *t'b*, see Ezek 16.25.

33 **There's no arbiter.** Many scholars are fascinated by and accept the reading of LXX, Syriac, and some Hebrew manuscripts, *lū yēš*, "if only there were," instead of MT *lō' yēš*, "there is not." It is true that *lō' yēš* occurs nowhere else, while *lū yēš* occurs in Num 22.29 and Job 16.4. On the other hand, *'ēn yēš*, "there is not," is in Ps 135.17 and perhaps in 1 Sam 21.9, which permits acceptance of *lō' yēš*. The negative contains and discards the thought that the arbiter might intervene on Job's behalf, whereas the conditional allows the thought to stand.

34 **My back.** "Take his rod off me."

1 **Give . . . free rein.** The expression (cf. 9.27) is "I will abandon my complaint upon myself," meaning something like "I will loose my complaint."
bitter throat. *Nepeš*; cf. 7.11.

2 **Condemn.** The same verb as in 9.29a, but in a different stem.

3 **Good to you.** *H*^{a}*ṭōb l*^{e}*ka* could also be read as a possessive: "Is it your good?"

7 **Because.** This use of the preposition *'al* with the infinitive is frequent, e.g., Exod 17.7; Job 32.2. Most translators render *'al* as "though," but the causal thought seems to me at least as true to the context. Moreover, the use in the same line of the verb *rš'* echoes vv. 2a ("condemn") and 3c ("the guilty," *r*^{e}*ša'īm*).

8 . . . *Yaḥad sabīb* might mean "together around," but I do not know what that says.

[29] I'll be condemned—
why do I struggle with the breeze?
[30] If I wash myself with snow water,
purify my palms with lye,
[31] then you'll plunge me into the muck,
and my clothes will make me disgusting.

[32] For he's not a man like me whom I could answer,
come together with him to trial.
[33] There's no arbiter between us
to lay his hand on us both,
[34] to take his rod off my back,
tell dread of him not to terrify me.
[35] I'd like to speak and not be afraid of him,
for that's not how I am in myself.

10 [1] My soul finds my life repulsive—
I'll give my complaint free rein,
will speak with bitter throat,
[2] say to Eloah, "Don't condemn me,
let me know of what you're accusing me.
[3] Is it good to you that you oppress,
despise your hands' toil,
and beam upon the counsel of the guilty?
[4] Have you fleshly eyes;
do you see as a man sees?
[5] Are your days like human days,
like a man's days your years?
[6] For you search for my fault,
for my sin make inquiry,
[7] because you know I'm not guilty,
and no one can rescue from your hand.

[8] Your hands shaped me, made me
. . . , yet you'd swallow me down?
[9] Recall that you made me like clay,
yet you're turning me back to dust?
[10] Did you not pour me out like milk,
curdle me like cheese,

12 **life and loyalty.** The verb *‘śh*, “to do, make, deal with,” does not fit comfortably with “life,” and many commentators emend the noun. I have to take “life and loyalty” adverbially, and it remains doubtful.

13 **This is with you.** The line is somewhat obscure. It might mean something like “I know this is what you are up to.”

14 **Guard.** Job used the same verb positively about the deity in v. 12b and a nominal derivative of it in 7.12b.

15 **Gazing.** I read *r*^{e}*’ēh* as a construct of the verbal noun *ra’eh*. It can also be taken as an imperative of “to see.”

16 **He is proud.** Scholars emend the verb *yig’eh* on the assumption that the last two lines of v. 15 and this line must refer to Job, and that the second-person verb must be part of this line. I take the last line of v. 15 as two and combine them with this one as an aside, addressed to the friends or muttered under Job’s breath, referring in the third person to the deity. With the next line, Job reverts to the second-person address to the deity. This entails some modification of the MT punctuation.

17 **Fresh squadrons.** I take “relievers and squadrons” as a hendiadys. *Ḥ*^{a}*lîpōt* seems to refer to replacements (see 1 Ki 5.28 [Eng. 14]) and is used in a military sense by Job in 14.14.

20 **Stop, stand off.** The Qere reads both verbs as imperatives, where Ketib has imperfects. I have turned MT’s two lines into three.

cheer up. See also 9.27.

21 **Deepest dark.** *Ḥōšek w*^{e}*ṣalmūt*, “darkness and deep darkness.”

22 The three lines are dominated by dark *o*-vowels.

like dusk. The words *k*^{e}*mō-’ōpel* are repeated in v. 22a and c. The latter line is a fine oxymoron.

2 **Gang.** “Multitude.”

gabby man. “Man of lips,” which suggests a very talkative man.

4 **You say.** What follows does not accurately quote Job, though it may allude to remarks like those in 9.21.

your eyes. The pronoun is masculine singular and presumably refers to the deity.

11 clothe me with skin and flesh,
weave me together with bones and sinews?
12 You've dealt with me in life and loyalty,
and your care has guarded my spirit.
13 And you've hidden these things in your heart;
I know this is with you.

14 If I sin, you put a guard on me
and don't acquit me of my fault.
15 If I'm guilty, woe upon me!
If innocent, I cannot lift my head.
(Gorged with dishonor,
gazing at humiliation,
16 he is proud as a lion.)
You hunt me down, repeat your wonders on me,
17 bring new witnesses before me,
increase your fury against me,
fresh squadrons against me.

18 Why did you bring me out of the womb?
I might have died, and no eye see me,
19 might be as not having been,
borne from womb to grave.
20 Are not my days few enough?
Stop, stand off from me,
and I might cheer up a bit
21 before I go and don't return,
to the land of deepest dark,
22 land of gloom, like dusk,
deep shadow, all disordered,
which shines like dusk."

11 1 Zophar the Na'amathite answered thus:
2 Is a gang of words not answered?
Is a gabby man innocent?
3 Does your chatter silence men?
When you deride, does no one rebuke?

4 You say, "My understanding is pure,
and I am clear in your eyes."

[6]**Sagacity is double.** A very difficult line in a verse that has given commentators much trouble. I accept JPS's "sagacity" for *tūšīyyah*, and I think *kiplayim* is best translated "double." Zophar does not spell out the duality he thinks of.

Know, then, etc. Gordis (*Book of Job*, p. 121) points out that *yaššeh* may come either from *nšh*, "to forget" (which I accept) or from *nšh*, "to demand payment" (which he accepts): "God is exacting less from you than your guilt demands." Either is possible.

[9]**Its stature.** The pronoun is feminine singular, and I take its antecedent to be *taklīt*, "boundary," v. 7b.

[10]**Sweeps past.** Job complained in 9.11 that the deity "sweeps on, and I don't discern him," perhaps an allusion to 4.15.

[11]**He knows.** The pronoun is emphatic.

but doesn't examine it? The sentence has no interrogative marker, though earlier we have seen indicative sentences with interrogative meanings. I take this sentence in that way because the indicative seems to me too drastic a lapse of logic even for Zophar. Jacob (p. 283) analyzes "examine" as Hitpolal, a passive, and gives the word a visual meaning: "und ist selber unsichtbar [invisible]."

[12]This couplet seems to quote a proverb.

hollow-headed. *Nabūb* means only "hollow." The sound play between it and the verb, *yillabēb*, "be intelligent" (cognate to *lēbab*, "heart"), underscores the reference to a stupid man. A paraphrase might be "The stupid man will become clever."

wild ass colt. Pope (*Job*, p. 86) draws the contrast in the proverb between *pere'* ("wild ass") and *'ayir* ("colt"), rather than between "wild ass" and "human," because *'ayir* is a domesticated ass, and *pere'* is a wild ass. He takes the phrase *pere' 'adam* ("wild ass, human") as equal to *pere' 'ᵃdamah* ("wild ass of the steppe"), for "when a wild ass is born tame." On the other hand, the phrase *pere' 'adam* echoes Gen 16.12, which calls Ishmael a "wild ass of a man," and I agree with Gordis (*Book of Job*, p. 123) that readers would recognize the allusion.

[13]**You.** The pronoun is emphatic in Hebrew, and it reverberates with the emphatic "he" in v. 11a.

[15]**From your fault.** The usual translation, "unblemished," takes the preposition *min* in a way I think not right. The metaphor in the couplet is dominated by the "molding" in v. 15b, and this line seems to suggest lifting the face from a flawed mold.

[2]**You.** The pronoun is masculine plural.

5 How I wish that Eloah would speak,
open his lips against you,
6 tell you the secrets of wisdom,
that sagacity is double.
Know, then, that Eloah lets some of your guilt be forgotten.

7 Can you discover Eloah's farthest edge,
or discover as far as Shaddai's boundary?
8 Heights of the sky—what can you do?—
deeper than Sheol—what can you know?—
9 longer than Earth its stature,
broader than Sea.
10 If he sweeps past, imprisons,
assembles, who can stop him?
11 For he knows empty men
and sees wrongdoing, but doesn't examine it?
12 "A hollow-headed man will be intelligent
when a wild ass colt is born human."

13 If you prepare your heart,
spread out your palms to him,
14 if guilt is in your hands, send it away,
and don't let iniquity dwell in your tents.

15 Then you'll lift your face from your fault,
become properly molded, and not fear.
16 You'll surely forget your toil,
remember it like water gone by.
17 Your life will rise above noon,
gloom will become like morning.
18 You'll trust that hope is there;
having been shamed, you'll lie down in trust,
19 stretch out, and no one will terrify,
and the great will beg for your favor.
20 But the eyes of knaves will be exhausted,
refuge perished from them,
their only hope to breathe their last.

12 1 Job answered thus:
2 In truth, you are the people,
and wisdom dies with you.

3 **Like these.** The friends' ideas, I think.

4 **His friends.** Eloah's friends, I think.

who called . . . answered him. The participle *qōrē'*, "called," refers to Job, and the antecedent of the accusative pronoun is *qōrē'*. Job refers to himself partly in the third person.

5 **Contemptuous torch.** The image is of someone shining a light on someone else's misfortune, which is assumed to come from the deity. *Mō'*^{a}*dē*, "wobbly," is a plural participle of *m'd*.

6 **Whom Eloah brings.** Another translation, "who brings Elohim in his hand," is syntactically problematic but possible. *La'*^{a}*šer*, "whom," is syntactically parallel to *l*^{e}*margīzē 'ēl*, "who stir up El," in the preceding line, and the referent of the possessive singular pronoun on "hand" is probably Eloah.

7 **Ask.** The imperative and the pronouns in vv. 7–8 are masculine singular. Does Job address one or other of the friends? The second-person singular usually signals an address to the deity.

Behemoth. An allusion to the monster of 40.15–24 is surprising, but the word may mean "cattle," though its verb, "teach," is singular. The next three lines refer to the three realms of creation in Gen 1: sky (*šamayim*), earth (*'ereṣ*), and sea (*yam*), a context larger in scope than "cattle."

8 **Plants.** Most commentators translate *śīaḥ* as an imperative, "speak to," parallel to "ask" in v. 7a, because of the preposition *l*^{e}, "to," or "with." It is possible but has more complaint in its connotation than the context seems to demand. I read "plant" (see Gen 2.5; Job 30.4, 7) because of the parallel expressions on either side of it, "birds of the sky" and "fish of the sea," and the preposition on *la'areṣ* can also signify possession.

9 **Yahweh's hand.** Only here in the poetic dialogue do we come across the divine name Yahweh. Some MSS have *'*^{e}*lōah*.

12 It is commonly supposed that this couplet is a proverb or proverbial saying. Perhaps Job attributes the proverb to the friends, in effect charging them with repeating outworn lore. The best reason to think so is that v. 13 rejects the platitude of v. 12.

19 **Well-established.** The word usually refers to watercourses that never run dry, though it can be used otherwise (cf. Num 24.21; Jer 5.15; etc.).

20 **Speech.** *Śapah*, "lip."

3 I too have a heart like you,
I've fallen no further than you,
and who has nothing like these?
4 To his friends I've become a joke,
who called to Eloah and he answered him,
a perfectly righteous joke!
5 Easy thought holds a contemptuous torch
ready for the wobbly foot.
6 Tents are tranquil for violent men,
secure for those who stir up El,
whom Eloah brings in his hand.

7 So now, ask Behemoth, who will teach you,
the birds of the sky, who will tell you,
8 or the plants of the earth, who will teach you,
and the fish of the sea will recount to you.
9 Who doesn't know all these things,
that Yahweh's hand has done this,
10 in whose hand is every living soul,
the breath of all human flesh?

11 Doesn't an ear examine words,
and a palate taste food?
12 "In age is wisdom,
length of days is understanding."

13 With him is wisdom—and power—
his are counsel and understanding.
14 Oh, he tears something down, it's not rebuilt,
shuts a man up, he's not opened;
15 he restrains the water, it's dry,
sends it out and it tosses the land about.

16 With him are strength and success,
his, deceived and deceiver alike.
17 Leads off counselors barefoot,
makes fools of judges,
18 undoes the discipline of kings,
binds a waistcloth on their loins;
19 leads off priests barefoot,
subverts the well-established;
20 deprives the trustworthy of speech,
takes discretion from the elderly;

[21] **Strong.** Another somewhat puzzling allusion, perhaps, to water. *'ᵃpīqīm* ordinarily means "water channels," but other meanings for similar terms turn up in other Semitic languages (see Pope, *Job*, p. 94).

[23] **Abandons.** Blommerde (*Northwest Semitic Grammar*, p. 64) points out that *nḥh*, "to lead," never has the negative meaning that the context seems to want. I repoint *yanḥēm* to *yannīḥēm* with Gordis (*Book of Job*, p. 140).

[24] **Mind.** *Lēb*, "heart."

the people's chiefs. *'Am ha'areṣ* seems to mean something like "people of the countryside."

[2] The first-person pronouns are emphatic in Hebrew. Note that v. 2b repeats 12.3b.

[3–4] I have not found a way to reflect the structure of this quatrain. Verses 3a and 4a begin with a more or less untranslatable particle, *'ūlam*, followed by an emphatic pronoun, "I" in 3a, "you" (masculine plural) in 4a. The effect is a stronger contrast between v. 3 and v. 4 than my translation brings out.

argue the case. *Hōkēaḥ*, a verb of legal action that occurs also in vv. 10a ("make a final decision") and 15b ("argue"). The cognate noun, *tōkaḥat*, appears in v. 6a ("argument").

godlings. *'ᵉlīl* is usually related to the negative particle, *'al.* I use it as a collective diminutive of *'ēl*, as in Lev 19.4; Isa 2.8; Hab 2.18; Ps 97.7, among other passages.

[8] **Weight the scales in his favor.** "Lift his face," an idiom for showing partiality in a case, sometimes involving bribery (e.g., Deut 10.17). Here and in v. 10b I shift the metaphor to that of the scales of justice. "Weight" in v. 11a (*śᵉ'ēt*) is cognate to the verb *nś'*, "lift," in this expression.

[12] **Your shields.** A notorious crux. With Pope (*Job*, p. 99), I take *gab* as in 15.26, referring to the bosses of a shield, knobs that increase the bearer's protection. Thus "bosses" is a synecdoche for the shield. I cannot resist Blommerde's quotation (*Northwest Semitic Grammar*, p. 66) of Ehrlich's German translation—if such it can be called—of v. 12b: "Zusammengeklaubten bröckelnden Lehmklüppchen gleicht das was ihr gegen mich zusammenkramt." All you need to know about that sentence is that it translates only three Hebrew words.

21 pours contempt on the noble,
looses the belt of the strong.

22 Who uncovers deeps out of darkness,
brings gloom to the light,
23 magnifies some peoples, then slays them,
disperses other peoples, then abandons them,
24 deprives of mind the people's chiefs,
makes them wander aimlessly in chaos.
25 They grope through lightless dark,
and he makes them wander like drunkards.

13 1 There, my eye has seen it all,
my ear has heard and understood it.
2 As you know, I know too,
I've fallen no further than you.

3 But I want to speak to Shaddai,
desire to argue the case to El.
4 Whereas you, you whitewashers of lies,
you're all healers by godlings.

5 How I wish you'd be utterly silent—
it might be wisdom for you.
6 Then listen to my argument,
attend to my lips' accusations.
7 Would you speak perversely for El,
speak deceitfully for him,
8 weight the scales in his favor,
accuse on El's behalf?
9 Will it be well when he searches you through?
As one tricks a man, can you trick him?
10 He'll make a final decision about you
if you secretly weight the scales for him.
11 Will not his weight terrify you,
his fear fall upon you?

12 Your memories are dusty proverbs,
your shields are shields of clay.
13 Be silent a while, and I will speak,
and whatever happens to me happens.

[15]**He's going,** etc. Perhaps the most famous line in the book of Job. KJV's religiously splendid "Behold though he slay me, yet will I trust in him" depends on three doubtful suppositions: (1) that one can take the imperfect *yqṭlny*, "kill me," as a subordinate clause; (2) that Ketib *lō'*, "not," is to be abandoned in favor of Qere *lō*, "to him"; (3) that the verb *yḥl* can mean "trust." Like most scholars and translators, I have taken *yqṭlny* as an indicative, "he will kill me." With many colleagues (Fohrer, *Das Buch Hiob*, pp. 238, 251, is a notable exception), I accept Ketib's negative. But I do not find the meaning "hope" in *yḥl*, as many scholars do. The verb has to do with waiting, tarrying (see Job's uses of it in 6.11; 14.14; 29.21, 23; 30.26). The second line, then, needs the feeling of urgency that is suggested in "I must argue" (*ykḥ*, see note to v. 3).

[16]**That.** Or "he," an emphatic pronoun.

[17]**Listen.** The imperative is masculine plural, as is the pronoun in v. 17b.

[20]**Don't do.** The verb is second-person masculine singular, an address to the deity. There is a disparity between this negative and the positive statement of the "two things" Job wishes not to be done: "remove" (v. 21a) and "call" (v. 22a). Some scholars identify "don't fall on me" (v. 21b) as the second of the two things. Blommerde (*Northwest Semitic Grammar*, pp. 67–68) and Habel (*Book of Job*, p. 225) read the negative *'al* as *'ēl*, a vocative: "El, do just two things." Job does not use vocatives to the deity otherwise, and the word order is odd in that reading. The lines are simply difficult.

[24]**Enemy.** More than one scholar has seen in *'ōyēb* a pun on Job's name, *'īyyōb*. Of course.

[26]**Write.** Dahood ("Northwest Semitic Philology," pp. 59–60) takes the expression "to write against" as a commercial idiom meaning "to debit the account." Job sometimes mixes metaphors, but v. 26b would lead one to expect an allusion to inheritance, and "to write about or against" seems sensible in that context too. Pope (*Job*, p. 102) compounds the mixture (if that is chemically possible) by taking the expression medically, for making a prescription for bitter medicine.

[28]The line begins with an emphatic pronoun, "he" (*hū'*), which points on to "humankind" (*'adam*) in 14.1 (so Gordis, *Book of Job*, p. 146).

[3]**Is this why.** I take *'ap-'al-zeh* as in Amos 8.8 and Lam 5.17, to mean "Is it even because of this?" *Zeh* is a demonstrative that could refer to Job himself: "upon such a one."

[4]**If clean,** etc. The expression *mī yittēn* is a wish formula: "Would that clean might come from dirty."

never. *Lō' 'eḥad*, "not one." Job is reduced, it seems, to an inarticulate exclamation.

[14] How long! I'll take my flesh in my teeth,
grasp my throat with my hand.
[15] He's going to kill me; I cannot wait,
but I must argue my ways to his face.
[16] That might even be my salvation,
for an impious one could not face him.
[17] Listen carefully to my word,
my report in your ears.
[18] There, now, I've marshaled a case,
I know that I'm innocent.
[19] Who is it who'll accuse me?

But now I'll be silent and die.
[20] Only don't do two things to me,
then I'll not hide from your face:
[21] remove your hand from me,
and don't fall on me with terror of you.
[22] Call, and I will answer,
or I will speak, and you respond to me.
[23] What scope has my fault and sin?
Let me know my guilt and sin.
[24] Why do you hide your face
and count me as your enemy?
[25] Do you make the drifting leaf tremble,
chase after dry straw?
[26] But you write bitter things against me
and bequeath me my youthful faults.
[27] You put my feet in the stocks,
watch all the paths I walk,
grave your mark on the soles of my feet.

[28] Worn out like something rotten,
like a garment that moths eat,
14 [1] humankind, born of woman,
few of days and sated with turmoil,
[2] comes out like a blossom and withers,
flees like a shadow and does not stay.
[3] Is this why you open your eyes,
bring me to trial against you?
[4] If clean could come from dirty—
Never!

[7] **Cease.** The same verb as in v. 6a.

[13] **Limit.** Presumably a limit of time, as in Mic 7.11; Zeph 2.2.

[14] **Term . . . relief.** The words are used together in 10.17 ("fresh squadrons"). The image is a military one.

[16–17] Verse 16a seems to contradict vv. 16b and 17b. Several translators continue the subjunctive sense that started in v. 13, turning these two verses into a strong hypothesis of a positive outcome. I think the strong "but now" in v. 16a tells against that, and I take "guard" in a preventive sense. Verse 17 suggests treasuring the guilt, smearing a waxen seal over it to keep it intact for later scrutiny.

5 If his days are determined,
the number of his months with you,
you've set him limits he cannot exceed.
6 Take your gaze from him and he'll cease,
until, like a laborer, he can enjoy his day.

7 But for a tree there is hope.
If it's cut, it will come new again,
and its shoots will not cease.
8 If its root ages in earth,
its stump dies in the dust,
9 at water's scent, it will send out buds,
make twigs as if planted.

10 A hero dies, is prostrated,
humans expire—and where are they?
11 Water drains from the sea,
a river dries entirely away.
12 A man lies down and doesn't get up;
till there is no sky, they won't awake,
won't rouse from their sleep.

13 I wish you'd conceal me in Sheol,
hide me till your anger stops,
set me a limit and remember me.
14 If a hero die, shall he live?
All the days of my term I would wait
until my relief should come.
15 You would call, and I'd answer you,
you'd long for the work of your hands.
16 But now you count my steps,
do not guard my sin.
17 My guilt is sealed in a bag,
and you smear across my fault.

18 Yet a mountain falls, sinks down,
a rock disintegrates from its place.
19 Water wears away stone,
freshets overflow earth's dust.
And you destroy a man's hope,
20 victoriously subdue him and he goes,
change his face and send him off.

[22]I cannot reproduce the parallelism of the statement, which comes to something like "His flesh hurts all over him / and his soul laments over him" (*'ak-b^eśārō 'alayw yik'ab / w^enapšō 'alayw te'^ebal*). The problem is the untranslatable *'ak*, which puts a sense of completeness, an unplaceable "only," into the first line.

[4]**Religion.** *Yir'ah*, "fear." See note to 1.1.
[5]**Multiplies.** With Dahood ("Hebrew-Ugaritic Lexicography," p. 294), I derive *y'lp* from the verb *'lp* II, "to make 1,000-fold," denominative from *'elep*, "1,000." The verb occurs otherwise only in Ps 144.13.
[12]**What . . . your eyes.** The verb *rzm* is a hapax legomenon, repaired variously by metathesis to *rmz*, producing "flash" or "blink," or by connecting the word with an Arabic cognate, "to dwindle away, become weak."
[13]**Blow your wind.** The verb form, *tašīb*, is transitive, "turn something." Most commentators think *rūaḥ* means "anger," but I prefer the more literal "wind."
[14]**What is a man.** Eliphaz alludes to his dream message in 4.17, but by way of Job's parody of Ps 8 in 7.17 and his allusion to the dream in 9.2.
[15]**He.** By reference to 4.18–19, the pronoun apparently signifies the deity.

[21] His children are honorable, and he doesn't know,
insignificant, and he doesn't understand it.
[22] All he feels is his flesh's pain,
and his soul laments over him.

15 [1] Eliphaz the Temanite answered thus:
[2] Does a wise one answer windy knowledge,
fill his belly with the east wind,
[3] argue with useless talk,
words without possible profit?
[4] But you are breaking up religion,
constraining complaint before El.
[5] For your mouth multiplies your guilt,
and you choose a guileful tongue.
[6] Your mouth condemns you, not I,
your lips testify against you.
[7] Were you born the first human,
brought forth before the hills?
[8] Do you listen in Eloah's council,
restrict wisdom to yourself?
[9] What do you know that we don't know,
understand that's not ours as well?
[10] Both graybeard and elderly are among us,
mightier of age than your father.

[11] Are El's consolations too slight for you,
the gentle word against you?
[12] What takes your mind from you,
what . . . your eyes,
[13] that you blow your wind at El,
spout talk from your mouth?
[14] What is a man, that he can be pure,
innocent, one born of woman?
[15] After all, he doesn't trust his holy ones,
and the sky is not pure in his eyes.
[16] What then of one horrible and corrupt,
a man who drinks wrongdoing like water?

[17] I'll tell you, listen to me,
I've seen this, and I'll recount it—

[18] **From their fathers.** The line seems illogical, and commentators have sought ways to reverse its meaning. One method is to move the preposition "from," *m* prefixed to *'ᵃbōtam*, back to the end of *kḥdw* as an enclitic particle, thus making "their fathers" the subject of the verb: "their fathers haven't hidden." I expound my difficulty with the enclitic *mem* in the "Indispensable Introduction." The logical problem will simply have to remain unsolved.

[22] The third-person plural perfect verb in the second line makes no sense.

[23] **His hand.** The referent of the pronoun might be either the deity or the victim.

[24] **Overwhelms.** The grammar is doubtful. The verb in the first line is plural, but this verb is feminine singular, its nearest possible subject *mᵉṣūqah*, "stress." To turn the verb into a plural produces an anomalous form.

[27] **Grease . . . fat.** Grease on the face is the ancient equivalent of suntan lotion. Only the rich could afford to waste olive oil by smearing it on their faces, and a greasy face and fat body were therefore signs of wealth.

[28] The change of tone might signal a new sentence. On the other hand, the parallel uses of *kī*, "for," in vv. 25a and 27a suggests that the subject swerves surprisingly.

[29] **Earth.** *'ereṣ* may signify "netherworld" here (so Habel, *Book of Job*, p. 248). "You can't take it with you," as Qoheleth said (Eccl 5.14 [Eng. 15]).

[31] **Vanity.** I take *šaw* in the first line as a defective spelling of *šaw'*, as the word is spelled in the second line. The couplet is not elegant.

18 what wise men make known,
haven't hidden even from their fathers,
19 to whom alone the land was given,
and a stranger did not pass among them.
20 All a knave's days, he's twisting about,
the whole count of years treasured for the ruthless.
21 Terrible sounds are in his ears;
when he's healthy, the destroyer arrives.
22 He doesn't think he will turn from darkness,
and . . . he to the sword.
23 He wanders about for bread—where is it?—
he knows that a dark day is ready in his hand.
24 Strain and stress terrify him,
overwhelms him like a king prepared to attack.

25 For he flings out his hand to El,
toward Shaddai plays the hero,
26 runs toward him, neck held high,
thick the bosses of his shield.
27 For he coats his face with grease,
loads his buttocks with fat,
28 lives in hidden cities,
houses that aren't inhabited,
that are destined for rubble.
29 He won't be rich, his wealth won't remain,
nor will his possessions reach the earth.
30 He won't escape from darkness,
flame will dry up his shoots,
and he'll escape with the wind in his mouth.
31 He should not trust in stumbling vanity,
for the exchange will come to vanity.
32 Before his time it will be filled up,
before his branch is green.
33 Like the vine, he'll thrust off his early grapes,
drop his blossoms like the olive.
34 For the band of the impious is sterile,
and fire consumes the bribers' tents,
35 conceiving toil and bearing guilt,
their womb fosters deceit.

[3] **Hurting you . . . you answer.** Quite unexpectedly, given the plural pronouns in vv. 2 and 4, these pronouns are singular. Job uses the second-person masculine singular elsewhere to address the deity.

[4] **Shake my head.** Presumably a conventional gesture of opprobrium.

[7–8] The second-person masculine singular verbs in vv. 7b and 8a, as in v. 3, probably address the deity. In v. 9, Job reverts to the third-person forms.

company. The same word as the one I translate "band" in 15.34.

[10] **They.** These plural forms no doubt refer forward to v. 11, since there are no plurals in what precedes.

[11] **The vicious.** I repoint *'awīl* to *'awwal.*

[12] **Neck.** *'ōrep* refers specifically to the back of the neck. JPS's "took me by the scruff" is accurate.

[15] **Horn.** A frequent symbol of power, doubtless derived from the horned bull.

16 1 Job answered thus:
2 I've heard so many things like these—
troublesome comforters, all of you.
3 Do windy words have an end,
or what is hurting you, that you answer?

4 I too could talk as you do
if you were in my place.
I could pile up words against you
and shake my head over you.
5 I could strengthen you with my mouth,
and my lips' condolence would assuage.
6 If I speak, my pain is not assuaged,
but when I stop, how much leaves me?
7 Surely now it exhausts me.
You've desolated my whole company,
8 have seized me to be a witness.
My emaciation rises against me,
testifies against me.
9 His anger tears—he despises me—
grinds upon me with its teeth.
My foe whets his eyes at me.

10 They open their mouths against me,
scornfully strike my cheeks,
mass together against me.
11 El abandons me to the vicious,
flings me to the hands of knaves.

12 I was once at ease, and he shook me up,
grabbed my neck and broke me apart,
raised me as a target.
13 His troops surround me;
he splits open my guts without pity,
pours my gall on the ground,
14 breaches me, breach upon breach,
runs against me like a warrior.

15 I sew up sackcloth over my skin
and thrust my horn in the dust.
16 My face is red from weeping,
and darkness is on my eyelids,

[19] **In heaven.** Ordinarily I take *šamayim* as "sky," because I find no clear evidence that ancient Israelites thought of a divine dwelling-place somewhere "up there." Here, however, the language seems to imply that the witness is in a place where he can have an effect on Eloah (vv. 20–21). Though the Book of Job does not locate the deity explicitly in the sky, let alone in any place analogous to later Christian pictures of "heaven," I borrow the idea to indicate the witness's presence with the deity.

[20] **My interpreter, my friend, to Eloah.** A very difficult couplet. I repoint the plural *m^e^līṣay rēʿay* to singular *m^e^līṣī rēʿī*, and take *'el '^e^lōah* with the first line. The short second line is an emotional aside in the midst of this very emotional outburst.

are sleepless. Alternatively, *dlp* I, "drip."

[21] This verse might be a resultative, jussive sentence from the foregoing, "that he may," etc., but the compound sentence makes as good sense.

between. MT has *ūben-'adam*, "and Adam's son." With some trepidation I adopt *ūbēn*, "and between," with some MSS and many commentators. It muddles the parallelism with the prior line a bit.

[22] **Cannot turn.** Or "cannot return" (*lō'-'ašūb*). The "road of no return" as a symbol of death had probably become a cliché by the second millennium B.C.E. See the translations in ANET of the Sumerian "Inanna's Descent to the Nether World," p. 54, lines 82–83, and of the Akkadian "Descent of Ishtar to the Nether World," p. 107, lines 5–6, and similar language in Job 7.9–10; 10.21.

[2] The sentence is, I think, a formula of self-cursing. The negative particle is implied in the second line.

[3] **You.** Masculine singular, and also in v. 4, hence an address to the deity.

clap my hand. The gesture used in concluding a bargain or contract (see, e.g., Prov 6.1). I repoint *yittaqēaʿ* to *yitqaʿ*.

[4] **Exalted.** MT *t^e^rōmēm* is active, and with Gordis (*Book of Job*, p. 181), I repoint to Polal, *t^e^rōmam*.

[5] With Gordis (*Book of Job*, pp. 181–82), I see this couplet as a proverbial saying.

[6] **He.** Job's speech to the deity is over, and he reverts to the third person.

spittle. Or Tophet, a place in the valley below Jerusalem where, according to passages like Jer 7.31, some Israelites burned children as sacrifices to Molek, a Canaanite god. That connotative reference of Tophet has a certain resonance with v. 5, but I leave it in a note because "spittle" seems more apt, and I am not happy with JPS's "of old" for *l^e^panīm*.

[10] **You.** Plural.

[17] though no violence is on my palms,
and my prayer is pure.

[18] Earth, do not cover my blood,
do not provide a place for my outcry!
[19] Even now, Ah! my witness is in heaven,
my supporter is on high,
[20] my interpreter, my friend, to Eloah—
my eyes are sleepless—
[21] and he will decide for a hero against Eloah,
between Adam and his friend.

[22] But years come by the number,
and I walk a path from which I cannot turn.
17 [1] My spirit is wrecked,
my days extinct,
I own the grave.
[2] If mockeries are not ever-present,
my eye does not lodge in their bitterness—

[3] Put up my guarantee against you!
Who is he who'll clap my hand?
[4] Because you've closed their minds to insight,
therefore, you'll not be exalted.
[5] "He tells his friends about his profits,
and his children's eyes are failing."
[6] He sets me out for peoples to taunt,
and I become spittle on the face.
[7] My eye is dulled by frustration,
and my limbs are all like a shadow.

[8] Moral people are astounded by this,
the guiltless rouses up against the impious,
[9] the innocent holds tight to his way,
and the clean of hands grows ever stronger.
[10] But you, bring them all and come,
and I won't find a wise one among you.

[11] My days are past,
my purposes shattered,
the desires of my heart.

[12] **Put night over day.** The usual interpretation of this line is the exact opposite: "they turn night into day." The expression could be so read, but because of the context, I prefer to take *śym* in its usual sense, "to put, set."

[15] **I mean.** I interpolate these words to reflect an emphatic tone both in the repetition of "my hope" and in the emphatic conjunction on the second use of the word (on the latter, see Blommerde, *Northwest Semitic Grammar*, pp. 82–83).

[16] **Beside me.** Repointing *baddē* to *bīday*, "at my hands, beside me."

do we descend. Repointing *naḥat* to *nēḥat*.

[2–3] The second-person pronouns and verb forms in these lines, oddly, are masculine plural. It seems that Bildad addresses the other two friends, though we expect him to address Job.

[2] **Put on a hunt.** For this sense of *qeneṣ*, see Pope, *Job*, p. 133. The word is a hapax legomenon, and Horst (*Hiob*, p. 268) rejects it.

[4] **Your account.** The pronoun is masculine singular.

disintegrates. Bildad quotes Job from 14.18, with the first two words in reversed order. The basic sense of the verb *ʿtq* seems to be "to become old," though most commentators translate it here "be moved." Both here and in 14.18, the best sense is that the rock is wearing out. I suspect that Bildad's tone is sarcastic.

[8] **Flung.** The pun between *šullaḥ* here and *tašlīkēhū*, "fling him," in the previous line leads me to translate them similarly. *Šlḥ* is "to send," *šlk* "to throw."

[13] The sentence is unusual in form but syntactically possible. The subject appears only in the second line, and the verb is repeated there. "Skin-covered limbs" renders the unusual *baddēy ʿōrō*, "limbs of his skin." Sarna ("Mythological Background," p. 317), among others, reads: "devours with two hands his skin," taking *baddēy* as a defective spelling of *bᵉyaddēy*, a dual. "Death," *Mot*, is a proper name, but no mythic material on Mot's offspring survives. Pope (*Job*, p. 135) accepts Michel's suggestion that *bakōr* and *mawet* are in apposition, "Death, the first-born," syntactically acceptable but not reflected in the mythic material we have. Umberto Cassuto first proposed the meaning "Mot's first-born" (in *The Goddess Anat* [in Hebrew: Jerusalem, 1951], p. 49). Sarna (p. 316) compares "Mot's first-born" to Namtar, the messenger and son of Ereshkigal, queen of the netherworld in Babylonian mythology, but he admits (*n*13) that the Ugaritic texts give no indication that Mot had offspring. It is like the presumed Rahab combat myth (see note to 9.13), to which we have several passing allusions but of which no account remains.

[12] They put night over day,
bringing light close to darkness.

[13] If I hope for Sheol as my home,
in darkness spread out my bed,
[14] to the muck say, "You're my father,"
"Mother, sister," to the maggot,
[15] where, then, is my hope?
My hope I mean—who will see it?
[16] Will they go down beside me to Sheol?
Do we descend together to dust?

18 [1] Bildad the Shuchite answered thus:
[2] How long will you put on a hunt for words?
When will you understand, so we can speak?
[3] Why are we considered as cattle,
presumed stupid in your eyes?

[4] He who preys angrily upon his soul,
will earth be abandoned on your account?
"A rock disintegrates from its place!"

[5] Surely knaves' light is snuffed out,
its fire's blaze doesn't shine,
[6] light goes dark in his tent,
the beacon above him is snuffed out.

[7] His strong strides themselves constrict him,
and his own plans fling him down.
[8] For he's flung into a net by his feet,
walks across a pit-cover,
[9] a snare snatches at his heel,
traps grasp onto him,
[10] hidden in the ground is a cord,
meshes are above the path.

[11] Terrors all around make him shiver,
chase after his feet.
[12] His strength is famine-ridden,
and disaster is ready for his stumbling.
[13] Devours his skin-covered limbs,
Death's first-born devours his limbs.

[14] **Marched.** I have no explanation for the t-prefix on *tṣʿydhw*, which some explain as an Amarna-type masculine t-preformative, others as an odd third-person masculine plural (vocalized *taṣʿīdūhū*). Gordis (*Book of Job*, p. 192) takes it as a feminine impersonal, but I see no referent.
king of terrors. It is hard to be sure of the mythic reference, but the Mesopotamian underworld god often has such characteristics. In Canaanite mythology, Mot is king of the underworld.
[15] **Not his.** A difficult phrase, *mibbᵉlī-lō* has given rise to many emendations, the most common of which is *līlīt*, the demon Lilith. Gordis's *mabbūl*, "flood of fire" (*Book of Job*, p. 193), or Dahood's *mabbēl*, "fire" ("Some Northwest-Semitic Words," pp. 312–14; see also Pope, *Job*, p. 136), are more acceptable, but I find Dhorme (p. 266) still more persuasive.
sulfur. As in *Odyssey* 22.480–81, 492–94, the sprinkled sulfur would magically prevent any resumption of habitation.
[20] **In the west.** Some scholars take *'aḥᵃrōnīm* and its parallel *qadmōnīm* as temporal terms, "latter and preceding generations" (see Gordis, *Book of Job*, p. 194). I could not reject this meaning, but the terms accord more closely with the geographical terms in vv. 17–19 and 21. The plurals suggest "westerners" and "easterners" (Pope, *Job*, p. 137), and I have modified that idea adverbially.
stand on end. Somewhat literally, "and easterners seize [their] hair." The feeling of astonished terror in the couplet leads me to the hair standing on end, but one might equally well picture people tearing at their hair.
[21] **Place that doesn't know El.** Most translations take *lō'-yadaʿ 'ēl* to mean "the person who does not know El." If MT read *yōdēaʿ*, the participle, I would be more amenable to it. Of course, "dwellings" and "place" might be metonymies for the dwellers and the occupants.

[3] . . . The verb *hkr* is a hapax legomenon, and its meaning is not known.
[5] The syntax of the sentence is confused by the fact that the accusative of both verbs, "my disgrace," turns up only at the end of the second line. The pattern recurs a number of times in Job.
[6] **Bent.** The same verb that Bildad used in 8.3, *ʿwt*.
[7] **Cry "Violence!"** The same words begin the complaint in Hab 1.2. Perhaps it is a convention of a heartfelt complaint. There is *ḥamas*, "violence," a certain component of what the law calls perjury, violence done to truth, perhaps, which reminds us of v. 6a.

[14] He's wrenched from the tent he trusted,
marched off to the king of terrors.

[15] What dwells in his tent is not his,
and sulfur is sprinkled on his shanty.
[16] Underneath his roots dry up,
and up above his twigs wither away.

[17] Memory of him perishes from the earth,
and he has no name along the street.
[18] They thrust him from light into darkness,
chase him out of the world.
[19] He has neither kith nor kin among his folk
nor survivor where once he lived.

[20] They shudder over his day in the west,
in the east the hair stands on end.
[21] Certainly these are the evil dwellings,
this the place that doesn't know El.

19 [1] Job answered thus:
[2] How long will you pain my soul,
pulverize me with talk?
[3] These ten times you've insulted me,
haven't been ashamed to . . . me.

[4] Have I truly strayed?
My straying stays at home with me.
[5] If you truly boast against me,
decide my disgrace against me,
[6] know then that El has bent me around,
circled his net over me.
[7] Ah, I cry "Violence!" and I'm not answered,
I call out, but justice is not there.

[12] **Construct their highway.** A strange statement in the context, which, as Gordis argues (*Book of Job*, p. 201), suggests preparations for siege. Pope translates "set siege" (*Job*, p. 138).

[14–15] I have abandoned the MT accentual punctuation of these lines, reading them as: *ḥdlw qrby wmyd'y / škḥwny gry byty / w'mhty lzr tḥšbny / nkry hyyty b'ynyhm.*

[17] **Stinking.** Wernberg-Møller was the first to argue that this verb is *zwr* III, "to stink."

my own children. Job's reference to his wife and children leads some scholars to argue that the poet did not trouble to achieve scrupulous consistency with the details of the pre-existing story. Still, the expression here is, to put it mildly, unusual: *libnē biṭnī*, "to the sons of my womb." Blommerde (*Northwest Semitic Grammar*, p. 87) turns the *y* suffix not just to third person, as he does frequently, but to third-person feminine, which is rarer. Actually, *y* can be a feminine verbal suffix (second person), and "sons [= children in that sexist society] of her womb" is distantly possible. It is difficult to know what Job might mean by "my womb." Is he proprietary over his wife's womb? Is "womb" a synecdoche for "clan," as a number of scholars think? I would sooner accept the former than the latter (in that sexist society). Terrien (*IB*, pp. 1046–47) takes *biṭnī*, "my womb," in 3.10 to mean "my mother's womb" and so justifies RSV's "brothers" (i.e., "sons of my [mother's] womb") here.

[23] **Inscription.** *Sēper*, "book, writing." The latter is the more accurate, as "books" in our sense of them did not exist in that world. See Gehman, "*Sēper*." Dhorme (p. 282) plausibly connects *sēper* with Akkadian *siparru*, "copper" (see also Pope, *Job*, pp. 143–44). The verb "engraved," *ḥqq*, points to something hard like metal or wood, and the parallelism of *sēper* with *lūaḥ*, "tablet," in Isa 30.8 (with the same verb as here) may suggest an inscribed object like a plaque.

[24] **Lead.** Pope (*Job*, p. 144) cites an inscription in which the incised letters were filled with lead, doubtless in the expectation that they would be both more visible and more permanent.

[25–27] This passage gives everyone fits, both of furious activity and of blank despair. In 35 years of trying to perceive sense in these verses, I have found it only in the first line. I can read each of the words. Except for v. 25a, I cannot with an acceptable degree of confidence construe the words in sensible sentences. Having declared myself opposed to rewriting to make the passage mean what I wish it meant, I leave the lines blank, and I will not use them in thinking about meaning. Here, however, I present the best sense I can make out of these lines, with the proviso that I find them much less meaningful in Hebrew than they may seem:

> [25] As for me, I know that my avenger lives,
> and afterward he rises upon dust.
> [26] And after they have flayed my skin, this—
> and from my flesh I perceive Eloah,

8 My road is blocked, I cannot pass,
and he sets darkness across my paths.
9 He has stripped my honor from me,
pushed aside the crown on my head.
10 He breaks me all around when I walk,
uproots my hope like a tree.
11 His anger burns against me,
and he considers me like his foes.
12 His gangs come in together,
construct their highway against me,
encamp all around my tent.

13 He has distanced my brothers from me,
those who know me are even alien from me,
14 my visitors and those I know have stopped,
15 strangers in my house have forgotten me,
my maids consider me an alien,
I've become a foreigner in their eyes.
16 I call my slave, and he doesn't answer,
with my mouth I must beg him.
17 My breath is stinking to my wife,
I am loathsome to my own children.
18 Even the young despise me,
I stand up, and they heckle me.
19 All my confidants abhor me,
and any I have loved turn against me.

20 My bones cling to my skin and flesh,
and I escape by the skin of my teeth.
21 Pity, oh pity me, you my friends,
for Eloah's hand has touched me.
22 Why do you pursue me, like El,
not satisfied with my flesh?

23 Would that my words were written,
would that they were engraved in an inscription,
24 with an iron stylus and lead
forever in rock they were incised.
25 As for me, I know that my avenger lives;
. . . . . . - . . . . . .
26 . . . . - . . .
. . . .

[27]whom I perceive to me,
and my eyes saw, and not a foreigner.
My kidneys are ended in my bosom.

[25] **Avenger.** The meanings attached to *gō'ēl* are legion. I take the basic metaphor to be the traditional function of the *gō'ēl haddam*, the "avenger of blood," as found in Num 35.19; Deut 19.6, 12; etc. When someone was killed by a member of another tribe or clan, the injured clan appointed one of its members to procure vengeance on behalf of the deceased by recourse not to courts but to plain old "frontier justice." That person was the *gō'ēl haddam*, or *gō'ēl*. The less violent sense of *gō'ēl* in the Book of Ruth, as a kinsman who buys back the clan's property, strikes me as less consistent with the context.

[29] **Trial.** Ketib is *šdyn*, Qere, *šaddūn*, neither of which reveals meaning to anyone. I read *šeddīn*, taking *dīn* not as abstract "justice" or "judgment" but as a legal proceeding. I am not utterly convinced of this decision.

[3] **Intellect.** *Bīnah* means something like "understanding." Perhaps Zophar thinks of his "wind" as interior to him as against the external "wind" in Eliphaz's dream (4.15).

[4] **Is this what you know.** The rhetorical question implies a negative answer. That is surely not Zophar's meaning, but it is not for me to repair his rhetoric and reasoning for him.

[9] **In his place.** See Tur-Sinai, p. 312, for this reading.

[10] **His wealth.** I do not know whose wealth this is.

[27] . . . .-. . .
. . . .-. . .
. . . .

[28] Because you say, "How we'll pursue him!"
and the root of the matter is found in me,
[29] fear for your lives before the sword,
for the sword is fury on wrongdoing,
so that you may know that there is a trial.

20 [1] Zophar the Na'amathite answered thus:
[2] Therefore my disquiet stops me,
and because of the haste that's in me
[3] I hear indication of an insult to me,
and a wind from my intellect answers me.

[4] Is this what you know from of old,
since Adam was put upon earth,
[5] that knaves' triumphal shout is short,
the joy of the impious but for the moment?
[6] Though his frame ascend to the sky,
his head reach into the clouds,
[7] he'll perish forever like his dung,
those who saw him will say, "Where is he?"
[8] Like a dream he'll fly off, not to be found,
flee away like a vision at night.
[9] The eye that glimpsed him won't do so again
nor any longer behold him in his place.
[10] His sons will beg from the poor,
his hands will restore his wealth.

[11] His bones may be full of lustiness,
but they will bed with him in dust.
[12] If evil gives his mouth a sweet taste,
he hides it under his tongue,

[15] Here and in vv. 20a, 23a, I have used "belly" for *beṭen*, which also means "womb" (and in that meaning gives some difficulty in 3.10 and 19.17).

[17] I ignore the MT punctuation of this rather strange statement, taking *nhry* from the second line into the first, and reading its form as a genitive: "streams of shining," i.e., "shining streams." See Pope, *Job*, p. 152; Blommerde, *Northwest Semitic Grammar*, p. 90. "Wadis of honey and butter" echoes the traditional description of Israel as "a land flowing with milk and honey."

[18] **Like.** The preposition is strange in the statement.

[23] **Food.** I take *laḥūm* as a passive participle of *lḥm* II, "to feed, eat."

[24] **Cuts him down.** That implies *ḥlp* II. One might read *ḥlp* I, "catches him." The image of a bow doing such damage is odd, the picture of a bronze or copper bow in actual use even odder.

[25] **Drawn sword.** *Šalap* means "he draws" (or drew). I repoint to *šalup*, "something drawn," in the context most naturally a sword. I wish the conjunction were not present on the following verb, though it may suggest that "the drawn sword" is appositional to (and a correction of?) the "bronze bow."

glittering. Taking *baraq*, "lightning," metaphorically, as in Deut 32.41.

horrors come. Bypassing the MT punctuation, I join *yhlk* to what follows rather than to what precedes.

13 treasures it not to abandon it,
keeps it close in his cheek.
14 His bread churns about in his innards,
the asp's bitter gall within him.
15 He swallows wealth and vomits it out,
El forces it on him from the belly;
16 he suckles the poison of asps,
a viper's tongue slays him.
17 He'll not look on shining streams,
wadis of honey and butter,
18 he'll stop his toil and won't swallow,
like the wealth of his trade, and won't enjoy it.

19 Because he has crushed the poor and left them,
seized a house he did not build,
20 because he's known no peace in his belly,
he'll not escape with what he holds dear.
21 There's nothing left for him to eat,
therefore his property cannot increase.
22 Even with plenty, he is constricted,
the whole power of toil comes upon him.
23 Does he act to fill his belly?
Furious wrath is dispatched upon him,
rains upon him with his food.

24 He flees an iron weapon,
a bronze bow cuts him down,
25 the drawn sword, and it comes out his back,
glittering out of his gall.
Horrors come upon him,
26 all the hidden darkness his treasures hold.
A fire not blown will devour him,
what's left in his tent will be damaged.
27 The sky itself will uncover his guilt,
earth revolt against him.
28 A storm will carry his house away,
flood it on the wrathful day.

29 This is the lot of evil humankind from Elohim,
the heritage that El bespeaks him.

[2] **Listen carefully**, etc. Identical to 13.17a. The imperative is plural, as are the pronoun in v. 2b and the imperative in v. 3a.

[3] **So I.** The separate pronoun is emphatic, and its use here is strange.

you can scoff. This imperfect is second-person masculine singular, which in Job's mouth otherwise signifies an address to the deity (unless 16.3 is an exception). One would expect the plural, and some scholars take the singular as addressing Zophar (see Gordis, *Book of Job*, p. 228; Pope, *Job*, p. 157).

[4] **Now for me.** Again the emphatic separate pronoun.

[5] **Lay your hands on your mouths.** Job uses nearly the same expression (*śym yad ʿal-peh*) of himself in 40.4b (*śym yad l*^{e}*mō-peh*) and of others in 29.9 (*kap śym l*^{e}*peh*). Gordis (*Book of Job*, p. 228) thinks that it signifies silence, whereas Pope (*Job*, p. 157) adduces a Mesopotamian seal to suggest that it means "awe and stupefaction."

[8] **Their people before them.** I have turned this verse into a tercet with two words in each line, and have repointed MT *ʿimmam*, "with them," to *ʿammam*, "their people."

[10] **His bull.** The singular pronouns in this couplet contrast with the masculine plurals in vv. 9 and 11. I have no explanation, but neither am I inclined to be nervous about it. A similar switch from plural to singular occurs between vv. 18 and 19.

[12] **Lift [their voices].** MT has only "they lift," and I assume an ellipsis of *qōlam*, doubtless for rhythmic reasons and probably not to avoid two uses of *qōl* in two lines.

with drum. MT has *k*^{e}*tōp*, "like drum." Most ancient translations and many Hebrew manuscripts and editions of the text have *b*^{e}*tōp* or its equivalent. In the presence of so much textual backing, as well as the ease with which copyists could (and did) confuse the letters *bet* (ב) and *kaph* (כ), I accept the variant.

[13] **Wear out.** This is the Ketib *y*^{e}*ballū*; Qere is *y*^{e}*kallū*, "they end" (see my comments on this reading in the "Indispensable Introduction").

are terrified at the moment of Sheol. The line, *ūb*^{e}*regaʿ š*^{e}*ʾōl yēḥattū*, allows two completely incompatible translations and a third that combines them. Gordis (*Book of Job*, p. 224) reads "And in peace they go down to Sheol." That reading connects *regaʿ*, usually "a moment, suddenly," to Arabic *rajaʿa*, "return to rest" (Gordis, p. 229, wants to include both meanings) and takes *yēḥattū* not as Niphʿal of *ḥtt*, "be terrified," but as Qal of *nḥt*, *yēḥatū*, "go down" (cf. Jer 21.13 in Qal). One might also combine the usual meaning of *regaʿ* with *yēḥatū*, as in Pope's "And quickly go to Sheol" (*Job*, p. 155).

[17] The particle "how often" (*kammah*) governs all three lines of the tercet.

[18] This couplet may continue the rhetorical question of v. 17.

[19] The first line has no interrogative sign, but I take it as one of those indicative-interrogatives that one finds here and there. Or we could, with Gordis (*Book of Job*, p. 231), take it as a quotation attributed to the friends.

21 [1]Job answered thus:
[2]Now listen carefully to my word;
you may get some consolation from this.
[3]Lift me up so I can speak,
and after I've spoken, you can scoff away.

[4]Now for me, is my complaint with humans?
Why shouldn't my breath be short?
[5]Face me and be appalled,
lay your hands on your mouths.
[6]If I recall it, I'm frightened,
and my flesh grasps a shudder.

[7]Why do the wicked live,
mature, and increase strength,
[8]their progeny established,
their people before them,
their offspring in their sight?
[9]Their houses are safe from terror,
and Eloah's rod does not hang over them.
[10]His bull unfailingly breeds,
his heifer calves and never aborts.
[11]They sire infants in flocks,
and their children dance about.
[12]They lift [their voices] with drum and zither,
rejoice at sound of flute.
[13]They wear out their days with good,
are terrified at the moment of Sheol.
[14]They say to El, "Get away from us!
Knowing your ways does not please us.
[15]What is Shaddai that we should serve him?
What the profit that we should beg of him?"
[16]Ah! their good is not in their hand;
the counsel of the wicked is far from me.

[17]How often is the beacon of the wicked snuffed out,
does their calamity come upon them,
does he apportion destruction in anger?
[18]Let them be like straw before the wind,
like chaff the storm wind steals.
[19]Eloah is treasuring up punishment for his sons?
Let him pay him directly, so he knows!

22 **Who judges.** The referent of the emphatic pronoun *hū'* may be El or the same "he" who has been the subject since v. 17. If the former, this line is a question in parallel to v. 22a: "Does he teach knowledge to El, and does *he* [the human?] judge the lofty ones?" The emphatic pronoun seems less apt for that interpretation. If El is the subject of this pronoun, the two lines of the couplet are sharply antithetic: "Does he [that human] teach knowledge to El, and *he* [that deity] judges the lofty ones?"

lofty ones. The plural can be taken adverbially, "on high" (so Gordis, *Book of Job*, p. 224), or as an epithet of the deity with the enclitic *mem* (so Blommerde, *Northwest Semitic Grammar*, p. 93; Pope, *Job*, p. 160—Blommerde also suggests that *ramīm* could be a plural of majesty). The reference is the same as Eliphaz's in 4.18; 15.15.

24 **His . . . .** The hapax legomenon *'ṭyn* is commonly emended to *'ṭmyw*, meaning something like flanks or haunches in comparison to Akkadian *eṣmu* (see Pope, *Job*, p. 161). JPS reads "his pails," on the basis of an assumed Arabic cognate that means camels' watering places. Tur-Sinai (pp. 330–31) quotes Jerusalem Talmud Mo'ed Qat. II, 1, 81a, for the meaning olive oil and redivides the words of the line to *'aṭīn yimmalē' wᵉḥalab*, for "he is full of oil and milk." Gordis (*Book of Job*, p. 233) suggests that a later Hebrew meaning, "olive," was used euphemistically for the testicles. Perhaps a word that can be made to mean so many things cannot be made to mean anything.

28 **Aristocratic house.** I accept Albertz's evidence (p. 361, *n*30) that *nadīb* denotes aristocracy, not royalty.

30 **Wretch.** *Ra'*, someone vile, not someone in misery.

33 **[Mourners].** I interpolate the word as being implied by the image of the funeral procession. The Hebrew has only "countless" (*'ēn mispar*).

4 **Because of your religiousness.** I take "your fear" in the same sense as in 1.1. The expression here is elliptical. "Because of" is the preposition "from" (*min*), slightly stretched.

come against you with your justice. Because *yabō' 'immᵉka*, "come against you," is elliptical for "enter a trial against you," I take *bᵉmišpaṭ* as parallel to *miyyir'atka* as the motive sarcastically imputed to the deity.

[20] Let him see his own distress,
drink from Shaddai's wrath.
[21] For what pleasure has he in his house after him
when the number of his months is cut off?
[22] Does he teach knowledge to El,
who judges the lofty ones?

[23] This one dies with perfect bones,
all secure and at ease,
[24] his . . . full of milk,
the marrow of his bones well watered.
[25] And that one dies with a bitter soul,
having never eaten good.
[26] They lie down together on the dust,
and the worms cover them.
[27] Oh, I know your schemes,
the tricks you're hatching against me.
[28] For you say, "Where is the aristocratic house,
where the tent where the wicked live?"
[29] Have you not asked those who pass on the road,
and do you not mistake their signs
[30] that on a calamitous day a wretch is spared,
on a day when fury is led forth?
[31] Who points out his way to his face?
When he has done something, who pays him back?
[32] But he is led forth to the graveyard,
and over his barrow is a wakeful watch.
[33] The clods of the wadi taste sweet to him,
everyone follows his procession,
and ahead of it are countless [mourners].

[34] How you console me with empty air,
and your replies leave only fraud behind!

22 [1] Eliphaz the Temanite answered thus:
[2] Does a man benefit El?
But even a wise one benefits only himself.
[3] Is Shaddai pleased that you are innocent,
or is it profit that your life is perfect?
[4] Does he charge you because of your religiousness,
come against you with your justice?

[6] **Because.** *Kī* governs all the clauses through v. 9.
stripped. *Tapšīṭ* may be a pun with *mišpaṭ*, v. 4b.
[8] **Strong man.** "Man of arm."
the one with status. *N^e^śū' panīm*, "lifted of face," generally one approved or accepted. Job uses the same expression in 13.8, 10 to signify the illicit skewing of a legal case.
[9] **Are crushed.** The verb is a third-person masculine singular passive, but its subject is a feminine plural, "arms."
[10] **Snares . . . terror.** This bad rhyme is as close as I can come to the sound play between *paḥ* and *paḥad*.
panic. The verb *bhl* has elements both of terrifying and of being hasty. Job uses the same verb in 23.15a, 16b.
[13] **Give order.** The verb *špṭ* is usually taken as "to judge." I think it also has to do with keeping order, including cosmic order (see the noun *mišpaṭ* in 40.8).
[15] **Ancient path.** One might, repointing *'ōlam* to *'alūm*, read "the hidden path." Either makes good sense. If "ancient," Eliphaz alleges a perennial human tendency to go wrong. If "hidden," he matches ridiculous efforts to conceal wrongdoing with Job's ill-conceived idea that the deity is "concealed" by distance and clouds (v. 14a). That connection is so suspiciously neat that I have chosen the *lectio dificilior*, "ancient."
[17] The first line repeats Job's words in 21.14a.
[18] **He.** An emphatic pronoun, which I take as an indignant answer to "What does Shaddai do about it?" in v. 17b.
the counsel, etc. Another repetition of Job's words, these from 21.16b.
[20] These two statements are self-curses by the "righteous" and "innocent" in the same form as the Prosecutor's in chaps. 1 and 2. Because v. 20b has no negative, I suppose that *'im-lō'* in v. 20a covers both lines.
[21] **Benefit.** In v. 2, Eliphaz denied that a human could benefit the deity.
your income. I repoint *t^e^bō'atka* to *t^e^bū'atka*.
[24] **Ophir's [gold].** MT does not have "gold," but Ophir, proverbially rich in gold and gems (see 28.16), may be a metonymy for it. There is a nice pun in Hebrew between "treasure," *beṣer*, and "among the stones," *b^e^ṣūr*, and another between *'apar*, "dust," and the name Ophir.

5 Are you not in fact greatly wicked,
with no end to your misdeeds?

6 Because you have taken your brother hostage for no reason,
stripped the clothes from the naked,
7 have given no water for the thirsty to drink,
have withheld bread from the famished;
8 to the strong man belongs the land,
the one with status governs in it;
9 you have sent widows away empty,
and the arms of orphans are crushed;
10 therefore, snares will surround you,
terror suddenly panic you.
11 Or you will fail to see darkness,
and the flood of water will cover you.

12 Is not Eloah the apex of the sky?
Look at how high is the topmost star.
13 And you say, "What does El know?
Does he give order through the thick cloud?
14 Clouds conceal him, and he does not see,
and he walks around on the circle of the sky."
15 Do you watch over the ancient path
that worthless men have trodden,
16 who were seized before their time,
the river pouring out on their foundation?
17 Those who say to El, "Get away from us!"
and "What does Shaddai do about it?"
18 He filled their houses with good—
the counsel of the wicked is far from me!
19 The righteous see and rejoice,
the innocent mocks it:
20 "If our adversary is not destroyed,
what's left of them the fire does not eat—"

21 Then benefit him, and regain your health.
Your income with them will be good.
22 Then take instruction from his mouth,
and settle what he says in your mind.
23 If you turn to Shaddai, you'll be rebuilt,
will remove iniquity far from your tent.
24 Lay treasure on the dust,
Ophir's [gold] among the stones of the wadi,

[26] **Lift your face.** This phrase is not the legal metaphor "lifted of face" as in v. 8, but the echo suggests a properly "lifted face" in contrast to the illicit one implied in v. 8.

[29] **But they will sink down.** A strange statement, without a clear antecedent for the plural. Perhaps it is just an impersonal, "some."
pride. Some translators take *wattō'mer gēwah* to mean "You will say, 'Get up.'" The association of *gēwah* with pride, however, suggests that Eliphaz predicts that Job, having experienced the humiliation of suffering, will recognize pride when he sees it.

[30] **Not-innocent.** *'ī-naqī* is an unusual term, for which I use an unusual English one. The negative *'ī* is amply documented, though Sarna's proposal of an indefinite pronoun *'ē* ("*Crux Interpretum*") is also possible.

[2] **My hand.** Nearly everyone emends *ydy* to *ydw*, "his hand," the "heavy hand" being the divine pressure on Job. I take the "heavy hand" as the discouragement of one who feels it too difficult even to lift a hand. For "groaning," see 3.24.

[6] **By an attorney.** I find Tur-Sinai's interpretation (pp. 353–54) of *rob kōaḥ* as a legal plenipotentiary convincing, but the phrase can equally well be read "with great strength."
attend. I take *yaśīm bī* as an ellipsis for *yaśīm [libbō] bī*, "set [his heart, mind] on me."

[7] **Bring forth my case successfully.** As in 21.10, the verb *plṭ* is a metaphor of birth (cf. Tur-Sinai, p. 355). Therefore I repoint *miššōpṭī*, "from my judge," to *mišpaṭī*, and understand *lnṣḥ* as "victoriously."

[8–9] The four points of the compass are, more literally, "in front," "in back," "to the left hand," and "to the right hand."

[12] **His lips' commands.** I take these words as parallel to "his way," v. 11b.
within my limits. The preposition *min*, "from," sometimes means "within a territory" (see Gen 11.1). *Mēḥūqī* is often taken as "in my bosom." But *ḥōq* signifies a limit or boundary in 14.5; Prov 30.8; Jer 5.22; and Isa 5.14, and Job uses it in the related sense of "decree, sentence" in v. 14a.

[13] . . . I cannot find an acceptable meaning of *b*^{e}*'eḥad*, "in one" (the numeral), without resorting to emendation.

25 and Shaddai is your treasure
and your choicest silver.
26 For then you will find pleasure in Shaddai,
will lift your face to Eloah.
27 You will pray to him, and he will listen to you,
and you will pay what you vow.
28 You will decide something, and it will stand,
and light will dawn upon your way.
29 But they will sink down, and you will call it pride,
and he delivers the lowly of eyes.
30 He rescues the not-innocent,
who are rescued by your pure palms.

23 1 Job answered thus:
2 Today, too, my complaint is bitter,
my hand heavy from my groaning.
3 Oh that I knew, and could find him,
could enter his throne room,
4 set out a case before him,
fill my mouth with arguments.
5 I would know the words of his answer,
understand what he says to me.
6 Would he prosecute me by an attorney?
No, he himself would attend to me.
7 There a moral person could argue with him,
and I should bring forth my case successfully.

8 Ah, I go east, and he's not there,
west, and I don't discern him,
9 north where he works, and don't perceive him;
he hides in the south, and I cannot see him.
10 Because he knows the way I'm on;
he'll test me, I shall emerge as gold.
11 My foot has stayed firm in his track,
I've kept to his way, have not turned aside,
12 his lips' commands, have not departed,
within my limits I've treasured his mouth's words.
13 And he . . . , who could change him?
His soul wishes something, and he does it.

14 **Come to terms with.** *Yašlīm*, "make peace with."
17 **Silenced.** A number of scholars (e.g., Gordis, *Book of Job*, pp. 262–63; Terrien, *IB*, p. 1084; see also Brown et al., s.v. *ṣmt*) take *nṣmty* as "annihilate, destroy," a quite acceptable sense. The Arabic cognate, signifying speechlessness, is also acceptable to K-B, s.v. *ṣmt*; Fohrer, *Das Buch Hiob*, p. 362; and me.
before the throne of gloom. None of the translations of this line that refrain from emendation is satisfactory to me. I have repointed *mippanay kissah*, "before (or from before) me he has hidden," to *mippᵉnē kissēh*, taking the two "before's" as parallel. *Kissē'*, "throne," is spelled *kissēh* in 1 Ki 10.19 (twice) and in Job 26.9, where I repoint to *keseh*.

5 **Searching the steppe for prey.** The plural construct followed by the preposition *lᵉ* can be found in Exod 38.11 and Ps 122.5 (see Gordis, *Book of Job*, p. 265).
* **for food.** MT *lō leḥem lannᵉʿarīm* makes no sense to me, and I have permitted myself to emend to *laleḥem*.
9 **Suckling.** Repointing *ʿal* to *ʿūl*.
11 **Rows.** I am persuaded by Gordis (*Book of Job*, p. 267) that *šūrōt* means "rows" in the Mishnah. The image is of pressing the olives in the orchard.
12 **Dying.** I repoint MT's *mᵉtīm*, "men," to *mētīm*.
thinks nothing amiss. MT's *tiplah*, "unworthy," suggests my translation (and cf. 1.22). Two Hebrew MSS and the Syriac read *tᵉpillah*, "prayer," meaning "Eloah pays no attention to [their] prayer," which is acceptable and entails only repointing.

14 But he will come to terms with my sentence;
many like it are in his mind.
15 Therefore I am in terror before him,
I ponder it, and I dread him.
16 El has weakened my mind,
Shaddai has terrified me.
17 But I am not silenced before darkness,
before the throne of gloom.

24 1 Why are not proper times treasured by Shaddai,
and those who know him don't see his days?
2 They snatch away boundary markers,
seize flocks and pasture them.
3 They drive off orphans' asses,
take a widow's ox for collateral,
4 shove the poor off the road;
the land's destitute huddle together in hiding.

5 See the wild asses in the desert,
they go out to their task,
searching the steppe for prey,
* for food for their young.
6 In the field by night they harvest,
quickly plunder a poor vineyard.
7 Naked they lodge, without clothing,
uncovered in the cold,
8 wet with mountain rain,
without shelter they hug the rock.
9 They seize an orphan from the breast,
take the suckling of the poor for collateral.
10 Naked they go about, without clothing,
famished, they carry the grain.
11 Between the rows they press oil,
tread the presses and are thirsty.
12 From the city the dying cry out,
the throats of the wounded call,
but Eloah thinks nothing amiss.

[13] **They—they**. The emphatic pronoun is matched by "he" in v. 18a.

[16] **Come daylight**. *Yōmam*, "by day."

they are sealed. The referent of this verb, like the next ("they do not know"), is the houses.

[17] **Him**. I.e., the adulterer, v. 15.

[18] **He, on the contrary**. The emphatic pronoun *hū'* refers to the deity, who seems to be the subject through v. 24.

[19] **Which never flow down to Sheol**. A free rendering of *š^{e}'ōl ḥaṭa'ū*, which, I think, means, "they miss Sheol," an ironic understatement, as snow water that has evaporated ("seized") can hardly make it all the way down to underworld Sheol.

[20] I ignore the MT punctuation, which would produce something like "The womb forgets him, his sweetness, / the worm is never remembered, / and wickedness," etc.

bought like wood. I take *tšbr* from *šbr* II, "to buy," which occurs about fifteen times, mostly in Genesis. To read *šbr* I, "to break," produces "wickedness is broken like a tree," which is very strange in this context.

[24] **They are exalted**. I take the ordinary meaning of *rwm*, "to be high." Gordis's interesting argument (*Book of Job*, p. 271) that this is *rwm*, "to wait," makes "They wait a little, and he's not there," a nice counterpart to 7.8b, 21d.

. . . . MT has *kakkōl*, "like all." We want a reference to a plant, but emendation to achieve "mallow" will not do, and I am uncertain of Gordis's *kōl* = "grass" in 2 Sam 17.3. See Grabbe, pp. 88–89.

[2] **Dreaded rule**. A hendiadys, "rule and dread."

[13] They—they are among the rebellers against light,
are unfamiliar with its ways,
have not sat along its paths.
[14] The murderer rises up at the light,
kills the poor and the needy,
and at night becomes like the thief.
[15] The adulterer's eye marks the twilight,
thinks, "Not an eye will spy me,"
and masks his face.
[16] He digs into houses in the dark;
come daylight, they are sealed around him.
They do not know light.
[17] Morning and deep darkness are the same to him,
since he is familiar with darkness's terrors.

[18] He, on the contrary, is swift across the waters.
Their plot of land is cursed,
he does not turn toward the vineyards.
[19] Dryness, like heat, seizes snow waters,
which never flow down to Sheol.
[20] The womb forgets him, the maggot is his sweetness,
and he is never remembered,
and wickedness is bought like wood.
[21] He pastures on the barren, on the childless,
and does no good to the widow.
[22] He draws out the mighty with his strength,
rises up, but does not assure life.
[23] He gives him security, and he is supported,
and his eyes are upon their ways.
[24] They are exalted a little, and he is not there.
They are brought down like . . . , are closed up,
and like the ear of grain they wither.
[25] If it is not so, who will prove me a liar
and bring my words to naught?

25 [1] Bildad the Shuchite answered thus:
[2] Dreaded rule is with him
who imposes peace on his heights.
[3] Is there any counting his troops?
On whom does his light not arise?

4–5 The sentiment is like Eliphaz's in 4.17–19, the statement even more like 15.14–16. Compare v. 4b, *ūmah-yizkeh yᵉlūd 'iššah*, with 15.14, *mah-'ᵉnōš kī-yizkeh wᵉkī-yiṣdaq yᵉlūd 'iššah*, and v. 5b, *wᵉkōkabīm lō'-zakkū bᵉ'ēnayw*, with 15.15b, *wᵉšamayim lō'-zakkū bᵉ'ēnayw*.

4 **Pure.** The image of moral purity comes from *zkh*, "to be clean."

2–4 The address in these lines is masculine singular, which usually marks Job's speaking to the deity.

6 **Abaddon.** A rather rare term for the underworld place of the dead, it is apparently derived from *'bd*, "to perish."

9 **Full moon.** With Pope (*Job*, p. 184), reading *keseh* for MT *kissēh*, "throne."

. . . . The quadriliteral *paršēz* is a hapax legomenon. Some scholars take it as an artificial combination of *prš* and *prz*, either of which would give a sense of "spread out."

10 **He inscribes a circle.** With many others, I repoint *ḥōq-ḥag*, "a limit he has circled," to *ḥaq ḥūg*.

11 **Blast.** The word is often translated "rebuke," but I am persuaded by Kennedy's argument (pp. 58–60) that it means a powerful or explosive blast. See also JPS.

13 . . . . Pope (*Job*, pp. 185–86) follows Tur-Sinai in reading *šiprah* as *siprah* (see Ps 56.9), and he divides *šamayim*, "Sky," to *śam yam*, "he put Sea in a bag." I would rather retain *šamayim*, because "Sea" is dealt with in v. 12a, but I want *šiprah* to be a verb, and I can find no candidate.

fleeing Dragon. Exactly the same phrase, describing Leviathan, occurs in Isa 27.1.

14 **Way.** I read Ketib, *darkō*; Qere is plural, *dᵉrakaw*.

his might. Ketib is singular; Qere, *gᵉbūrōtaw*, presumably a plural of abstraction. Either is satisfactory.

2 **As El lives.** Unusually, Job swears by the deity. The oath itself, lacking a result clause as usual, occurs in v. 4.

[4]How is any man righteous with El,
how is one born of woman pure?
[5]Oh, even the moon is not bright,
nor are stars pure in his sight,
[6]much less a man, that maggot,
child of Adam, worm that he is.

26 [1]Job answered thus:
[2]How helpful you are to the powerless,
bringing deliverance to the arm without strength!
[3]How you advise one lacking wisdom,
effusively propound knowledge!
[4]By whose help do you declare these words?
Whose breath comes out from you?

[5]The shades below writhe in agony,
the waters and their inhabitants.
[6]Sheol is naked before him,
Abaddon has no covering.
[7]He stretches the North over the void,
hangs Earth upon nothing.
[8]He binds up the waters in his clouds,
but the cumulus does not burst with their weight.
[9]He covers the face of the full moon
. . . the cumulus over it.
[10]He inscribes a circle on the waters
at the border of light with darkness.
[11]Sky's pillars tremble,
stunned by his blast.
[12]By his power he stilled Sea,
by his understanding smashed Rahab,
[13]by his wind Sky . . . ,
his hand pierced the fleeing Dragon.
[14]Oh, these are but the edges of his way.
What whispered word do we hear of him,
and the thunder of his might who understands?

27 [1]Again Job took up his discourse:
[2]As El lives, who has turned away my case,
Shaddai, who has embittered my soul,

5 **I'm damned.** The expression *ḥalīlah lī* seems stronger than its conventional translation, "Far be it from me."

integrity. The word is *tummah*, as it has been so often.

6 **Rightness.** An awkward effort to echo "right" (*'aṣdīq*) in v. 5a without saying "righteousness" for *ṣ^{e}daqah*.

7 **Considered.** *Y^{e}hī k^{e}raša‘ 'ōy^{e}bī*, "Let my enemy be as [like] a wicked one." That is a real wish, perhaps even an addition to the curse in vv. 2–4, but I take *y^{e}hī k^{e}* as mental, not physical: "Let my enemy be thought of [not 'treated'] as a wicked one."

8 **Godless.** I dislike both "godless" and "impious" (see 15.34; 20.5) as translations of *ḥanēp*. The word seems to have more to do with ritual pollution and impurity than with irreligion or disbelief.

carries away. Gordis (*Book of Job*, pp. 288–89) neatly summarizes the options. I repoint *yēšel* to *yašōl*, from *šll*, which occurs in Ruth 2.16 meaning "carry off sheaves." It is a nice counterpart to *bṣ‘*, "snipped off," in v. 8a.

12 **Utterly vapid.** *Hebel tehbalū*. The metaphor in *hebel* is "a puff of wind, vapor"; hence "vapid" in its proper sense. To combine verb and cognate noun is emphatic, matching the emphatic pronoun *'attem*, "you" (plural), at the beginning of v. 12a.

13 **Receive.** I take the verb at the end of the second line to govern the entire couplet. The couplet is a somewhat skewed quotation of Zophar's statement at 20.29.

14–17 The uses of the particle *'im* in vv. 14 and 16 suggest the possibility that these lines present complete curse formulae, which might be rendered thus:

> 14 If his children grow up to the sword,
> and his issue have not food enough,
> 15 may his survivors be buried with Mot,
> his widows not weep.
> 16 If he heaps up silver like dust,
> piles up clothing like clay,
> 17 may he pile it up, and the righteous wear it,
> the innocent divide the silver.

15 **With Mot.** The allusion may be to an episode in the Ugaritic Baal-Anat myth, in which Anat chops Mot up into little bits and flings them about the landscape. See ANET, p. 140.

widows. The Hebrew word is plural. Polygyny was never against law or custom in ancient Israel.

3 as long as I still have breath,
Eloah's wind in my nostrils,
4 if my lips speak viciousness,
my tongue, if it mutter deceit—

5 I'm damned if I'll say you are right;
until I perish, I'll not turn away my integrity.
6 To my rightness I hold fast, will not weaken it;
my heart finds nothing from my days to taunt.
7 Let my enemy be considered wicked,
the one who rises against me, vicious.
8 For what hope has the godless when he is snipped off,
when Eloah carries his life away?
9 Does El hear his cry
when trouble comes upon him?
10 Or does he find pleasure in Shaddai,
meet Eloah constantly?
11 I'll teach you what is in El's hand,
will not conceal what Shaddai has.
12 You, of course, have all seen it,
and why, then, are you so utterly vapid?
13 They receive this lot of evil humankind with El,
this heritage of oppressors from Shaddai.

14 If his children grow up, it is to the sword,
and his issue have not food enough.
15 If his survivors are buried with Mot,
his widows will not weep.
16 If he heaps up silver like dust,
piles up clothing like clay,
17 he may pile it up, and the righteous will wear it,
the innocent divide the silver.
18 He builds his house as does the moth,
like a lean-to a watchman makes.
19 He lies down rich, but has no harvest,
opens his eyes and is no more.
20 Terrors overwhelm him like torrents,
the tempest kidnaps him by night,
21 the east wind lifts him and he is gone,
sweeps him off from his place,
22 drives upon him without pity,
though he flee headlong from its hand.

[23] **It claps its hands.** The implied subject is the east wind in v. 21a, an identification strengthened by "his place," from which the wind "swept" the unfortunate human away, v. 21b, and from which it now whistles its derision. On the other hand, the subject might be the deity: "He claps his hands over him [the victim]."

[3] **He.** The verb is third-person masculine singular, and I take its subject as the generalized human miner. If the lines signify the deity's limit on humans, the singular verb beginning v. 4 must be taken as a plural.

[6] **To him.** This masculine pronoun suddenly appears where we expect a feminine, referring, like "it," v. 5a and "its," v. 6a, to the feminine "earth" (*'ereṣ*). The antecedent of "him" has to be the miner in vv. 3–4.

[8] **Proud beasts.** "Sons of pride" (*b^{e}nē šaḥaṣ*) is a phrase we see again in 41.26. I refer to beasts only because other animals are in the context.

[9] **He.** Again we have only the masculine singular verb form to suggest that the human miner is the subject. Conceivably the deity is meant.

[11] **Ties up.** This is a curious image for dealing with water, and some scholars have emended *ḥbš* to *ḥpš*, "search out," or have argued the interchangeability of *p* and *b* in Semitic and read *ḥbš* as meaning "search out." I am not willing to give up the intriguing image of "tying" or "binding" springs. Grabbe (pp. 96–98), demonstrating the limitations on the *b-p* shift in Semitic languages, shows that this instance does not fall within them.

[12] **She.** The pronouns are feminine because *ḥokmah*, "wisdom," is a feminine noun, though it is possible that, as in Prov 1–9, Wisdom is personified in the poem.

[15–17] Four different words for gold are used in these six lines: *s^{e}gōr*, v. 15a; *ketem*, v. 16a (repeated in v. 19b); *zahab*, v. 17a; *paz*, v. 17b. Moreover, it is uncertain what gems or precious materials are designated by the words translated in vv. 16 and 18 as "onyx," "coral," "crystal," and "rubies."

23 It claps its hands over him,
whistles derisively at him from his own place.

28 1 For there is a mine for silver,
a place where they refine gold.
2 Iron is taken from the dust,
and rock is smelted into copper.
3 He puts an end to darkness,
digs down to the furthest bound
through dim and gloomy rock,
4 sinks a shaft far from human habitation,
forgotten by any foot,
dangling far from men they sway.
5 Earth—out of it comes bread—
is overturned below as by fire.
6 Its rocks are a place of sapphire,
and gold dust comes to him.

7 The path no bird of prey knows,
nor has the falcon's eye seen it.
8 Proud beasts have not trodden there,
nor has a lion passed over it.
9 He forces his hand into the flint,
overturns mountains from the root,
10 cleaves channels in the rocks,
and his eye sees everything precious,
11 ties up the springs of the rivers,
and brings concealed things to light.

12 Wisdom—where can she be found?
Where is understanding's place?
13 No human knows her dwelling,
nor is she found in the land of the living.
14 The Abyss says, "She's not in me,"
and Sea says, "Not with me."

15 Bullion cannot be given for her
nor silver weighed as her price.
16 She cannot be bought with Ophirian gold,
precious onyx, or sapphire.

27 **Made her fast.** The sense is "made her firm, fastened her."

28 **Fear of Adonai.** Adonai is used of the deity only here in Job. The word is usually translated "Lord," and it is also an honorific addressed to a human ("sir," for example). In the Jewish tradition, wherever the biblical text has the divine name YHWH (Yahweh), the word *Adonai* is pronounced (some modern groups read something different); in those passages many English translations read "the LORD" with capital letters. "Fear" is the word I have been translating "religion" or "religious" (*yir'ah*).

5 **My youngsters.** I take *ne'arīm* as in 1.19. The word recurs in v. 8a as "young people."

6 **Milk.** This meaning depends on the common reading of *ḥēmah* as a misspelling of *ḥem'ah*. Otherwise the word would be *ḥēmah*, "hot anger" or "poison" (as in 6.4).

. . . . "And rock was poured with me streams of oil" is unintelligible, and no reconstruction I have found satisfies me.

[17] Gold and glass cannot match her,
nor vessels of fine gold be bartered for her.
[18] Coral and crystal deserve no mention,
wisdom's value exceeds that of rubies.
[19] Ethiopian topaz cannot match her,
nor can she be bought with pure gold.

[20] Wisdom—whence does she come?
Where is understanding's place?
[21] She is concealed from all living eyes,
hidden from the birds of the sky.
[22] Abaddon and Death say,
"A rumor of her has reached our ears."

[23] Elohim understands her way,
he it is who knows her place.
[24] For he looks out to earth's edges,
sees everything beneath the sky,
[25] giving weight to the wind,
measuring out the waters.
[26] When he made a channel for the rain,
a road for the thunderclap,
[27] then he saw her and recounted her,
made her fast, even dug her out.
[28] And he said to humankind,
"Now, the fear of Adonai, that is wisdom,
and avoiding evil is understanding."

29 [1] Job again took up his discourse thus:
[2] Would that I were as past months,
the days when Eloah watched over me,
[3] when his lamp shone over my head,
and I walked the dark by its light;
[4] as I was in my autumn days,
when Eloah's friendship was over my tent,
[5] Shaddai was still with me,
my youngsters surrounded me,
[6] my steps were washed with milk,
and rock . . . streams of oil.

[7] When I went out the gate of the city
to take my seat in the square,

[8] **Stood in their places.** *Qamū 'amᵉdū* is asyndetic, "rose stood," which is syntactically unusual. Dahood ("Northwest-Semitic Philology," pp. 68–69), arguing that *qwm* is a verb of inchoate action, interprets it as "began to stand." I derive my translation from the fact that *'md* sometimes means "to stand still."

[10] **Hidden.** I take *qōl*, "voice," in a collective sense. I'm not sure how you "hide" a voice.

[15] **Feet . . . was I.** I include the awkward last two words because the Hebrew has the emphatic pronoun in a somewhat awkward place.

[16] **The case I did not know.** The object of "I did not know" (*lō' yada'tī*) may be either "case" (*rīb*), as I have taken it, or an implicit person, "the case [of someone] I did not know," as JPS has done ("the case of the stranger"). In either case, the pronominal suffix on *'eḥqᵉrēhū*, "I investigated (dug) it," refers back to "case."

[18] **Like sand.** I am persuaded by Pope's argument (*Job*, pp. 214–16) against Dahood's suggestion that *ḥōl* means "phoenix," and Grabbe (pp. 98–101) does not change my mind. Nor does Ceresko's reference (*Job 29–31*, p. 23) to Old Canaanite *ḥl* in a lexical list from Ebla, with a Sumerian logogram indicating the name of a bird. The phoenix is not merely a bird, and the evidence is too vague to be convincing. The reference to "nest" in v. 18a makes "phoenix" attractive, but sand as an image of the countless and immeasurable, as in Gen 22.17, is equally apt. Moreover, we know the phoenix myth only from Greek sources, not at all from Near Eastern ones.

[20] **Successful.** Cf. Isa 9.9 for this sense of *ḥlp* Hiph'il. The verb often has to do with changing or even exchanging.

[21] **Listened expectantly.** Another hendiadys, "listened and waited."

[22] **Dropped.** The verb *nṭp* has to do with the dropping of dew in Deut 32.2 and with the dripping of honey and myrrh in Song of S 4.11; 5.5. The image of life-empowering rain continues in v. 23.

[24] **Treasured.** "Did not let fall."

[25] **Like a happy person.** I accept Ceresko's repointing (*Job 29–31*, p. 32) of *kaʾᵃšer* to *kᵉ'ašēr*.

8 young people saw me and hid,
old ones stood in their places,
9 princes restrained words
and laid their hands on their mouths,
10 the voices of leaders were hidden,
and their tongues stuck to their palates.

11 For ear heard and commended me,
eye saw and testified for me,
12 that I rescued the poor who cried out,
the orphan with no helper.
13 The blessing of the destitute came to me,
and I made the widow's heart sing for joy.
14 I dressed in righteousness, and it dressed me,
like robe and turban my justice.
15 Eyes I was to the blind,
feet to the lame was I.
16 I was father to the needy,
and I investigated the case I did not know.
17 I broke the jaws of the vicious,
flung the prey from his teeth.

18 And I thought, "I'll die with my nest,
multiply days like sand,
19 my root opened out to water,
dew lodging on my twigs,
20 my vigor ever new,
my bow successful in my hand."

21 People listened expectantly to me,
were silent for my counsel,
22 added nothing after I spoke.
My word dropped upon them;
23 they waited for me as for rain,
opened their mouths as for showers.
24 If I smiled at them, they did not believe it,
they treasured the light of my face.
25 I chose their way, sat at the head,
lived like a king among the troops,
like a happy person who consoles mourners.

[2]**Whose vigor is gone.** I take the referent of the singular pronoun as Job: "to me, upon him [whom] vigor has perished." It could refer collectively to "them" whose hands are mentioned in v. 2a.

[3]The verse is difficult. I think that it continues v. 2, and Job is describing himself as sterile. The plural participle *ha‘ōr*^{e}*qīm*, "which gnaw," in v. 3b has "want" and "hunger" as subjects, and v. 3c is in apposition to "dry." Verse 3c might also mean "a yesterday of desolation" (the phrase occurs also in 38.27).

[4]The antecedents of the plurals in this verse are still "want and hunger." *Haq-qōṭ*^{e}*pīm*, "pluck," is parallel to *ha‘ōr*^{e}*qīm*, "gnaw," in v. 3b.

[5]**Community.** Ceresko (*Job 29–31*, p. 53), Gordis (*Book of Job*, p. 331), and Pope (*Job*, p. 220) give persuasive evidence for this meaning of *gēw*.

[7]The referent of the plurals here and in v. 8 is problematic. In v. 5, the chaser is plural ("they cast out, shout") and the chasee singular ("over him"), but suddenly in vv. 7–8 the chasee has become plural ("they bray, huddle"). It is as if the poem has imperceptibly shifted from describing someone respectable who is hounded from the community to describing the no-goods to whom Job referred disdainfully in v. 1. Those people in their turn are the ones to whom, in v. 9, Job becomes an object of derision.

[8]**Nobodies.** "Sons of not names."

[11]**His bowstring.** So Ketib; many commentators prefer Qere, "my bowstring." "Bowstring" could also be "tent cord."

[12]. . . . Hebrew *prḥḥ* is an unexplained hapax legomenon.
put off my feet. I rather like Gordis's "send me sprawling" (*Book of Job*, p. 333), but the line is uncertain in view of the shift of the metaphor in the next line to military road-building, an echo of Job's complaint in 19.12b.

[13]**No help to him.** I read *‘ēzer* for MT *‘ōzēr*, and I am no more pleased with it than with other proposals.

[14]**Breach.** Specifically in a wall.
amidst. Ceresko (*Job 29–31*, pp. 55–56) suggests this meaning of *taḥat* rather than "under."

[15]**Are dumped.** The verb form is masculine singular (*hohpak*), but the apparent subject, *ballahōt*, is feminine plural. GK, par. 145o (p. 465), gives other instances of masculine singular verbs with following feminine plural subjects.
standing. I.e., social standing. See Albertz, p. 361.
is driven off. The verb *tirdōp* is singular, and I take its subject to be the feminine singular noun *n*^{e}*dībatī*, "my standing," which suggests its passive sense.
safety. Pope (*Job*, p. 222) compares Isa 32.8 for the rendering "dignity."

[17]**My bones.** I have been unable to think of a way to translate *mē‘alay* without extra verbiage. The line is "At night he bores [digs] my bones from upon me"; i.e., bores through the bones without removing them from the sufferer's body.

30 [1] And now they laugh at me,
those much younger than I,
whose fathers I disdained
to station among my sheepdogs.
[2] What is their hands' strength to me,
whose vigor is gone,
[3] sterile by want and hunger
which gnaw on what is dry,
a desolation even yesterday,
[4] pluck off saltweed on the bush,
broom-root their bread?

[5] From the community they cast out,
shout over him as over a thief,
[6] to live in the gullies of the wadis,
holes in the dirt and rocks.
[7] Between the bushes they bray,
huddle together under the nettles—
[8] churls, nobodies,
whipped out of the land.

[9] And now I am their song,
I've become the word for them.
[10] They detest me, keep their distance,
don't hesitate to spit at me.
[11] Because he has loosened his bowstring and humiliated me,
they put off the bridle in my presence.
[12] At my right, . . . they rise,
put off my feet,
build up against me their ruinous roads,
[13] break up my path,
promote my destruction—
no help to him.
[14] They come like a wide breach,
roll along amidst the desolation.
[15] Terrors are dumped over me,
my standing is driven off like the wind,
my safety sweeps away like a cloud.

[16] And now my life is poured out over me,
miserable days grab hold of me.
[17] At night he bores out my bones,
my gnawing pain never lies down.

[18] The most I can make of this couplet is an image of clothing. The phrase "with great power" (*b*^{e}*rob-kōaḥ*) in 23.6a may mean a plenipotentiary, an "attorney."

[19] **I'm a cliché.** The verb *mšl*, related to the noun *mašal*, a saying or proverb, can mean in Qal "to utter a proverb." This is the only occurrence of the Hithpaʿel of the verb.

[20] **You.** The pronoun is masculine singular, and through v. 23 Job addresses the deity.

stand. Most commentators take the negative in the prior line to govern *titbōnen*, "examine," in this one. I think not, though the phenomenon is known. Job is complaining of inconsistency: when he is noisy, the deity does not answer; when he stands mute, the deity has many questions. The text, to be sure, says only "stand" (*ʿamadtī*), but the analogy with the same verb in 29.8b suggests that silence is implied.

[21] **Powerful.** The relation between *ʿōṣem*, used here, and *ʿeṣem*, "bone," suggests the image of a "bony" hand.

[22] **Level.** Qere is *tušīyyah*, "sound wisdom"; Ketib *t*^{e}*šuwwah* is usually analyzed as Puʿal of *šwh* II, "to place before." I read *t*^{e}*šawweh*, Piʿel of *šwh* I, "to level something." The pronominal suffix on the foregoing verb is to be understood on this one as well.

[24] **He.** Job resumes speaking of the deity in the third person.

. . . . The line begins promisingly, but *lahen*, "to them" (feminine plural), has no referent, and the meaning of the noun *šūaʿ* is unknown. It might be connected to the verb *šwʿ*, meaning "cry for help," which Job uses in vv. 20a and 28b.

[25] Another self-curse without a result clause.

[27] **Boiled.** We might take the two verbs, *rutt*^{e}*ḥū w*^{e}*lō'-damū*, as a hendiadys: "boiled unsilently" or something more elegant.

[28] **Dark I go.** "Dark," *qōdēr*, is a participle, and therefore I think it refers to Job himself, though ambient "gloom" (Pope, *Job*, p. 218) is a possible meaning.

cry for help. The same verb Job used in v. 20a.

[29] **Jackals.** The word may be either singular, *tannīm* (sometimes *tannīn*), "sea monster," or masculine plural, *tannīm* from *tan*, "jackal."

[30] **Black upon me.** Ceresko (*Job 29–31*, p. 97) quotes Dahood's attractive proposal to repoint *mēʿalay*, "upon me," to *mēʿalī*, for "My skin is blacker than a cauldron." I wish the evidence were closer to Hebrew.

[31] **Lyre.** I suspect that a *kinnōr* was some sort of zither, but the word is less euphonious than "lyre."

[1] **Virgin.** I agree with Ceresko (*Job 29–31*, p. 107): this is no mere disclaimer of lustful thoughts; the virgin is the Virgin—the Canaanite goddess Anat. The idea is connected with the later curse about worship of the moon, vv. 26–27. Jeshurun first proposed the connection with Anat in 1928.

[18] With great power . . . . ,
. . . .
[19] He has flung me to the muck,
and I'm a cliché, like dust and ashes.

[20] I cry out to you, and you don't answer me,
I stand [silent], and you examine me.
[21] You have been changed to cruelty toward me,
with your powerful hand you attack me.
[22] You lift me to the wind, make me ride,
you dissolve me, level me.
[23] For I know you will return me to Death
and the house appointed for all who live.
[24] Surely he does not put out his hand to a ruin,
if in its extinction . . . .
[25] If I did not weep for a difficult day,
or my soul grieve for the poor—
[26] But I hoped for good, and evil came,
waited for light, and darkness came.
[27] My bowels are boiled, they are not silent,
days of affliction stretch out before me.
[28] Dark I go without the sun,
rise in the assembly, cry for help.
[29] I have been brother to jackals,
companion to ostrich's daughters.
[30] My skin is black upon me,
and my bones burn from heat.
[31] And my lyre has become mourning,
my flute a weeping voice.

31 [1] I made a covenant with my eyes,
and how could I pay attention to the virgin?
[2] What is Eloah's portion from above,
Shaddai's inheritance from on high?
[3] Is it not disaster for the vicious,
calamity for evildoers?

[5]Here begins a series of self-curses by Job, some of which are, unusually, accompanied by the result clause. The series of curses is intermingled with statements and, in vv. 14–15, questions. Toward the end of the chapter the curses are interrupted by a challenge to the deity to appear and answer the complaint (v. 35). I present those curses that omit the result clause as "if" clauses closed by a dash, and those that include the result clause as "if" clauses continued with finite verbs after commas. I separate the statements and questions from the curses by spacing.

[6]This sentence could be read as a result clause, following the curse formula in v. 5. I think it is an independent statement, because the result clause of a curse calls down a punishing calamity, not a preliminary procedure.

[10]**Woman.** As in many languages, "woman," *'iššah*, may mean "wife," just as "man," *'īš*, can mean "husband." Because v. 9a is ambiguous as to whether "woman" is the neighbor's wife, I leave the ambiguity here in order to make clear the verbal connection between curse and result clause.

others. The noun has an Aramaic plural ending.

[11]**That.** Gordis (*Book of Job*, p. 347) points out that the two "that's" present a little puzzle of Qere and Ketib. The first is written *hw'*, masculine, but the Qere is *hī'*, feminine, in agreement with the following noun, *zimmah*. The second is written *hy'*, feminine, but the Qere is *hū'*, masculine, in agreement with *'awōn*.

intended crime. *Zimmah* is a technical legal term, sometimes for sexual misconduct (e.g., Lev 18.17; 20.14), sometimes for other kinds (Ps 26.10; Hos 6.9). The noun is derived from *zmm*, which has to do with intending, and its use in the plural in 17.11 apparently has the meaning not of a crime but simply of an intention or purpose.

actionable offense. I repoint *'awōn* to the construct. The expression means "a crime of judges"; i.e., one that calls for legal action.

[12]**Abaddon.** See the note to 26.6.

[13]MT's line accents make my first two lines only one, which is extremely long. My solution produces an enjambment, which troubles me less.

maid. *'amah* means a slave woman, not a hired woman.

[16]**Exhausted.** For the expression *klh 'ēnayim*, "exhaust the eyes," see 11.20; 17.5.

[18]. . . . The verb *g^{e}dēlanī*, "he became large (with) me," taking "orphan" as its subject, makes no sense, and taking the subject as the deity is confusing in the context. If I were given to emendation, I would solve the problem by reading *'agadd^{e}lennū*, "I reared him."

her. The antecedent seems to be the "widow" in v. 16b. The construction is awkward (see Boadt, p. 69).

[4] Does he not see my ways,
number all my steps?

[5] If I have walked with worthlessness,
my foot has hurried upon fraud—

[6] He will weigh me on accurate scales,
Eloah will know my integrity.

[7] If my step has strayed from the way,
my heart has gone after my eyes,
a stain has stuck to my palms,
[8] may I sow and another eat,
and my descendants be uprooted.

[9] If my heart has been fooled over a woman,
and at my neighbor's door I have lain in wait,
[10] may my woman grind for another,
others kneel over her.

[11] For that is an intended crime,
that an actionable offense,
[12] that is a fire consuming to Abaddon,
uprooting all my produce.

[13] If I have despised justice
for my slave and my maid
when they complained against me—
[14] What do I do when El rises up,
when he calls to account, what do I answer him?
[15] Did not the one who made me in the belly make him,
one establish us in the womb?

[16] If I have kept the poor from pleasure,
have exhausted the widow's eyes,
[17] eating my bread alone,
the orphan not eating it too—

[18] For from my youth . . . like a father,
and from my mother's womb I led her.

[19] If I see someone perishing without clothing,
a poor person without covering,
[20] if his loins do not bless me
as he warms himself with fleece from my sheep—

[21] If I have shaken my fist at the orphan
because I saw my helpers in the gate,

[23] **Disaster.** The same word as that in v. 3a.

I cannot bear his partiality. The expression is strange: "I am unable from his lifting." The verb *ykl* often simply means to overcome (negatively) or to succeed (positively) in something, and the question is what Job cannot overcome. *Śᵉʾētō*, from *nśʾ*, "to lift," understood as the deity's "loftiness, majesty" (see S. R. Driver and Gray, Pt. I, p. 268; Habel, *Book of Job*, p. 426), makes little sense to me, unless the clause means "I cannot endure his majesty." That does not explain the preposition *min*, "from," which Gordis (*Book of Job*, p. 350) thinks must mean "because of." With a good deal of doubt, I take *miśśᵉʾētō* as an elliptical expression for *nśʾ panīm*, "lift the face, show partiality" in a legal case.

[27] **Fooled.** See the similar expression in v. 9a.

my hand kisses on my mouth. This must be a forbidden ritual gesture. Albertz (p. 359, *n*24) identifies the gesture as the Babylonian *laban appi*, where the uplifted hand touches the nose in a gesture of obeisance to the god. The expression would be trouble-free if only it said "My mouth kisses my hand" (*wattiššaq pī lᵉyadī*). I take *nšq* in an analogous or metaphorical sense, the raised hand quickly and furtively brushing against (kissing upon) the mouth.

[28] **Actionable offense.** In v. 11b, the word is *pᵉlīlīm*, but here it is *pᵉlīlī*, an abstract adjective. I see no significant difference of sense.

[32] **Wayfarer.** With Gordis (*Book of Job*, p. 353), I take *ʾōraḥ* as a participle, not as the noun, "way." The latter would not seriously impair the sense: "I open my door to the road."

[35] **Mark.** The *taw* is the X, the signature. The order of lines in this verse is strange, and were I rewriting it, I would put this line third. The dashes are there to show its intrusive quality and also the syntactical parallel between "someone to hear" (*šōmēaʿ*) in the first line and "inscription" (*sēper*) in the third, which seem to be accusatives to "Oh that I had" (*mī yittēn lī*). The alternative is to take the third line as accusative to "answer" in the second. But Job does not have the written charge, which is apparently what he means by "inscription."

[37] **Number of my steps.** Compare v. 4b.

imprint. More nearly, "inform, instruct him." My translation is intended to reflect the pun between *ʾaggīdennū* and *nagīd*, "prince," in the next line.

[39] **Baals.** The "Baals" of a piece of land are the divine powers that fructify it, and Job claims that he has not hindered their proper function.

22 may my arm fall from my shoulder,
my forearm be broken at the elbow.

23 For El's disaster is frightful to me,
I cannot bear his partiality.

24 If I have put my confidence in gold,
have called fine gold what I trust—
25 If I rejoice because my wealth is great,
because my hand has found power—
26 If I see the light that shines,
the gorgeous moon going by,
27 and my heart is secretly fooled,
and my hand kisses on my mouth—

28 That too is an actionable offense,
for I had lied to El above.

29 If I rejoice at my enemy's ruin,
am stirred because he finds evil—

30 I have not given my palate to sin,
asking his life with a curse.

31 If the men of my tent have not said,
"Would that we were not well fed by his meat"—

32 The foreigner has not spent the night outside,
I open my door to the wayfarer.

33 If I have concealed my iniquities like Adam,
hiding my guilt in my pocket,
34 because I am alarmed at a great uproar,
and the contempt of relatives shatters me,
and I am silent and do not go out the door—

35 Oh that I had someone to hear me—
Here is my mark; let Shaddai answer me—
and the inscription my accuser has written!
36 If I do not carry it on my shoulder,
tie it on me like a wreath,
37 the number of my steps imprint upon him,
like a prince approach him—

38 If my ground cries against me,
its furrows weep together,
39 if I have eaten its strength without silver,
made its Baals gasp,

40 **Spent.** Perhaps this formula ought not to be taken too seriously. Yet the verb, *tammū*, an unusual one for "completion," is cognate to *tam*, "perfection," and *tummah*, "integrity," which are repeatedly attributed to Job (see, e.g., v. 6b). The verb sometimes also has the connotation of being used up (Gen 47.15, among a good many other passages).

2 **Elihu.** It is often pointed out that Elihu's name (*'lyhw'*) adds only a final *aleph* to that of the prophet Elijah (*'lyh* or *'lyhw*). However unlikely it is, Elihu's name does remind the reader of Elijah.

angry. The expression, *ḥrh 'ap*, "his nose burned," is probably a dead metaphor.

3 **Job.** A strong tradition that this word is one of the *tiqqūnē sōferīm*, "corrections of the scribes," leads some translators to change it to *'ᵉlōhīm*.

6 **You.** Masculine plural in both places in this verse.

decrepit. *Yašīš* may point not only to age but also to its weakness.

crawled about. Holladay (s.v. *zḥl*), distinguishing two roots with these consonants, identifies this passage as the only occurrence of the second. I prefer the first.

8 **Wind.** One never knows whether *rūaḥ* means "wind" or "spirit." I think here of the wind at creation in Gen 1.2.

10 **Listen.** The imperative is singular, perhaps addressed to Job.

11 **Speeches.** Reserving "words" for *millīn* in v. 11c. Through v. 14 the second-person pronouns are plural.

listening for. See S. R. Driver and Gray, Pt. II, p. 236. *'azīn* is usually analyzed as a contraction of *'a'ᵃzīn*.

while you were digging. A somewhat odd use of *'ad*, a preposition usually meaning "to, up to." The verb is the same one used in 28.3, 27.

12 **Arbiter.** In 9.33, Job said he had no arbiter (*mōkīaḥ*), but in 40.2 Yahweh challenges the *mōkīaḥ* to answer.

14 **Refute.** *'ᵃšībennū*, "turn him back."

15 **They.** Elihu apparently refers to the friends in the third-person plural.

[40] instead of wheat may thorns come up,
instead of barley, stinkweed.

Job's words were spent.

32 [1] These three men stopped answering Job, for he considered himself
right. [2] Elihu, son of Barachel, the Buzite from the clan of Ram, was
angry. He was angry with Job, because his soul was more right than
Elohim, [3] and he was angry with his three friends because they found
no answer, while condemning Job. [4] Elihu waited for Job with words,
because they were older than he. [5] Elihu saw that no answer was forthcoming from the three men, and he was angry.

[6] Elihu, son of Barachel, the Buzite, answered thus:
Young am I of days,
and you are decrepit;
therefore I have crawled about, afraid
of imparting my knowledge to you.
[7] I said, "Days will speak,
and many years will make wisdom known."
[8] Yet the wind is that in a man,
and Shaddai's breath, that makes them understand.
[9] Not the great are wise,
or the elderly understand justice.
[10] Therefore I say, "Listen to me,
I will impart my knowledge, I myself."

[11] Here, I waited for your speeches,
listened for your understandings
while you were digging for words.
[12] And I examine you,
and there! Job has no arbiter,
one answering his statements, among you.
[13] Lest you say, "We have found wisdom,
El, not a man, will drive him off,"
[14] he has not arranged words to me,
and with your statements I will not refute him.
[15] They are terrified, they answer no more,
words move away from them.
[16] And I waited, because they did not speak,
because they stood around, answered no more.

17 The couplet is as awkward and overblown in Hebrew as it is in English.
18 **Wind.** Or "the spirit [*ruaḥ*] presses on me—in my belly."
21 **Partial.** The expression, "to lift the face," signifies partiality in a legal context. **give honor.** Staples (p. 28) translates the phrase nicely, "to give flattering titles." *'adam* may be either the proper name Adam or the generic term for humankind.

1 **Words, speeches.** The same pairing of *millīn* and *d*^{e}*barīm* as in 32.11.
3 **Plainly.** *Barūr* has a connotation of purity, ritual cleanliness, but the verb *brr* also once refers to a polished arrow (Isa 49.2).
5 **Draw up before me, take your position.** A military image. "Draw up" (*'rk*, "to arrange") is often used of an army mustered in battle order (e.g., Gen 14.8; 2 Sam 10.8; but notice its use of discussion in "arranged" in Job 32.14a), and "take position" (Hithpa'el of *yṣb*, "stand, take a stand") frequently means "taking a military station" (e.g., 1 Sam 10.19; Hab 2.1).
6 **Jar.** MT *k*^{e}*pīka*, "like your mouth," makes no sense. Blommerde (*Northwest Semitic Grammar*, pp. 117–18) reads *pīk* as "a little jar," and *pak* is used in 1 Sam 10.1 and 2 Ki 9.1, 3 to mean a jar or juglet.
9–11 For all Elihu's pretense at accurate reporting ("I heard the sound of the words"), v. 9 is only faintly like 13.23 (and cf. 16.17), in part more like Bildad's words in 8.6 and Zophar's in 11.4 (wrongly attributed to Job). Verse 10a has no connection to anything, but v. 10b alludes to Job's pun between his name and "enemy" (*'ōyēb*) in 13.24b, and v. 11 quotes Job in 13.27.
10 **Frustration.** Loewe makes a persuasive case for this rendering of *t*^{e}*nū'ah*, both here and in Num 14.34.
13 **That . . . words.** Or "that, for all his words, he does not answer?" My rendering leaves the source of "his words" uncertain.

[17] I, I myself, will answer for my part,
I will impart my knowledge, I myself.
[18] For I am full of words,
the wind in my belly pushes on me.
[19] Ah! my belly is like unopened wine,
like new wineskins, it will burst.
[20] Let me speak, and I will get relief,
open my lips and answer.
[21] I would not be partial to a man,
to Adam would not give honor.
[22] For I do not know how to give honor,
very shortly my maker would lift me up.

33 [1] But now, listen, Job, to my words,
and give ear to all my speeches.
[2] Now then, I have opened my mouth,
my tongue has spoken in my palate.
[3] My straightforward mind, my statements,
my lips' knowledge talk plainly.
[4] El's wind made me,
and Shaddai's breath gave me life.
[5] If you can, refute me,
draw up before me, take your position.
[6] After all, I am like a jar to El;
I too was pinched from clay.
[7] After all, fright of me does not terrify you,
and my pressure on you is not heavy.

[8] But you have said in my ears
(I heard the sound of the words),
[9] "I am pure, without transgression,
I am clean, have no iniquity.
[10] Oh! he finds frustration over me,
considers me to be his enemy.
[11] He puts my feet in the stocks,
guards all my paths."

[12] Ah, but you are not right about this, I answer you,
for Eloah is greater than a man.
[13] Why do you accuse him
that he does not answer all his words?

[14] **He does not regard it.** It seems that Elihu reverses himself, though the referent of the feminine pronoun "it" is not clear. Most translators take the subject of the verb to be the human recipient of the divine speech, e.g., "though no one may see it" (Habel, *Book of Job*, p. 455; cf. Pope, *Job*, p. 245); "—Though man does not perceive it—" (JPS; cf. Weiser, p. 219; Guillaume, *Studies*, p. 61); "—if only man noticed" (Gordis, *Book of Job*, p. 362, repointing *lōʾ*, "not," to *lūʾ*, "if"). The thought is difficult, but I take the deity as the subject.

[15] **When deep sleep falls upon men.** Quoted from Eliphaz, 4.13b. Like Eliphaz and the rest of the ancient (and not so ancient) world, Elihu takes dreams as communications from outside one.

[17] **An arrogant deed.** I take *maʿ*^{a}*śeh w*^{e}*gēwah* as a hendiadys, "deed and arrogance" = "an arrogant deed." That forces acceptance of enjambment, of which there are other instances in Job.

hero. I have unsuccessfully looked for a better translation of *geber*.

[18] **The Pit.** The netherworld, place of the dead. See the note on "muck," 9.31, the same word as here.

crossing the channel. So Dhorme (p. 496), followed by both Pope (*Job*, p. 250) and Gordis (*Book of Job*, pp. 375–76). Perhaps "channel," like "Pit," ought to be capitalized, if it coheres with other rivers that the dead must cross, Hubur in Mesopotamia, Styx in Homer, Cocytus and Acheron in Virgil. There is very little evidence for this idea in the Hebrew Bible, but Tsevat ("The Canaanite God Šälaḥ") and Loretz ("Der Gott *šlḥ*") present Canaanite sources for it. The same language recurs in 36.12.

[19] **On trial.** I accept Ketib, *rīb*; Qere is *rōb*, "many."

[20] **Throat.** *Nepeš*, often "soul" (e.g., v. 22).

[21] **Not . . . .** Gordis (*Book of Job*, p. 376) analyzes MT *ruʾū* as Qal passive plural; S. R. Driver and Gray (Pt. II, p. 247) as Puʿal. Neither makes good sense in the context. Pope's "And his bones which were not seen are laid bare" (*Job*, p. 251) strikes me as stretching it.

[22] **To the executioners.** MT *lam*^{e}*mitīm*, Hiphʿil plural participle of *mwt*. If I were given to emendation, I would change it to *l*^{e}*mō mētīm*, "to the dead."

[23] **Interpreter.** *Mēlīṣ* may have a derisive connotation of someone who repeats what someone else says (see Prov 19.28). Job uses the word seriously of his "witness" in 16.20a, however, and perhaps Elihu alludes to that passage.

morality. *Yašar*, as in Job's morality, 1.1, etc.

[24] **Redeem.** *Pdʿ* may be an Aramaic loanword; it occurs in this sense only in the Jerusalem Talmud, Kiddushin I, 61d, a passage that may refer to this one. *Pdʿ* otherwise means "wound."

[25] **Plumper.** Pope (*Job*, p. 252) analyzes the word as an infix-*t* form cognate to Akkadian *rapašu*, "be wide."

boy's. Reading *naʿar* for MT *nōʿar*.

[26] Hebrew style frequently mixes together unreferenced pronouns, and the reader must simply disentangle them. The first "he" in v. 26a might refer either to the human being who is the subject of v. 25 or to the "angel" in v. 23.

14 For El speaks once,
and twice he does not regard it.

15 In the dream, a vision at night,
when deep sleep falls upon men,
in slumbers upon the bed,
16 then he uncovers men's ears,
and seals up with chastisement,
17 to turn a human, an arrogant
deed from a hero, he covers.
18 He restrains his soul from the Pit
and his life from crossing the channel.

19 He is reproved by pain on his bed,
his bones constantly on trial;
20 his life makes bread loathsome to him,
his throat, the food of craving.
21 His flesh vanishes from sight,
and his bones are bared, not . . . .
22 His soul approaches the Pit,
his life to the executioners.

23 If there's an angel over him,
one interpreter out of a thousand,
to tell a human his morality,
24 and he favors him and says,
"Redeem him from descending to the Pit,
I have found a ransom."

25 His flesh is plumper than a boy's,
he returns to the days of his youth.
26 He entreats Eloah, and he accepts him,
sees his face with a shout,
and he returns a man's righteousness.
27 He sings before men and says,
"I sinned, perverted morality,
and he did not requite me.
28 He redeemed my soul from crossing into the Pit,
and my life sees the light."

---

27 **Sings.** Reading *yašīr* for MT *yašōr*.
requite. With Pope (*Job*, p. 252), I repoint *šawah* to Pi'el *šiwwah*.
28 **My soul, my life.** I accept Ketib; Qere has a third-person masculine singular suf-

fix. Qere seems to imply that the quoted speech is only in v. 27, whereas Ketib carries the quotation through v. 28.
[29] **Man.** *Geber.*
[33] **Familiarize.** The Hebrew expression is as pretentious as the sentiment.

[3] This couplet quotes 12.11 with *kī*, "for," instead of *h*^{a}*lō’*, "does not?" in the first line and a slightly different word order and the omission of *lō* in the second.
food. Repointing MT *le’*^{a}*kōl*, an infinitive, to *l*^{e}*’ōkel*, a noun.
[4] The verbs have lengthened forms, *nibḥ*^{a}*rah*, "decide," and *nēd*^{e}*‘ah*, "know," which many translations (e.g., JPS) take in the cohortative plural sense: "let us decide," "let us know."
[5–6] Again Elihu misquotes Job. In 9.15 and 10.15, Job used *ṣadaqtī*, "I am innocent," but both were preceded by the particle *’im*, "if." In 27.2, *’ēl hēsīr mišpaṭī*, "El has turned away my case," is preceded by *ḥay*, which turns that statement into an oath, "As El lives, who has turned away my case." Verse 6a is not a quotation from Job; he uses the verb *kzb*, "to lie," in 6.28 to deny that he has lied to the friends—not at all the issue here—and with a completely different form in 24.25. In 6.4, he refers to Shaddai's poisoned arrows, but here (see next note) the arrow is Job's.
[6] **My arrow.** One would expect "his arrow," *ḥiṣṣō*, and many commentators make that change. I almost wish I could accept the third-person masculine singular *yod* suffix here. See Boadt, pp. 64–65.
[9] Another quotational malfeasance, closer to what Eliphaz says in 22.2 than to anything Job says. Job never uses the verb *skn*, "to get benefit"; only Elihu (here and 35.3) and Eliphaz (15.3; 22.2 [twice], 21) do.
[10] **Intelligent men.** "Men of heart." Since v. 2, Elihu has been addressing and referring to "men," always with *’īš* in one of its forms. I use the word "man" or "men" only where the Hebrew has some specific term for male humans and in a few places where an adjective in a masculine plural form seems to refer to human beings.
[11] **Humans . . . them.** The Hebrew is singular, *’adam*, and I have turned it into a reference to the human race. See also v. 15.
[12] **Shaddai does not bend justice.** Close to what Bildad says in 8.3.
[13] **Who appointed him.** I follow Tur-Sinai's solution (p. 479) to the odd syntax of the sentence.
set him over. The *‘alayw* of the first line is understood in the second.

29 Ah, El does all these things
twice, thrice with a man,
30 to turn his soul back from the Pit,
to shine with the light of life.

31 Pay attention, Job, listen to me,
be silent, and I will speak.
32 If there are words, refute me,
speak, for I wish to see you right.
33 If not, you listen to me,
be silent, and I'll familiarize you with wisdom.

34 1 Elihu answered thus:
2 Hear my words, you wise people,
you who know, give ear to me,
3 for the ear tests words,
and the palate tastes food.
4 Justice we will decide for ourselves;
we know among us what is good.
5 So Job has said, "I'm innocent,
and El has turned aside my case.
6 For the sake of my case, I have to lie?
wounded by my arrow, I'm guiltless."
7 Who is such a man as Job?
He drinks derision like water,
8 wanders in company with evildoers,
walks with wicked men.
9 Indeed, he says, "A man gets no use
out of friendship with Elohim."

10 Therefore, intelligent men, listen to me:
Far be El from wickedness,
Shaddai from wrongfulness.
11 For what humans do, he pays them back,
whatever a man's path, he makes him find it.
12 Of course, El does not cause wickedness,
Shaddai does not bend justice.
13 Who appointed him over the earth,
who set him over the whole world?
14 If he sets his mind to it,
he can gather in his wind and his breath.

[15] **Humankind.** Elihu alludes to what Job said in 10.9, changing its sense a bit. The question is whether *'adam* is the proper name, alluding to Gen 3.19, or the generic term for the human race. See also v. 11.

[16] **Understanding.** I differ from most translators in thinking that *bīnah*, a feminine noun, is the subject of the feminine verbs in vv. 16–17.

[17] **Rule.** The masculine verb form corresponds to the participle *śōnē'*.
she. "Understanding," v. 16a.

[18] **Aristocracy.** Albertz (p. 361, *n*30) explains *nadīb* persuasively.

[19] **Play favorites.** I am uncertain whether the subject of this verb is the deity or someone human.

[20] **He touches nobles.** I redivide and repoint the impossible *y^{e}gō‘^{a}šū ‘am* (Gordis, *Book of Job*, p. 389, and Pope, *Job*, p. 258, take *‘am* as "gentry, upper classes") to *yigga‘ šō‘īm.*
they remove. I do not know who "they" are.

[23] **Given a man permission.** A difficult phrase, *lō' ‘al-'īš yaśīm* is literally, "he has not set (laid) upon a man." Taking the verb as an ellipsis for "set the heart upon" (i.e., think about a person), I suppose, with no clear parallel to adduce, that thinking about someone might involve "giving permission."
for a trial. Or "with a case."

[24] **Unscrutinized.** See 5.9; 9.10; and 36.26 for something like this sense of *lō'-ḥēqer.*

[26] **Jeers.** A verb peculiar to Elihu (here and v. 37; the cognate noun *sēpeq* is in 36.18). It seems to mean "to clap the hands," and comparing Lam 2.15, I take it as a derisive gesture.
onlookers. "Those who see." I think the word is less casual than "onlookers" may suggest.

[28] **And he hears.** I insert a dash at the end of the previous line because this one seems to contradict it.

[30] **From being the snares of a people.** Tur-Sinai's comment (p. 484) that this is "an unlikely expression even in Elihu's peculiar style" comforts me. The syntax of this and the two lines preceding escapes me, as does their relation to the couplet before them, though I think that there is a connection.

[31] **Can one say.** MT *he'amar* is interrogative. The question ends at v. 32b.
I lift. This line seems to me a defense of the speaker's virtue. "Lift" (*nś'*) might mean something like "I accept, show favor."

[32] **You teach.** The form is second-person masculine singular imperative, preceded somewhat oddly by the independent pronoun.

15 All flesh would expire together,
and humankind revert to dust.

16 If understanding hears this,
gives ear to the sound of my words,
17 can a hater of justice rule?
If she condemns a righteous or powerful one,
18 is that saying "Knave!" to a king,
"Wicked one!" to aristocrats,
19 who does not play favorites with princes
or consider the noble before the poor?—
but they are all the work of his hands.
20 Suddenly they die when it's midnight,
he touches nobles, and they pass on,
and they remove a mighty one without a hand.

21 For his eyes are on a man's ways,
and he sees all his steps.
22 There is no dark, no deep gloom,
where evildoers can hide.
23 But he has not yet given a man permission
to go to El for a trial.
24 Unscrutinized, he breaks the powerful
and sets successors in their stead.

25 Therefore he investigates their deeds,
overturns the night, and they are crushed.
26 Where the wicked are, he jeers at them
in the onlookers' place;
27 that is why they turn from following him,
and do not attend to all his ways,
28 to bring to him the outcry of the poor—
and he hears the outcry of the oppressed.
29 He gives content—and who finds that bad?—
hides his face—and who can see it?—
and upon nation and race alike
30 the godless from ruling the race,
from being the snares of a people.
31 For to El can one say,
"I lift, I do not mistreat;
32 except what I see, you teach me;
if I have done evil, I will not do it again"?

[33] **Yours.** This and the other second-person pronouns in the tercet are masculine singular.
what do you know to speak? I take the particle *mah* as an interrogative and *dabbēr* as Pi'el infinitive construct. But *mah* could also be a pronoun and *dabbēr* a Pi'el imperative: "Speak what you know."

[36] **Constantly.** *'ad-neṣaḥ*, "for ever" (or for a very long time).

[2] **You consider.** The second-person forms in this chapter are masculine singular.
more righteous than El. The closest to this statement Job has come is 9.2b: "How can a man be innocent with El?" Both that statement and this are somewhat similar to Eliphaz's "Is a man more righteous than Eloah?" (4.17a), but neither Job's nor Eliphaz's question implies the positive statement Elihu gives here. His quotational accuracy is not improving.

[3] **Of use.** See note to 34.9.
sin. Tur-Sinai (p. 489), translating "appeasing," implies that *ḥaṭṭa'tī* means "my sin-offering," a very intriguing idea.

[4] **Refute your words.** *'ᵃšībka millīn* might also mean "I will refute you with (your own) words."

[8] **Human being.** "Son of Adam."

[9] **They.** I do not know who is the referent of this implied pronoun.

[11] **Beasts of the earth.** *Bahᵃmōt*, construct of *bᵉhēmōt*. The use of the construct shows that this is not the mythic Behemoth of chap. 40. But Elihu alludes to Job's advice to the friends in 12.7–8, to consult these creatures for knowledge, and it goes somewhat against Job's point. Perhaps he does not realize the allusion. In that case, not only does Elihu misquote Job, but he quotes him without knowing it.

[13] **Surely it's false,** etc. Gordis (*Book of Job*, p. 402) argues this sense of the line, and JPS also adopts it. Habel (*Book of Job*, p. 487) and Pope (*Job*, p. 262) prefer "El does not give deceit a hearing," and Guillaume (*Studies*, p. 64; cf. RSV) has the similar "God will not hear vanity." The syntax allows both readings.

[33] Does he repay out of what is yours because you despise?
For you choose, not I,
and what do you know to speak?
[34] Intelligent men will say to me,
the wise man who listens to me:
[35] "Job does not speak with knowledge,
and his speeches are uncomprehending.
[36] Oh that Job might be tested constantly
about his returning among bad men.
[37] For he adds to his sin,
in transgression jeers among us,
multiplies his words to El."

35 [1] Elihu answered thus:
[2] Is this what you consider justice,
that you say, "I am more righteous than El"?
[3] For you say, "How is he of use to you?
How do I profit from my sin?"
[4] I will refute your words,
and your companions with you.

[5] Look to the sky and see,
spy out the dust clouds—they are higher than you.
[6] If you sin, what have you done to him?
Multiply transgression, what do you accomplish with him?
[7] If you are innocent, what have you given him?
Or what does he take from your hand?
[8] Your wickedness is confined to a man like yourself,
your innocence to a human being.

[9] They cry out at great oppression,
call for help at the arm of the great.
[10] But he does not say, "Where is Eloah, my maker,
who gives me songs in the night,
[11] who teaches us by the beasts of the earth,
makes us wise by the birds of the sky?"
[12] There they cry out, and he does not answer,
before the pride of the evil ones.

[13] Surely it's false that El does not hear,
that Shaddai does not look at it,

14 **Before *you**. I have broken my rule against emendation. MT's *l^e^panayw*, "before him," makes no satisfactory sense in the light of the second-person singular verbs in both lines of this verse, and I change it to *l^e^paneyka*. But I will base no conclusions on this reading.

dancing around it. An odd image and, many may think, a bizarre translation. I take *t^e^ḥōlēl* as a Pilpel of the verb *ḥyl* or *ḥwl*, which has to do with both childbirth and a whirling dance (perhaps originally a mimetic dance accompanying childbirth). Efforts to make the word mean "wait" are not morphologically persuasive.

15 . . . . *Paš* is a hapax legomenon. MT *bpš* is usually emended on the basis of LXX, Symmachus, and the Vulgate to *b^e^peša'*, "in (or with) transgression." Grabbe (pp. 110–12) finds some Semitic cognates that add up to "overflowing" in some sense or other, but the case for this is not satisfactory.

2 **Wait . . . you**. The imperative and the pronoun are masculine singular.

Eloah still has words. This could also be read "There are still words for (on behalf of) Eloah."

5 **Mighty**. Tur-Sinai (p. 494) argues that *kabbīr* is a judge, as in 34.17, 24, but Ceresko (*Job 29–31*, p. 156) wants it as a divine title, "the Old One."

7 **Withdraw**. *Gr'* appears again in v. 27a, but whether these are two different verbs (so Holladay, s.v.) is unclear.

12 **Channel**. The same expression as in 33.18.

14 even though you say, "You're not looking at it;
the case is before * you, and you're dancing around it."
15 Now because no one calls his anger to account,
and he does not know . . . much,
16 Job opens his mouth with vapor,
without knowledge increases words.

36 1 Elihu added this:
2 Wait a little for me, and I'll inform you
that Eloah still has words.
3 I'll display my knowledge afar,
show my maker's righteousness.
4 For certainly my words are not lies,
faultless knowledge is in your presence.

5 Now, El is mighty, does not despise,
mighty, strong in his heart.
6 He does not give the wicked life,
and he grants justice to the wretched.
7 He does not withdraw his eyes from the innocent,
and as for kings on their thrones,
he seats them permanently, and they are exalted.

8 If they are bound in fetters,
trapped in cords of misery,
9 he is telling them their deed
and their transgressions, that they have outdone themselves.
10 He opens their ear to discipline,
says they must turn back from evil.
11 If they hear and serve,
they spend their days in good,
their years in pleasantness.
12 And if they do not hear,
they will cross the channel,
die without knowing.

[13] **Set their faces.** The expression is "to set (the) nose." Tur-Sinai (p. 497) notes the parallels in 2 Ki 12.18 (Eng. 17) and Jer 42.15.
because. *Kī* might mean "when."

[14] **Holy males.** *Q*^{e}*dēšīm*, male cultic prostitutes. The word is unexpected, to say the least, though it actually fits rather well.

[15] **In their misery.** The preposition *b*^{e} in both lines of v. 15 might signify agency: "by their misery, by their torment."

[16–20] More than one commentator has remarked on the near unintelligibility of these verses. I find each sentence relatively understandable in itself, but perceiving how they go together in a sensible sequence is another matter.

[16] **You.** The second-person forms in vv. 16–21 are masculine singular.

[17] **Taken up.** Taking *yitmōkū* as a passive sense of Qal.

[18] **Look out.** Repointing *ḥēmah*, "wrath," to *ḥ*^{a}*mēh*, the imperative of *ḥmh[y]*, "to see."

[19] **Arrange your wealth.** The verb *'rk* probably does not have the military sense it has elsewhere. I take *šūaʿ* as "wealth" by analogy to *šōaʿ*, "noble, aristocrat," in 34.19b among other passages.

[24] **Remember to extol.** "Remember that you [singular] extol," with imperfect.
sing. Taking *šōr*^{e}*rū* from *šyr*; others derive it from *šwr*, "to see."

[25] **Gazes.** An object is understood; e.g., "at it."

[26] **Exalted.** The word is a nominal cognate of the verb translated "extol" in v. 24a. Notice the enjambment in this couplet.

[27] **Flood.** *'ēd* also occurs in Gen 2.6 (there sometimes mistranslated "mist"). The meteorological theory behind vv. 27–28 escapes me, but the "flood" might be the cosmic waters outside the barrier of sky and abyss. See v. 30.

[28] **Clouds.** A somewhat unusual noun, *š*^{e}*ḥaqīm* may suggest not rain clouds but dust clouds (see, e.g., Isa 40.15 and the cognate verb in Job 14.19a: "Water wears away [i.e., grinds down] stone"). The same noun occurs in 37.18a, 21b.
continually. Taking *rab* adverbially, "a long time."

[29] **Cloud.** *'ab*, different from the word in v. 28a. It also occurs in 37.11a.
canopy. The image is of the clouds as a woven covering.

[30] **Roots of the sea.** The phrase seems odd because the imagery since v. 27 has been of clouds and sky. Tur-Sinai (p. 505) argues that the "sea" is the cosmic water above the bowl of the sky, "the waters that are above the firmament" of Gen 1.7. The "roots" of that sea, then, are to be found in the sky.

13 The godless of mind set their faces,
do not cry out because he binds them.
14 Their soul dies in youth,
their life among the holy males.
15 He rescues the miserable in their misery,
opens their ears in their torment.
16 He even draws you back from distress's mouth,
a wide place, your steps not narrowed,
a rest, your table filled with fat food.

17 You are full of a wicked case;
the case and justice will be taken up.
18 But look out lest he draw you back with jeering,
and don't let a large bribe divert you.
19 Will he arrange your wealth when there is no distress,
no matter how strong your exertions?
20 Don't pant for the night
when peoples disappear from their place.
21 Be careful, don't turn toward evil,
because this you have preferred to misery.
22 Oh, El is inaccessible in his strength;
who is a teacher like him?
23 Who appoints his ways for him,
who says, "You've done a bad thing"?
24 Remember to extol his deed,
of which men sing,
25 which the whole race has perceived,
a man gazes from afar.

26 Oh, El is exalted, and we do not know
the number of his years, and cannot search them.
27 For he draws up drops of water,
which distill rain in the flood,
28 trickle down from the clouds,
drip continually upon humankind.
29 Even if one understands the spreading cloud,
the crashing from his canopy,
30 Ah! he spreads his light over it,
and it covers the roots of the sea.
31 For with them he judges peoples,
gives food in plenty.

32 **Light covers his hands.** I take the masculine *ʼōr* as the subject of the masculine verb "covers." Job used the expression *ksh ʻal*, "covers over," in 21.26. Habel (*Book of Job*, p. 499) takes the deity as the subject.
accuser. I like Pope's "sure aim" (*Job*, p. 276), but v. 33 leads me to think that the Hiph'il of *pgʻ*, which in Qal frequently means "to assail, press upon," might be taken as pressing a legal accusation.
33 **Wickedness.** Reading *rōʻō* instead of *rēʻō*.
extending. Repointing *miqneh*, "possessions, cattle," to *maqneh*, Hiph'il participle of *qnh*, "to acquire" (see Zech 13.5 and Ezek 8.3).
iniquity. A third repointing, from *ʻōleh*, "one who rises," to *ʻawlah*.

1 **Starts up.** Taking *yittar* as a Qal imperfect from *ntr* II.
2 **Listen.** The form is masculine plural.
rumble. Staples (p. 35) thought of that for *rōgez*, and I snatched it.
3 **Looses it.** A doubtful reading, given the uncertainty about the root *šrh*.
6 **Fall.** So Vulgate, *descendit*. An Arabic verb *hawa* means "to fall or descend," but Tur-Sinai (p. 508) denies any such verb in Hebrew or Aramaic. One must neither invent words nor disagree lightly with Tur-Sinai, but Gordis (*Book of Job*, p. 426) demonstrates occurrences of the verb and cognate nouns.
rain. I take *w*^{e}*gešem maṭar* in parallel to the first line, with the verb *y'mr* there governing this line too. I understand the preposition *l*^{e} on *gešem* in parallel to *lašeleg* and repoint *maṭar* to the imperative, *m*^{e}*ṭar*.
7 **On every human hand he puts a seal.** Some take "put a seal" as to close up something, and that sometimes leads to emendations of *b*^{e}*yad*, "on the hand." I have taken it as stamping a seal on the hand with Habel (*Book of Job*, p. 513) and Dhorme (p. 562), without the emendation.
so all the men he has made may know. The question is whether "to know" (*ladaʻat*) is something the "men he has made" (*ʼanšē maʻ*^{a}*śēhū*) do or something the deity does. If the latter, the couplet pictures the deity sealing up humankind so that he may come to know them, introducing the unusual notion that the maker is not acquainted with what he has made. If the humans do the knowing, the couplet follows the notion of the storm as somehow instructive.
9 **Rain-presses.** I am persuaded by Pope (*Job*, pp. 281–82).
11 **Moisture.** *Rī* is a hapax legomenon, and I would almost prefer to take *b*^{e}*rī* (so Blommerde, *Northwest Semitic Grammar*, p. 31) as a form of *bar*, "brightness, purity." But "moisture" is sensible in the context, and the presumed root *rwh* has to do with drinking and being wet.
12 **Things that whirl.** Taking *mithappēk* in the same sense it has in Gen 3.24 (to which it may be an allusion). I wish the word were plural, but that is the least of what I wish for this quatrain. Mere intelligibility would be pleasant.

[32] Light covers his hands,
and he commands it by an accuser.
[33] He tells him of his wickedness,
extending anger against iniquity.

37 [1] Oh, at this my heart trembles,
starts up from its place.
[2] Listen carefully to his voice's rumble,
the growl that comes out of his mouth.
[3] Under the whole sky he looses it,
and his light over the wings of the earth.
[4] After it roars his voice,
he thunders with his majestic voice,
and he does not restrain them when his voice is heard.
[5] El thunders marvels with his voice,
does great things we do not know.
[6] For to the snow he says, "Fall to earth,"
and to the downpour, "Rain,"
and the downpour is his strong rains.

[7] On every human hand he puts a seal
so all the men he has made may know.
[8] And the beast enters its lair,
lies down in its den.
[9] From the chamber comes the storm wind,
from the rain-presses the cold.
[10] From El's breath frost is formed,
and the wide water is narrowed.
[11] He also loads the cloud with moisture,
his light scatters the cloud cover.
[12] And he turns over the things that whirl
with his guidance to their deed,
to everything he commands them
across the inhabited earth.

[13] **Find [its goal].** I interpolate "its goal" as a guess at the implied object of "find," in a sentence that seems at least odd in its surroundings.

[15] **Considers.** I take *b*^{e}*śūm . . .* *ʿ*^{a}*lēhem* as an ellipsis for *śūm lēb ʿal*, "set the mind on."

cloud. *ʿanan*, different from the two words for "cloud" in 36.28, 29, noted above.

[18] **Strong as a cast-metal mirror.** That this clause modifies the foregoing one is shown by the agreement of "strong" (*ḥ*^{a}*zaqīm*) with "clouds." It would be nice to know more about the metallurgical technologies to which Elihu alludes, and whence comes the strange image of "cast-metal mirrors" as representing strength. On the other hand, *ḥazaq* can signify hardness as well as strength. "Mirrors" still seems a strange image.

[19] **Make known.** The imperative is singular, addressed to Job.

drawn up. I have suggested the military sense of *ʿrk* before.

[20] **To him.** To the deity.

swallowed up. It is also possible to read this line, "Does a man say he is confused?" taking *yebullaʿ* from *blʿ* II.

[22] **North.** Perhaps not north in general but Mt. Zaphon ("North Mountain") where, according to Canaanite mythology, Baal lived.

[23] **Just power.** Another hendiadys among my many examples: "strength and justice."

[3] **Real man.** A translation of *geber* that I like no better than "hero."

[4] **Know so much.** "If you know understanding."

[5–6] **Its.** These feminine singular pronouns agree with "earth."

pedestals. The *ʾeden* is the pedestal or base on which a pillar stands, but whether the pillars are conceived as holding up the earth is unclear.

[13] Whether for a tribe or for his land
or for loyalty, he makes it find [its goal].

[14] Listen to this, Job,
stop and pay attention to El's marvels.
[15] Do you know when Eloah considers them,
makes light shine in his cloud?
[16] Do you know about the cloud rolls,
marvels of perfect knowledge,
[17] you whose clothes are hot
when the land lies still from the south wind?
[18] Can you hammer out the clouds with him,
strong as a cast-metal mirror?
[19] Make known to us what we say to him;
we are drawn up before darkness.
[20] Is it said to him, "I'll speak"?
Does a man say he will be swallowed up?

[21] Now they do not see light,
however bright he is in the clouds
when the wind has passed and cleaned them.
[22] From the north gold comes forth,
over Eloah is fearful splendor.
[23] Shaddai—we cannot find him;
exalted in just power,
greatly righteous, he does not oppress.
[24] Therefore men are afraid of him,
he does not see any who are wise of heart.

38 [1] Yahweh answered Job from the whirlwind:
[2] Who is this who darkens counsel
with ignorant words?
[3] Gird your loins like a real man.
I will ask questions, and you instruct me.

[4] Where were you when I laid earth's foundations?
Tell me, if you know so much.
[5] Who set its measurements—surely you know!—
or who stretched the line out on it?
[6] Upon what were its pedestals sunk,
or who laid its cornerstone

[8] **He blocked.** Vulgate *quis conclusit* encourages some commentators to change *wayyasek* to *mī sak*, "who blocked," and LXX *ephraxa de* permits others to change it to first-person singular. I should like to take the Qal of *skk* in a passive sense but have not found the necessary evidence.

[10] **Set my limits.** The verb *šbr*, "break," is so strange here that K-B lists this citation with only a question mark. Many have been the emendations and explanations by comparative philology or by a hidden logic of Hebrew. I am unhappy with "set" or "put," but I find nothing better.

[11] **The end.** *Yašīt* has given interpreters fits. One might wish to interchange this verb with *'ešbōr* in v. 10, for this one would fit well there, and *šbr* would make good sense here. "To set," then, suggests setting a boundary, an end (see also Pope, *Job*, p. 294, "halt").

[12] **Instructed dawn.** Following Qere, *yiddaʿtah haššaḥar*.

[13] **Skirts.** *K*^{e}*napōt*, "wings."

[14] **Do you change.** The interrogative in v. 12 is still in force.

as if in uniform. "As one (or something) clothed." *Yṣb* often means to take a military station, and the image seems to be of the earth taking station at dawn. The implied uniform may be the dawn's light.

[24] **Light is allotted.** Translators seem to look for excuses to read something other than "light." I take the "division" implied in *yḥlq* as deliberate, rational allotment.

7 when the morning stars sang together,
and all the sons of Elohim shouted?

8 He blocked the sea with two doors
when it burst out of the womb,
9 when I clothed it in cloud,
swaddled it in dense cloud,
10 and I set my limits upon it,
put up the bar and doors,
11 And I said, "So far you come and no farther,
here is the end for your lofty waves."

12 During your days have you commanded morning,
instructed dawn of its place,
13 snatched the skirts of earth,
when the wicked are shaken out of it?
14 Do you change it like clay for a seal,
when it stands forth as if in uniform?
15 Their light is withheld from the wicked,
and the upraised arm is broken.

16 Have you entered Sea's springs,
walked around in the Deep's recesses?
17 Have Death's gates been uncovered for you,
and have you seen the gates of deep darkness?
18 Have you examined the earth's expanses?
Tell it, if you know all this.

19 Where is the road where light lives,
darkness, where is its place?
20 That you may take it to its territory,
perceive the way to its home.
21 You know, for you were born then,
the number of your days is many.

22 Have you entered the snow's treasury
and seen the hail's treasury,
23 which I store up for a troubled time,
a day of attack and battle?
24 Where is the road where light is allotted,
the east wind is scattered over the earth?
25 Who cut a channel for the flood
and a road for the thunderclap,

[26] **With no one.** *Lō' 'īš*, "not a man."

[27] **Desolate desert.** The expression, *šō'ah ūm^eš ō'ah*, also occurs in 30.3. It may be a hendiadys, but I add "desert" to reflect the alliteration.

in its spot. I take *mōṣa'* as the "place of its coming up."

[30] . . . . Many ancient versions, and most modern ones, read something like "congeal, freeze, harden," for a verb that means "hide" (*ḥb'*). Scholarly explanations are very thin, as Grabbe (pp. 118–20) has persuaded me.

[31–32] Except for Mazzarot, which occurs nowhere else, these constellations are referred to in 9.9. *'aš*, Lion, there is spelled *'ayiš* here, and I call it Lioness because of *baneyha*, "her cubs." G. R. Driver ("Two Astronomical Passages"), following Schiaparelli, identifies the "cubs" as the Hyades (see also note to 9.9). The masculine singular suffix on *b^e'ittō*, "at its time," v. 32a, is somewhat troubling with Mazzarot, a feminine plural noun.

[33] **Its rule.** The basic sense "rule, order" for *mišṭar* seems now fairly well agreed. "Its" refers to *šamayim*.

[36] **Thoth.** The Egyptian god of wisdom. The name was probably vocalized as *ṭaḥūt*. *Baṭṭuḥōt*, as in Ps 51.8 (Eng. 6), was assumed to mean "in secret."

Sekwi. A proper name, which Freedman reports ("Orthographic Peculiarities," p. 44) is attested on a Phoenician seal as Shekwi. What the name signifies I do not know, nor does he say. On both of these names, and the various interpretations of them (e.g., Sekwi as a cock, "Thoth" meaning Thoth's bird, the ibis), see Pope, *Job*, pp. 302–3.

[37] **Tilts.** *Yaškīb*, Hiph'il of *škb*, "to lie down." The image is of rain pouring from the tilted jars upon the parched ground. Another possibility is Orlinsky's suggestion, quoted by Barr (*Comparative Philology*, p. 137), that a homonymous *škb* is cognate to Arabic *sakaba*, "to pour out."

[2] **Know the season,** etc. This line is as repetitious of v. 1a as it seems.

26 to rain on a land with no one,
desert where no humans are,
27 to satisfy the desolate desert
and make the grass sprout in its spot?

28 Has rain a father?
Or who begot dewdrops?
29 From whose belly comes the ice?
The sky's hoar, who bore it?
30 Water . . . like a stone,
and the face of the deep sticks together.

31 Can you tie up the Herd with fetters
or loose the Fool's chains?
32 Can you bring out Mazzarot at its time
or lead the Lioness with her cubs?
33 Do you know the sky's statutes
or effect its rule on earth?
34 Can you raise your voice to the cloud
so that a flood of water covers you?
35 Can you send off lightnings, and they go,
and say to you, "Here we are"?
36 Who put wisdom into Thoth,
who gave understanding to Sekwi?
37 Who counts clouds with wisdom,
and the jars of the sky, who tilts them
38 when the dust is molded in a cast
and clods are stuck together?

39 Can you hunt prey for the lioness,
fill the bellies of young lions?
40 For they crouch in lairs,
stay covered in ambush.

41 Who provides food for the raven
when its young cry out to El,
frantic for want of food?

39 1 Do you know the birth season of rock goats,
watch the fallow deer calve?
2 Can you count the months they fulfill,
know the season they give birth,

[3] **Their cords.** I take *ḥeblēhem* from *ḥebel* I (K-B), meaning here, I think, umbilical cords, rather than from K-B's *ḥēbel* II, "fetus," the only citation of which is this passage. The masculine plural suffix is troublesome, since the antecedents are all feminine plurals, but the shift from one to the other occurs fairly frequently.

[10] **Wild ox.** It would be more elegant if *rēm* were not repeated from v. 9a. The animal is the ancient aurochs, a particularly large wild ox.

[12] **Return.** I accept Ketib; Qere's *yašīb* is the transitive "return."

threshing floor's grain. A nice example of the ever-present hendiadys: "your seed and your threshing floor." Only as a hendiadys does the phrase make sense.

[13] **If pinions . . . .** The line says, "if pinions [noun] a stork and a falcon." Anyone who can find meaning in that is welcome to do so.

[16] **Being harsh.** *Hiqšīaḥ* is a masculine verb form for a feminine subject. I prefer to repoint to the infinitive construct, *haqšīaḥ*.

[19] **Thunder.** Some commentators actually prefer "mane"!

[21] * **He paws.** I break the emendation rule again. The verb is a plural with no antecedent, and its subject is so evidently the horse that eliding the final *waw* seems better than being excessively principled. LXX, Syriac, and Vulgate have singular verbs, but that is no proof of singulars in the Hebrew texts that they read.

3 crouch down, press out their young,
expel their cords?
4 Their children are strong, grow in the open,
they leave and do not return.

5 Who sets the wild ass free?
Who opens the onager's bonds,
6 whose home I have put in the desert,
his dwellings the salt barrens?
7 He laughs at the city's uproar,
does not hear the driver's shouts,
8 roams the hills for his pasture,
seeks after any patch of green.

9 Does the wild ox consent to serve you,
bed down by your crib?
10 Can you hold the wild ox in the furrow with a rope?
Will he harrow the valleys after you?
11 Can you trust him because he is very strong,
leave your labor to him?
12 Can you believe that he will return,
gather in your threshing floor's grain?

13 The ostrich's wings are glad,
if pinions . . . .
14 For she leaves her eggs on the ground,
has them warmed on the dirt,
15 forgets that a foot may crush it,
a wild beast trample it,
16 being harsh to her young, as if they're not hers,
vain her labor, without caring.
17 For Eloah deprived her of wisdom,
apportioned her no understanding.
18 Time comes, on the heights she spreads her plumes,
laughs at horse and rider.

19 Do you give the horse his strength,
clothe his neck with thunder?
20 Do you make him shake like a locust,
his majestic snort a terror?
21 * He paws in the valley, exults in his strength,
charges out to meet the battle,

[25] **Retreat.** This is, I admit, a bit whimsical. Hebrew reads *b^{e}dē šōpar*, which I take as "at 'Enough' of the trumpet," and postulate "Enough" as the title of a bugle call. That puts me right athwart Gordis (*Book of Job*, p. 463), who interprets *dē* as "faint sound," like Arabic *daway*, meaning the first, distant intimation of battle. I think it is at the height of battle. Alternatively I would take Pope's reference (*Job*, p. 313) to Ugaritic *bd*, "song," and read *baddē šōpar*, "songs (calls) of the trumpet."

he has the reek. I am persuaded by DeBoer that *yarīaḥ* means "to give out a smell" and not the active "to smell." This understanding throws the syntax of the sentence into a disarray that I solve in the way every writing teacher forbids—with dashes.

[27] **Vulture.** See Pope (*Job*, p. 314) for this reading.

[28] **Sharp, craggy fastness.** "On the tooth of rock and stronghold."

[30] . . . . The meaning of the verb *y^{e}'al'ū* is unknown.

[2] **Will an accuser of Shaddai yield.** I repoint two words in the line: *rōb*, an infinitive, I read as *rab*, Qal participle of *ryb*, "accuser"; and *yissōr*, a noun meaning, perhaps, "faultfinder," I point *yasūr*, Qal imperfect of *swr*, "yield." See Pope, *Job*, p. 318; and Terrien, *IB*, p. 1182. Fullerton ("On the Text") gives an impressive argument in favor of the text as it stands.

answer it. "It" is feminine singular, and I take its referent to be the prior speech.

[4] The first line is translated as most commentators understand it. I suggested (*Irony*, p. 236) that it is a feisty, defiant retort: "Oh, I have trifled, how could I change you?" Multiple meanings are always possible.

[7] The couplet is identical to 38.3.

[8] **Order.** I argued ("Job and the Literary Task," pp. 479–80) that *mišpaṭ* here signifies not merely "justice," its usual meaning, but order, both social (Deut 33.10) and cosmic (Jer 8.7). See also John Gray, "Book of Job in the Context of Near Eastern Literature," p. 253; and the "Indispensable Introduction," above.

treat me as guilty. The Hiph'il of *rš'* is often used of a legal decree, in which the defendant is found guilty of the charges.

[10] **Pride and puissance,** etc. The alliterations in these two lines reflect alliteration in the Hebrew.

22 he laughs at fear, is not terrified,
does not turn away from the sword.
23 The quiver rattles upon him,
flame of spear and battle sword.
24 In clatter and clamor he swallows the ground,
does not heed the trumpet call—
25 at “Retreat,” he says, “Aha!”
even afar he has the reek of battle—
princes in panic, alarm signal.

26 Does the peregrine soar by your wisdom,
spread his wings to the south?
27 Does the eagle soar at your command,
the vulture build his nest up high,
28 dwelling on rock, lodging
on the sharp, craggy fastness?
29 From there he spies out food,
his eyes look forth from afar,
30 his nestlings . . . blood,
and where corpses are, there is he.

40 1 Yahweh answered Job thus:
2 Will an accuser of Shaddai yield,
Eloah’s arbiter answer it?

3 Job answered Yahweh thus:
4 Oh, I am small, what could I reply to you?
I put my hand to my mouth.
5 I spoke once, and I will not answer,
twice, and I will add nothing.

6 Yahweh answered Job thus from the whirlwind:
7 Gird your loins like a real man.
I will ask you questions, and you instruct me.
8 Would you even annul my order,
treat me as guilty so you may be innocent?

9 If you have an arm like El’s,
and with a voice like his you thunder,
10 deck yourself with pride and puissance,
with glory and grandeur clothe yourself.

11 **Everyone.** There is no way to be sure whether *kōl* here and in the next line, and *r*^{e}*šaʿīm* in v. 12b, refer to persons or to things. I tilt toward persons, and "faces," v. 13b, is a further justification.

them. The pronouns here and in the next line are third-person masculine singular collectives. English ordinarily uses plural pronouns for collective nouns, and I have followed the English convention, even pretending that "everyone" is plural.

12 **Trample.** The verb is a hapax legomenon. Habel (*Book of Job*, p. 553) points to "crush" as the common ground of the roots *dk'*, *dky*, and *dkk*, and "trample" may be too precise a variant on that. A post-biblical Hebrew cognate is "crush" (so Dhorme, p. 618), and an Arabic cognate has to do with razing a building. In any case, the word has the display of force in it.

14 **Even I, I.** The prolixity reflects the presence of an emphatic pronoun along with a first-person verb form.

15 **Behemoth.** The word might be—but surely is not—the plural of *b*^{e}*hēmah*, "cattle, domesticated animals." Its singular verbs and masculine singular pronouns in the verses that follow strongly suggest that the word is a name, whether of a cosmic monster, a hippopotamus, a dolphin (Eerdmans, pp. 29–30—unpersuasive to me), or a crocodile (G. R. Driver, "Mythical Monsters"—much better if we must have a real animal). Keel (p. 127) points out that the identification of Behemoth as hippopotamus (and Leviathan as crocodile) was first made in Samuel Bochart's *Hierozoicon* of 1663, and since then it has become a virtual consensus.

grass. Three nouns *ḥaṣīr* are listed in the lexica: one means grass or plants in general, one apparently refers specifically to leeks, and a third means reeds or cattails. I prefer the first, more general one.

17 **Stiff.** The verb *ḥpṣ* is a hapax legomenon, and "to be stiff" is an uncertain meaning. The tail as a sign of overpowering strength does not apply to the hippopotamus. That impressive animal has a most unimpressive tail. It would make better sense if Behemoth were a crocodile.

intertwined. The physiological description offered here escapes me.

18 **Rods.** The noun *m*^{e}*ṭīl* is a hapax legomenon, connected by some Arabic cognates to ironworking.

19 **Ways.** A somewhat odd use of the noun *derek* in a passage that we might expect to refer to a product of creation. The same expression (in the singular) is used of wisdom in Prov 8.22, with which this passage may be connected.

his maker. The form is anomalous, having a definite article that ought not be there on a noun with a pronominal suffix.

20 **The mountains bear him wood.** A strange idea, to say the least. The verb *nś'*, "bear," can be used to mean both to lift or carry and to bear fruit (Ezek 36.8). *Būl* is used of wood only in Isa 44.19 (*būl ʿēṣ*). Habel (*Book of Job*, p. 553) takes *būl* as a short form of *y*^{e}*būl*, "tribute," which would make sense but is without parallel. Several scholars (e.g., Pope, *Job*, p. 325; G. R. Driver, "Mythical Monsters," p. 237, *n*3) find in *būl* a cognate to Akkadian *būlu*, "cattle, beasts." That does not help a great deal with "bear, lift." Kinnier Wilson (p. 9) adds to that reading of the noun the suggestion that "lift" is elliptical for "lift the voice" (*nś'*

[11] Strew about the furies of your anger,
see everyone proud, bring them low,
[12] see everyone proud, humiliate them,
and trample guilty people where they stand.
[13] Conceal them in the dust together,
bind their faces in concealment.
[14] Even I, I will praise you,
for your right hand won you victory.

[15] Ah, then! Behemoth,
whom I made with you,
eats grass like cattle.
[16] Ah, then! the strength in his loins,
potence in his belly's muscles,
[17] his tail stiff like a cedar,
the sinews of his thighs intertwined,
[18] his bones tubes of bronze,
his limbs like iron rods.
[19] He is first of El's ways—
his maker brings out his sword!

[20] The mountains bear him wood,
all the wild animals play there.
[21] Under the thorn-lotus he lies down,
in covert of reed and marsh,
[22] thorn-lotus covers him with its shade,
wadi-poplars surround him.
[23] Oh, the river presses, he does not flee,

---

qōl), which is otherwise known (e.g., 21.12), and proposes that the mountain beasts (*būl harīm*) "howl" at Behemoth. See Chapter 8.

play. *Śḥq* has a number of connotations, including that of sexual intercourse (see, e.g., Gen 26.8; Exod 32.6) and, more commonly, of laughter (e.g., Gen 17.17; 18.12–14). Any of them are possible here.

[21] **Thorn-lotus**. Generally identified as *zizyphus lotus*, a thorny shrub found from Syria to North Africa. See Pope, *Job*, p. 326.

[22] **Wadi-poplars**. Probably *populus euphratica*, a tree common in Palestine. See Pope, *Job*, p. 326.

[23–24] These two verses are extremely obscure, both in meaning and in syntax. Some commentators think that the Leviathan section begins at v. 24.

[23] **Presses**. Job uses the same verb in 10.3 to mean "oppress." Its basic meaning seems to be to apply physical pressure.

flee. I take this verb in its usual sense of hurrying away from something.

secure. "He trusts." Several commentators, especially Guillaume (*Studies*, p. 136) and G. R. Driver, quoted by Barr (*Comparative Philology*, p. 91), adduce an Arabic cognate meaning "lie still" or "lie extended." The suggestion is attractive, and the verb may occur with that sense in Prov 14.16 and Jer 12.5.

Jordan. Perhaps, as Pope (*Job*, p. 327) argues, *yardēn* does not mean the river Jordan but more generally a swift stream.

bursts forth. See the use of the same verb for water bursting out of confinement in 38.8.

takes him by the eyes. A number of commentators interpolate *mî hû'*, "who is he who will?" at the beginning of a line they find unusually short. Others read the couplet interrogatively, "Will one take him by the eyes," etc. I take the two lines to continue the sentence of v. 23, as *yardēn* provides a masculine singular subject for the verbs. But the images are difficult. "Nose" (*'ap*) has no possessive pronoun, and I insert "his" because both "mouth," v. 23b, and "eyes," v. 24a, have possessives.

25 In the chapter-and-verse numbering of Christian Bibles, derived from LXX and Vulgate, this is 41.1. I hew to the numbering in the Hebrew Bible.

Leviathan. The more powerful of the two monsters in these chapters (and cf. 3.8). Those who identify Behemoth as a hippopotamus usually think of Leviathan as a crocodile (see the note on Behemoth at v. 15 above). But G. R. Driver ("Mythical Monsters"), thinking that Behemoth is a crocodile, identifies Leviathan as a whale. In Chapter 8, I explain why I think that, though such animals as the crocodile, the whale, and perhaps others may have furnished some images for these descriptions, Behemoth and Leviathan are imaginary monsters.

28 **Perpetual slave.** A reference to a law in Deut 15.17.

30 **Salesmen.** The word means "companions" or perhaps "partners," and I see a somewhat whimsical picture of salesmen or buyers haggling over the goods.

merchants. "Canaanites," a gentilic that came, by popular perception of a typical occupation, to mean those who pursue that occupation. Another biblical instance is "Chaldeans," which in Dan 2.2 means "astrologers."

1 **Any expectation of him.** I take the pronominal suffix as objective and add "any" to clarify what is being said.

is El himself thrown down. With Pope (*Job*, pp. 336–37) I repoint the preposition *'el*, "to," to *'ēl* and take *gam* emphatically. The sentence is a rhetorical question expecting a negative answer.

2 **Before me.** One might expect "him," which several MSS read. The first-person forms in the next line justify a first-person singular, and v. 3b makes a contrast between the deity and Leviathan. The parenthesis points up the fact that vv. 1–2a and 3b–4 are tercets on either side of this couplet.

4 . . . The ellipsis covers a hapax legomenon, *ḥîn*, followed by *'erkō*, "his valuation, array," or something like it.

5 **Double bridle for him.** Several commentators follow LXX in a metathesis of

is secure, though Jordan bursts forth to his mouth,
24 takes him by the eyes,
pierces his nose with traps.

25 Can you drag out Leviathan with a fishhook,
press down his tongue with a rope,
26 put a line in his nose,
pierce his jaw with a barb?
27 Will he beg you abjectly for mercy,
speak weakly to you?
28 Will he make a covenant with you,
and you take him as perpetual slave?
29 Can you play with him like a bird,
put him on a leash for your little girls?
30 Will salesmen haggle over him,
divide him among the merchants?
31 Can you fill his skin with harpoons,
his head with fish spears?
32 Put your hand upon him—
think of the fight; don't do it again.

41 1 Oh, any expectation of him is false.
Is El himself thrown down at sight of him?
2 None is fierce enough to rouse him.
(Then who will take a stand before me?
3 Who confronts me? I'll repay him!)
Under the whole sky, he is mine.
4 I will not silence his boasting,
word of his exploits, and . . . .

5 Who would snatch off his outer garment,
who would come with a double bridle for him?

risnō, "his bridle," to *siryōnō*, "his mail coat," attractive if Leviathan be considered a crocodile. I take the pronominal suffix objectively.

[6] **Terrifying teeth.** The Hebrew is not alliterative.

[12] **Boiling pot and . . . .** In 40.26, *'agmōn* seems to mean reeds or rushes put together to make a rope. I cannot fathom what "a boiling and reedy pot" might mean.

[14] **Languor.** Perhaps the last word one would expect as the subject of "leaps." Frank M. Cross ("Ugaritic *DB'AT*," pp. 163–64) first proposed, and several commentators accept, a metathesis of *d*^{e}*'abah*, "languor," to *d*^{e}*ba'ah*, "violence." The unexpected image of Leviathan galvanizing languor into hasty motion is poetically rather more forceful.

[17] **Crashing down.** The word is *š*^{e}*barīm*, "breakings." In contrast to "rising" (*śētō* = *ś*^{e}*'ētō*), a sudden falling seems to be the meaning. For *yitḥaṭṭa'ū* meaning "to shrink away," see Pope, *Job*, p. 345.

[20] **Bow's child.** A literal translation of *ben-qešet*, perhaps meaning an arrow.

[21] **Seems to him.** With Blommerde (*Northwest Semitic Grammar*, p. 139) I repoint *neḥš*^{e}*bū*, "they seem, are considered," to *neḥš*^{e}*bō*.

[22] **Sharpened shards.** The Hebrew is alliterative.

[24] **Tehom.** Usually the cosmic abyss, the word seems to be a proper name here. **white-haired.** If Leviathan is the subject of the verb, *śēbah* probably suggests weakness or senility. I am unsure of that meaning, and the impersonal "one might think" allows "white-haired" to be merely descriptive.

[6] Who would open his face's doors,
ringed with terrifying teeth?
[7] His pride is his rows of shields,
closed with a flinty seal,
[8] one touching another,
and wind can't come between them.
[9] Each clings to its brother,
clasping inseparably.
[10] His sneezes flash with light,
his eyes are like dawn's eyelids,
[11] from his mouth come flares,
fiery sparks fly out.
[12] From his nostrils spurts smoke
like a boiling pot and . . . .
[13] His throat kindles coals,
and flame spurts from his mouth.
[14] In his neck resides power,
before him leaps languor.
[15] His sagging flesh clings together,
cast upon him, immovable.
[16] His heart is cast like stone,
cast like a nether millstone.

[17] Gods are frightened at his rising,
at his crashing down, they shrink away.
[18] At his onslaught, a sword is no avail,
nor spear, catapult, or arrow.
[19] He considers iron as straw,
bronze as rotted wood.
[20] Bow's child cannot put him to flight,
sling stones are turned by him to stubble.
[21] A cudgel seems to him like stubble,
he laughs at the battle sword's clatter.

[22] His underbelly is sharpened shards,
he stretches out, a threshing sledge on the mud.
[23] He boils the deep like a pot,
makes Sea like an ointment pot.
[24] His wake behind him is bright,
one might think Tehom white-haired.
[25] Upon the dust is not his ruler,
made as he is without terror.

26 **Proud beasts**. The phrase, *b^e^nē šaḥaṣ*, "sons of pride," occurs in 28.8, apparently of animals.

2 **I know**. The reading is Qere, and the ancient versions agree with it. Ketib is *yada'ta*, "you (masculine sing.) know," which I discuss in Chap. 8.
plan. Hebrew *m^e^zimmah* has a certain connotation of scheming (see Habel, "Naked I Came," p. 388).

3 **Who is this**, etc. The line alludes to, though it does not exactly quote, 38.2. There it was "darken" rather than "obscure" counsel, and "ignorant words" (*b^e^millīn b^e^lī-da'at*) rather than "ignorantly" (*b^e^lī-da'at*). Job is thinking about what Yahweh said to him.
therefore, etc. The syntax of these two lines is unusual. "Wonders beyond me" is the accusative of "I told," and the verbs "I didn't understand" and "I didn't know" are parallel to each other.

4 The first line is not a quotation, but the second exactly quotes 38.3b and 40.7b. I have put quotation marks around the entire couplet because it feels like a quotation.

5 **I hear you**. It is possible that *š^e^ma'tīka* means "I heard of you." That reading would make a contrast with the next line, as the difference between secondhand and firsthand acquaintance. But *'attah*, "now," in v. 5b need not be interpreted as temporally subsequent to v. 5a, and the verbs in both lines are perfect.

6 **Despise and repent**. Patrick ("Translation") has demonstrated two things to my satisfaction: *m's*, "despise," is transitive, and reflexive translations of it, as in RSV ("despise myself"), are mistaken; *nḥm 'al* never means elsewhere to "repent in or on" a place but always means to "repent of" something. "Dust and ashes" (*'apar wa'ēper*), then, is the accusative of both verbs.

8 **Accept him**. The legal phrase, *nś' panīm*, "lift the face."
doing anything foolish to you. The statement, *l^e^biltī ^a^śōt 'immakem n^e^balah*, is strange, and Gordis (*Book of Job*, pp. 494–95) may be right in thinking that it means "not exhibiting you as fools." On the other hand, *'śh n^e^balah* refers a number of times in the Hebrew Bible to a serious crime, where "foolishness" would be an understatement. When *'śh* has an object, it is always, except here, preceded by the preposition *l^e^*.

10 **Reversed Job's fortune**. The expression *šwb 'et-š^e^būt* is "turn the turning," a somewhat pleonastic way of saying "turn things around." I willingly accept the double sense of "fortune."

11 **That Yahweh had brought**. There is no reference to the Prosecutor's agency, and the language differs from that of 2.11, where the friends hear of "this evil."
qesitah. A unit of exchange found only in Gen 33.19, where Jacob pays a hundred *qeśiṭas* for a piece of land, and in Josh 24.32, which refers to the same episode. As Pope (*Job*, p. 351) points out, a *qeśiṭah* is no trivial present, but its value is unknown. An Arabic weight, *qiṣṭ*, is estimated to be over three pounds (O. R. Sell-

[26] He looks on everything lofty,
he, king over all proud beasts.

42 [1] Job answered Yahweh thus:
[2] I know that you can do everything,
no plan is inaccessible to you.
[3] "Who is this who obscures counsel ignorantly?"
Therefore I told, and didn't understand,
wonders beyond me, and I didn't know.
[4] "Hear, and I will speak,
I will ask you questions, and you instruct me."
[5] With ears' hearing I hear you,
and now my eye sees you.
[6] Therefore I despise and repent
of dust and ashes.

[7] After Yahweh had spoken these words to Job, Yahweh said to Eliphaz
of Teman, "I am very angry with you and your two friends, because you
have not spoken truth of me, as has my servant Job. [8] Now, get yourselves
seven bulls and seven rams, go to my servant Job, and make a burnt offering for yourselves. My servant Job will pray over you. I will certainly accept him without doing anything foolish to you, for you have not spoken truth of me, as has my servant Job."

[9] Eliphaz of Teman, Bildad of Shuach, and Zophar of Na'amah went
and did as Yahweh had told them, and Yahweh accepted Job. [10] Yahweh
reversed Job's fortune when he prayed for his friends, and he increased Job's holdings twofold.

[11] All his brothers and sisters and acquaintances came to see him and ate a meal with him in his house. They consoled and comforted him about all the evil that Yahweh had brought upon him, and each gave him one *qesitah* and one gold ring.

[12] Yahweh blessed Job's later life more than his earlier life: he had fourteen thousand sheep and six thousand camels, a thousand span of oxen

---

ers, "Weights and Measures," *Interpreter's Dictionary of the Bible*, 4: 832). Precious metal of that weight would be an extremely expensive present. LXX reads *amnas*, "lamb," which might mean either that someone thought a *qeṣiṭah* was the price of a lamb or that someone misread the word *mina*, a well-known Hebrew weight, to *amnas*.

[12] Job now has double the number of animals he had in 1.3 but apparently no slaves.

[13] **Seven.** The odd form of the numeral, *šibʿanah*, has been explained by some as a dual (= twice seven). The doubling of Job's former fortune in v. 12 makes the idea attractive, but it founders on the three—not six—daughters. Sarna ("Epic Substratum," p. 18) suggests an adverbial form: "There were sons to him seven times."

[14] The daughters' names have meaning: *y*^{e}*mīmah* is "dove"; *q*^{e}*ṣīʾah* is "cassia" (used for perfume or incense); and *qeren happūk* is "antimony horn" (antimony was used in antiquity as mascara is used today, and the horn is the container). Sarna ("Epic Substratum," p. 24) refers for Jemimah to the Ugaritic *ymmt limm*, an epithet of the goddess Anat, and to Ugaritic *qṣʿt*, a bow, for Qeziah (for the latter, see also Gordon, *Ugaritic Textbook*, 3: 349). Sarna does not deal with *qeren-happūk*, nor does he explain what *y*^{e}*mīmah* means. The word is difficult, perhaps indicating "progenitress," if *ymmt* is the same as *ybmt*. Kapelrud (pp. 31–33) gives up on interpreting the Ugaritic.

[15] That daughters would inherit along with sons is unusual.

[16] **One hundred forty years.** Twice the 70 years that Ps 90.10 says is the standard span of life, and longer than Moses' 120-year life (Deut 34.7).

[17] **Sated.** Hebrew *śbʿ*, "fed full," may be a dead metaphor for satisfaction, as English "satisfied" (etymologically "made full") is. It may be significant (Sarna, "Epic Substratum," p. 14, argues that it is) that the same expression is used of the deaths of Abraham and Isaac (Gen 25.8; 35.29).

and a thousand female asses. [13]He had seven sons and three daughters.
[14]He named the first Jemimah, the second Qezi‘ah, and the third Keren-
happuk. [15]Nowhere in the whole country could women be found as beautiful as Job's daughters, and their father gave them inheritance among
their brothers.

[16]Job lived after this one hundred forty years and saw his sons and
grandsons, four generations. [17]Then Job died, old and sated with days.

A Reading of Job

I

On Reading

> The vision of the whole has become to you like the words of a sealed book, which they give to one who knows how to read, saying, "Read this, please." He says, "I can't, because it is sealed." The book is given to one who does not know how to read, saying, "Read this, please." He says, "I don't know how to read." —Isaiah 29.11–12

Like so much of what used to be taken for granted, reading has become problematic. Not, of course, for everyone. People who devour ten romance novels every week do not think that reading is problematic—for them it is avowedly a form of daydreaming. Those who read only texts that give them irreproachable facts to ingest do not think that reading is problematic—but they may not realize how problematic those irreproachable facts are.

For those who read for a reason other than to give rein to fantasy or to amass mere facts, however, reading has disintegrated. We have become uncertain about what a text is and about why we read. According to the semioticians, a text is a congeries of codes to be cracked. To the structuralists, it is a system of signifiers. The deconstructionists tell us that a text has already undermined itself and means a whole host of contraries. The hermeneuts are sure that a text is (1) something that means or (2) that properly means only what its author meant or (3) that probably never means what its author meant. The reception theorists tell us that it means what *we* think it means. The psychoanalytic critics deny this, on the grounds that we do not know what we think. The political critics have decided that a text means what "they" think it means, because a text is always a product of those in power. Historical critics may insist that the text means only what it used to mean.

I admit the parodistic rhetoric of that paragraph, and I will shortly take some of it back. If reading is the search for meaning, perhaps meaning has broken apart (hence the necessity, some years back, of I. A. Richards's *The Meaning of Meaning*). But perhaps reading is not the search for meaning. Why do we read? To come closer to the point, why do we read the Book of Job? Or, even closer, why are you reading this book about the Book of Job? (If your answer is that you are reading my book in order to find the truth, I thank you for your donation. And I will never again believe a word you say.)

In preparing the first part of this book, I had to make unitary decisions. I had to decide how to translate words in order to achieve a readable, comprehensible text. I could not always reflect the ambiguities or double meanings of the Hebrew text, except by referring to them in the annotations. If, as in chaps. 1–2, the Hebrew verb *brk* could mean either "bless" or "curse" or both, I could not write "bless/curse" or "curse/bless" or "blurse" or "cess." It had to be either "bless" or "curse." The translation presents the text as I see it when I am willing to make decisions, and the annotations give other options and demonstrate the need for wariness and uncertainty.

In this part, "A Reading of Job," my methods of proceeding change drastically. The game goes in the opposite direction. I examine the text of Job as closely as possible, and the reader watches over my shoulder, making constant reference to the text itself, shaking her head in exasperation as I misunderstand sentences and draw illogical conclusions, play with double and triple meanings and with allusions to earlier and later parts of the text. My wish is not to close down options of understanding but to break them open, not to decide definitively that one alternative is to be adopted but to allow the alternatives free rein as I ask how the text plays itself.

This "reading" of Job does not pretend to discover Truth about or in the book. I neither find that truth for myself nor uncover it for the reader. I am reading in order to see what I can see. "We joined the Navy to see the sea," went a humorous song in my childhood. "And what did we see? We saw the sea." The song went on to observe that the "Atlantic isn't romantic," the "Pacific isn't terrific," and the whole thing "isn't what it's cracked up to be." That may happen with the Book of Job too. Not only do I avoid claiming that I have found the truth about Job, I claim that it cannot be found. There is no single correct understanding of the Book of Job.

Readers are too ready to think that, if someone will make the decisions for them—tell them the real truth and show how to arrive at it—

they will have no more worries. That is what an Expert, an Authority, is. Even if we need to tinker with the Authorized truth, we can still feel warmly contained in it.

I decline to be your Authority and hold you hostage to my perceptions. We must "see the sea" for ourselves, and we may discover that it "isn't what it's cracked up to be." In the past I pursued what I supposed was an acceptable, arguable, and possessible—even correct—truth about Job.[1] In writing this book, I found that I could no longer do that. Just as reading in general has become problematic, reading the Book of Job has for me become newly problematic. The title of this part, "A Reading of Job," is precise: it is *a* reading, not *the* reading. It is a reading impressed with how the book continually dissolves into multiple alternative meanings, and, as it proceeds, it poses more questions than answers. Indeed, every time I think I have found an answer, it shades off into ambiguity and several more questions. Finality, the definitive solution, is not to be found.

The Book of Job is, in the sense suggested by critics like Umberto Eco and Roland Barthes, an "open" text, not a "closed" one.[2] Or, perhaps more accurately, I read it as open, not closed. A "closed" text is the sort that we in the Western tradition always thought any text was: a complete, completed literary object containing a defined set of words in a specific order with a single definitive, discoverable meaning. The relatively modern assumption, moreover, has been that an author determines the meaning of the text in creating it. Even if a text is anonymous, someone composed, created, *intended* a coherent meaning and embodied it in the text.[3] That coherence intended by the author is the true meaning. In this view, "author" is not merely the writer, the composer, the mind behind the text, but *authority*. We have been expected, if possible, to discover the author's expressed intention. Failing that, we were to make the case for the most plausible intention we could discern and connect that intention and what the author might reasonably be supposed to have said, thought, or implied, given everything else we can discover that that author said, thought, or implied. On this assumption, the text is an inert, passive object, the container for the author's thoughts, which we disclose by our examination. The text itself has no role to play except to suffer our penetration, and the purpose of the penetration is to recreate as nearly as possible the thoughts and intentions of the author.

It sounds like—and is—a parody of an insensitive male sexuality, which takes its pleasure in penetrating a passive, female object in imitation of creation by a cosmic, powerful, and masculine deity. The female object is valuable only as a bearer of the thoughts and intentions of its—assumedly both divine and masculine—author. The object, moreover, belongs absolutely to its author, and the pursuit in it of anything but the author's wishes constitutes adultery, punishable under the Author's law.

Enough of parodies.[4] I am reading an "open" text, but I think of that somewhat differently from the way, say, Eco does. He is especially fascinated with "the role of the reader," as his book is titled, and he describes that role as "cooperating" with the text.[5] The text for him comes into being, in a serious and interesting way, only as it is received by a reader. The receiver of the text plays a part in generating the text.[6] There is another sexual image, and we see it again and again in writing about literature, in words like "creation," "creativity," "conception," "generation." Someone has created or conceived or generated the work, and the reader has only to recreate or reconceive or regenerate in order to uncover its meaning.

But an "open" text is not closed; it is not a lidded container of meaning. An open text may propose many meanings or few, or none, but it is not inert and passive. A sexual analogy to this kind of text and this kind of reading has much more to do with a playful eroticism that is bent neither on one's being mistress or master over another nor on some purpose external to the play itself. "Conception," "generation," and "creation," whether by author (or Author) or by reader, are just such external purposes, justifications that our society, culture, history, and tradition require in order to legitimate the play. Indeed, it is as if we must apply for permission to play, whether at reading or at the erotic. But if texts are "open," the only way to approach them is in play, and permission by some superego is redundant.

This kind of reading promotes a certain purposelessness. Some may think it is unserious, because it ignores such grave intentions as those of Finding the Truth. In many ways play is the best analogy. I like the erotic image, because the purpose of play, especially erotic play, is the play itself. The purpose of reading is to read, to see what one can see, to let the text play openly on us and we openly on it—or, perhaps better, that we and the text play with each other—so that we close off no possibility.

That requires both an insouciance about the text, a willingness to trust the text in the play, and a certain courage about not imposing closings upon it. We need courage in the face of our own fears about letting texts get out of hand, of losing sight of truths or Truth, of feeling nakedly exposed if our interpretation does not put us fully in control of the text.[7] At times in the chapters to follow, the reader may feel vertigo, a loss of secure foothold and certainty of direction, an intellectual weightlessness. But the freedom of relinquishing mastery—of refusing to be the tyrant of the text or of the play with it—allows us to range across a greater territory, to perceive both the text's world and our own world as much larger than we had thought. If Job turns out not "all that it's cracked up to be," that may well be gain, not loss.

Readers who know something of recent literary theory and criticism may perceive elements of "deconstruction" in this discussion. I have found deconstructive criticism, with its pleasure in indeterminacy, a helpful stimulus in breaking open my own lifelong critical habits and nervous mental constrictions.[8] Once one has allowed the possibility of that kind of approach, everything else comes to feel bound. One longs for the wide skies, the prairies, and the oceans of the open text, the many-branched canyons and arroyos of deconstructive indeterminacy.

Let me assure readers inclined to translate "deconstruction" into "destruction" that the element "con" is of the essence. "Con"—*cum*—"with": I have already discussed playing *with* the text, and I find that deconstruction has to do far less with smashing things with sledgehammers than with slipping playfully out from under the walls and fences that the search for Truth has erected around us. The deconstructionist searches for the text's multiple possibilities, its fascinating and liberating inconsistencies, its simultaneous contraries—the ways the mind and the text play their mutual games.[9] That indeed is recreation, both at play and at the business of recapitulating creation. But the play is more important than the creation.

Deconstruction is emphatically not destruction, not the removal of truth. It is the assertion that the open text has already undone its own tendencies to closure, already is playing with breaking its unities into multiplicities. And the deconstructive critic joins the game with the text in order to help the text further play its indeterminate truths and to let it help him crack the armor he has clamped around his own mind, to the end that the game may become ever freer.

Some may write me off as an outlandish critic concerned only with what the jargon now calls synchronic study,[10] someone totally uninterested in the past. For the record, I am not uninterested in the past. I am, however, uninterested in the kind of historiographical criticism that insists that knowing the external, past circumstances of a text is the necessary prologue to understanding the text. As for *historical* criticism, I am committed to it. My play with the Book of Job is with that book, not with some phantasm of my own mind. Among other things, that requires that I take seriously that the Book of Job is an ancient Hebrew book, not a modern English one, and that I read it in its antiquity and with awareness of the character of that antiquity. The very translation of the book from Hebrew into English acknowledges the antiquity. But the translation was a unitary undertaking, attended by all the illusions of such an activity, whereas the reading here is frankly an undertaking of indeterminacy. In the reading too, I must take seriously Job's antiquity, and, in my judgment, I do. There are assumptions around the book, belonging to the book's original age, that cannot be swept aside. At the same time, if there were no similarity between ancient persons and modern ones, no modern could remotely read, let alone understand, any ancient book.[11] The book's very antiquity, however, means that we must try to understand without knowing all we might like to know about the ancient culture and its ways of thinking and telling.

For a long time, the central issue of scholarship on the Hebrew Bible was historical reconstruction. This was, I suspect, the only way biblical scholarship could gain a hearing in European universities in the nineteenth century. That was a great time of pushing back the frontiers of knowledge of the past, and scholarly practitioners took as the key to understanding anything a knowledge of its past circumstances as a way out of our own provincialisms and into understanding the past on its own terms, if possible. One result of that enormously important historiographical tutelage has been the doubtful supposition that arriving at the historical facts is the essence of the matter, that in scholarship of the Hebrew Bible every question is a historical question. There are, of course, historical questions to pursue in and about the Book of Job. But that one must have firm answers to historical questions such as the work's date, authorship, and process of compilation before one can go on to anything else strikes me as both theoretically nonsensical and practically impossible. We cannot await a by-your-leave from the poser of historical questions before we read the book.[12]

Of course, historical questions extend beyond questions about temporal sequences and the events of human experience. They have also to do with language, for example, and with the stages in the composition of works and the copying of texts. In one sense, every question about something that happened in the past is a historical question. What troubles me about many studies of the Book of Job is that they see every problem as nothing but a historiographical question. An apparent logical lapse between two lines becomes an occasion for deciding that the text "originally" (at some time in the past) must have contained different words. An apparent grammatical error or an infelicity in syntax is handled the same way, by working toward the "original." A difference of ideas between one passage and another becomes an occasion for proposing different authors for different parts of the text. To understand a text by this method becomes an attempt to reconstruct a sequence of events in the life of the text, and without a sense of that sequence, we think we cannot go on to understand. This reduces a work to a series of events outside of the work, which we clamp deterministically upon the work.

Some scholarly energy has gone into deciding, for example, that the prose tale in chaps. 1–2 and 42.7–17 is actually two tales, and into solving the problem of what seems an incoherence between 42.7–9 and 42.10–17 by saying that those two sections stem from the minds of two different authors.[13] The result is the conclusion that, having identified the incoherence and explained its cause in terms of historical events, we need pay no further attention to it. To be sure, we think we cannot leave the incoherence unexplained. Incoherence is incompatible with the notion, derived from our entire tradition, that by definition a text is the coherent presentation of an author's views on something.

That idea goes in two directions. On the one hand, it takes texts of fiction, drama, or poetry as vehicles for authors to express their opinions about truth external to the works.[14] Thus the interpretation of literature has often centered upon the discovery of the truths, moral teachings, and opinions the author couched in the fictional or poetic mode. Content is all, form is mere carrier, and every assertion conveys the author's views. The value of a work, then, has often been felt to lie in the truths it conveys and the agreements between those truths and other truths, moral teachings, or opinions the interpretive community found acceptable or orthodox.

On the other hand, coherence is essential in this authoritarian world to the definition of Truth. An incoherent text cannot be true and by definition is not worth reading. Our common scholarly practice solves any incoherence in one of two ways. We can remove it historically by showing that, because the parts of the incoherence originated at different times and places, we need not consider them at the same time; they therefore cease to be incoherent for us. Or we can solve it textually, by changing whatever in the text makes it incoherent, to restore a coherent "original."

An example of the former practice is the conclusion, probably held by 95 percent of all scholars of Job, that chap. 28 was not part of the original dialogue.[15] It is, indeed, a bit odd, having read in chap. 27 a discussion of the plight of the wicked and their destruction by the deity, to find suddenly, in 28.1–6, a poetic disquisition about mining technology that leads to a beautiful, well-structured inquiry into wisdom. Most commentators see chap. 28 as an independent poem that is unrelated to the rest of the book.[16] Having concluded that chap. 28 was interpolated, they seldom ask why it was put here, unless it be to point out how inept the placement was. To say that it was not originally here is reason enough to say no more about its presence.

That seems to me a pseudo-historical answer to a historical question. Because the "original" book supposedly did not contain the poem, people who hold this view of texts find it self-evidently stupid that someone inserted it. But if the historian's task is to explain historical change, to satisfy oneself with merely noting historical change ("This poem was not present in the original Book of Job") is to do only half of the historian's task ("This poem is now present in the Book of Job because—").

I distinguish, then, a necessary *historical* criticism, which reads the book critically in the light of its language, style, and cultural assumptions, from *historiographical* criticism, which is content with answers to questions of date, provenance, authorship, compilation, with all the information that good answers to such questions might give of historical and biographical settings and the process by which a book achieved its present form. I do not find answers to those questions necessary or helpful to reading the text, even if indubitably factual answers to them are available.[17]

The other way of dealing with incoherence is to repair it. Scholars of the Bible have the bad habit, ingrained through several generations of Ph.D. training, both in North America and in Europe, of solving the problems of the text by rewriting. They do not, of course, call it that. The scholarly word is "emendation" and sometimes "correction" (for example, in the footnotes to the RSV translation, where the abbreviation "Cn" means "correction"). That is an interesting image: the text is "mistaken," and the scholar "corrects" it. A euphemism is a euphemism in any language or occupation, and both "emendation" and "correction" are a screen in front of "rewriting."

The scholar finds for some reason (and sometimes the reasons are of the best) that the text is incomprehensible or violates some structure of coherence the scholar thinks must apply. In order to make it compatible with that structure, the scholar "repairs," "corrects"—rewrites—the text. Now the scholar can be comfortable that the "corrected"—rewritten—text permits interpretation, and he (I use that pronoun deliberately, because this is a very male way of dealing with texts and the notion of authorship) almost always argues that the emended—rewritten—text is closer to the "original" than the "erroneous" one. He generally forgets that the grounds on which the text achieved its interpretable condition were his own supposition that it would cohere with acceptable meaning if only it said something else. The result is that the scholar proceeds to interpret not the text but his own rewriting of the text.

The point is twofold: biblical scholars have been far too quick to turn the text to be interpreted into a text that the scholar has composed; and biblical scholarship has believed that every problem in the text must be solved in order for interpretation to proceed. It has therefore taken every difficulty in the text as an error to be repaired. The fiction that issues from these suppositions is that the scholar has restored the original. Nothing could be further from the fact. The scholar has produced a new text, one the world has never seen before.

My impatience with this comes from two sources. First, my training, too, involved those suppositions, and I spent more energy in the past doing that sort of scholarship than I like to admit.[18] My teachers were better than most, because they taught me to be leery of rewriting the text (though they did not call it that). Second, in working over the years on the scholarship of the Book of Job, I have wasted much time and energy poring through highly regarded works of scholars who rewrote the Book of Job and whose interpretations were therefore interpretations of something other than the Book of Job.

Perhaps it is impolite to name names, but unless I do, my point may be missed. One of the thickest, most complete, most influential commentaries on the Book of Job is Georg Fohrer's 565-page (in small print) *Das Buch Hiob*. Fohrer has written not only that huge volume but many other articles on Job.[19] In the name of responsibility to the scholarly tradition, I have had to work closely with Fohrer's work, which is extremely impressive in its eloquence, massive in its coverage of the other scholarly literature, and shrewd in its interpretation, both in general and in particular. But Fohrer follows the great German scholarly tradition in feeling quite free to "correct"—rewrite—the text. To take only one example, Fohrer decided at some point that Hebrew poetry proceeds in couplets only, never in tercets. Therefore, wherever the Hebrew text presents a tercet, Fohrer must decide which of the three lines is to be eliminated or to which of the three a fourth line must be added. And he succeeds every time! In chap. 3, for example, Fohrer eliminates the first line of verse 4, the second line of verse 5, the first line of verse 6, and the second line of verse 9 (he also deletes verse 16 because he thinks it upsets the context).[20] Georg Fohrer is a learned, eloquent scholar. But the man has the nerve to claim that he is interpreting the Book of Job. He is not; he is interpreting a book he has written himself. I object to that, no matter who does it.[21] And the scholarly tradition has taught us that it is acceptable.

I object to it when I do it. And I have done it in this book three times (24.5; 35.14; 39.21). Each word that I have changed appears in the translation with an asterisk (see the "Indispensable Introduction"). That is much more conservative than even my teachers were. But it is a way of saying that problems in the text are simply problems in the text. They are not excuses for rewriting it to say what we think it should. When the problem is intractable, I have no compunction about throwing up my hands, saying "I can't solve this one," and leaving a blank space. I refuse to write the text over again and pretend that I am reading the original. Why not just admit that we cannot solve a problem? (But what will my colleagues think?)

If the Book of Job belongs to a category of "open" texts, as I argued above, that indicates nothing more than how we may most productively and entertainingly read it. We find meaning in cooperative play with the text itself, not by jamming a theoretical or critical approach over it. The question is What sort of book is the Book of Job? In one sense, we could wait until the rest of the work has been done to pursue that question. Only careful examination will tell us what sort of book Job is. But I raise the question here instead of at the end in order to clear some ground.

A preliminary response is that the Book of Job combines prose and poetry into something like a drama, a story about Job and a series of poetic speeches by Job and the other characters. To read the Book of Job is to immerse oneself in a dialogue of great scope and complexity, to follow arguments that are not organized in the neat ways philosophers are expected to organize their arguments. We see, that is, how *characters* do what they do.[22] That entails relating what they are saying at any time to their previous speeches, as well as seeing how one character responds or does not respond to another. Most of the Book of Job is anything but a gripping narrative. But the dialogue, as the implied narrative of what is happening with and among persons, is as gripping as can be, however difficult it is.

I am concerned therefore about the questions that arise from the fact that the Book of Job is a *book*. Because I do not think that set of questions necessitates consideration of the historiographical questions, I leave the latter unsolved. One can find decent accounts of the variety of solutions to them in any good commentary to the book.[23]

My working assumption about any text is that it is a pattern of words that means itself. Some texts intend to mean beyond themselves, and some texts mean beyond themselves without intending to. A newspaper report means the events that it reports. But a newspaper, like any text, also means itself as a pattern of words, as a presentation and representation. The scholarly report of an historical epoch means a presentation of that epoch, but it also means itself as a pattern of words that presents not merely facts external to itself but also an interpretation internal and peculiar to itself. No text does not mean itself. Some texts, especially poetry, I think, mean only themselves. It is the business of the literary critic to examine texts in the terms in which they mean themselves. The historian, the linguist, the philosopher, the theologian, may all examine texts in the terms in which they mean something beyond or other than themselves. The historian looks for useful perceptions of the actual past, the linguist for structures and usages of language, the philosopher for considerations of ideas and relations to other ponderings of the same or similar ideas, the theologian for perceptions of the deity. Perfectly valid, interesting, worthwhile questions, those—but not literary ones.

The literary question, I think, asks how the text plays, how it discloses its patterns of words in all their multiple possibilities. A literary text is a game of language, a play of the linguistic imagination. That may involve it in sound as well as in sight, in rhythm as well as in grammar, in patterns of recurring words and syllables as well as of recurring thoughts and ideas. It may entail images with many possible referents and pictures, words with double or triple meanings, words, phrases, and sentences used in ways that deny conventional meanings or include and surpass them. It cannot be emphasized too much that a literary text is a play of imagination, not a mere purveying of fact. That is why some readers become impatient with literary works, because the games literary works play are more surprising and jocular than they can handle. That is why so many critics are so dull, especially if their criticism cannot find its way to the other side of fact. Such critics may demolish both imagination and play in the text. But the critic need not do so, ought not do so, for to demolish imagination or play is destruction, not deconstruction, and it undermines understanding.

I do not wish by interpretation to make of the "open" Book of Job a "closed" Book of Job. I am not out to exclude "wrong" or "alternative" understandings of Job. There may be times in the chapters that follow when I deny certain understandings, when I make so bold as to say, "No, the text could not signify *that*, it must signify *this*." If I do, and forget to qualify such a statement, I hope the reader recalls that I said earlier—and say now—that such exclusions and denials of possibility claim not the absolute falsehood of what they reject but only its relative distance from the text's fullness of possible meanings.

To be sure, I sometimes argue that the syntax and grammar of Hebrew do not permit some construction of meaning. Any language has rules within which multiplicity of meaning takes place. No sentence can mean everything without limit. Possible meaning is limited by the number of different ways in which words in a sentence (or a phrase, paragraph, chapter, or entire text), given their order and forms, can be related to one another within the system of the language. For some complex texts, the number of possible meanings may be beyond our ability to articulate, but it is never theoretically limitless. In even a complex sentence, the number of possible constructions of the pattern of words is limited. I even think—and I know people who are sure that no deconstructionist can say this—that some interpretations are better than others.

It is now time to plunge into the joys and hazards of reading. It is fair to warn you that one of the hazards is that the going is heavy. The Book of Job is a dense text, and the reading must sometimes be correspondingly thick-textured. You must find your own pleasures in the density; I know what mine are. But Job is there waiting for the game to begin, and that is far more interesting than discussions of the theory of reading and understanding. Let us rather read and play and, more broadly than we might have thought, understand.

2

"Is Job Religious for Nothing?"

> Someone must have been telling lies about Joseph K., for without having done anything wrong he was arrested one fine morning.
>
> —Franz Kafka, *The Trial*

Perhaps Job 1–2 is a folktale. In some respects it reads like one: the "once upon a time" beginning, with its quick, deft encapsulation of the hero's circumstances and character, the formulaic structural points ("It was the day when," 1.6, 13; 2.1), the refrains of the messengers' speeches ("And I escaped all alone to tell you," 1.15, 16, 17, 19), the formal greetings between Yahweh and the Prosecutor (1.7; 2.2), the repeated formula defining Job, given by the narration and twice by Yahweh ("scrupulously moral, religious, one who avoids evil," 1.1, 8; 2.3).[1]

The only reference to Job outside the Book of Job might suggest that he was the subject of a folktale. The prophet Ezekiel refers to him twice as one of the three most righteous ancient worthies: "Even if these three men—Noah, Daniel, and Job—should be in [Jerusalem], they would by their righteousness save only themselves" (Ezek 14.14; JPS). Yahweh goes further in 14.20, saying that Noah, Daniel, and Job "would save neither son nor daughter." Noah saved his sons from the Flood (Gen 6–9), and if daughters-in-law counted in those days as daughters, he saved daughters too. Daniel we know not from the Book of Daniel in the Hebrew Bible but from Canaanite epic texts recovered since the 1920's from the ancient city of Ugarit (modern Ras Shamra) in Syria containing a tale about a king named Dan'el who has, but does not save, a son.[2] For Ezekiel, Job is the epitome of "righteousness" in the culture's lore. In our story, however, Job does not "save" either son or daughter but loses them all. There is some incongruity between Ezekiel's perception of Job and what happens in the book.[3]

Perhaps, because we are dealing with a folk hero, we are engaged not with a folktale but with an epic. Nahum Sarna has argued that the original tale was written in poetry, a characteristic of ancient epics.[4] Job's high social stature and gravity of circumstance, moreover, are comparable to those of an epic hero. The presence of prose, together with the brevity of these opening chapters, is the major difference between the Hebrew story and the Canaanite epic tales from which Sarna derives his analogy, and both characteristics may make us think of folk story rather than epic. The style of Job's story is pure in its simplicity, and I remain unpersuaded that it was ever poetry.[5] As we will see later in this chapter, we are not dealing with naive, unsophisticated storytelling. If calling the story a folktale makes readers expect naiveté (and some scholars who have called it a folktale have thought it naive),[6] it is best to call it something else. But I do not feel required to designate the genre more closely than to call it a story or narration.

The story has six episodes, the first of which is general and introductory.

1. Job's character and circumstances (1.1–5)
2. First scene in Yahweh's court (1.6–12)
3. Job's first calamity (1.13–22)
4. Second scene in Yahweh's court (2.1–7a)
5. Job's second calamity (2.7b–10)
6. The coming of the friends (2.11–13)

Episodes 1 and 6, told as omniscient narration, present a certain symmetry. The first portrays Job's character and habitual activity, including a ritual of sacrifice, and the last shows a stereotypical, ritual action of the friends.

The middle four episodes alternate between Yahweh's court and Job's troubles in the land of Uz. All four are carried by dialogue:[7] the two scenes in Yahweh's court consist of two sets of questions and answers between Yahweh and the Prosecutor followed by an imperative spoken by Yahweh. They are framed by date- and scene-setting sentences at the beginning (1.6; 2.1) and exit sentences at the end (1.12b; 2.7a). The two scenes of calamity are presented in a simpler frame: in 1.14–19, the messengers' reports form one cumulative speech, to which Job responds hymnically (v. 21); in 2.9–10, Job and his wife have one speech each. Yet these two episodes are also asymmetrical. The first calamity is told from the point of view of Job's own position, sitting at home learning the story from successive messengers. By contrast, the second calamity proceeds by objective narration combined with dialogic comment.

The balance of these middle episodes is disrupted in the move from episode 4 to episode 5. Episodes 2–4 begin with the same formula, which suggests a customary occurrence: "It was the day when" (*wayᵉhī hayyōm*). They also end with similar conventional formality. The Prosecutor makes his exit from Yahweh's presence in 1.12b and 2.7a, and Job engages in conventional mourning behavior in 1.20–22. But episode 5 plunges abruptly into action with no structural prelude, dropping the regularity maintained through episodes 2–4. The new narrative technique signals that Job's second calamity presents a new set of circumstances.

Within its apparent symmetry, then, the tale drives from one situation to a wholly different one, from a beginning in what seems stability to an end in change and uncertainty. At the beginning and in both scenes in Yahweh's court, Job is described as "one who avoids evil" (*ra*ʿ, 1.1, 8; 2.3). At the end, the friends come because of "all the evil [*ra*ʿ*ah*] that had come upon him" (2.11). The recurring "days" also point to changed circumstances. The "feast days" in episodes 1 and 3 (1.4, 5, 13) and the customary meeting "days" of Elohim's sons in episodes 2 and 4 (1.6; 2.1) give way at the end of episode 6 to seven days of silence (2.13), a number that echoes the annual feasts of the seven sons (1.4). The feast days have turned into death—deeply ironic if those parties of Job's children were birthday dinners—the meeting days have produced Job's suffering, and now the days pass in silence. We find not a resolution of the problem but its intensification. Evil formerly avoided is now present; days have reversed their character.

On the other hand, we might seem to see a resolution. A recurring motif in the tale is blessing (see the annotation to 1.5). Job's religiousness, a question on which much turns, consists partly in his scrupulous sacrificing on the chance that his children have sinned in blessing the deity (1.5) and partly in a conventional piety that blesses Yahweh's name and avoids sin thereby (vv. 21–22). The first scene between Yahweh and the Prosecutor turns on two allegations of the Prosecutor: that Job is religious because Yahweh has blessed him with prosperity (1.10), and that if Job should come to think that Yahweh has stopped blessing him, he will bless Yahweh in another sense (v. 11). In fact, with the calamity, Job does "bless" Yahweh (v. 21), and he avoids sin by doing so (v. 22). The second scene in Yahweh's court, like the first, centers on the Prosecutor's expectation that Job will bless Yahweh (2.5), and with Job's second calamity in episode 5, his wife urges him to "bless Elohim and die" (2.9). Job does not bless anyone and again avoids sin (2.10).[8]

From that point of view, it seems that Job has decisively avoided whatever problem has been posed. Yet the means by which he does so is strangely reversed. Twice the Prosecutor has put Job in a situation where he is sure he will bless Yahweh; once Job has avoided difficulty by blessing, and once, it seems, he has avoided difficulty by not blessing. It is not yet clear what the problem of the story is. If it is that of an evil that a good man wishes to avoid and does not, the story deepens the problem and does not resolve it. If it is the problem of a good man who is given a religious test, the problem is resolved, or seems to be resolved. We need to circle back over the story for a closer look.

The first paragraph underscores Job's extraordinary qualities. He is fecund and rich, which in his culture signified excellence. Many children—ten are many and in a decimal system are symbolically "perfect"—promise prosperity in old age. Children assured retirement security in those days, unless one had much wealth of one's own. Job has it, expressed again in stylized perfect numbers: thousands of sheep and camels that add up to ten thousand, hundreds of oxen and asses that add up to ten hundred, and—a nice breaking of the numerical symmetry—"a great many slaves."

There is more than external wealth and prosperity. We know that Job is "scrupulously moral, religious, one who avoids evil" (1.1), and in the second paragraph we see something of what that means. His family is unusual. That seven brothers would enjoy one another's company enough to have regular parties together might not seem surprising, though the fact, stated baldly, proposes a familial harmony that cannot be unremarkable. Quite exceptionally, the parties include the sisters. In those days one did not, it seems, deal socially with women, even one's sisters, as equals. The siblings' harmony appears nearly revolutionary.

Yet the oddly negative factor turns up. Job is so scrupulous that he wishes to forestall any religious fault that his children might incur in their feasts. "Perhaps my children have blessed Elohim sinfully in their hearts" (1.5). For the ancient Hebrews as for the Greeks, the heart was the seat not of emotion but of thought, decision, and intention.[9] It had what we think of as the brain's function (the emotion we feel in the heart, they located in the bowels). They did not, moreover, distinguish an inner, genuine self (the heart) from an outer, ostensible self (the body, perhaps). Job worries, then, not about internal sin as opposed to external but about intended sin as opposed to inadvertent sin.[10] The children may be purified of such thoughts by the religious intervention of the proper sacrifice.

What does that mean? Evidently Job is, in our day's jargon, a caring father. Equally evidently, he is entirely confident only of his own piety, not of his children's. If inadvertent sin concerns him, he need only remind his children to make the proper sacrifices. But he does it for them, apparently not trusting them to think of such precautions or to safeguard their intentions. His only thought about their intention is that they might "have blessed sinfully." An ambiguity is present. "Bless," as I said in the annotation, is only one possible meaning of the word (*brk*). Another is "curse," which, combined with "sin" (*ḥṭ'*), seems on the surface the better meaning. We are faced here, and in several places in this part of the story, by a crucial word with diametrically opposed, simultaneous meanings.

Job further assumes that his sacrifices, the expiations of a scrupulously moral and religious father, will ward off the punishments for intentional sin from his children. The father's religious deed produces the religious effect on the children, without their needing to do anything of their own. That means, I think, that Job's religion is a magical one. I do not criticize that but only label it.[11] Every religion I know anything about is magical, assuming that certain religious actions, whether external or internal, physical or spiritual, if done properly, produce certain religious effects.

The first episode, then, exhibits a hero remarkable spiritually and materially, and religiously conventional, however profoundly if not excessively scrupulous. The religiosity that Job employs in 1.5 sets up the situation that arises in the next episode.

The scene changes to the divine court on assembly day. Just as Job's sons are in close contact with their father, so are the "sons of Elohim,"[12] especially the one with the Hebrew title *haśśaṭan*, "the Satan," which I have translated "the Prosecutor" (see the annotation to 1.6). He is not the Devil, not a principle of evil, but a member of the divine court whose apparent duty is to bring malefactors to the bar of divine justice. He is, then, no interloper in the assemblage of Elohim's sons but someone with every right to be there.[13]

Yahweh evidently thinks so. He asks pleasantly after the Prosecutor's career, and the latter gives a curiously evasive answer. Can he conceal anything from Yahweh? Well, yes. Not only does this story imply polytheism, it also assumes no divine omniscience. Yahweh is interested less in the details of the Prosecutor's comings and goings than in one fact: there is a person with whom the Prosecutor will never have professional dealings. Yahweh incautiously boasts: "Have you given thought to ['set your heart on'] my servant Job? There's certainly no one like him on the earth, a scrupulously moral man, religious, one who avoids evil" (1.8). The description advances beyond what we have seen before. In 1.3 Job was "one of the greatest people of the East"; here there is "no one like him on the earth."[14]

Both Yahweh and Job deal with hearts. Job made sacrifices on the possibility that something untoward had happened in his children's hearts, but he did not ask them about their hearts. Yahweh asks the Prosecutor about his heart: "Have you set your heart on my servant Job?" The Prosecutor's function is to think about people, to decide whether their faults, including those most concealed, deserve punishment. Yahweh wonders whether he has done his job and suggests that someone is proof against his investigations.

The Prosecutor responds with some heat. "Is Job religious for nothing?" (1.9) The rhetorical question implies a negative answer: "Of course not; he is religious for some reason." Yahweh has made sure that he would be religious by "hedging around him" with protection, by "blessing" him (*brk*—that word again), so that "his possessions burst out over the earth" (v. 10). The Prosecutor exaggerates Job's situation with the contradictory images of a protective hedge and of possessions bursting out. It is unfair of Yahweh to ensure by his own efforts so responsive a piety and then to boast about Job as if the man were responsible for it. The whole basis of the divine government of the world is challenged. If Yahweh is really in charge—and the crucial verb "bless" underscores that he is—then human beings have no possibility of responsibility. If they can be responsible, Yahweh is not in charge.

The Prosecutor has a still more powerful way of challenging the divine claims. He proposes that the deity "touch all [Job] has" (v. 11) and goes on: "If he doesn't curse you (*brk*) to your face—." Rhetorically, that clause is a curse upon the speaker, with the result clause omitted. Yahweh's hand is drastically forced. Faced with a curse (If A does not happen, may a horrible B happen to me), Yahweh has no choice. In that world, a spoken curse was an objective event, which ineluctably and with no moral entailments set in train a succession of events that had to work itself out to its end. By the risky expedient of putting himself under a curse, the Prosecutor has tied Yahweh in a knot from which only Job can extricate him. It is a crucial addition to the chain of curses and blessings I noted above.

This reading overturns the long interpretive tradition around this transaction between Yahweh and the Prosecutor, which has seen the transaction either as a test that Yahweh is persuaded to permit or as a wager between him and the Prosecutor. The tradition has been bedeviled, moreover, by reading the Prosecutor's remark in terms not of its own rhetorical form but of its paraphrase into an "equivalent." "If Job does not curse you to your face" equals "Job certainly will curse you to your face." For reasons that escape me, most interpreters have missed the additional meaning present in the sentence: "or else I will be cursed."[15] If inflicting suffering upon Job is a test, it is meaningless, because Yahweh was seduced by the Prosecutor into permitting it (which lends a certain plausibility to identifying him as the Devil). If Job suffers because of a mere wager, the suffering is even more meaningless. Betting plays too close to the edges of blind chance, and our culture distrusts that. Suffering resulting from an illegitimate test or from a wager is by definition unjust. Nothing with the deity's fingerprints on it is supposed to be unjust.

When the sufferings result from the Prosecutor's curse *upon himself*, the situation is changed. The curse does not bind Yahweh in moral problems at all; Yahweh is helpless to stop the working of the curse, though he can, it seems, put limits on the worker ("but on him don't put your hand," 1.12).[16] And the Prosecutor puts himself at hazard with his curse. We are not dealing with an underhanded trick of a Devil or with an unobservant deity who allows his most faithful servant to be the object of an experiment. We are dealing with a frontal challenge to magical religion, a religion that allows Yahweh's favorite to be religious for his own ends, not for Yahweh's. In one sense, the Prosecutor is angry not at the righteous Job but at Yahweh's system of order.[17]

I cannot overemphasize the point that the transaction between Yahweh and the Prosecutor is not "I bet he'll do it" or "Let's see if he flunks." The Prosecutor could take no more serious step than the curse, and he himself stands to lose the most. He leaves unspoken the specific result that he calls down on himself, as is usual in such self-curses, but it cannot be trivial, and the lack of a stated result may be more powerful than its presence.[18] The next loser is likely to be Yahweh, if Job hurls a curse in Yahweh's face. We do not yet know what Job stands to lose.

We must pause here over two things. I have spoken as if the Prosecutor expects from Job a *curse* similar to his own. We are faced again with that ubiquitous word *brk*, which inconveniently refuses to bear but one meaning. The Prosecutor says, "If he does not *brk* you to your face—." Everyone thinks that *brk* here is a euphemism for "curse," just as everyone thinks the word had to mean that back in verse 5. But no one blinks at interpreting the same verb as "bless" in the preceding sentence. We must relax our certainty that we know what this word means.

The other point is that the ambiguous, indeterminate *brk* appears in a sentence that is formed as a curse. Of that there is no question. We may not with the same confidence be able to assert the English equivalents of all of the words. "If he does not *brk* you to your face—."

Observe the next exchange. "Put out your hand and touch all he has," says the Prosecutor (v. 11). "All that he has is in your hand," replies Yahweh (v. 12). The Prosecutor wants Yahweh's hand to do the deed, but Yahweh shifts it to the Prosecutor's hand and imposes a limitation: "On him don't put your hand" (v. 12). The limitation is formal, indeed redundant; the Prosecutor has already specified what is to be touched: "all he has" (v. 11). Perhaps Yahweh states the limitation to remind the Prosecutor who gives the orders in this universe. The command might seem a bit hollow, given that Yahweh and his power are under constraint of a curse. Still, the formality of rank is observed, and the universe is not yet absurd.

Are we sufficiently on our guard to realize how ominous the opening of episode 3 is? "It was the day" (v. 13)—the formula that began episode 2. It is the prime heir's feast day. We can easily let the fact pass as mere fact, the formulaic beginning lulling us into inattention and its significance not sinking in until the terrible message of verse 19. Yet the narrative technique continues to mask the fact. We, the readers, hear the series of messages from Job's point of view, know only what Job knows. We are drawn inside the story and into its ignorances.

The series of messages, bursting over Job like those fireworks where one shower of stars explodes into another and that into a third, is notable both for its patterned formality and for its completeness. In the first and third messages, the agents of destruction are marauding neighbor peoples; in the second and fourth, they are natural phenomena thought of in that world as being under the deity's control. The messenger calls the lightning that burned up the sheep and the servants "Elohim's fire" (v. 16); the messenger cannot know that it is from the Prosecutor, and I suspect that we, being immersed in the story, forget it. The first and fourth messages have identical structures: (1) description of the situation; (2) narration of the catastrophe; (3) death of the *n*[e]*'arīm*; (4) escape. The second and third messages omit the description and begin immediately with the catastrophe. Such crossing and interlocking repetitions are the force of this formulaic style. The repetitious patterning makes the statements so terrible.

The catastrophes are total. In the first three, Job's wealth is taken, category by category (the elimination of his slaves is spread over all the events), in the fourth, his posterity is wiped out. Only in the fourth is the messenger allowed the exclamation of emotion: *hinnēh*, "Ah!" (v. 19). The very formula leaves us with a momentary ambiguity: "It [the house] fell on the *ne'arīm*, and they're dead." Each successive messenger has used *ne'arīm* to mean Job's slaves who were killed (vv. 15, 16, 17). The fourth messenger has stated the circumstance, that Job's sons and daughters were having their feast, and when he says that the house fell on the *ne'arīm*, perhaps we are at first relieved: "Oh, only the slaves." The relief is momentary, for we quickly realize that *ne'arīm* can include the sons, and we must then assume that here, unusually, it also includes the daughters. On further reflection, we may be ashamed that we have underplayed the humanity of slaves. Perhaps the messenger is being kind to Job, muting the impact of the bald statement by his formulaic repetition.[19]

Are we prepared for Job's response? It is so utterly conventional, and the little hymn he sings (v. 21) is so banally repetitive.[20] Verbal repetition ("Naked . . . and naked") and the repetitive word order (adjective–verb–adverbial expression) call attention to the opposed verbs ("came out . . . return") in the first two lines. The antonymous verbs in the third line ("gave . . . took") emphasize the repeated divine name. The final blessing formula, at last, puts the lie to the Prosecutor's curse in the same terms. "If he does not *brk* you—" said the Prosecutor. Job says, "May Yahweh's name be *mebōrak*." There is that verb again, and perhaps we are too sure that it means "blessed" here.

Job's actions and words are completely appropriate. He fulfills all of the acts expected of a mourner, tearing his robe, shaving his head, falling prostrate on the ground, singing a hymn. It is exactly what he ought to do. Conventionalities are the most important religious acts, because they channel responses to unusual events and prevent them from overwhelming people. That is what religion is for. Job's mourning behavior, however formalized and conventional, has stood him in the best possible stead. He has avoided "sin" (v. 22), and Yahweh's boast has been vindicated. Now perhaps we will find out the unspoken result clause of the Prosecutor's curse.

Instead, we find the Prosecutor among Elohim's sons on the next assembly day (2.1). The god[21] still has his sons, though Job has lost his. What happened to the curse? Was its unspoken result so mild as to leave its object undamaged? Or did the catastrophe drop between the two senses of *brk*? "If he does not *brk* you to your face—" said the Prosecutor. When Job said, "May Yahweh's name be *m^ebōrak*," he did *brk* Yahweh, whatever the Prosecutor might have meant. Magic is magic, the right word was said, and no catastrophe need befall the Prosecutor.

The preliminaries identical to those in 1.6–8 passed, Yahweh adds to his previous description of Job the triumphant statement of his success: "He is still holding to his integrity, even though you urged me against him to swallow him up for nothing" (2.3). Three points of this speech need attention. Job's "integrity" (*tummah*) is etymologically related to his scrupulosity (the *tam* half of the hendiadys *tam w^eyašar*, 1.1, 8; 2.3). Job's basic character has not changed, and Yahweh still boasts about him. Second, Yahweh talks as if *he* had done the deed against Job at the Prosecutor's instigation, doing so with a nice pun on *haśśaṭan* in "you urged me" (*t^esītēnī*). Third, it was "for nothing" (*ḥinnam*), a word the Prosecutor used in 1.9: "Is Job religious *ḥinnam*, for nothing?" Repeating the word, Yahweh turns it back on the Prosecutor: Job did not do his religion "for nothing," but you did something against him "for nothing."

The Prosecutor's response, like his earlier one, is heated. "Skin up to skin!" There seems to be scorn in that strange, probably proverbial statement, and beyond that it is difficult to determine what is in it. Most scholars propose variants on the notion of equal exchange.[22] The preposition (*b^eʿad*, "up to") refers to boundaries, signifying a different idea of exchange. The Prosecutor uses it in his next sentence: "Everything the man has he will give over, right up to [*b^eʿad*] his life." It is not merely equal exchange. Job cannot give anything equivalent to his skin, for there is nothing equivalent to it. The limit on what Job can give in exchange for his life is his life. "Skin up to skin," then, means that the point at which you stop paying for skin is the point at which the price demanded is skin. Job will give anything short of life to remain alive—to give up life to stay alive is self-evidently absurd.

Now the Prosecutor's proposal is more drastic: "Touch his bone and his flesh"—his very person, his boundary of possible exchange, his life. And again the same self-curse: "If he doesn't *brk* you to your face—."

For the second time, the Prosecutor lays himself on the line, and again the operative word is that ambiguous *brk*. Again the situation is not tainted with morality or its absence; a curse on oneself is too serious for that. Does Job's earlier survival with his piety intact make us expect that it will triumph a second time, or do we expect him to fail? Either is possible.

As before, Yahweh shifts the deed to the Prosecutor's hands and emphasizes his own proviso, implied in "right up to his life." "Protect his life" is more than the rather inactive "spare his life" in most translations.[23] The verb *šmr* has to do with guarding, and the Prosecutor is being told not merely to avoid killing Job but positively to guard him, indeed, to watch over him. That may be a kindly proviso. At the least Job is to remain alive. Yet we will see later that Job thinks the god watches him more closely than he likes, and he objects to the scrutiny.[24] The lurking feeling remains that, though Yahweh cannot refuse the curse, his limitation on the Prosecutor's execution of it can be interpreted ironically as an effort to maintain the show of his own scrupulosity. He does not refuse to allow Job's suffering, and he surely does not expect the Prosecutor to slide away from the issue. Given the miscarriage of the Prosecutor's prior curse, a second following on it is nearly predictable. At least, if Yahweh cannot predict it, we must dismiss any notion of divine omniscience from the story. In any case, he does not object to the Prosecutor's touching Job's "bone and his flesh."

The catastrophe occurs, and Job is smitten with personal suffering. We might think the order of events curious, tending as we do to think of physical suffering as having less magnitude than mental or psychic suffering. Yet the story clearly proposes a crescendo of difficulty, and Job's suffering in his own person implies a greater pain than the psychic suffering he has endured at the deaths of his children.

Mental suffering is also involved, however. Job's scraping himself with a broken sherd of pottery to alleviate his pain (v. 8) is one sign. There is very little dignity in scraping one's horrid sores with a dirty potsherd. Moreover, he sits not in the midst of loving family and attentive friends, but as an outcast from social contact, in the ash heap, the garbage dump (he will lament that with vivid images in chap. 30).[25] There are no hymns in Job's mouth this time.

Now we hear, for the only time, a character whose implied presence is very strong, both in this part of the story and at its end: Job's wife (2.9). Her explicit presence is rather meager. Job will refer to her in 19.17 as disliking his breath, and she is a strange part of one of his self-curses in 31.10. Otherwise, she is the mother finally of twenty children. Her one line of dialogue has not made her a favorite with readers of the book: "You're still holding to your integrity? Curse [*brk*] Elohim and die!"[26] The question repeats word for word what Yahweh had said about Job to the Prosecutor (2.3), and the imperative urges Job to do both what the

Prosecutor has cursed himself about and what Job worried in 1.5 that his children might have done, to "*brk* Elohim."

The first sentence, which most interpreters translate as a question, contains no interrogative mark and could as well be the statement "You're still holding to your integrity." If the sentence is understood positively, as it is when Yahweh says it, the imperative *barēk* might very well mean something positive. If the first sentence expresses sarcasm, *barēk* is negative. That ambiguous verb allows several alternative readings of the second sentence: farewell: Say goodbye to Elohim and die; rebellion: Throw the whole thing in Elohim's face and take the consequence of death; encouragement: Go on holding to your integrity, stand fast in your piety even to death; pity: Curse Elohim and be released from your suffering.[27]

Job's response makes clear that he hears a negative meaning: "You're talking like a fool" (v. 10).[28] He would not say that if he thought his wife were being supportive—unless his own mind has changed drastically since he said, "May Yahweh's name be blest" (1.21). Given the pain that has intervened since that hymn, it is quite possible that he has changed. We must investigate the next sentence: "We receive good from Elohim and do not receive evil."

As far as I know, I alone have translated this sentence as an indicative. Everyone else makes it an interrogative: "Should we accept only good from God and not accept evil?" (JPS)[29] That is an interpretive decision, not a translational one. The Hebrew sentence has no interrogative marker, but one may legitimately translate it interrogatively if one thinks that the question gives the most sensible meaning.

The sentence allows at least three understandings. As a rhetorical question it has one meaning, and as a statement it acquires two more. The question proposes that it is irrational to accept what is pleasant from the deity and to refuse what is unpleasant. Both "good" and "evil" are to be expected and accepted, and one does not "curse Elohim" but "blesses" him for either, as Job did in 1.21.[30] Self-evidently, the deity is the author of both good and evil, and one ought not be surprised to receive either at his hands. According to the interrogative interpretation, the world and the god's actions have no clear moral structure, but the god is in charge of all that happens in the world.

If the sentence is a statement, it may have two other meanings. Statement 1 is that, because humans receive only good from the deity and not evil, such evil as there is must come not from the deity but from some other source. There is no single origin of all events, and the god is not in command. Statement 2 is that, because everything humans receive from the deity is good, not evil, any unpleasantness, being from Elohim, is good, however contrary to appearances. In either case, there is no reason to "curse Elohim" for it. Under Statement 1 Elohim is not responsible for the evil; under Statement 2 the apparent evil is not to be understood as evil. The two statements hold as self-evident that the deity has nothing to do with evil. Statement 1 maintains the god's moral purity but denies him total control of the world. Statement 2 maintains that, despite evidence to the contrary, the god controls the world, and the world is nothing but good.

That everything that happens comes from the deity was a common assumption in the book's world. If Job intends the question or the second statement, he shares that assumption. Yet the story lays a question against it, by showing us what Job does not know, that this evil has come not from Yahweh but from the Prosecutor. What has happened as a result of the Prosecutor's self-curse is not necessarily attributable to Yahweh, even if Yahweh accepts the blame, as he does implicitly in 2.3.

Whatever may be the import of Job's statements, the narration shows that he avoids sin again—with his lips. I have already referred to the question whether that specification glances sidelong at the integrity of his inward disposition. "Job did not sin with his lips" may suggest that he sinned with something else.[31] On the other hand, the only thing Job is portrayed as doing besides talk is scraping himself with a potsherd. Surely he could not sin doing that. Thus "Job did not sin with his lips" refers to the only significant thing he has done, and it could mean that he did not sin at all. To be sure, Job might have had a sinful thought that did not pass his lips as words. Yet the story's only apparent reference to Job's inner thoughts, in 1.5, does not specify that Job "said" those words within himself. It seems that the story is not concerned with the hero's inward, unexpressed thoughts. But suddenly that casual, passing phrase "with his lips" has become centrally important, and ambiguous in terms of the Prosecutor's curse, which galvanized all of this action.

At least Job has not cursed Yahweh to his face, though his wife has urged him to do so, and the provocation has been great. More than that: in this episode he has not used the crucial verb *brk* at all, in any of its senses. The Prosecutor, it appears, has failed, and because we see and hear no more of him, we may suppose that whatever catastrophe he called down on himself in his curse came about. His disappearance has greatly troubled some interpreters.[32] But if we take his self-curse seriously, as I believe we must, his absence is not strange. The curse eventuated, by implication, in his banishment or destruction.

It is necessary to look back at the problem of blessing and curse, especially but not solely as it is embodied in that ambivalent Hebrew word *brk*. The fact that at every occurrence the verb may mean "bless" or "curse" or both at the same time strains every unambiguous interpretation of the story. The blessing/cursing is central to it, carries the episodes from one place to another, motivates nearly everything that is done, both as to the words that appear in the text and as to the verbal actions the characters take. For example, the conjunction of *brk* with *ḥṭ'* in 1.5 might require that *brk* mean "curse," yet I think it plausible to join *ḥṭ'* and *brk* in a hendiadys meaning something like "sinful blessing," intending the wrong deed despite using the right words, or using the wrong words while intending the right deed. If *ḥṭ'* means "to miss," as it sometimes does (Prov 8.36; Job 5.24), the sentence might be translated, "Perhaps my children have missed blessing [failed to bless] Elohim in their hearts." It seems possible to consider all three ideas simultaneously.

It is easy to take as self-evident that *mᵉbōrak* in the hymnic context of 1.21 must mean "bless." Indeed, that is the sense that the line takes best. Still, the hymn emphasizes the duality of the divine activity, "giving and taking," and the duality of *brk* mirrors on the human level the deity's duality. I twist about through this difficulty not to propose that the meaning of *brk* evaporates into nothing, but rather to help readers liberate their imaginations, wherever the word appears, to focus on its depth, not its shallowness, on its multiplicity, not its illusory simplicity. The very centrality of *brk* prevents smug certainty that we know the meaning of this story. It means in addition to our knowing, and perhaps in spite of and in opposition to it.

Some interpreters believe that Eliphaz, Bildad, and Zophar were introduced into the story when the poetic dialogue was composed, in order to provide a transition to the dialogue.[33] They must somehow be gotten on stage. To say that the friends appear in the story only to be in the dialogue, however, is to attribute more than we can be sure of to the intention of an author whom we cannot consult. I do not know whether Eliphaz, Bildad, and Zophar were in the original story or not, having no access to that "original." The story we read now introduces them by the device of their hearing about evil (*ra'ah*) and, being friends (*rē'īm*), deciding to come. The pun is justification enough, and we need no permissions from an author's supposed intention.

What kind of gesture do they make toward a man otherwise isolated from human contact, who sits on his ash heap with only a seemingly unsupportive wife for company? Surely their coming to "console and comfort him" is friendly. On the other hand, their gestures in verse 12, weeping, tearing their robes (compare 1.20), and sprinkling dust on top of their heads, are those of mourning the dead, which would hardly encourage a man in pain. If Moses Buttenwieser is right that these gestures ward off from the friends the curse they perceive has fallen on Job, the ritual puts distance between the friends and Job.[34] And though they are at least present for those seven days and nights of silence, the silence itself may signify another funeral rite.[35]

Still, they have come because of evil (2.11), and evil was what Job so assiduously avoided. Now he has it, and the formalities of mourning underscore the fact. They have "raised their eyes" to see, and seeing have not recognized, so they have "raised their voices, weeping." Job is, it seems, as good as dead, even though he has not cursed Elohim.

The story, then, both resolves and does not resolve the issue it raises. The danger that Job might curse Yahweh is past. The Prosecutor has been defeated, and his forthright challenge, "Is Job religious for nothing?" (1.9) has been met. Job, it seems, *is* religious for nothing, holds to his integrity and to his piety even when the magic goes out of his life. He apparently requires neither special hedges as protection nor evidences of wealth and prosperity to persuade him to do religiously what he is supposed to do. With the Prosecutor's disappearance, the debate in Yahweh's court about Job's piety appears to be settled.

Yet not every loose thread is tied. Evil, formerly absent from Job's life, is now present. The friends have yet to begin their consoling and comforting, and there is the rising tension of those seven days and nights of silence. The debate in the land of Uz about the divine control of the world has barely begun.

3

"Turmoil Comes"

> Nobody is ever ready for the feel of the raw edge
> between being and nothing, the knowledge
> that abrades the palm, refusing to lie easy.
>
> —Amy Clampitt, "Burial in Cypress Hills"

The Curse (Chapter 3)

Job refused to curse God, though the provocation was serious. Now after seven days and nights of silence, he is ready to curse (3.1), and by no weaseling ambiguity that might mean bless or curse interchangeably. Here it is *qll*, indubitably cursing. Yet Job curses not the deity but "his day," which, verse 3 shows, is his birthday and night of conception. Those cannot be the same day, and we are already in a tissue of complexity. There is an oddity about the usage of the verb *qll* here. Dermot Cox shows that only here does it have an impersonal object; everywhere else it has a personal one.[1] Any ancient reader of Hebrew, seeing the verb after the preceding story, would be surprised that the words "his day" follow, fully expecting that Job would now curse the god.[2]

As Job continues, he interweaves images of day and night, light and darkness, and life and death. The paradoxical opening, "Perish the day on which I was born," demanding the death of life, begins the movement among those images. It is not irrelevant that Job mentions the day of birth and the night of conception in reverse chronological order. He is doing two things. First, he mentions "day" and "night" in their conventional order in parallel lines; seldom is "night" in the first line of a couplet paralleled by "day" in the second.[3] Second, he moves temporally backward from that particular "day" to that particular "night,"[4] a mythical order that becomes clear when, after the introductory curse (v. 3) on the day and the night, he goes on to deal with them one at a time: "that day" in verses 4–5, "that night" in verses 6–7.

With the opening of the curse on his birthday at verse 4, what is really happening begins to come clear. The first line parodies Genesis 1.3: "And God said, 'Let there be light [*y*^{e}*hī 'ōr*].'" "That day," Job says, "let there be darkness [*y*^{e}*hī ḥōšek*]." By the allusion to Genesis 1, Job extends the curse on his birthday back to the first of all days and therefore to the creation itself, and by turning creation's "light" into the curse's "darkness" Job wishes away all vestiges of that light. The imagery of the rest of these curses points to the absence of the deity and of light, to darkness dominating, avenging, and terrifying day. Job wishes to reverse the first process that the deity's creating set in train.

The same reversal characterizes the curse on his night of conception, its absence among days and months (v. 6), its conceiving turned to barrenness, its cry of pleasure choked (v. 7). The curse, then, falls not on an abstract day and night, not even on the specific day and night alone, but on ordinary human actions as well as on divine and extraordinary actions. Job wishes to cancel by curse the entire creation and all that belongs to it.

The second part of this section underscores the reversal, as Job calls upon those who by magic can control the deity's cosmic enemies, Sea (Yamm) and Leviathan (v. 8). These lines are unified poetically by the play on the consonant combination *'r*: "put spells on" (*'ōr*^{e}*rē*, v. 8a, a nice pun on *'ōr*, "light"), "light" (*'ōr*, v. 9b), and "sight" (the verb form *yir'eh*, v. 9c).[5] Sea and Leviathan signify the opposite of creation,[6] and Job wishes them conjured into action, "roused" from sleep to turn the created order back to disorder and chaos, to interrupt the ordinary progression from evening to dawn, from dark to light (v. 9). But light was not twisted into dark for Job, and that is why he curses: "Because it [the night, or the day] did not close the belly's doors / or hide toil from my eyes" (v. 10). Light itself, the first product of the divine creation, has become the equivalent of "toil," the drudging meaninglessness of a life under a burden, real or metaphorical (see also v. 20).

Is this implicit curse on the creation actually a curse upon the creating deity? The emotion reaches its highest level in the entire chapter here. By verse 10 Job has not in so many words cursed the deity, as the Prosecutor predicted and his wife urged. Yet he has cursed the entirety of what the god has done, from the first action of creation to the cry of pleasure at the instant of human conception, encompassing every influence and activity attributable to the god. To our way of thinking, Job can hardly exempt the deity from the curse on the deity's acts. In a word-centered culture and style like Job's, however, perhaps a verbal reference to the god would make a difference.

Job now brings the focus of his complaint down to himself. The rest of the speech consists of two stanzas, each of which begins "Why?" (*lammah*, vv. 11, 20). In the first, Job expands on the last observation in the first stanza, that the cursed day did not prevent his birth. He wonders why he was not stillborn (vv. 11–12), for that would have put him pleasantly to sleep with the dead (v. 13), a contrast to the "toil" (v. 10) of his life. But death is not only restful; it is also the leveler; one sleeps in company with kings, counselors, and princes (vv. 14–15), a common sentiment in the ancient Near East. The yes-man slave in the hilarious Babylonian dialogue of slave and master,[7] giving his master good reason not to do something immediately after giving him equally good reason to do it, suggests that he climb the burial mounds and gaze at the skulls of the dead. "Who among them was the villain, who the benefactor?" All are the same in death, and the deeds of the great add up to nothing. Princes "possessed gold, / filled their houses with silver" (v. 15), but in the end, kings and counselors built "ruins" (v. 14).[8]

The stillborn or miscarried child (v. 16) is the hinge between these "great" people and the freed lesser ones. The miscarried fetus is on a level with the great, not having had to endure the toil necessary to achieve greatness. And in "never seeing light" (v. 16), it achieves what Job wishes his "day" had (note the echo from vv. 9–10). That leads him to the view (vv. 17–19) that death is freedom. Wicked people are free of their turmoil (*rōgez*), powerful ones of their exertions (*nwḥ*, as in v. 13b), prisoners of ceaseless labor, slaves of masters.

This is a remarkably un-Israelite sentiment. Wishes for death are rare in that world (Jeremiah's curse on his birthday, Jer 20.7–18, is quite similar to this chapter). The culture put no stricture on suicide—Saul's is a notable example (1 Sam 31.4). But Job is not thinking of suicide. The culture valued long and prosperous life and expected no future life preferable to this one. One finds now and again in Egyptian literature a wistful longing for death, but Egyptians believed in an afterlife.[9] In Job 3.13–15 and 17–19 Job describes not life but its cessation, the absence of possession and poverty, power and oppression. Nothing remains but sleep, rest, freedom from exertion, and the ubiquitous darkness, objects of desire to one whose possessions are gone, whose power is vanished, whose very breathing is a struggle. Indeed, because Israelites thought that the deity never visited the realm of the dead (Ps 139.8 and Amos 9.2 are startling exceptions), Job's description of death as freedom must include the thought of liberation from the god.

Though in 3.20–23 Job broadens his subject to "bitter souls" in general, he clearly thinks of that category as he himself fits it. He lamented (v. 10) that "toil" is not hidden from his eyes, and now he wonders why there is "light for a toiler" (v. 20a). Bitter souls long for Death, who is "not there" (*'ēnennū*, literally "none of him"), just as Job had wished (v. 9b) that the evening stars might "wait for light and see nothing" (*'ayin*, the same word). Those bitter souls dig for "concealed treasure" (*maṭmōnīm*), as he wished he had been a "concealed" (*ṭamūn*) abortion (v. 16a). And it is clear from his wish for death in verses 11–19 that he too will "rejoice over the burial mound, / gladly discover the grave" (v. 22).

Resuming his sentence with "man" (*geber*, v. 23), a beautiful pun on "grave" (*qeber*),[10] Job brings out still more reminiscences of what he has said before, with the "hidden" way (*nistarah*), unlike the "toil" that his birthday did not "hide" (*yaster*) from him (v. 10b), or the doors of the womb that it did not block (v. 10a). A more distant allusion is somewhat concealed. The deity has "hedged around" (*yasek ba'ᵃdō*) the "hidden way," an image of blocking constriction (v. 23). In 1.10 the Prosecutor used the same verb, spelled with *śin* rather than *samek* to characterize Yahweh's protection of Job: "Have you not hedged around [*śakta ba'ᵃdō*] him and his family?" Job perceives that "hedging" in a very different light.

Thus Job's description of suffering humanity makes constant implicit reference to himself. At 3.24, even the appearance of discussing other people is dropped, as the connecting word "for" (*kī*) brings the discourse back to himself. He likens himself not to a human being in distress, as he had in wishing for the peace of death, but to an animal who "bellows" (v. 24b).

Then in verse 25 comes the most astonishing statement of all:

> For I was terrified of something,[11] and it arrived,
> what I feared comes to me.

Job the righteous, who refused to curse the deity for his suffering, who blessed Yahweh for giving and for taking, has long been afraid precisely of this outcome. His remarkable piety has accompanied the image of just such suffering as he now has, and avoidance of it has motivated all he has done. That seems almost incredible, given the portrait of the scrupulous, profoundly religious man in the first two chapters. Yet at this climax Job reminds us of the Prosecutor's crucial question in 1.9: "Is Job religious [does he 'fear Elohim'] for nothing?" His religion has been based not merely on fear (*yir'ah*), in a conventional sense of obligation and responsibility, but, he now tells us, on something even deeper, on terror (*paḥad*). Fear of the deity now has another dimension: to the fulfillment of obligation without expectation of reward that seemed the burden of chaps. 1–2 is added the need to fend off terrible results. Job fears the god because he fears something else more.

The emotion is draining away now, and the last couplet (3.26), packed though it is, is understated in tone. It underscores the focus on Job's own situation, for of four important words, "tranquil," "quiet," "rest," and "turmoil," three are repeated from verses 13 and 17. In verse 13, Job wished to lie down "quietly" in death and have "rest" there. In verse 17, those weary of exerting power have "rest" in death, and wicked people cease their "turmoil." But Job has just the opposite: not the quietude or rest of death, but the turmoil of life.

This outburst descends from the highest emotion to the lowest, from "Perish the day," uttered in as shrill a tone as we can imagine, to "turmoil comes," said in the monotone of exhaustion. But Job has not asked, "Why has this happened to me?" He begins not with a question but with a curse. Only farther on does he ask why, and then the questions are Why am I alive? and Why is anyone alive who would prefer to be dead? Those questions emanate from the implications of the curse on the creation. Job addresses himself to life, not to justice.

Eliphaz (Chapters 4–5)

As Eliphaz begins to speak and monologue becomes dialogue, it is worth pausing to ask what kind of discussion this is. Are four friends sitting around talking about what has happened to one of them? Has a petitioner for divine comfort sought out not one but three pastoral counselors?[12] Is the dialogue a philosophical debate—what biblical scholars call a "wisdom" debate—where the wise discuss the finer points of living the good life, thinking through problems to their solutions? Or is it more like a trial, in which Job is the plaintiff (or the defendant), the deity is the accused (or the judge), and the friends appear to be the counsel for the defense (or prosecuting counsel)?[13]

The question of the genre of the dialogue has received much attention from scholars who wish to establish that it has but one. Hans-Peter Müller's division of the proposals into psalmodic, wisdom, and juridical genres neatly covers the options, and each works well for certain passages and badly for others. To see the whole as a series of laments in the pattern of the complaint psalms makes one think of the friends as pastoral counselors to the sufferer. To insist on a background in the wisdom schools leads one to think of a disputation, and to conceive of the language as legal emphasizes the senses in which it is a trial scene. All three genres, and others as well, are to be found in one place or another in the debate, as indeed are parodies of those typical language patterns. In the latter part of the second and the third cycles of speeches, Job, especially, turns increasingly to the language of the law court and the trial, but that is insufficient reason to pronounce the genre of the entire discussion to be the juridical one.[14] So complex a work as this dialogue outruns the limits of any single genre.

Eliphaz's first speech is the longest and most elaborate of the friends' speeches.[15] After a rather gentle opening, praising Job for his past strengthening of others in trouble (4.2–5), Eliphaz assures Job that, being religious, he will never undergo the troubles of the wicked (vv. 6–11). His frightening vision (vv. 12–21), however, has taught him that no human being is exempt from error. Challenging Job to turn anywhere but to the deity for help (5.1), Eliphaz brings up the typically brief career of the "fool," who will go under suddenly, along with his children (vv. 2–5). Reiterating the universality of wickedness among humans ("The race is born to toil," v. 7a), Eliphaz indirectly counsels Job to turn to the deity, who puts down the strong and raises the weak (vv. 8–16), and he finally assures the sufferer that the "discipline" (*mûsar*, v. 17b) of suffering will bring him to a satisfying end (vv. 17–26).

> Oh, we have explored all this, it's true.
> Hear it, and know for yourself. (v. 27)

David Clines is sure that Eliphaz wishes to encourage Job in a difficult but not hopeless situation and that he begins with the assumption that Job is innocent of any sin more serious than that to be expected in any normal human being.[16] Several of Eliphaz's statements suggest just that: the praise at the beginning (4.3–4), the identification of the source of Job's assurance (v. 6), his putting himself in Job's place in order to give advice (5.8), the certainty that the suffering the god gives good people is but "correction" and its outcome finally positive (vv. 17–26). Clines stresses two "nodal" sentences, which in his judgment most centrally illuminate what Eliphaz is saying: "Is not your religion your confidence, / your hope, and the integrity of your ways?" (4.6);[17] and "If it were I, I would seek for El, / to Elohim commit my cause" (5.8).

I think that Eliphaz is not so self-consistent as Clines believes, and I find Kemper Fullerton's arguments about "double entendre" more persuasive.[18] Indeed, the first of Clines's "nodal sentences" seems to me a case in point (though not one mentioned by Fullerton). In 4.6 Eliphaz cites as sources of Job's "confidence" (*kislah*) two crucial terms used to characterize Job in chaps. 1 and 2: "fear" (or "religion," *yir'ah*) and "integrity" (*tōm*, cf. *tam w^{e}yašar*, 1.1). Apart from the seeming paradox that "fear" (that fear, intensified to "terror," that Job has only now described as his motivation) should be the ground of "confidence," the word *kislah* and its cognate *kesel* in other passages, both in Job (8.14; 31.24) and elsewhere (Ps 85.9 [Eng. 8]), appear to point to misplaced confidence. They are, moreover, related to the noun *k^{e}sīl*, "fool, stupid." When we come to Eliphaz's rather brutal denunciation of the fool in 5.2–4 (*'^{a}wīl*, a different word, to be sure), it appears that "confidence" has come to mean its own opposite. Even while praising Job's religion as the source of his confidence, Eliphaz suggests sarcastically that fear is stupid. Whether or not 4.6 is a "nodal sentence," its effect is at best ambiguous.

It is not the only ambiguity. If Eliphaz mentions the notion of retributive punishment in order to reassure Job that he does not belong among the wicked, he demonstrates a curious inattention to Job's words. "As I have seen," he says, "those who plot iniquity [*'awen*] / and sow toil [*'amal*] harvest it too." (4.8) The parallelism suggests a connection, if not a similarity, between "iniquity" and "toil." Job said in 3.10 that he has received "toil" (*'amal*, and note "toiler," *'amēl*, 3.20a). Eliphaz must think, then, that he has also "plowed iniquity." His later suggestion (5.7) that "toil" is the inevitable lot of the race does not remove this logical difficulty, because he seems in the same breath (5.6) to think humans are responsible for that toil. It is at least unkind of Eliphaz to say that these bad people are "finished by [the deity's] nostril's wind" (*rūaḥ*, 4.9) in light of the "great wind" that smashed the house where Job's children were feasting (1.19), but perhaps he has not heard the details. Only some such assumption could excuse Eliphaz's unfeeling remark in 5.24, that when the present calamity is over Job will visit his "fold" (*nawah*) and not miss anything.

Eliphaz is, moreover, not only tactless but illogical in turning on the "fool" (5.2–5). Eliphaz suddenly curses his poor "shanty" (*nawah*, v. 3). And Job can hardly avoid identifying himself with the father of the fool's sons, who

go far from safety,
are crushed in the gate, no rescuer near. (v. 4)

Eliphaz may mean to show how the fool differs from Job, but he actually shows the opposite. Job has suffered just as Eliphaz says the fool will suffer, and therefore Eliphaz must think him like that fool.[19] What is more, both of these bits of illogical unkindness, 4.8 and 5.2–5, rest on Eliphaz's assurance of firsthand experience: "I have seen" (*ra'ītī*). When Eliphaz claims to have seen, he is not to be trusted.

Eliphaz's account of the universality of human weakness ducks the issue. He received the message from his revelatory vision: if even the god's special associates are in error (4.18), then no mere human, resident in a "clay house" (v. 19), can be exempt from the expectation of punishment (vv. 20–21). But if Eliphaz is trying to assure Job that everyone is in the same situation, it does not help to suggest that humans are not responsible for their own behavior.

For iniquity does not spring from dust,
nor does toil sprout from the ground [*'ᵃdamah*],
but the race [*'adam*] is born to toil,
and Reshef's sons fly high. (5.6–7)

The pun between *'ᵃdamah* and *'adam* is a nice allusion to Genesis 3.17–18, a passage about responsibility for behavior. Yet Eliphaz, denying in Job 5.6 that sin is inevitable, contradicts himself in verse 7a with the passive "is born" and with the claim in his dream-message of the universality of sin (4.17). Underscoring the message of his vision, Eliphaz trivializes his emphasis on its privacy ("stolen" is the strange word he uses in 4.12).[20]

On the other hand, if the vision explains punishment, the question becomes what kind of punishment. In 5.17, Eliphaz calls it "correction" or "discipline" and suggests that punishment is an occasion for the solution. In that case, however, he trivializes the punishment and contradicts himself in the process:

In six troubles he will rescue you,
in seven, evil will not touch you. (5.19)

Evil *has* "touched" Job, for the Prosecutor successfully urged Yahweh to "touch" Job's goods and Job's person (1.11; 2.5). Eliphaz himself said it had touched him:

But now it comes to you, and you falter,
touches [*tigga'*] against you, and you've panicked. (4.5)

The promise that the deity will help Job avoid the effect of the scourging tongue (5.21a) will be shown in all its fatuity in chap. 22, when Eliphaz himself leaps upon Job with slanderous accusations.[21] His apparent solicitude dissolves as we look beneath what he says in chaps. 4–5, and ironically Eliphaz is himself the exemplar of his own false promises and premises.

Clines is certainly right, however, that Eliphaz's indirect counsel at 5.8 puts him into Job's shoes, if only temporarily, and emphasizes a positive way for Job to reverse his curse in 3.4b. Job had wished that the deity not "seek" (*drš*) his day, but Eliphaz suggests that Job "seek" (*drš*) the deity. To the negative agricultural images of the wicked in 4.8 and of the fool in 5.5, he adds the ambiguous ones of the origin of sin in 5.6 and the positive ones of his expectations for Job's satisfying end in 5.25–26; to the frightful image of the destruction of lions in 4.10–11, he counterposes the assurance of peace with wild beasts in 5.22–23. He alludes to Job's admission of terror (3.25) in mentioning his terror at receiving the vision (4.14), almost as if to say, "I too have been terrified."

And at the end, Eliphaz's tone is mainly encouraging:

> Oh, we have explored all this, it's true.
> Hear it, and know for yourself. (5.27)

Yet we saw reason above to think that Eliphaz's "exploration" of the meaning of things is not always trustworthy, and we emerge in ambiguity.

Eliphaz introduces a subject that will occupy us throughout the dialogue. I noted above that Job has not asked about justice. Eliphaz does:

> Think, who that was innocent [*naqī*] has perished,
> where have moral people [*y^{e}šarīm*] been destroyed? (4.7)

The expected answers to these rhetorical questions are, respectively, "no one" and "nowhere," though they do not cohere with Eliphaz's notion that all human beings sin by virtue of their human weakness.

Eliphaz states in 4.7 the idea of a divine retributive justice, found throughout the Hebrew Bible. On this theory, life is just. The deity rewards righteous people with happiness and prosperity in life and punishes wicked ones with calamity and suffering.[22] "Innocent" folks do not "perish," nor are "moral" ones "destroyed." The idea of a divine retributive governance of the world has raised for our culture the difficult question of theodicy, the problem of explaining divine justice. The suffering of someone who is a model of moral goodness is a common problem. "What have I done to deserve this?" The familiar question implies the idea of retributive justice. If suffering is punishment for or a symptom of badness, a good person's suffering is an injustice. Because our culture has appealed to the biblical roots of that idea, the problem of divine providential justice in the question of suffering has bulked large in our debate.

Job did not raise the issue of justice. In 1.21 he walked around it, supposing that Yahweh both gives and takes and is to be blessed for it. He avoided it again in 2.10, whether that verse is read as a question ("Do we receive good from Elohim and not receive evil?") or as a statement. If it is the latter, either the evil comes from elsewhere than from the god or nothing the god sends can be defined as evil. In his curse in chap. 3, he damned all creation, wondering why he was alive. But he did not wonder why, being good, he received this evil.

Eliphaz raises that question for the first time, and it takes us a long way in this dialogue.[23]

Job (Chapters 6–7)

Any doubt that Job would take Eliphaz's animadversions against the fool personally is abruptly removed as Job begins to speak:

> If only my passion [*ka'aś*] could be weighed,
> my disaster laid with it in scales. (6.2)

"Passion" (*ka'aś*), Eliphaz said (5.2), "murders the fool." Job makes other allusions to Eliphaz's speech. He has been attacked by Shaddai (6.4), a divine name Eliphaz used in 5.17 in describing suffering as "Shaddai's discipline."[24] Eliphaz proposed that the god "wounds" in order to heal (5.18); Job thinks that Shaddai's "poisoned arrows" (6.4) make him more vicious than that. He wishes the deity would "give me my hope," to

> crush me,
> free his hand and cut me down. (6.8–9)

Eliphaz had defined Job's hope as his "religion" (*yir'ah*, "fear," 4.6), but Job redefines it as "crushing" (*dk'*), using a word Eliphaz had used twice: in 4.19, to characterize human beings as "disintegrating" (*y^{e}dakk^{e}'ūm*) before a moth, and in 5.4 of the fool's sons as "crushed [*yiddak^{e}'ū*] in the gate." That passage on the fool did get under Job's skin![25]

When Job, describing his disaster as "heavier than sea sand" (6.3), explains why his "words are wild," we must emphatically agree. The shifting images and metaphors in this speech are extremely difficult to follow. The metaphor of weighing (6.2–3) is followed by a military image of attack by poisoned arrows (v. 4). An image of inedible food (vv. 5–7) has some coherence with the poison in v. 4, but it is succeeded by a dual image of crushing and cutting (v. 9), neither of which seems related to food. Strength (vv. 11–12) is put in terms of rock and of bronze, two images related to one another but not to anything around them. An extended simile of the drying up of water-carrying wadis (vv. 14–20) gives way (vv. 22–27) to terms of legal and extralegal dealing. Then (v. 30) we return to eating, but we abruptly shift (7.1) to corvée labor, drifting into inheritance (v. 3), to a mixed metaphor of measuring and eating (v. 4), to the image of skin disease (v. 5), and to weaving (v. 6). "Therefore my words are wild." They certainly are.

Is this character portrayal? The speech throws out not only many ill-connected images but also a number of ideas, almost as if it were a stream-of-consciousness depiction of Job's "tossing till dark" (7.4). It is believable as a portrait of a man trying to think in the throes of pain.[26]

Beginning with the deity's poisoned-arrow attack (6.4), which leads to the passage about food (6.5–7), in which the reference to animals echoes his "bellowing" in 3.24b, Job now wishes that the god would attack him and put him out of his misery (6.8–9). The wish differs from the impossible one in chap. 3, that his life since before birth might be canceled. The image of Shaddai's poisoned arrows identifies the agent of his trouble, and Job calls on Shaddai to complete the assassination. Just as he described the pleasure of "bitter souls" at the discovery of Death in 3.22, so in 6.10 he expects "consolation."

Being "flesh" and not "bronze" (v. 12b), he sees every reason to wish for death. The absence of "help" (v. 13) leads into the wonderful picture of life and death in the desert in verses 14–20. Job elaborates the metaphor of the melting of loyalty (v. 14a) into the image of wadis that flow with water in winter rains, store water in the ice of winter cold, but suddenly go dry in the hot season, bringing death to caravans forced from the road into the desert in search of water.

> But now you act that way:
> you stare [*tir*^{e}*'ū*] at ruin, and you're scared [*tīr*^{e}*'ū*]. (v. 21)

What sort of help can he get from such friends? The healthy, sure that suffering is punishment, must have in mind that it might happen to them too. Perhaps this is the first indication that Job has begun to think in terms of justice. Or it may be the same fright (Job uses a different word here) as in 3.25. There he was afraid of something that came; here they see that it has come to him, and they are afraid of it.

It is important that just at this point Job talks in legal terms for the first time. He denies by his rhetorical questions in 6.22–23 that he asked for illegal assistance. But in verses 24–27, he suspects that the friends are planning an accusatory indictment. The issue of his guilt has surfaced in his own mouth, and he sees that his "innocence" (*ṣedeq*) is at stake (v. 29).[27]

In fact, the wording seems to imply a little flurry of activity: "Make up your minds, face me," he demands (v. 28a), and then, twice, "come back" (*šūbū*, v. 29). Perhaps his sarcasm about their response to his "honest words" (v. 25a) and their planned indictment (v. 25b–26), and his implicit accusation that they are undertaking shady deals (v. 27), have so insulted the friends that they have gotten up to go away. But *šwb* can also signify relenting or changing the mind, and Job may refer to both an outward and an inward motion.[28]

Job reverts to his earlier image of food (vv. 5–7):

> Is any wrong upon my tongue?
> Does not my palate understand a disaster? (v. 30)

Because Job has said nothing "wrong," the friends ought not to do wrong (v. 29a). Yet the tongue is not only for speaking but also for eating, and in that respect the bad food of which Job has already complained is a "wrong" on his tongue, and his palate recognizes what he had first described in this speech (v. 2b). His situation calls for help that the friends are unable or unwilling to give.

Perhaps that is why Job turns at 7.1 to address the deity.[29] Having failed to persuade the friends of his case, he may as well turn to the god, who could solve his problem if he wished (6.8–10). He sets it forth again, lodging the description in terms of the laborer's (7.1–2) and the sufferer's (vv. 3–4) contradictory "days," which drag out into months (v. 3a) but also "go faster than a shuttle" toward a too-quick end (v. 6). Even so, the singular "day" of his curse in chap. 3 is now plural.[30]

But there are limits: "Consider that my life's a wind" (7.7), and later, "Leave me alone, my days are a puff" (v. 16b). Job emphasizes his ephemerality. His flesh is not bronze (6.12), and his life goes past more quickly than a weaver's shuttle (7.6a). His days "are finished [*yiklū*] at the end of hope" (v. 6b), as "a cloud is finished [*kalah*] and goes" (v. 9a), and the human who "descends to Sheol, does not come up" (v. 9b). Just as good is invisible to his eye (v. 7b), Job thinks of himself as invisible to other eyes (v. 8a), even the god's:

> Your eyes will be on me, but I'll not be there. (v. 8b)

And at the end of the speech:

> For now I lie down in the dust;
> you'll search for me, but I won't be there [*'ēnennī*]. (v. 21c–d)

Perhaps it is an ironic allusion to the ancient hero Enoch, who, as Genesis 5.24 has it, "walked with Elohim, and he was not [*'ēnennū*], for Elohim took him." Job will later claim (e.g., 23.11) that he too has walked with the deity, but his "not being there" is unlike Enoch's absence, which, as Norman Habel suggests, implies presence somewhere else.[31]

The god is dealing with him not as if he were a cloud that evaporates but as if he were the enemy in a cosmic combat myth. He guards him like "Sea or a sea monster" (v. 12a), creatures that stand up to the deity on equal terms. Let him try to get a little rest—what he longed for in death (3.13)—and the deity comes to him in terrifying dreams (7.13–14). Eliphaz's dream is frightening enough, but Job taxes the deity himself for sending the judgmental dream, for being so consistently present. He would rather suffocate in his own way (v. 15a), and he rejects these attentions: "Leave me alone" (v. 16b).

Finally, as in chap. 3, Job starts to talk about the human being in general as a way of talking about himself.

> What's a man, that you magnify him so,
> set your mind on him,
> visit him every morning,
> test him every moment? (7.17–18)

Job partially answered his own question in verse 1: "Is not a man [*'ᵉnōš*, the same word as in v. 17a] conscripted on earth?" It is reminiscent of the Mesopotamian view of the human race as the gods' menials.[32] Yet in verses 17–18 Job equates a man with the oceanic enemies, who are the objects of the god's constant opposition. The bitter parody on Psalm 8 reiterates that this attention is overdone. Yahweh had wondered if the Prosecutor had set his "mind" (*lēb*, "heart") on Job; now Job wonders why the god, the "watcher" (*nōṣēr*, v. 20b), sets his mind on him. Thinking before that the god would one day look unsuccessfully for him (v. 8b), he now wants him to stop looking at him at all: "Let me be till I swallow my spit" (v. 19b). Job wished in 6.8–10 that the god would crush him and let him go, but instead he is standing over him.

And why? For the first time Job asks that question. In chap. 3 it was "Why am I alive, when I would rather be dead?" Now comes a series of questions to the god: "Is not a man conscripted?" (7.1); "Am I Sea or a sea monster?" (v. 12); "What's a man?" (v. 17); "How long?" (v. 19); "What have I done to you?" (v. 20a). And at the end of the series: "Why have you set me up as your target?" (v. 20c); "Why not lift my guilt?" (v. 21a) The questions come more and more quickly, and the only one that is repeated is "Why?"

At last the issue has emerged. Job's condition, exacerbated as it is by the friends, is the deity's doing. In chap. 1 Job thought the god's responsibility acceptable and positive, and he was able to neutralize it in chap. 2. Now he perceives the god's responsibility as enmity and guilt, as if Job were an enemy. Why? The first "why" question brings back the image of the poisoned arrows (6.4) at the beginning of the speech:

> Why have you set me up as your target? (7.20c)

Job has already answered his own question, yet in such a way as to dismiss the answer.

> I sin. What have I done to you,
> you watcher of men? (v. 20a–b)

It is as if he had accepted Eliphaz's contention, proposed as a special divine revelation, that all human beings are imperfect and ephemeral, "born to toil." Job is but a human, unimportant in the grand scale of things. In that case, why the deity's grand reaction? Given Job's swift passage across the days and his likeness to an evanescent puff of wind, it would hardly be too much for the god to overlook whatever sin he might have committed. It is inconceivable that it has any real impact; surely not enough to make him a target for archery practice or a "burden" (*maśśa'*, v. 20d). There is a thought: Why not "lift" it (*tiśśa'*, v. 21a)? Just forgive, carry the iniquity away. If Job is so ephemeral, his guilt must be very light as well.

But soon it will be too late: "I won't be there" (7.21d).

Bildad (Chapter 8)

Bildad is given to shorter prefaces than are the other friends. After one sarcastic couplet (8.2), extending Job's complaint that the friends blow like wind at his words (6.26) to call Job's "words a gusty [*kabbīr*] wind," he leaps immediately into his doctrinal position, framed as a rhetorical question, and his conclusion from it, framed as a statement:

> Does El bend justice,
> Shaddai bend the right?
> If your sons have sinned against him,
> he has sent them off in custody of their guilt. (vv. 3–4)

The "if," Clines points out, is not hypothetical.[33] Nor is Bildad's statement considerate: Job's children died because they deserved to. There is a bluntness, an absence of rhetorical artifice, in Bildad that could be refreshing if the man but showed some ordinary kindness.[34] One knows people like that, people with kind hearts and rough tongues, whose deepest sympathy sounds like harsh criticism.

Bildad comes close in verse 3 to proposing that whatever the deity does is just, which may remind us of one of the interpretations of Job's remark in 2.10 about good and evil.[35] At least Bildad thinks it impossible that the deity should be unjust, however much like a captain of police he may be.[36] That definition determined, the conclusion follows: because the god is in charge of what happens, what happens is just. Suffering and death are punishment; prosperity and long life are reward. The power of the deity who is in charge of what happens is conjoined with the justice of what happens with no conceivable incoherence between them. That Job's children died untimely is sufficient evidence that they deserved death.

Job in his turn, insofar as he is "pure and moral" (*zak w^{e}yašar*, 8.6), will find his lot improved.[37] He must reverse himself: instead of expecting the deity to come searching for him (7.21d), he must search for the deity (8.5a—*šḥr* in both lines).[38] If he does that, and if his character justifies it, the god will reverse himself. But the "if's" in verses 5–6 are hypothetical, and so too perhaps is "innocent," as it is applied to Job's dwelling.

> Though now he rouses up against you,
> he will repay your innocent dwelling. (v. 6b–c)[39]

Job's future will reverse his past (v. 7). The apparent hopefulness of the sentiment justifies the thought that the friends are not so negative to Job as is sometimes thought. William Irwin was certainly not mistaken when he insisted that, though the friends are interested both in the differing fates of the wicked and the righteous and in Job's wrongful conduct, they also wish to show Job how to escape his suffering.[40] At the same time, however, Bildad does not perceive the contradiction between the god's unbending justice and his "rousing himself up against" the "innocent dwelling" of a man who is "pure and moral," and he seems not to have attended to Job's bitter complaints that the deity is all too present with him.

He now appeals to the past for the way out:

> Ask, then, a past generation,
> adhere to what their fathers found. (v. 8)

It is an interesting balance to the first stanza (vv. 2–4). The "future" generation, the sons, has already gone down in guilt (v. 4), and truth is to be found with a "past" generation of fathers. Those fathers can "talk" (*'mr*, v. 10a; cf. *'imrē-pīka*, "your mouth's words," v. 2), "bring forth words" (*millīm*, v. 10b; cf. *temallēl*, "prattle," v. 2), as Job cannot, because their words come from their "mind" (*lēb*, v. 10b), whereas Job's come only from his "mouth" (v. 2b). The correspondences between the first and third stanzas, furthermore, are in reverse, chiastic order: verse 10 corresponds to and corrects verse 2, and verse 8 corresponds to and corrects verse 4. Such a structure suggests that verses 2–10 are a subunit of Bildad's speech.[41]

One may wonder about coherence when Bildad suddenly turns in verse 11 to a proverb about the necessity for water in growing papyrus. The verb in the second line of that couplet, *yiśgeh*, "increase," is repeated from verse 7b, where Bildad promised that Job's future would grow. The plant image may owe something to the agricultural themes at the end of Eliphaz's speech (5.23–27) and may allude to Job's plea of his ephemerality in the image of reeds drying up quickly when water is withdrawn (v. 12).[42] Just so, says Bildad, mixing his metaphors badly, are the "paths" and the "hope" of bad people. Any walker prefers a dried-up path, if not a dried-up reed, and the image is not a very happy one. As for "hope" (*tiqwah*) perishing (*'bd*), Job wished, back in 3.3, that his "day" would "perish" (*'bd*), and, in 6.8, that the god would give him his "hope" (*tiqwah*), namely, death. Bildad's remark is another convoluted reversal, like the one we saw in 8.5a and will see again.

His second image of ephemerality, the spider's web (v. 14b), casts another negative shadow across Job's "innocent dwelling" (a different word) in 8.6c. Just as a spider's web collapses when one leans against it, so what the wicked person "trusts" is insubstantial, even if one tries to "strengthen" (*ḥzq*) it. It is unfortunate that the meaning of the crucial word in verse 14a is unknown,[43] for whatever it is, it is a source of "confidence" (*kesel*), a word that in Eliphaz's mouth (4.6a), as here, pointed to a misplaced confidence.

The middle stanza of this section (vv. 16–17) seems more positive than the rest, with its interesting conjunction of the metaphors of the plant ("well watered," "shoots," "garden," "roots," "pool") and the house ("house of stone"). Just that positivity, however, suggests that this stanza and the next emerge from the double image of the house both strengthened and ephemeral in verse 15. Verses 16–17 expect permanence in the strengthening, while verses 18–19 present ephemerality all the more powerfully for the interlude of optimistic hope. It is the same irony as the reeds in verses 11–12. Bildad, then, emphasizes not simply temporariness but the ironic disparity between expectation and reality.

The irony is perhaps clearest in verse 19a: "Oh! that's the joy [*meśōś*] of his way." But the ironic oxymoron in the perishing of hope (v. 13b), which reminds us that Job hopes to perish (6.8–9), is equaled by the disparity in "what he trusts is a spider's house" (8.14b) and the deadly thrust of the denial by "his place": "I've never seen you" (v. 18b). The last is a telling allusion to Job, who, describing his own transitoriness under the image of the cloud, said,

> So one descends to Sheol, does not come up,
> never returns to his house,
> and his place never recognizes him again. (7.9b–10)

Bildad's allusion makes clear that his images of plants and houses are variations on the theme of ephemerality that Job had sounded in chap. 7. He makes it less clear that he is encouraging Job.

I have come to think that this discussion among Job and the friends is more of a discussion than most scholars have recognized. Perhaps we are too sure that a discussion is a constant give-and-take, a reply to this point and a refutation of that one. These speeches contain some of that kind of discussion. But the dialogue is carried more by a series of understated, crossing allusions, in repeated words and images, to what the other party said. It is not a debate or a disputation on our usual model, but it is, however much at arms' length, a dialogue, and it requires close attention of its readers.

We see more echoes in the last stanza, 8.20–22. Bildad assures Job that "El does not reject [*m's*] a perfect person [*tam*]." Bildad cannot know, though we can, that "perfect" is a word Yahweh used in 1.8 to describe Job. But he knows that in 7.16, Job's vexation with the deity had led him to cry out, "I refuse [*m's*]! I won't live forever." Job has perhaps "refused" the deity; Bildad calmly tells him that the deity will not refuse him, if he is "perfect," or at least "pure and moral" (8.6a). Eliphaz, of course, was certain that no one is good enough (4.17–19), but Bildad need not agree with everything Eliphaz says.

Bildad seems to suppose that Job is good enough to make it. The deity does not, Bildad insisted in 8.3, "bend" justice or right, and verse 20 portrays justice as neither rejecting a good person nor upholding an evil one. Job's situation will change for the better in the end:

> He will yet fill your mouth with laughter,
> your lips with festal shout. (v. 21)

Job can look forward to genuine joy, not the kind ironically promised the wicked (v. 19a).

Bildad closes with one last poetic outburst that combines a nice alliteration with another allusion to what Job had said:

> Those who hate you will be dressed in shame [*yilbᵉšū bōšet*],
> and the tent of the wicked will not be there. (v. 22)

"Tent" subtly recalls the image of the house and completes the theme of ephemerality. But the positive encouragement abruptly dissipates. The tent of wicked folks "will not be there" (*'ēnennū*, "none of it"), he says. "You'll search for me," Job assured the god in 7.21d, "but I won't be there" (*'ēnennī*). In a neat rhetorical touch, Bildad ends his speech with the same word as Job in his prior one. But what sort of comfort is it? The "tent of the wicked" becomes the analogue of the suffering friend.

Job (Chapters 9–10)

Job's third speech may seem the best testimony to the idea that the participants in the debate respond to the last speech but one.[44] Eliphaz asked (4.17a), "Is a man more righteous than Eloah?" (*ha'ᵉnōš mē'ᵉlōah yiṣdaq*) Job begins with a near-quotation: "How can a man be innocent with El?" (*ūmah-yiṣdaq 'ᵉnōš 'im-'ēl*) (9.2b) It is different from what Eliphaz said, to be sure. Eliphaz used the verb "to be righteous" (*ṣdq*) in a moral sense, and I believe that Job shifts its reference to the legal sphere, as the succeeding couplet shows. But 9.2b clearly responds to 4.17a. What is more, 9.10 directly quotes 5.9, and "sweeps on" in 9.11b repeats the verb from 4.15a. It is more difficult for the reader of English to see that Job's style of description in 9.5–10, a series of Hebrew participles, echoes Eliphaz's use of the same stylistic device in 5.9–13.

This speech also alludes, however, to Bildad's speech. The use of "be innocent" (*ṣdq*) in 9.2b echoes 8.6c and perhaps 8.3b, and Job complains in 9.15 that he must "beg mercy" (*'etḥannan*), which Bildad had urged him to do (*titḥannan*, 8.5b). Bildad's certainty (8.20) that "El does not reject a perfect person [*tam*], / or strengthen the hand of evil ones [*mᵉrē'īm*]" is rejected by Job: "He finishes off both perfect [*tam*] and wicked [*rāša'*]" (9.22). Though the reply to Eliphaz stands out at the very beginning, chaps. 9–10 do not give good evidence that the speakers refer back to the speech before the latest one.

This speech is, if anything, even more complex than Job's previous one (chaps. 6–7), and its complexity arises from Job's intertwining a remarkable multiplicity of images around a central thread of argument. That argument, which we have not seen before, turns on the language of law and legal procedure—a theme that will occupy Job more and more as the dialogue proceeds.

Indeed, just that theme characterizes Job's skewing of Eliphaz's language in 9.2b. Eliphaz's vision in 4.17–21 began with the question "Is a man more righteous than Eloah?" and he said, in effect, that the human not only is not more righteous than the god but is doomed to be unrighteous, an inevitable sinner who, being morally less than the god, is for that reason morally in contrast to the god. Job's rhetorical question "How can a man be innocent with El?" implies the answer "He cannot be innocent." The question points to someone accused and found guilty before the law. Eliphaz talked morality, and Job talks law. But they use the same words, and because words can always mean more than one thing, they talk both to and past each other.

Job's problem is that the deity, being the force behind the law, has all the power on his side.

> If one wished to enter a case against him,
> he couldn't answer him once in a thousand. (9.3)

The pronouns are confusing. "To answer" in the legal sense is to defend oneself against a charge. It makes sense to take both "him's" to refer to the deity, and "he" as the human litigant. The divine power that bothers Job prevents human success. That is a familiar sentiment today, one that today's elderly find hard to take from today's young, when they claim that the whole system of social institutions, on which we have always depended to provide justice and honesty and all those high values, actually represents injustice or unacceptable morality. The very deity comes under doubt here:

> Wise of mind and powerfully strong,
> whoever is stubborn to him, and safe? (v. 4)

One might think that a wise, strong deity is what is wanted. Seeing both wisdom and strength directed against him without justification, Job thinks that neither is clearly in league with justice. But the god possesses both wisdom and strength, and he is also supposed to be responsible for justice. Job feels himself in a dangerous bind. Yet the question of justice may also point in another direction. If "he" in verse 3b is the god and "him" the human, the tone of the complaint is rather different. In that case, the problem is the deity's incapacity for justice, the impossibility that he could deal justly with a legal suit. Job may be arguing simultaneously that the god is incapable of justice because he is so powerful and that the god is incompetent to do justice.

Perhaps Job picked up the question of justice from Bildad's "Does El bend justice [*mišpaṭ*]?" (8.3a) Job is not yet using that word, but soon he will. First he combines two themes, one from himself and one from Eliphaz in a long section on the activity of the god (9.5–12). The style is the language one finds, for example, in the narrative of Psalm 136 (I omit the antiphonal refrains):

> Who alone works great marvels,
> Who made the heavens with wisdom,
> Who spread the earth over the water,
> Who made the great lights. (Ps 136.4–7; JPS)

Or in the rolling periods of the Second Isaiah (Isa 40–55):

> Who measured the waters with the hollow of his hand,
> and gauged the skies with a span,
> and meted earth's dust with a measure,
> and weighed the mountains with a scale
> and the hills with a balance? (Isa 40.12; JPS)

It is the participial language associated with the hymnic praise of a god who does wonderful things in nature.[45] In Job's mouth that language emphasizes the raw power that makes it unsafe to act stubbornly toward the god (Job 9.4b), the power that removes mountains (v. 5), shakes earth (v. 6), prevents the sun from rising and the stars from shining (v. 7). It is chaotic power, which undoes the world's order, the kind of power one would expect from the great enemies of creation, Leviathan, Sea, Death, Tiamat. Yet without changing pace or mood, Job shifts to the kinds of words the Second Isaiah uses in describing the creative God: he "stretches out the sky" (v. 8a; cf. Isa 40.22; 42.5; 44.24, among other passages).[46] And the image of the god's treading on Sea (Yamm, Job 9.8b), implying the triumph of fertile order over the disorder of oceanic chaos, reverses the chaotic impression. Having talked of the god's putting "a seal on the stars" (v. 7b), he turns around and refers to his having "made" the constellations (v. 9).

In verse 10 Job directly quotes Eliphaz from 5.9:

> who does great things, even inscrutable,
> wonderful things innumerable.[47]

Eliphaz made that participial, hymnic statement in order to persuade Job to seek out the deity. Job uses it to explain why he cannot do so: the deity is too powerful, too inconsistent in handling the creation. He uses his power to frustrate the very perception by humans that Eliphaz proposes:

> Ah, he passes me by, and I don't see him,
> sweeps on, and I don't discern him. (v. 11)

In verse 12, repeating the ejaculatory *hēn*, "Ah!" of verse 11, Job's complaint of brutal treatment puns on the prior line: "he seizes" (*yaḥtōp*) echoes *yaḥlōp*, "sweeps on," a word used by Eliphaz in 4.15a of the wind sweeping across his face in his vision. Perhaps he "discerns" the deity as he "sweeps on," but Job cannot. Traditional hymnic language in praise of the god emerges from Job's mouth as bitter grievance against the god.

From hymnic parody Job turns to legal language. He begins in verse 13 by alluding to the Rahab myth, a combat myth of creation.[48] The analogue to Job's trial is the battle between chaos and order, as it was in 7.12, when Job wondered whether he were "Sea or a sea monster," similar chaos figures. This analogy of trial to combat emphasizes what a charade the proceeding must be. If the god so easily put down Rahab, a mere human, inferior and ephemeral as Eliphaz and Bildad described him, cannot hope to respond to the charges (v. 14) but will be forced to "beg mercy" of the god.

It is the old problem of power and justice. To those who have not run afoul of power, it seems sweetly reasonable that power is secure enough to offer justice. Bildad proposed that to "ask mercy" of the god (8.5b) would simply solve the problem. To Job, whose experience of power is its brutality, the appearance of justice is not believable:

> If I summoned him and he answered me,
> I wouldn't believe he was hearing my voice,
> he who tramples me down with a whirlwind,[49]
> enlarges my wounds for no reason. (9.16–17)

Job faces the problem that the judge in his trial is also the prosecutor.[50] He uses some intricately interconnected words. No one can "turn back" (*y^ešībennu*, v. 12a) the god, who will not "turn back" (*yašīb*) his anger in the creation combat (v. 13a), and who does not let Job "catch" (*hašēb*, v. 18a) his breath. His power is uncaring, extending even to force-feeding (v. 18b). Judge, jailor, and district attorney are all combined into one.

Innocence gives no assurance. Job's emotion rises nearly to hysteria:

> If it's a case of strength, Oh!—
> and if of justice, who'll docket my suit?
> If I'm innocent, my own mouth condemns me;
> if I'm perfect, he'll do me fraud.
> I am perfect—
> I don't know myself—
> I despise my life. (vv. 19–21)

"Perfect" (*tam*) is the word the narrator used of Job in 1.1 and Yahweh used of him twice, in 1.8 and 2.3. Bildad used it, ostensibly of Job, in 8.20, and Eliphaz called the "integrity" (*tōm*) of Job's ways one of his sources of confidence (4.6). For the first time Job uses the word of himself, first hypothetically as a contrast to the fraud that the judge will perpetrate on him, and then, without changing the words (*tam 'anī*), as a powerful affirmation: "I am perfect!" Immediately he almost withdraws it: "I don't know myself" (*lō' 'ēda' napšī*), and he rejects the whole situation: "I despise [*m's*] my life," just as he had "refused" (*m's*), thinking about ephemerality in 7.16.

The thing has slipped out, then, in the midst of a very emotional outburst. Job thinks himself "perfect," *tam*, as had Yahweh (Job does not know that) and his wife (*tummah*, 2.9) and Eliphaz and Bildad. He does not deserve the suffering, and the justice being worked on him is unjust.

It is sometimes suggested that the friends have pushed Job to this conclusion by harping on the implication that Job's suffering gives evidence that he must be immoral. To be sure, both Eliphaz and Bildad have implied that idea (4.7–8; 5.2–7; 8.4) by means of some sharp barbs beneath their seemingly friendly remarks, and Eliphaz introduced the idea into the discussion. But Job comes to this point through his own pondering of the question of justice. Having begun the discussion with the creation (chap. 3), he now draws a connection between the creator's power and the justice of the creature's situation. Job began in 9.2 with legal language, linked it to strength in verse 4, extended strength to the power of creation in verses 5–10, and suggested injustice to himself in verses 11–12. Resuming legal language in verse 14, Job has already given up on the trial because of the brutal power of the judge, and in verses 19–21, the impossibility of a fair trial, as Job has come to conceive it, leads him to set himself up as *tam*.

Job concludes that there is no connection between the deserts of a human being and that person's treatment by the god.

> It's all the same. Therefore I say,
> he finishes off both perfect and wicked. (v. 22)

It is a claim of amorality. The god does nothing with people but "finish them off." Uppermost in Job's mind is brutality, and his reference to the deity's scoffing at the "guiltless" (*naqī*) in the flood (v. 23) typifies the way in which he has inextricably linked the themes of law and power. Here Job gives us the other half of the equation that began "I am perfect" in verse 21:

> Earth is given over to a wicked hand;
> he covers its judges' faces—
> if not, then who is it? (v. 24)

Only the god can be the subject of that extraordinary statement. Job's style has shifted from the emotional outburst of verses 19–21 to a calculating logic. Might corrupts legal power into brutality and "wickedness" (*raša'*). Such wickedness destroys both its own kind and its opposite, "both perfect and wicked" (v. 22), and sees to the "condemnation" (*yaršī'ēnī*, a "causative" form of the verb *rš'*) of the "innocent" (*ṣdq*, v. 20a). That remarkable series of words forms a high point of the dialogue. It begins in verse 20 with a normal term for the legal declaration of guilt, goes on to define the destruction as amoral, falling indiscriminately upon both good and bad (v. 22), and identifies the perpetrator of the destruction as not merely amoral but immoral (v. 24).

The images of speed and ephemerality in verses 25–26 suggest exhaustion and despair. Job's days pass quickly (as in 7.6), they "sweep" (see 9.11b) like reed skiffs. He takes another sidelong glance at distasteful power and at death with the image of his days' swooping (the Hebrew has no pun with "sweeping") like a vulture. Where can he go from here?

He does what he did at the beginning of chap. 7: surprisingly, in view of the accusations he has just leveled, he turns to speak directly to the deity. He says just what he has said to the friends: the pain frightens him because it symbolizes guilt (vv. 27–28), and he has no hope of a fair outcome to the trial. "I'll be condemned" (*'anōkī 'erša'*, v. 29, "declared wicked")—one hears "I'm already condemned," already determined wicked (cf. vv. 20, 22, 24). Pure human hands cannot stand up against the "wicked hand" into which the earth, Job said, is given (v. 24). There is no way Job's cleanliness (v. 30) can hold out against the deity's wish to dirty him (v. 31). And the dirt is not happy, playful, child-in-a-mud-puddle dirtiness. It is "disgusting," putrescent, third-circle-in-Hell muck.[51] Thinking about it, Job turns away from speaking to the deity.

Only here in the dialogue does he begin to address the god, stop and talk of him in the third person, and then (10.2) resume speaking to him—though 10.2–22 is a report of what he intends to say. The third-person stanza about the deity (9.32–35) is most important. The distinction between human and divine is common coin in the Hebrew Bible, though the terms in which Eliphaz stated it in chaps. 4–5 are unusual. Unlike the ancient Greeks, the Hebrews never placed the divine and the human on a plane.[52] So no theological surprise is implied by the first line of verse 32: "For he's not a man like me whom I could answer." "Answer" may surprise us a bit, because we have suddenly left the water and dirt images of verses 30–31 and have returned to legal language. Job implicitly defines a trial as a procedure between two equal parties. If the deity is not human,

Job seems to say, no trial is possible, and the arbitrary dumping into filth that verse 31 portrays is the way the god acts. Is there any legal recourse?

No, says Job, unless a third party could bring the two contending parties together, an arbiter (*mōkīaḥ*) "lay his hand on us both." What kind of pipe dream is that? Clearly it is not a dream; Job dismisses the thought as soon as he has it: "There's no arbiter" (v. 33).[53] Any third party who might "lay his hand on us both" would necessarily be more powerful than the god, and Job cannot imagine that. He is doomed to his fear (vv. 34–35). But we must keep the *mōkīaḥ* in mind, because we will see him again.

Because the trial is impossible, Job can do only what he complained earlier he would have to do, to beg for mercy (see 9.15): "Don't condemn me, let me know of what you're accusing me" (10.2). It seems a pointless demand, for Job thinks he is hopelessly condemned (9.20a, 29a). Sarcasm is understandable:

> Is it good to you that you oppress,
> despise your hands' toil,
> and beam upon the counsel of the guilty [*rᵉšaʿīm*]? (10.3)

The "toil" (*yᵉgīaʿ*) is the kind that exhausts the toiler,[54] and Job wonders whether the god finds pleasure in despising (*m's*; cf. Job in 7.16 and Bildad's use of the same verb in 8.20a) what had cost him so much of weariness. He wonders whether to reverse his denial in 9.32 of the equality between deity and human:

> Have you fleshly eyes;
> do you see as a man sees?
> Are your days like human days,
> like a man's days your years? (10.4–5)

One might expect a human to act that way. The god "searches" (*bqš*, v. 6) for his shortcomings

> because you know I'm not guilty,
> and no one can rescue from your hand. (v. 7)

Knowledge of Job's innocence motivates the search for his guilt. It is a "sting," an "entrapment" operation. Power has become the bending of justice that Bildad denied it could be.

Power brings Job back to the theme of creation. In 9.5–10, he pointed out the incongruity of the creator's dismantling the creation. Now he applies the same incongruity to himself:

> Your hands shaped me, made me . . .
> Recall that you made me like clay,
> yet you're turning me back to dust? (10.8–9)

As in 9.5–10, Job both describes the god's introduction of dissolution into the creation and talks more positively about the creation. But the positive terms of 10.10–12 are turned askew by the reversal in verse 9, and even verse 12, which seems to acknowledge a kindly providence, is made ironic by the fact that "your care has guarded [*šmr*] my spirit" (v. 12b) echoes 7.12:

> Am I Sea or a sea monster
> that you station a guard [*mišmar*] over me?

The irony deepens as we recall that "guarding, watching" echoes what Yahweh instructed the Prosecutor to do (2.6).

It is fascinating how, in two major stanzas in this speech, Job reverts to the issue of the creation, so significant a subject in chap. 3. These recurrent themes, gliding into and out of the discourse, look to a musician like a fugue, constantly weaving its themes around each other. There is more yet.

Having decided that he has no hope of anything but condemnation from a trial, Job now comes as close as he ever does to admitting that he has done something wrong and echoes the words about the god's guarding him:

> If I sin, you put a guard [*šmr*] on me
> and don't acquit me of my fault.
> If I'm guilty [*rš'*], woe upon me!
> If innocent, I cannot lift my head. (vv. 14–15)

The echo also goes back to verses 6–7, where he had accused the deity of searching (*bqš*) for his fault (*'awōn*), inquiring after his sin, because the god knew he was not guilty. Those verbal connections suggest that the "if's" in verses 14–15 are completely hypothetical, especially in the light of Job's ambiguity in the intervening stanza about his treatment by the deity. And the parenthesis in verses 15–16a likens the god to a lion:

> Gorged with dishonor,
> gazing at humiliation,
> he is proud as a lion.

One is reminded of verse 7b: "And no one can rescue from your hand." Job enters a bewildering thicket of metaphors:

You hunt me down, repeat your wonders on me,
bring new witnesses before me,
increase your fury against me,
fresh squadrons against me. (vv. 16b–17)

The lion metaphor, contained in "hunt me down," switches to an allusion to the "wonders" of the theophany (the verb *pl'*, cf. "wonderful things," *nipla'ōt*, 9.10b), to the legal sphere in "witnesses," to passionate fury (*ka'aś*, cf. 6.2a), and finally to a military attack (cf. the image of the poisoned arrows in 6.4 and Job's complaint about being a target in 7.20). Such a tangle of images is difficult to comb into neat strands of rationality. Perhaps it portrays again the sufferer speaking through pain.

Now, completing his part of this cycle of speeches, Job reverts both to the issue of the creation from chap. 3 and to his question there: "Why did you bring me out of the womb?" (cf. 3.11) We hear again that death is preferable and he is ephemeral (10.20), the wish that the god would leave him alone (cf. 7.16, 19), and the certainty that he is about to depart with no possibility of return (cf. 7.10) to

the land of deepest dark,
land of gloom, like dusk,
deep shadow, all disordered,
which shines like dusk. (10.21b–22)

Reverting to the images of darkness from chap. 3, Job's splendid closing oxymoron, "which shines like dusk," is the mirror image of "That day, let there be darkness" (3.4a).

He is nevertheless at a different place from where he was when he cursed his day. There he wanted to be dead because to be alive was terrible, nothing but a "toil" (*'amal*) too much to be borne. Here he wants to be dead because the structure of things has fallen apart. He had thought that divine power and divine justice were positively related, and that divine power supported those weak ones who deserved divine justice. Sure that he deserves justice, he is also sure now that, like those wicked people who ought not to be supported, he is being attacked by the divine power. Distinction has dissolved into darkness, and Job would rather be dead.

Zophar (Chapter 11)

Job began his last speech with a number of references to answering (9.3, 14, 15, 16), alluding to legal procedure. Zophar begins with one such reference, which seems to allude to Job's problem about legal procedure:

> Is a gang of words not answered?
> Is a gabby man innocent?
> Does your chatter silence men?
> When you deride, does no one rebuke? (11.2–3)

It is almost as if Zophar were saying, "Do you expect an answer with that kind of babble? Will there ever be a trial if you refuse to be serious about it?"

Zophar is sure that if the god answered Job directly (v. 5), Job's unwarranted arrogance that he is right (*zak*, "pure," *bōr*, "clear," v. 4) would crumble away. It is difficult to find in Job's mouth anything like what Zophar attributes to him. "I am perfect" (9.21) comes closest to it. Yet Zophar's thought leads him to a sharp contrast between Job's and the god's wisdom. Divine speech, unlike Job's chatter, would take him further into wisdom than he can go unaided by the revelation. In the "gang of words" that claims pure understanding, Job shows how far he is from a god who holds wisdom's secrets, a god who *knows* (11.11) in ways that Job cannot know (v. 8). But Zophar also knows, and he is willing to let Job in on it: "Eloah lets some of your guilt be forgotten" (v. 6c). That translation is only one possible meaning of a difficult sentence. The most popular alternative is: "God exacts from you less than your guilt deserves."[55] In either reading, Zophar claims that Job is getting off too lightly for the enormity of his guilt.

Zophar begins, then, by seeing Job's situation with the deity as the opposite of what Job thinks it is. Job *thinks* he is pure (v. 4), but Zophar *knows* he is guilty (v. 6c). Zophar does not say how he has come to know that, and Clines's assumption, that Zophar starts "from the same presupposition as the friends, that suffering is deserved," interestingly plays no part in the way Zophar argues.[56] He disputes Job's understanding of his suffering more than the objective reason for it. Job blames the god for transgressing the bounds of moral decency, but Job is incompetent to judge that. If the god would only speak, wisdom would be available to Job. If the god does not reveal himself, he remains so far beyond Job as to be unknowable (vv. 7–9).

Zophar's is not quite the same account of divine transcendence that Eliphaz had received in his vision (4.17–21), which had more to do with moral than with physical transcendence. The divine moral transcendence, Eliphaz said, renders every human guilty. Zophar seems willing to assume divine wisdom and human limitation, and even more, divine power and human weakness on the basis of divine transcendence beyond the sky above and Sheol below.[57] The deity does what he wishes, with no possible hindrance (11.10), knows everything beyond possible contradiction (v. 11) from a human race invincibly and intrinsically stupid. Zophar assumes, with Job, the god's power and distinguishes human weakness from it as lack of intelligence rather than as moral failure. That, at least, seems the implication of the rather odd proverb Zophar quotes:

> A hollow-headed man will be intelligent
> when a wild ass colt is born human. (v. 12)

Just as the animal's intelligence does not approach that of the human, so the human's cannot be compared with the deity's. Yet it looks as if Zophar appropriates the wrong proverb for saying that. Having earlier offered Job a share in what he himself knows (v. 6c), he seems here to imply also that Job is "hollow-headed" and can never approach the intelligence Zophar possesses. The context makes the first reading necessary, but the application to Job lies just beneath the surface.

It pops up to view when, in verse 13, Zophar begins his remedial suggestions with Job's "heart" (*lēb*). In the proverb he used the denominative verb *lbb*, which I translate "be intelligent." The heart, we have seen, is the seat of intelligence, thought, and intention. Having proposed that the problem with the "hollow-headed" is a problem of the heart, Zophar's suggestion that Job "prepare [his] heart" can hardly be anything but a solution to the problem of verse 12. The ostensible goodwill of still another friend masks a will not entirely friendly.

Zophar's proposal is both short and unhelpful. Prepare the mind (v. 13a), pray (v. 13b), get rid of fault (v. 14). Just like that: "remove it," distance it from you, don't let it reside in your tent. Zophar does not identify or offer assistance in identifying Job's fault; he simply assumes that Job has one and counsels him to rid himself of it. He goes on to proffer a conventional procession of promises about a good outcome for the righteous (vv. 15–19) and a bad one for the wicked (v. 20).[58]

We may pause over the latter:

> But the eyes of knaves will be exhausted,
> refuge perished from them,
> their only hope to breathe their last. (v. 20)

The first line implicitly answers Job's outburst in 9.22, that the god "finishes off [*m*ᵉ*kalleh*] both perfect [*tam*] and wicked [*rašaʿ*]." No, says

Zophar, only knaves (*r^e^šaʿīm*) will be "ended" (*tikleynah*, the same root as in 9.22). Having in 11.6 estimated Job's guilt (*ʿawōn*) as more than what the deity counts, though in verse 14a he put a conditional "if" around Job's possession of guilt, Zophar has given the game away. Perhaps there is hope for Job, if he can get rid of the guilt, but he must watch out.

As for Job's wish for escape to Sheol and the dead, that too is blocked. In the second line of v. 20, Zophar uses the unusual word *manōs*, "refuge," with the verb *'bd*, "perish," the verb Job had wished in 3.3 upon his birthday. Because Job finished his last speech (10.18–22) with this very motif, Zophar's reference to the perishing of refuge sounds very like an allusion to Job's death wish.

The closing line, "their only hope to breathe their last," is the clincher. Exactly that is what Job had hoped:

> Would that what I ask would come,
> that Eloah would give me my hope,
> would make up his mind and crush me,
> free his hand and cut me down. (6.8–9)

It is becoming usual that the parting shots in the friends' speeches are not calculated to assure Job that the friend cares about his well-being. Job is being identified, intentionally or inadvertently, with the knaves of this world.

4

"Earth, Do Not Cover My Blood"

> I am sometimes visited by a suspicion that everything isn't right with the Righteous; that the Moral Law speaks in oddly equivocal tones to those who listen most scrupulously for its dictates.
>
> —Logan Pearsall Smith, *Trivia*

In the first cycle, the friends, unlike Job, had no opportunity to develop their arguments. He spoke three times, each of them only once. Eliphaz introduced the issue of justice, the morality of the world's governance. People's situations mirror their deserts, though every human, being less than the god, is to some significant degree morally the deity's opposite. Bildad's view is simpler: if Job is guilty, he had best set the matter right as soon as possible, for the deity is just and will punish. Zophar, on the other hand, apparently thinks that Job is not being punished as he ought to be.

Not until the friends raised the issue of justice did Job begin to interpret his situation in terms of it. At the beginning of the dialogue, he simply wanted to be out of life, and the heartfelt curse on his birthday, and with it on the creation as a whole, initiated a major theme that runs through Job's speeches: an appeal to the created order. But as the problem of justice impinged more and more on Job's consciousness, he shifted the ground from his death wish, though he reverted to it several times. In the third speech, legal language became central (chaps. 9–10).

Job wanted a trial against the god, because he realized that his situation, far from demonstrating the god's justice and morality, implied its opposite. Agreeing with the friends' assumption that the god rewards what pleases him and punishes what displeases him, Job saw no logic in his situation. If the moral order decrees that goodness produces health and prosperity and wickedness brings about pain and desolation, something has gone wrong with the administration in Job's case. Some heavenly archivist failed to file the fact that Job is good, and he began his wish for a trial with the supposition that he had already been found guilty. Zophar's certainty that wicked people can hope only for death—just what Job had been hoping for—ended the first cycle with a profound impasse between the sufferer and his friends.

Job (Chapters 12–14)

Job's opening salvo of the second cycle is his longest speech next to the one that closes the entire dialogue (chaps. 26–31). This speech falls into two nearly equal parts. From 12.2 to 13.19a, Job addresses the friends, and from 13.19b to 14.22, the deity.

Perhaps we should not be surprised at the tone of the beginning, a textbook example of sarcasm.

> In truth, you [plural] are the people,
> and wisdom dies with you. (12.2)

Job's sarcasm goes in two directions: wisdom as a human capacity will die when the friends die; and, with even heavier sarcasm, if they are wisdom's representatives, it is already dead. The reference to wisdom responds to Zophar's equally sarcastic certainty of Job's intellectual limits:

> Can you discover Eloah's farthest edge,
> or discover as far as Shaddai's boundary? (11.7)

In the face of Zophar's claim to know the divine secrets, Job insists that he is as intelligent as the friends (12.3). They fail to understand, both by not taking him seriously (v. 4) and by their principled contempt for any sufferer (v. 5). At last, with a mordantly personal attack, he implies that Zophar criticized Job's "tent" for allowing "iniquity" a berth in it (11.14) because Zophar's own "tent" possesses the tranquillity available to the violent (12.6). We have seen that pattern of reply by understated allusion before.

Alluding to Bildad's advice to ask past generations for the truth (8.8), Job proposes that the friends inquire even further back, to the creation itself, to Behemoth (whom we will meet again in chap. 40) and to the inhabitants of the realms of creation, "the birds of the sky," "the plants of the earth," and "the fish of the sea" (12.7–8; cf. Gen 1.28).[1] Just being a creature qualifies a being to know about the god's governance of the world. "Who doesn't know all these things?" (Job 12.9; cf. v. 3c) The deity's "hand" governs all (vv. 9b, 10a), as Job had insisted with his negative picture of its government in 10.8–17. There too, the god's "hands" had "shaped, made" him (*'śh*, as also in 12.9b), and that was the "wicked hand" into which the world is given (9.24a), over which the absent or nonexistent "arbiter" (*mōkīaḥ*) cannot lay his own hand (9.33). The god is surely in control, but the friends persist in the illusion that the control is fair and just.

Job now makes his contrary understanding more explicit. He moves from the wisdom of creation's creatures to human wisdom, expressed in the banal proverb, "In age is wisdom, / length of days is understanding" (v. 12), perhaps another allusion to Bildad's appeal to past generations (8.8–10). Job asserts that wisdom belongs not to humans but to the deity:

> With him is wisdom [*ḥokmah*]—and power [*gᵉbūrah*]—
> his are counsel and understanding. (12.13)

There is the new point about the nature of the control this god exerts. Wisdom is connected with power, not with justice, and power dominates in Job's description. Normal prophetic oppositions, such as tearing down and rebuilding (cf. Jer 1.10), do not apply. When this god tears down, no rebuilding happens; when he shuts, no opening occurs; when he dries, there is no water; when he soaks, dryness is permanently gone (Job 12.14–15).

This power reverses other power, removes might from the mighty, influence from the influential, rule from rulers. Like Eliphaz's description (5.11–16) of the god's reversals of human power, it reminds us of prophetic denunciations of ill-applied power. Yet 12.16–25 is unlike Eliphaz's discussion in using language not of "frustration" (*mūpar*, 5.12) or of trapping (*lōkēd*, 5.13) but of subversion (12.19b), deprivation (v. 20a), and contempt (v. 21a). "They grope [*yᵉmašᵉšu*] through lightless dark" (12.25a) echoes Eliphaz's "they grope [*yᵉmašᵉšu*] at noon as at night" (5.14). But where Eliphaz's image is of ordinary blindness, Job uses it in the context of cosmic disorder, of "deeps" (*'ᵃmuqōt*) that emerge from darkness (v. 22a) and people who wander in pre-creation "chaos" (*tōhū*, v. 24b; cf. Gen 1.2) and grope in pre-creation "dark" (Job 12.25a).

The disorder is both cosmic and social. The god deprives the powerful of power, the "trustworthy" of influence, the "elderly" of wisdom, the noble of respect (12.20–21). Control has run wild, and power is exerted for its own sake alone. The god plays arbitrary, unmotivated games with "peoples" (vv. 23–24) in "lightless dark" (v. 25). Far from sustaining the creation and its inhabitants, this power dissolves and disintegrates them. Of that the friends have no idea.

Remarkably, Job has discerned these scenes in the dark (13.1), and he repeats his claims (12.3, 9) to knowledge. If Eliphaz knows the ways in which the deity overturns illicit human power, Job does too—but not merely illicit power is affected.

Yet Job turns again for nearly the rest of the speech to the wish for a trial.

> But I want to speak to Shaddai,
> desire to argue the case to El. (13.3)

The verbs are legal ones, and they picture the god as the judge presiding over the case. It is surprising and puzzling that Job, who has just described this deity as overthrowing, apparently without reason, the practitioners of human law (12.17), wishes to apply for a trial under that very deity's supervision. Is he not thinking clearly? Or does he see no alternative? Such questions are made no easier to answer by the ways in which Job continues with the image of the trial.

Clearly he is fed up with arguing with the friends, though he will continue doing it for some chapters yet. They cannot dispose of the case as the god can, and they are unacceptable judges and counselors, "whitewashers of lies" and "healers by godlings." The former phrase can mean both that the friends daub rhetorical whitewash over the lies to hide them, and that they use lies as whitewash to cover up other lies. The latter phrase suggests that the healing the friends attempt derives from weak sources and is therefore incompetent.[2]

Job will speak to the deity about the trial in verse 19b. First he castigates the friends about it, using images of speech and silence mixed with additional terms of legal procedure. He wishes to "speak" and "argue" (*ykḥ*, an important legal term) to the god (v. 3), so that his "argument" (*tōkaḥat*, derived from *ykḥ*) and his "accusations" (*rībōt*) may be heard (v. 6). On the other hand, he enjoins the friends to silence (*ḥrš*) as a sign of wisdom (v. 5), for they speak only "perversely" and "deceitfully" (v. 7), illegally in partiality (v.8a),[3] wrongly in accusation (v. 8b). They are in danger, indeed, of trials of their own (v. 9), with unfavorable and fearful outcomes (vv. 10–11).[4] Job must speak because he is the defendant, whereas the friends have reason only to remain silent.

He now puts his advice of silence into the imperative (v. 13a). Because their "memories" (v. 12) are useless,[5] they must "listen carefully" to what he has to say (v. 17). Job is desperately urgent about arguing the case. The time is short, because the god is about to destroy Job as he destroys the powerful and influential (12.16–25), and Job must muster all of his courage to meet the threat (13.14). It is a moment of the most powerful intensity:

> He's going to kill me; I cannot wait,
> but I must argue my ways to his face. (v. 15)[6]

The proud declaration that he has "marshaled a case" (*'araktī mišpaṭ*) concludes the prologue to the demand for a trial.

> I know that I'm innocent [*'eṣdaq*].
> Who is it who'll accuse [*yarīb*] me? (vv. 18b–19a)

Yet as he begins to address the deity, the tone changes, his pride vanishes, and his approach is strangely understated.

> But soon I'll be silent and die. (v. 19b)

He summarily told the friends to be silent, but he now predicts his own silence. He has told them that the god will shortly kill him, and he now expects to die soon in any event. Though the next sentences are imperatives to the god, they are not exactly imperious:

> Only don't do two things to me,
> then I'll not hide from your face:
> remove your hands from me,
> and don't fall on me with terror of you. (vv. 20–21)

There is more request than demand in Job's setting the conditions for the cross-examination: the deity must lift the punishing hand (cf. 12.9b–10a) and not terrorize the defendant.[7] It is almost as if Job invites the god to begin, then thinks better of it and starts himself:

> Call, and I will answer,
> or I will speak, and you respond to me. (v. 22)

The rest of Job's speech falls into two main parts with several points of connection between them. Verses 13.23–14.6 are the cross-examination. In 14.7–22, Job ponders life and death, permanence and ephemerality, hypothetical hope and actual decay.

To call the first part "cross-examination" stretches the term a bit. The section is carefully organized, but it is not merely a series of questions. The questions about Job's situation and the deity's activities in 13.23–25, ending with an image of pursuit after dead plants, lead to Job's statements about legal procedure and public punishment in verses 26–27. The statements about the human condition in general in 13.28–14.2 close with an image of plant growth and decay, recalling 13.25. The general statement about human ephemerality (*'adam*, 14.1) turns into another question about Job and his trial in 14.3. At verse 5, another statement about human limitation (the singular pronoun doubtless refers to the singular *'adam* in v. 1) leads to an imperative to the deity in verse 6.

Job's beginning question (v. 23) assumes what the friends have assumed all along, namely that he is being punished for guilt. Wanting to know its magnitude (*kammah*, "like what"; JPS "how many?"), he presumes its actuality. He asks immediately to "know" what he has done wrong, why the deity acts in secret (*str*, v. 24a) as the friends do (v. 10b), why he turns language around (v. 24b), transforming *'Iyyōb*, "Job," into *'ōyēb*, "enemy." Questions about the pursuit of drifting leaf and dry straw (v. 25) open a series of images of dead or dying plants (14.2, 7–9), to which Job explicitly compares himself.

The statements in verses 26–27 turn to legal metaphors: wills and bequests (v. 26) that contain no desirable provision,[8] but reinstate "youthful faults" (*'ᵃwōnōt nᵉ'ūray*), which he long ago gave up; and public humiliation in the stocks,[9] constant divine surveillance, and the mark on his foot that designates him the deity's slave property (v. 27). Job the "enemy" has become the outmatched prisoner-slave.

The next statements (13.28–14.2), ostensibly about humans in general but, as the transition to the question of 14.3 shows, actually about Job, turn humiliation into the ephemerality of garbage and moth-eaten cloth (13.28), of withering blossoms and fleeting shadows (14.2). The emphatic opening pronoun *hū'* (13.28) leads us to expect a strong statement about "him," and we discover its referent only in *'adam* in 14.1. But the statement is not at all strong; rhetorical gesture is ironically opposite to substance.

Job points up that irony in the question to which the statements lead:

> Is this why you open your eyes,
> bring me to trial against you? (v. 3)

It is as if the god came drowsily awake in the presence of this utterly uninteresting being and entered suit.[10] We have returned to the unfair trial and the judge/prosecutor who terrorizes the defendant (13.21) and who litigates *because* the case is evanescent. It looks now much less attractive to Job in the light of the relation between legal and actual power. The strange emotional exclamation in v. 4, reminding us of the "muck" in 9.31, makes one wonder if Job thinks that the case is already decided. Yet what that "dirty" (*ṭamē'*) is, from which Job wishes "clean" (*ṭahōr*) might come, is not clear. If he tacitly admits guilt that the trial will not clear him, it is much stronger than his formal acknowledgment that no human is "innocent with El" (9.2). If he angrily charges that a corrupt judge cannot produce a fair verdict, it is quite like the despair before divine wickedness governing earth (9.24) that led him to

> I'll be condemned—
> why do I struggle with the breeze? (9.29)

Control is the watchword: inevitable human decay and inevitable trial, days "determined" and months numbered, "limits" set that cannot be passed (14.5). But humans are confined not merely by time or space. "Limit," *ḥōq*, also means "statute, regulation." We are simultaneously in the languages of law and of creation—those two realms of thought to which Job turns so repeatedly: "You've set him limits / laws that he cannot [or 'will not' or 'does not'] exceed / transgress [*'br*]" (v. 5c). The combination of evanescence and determined time suggests that here, too, we are in the realm of necessity, a relation between law and order, justice and power, that is not at all hopeful for the human caught in it.

All the more reason, then, for the imperative requesting relief, "Take your gaze away from him" (v. 6). The word is stronger than just "look away," and Job complained before that the god's gaze is not turned away (7.19). There it seemed that the gaze might cause his death; here he wishes that turning away the gaze might facilitate death ("cease," *ḥdl*—more than JPS's "be at ease," as its use in 14.7c shows). More yet: death becomes, as it was in chap. 3, the realm of pleasure, the place where the wage-laborer (*śakīr*) can "enjoy his day."[11] As in 7.1–2, which likens the laborer's "day" to a military draft, endured in eager anticipation of its end, the conjunction of "cease" and "enjoy" in 14.6b reverts to the wish for death, an ironic reflection on the "determined" days in 14.5a. Only in death can humans be joyful about a day—our minds go back to chap. 3, and farther back to chaps. 1–2.

The irony deepens after Job finishes his cross-examination. He ruminates to the god about life and death as he completes the images of shriveled and tossed plants.

> But for a tree there is hope.
> If it's cut, it will come new again,
> and its shoots will not cease. (v. 7)

Zophar told Job that he would "trust that hope is there" (11.18). So he does—but only for a tree. Earlier plant images (13.25; 14.2) were similes or metaphors of the human. The analogy of the felled tree that renews itself and grows again is opposed to the human who, as verses 10–12 put it, "lies down and doesn't get up." The tree is precisely unlike the human being, for its apparent death is not a "ceasing" (v. 7c), as is the human's (v. 6a). Even the water "drains away" for the human (v. 11), while it provides life for the tree. Human sleep is permanent (v. 12), but the tree ages to grow anew (v. 8a). The earlier images of dead plants are reversed, from being analogous to the weak, ephemeral human to being its exact, vital opposite. In verses 7–9, the dead tree is a symbol of life.

A new thought strikes Job. Might the god deal with mortal humans as with trees? Might there be some interim, some "decompression period," during which the offender is taken out of circulation, "put on hold," until a fair disposition of the case could be made? It is a bold thought. Apparently dead trees rest in the earth. By analogy, might apparently dead humans rest in Sheol (the place of the dead) until later?

Job gives verses 13–15 to this revolutionary idea in what seems mounting excitement and with language full of allusions and oppositions to ideas he has expressed before. This death could be the opposite of what he wished in 10.19–22, which was the kind of cessation he mentioned in 14.6. It might be a temporary concealment (*str*), the opposite of the deity's "hiding" his face from Job (13.24a), might involve a different "limit" or "statute" (*ḥōq*, 14.13c; cf. v. 5c), which would help the deity to "remember" rather than to "take his gaze away." Because "remember" may have some legal connotation (cf. 13.12), as *ḥōq* certainly does, Job might even speculate about a new legal basis for his relationship to the deity. He stops to wonder at this new thought: "If a hero [*geber*] die, shall he live?" (14.14a) Death was the first point of contrast with the tree (v. 10a). Might life succeed death, the human be like the tree after all, the reversed image turned back on itself yet once more? It is an old, old human question, answered in dissimilar ways by different cultures and religions. Ancient Israel consistently answered it in the negative.

Job will do so too, shortly, but not until he ponders further this possibility (vv. 14–15). His "days" would lose their hopelessness (contrast vv. 1, 5, and 6), his "term" of military service (*ṣaba'*; cf. 7.1) become a mere interim. He would be able to "wait" (14.14b) as he thought he could not in 13.15, when death looked like finality. His "relief" (*ḥalīpah*, 14.14c) could be awaited eagerly, unlike the "relief troops" that the god sent to attack him in 10.17. Real responses of communication, "calling" and "answering" could take place (14.15a) instead of mere formal anticipations of them, as in 13.22. The god might "long for the work of [his] hands" (*ma'aśēh yadeka*, 14.15b), unlike the charge that he "despised [his] hands' toil" (*yegīa' kappeka*) in 10.3. The differences of the terms in these two passages underscore their difference of tone. The idea of a peaceful interlude intervening before the conflict's resolution, analogous to the tree's root aging in the soil (v. 8), is entirely positive.

But Job returns with a thump to reality. He remembers that he was "guarded," his steps watched (13.27), his presumed guilt carefully hoarded (14.16–17). Positive "concealment" (v. 13) is not to be expected from the deity he has been describing, who treasures up guilt. Job recalls, in an imperfectly chiastic order, all of the sins for which he had asked evidence at the beginning of the cross-examination (13.23). There he used "sin" (*ḥaṭṭa't*) twice:

> What scope has my fault ['*awōn*] and sin [*ḥaṭṭa't*]?
> Let me know my guilt [*peša'*] and sin [*ḥaṭṭa't*].

In 14.16–17, the order of the sin words is reversed:

> But now you count my steps,
> do not guard my sin [*ḥaṭṭa't*].
> My guilt [*peša'*] is sealed in a bag,
> and you smear across my fault ['*awōn*].

Job's idea of an interim after death has vanished under the pressure of presumed guilt.

He now sees how things greater than trees have an end. However contrary to appearance, mountains and rocks too are limited (vv. 18–19). Mountains "fall," the water that gives new life to the tree (v. 9a) "wears away stone" (v. 19a) and overflows the "dust of earth" ('*apar-'ereṣ*), where the tree is renewed (see *'ereṣ* and '*apar*, v. 8), and it "destroys a man's hope" (*tiqwah*, cf. v. 7a). "Water," "dust," and "hope" in v. 19 are in reversed order of the same words in verses 7–9, emphasizing how negative the analogy of the tree has now become, how brief was the thought that the human might be more like a tree than Job had first supposed. Zophar was wrong when he assured Job that he could "trust that hope is there" (11.18).

The hopeless human is subdued and sent off, kept in ignorance of the future. His flesh, as Job said neither positively nor negatively in 12.10, is in the deity's hand. Now that hand gives only pain. To be in the hands of the god is to be not only in contrast but in opposition to the god. Job is the god's enemy; *'Iyyōb* has definitively become *'ōyēb*.

Eliphaz (Chapter 15)

Eliphaz is more concerned with language here than he was in his first speech. He has heard "windy knowledge," and he will not respond with the hot air of a primal belch (the east wind in Palestine is hot off the desert). Job's legal talk (*ykḥ*, "argue," v. 3a) is profitless, and his guileful mouth increases his culpability (v. 5). Indeed, Job's wish for a trial is self-defeating, because Job himself is the prosecution's star witness, ensuring a guilty verdict with every word he speaks. Eliphaz thoroughly agrees with Job's complaint about the prospective trial in 9.14–20, except that Job was sure the perception of his guilt was mistaken, and Eliphaz finds it entirely correct.

Eliphaz has changed his tune since 4.6, when he was sure that Job's "religion" (*yir'ah*) was ground for confidence. He criticizes Job's language now not merely because it demonstrates guilt, but because it "breaks up" (*tapēr*) religion (v. 4, *yir'ah*, "fear [of the god]," as in 1.1; 4.6, and elsewhere) and undermines what Eliphaz calls "complaint" (*śīḥah*). Job uses cognates of that word several times,[12] but only here does anyone else. The basic notion in the word is concern, being busied with something, interested in it. Sometimes the noun signifies "meditation" or "pondering,"[13] and in Ps 55.18 (Eng. 17) the verb, in tandem with *hmh*, "to moan," points to something like "complain." I translated it so in Job's bitter outcry in Job 7.11 and 13, and that connotation is present here. If Job casts these religion-destroying complaints at the deity, normally pious people will find it more difficult, Eliphaz thinks, to have their just objections heard.

Bildad suggested (8.8–10) that Job consult past generations, and Job responded by proposing to go even further back, to the beasts of creation (12.7–10). In 15.9–10, Eliphaz alludes to Bildad's thought, counting himself and the other two in those earlier generations. Before that, he asks the question, both sarcastic and portentous:

> Were you born the first human,
> brought forth before the hills?
> Do you listen in Eloah's council,
> restrict wisdom to yourself? (vv. 7–8)

Eliphaz wonders whether Job claims to be the primal human, living before the creator had completed the landscape. Adam is the exemplar most familiar to us of this widespread myth. Eliphaz's scorn suggests that it is silly for Job to entertain such grandiose thoughts about himself.

When Eliphaz asks (v. 8) whether Job sits in the divine council, he points to the assembly in chaps. 1–2, in which we heard the discussion between Yahweh and the Prosecutor. Some of the prophets claim to listen in it.[14] Eliphaz is asking whether Job thinks of himself as a prophet, who confines wisdom to himself.[15] He is still on the subject of language: the prophet communicates the word that the divine council commissions, and the wise deal conventionally in language.

Moreover, by comparing his own knowledge and that of the friends favorably to Job's knowledge (vv. 9–10), Eliphaz both indulges in mockery of an "anything you can do I can do better" sort and continues his talk about language. He criticizes Job for not taking seriously what the god is telling him.

> Are El's consolations too slight for you,
> the gentle word against you? (15.11)

Does Eliphaz actually mean that question, or is it ironic? If it is irony, Eliphaz knows that "consolations" ill defines what both he and Job assume the deity has done to Job. Not only does the situation present no "gentle word" to Job, even though Zophar proposed in 11.6 that it is gentler than Job deserves, it presents no "word" at all. It is hardly surprising that Job talks wildly and windily (15.13). If this is irony, Eliphaz is simply insensitive.

But if he seriously proposes that the deity is both consoling and kind to Job, he is witless, while accusing Job of irrationality. Edouard Dhorme suggests that Eliphaz accommodates all the deity's words to the "whisper" that he himself heard and recounted in 4.12, when he heard Job's bellowing (3.24) as an excessive reaction.[16] In Eliphaz's next speech (chap. 22), we will see that he overreacts. Here perhaps he underreacts.

He reverts to the kind of generality that we have heard from him before. Verses 15.14–15 are very like the vision in 4.17–18 and the reference to the "holy ones" in 5.1. The issue is again "innocence" (*ṣdq*) and "purity" (*zkh*). But 15.14 alludes to Job's parody in 7.17 of Psalm 8 and the divine attention to humans: "What is a man?" (*mah-'ᵉnōš*). The deity does not trust even "his holy ones,"[17] and the sky itself is not "pure" (15.15). It is hard to think that Eliphaz would hold that the god is contemptuous of the creation, yet he says something very like it, both here and in chap. 4. Difference from the god, inferiority to the god, both are somehow opposition to him. The idea approaches the depravity in certain forms of the Christian idea of Original Sin, and it poses the same problem for the human object of the divine contempt: no one could want intimacy with a deity like that.

Clutching to himself the generality that human purity and innocence are ridiculous, Eliphaz tries to make Job a special case, "horrible and corrupt," worse than what usually arouses the deity's contempt (15.16). It seems that Eliphaz has begun once more to overreact. When he promises again to tell Job the results of his "seeing" (v. 17b), we must recall how, when he claimed in 4.8 and 5.3 to have "seen" the truth, it turned out on examination to be untrustworthy. Nothing in Eliphaz's performance so far encourages us to expect anything different here.

Indeed, we are treated to another instance of the topos of the anguish of the wicked (15.20–24). Everything goes wrong for them: "terrible sounds" (v. 21a), destruction just when health is restored (v. 21b), constant darkness (vv. 22a, 23b), hunger (v. 23a), and "strain and stress" (*ṣar* and *m^eṣūqah*) and imminent attack (v. 24). It is a terrible life, and much too long (v. 20b).

Suddenly, at verse 25, Eliphaz drastically changes the texture of this life. He shifts from passive images (vv. 20–24) of unpleasant things suffered by the "knave" to active images of aggressive rebellion. The wicked person dashes into battle against the deity, "neck held high" (vv. 25–26), lives amid the signs of overweening prosperity, greasy-skinned and obese (v. 27). What that prosperity is temporary (vv. 28b–c, 29), that the reckoning will come (v. 30)? Even if well-being is but an interlude, it is not at all the unrelieved suffering that verses 20–24 present. Eliphaz confounds himself in verse 30 by saying almost simultaneously that the wicked will not escape from darkness (v. 30a) and that he will escape "with the wind in his mouth" (v. 30c), either battling into the face of a gale or with no possession but his breath.[18] Eliphaz proves to be consistent: when he claims to have seen, he is not to be trusted.

The "escaping" seems to lead Eliphaz to describe the outcome as "stumbling vanity" and an "exchange" that comes out to emptiness (*šaw'*, v. 31b), which he ironically suggests will be prematurely "filled" (v. 32a). He labors toward his close through a tangle of uncomfortable metaphors, similes, and images. The prematurity in verse 32 allows him the image of plants sloughing off their early fruit (v. 33), which justifies a metaphor of "sterility" and thus the cliché of tents consumed by fire (v. 34). The cliché is gratuitous, for in verse 35 Eliphaz reverses the metaphor of sterility, with "conceiving" toil (*'amal*; cf. his unhappy use of the word in 4.8b), "bearing" (*yld*, "childbirth") guilt, and nurturing ("foster," *takīn*) deceit.

The entire speech contains not a single word of encouragement, comfort, or hope. In his earlier speech, Eliphaz took pains to assure Job—ambiguously, I argued—that his situation was not hopeless. Nothing here can be construed to mean that. Not only does he criticize directly the bad results Job obtains for others (v. 4) and for himself by his talk (vv. 5–6), he even makes Job the outstanding instance of corruption in a corrupt universe (v. 16). It appears that Eliphaz has given up on Job's rehabilitation.[19]

Job (Chapters 16–17)

In the second cycle, the speakers do not allude to each other as much as they did in the first cycle. There I noted a dialogue, somewhat submerged, in which the friends and Job responded to each other by indirect allusion and reference to what others had said.

It is not that there is none here. In 16.2–3, Job turns Eliphaz's description in 15.35a of wicked folks as "conceiving toil" (*'amal*) back on him, castigating the friends as "troublesome [*'amal*] comforters." Calling their words "windy" (v. 3) echoes Eliphaz's implicit condemnation in 15.2 of his wisdom as "windy." Job makes his physical condition a witness in his trial:

> My emaciation rises against me,
> testifies against me. (16.8b–c)

It seems a direct rejection of Eliphaz's cutting statement:

> Your mouth condemns you, not I,
> your lips testify against you. (15.6)

Job's suffering is evidence of the injustice of the attack upon him, and he will not agree that his own words are the best evidence of his guilt. He admitted earlier that what he says, no matter what it may be, effectively condemns him:

> If I'm innocent, my own mouth condemns me;
> if I'm perfect, he'll do me fraud. (9.20)

It is not right, however, that that should be so.

Again, Job's description in 16.14b of the god's "running against" (*rwṣ 'al*) him "like a warrior" is the direct opposite of Eliphaz's image of the rebel, "playing the hero," who "runs toward" (*rwṣ 'el*) the god (15.26). And his claim in 16.17b that his "prayer is pure" (*zakkah*) denies Eliphaz's implication in 15.14:

> What is a man, that he can be pure [*yizkeh*]?

Perhaps Job's "witness" (16.19–21) also alludes to Eliphaz. That personage will, Job hypothesizes,

decide for a hero against Eloah,
between Adam and his friend. (v.21)

We shall consider later the relation between this Adam and Eliphaz's primal human:

Were you born the first human,
brought forth before the hills? (15.7)

Finally, Job may allude to Zophar's parting shot in 11.20, that wicked people's "only hope is to breathe their last." We have seen how 14.7, "for a tree there is hope," refers to the idea. But discouragement sets in at the end of this speech when he "hope[s] for Sheol as [his] home" (17.13), an ironic reversal that may refer to Zophar.

These references and allusions are fewer in number and less subtle and powerful than were the earlier ones. Perhaps in the second cycle Job and the friends increasingly talk not to each other but past each other. Many scholars argue that the entire dialogue is presented in just that fashion, but if the first cycle is more nearly dialogical than the second, it is another indication that the poem is not conceptually or dramatically static.

The other noticeable factor in this speech is the paucity of Job's remarks to the god. In earlier speeches, except for chap. 3, he always speaks directly to the deity, usually at about the middle of the speech, complaining or requesting some special attention. This speech has one couplet of address at 16.7b–8a:

You've desolated my whole company,
have seized me to be a witness;

and a quatrain in 17.3–4 (the proverb after it does not address the god):

Put up my guarantee against you!
Who is he who'll bargain with me?
Because you've closed their minds to insight,
therefore, you'll not be exalted.

I take these as statements to the deity because they are in the second-person singular. But, however important they are, they are much less in scope and extent than what we have heard before. There is another one-line address to the god, invisible in English because we gave up "thou" as a second-person singular. In v. 3b, Job wonders how much the god hurts. Given Job's pain and the god's total silence, the question, flung at him and dropped, is devastatingly sarcastic. From this speech on, except for a brief address to the god almost exactly in the middle of his last speech (30.20–23), and the two responses to Yahweh's speeches in 40.4–5 and 42.2–6, Job addresses the god very seldom and only in quick snatches, sometimes no more than a single line.[20]

Job begins this speech by talking about talk, as Eliphaz had done before. He discusses the friends' talk (16.3–4), how he would talk were they where he is (vv. 4–5), and his actual talk and silence (vv. 6–7a). The disparities among these various kinds of talk point up the irony of the entire dialogue. They are "troublesome" comforters, their words are "windy." But if Job sat where they sit, he would on the one hand talk as they do ("I could pile up words against you," v. 4c), but on the other hand he would do what their talk fails to do, "assuage" pain, "strengthen" them (v. 5). But perhaps verse 5 is ironic, and Job realizes that in their place his words would be as windy as theirs are. His own speech and silence work no miracles to assuage his pain.

At verse 7b, Job stops talking about talk and addresses the god in legal terms. The "desolating" of his "company" is the basic accusation, to which Job will return later. The phrase doubtless refers to the destruction of his family as well as to his alienation from other people in the community (e.g., 16.10–11; 17.2, 6–9; and, more powerfully, 19.13–19). The context seems to be the trial that Job both wants and does not want, in which he will be forced to be a witness. "[You] have seized me to be a witness" (16.8) surely indicates involuntary testimony.

That brings him to abandon legal language for images of attack, not merely psychic but physical (vv. 9–14). The unassuageable "pain" is doubtless the source of these images, along with the god's painless "hurt" (v. 3b), and they continue the ways in which the friends cause him pain (vv. 2b, 4) and in which his own talk increases it (v. 6). He describes the god's attack first in the metaphor of the wild animal (v. 9a–b), who "tears" as a beast of prey (*ṭrp*; cf. Gen 37.33 among many passages), and then in the astonishing picture of the attacker "whetting his eyes" (v. 9c).[21] The metaphor shifts to mob violence by the hands of "knaves" (*r^e^šaʿîm*, vv. 10–11) and to the god's direct military assault (vv. 12–14) upon the victim. The attacker must be the deity: the verbs are singular, and the surrounding troops are mere silent onlookers. The god personally damages Job, his neck (v. 12) and his guts (v. 13); he is a charging warrior (v. 14b).

This assault is, to say the least, vicious, and Job's passive response (vv. 15–17) is surprising. But it is consistent with his exhaustion (v. 7a), and the imagery takes us back before the picture of the attack. The "horn" (v. 15b) is a conventional symbol of strength, doubtless derived from conventional symbols of power such as the bull or the wild ox,[22] and its relation to the animal images reminds us, by the very opposite significance, of the animal metaphor in verse 9a–b. Here the horn is "thrust . . . in the dust," the strength rendered weakness. By the same token, Job's darkened "eyelids" (v. 16b) are the opposite of the enemy's "whetted eyes" (v. 9c). His statement of innocence in verse 17 completes a chiastic structure in verses 7b–17, diagrammable as follows:

A. Job as witness in trial (vv. 7b–8)
B. The god as animal (v. 9)
C. Mob violence (vv. 10–11)
C′. The god on the attack (vv. 12–14)
B′. Job's animal passivity (vv. 15–16)
A′. Job's legal statement of innocence (v. 17)

This divine attack pushes Job to a new high point in his wish for vindication. In an apostrophe he calls on Earth (*'ereṣ*) not to conceal evidence of his unjust murder. The thought is that, by preserving the trace of the murdered person's blood, Earth herself gives evidence of the event. Just as Yahweh says to Cain in Genesis 4.10: "The voice of your brother's blood is crying out to me from the ground," Job asks Earth not to hide his blood's evidence nor to permit his "outcry" (*za'ᵃqah*) to rest.[23] The attack upon the hero may provide evidence contrary to that of the victim's condition (Job 16.8), which could turn the trial to justice.

But Earth is not the sole witness. Job makes the remarkable affirmation that another witness is available to him, a "supporter" in the very presence of the god who can deal with the god on Job's behalf.[24] This passage is an advance on the earlier third party, the "arbiter" (*mōkīaḥ*) whose presence Job denied in 9.33 (see Chapter 3 above). "Even now" (*gam 'attah*), he says, the witness is there, and he not only can "interpret" Job (v. 20a) but is empowered to decide in the case (v. 21). The verb is *ykḥ*, a term we have met before denoting both arguing cases and deciding them.[25]

The case has some ambiguities. The "hero" (*geber*) for whom the witness decides "against Eloah" (*'im-'ᵉlōah*) seems clearly to be Job. But the parallel line, "between Adam and his friend" (*ūbēn-'adam lᵉrē'ēhū*), appears to imply two different cases, for in verse 21a the case is decided "for" the *geber* and "against" (*'im*) the god, whereas in verse 21b, it is decided "between" Adam (or a human being or humankind) and "his friend" (*rē'ēhū*).[26] Three questions surface immediately:

1. Is the referent of "Adam"
   a. the Adam of myth (Gen 2–4),

   b. the human race (*'adam*), or
   c. an unspecified (or specified) human being?
2. Is "his friend"
   a. "Adam's" in any of the three senses above,
   b. Job's,
   c. Eloah's, or
   d. the witness's?
3. Is that "friend"
   a. a companion, associate, fellow, or
   b. a "partner" in the wished-for trial, in other words, not a friend but the "opponent"?[27]

Problems enough to keep one occupied for a long time and, were it necessary to conclude firmly and finally for "the truth," a daunting prospect.

One can make sense of most of the options above in their various combinations. Let me try just a few:

1. "Between a human, any human, and his fellow." Banal, and, I think, the consensus of scholars, but acceptable. The "witness" decides about the *geber* against the god just as he would decide an ordinary human dispute. That is a banal trivialization of the witness, because in verses 18–20 Job urges a quite special connection between himself and this supporter and interpreter.

2. "Between Adam and his friend." Here Job seems to accept Eliphaz's mocking identification of him in 15.7 with the "first human" and turns it back on Eliphaz. The witness will decide not only the dispute between the human and the god but also that between the Primal Human, Job himself, and his mocking friend, Eliphaz (and, by extension, the other two). Alternatively, if "his" refers to Eloah, then presumably Eliphaz and the other two are meant, and the sense is approximately the same.

3. "Between a human and (the witness's) friend." Job is the witness's friend, as he claimed in verse 20a. The witness, then, will again decide between those humans present (one or all) and his special friend. If Eliphaz and the others think that they have special standing with the god, they are in for a surprise when Job's witness brings them to their own trial.

4. "Between Adam and his opponent." We know who the opponent must be: the deity. The question is whether this "Adam" is the same as the "hero" in v. 21a, namely Job, or not. If it is, Job adopts the Primal Human reference to himself. If not, he generalizes his dispute against the god to the human race, and "Adam" stands for the problems all human beings have with that deity's justice.

Doubtless other readings of the line are conceivable. I rule out very few, but it seems unnecessary to expound every possibility. Nor will I choose among those noted above. Even the most banal of them, the first, is a real choice. But on any of these readings of the witness's functions, this party clearly has power exceeding that of the deity. It was also the case with the "arbiter" in 9.33, who could "lay his hand on us both." But the thought of the arbiter disappeared as soon as it appeared. The witness is "even now" up there at work. We will see the theme again.

The high emotion of verses 18–21 drains quickly away to deep discouragement in 16.22–17.2. The language of time running out (16.22a; 17.1), years and days and the one-way path to the grave, recalls the feeling of chap. 3, though 17.2 leaves it unclear whether Job wishes for death. That couplet is an oath formula, which appears to be a solemnized description of Job's situation.

In verses 3–4, Job addresses the god again, demanding a guarantee (v. 3a). Exactly what the guarantee is remains uncertain, though analogous uses of the verb suggest something similar to a bail bond (e.g., Gen 43.9; Prov 11.15).[28] Job's memory seems to be short when he asks, "Who is he who'll clap my hand?" (v. 3b) The question seems to mean "Who else (than the deity) would make an agreement with me?" and it stems from the complaint about ever-present mockeries and bitterness (v. 2). Has Job forgotten his "witness"? The description in 16.19–21 would make us expect that he would rush to Job's aid in just this way. But the quatrain in 17.3–4 has the tone of a demand with no real strength behind it, a sort of formulaic feistiness. Job's heart seems not to be in it.

His criticism of the deity in verse 4 for closing the friends' minds appears at the least impolitic if it demands that the god give him legal guarantees. He has postulated a witness to overcome the god at his own legal game. Still, the statement is forthright in content, and the threat of withheld "exaltation," set about with the logical marker "therefore," may allude to the "witness's" hypothetical success. Had the god not sent the dim-witted friends as his emissaries to argue the matter out, he might deserve better at Job's hands. Anyway Job has no high opinion of the consistency or quality of the god's activity, and I think the odd proverb in verse 5 points to just that assessment:

> He tells his friends about his profits,
> and his children's eyes are failing.

The couplet has engendered much comment, and no one sees it just as I do,[29] as the heedless inconsistency of a man who brags about his winnings in the stock market while his children starve at home. The god fails to perceive reality.

This address to the god is soon over, and Job speaks to him very rarely from this point on. At verse 6 he reverts to third-person description of the god in the theme of mockery from verse 2. It is interesting that both here and after the earlier brief address to the god (16.7b–8), Job turns immediately to a description of the deity's attacks upon him. In 17.6b–7 as in 16.15–16, Job couches his response in terms of parts of his body ("skin," "face," "eyelids" in 16.15–16; "face," "eye," "limbs" in 17.6–7).

Job's sarcasm against the friends rises in temperature in verses 8–10.[30] Referring to people in general, he clearly aims first of all at the friends. Good people are not only shocked at Job's distress but are moved to oppress those who, as they think, deserve to suffer. When a man like Job suffers, dogmatically pure folks harden their dogmatism. It is the same contempt for the sufferer that Job has noted before (12.5), and it rests on the same fear that Job perceived in the friends' eyes (6.21).[31] More useful to Job than such "moral," "innocent," "cleanhanded" people would be only one wise one. But he knows better than to expect to find one (v. 10).

Now discouragement takes full control. Job has roused himself several times in this speech from what seems almost lethargy, and in the middle, at 16.18, he rose to high energy. But in 17.11–16 he echoes the time language of verse 1, the dispirited wish to be alone of 10.20, the reversal of creation of chap. 3, the oxymoronic hope for death of chaps. 6, 7, and 10. The profoundly ironic references to "hope" (vv. 13, 15) dominate the expectation of death in 17.13–16 and underscore the chilling intimacies of calling the "muck" (cf. 9.31) "father" and welcoming the grave's maggots as "mother, sister." This image of death as dust and darkness, present at the ends of Job's preceding three speeches (7.21; 10:21–22; 14.18–22) seems somehow further down here, closer to despair if not given over to it.

Bildad (Chapter 18)

Job predicted in 17.8–9 that his outburst would anger the friends. It is harder to think that it would utterly confuse them, but Bildad begins almost unintelligibly. The verbs in verse 2 and the second-person pronoun in verse 3b are plural.[32] Bildad criticizes his unspecified interlocutors for delaying the friends' speaking ("we," v. 2b) by an uncomprehending babble (v. 2) and for acting as if those friends ("we," v. 3) were stupid animals. That Bildad would say something like that to Job is understandable, but we expect him to address Job in the singular. Perhaps he is so upset that he forgets his grammar and the number of persons before him.

If he is addressing the other two friends, the "we" in verses 2b and 3a is difficult. Angry perhaps that they have not so demolished Job's arguments as to prevent Job's reaching the outlandish position he has just stated, Bildad criticizes the way Eliphaz's and Zophar's arguments have delayed his own intervention and castigates their supercilious attitude toward himself (we must postulate an editorial plural on this reading, unless Bildad includes Job with himself in v. 3). If Bildad is talking to Eliphaz and Zophar in this rather surly beginning, he demonstrates a rift in what has seemed unanimity among the friends.[33] They have not directly disagreed among themselves, though examination of the position of each would suggest that they might find some points to argue about.

The strangeness of the opening is emphasized, not diminished, by Bildad's addressing Job in the singular in verse 4, though only in the second line is it evident ("on your [singular] account"). The first line is in the third person. It is as if Bildad must push Job off into third-person distance before he can allow himself the second-person pronoun in the second line. That pronoun, moreover, is Bildad's only direct address to Job in the entire speech. Everything else is descriptive, including Job only by contextual implication. This failure to speak to Job is eloquent of the friends' inability or unwillingness to come directly to grips with his reading of reality.[34] Like Eliphaz, Bildad proffers not a word of assurance or of positive expectations for Job.

He picks up interestingly on his image of the stupid cattle in verse 4, when he describes Job as a beast of prey (*ṭōrēp*) that preys upon itself (*napšō*) in its anger. The description echoes Job's complaint about the god in 16.9: "His anger tears" (*'appō ṭarap*). "No," says Bildad, "your own anger tears at you, and you do all the damage to yourself." The rhetorical question that follows rather obliquely continues the thought and the image. A beast of prey on the rampage would cause a territory to "be abandoned," but Job, tearing only at himself, would not empty even a small area, let alone "earth." Bildad quotes Job (14.18) to extend his ridicule of Job's pretensions: "A rock disintegrates from its place!" Job ought not to dignify himself by the metaphor.

This denigration of the sufferer, I think, explains the sudden shift to the image of extinguished lights in 18.5–6. The image proposes the same limitations upon Job's magniloquent claims as those of the beast of prey and the rock in verse 4. Job is not as important as he makes out. Eliphaz made the point when he asked whether Job were "born the first human"

(15.7). But Bildad is still having trouble distinguishing plural from singular. "Knaves" in 18.5a is plural, but the confusing relations among "fire" (v. 5b), "tent" (v. 6a), and "beacon" (v. 6b) throw the images into disarray. "His" tent in verse 6 might turn the plural knaves in verse 5 into only one, who might be Job. Just as Job sometimes generalizes his situation into a human one, so perhaps Bildad's abstract account wishes to particularize it to Job. But he does it without clarity.

He returns implicitly to the metaphor of the beast of prey with an elaborate conceit (vv. 7–10) on trapping. Beginning with the theme that the sufferer brings suffering on himself (v. 7), he proceeds to list every term for an animal trap of which he can think.[35] A rather unsuccessful pun between *šlk* and *šlḥ* ("fling" and "flung," vv. 7b, 8a) interrupts a series of images of walking, bracketed by the noun *ṣaʿad* ("strides") in verse 7a and the verb *ṣʿd* ("marched off") in verse 14. Between them are "feet" (vv. 8a, 11b), "heel" (v. 9a),[36] and "limbs" (v. 13), and verbs of "walking" (v. 8b), "chasing" (v. 11b), and "stumbling" (v. 12b). Bildad transmutes the image of walking, which the Hebrew Bible often uses for the conduct and character of life, into a musing on entrapment and death.

The image of trapping is interrupted by "shiver" (v. 11a), an image of sickness that leads into death (vv. 12–14). The dead person's absence lends poignance to the picture of the tent occupied by someone else (v. 15a) and the "shanty" (*naweh*, see 5.3b) ritually purified and rendered uninhabitable by sulfur. Bildad spices up still another metaphor of the wicked person as a dying plant (18.16) with alliteration:

mittaḥat šorašaw yībašū	Underneath his roots dry up,
ūmimmaʿal yimmal qeṣīrō	and up above his twigs wither away.

The dying plant merges in verses 17–19 with the dying wicked person, who is the subject of all of this. Bildad's images of dead plants, unlike Job's in chaps. 16–17, do not move between negative and positive but are only negative. The very "memory" (*zēker*) of this dead person perishes from earth. Earth, then, is precisely not "abandoned on [his] account" (v. 4b), but he is forced to abandon earth, is eliminated from memory, nameless, chased from the world (*tēbēl*), deprived of survivors. A more hopeless picture of human desolation is hard to imagine. The ancient world, expecting no future life, laid all hope for the future on one's descendants' memory, and Bildad summarily rips that hope away from Job.

Beginning at 18.5 with the extinction of light, this speech sets out a series of images of disintegration: light turning to darkness, the strong animal trapped, the strong man enfeebled by sickness and marched to death, dwelling and memory dissolved. "A rock disintegrates from its place!" It seemed at 18.4c that Bildad exhibited Job's statement in scorn, but as his speech goes on, he seems the more to illustrate it.

Finally, as he alludes in verse 20a to Job's opening curse on "his day" (3.1), he contradicts his preceding picture of the loss of memory and survivors. His subject's dissolution has suddenly become notorious worldwide, from west to east, and throughout time, from future to past.[37] The "dwellings," dissolved in verses 15–16, suddenly return as "evil dwellings." Multiple images are wonderfully intelligible if they move interestingly from one angle of vision on the subject to another. But Bildad's images blatantly contradict one another.

This is all the more visible when Bildad closes with "the place that doesn't know El" (v. 21b). On the surface, the "place," echoing that "place" from which "the rock disintegrates" (v. 4c), is a metonymy for persons in the place who do not know the god. But we are reminded of the strange plural address at the opening, which, it seemed then, referred at least in part to the friends. "When will you understand?" he said. He comes perilously close to admitting that the friends fall under the dissolution he has so vividly portrayed.

Job (Chapter 19)

I pointed out above how seldom in this cycle of speeches one speaker alludes or refers to something another speaker has said. But Job begins (19.2) with a repetition of Bildad's opening particles: *'ad-'an* (8.2) and *'ad-'anah* (18.2), "How long?" One can well imagine Job's using a parodying tone of voice, for his prefatory quatrain is both querulous and indignant. It is also exaggerated: "These ten times you've insulted me" (v. 3a). The nitpicker will say it has been only five times.[38] At any rate, Job is feeling put-upon: "pained, pulverized, insulted," and something else that we cannot be sure of.[39]

Much of the rest of this relatively short speech revolves around images of distance and closeness, of travel and staying at home. Job begins with a curiously mixed, self-contradictory metaphor of travel:

> Have I truly strayed?
> My straying stays at home with me. (v. 4)

"To stray" (*šgh*) is often a metaphor for error, and Job asked the friends in 6.24 to show him wherein he had strayed, how he was in error. Here, provisionally accepting the notion that he has strayed, he adds to it the unusual image of "lodging" (*lyn*), as if his own "error" were his house guest.

The next stanza (vv. 8–12) piles up the travel images, with "blocked" roads that one cannot pass (v. 8), the divine devastation around the walker (v. 10a), the "gangs" and their highway building (v. 12), conjoined with their encampment "all around" (*sabīb*, cf. v. 10a) his tent, the image of home again juxtaposed with images of the journey. Job experiences the god's attacks again, as he did in 16.11, 13, feeling his anger and being the object of his platoons.[40] "He considers me like his foes" (v. 11b), a sentiment like the plaintive question in 13.24b, which has ceased to be plaintive. The image of travel in the building of the highway by those gangs who "encamp all around my tent" (19.12) becomes an image of military operations, clearing a track for the army to pass in order to undertake siege operations against the enemy. But the object of all these military attentions, Job points out, is merely his "tent."[41]

Job even absolves the friends from being the source of his difficulties. After the indignant opening, he glances ironically in passing at their "boasts" and their easy "decision" about his disgrace (v. 5). El is the one who has "bent" him,[42] who has "circled his net over" him (v. 6; cf. Bildad's trapping images, 18.8–10). His outcry "Violence!" (*ḥamas*), appropriate in reference to the legal language about the friends in 19.5b,[43] has at least as much to do with the hunting and trapping god, who neither answers nor provides justice (v. 7). He deprives Job of "honor" and its emblem, the "crown" (*ʿaṭeret*, v. 9). The symbol may be an exaggeration, though later Job describes himself as a king among troops (29.25) and claims something like a crown (*ʿaṭarōt*, 31.36b). At the least, such status as he has is "stripped" from him. In the metaphor of his hope's being uprooted (19.10b), he reverses his earlier image of the tree as a sign of hope (14.7–9).

The images of distance take a psychic turn in the remarkable complaint of 19.13–19. Job begins with the "causative" (Hiphʿil) stem of the verb *rḥq*, "to be distant," in verse 13a, making "distance" not a noun but a transitive verb. Associates, relatives, and inferiors who were once close—brothers, acquaintances, and visitors (vv. 13–14), strangers given hospitality (v. 15a), male and female slaves (vv. 15b–16), immediate family (v. 17), social inferiors (v. 18) and social equals (v. 19)—are now, by the god's agency, far.

Perhaps such a list of persons alienated from the sufferer was a convention of lament. The Babylonian poem *Ludlul bēl nēmeqi* (I will praise the lord of wisdom) contains the following lament:

To my many relations I am like a recluse.
If I walk the street, ears are pricked;
If I enter the palace, eyes blink.

My city frowns on me as an enemy;
Indeed my land is savage and hostile.
My friend has become foe,
My companion has become a wretch and a devil.
In his savagery my comrade denounces me,
Constantly my associates furbish their weapons.
My intimate friend has brought my life into danger;
My slave has publicly cursed me in the assembly.
My house . . . , the mob has defamed me.
When my acquaintance sees me, he passes by on the other side.
My family treat me as an alien.
The pit awaits anyone who speaks well of me,
While he who utters defamation of me is promoted.
(Tablet I, ll. 79–94)[44]

The poem continues with more complaint. Analogous passages appear in what scholars call "individual lament" psalms,[45] but Job's outburst is more elaborate.

Job's complaint is full of rhetorical touches. His acquaintances ("those who know me") have become foreign (*zwr* II, 19.13), whereas "strangers in [his] house" have forgotten him (having presumably known him before, v. 15a). But the maids think of him as "alien" (*zar*) and a "foreigner" (*nokrī*, v. 15c), which they would be expected to think of the "stranger (*gēr*) in the house." The slave reverses his relationship with Job by refusing his commands (v. 16), as do the "young," who "despise" and "heckle" him rather than respecting him (v. 18). His wife recoils from his "stinking" breath (*zwr*, a pun with the similar verb in v. 13b). Most surprising of all, Job refers to his "children" (v. 17b). Has he forgotten that they are dead? Does the convention of the lament require reference to them regardless of the facts? I know of no way to decide between those alternatives, and I can think of no third.[46]

The distance of which Job complains is suddenly replaced by three images of unbearable closeness: bones "cling" (*dbq*) to skin and flesh (v. 20);[47] the god's hand "touches" (*ngʿ*, v. 21);[48] both the friends and the god "pursue" Job (v. 22). Yet in the midst of these images is the poignant plea to the friends for a human closeness that has been missing:

Pity, oh pity me, you my friends. (v. 21a)

Job has virtually stopped talking directly to the god, and sarcastic invective is nearly all he has to say to the friends. But he so desperately needs a touch of kindness that he even drops his independence for a moment in quest of it. The lapse is brief.

But the emotion remains high. Job repeats the formulaic "Would that" in the two lines of verse 23 and adds to the first the emphatic and untranslatable particle *'ēpō*. The expression "would that" is originally the question "Who gives?" (*mī-yittēn*). Doubtless that sense of *mī-yittēn* dropped from Israelite minds long before the Book of Job was written.

The images of motion taken and blocked (vv. 4–12), the psychic distance of human associates (vv. 13–19), and the poignant lament over painful interior and exterior closeness (vv. 20–22) point to a profoundly changed situation and to change itself as the essence of Job's suffering. He shifts radically to an image of permanence:

> Would that my words were written,
> would that they were engraved in an inscription,
> with an iron stylus and lead
> forever in rock they were incised. (vv. 23–24)

Notice the ascending order of permanence. Writing is not necessarily permanent, but it persists longer than speech, which dies away in the air. Writing "engraved [*yuḥaqū*] in an inscription [*sēper*]" is more permanent than what is written on the surface of perishable leather, wood, or papyrus.[49] And this writing is to be "forever" (*la'ad*): "incised" (*ḥṣb*) in rock with an iron tool (*'ēt*), with the incised letters filled with lead.[50] Job wants a massive, public inscription, legible from great distances and impossible to efface. He is anxious, as he was in 16.18, that his complaint not be lost. There he called on Earth itself to testify to the blood of the slain martyr. Here he wants the "words" never to be lost, the testimony not of a mute fact but of the unmistakable meaning of his story. If words are to last, they must be written, not merely spoken.

The irony is, of course, that Job's words *are* written, are nothing but written. The thought of reclaiming an "original," spoken Job is impossible, an unthinkable thought. But the second irony of the writing is that, however permanent the words may be, they remain as ambiguous as ever. Incise them, engrave them, fill the hollow spaces of the letters with lead—or with gold or cinder slag—and the meanings of the marks will go on eluding everyone who reads. That is the case, even though Job has his wish, that his words be permanent, written, engraved, incised.

The irony deepens when we come to what he says next. If only we could decipher verses 25–27. Without rewriting what is written, I cannot, except for the first line:

> As for me, I know that my avenger lives.

Even so, the hazard is to think one can say too much. Most readers will recognize the line as "I know that my Redeemer liveth," familiar from

Handel's *Messiah*. The familiarity is much of the problem. Not only is the following context lost to me, but the line is heavily invested with meaning and associations by generations of a cultural tradition.

For reasons I explain in the annotation, the central word is not "redeemer," and especially it is not "Redeemer." Some may not distinguish the former from the latter, though the lowercase word may entail a less direct allusion to Jesus than does the capitalized version. At least in our culture, a "redeemer" might signify anyone who redeems anything, whereas "Redeemer" would naturally be taken unambiguously. But Christian theology can hardly be called in to pronounce on this statement for the reason that in Job's sentence the *gō'ēl* furthers the terrible opposition between Job and the god. Christianity classically understands its Redeemer as restoring guilty humans to unity with their god. Christians who wish to use Job 19.25 can do so only by taking it as at best a misunderstanding of the Christian Redeemer, at worst an anti-Redeemer, exhibiting what Christians believe in by its opposite.

Not only has Job admitted no guilt, he has hardly contemplated that such guilt as he might have is in any degree significant. His problem, as we saw in chaps. 16–17 and in the earlier part of this one, is not that the god has attempted to woo him back but that he has viciously attacked him, "circling his net over" Job (19.6), "pouring [his] gall on the ground" (16.13). It would be strange indeed if, just here, when the height of his emotion is expressed in the desire for a permanent monument to the god's injustice, Job should turn to a thought incompatible with his entire set of mind.[51]

Yet any interpretation, no matter what its religious orientation, that identifies the *gō'ēl*, the "avenger," with the deity falls afoul of the same problem. If Job reverses his direction now, of all times, he stands to lose not only our comprehension but also our respect. No, the avenger is a figure born of the desperation of Job's sense that the god "considers me like his foes" (19.11b), a figure who reminds us of two earlier ones:

> There's no arbiter [*mōkīaḥ*] between us
> to lay his hand on us both. (9.33)

And:

> Even now, Ah! my witness is in heaven,
> my supporter is on high,
> my interpreter, my friend, to Eloah—
> my eyes are sleepless—
> and he will decide for a hero against Eloah,
> between Adam and his friend. (16.19–21)

The "arbiter" could intervene between the two parties to the dispute, treat them as equally subordinate to himself ("lay his hand on us both"), and solve the problem. But the arbiter was a wisp of imagination, for all Job said of him was "There's no arbiter between us." The "witness" is more serious, for immediately after the apostrophe to Earth not to cover up his unjustly shed blood, Job affirms that his "witness, supporter, interpreter, friend" is there in the very presence of the god, possessed of the power to decide in the controversy. Job cannot imagine that the decision could go in any direction but his own. He makes a more serious move with the *gō'ēl*. This is an "avenger of blood," who will take vengeance on the enemy for the damage done to the sufferer. The *gō'ēl* is the opposite of the god who, Job said, "runs against me like a warrior" (16.14b).

It is an astonishing development of thought in a religious culture that saw only danger in dealing with any but a single deity. Job's exploration of the divine justice has brought him to this pass. Because the god's justice is injustice, the only possible solution to the impasse is neither arbitration nor legal controversy, but revenge. To be sure, we cannot tell what Job might have said about the avenger in the six or so lines following, and therefore our understanding of the word and the line are truncated. On the other hand, he turns in a different direction in his coming speeches.

Two further observations. First, Job assures us forthrightly that he knows about the avenger. Both Job and the friends often claim knowledge. But except in the weakened sense of the passive participle that he uses in verse 14 (*mᵉyudda'ay*, "those known by me"), Job has not claimed to know since 13.18, when he said he knew that he was innocent. All the more emphatic is it, then, that he comes out with both the first-person verb and the very strong independent first-person pronoun, "*I*, I know."

Second, he asserts that the avenger "lives." Several scholars have quoted the surprisingly similar statement in one of the Baal texts from Ugarit: "And I knew [or know or will know] that Aleyan Baal is alive."[52] It is hard to know whether this is a conventional Canaanite way to express assurance in ritual. The poem refers to the return to life of the slain fertility god, a theme that one might find beneath Job's situation.[53] Perhaps the certainty that the avenger is alive contrasts with Job's despairing weakness before the god's attacks and his expectation of quick death. Whatever the sufferer's imminent destiny, the avenger will take charge. Indeed, the avenger almost needs to await the death of the one who is to be avenged, and it would be metaphorically sensible to underscore the contrast of Job's death and the life of his *gō'ēl*.

A recent account of this passage plays with a kind of audience-reception approach. Peggy Day argues that Job's reference to this powerful third party against the deity will be perceived ironically by an audience that knows, as Job does not, about the Prosecutor.[54] The *gō'ēl*, she says, will "stand upon my grave" (v. 25b: *'al-'apar yaqūm*),[55] as the ancient personal god would have done, and rescue Job from death. But the audience already knows that a member of the divine court, the Prosecutor, has undercut Job, and his wild certainty about the intervention of a heavenly Avenger is impossible.[56] The irony in this view of the *gō'ēl* is interestingly fresh.

When the text returns to intelligibility in 19.28–29, Job is warning the friends of danger to themselves. He reiterates that they "pursue" him (v. 22a), in a sentence that makes them sound like conspirators. What he means by "the root of the matter" (*šōreš dabar*, perhaps "the root of a matter"), however, is quite unclear; a metaphor of the tree or the plant seems out of place. What is made the clearer by being repeated is that the friends are threatened by the "sword." We must wonder whose sword he has in mind. Will the friends, too, receive the avenger's attentions? Finally, they will come, he seems to think, to their own knowledge (v. 29c), knowledge perhaps not strictly analogous to what he claimed in verse 25a but related to what he had given them in verse 6. "There is a trial." The question of a legal procedure is still in Job's mouth as he ends his part of the second cycle.

Zophar (Chapter 20)

Zophar can hardly wait to leap into the discussion. He starts with a "therefore" that one would expect in the middle of a sentence, not at its beginning, and his first quatrain has scarcely a pause in it. We come very breathlessly to the end of verse 3.

Clearly, Zophar takes the matter personally. He repeats the word "insult," of which Job had complained in 19.3, in a phrase (20.3a) that might mean not only "indication of an insult" but perhaps almost "a disciplined [*mūsar*] insult." He seems not to notice that the way his "disquiet stops" (*yašīb*) him is not exactly compatible with his "haste" (v. 2). The sentence is not only breathless but somewhat irrational, however much Zophar attributes it to his "intellect."

As he proceeds with the answer his intellect has given him, he manifests the same approach the other friends have taken in this cycle: like them, Zophar has not a word of reassurance or positive support. In the second cycle the friends exhibit nothing but the pains of the wicked. Zophar emphasizes images of radical and sudden reversal. The "triumphal shout" and "joy" of the wicked are short (v. 5), they disappear like dreams (v. 8). Ascent to the sky (v. 6), reminiscent of the Tower of Babel myth (Gen 11.1–9), is supplanted by "perishing like dung" (Job 20.7a), opposing an image of the low to the image of the high. What is seen becomes unseen (vv. 7b, 9), the wretched beg even "from the poor" (v. 10a), being unable to reach the rich. The lusty bones of the apparently healthy will "bed" (*tiškab*) in the dust (v. 11), an image that begins with an ironically inappropriate description of Job, whose bones are anything but lusty, continues with the irony of lust's consummation in dust, and, in a third level of irony, echoes Job's expectation of descending with his hope to the dust of Sheol (17.16). The images are mixed, but their structure of reversal is consistent.

In verses 12–23, Zophar centers on images of eating and food, with the opposition of sweet and bitter (vv. 12, 14), the good-tasting evil savored and treasured in the mouth (vv. 12–13) and wealth (*ḥayil*), which ought to be pleasant, being vomited up (v. 15). The gall and poison of asps (vv. 14, 16) are opposed to the "wadis of honey and butter" (v. 17), though the wicked person does not see the latter (v. 18). Zophar introduces a moral principle into all this misery:

> Because he has crushed the poor and left them,
> seized a house he did not build,
> because he's known no peace in his belly,
> he'll not escape with what he holds dear. (vv. 19–20)

Putting down those who are down, taking what is not one's own, having ulcers—all are signs, symptoms, causes wrapped together, of a person's wrongs. Like Eliphaz (5.11–16), Zophar proclaims the reversal of the reversal, the justice that corresponds to injustice:

> There's nothing left for him to eat,
> therefore his property cannot increase. (20.21)

The principle is impeccable. Without food, one cannot expand one's holdings. With food (v. 22a), the constriction remains in place, and the wicked receives the "toil" (*'amēl*) that Job lamented (3.10, 20), Eliphaz threatened (4.8; 15.35), and Zophar himself dismissed (11.16).

The image is not strongly consistent but seems to cover the range of possibilities. In 20.21, the wicked has nothing to eat, in verse 22 he has plenty to eat, in verse 23 he has something, apparently enough, to eat.

Unlike Eliphaz, who exaggerated the case and contradicted himself in it (15.20–21), Zophar may recognize that at any given time one cannot necessarily identify the sinner by the external circumstances. Yet the certainty of identification lies at the center of the friends' claim about the correlation between badness and suffering, goodness and prosperity. That they are forced to contradict themselves may suggest that, at least in application, the principle itself is self-contradictory.

Zophar is not quite finished. He has yet some images of battle to complete his gloomy painting of the fate of the wicked. Again he is less than meticulously careful about them. One can recognize, I think, what he is saying in verses 24–25:

> He flees an iron weapon,
> a bronze bow cuts him down,
> the drawn sword, and it comes out his back,
> glittering out of his gall.

It is not unlike the irony of Amos's description of the "day of Yahweh":

> As if a man should run from a lion
> and be attacked by a bear;
> or if he got indoors,
> should lean his hand on the wall
> and be bitten by a snake. (Amos 5.19, JPS)

But Zophar's image falls apart. What good, after all, is a bronze bow? The world has never seen one, except in sculpture, where it need not function as a weapon.[57] Zophar's crescendo from iron to bronze would be effective if he took care with the objects to which he refers. A bow does not "cut down" people, unless the word is a synecdoche for a bow and arrow.

Am I too hard on Zophar? He began the speech in an agitated state, and perhaps we cannot expect righteous indignation, personal defensiveness, and crisp precision all in the same breath. Yet for all the winded emotion of the first quatrain, the rest of the speech passes across some more or less consistent pictures of reversal of opposition, has a nicely developed bit on the shift from sweet to bitter, and at last proposes a reversal that pretends precision but fails to deliver it. To be sure, Zophar doubtless remembers Job's complaints about the divine attacks in 16.10–14, and he suggests that Job deserves them.

The very cosmos does battle against the sinner. "A fire not blown" (20.26b) already affected Job when "Elohim's fire" burned up his sheep

(1.16). The sky and the storm act similarly, it seems, to "uncover" or "carry away to exile" (*glh*, 20.27a, 28a) his property and his character, and Earth revolts against him (v. 27b). Earth and sky, in collusion against him, do just the opposite of what Job had asked in 16.18–19.[58] Zophar sounds very like a hellfire preacher or a Hebrew prophet. "On the wrathful day," *b^eyōm 'appō*, refers, it seems, to the god's angry intervention, an idea that turns up in the prophets.[59]

Zophar's final summary turns on the ironic reversal of two positive terms of the reception of goods or even of food:

> This is the lot [*ḥēleq*] of evil humankind from Elohim,
> the heritage [*naḥ^alah*] that El bespeaks him. (v. 29)

"Lot" or "portion" is often what one eats in a special banquet (see, e.g., 1 Sam 1.4–5), and "heritage" is frequently a bequest. The images of food in Job 20.12–23 and of property in verses 19–21 climax with this ironic promise. Zophar, consistently, thinks that the wicked person—Job's category, as the allusions have shown—has no positive gift from the god to look forward to. In this cycle, the friends close off discussion. We will see how, in the third cycle, they go even further.

5

"Let My Enemy Be Considered Wicked"

> But I remember now
> I am in this earthly world, where to do harm
> Is often laudable, to do good sometime
> Accounted dangerous folly.
>
> —Shakespeare, *Macbeth*, IV, 2

As the friends turned distinctly unfriendly to Job in the second cycle, Job turned unfriendly to the god. The friends' speeches concentrated upon their vision of the wickeds' punishment. It may be debated whether those negative descriptions reassure Job that he will not receive the lurid punishments or imply that Job is undergoing punishment and therefore deserves what is happening to him. I incline to the latter view, for reasons stated in Chapter 4.

Job himself did two new things in the second cycle. First, he addressed the deity less. In the first cycle, except in chap. 3, he turned near the middle of each speech to speak directly to the god. In the second cycle, he spoke at length to the god in 13.19b–14.22, but after that he made only brief, passing remarks to him in 16.3b (perhaps), 16.7b–8, and 17.3–4. In chap. 19, as I read it, he said nothing directly to the god. Second, Job twice asserted his assurance of third parties to his dispute with the god: a "witness" whose presence with the deity he stated in 16.19 and an "avenger" who, Job says in 19.25, he "knows" is alive. These figures, who are, as it were, anti-Prosecutors,[1] are an advance on the "arbiter," whose existence Job denied in 9.33.

Job turned away from the god and toward other personages, then, in a controversy that was not at all less intense in the second cycle than in the first. He described in vivid and horrific terms the god's vicious attacks on him and his separation from all those who might be thought his supporters.

The argument takes some interesting and unexpected turns in the third cycle.

Job (Chapter 21)

Eliphaz wondered sarcastically whether Job found the deity's "consolations too slight" (15.11). Job suggests, as he opens the third cycle, that if the friends listen carefully, they may receive some "consolation" (21.2). The tone of the entire conversation allows us to suspect sarcasm. Job doubtless expects that what he is about to say will harden the friends' supposition that he is hopelessly guilty, a position they have implied if not stated throughout the second cycle.

We may have a little scene of action here, as I suggested we did in 6.29, when Job asked the friends to "come back," as if they had turned away. Here he requests them to "lift me up so I can speak" (21.3a). Most translations take that as a mildly ironic "bear with me," a somewhat weakened sense of the legal term, "to lift the face," to accept or acknowledge someone. At the same time, a request to the friends to lift Job up from his prostrate position so that he might speak more readily would not be surprising.

Then comes a sudden, strange, singular address in verse 3b: "And after I've spoken, you [singular] can scoff away." Is he addressing Zophar, who has just spoken, or Eliphaz, who, Job knows from the dialogue's pattern, is next in line to speak? Or, as with the other singular addresses in Job's mouth, does he make a sudden thrust toward the deity? Of the three, the address to Zophar, most popular with scholars,[2] strikes me as the least likely, though possible. Elsewhere in the dialogue we find allusion to prior speeches but not address to a specific earlier speaker. If the addressee is Eliphaz, the line is somewhat humorous and self-deprecatory. If Job addresses the god, it has more than a hint of truculence—"You up there!"

Perhaps the latter is implied as Job goes on to two rhetorical questions:

> Now for me, is my complaint with humans?
> Why shouldn't my breath be short? (v.4)

Job implicitly claims that his complaint about humans is a mere conventional formula with which each speech begins. Insofar as the focus of his complaint is the deity, Job's second question takes on greater force. The friends seem not to have understood that the problem does not originate with the sufferer. It originates, as Job has said before and will say again—and again—with the punishing deity.

He invites the friends to hold that thought in mind as they "face" him (*pᵉnū*, "to turn toward," but, more specifically, to "turn the face [*panīm*] toward"). "Be appalled, / lay your hands on your mouths" (v. 5). The appalling thing is not merely his condition, which is frightful enough, but the concept it necessitates: the god has done this, and without good reason. If suffering is divine punishment—and both Job and the friends think it is[3]—one ought to be able to identify a cause for the effect, a deed or a thought or a mode of living that opposes or evades the god's orders. Without ever identifying the cause, the friends have vaguely urged Job to remove it and have attempted to motivate him by lurid images of the terrible life endured by people who deserve punishment. Job has insisted that all possible causes he can perceive in himself are out of proportion to the effect, minor in scope compared to the depth of his suffering. Or else, he says, they are not there at all. Not only has he not done enough to justify this divine reaction, he has done nothing whatever that would justify it.

That is appalling enough. Job wants to know if the god in charge of the universe punishes people without cause. Ought one who has done everything the god ordered not be shocked at a sudden, inexplicable blow from the back of the divine hand? What Job has received is deeply, devastatingly frightening. The entire system of laws, assumptions, assurances, truths, behind his comfortable life has been snatched rudely away, leaving behind—what? "My flesh grasps a shudder" (v. 6b). A strange expression; perhaps Job's flesh can find nothing but a shudder to grasp. Nothing solid is there any more.

That appalled, shuddering terror points toward what Job is about to say. It is fearful enough to see your whole worldview evaporate, leaving nothing in its place. It is at least as fearful to find in its place a new interpretation of the world exactly opposite to the one that has gone. In the rest of this speech, Job propounds an understanding of life that reverses what he and the friends held before.

If the god rewards with prosperity those human beings who please him and punishes with suffering those who displease him, two scenarios are possible. According to the one that Job and the friends have adopted all this time, prosperity rewards virtue, and suffering punishes vice. Job's radical proposal is that turning that scenario upside down gives a more accurate view of the world.

> Why do the wicked live,
> mature, and increase strength,
> their progeny established,

their people before them,
their offspring in their sight? (vv. 7–8)

Job does not ask *whether* the wicked live this way, he asks *why* they do. It is not in question that the wicked prosper, and Job describes their fortune in a series of images centering around fertility, with the offspring in verse 8, the "safe" (*šalōm*, "healthy, peaceful") houses (or households) in verse 9, animal husbandry in verse 10, flocks of happy children in verse 11, joyous singing and playing of instruments in verse 12. Especially with verses 8, 9, and 11, the picture is exactly and ironically opposite to what Job, the model of virtue, experiences. Job's progeny are disestablished, his herds and flocks are destroyed or stolen, his children neither dance nor sing. He is virtuous, but he is living through appalling suffering, while those morally his opposites enjoy the blessings of the deity.

But a sudden, strange turn comes over the text at verse 13.

They wear out [*y^eballū*] their days with good.

"Wear out" is the Ketib reading, the word in the consonantal Hebrew text. The marginal Masoretic notes substitute as Qere *y^ekallu*:

They finish their days in good.

The consonants *beth* ב and *kaph* כ are easily mistaken for each other. The Qere reading continues the image of happiness in the foregoing lines. The Ketib can be understood as doing the same, but with a twist of ironic wry. Anyone might wish her days to "wear out" among such scenes as those. In any case, "good" here denotes not the moral but the pleasant, and death is fundamentally congruous on both readings with the idyllic picture that precedes it.

That congruity is not quite so certain in verse 13b. I refer in the annotation to this verse to the two opposite readings of these words:

[they] are terrified at the moment of Sheol

or:

[they] go down to Sheol in peace.

The latter reading is of a piece with what goes before, especially if we accept the Qere reading. The former introduces a shift that is less abrupt if we take the Ketib. The reference to death in the second line is more obvious than in the first, but the former reading arouses the sense of terror that verse 9 had mentioned as absent. Its very absence in verse 9 makes its presence in verse 13 more powerful, which suggests that the pleasures of verses 9–12 mask their opposites or are flimsy barriers against the terror that lurks outside. It is not unlike Job's admission (3.25) that his fears had materialized, with its connection to the positive descriptions of him in chaps. 1–2 as "religious," one who "fears Elohim."

Verse 21.13, then, introduces the theme of death into Job's discourse, simultaneously continuing in harmony with the descriptions of life (v. 7a) and entering an underlying discord with it, a terrifying moment of death that clashes with the life of amiable fecundity in verses 7–12. I refuse to choose between these two readings. Both are there, both euphony and dissonance. Death in verse 13 is terrifying and peaceful, and neither cancels the other out. We *must* have it both ways.

In its turn, the duality affects the following lines. These wicked folks push the god away, being displeased with knowing his ways (v. 14b), dissatisfied with serving him (v. 15a), disgusted with the prospect of "begging" from him (v. 15b): "Get away from us." Given the idyll of prosperity in verses 7–12, we can understand why. If those who wish to know the god's ways, to serve him, and to beg from him receive the rewards Job has received, anyone with an eye to a bearable life, let alone a pleasant one, could hardly be blamed for remaining distant from the source of unpleasantness. On the other hand, if death is so terrifying an end to prosperity, people will identify it with the god who ordains the structures of life and death and will prefer to keep both death and deity distant as long as possible, especially if life has its pleasures even in the light of death and if the rewards of virtue are a life like Job's.

But verse 16 is, to say the least, odd. The "good" here is not the usual *ṭōb* but a variant, *ṭūb*, which Zophar used in 20.21, meaning something like "property, goods." Hence the RSV's "prosperity" (and cf. Prov 11.10). But a phrase like *ṭūb lēb*, "good or happiness of heart," in Isaiah 65.14 and Deuteronomy 28.47 suggests not material but emotional prosperity, hence JPS's "happiness." What is more, we might take the first line of Job 21.16 either as a statement, as I have done ("Ah, their good is not in their hand"; cf. JPS), or as a question, as the RSV does ("Behold, is not their prosperity in their hand?").[4] The two senses are opposed to each other. The rhetorical question expects the affirmative answer that good does lie in the power of these poeple who keep the god at arm's length, whereas the statement asserts that prosperity or happiness is not in their competence.

Some scholars accept the LXX reading of the second line, "The counsel of the wicked is far from him," that is, from the god,[5] though it is banal in view of wicked people's desire to be far from the god in verses

14–15. The Hebrew text says "far from me." Job might mean that because the happiness of wicked people is not within their power, they are in for a rude shock from the deity within whose power it is. He therefore wishes no connection with their "counsel" (*'ēṣah*, "plan, scheme, advice") and prefers not to be there when the reckoning comes. Or he may wish ruefully that their counsel were not so far from him. Their prosperity, on one reading, is in their hold, and they succeed in achieving distance from the god who is all too close to Job.

Perhaps he could have more light and tranquillity if he could come closer to them. But he is not sure he wishes to do so. Granted, the happy, prosperous wicked seem to have little trouble. "How often," he wants to know (v. 17), is Bildad's confident assertion true?

> Surely knaves' light [*'ōr*] is snuffed out,
> its fire's blaze doesn't shine,
> light goes dark in his tent,
> the beacon [*nēr*] above him is snuffed out. (18.5–6)

Job's rhetorical questions combine Bildad's first and last lines and propose that the "calamity" of divine "destruction" among the wicked is rare. Verses 21.18–20 imply that he wishes it were not so rare,[6] and he lambasts the notion that the god might visit someone's punishment on that person's descendants (cf. Exod 20.5). It is not clear whether Job attributes that idea to the friends or, if he does, that he reports their views accurately. Bildad said something quite different about Job's sons in Job 8.4. The notion that retribution might be deferred until later generations was abroad in Israel, however, as Exodus 20.5 and Ezekiel's detailed refutation (Ezek 18 *passim*) demonstrate. Job dislikes the idea, thinking that people care only about their own pleasures and not about the destiny of later generations (Job 21.21).

He reverts to the idea of death in "When the number of his months is cut off" (v. 21b).[7] And the question in verse 22, "Does he teach knowledge to El?" with an implied negative answer, may explain why a person loses interest in the fate of descendants. It is the deity's business, not the human's, to do the judging. Besides, if the humans have been busy shooing the god away, as Job portrayed them in verses 14–15, their opportunity to instruct him diminishes.

Job's interest in the question is still contained in the theme of death as it appears this second time. We saw terror and peace, the two reactions to death, in the one statement in verse 13. In verses 23–25, the same reactions are set side by side to describe two dying persons, the one "all secure and at ease" with juicy marrow in the bones, the other "with a bitter soul" and a bad taste in the mouth. Both come to the same end, as Job has described death before: lying in dust in company with worms (7.21; 17.13–16). That conclusion seems to clash with Job's argument about the advantages the wicked have. In chap. 3, on the other hand, Job thought that the commonality of death overcomes the disparities in life, as he portrayed the equality of lowly and lofty (3.13–15, 17–19). Perhaps his argument has gone a bit astray. He wishes (21.17–20) that bad people would see the desperate fruits of their badness for themselves. Following on that thought, the equality of happy and miserable people in death is unfair to the unhappy good ones, who have no better future to anticipate than the joyful bad ones.[8]

The theme of death has taken two forms. In verse 13, it was both peaceful and terrifying to those who contemplated its coming. In verses 21–26, it is the dissolution of two different kinds of life, one pleasurable and the other miserable. The two faces of death are two, not one. There remains a third element.

Job must forestall the friends' predictable argument, and he does so with luxuriant invective (v. 27). Their ideas are "schemes" (*maḥšᵉbōt*), with which they are "hatching tricks against me" (*mᵉzimmōt ʻalay taḥmōsū*). They will try to bring up contrary evidence (v. 28), but Job wants them to consult other, unaccustomed sources of information. Wayfarers, "those who pass on the road" (v. 29), nomads, or at best traveling caravaneers—people not welcomed in the polite society of Job and his friends—have a sense of the world better attuned, Job suggests, to reality:

> that on a calamitous day a wretch is spared,
> on a day when fury is led forth.
> Who points out his way to his face?
> When he has done something, who pays him back? (vv. 30–31)

The last rhetorical question, implying that no one "pays back" (*yᵉšallēm*) the doer of the wrong deed, echoes Job's wish in verse 19b, that the god "pay" (*yᵉšallēm*) the wicked person directly.

The impunity of these despicable people is shown even better, Job suggests, at death than in life. Verses 32–33 present a vivid picture of the honorific funeral procession of one such vile wretch. He suffered no damage whatever "on a day when fury is led forth"(*yūbalū*, v. 30b); therefore at his death "he is led forth" (*yūbal*, v. 32a)[9] in a great procession, his grave guarded from robbers (v. 32b), the honored corpse preceded and followed by crowds of mourners (v. 33b–c), his very place in the dirt, among "the clods of the wadi" (v. 33a), the source of "sweetness" (*mtq*).

This third image of death is different from the other two, unless the positive side of the first image (v. 13) is independent of its negative side. In the latter case, we would move from the peaceful death of verse 13 to the dual and ambivalent deaths in verses 23–26 to the happy funeral of verses 32–33. If verse 13 is simultaneously double, we go from that combination of peace and terror to the more equable duality in verses 23–26, without so stark a difference between happiness and misery, to the unambiguous peacefulness of verses 32–33. In any case, the theme and images of death make concrete the basic and revolutionary direction of Job's thought in this speech. It has to do primarily not with death but with life. He begins with life (v. 7a), describing the experience of the wicked both in the positive terms in which he, like his traveler-informants, sees it and in the contrast of the negatives that he wishes upon them but cannot ascertain (vv. 18–20). Yet somehow the images of death constantly put the cap on the images of life.

Job has turned the usual account of divine retribution upside down. Yes, the god rewards those who please him and punishes those who displease him. But his friends have been completely mistaken about whom he rewards; the truth is the opposite of what they thought. The deity rewards the wicked and punishes the moral. Job cannot imagine that the friends could be more wrong.

> How you console me with empty air,
> and your replies leave only fraud behind! (v. 34)

He started the speech with the thought that the friends might receive some "consolation" (*tanḥūmōt*); he closes it with the charge of fraud and the irony that they console him (*t^{e}naḥ^{a}mūnī*) with puffs of wind (*hebel*).[10]

Eliphaz (Chapter 22)

Eliphaz begins by following the lead he had set in chap. 15, both in several of his terms and in the content of his introduction (22.2–5). He wonders how a deed may be of "use" or "benefit" (*skn*, 22.2a–b and 15.3a), he refers to an "argument" or "charge" (*ykḥ*, 22.4a and 15.3a) and to religion (*yir'ah*, "fear," 22.4a and 15.4a), and he notes Job's "guilt" or "misdeeds" (*'awōn*, 22.5b and 15.5a). So many verbal repetitions from the earlier stanza (and almost in the same order) might suggest either a deliberate echo or a mind not well stocked with ideas.

This time Eliphaz is concerned to arrive swiftly at the climax of his accusation that Job is "greatly wicked" (*ra'atka rabbah*, 22.5a; cf. "condemns," *yaršīa'*, 15.6a). The process of the argument is very interesting.

The opening rhetorical question, "Does a man [*geber*] benefit El?" expects a negative answer, and the second line of the couplet states that the benefit is limited to the self. We discover in 22.3 why Eliphaz began there, for he is sure that Job's alleged innocence (*ṣdq*) has no effect on the deity. The human's uselessness to the god is double-edged, then: not only does the human not "benefit" the deity (v. 2a), but even what might be thought of as pleasing (*ḥēpeṣ*, v. 3a) to the god arouses only indifference. It is no "profit" (*beṣaʿ*; cf. *yōʿīl*, 15.3b) to the god that Job's life (his "way," *derek*, 22.3b) is perfect.[11] Eliphaz appears to grant Job's innocence:

> Is Shaddai pleased that [*kī*] you are innocent?

He could have found ways of saying "*if* you are innocent" and did not.

That allows him to change the slant a little, appearing to assert Job's goodness while implicitly denying it.

> Does he charge you because of your religiousness,
> come against you with your justice? (v.4)

We surely think "No, of course the god is not accusing Job for being religious and just."[12] But two memories come to the surface. First, Eliphaz was quite sure in chap. 15 that Job was guilty, indeed, worse than the usual (15.16), which suggests the same thought here: "The god accuses you not for piety but for its opposite." That thought quickly becomes "If he accuses you, you must be guilty, your piety, if any, fatally defective," and we realize that Eliphaz is also saying the opposite of what he seems to be saying. Second, Job's last speech (chap. 21) turned the structure of rewards and punishments and their causes upside down. On the basis of that reversal, he would therefore answer Eliphaz's questions in the emphatic affirmative. The situation demands simultaneous negative and affirmative answers to the same pair of questions, both of which arise from the systematic structures of Eliphaz's and Job's ordering of the world. But we know, from chaps. 1–2, that there is no accusation, no charge, and that the situation has in fact arisen from Job's "religiousness" (1.9).

Having implicitly denied Job's moral and religious standing, Eliphaz can quickly and logically say exactly what he thinks, retaining the form of the rhetorical question:

> Are you not in fact greatly wicked,
> with no end to your misdeeds? (22.5)

The question "Are you not?" demands an affirmative answer: "Yes, I am." That was Eliphaz's end in view all along, and he arrived there both quickly and disingenuously.

Now no rhetorical barriers restrain Eliphaz from a series of straightforward accusations, forming something more than half of the speech (vv. 6–20). They fall into two parts: verses 6–11 specify Job's moral crimes, and verses 12–20 describe theological faults that seem to merge into moral ones. The concluding section, verses 21–30, proposes at last a solution for Job's dilemma.

The astonishing thing about verses 6–11 is Eliphaz's utter certainty in his accusation, which is, in fact, a tissue of invention. Job has done none of what he is accused of in verses 6–9, and in chap. 31 he will take some very solemn oaths about it. As Gordis nicely says, "Finding his theory of Divine justice contradicted by the facts, Eliphaz proceeds to the time-honored device of adjusting the facts to the theory."[13] Eliphaz has been sure ever since 4.7 that righteous people do not suffer and wicked people do, and he wishes to believe in a god who is in that respect just, consistent, and powerful. And the equation is reversible. Not only do the wicked suffer punishment, as he assured Job at length in chap. 15, but suffering is sufficient evidence that sufferers are receiving the punishment proper to their wickedness. Eliphaz may be unable to identify the deeds that brought on this reaction, but he is quite willing to make them up, because he is certain that he can be mistaken only about mere technicalities. If Job has not actually crushed any orphans' arms, he must have done something just like it.

It is interesting that this series of accusations is structured exactly like certain oracles of the prophets.[14] Eliphaz begins with a "because" (*kī*), which governs everything through verse 9 and sets out the accusation, and introduces the resulting punishments by "therefore" (*lakēn*). One can point to prophetic passages like Hosea 2.7–8 (Eng. 5–6):

> Because [*kī*] their mother is a harlot,
> shameful she who conceived them,
> because she said, "I will go
> after my lovers,
> who give me my bread and water,
> my wool and flax,
> my oil and drink,"
> therefore [*lakēn*] I will hedge
> her path with thorns,
> and I will build her wall,
> and she will not find her tracks.

Or Isaiah 8.6–7:

> Because [*ya'an kī*] this people refused
> Shiloah's waters

which flow lightly
and rejoice at Rezin
and Remaliah's son,
and therefore [*lakēn*], oh, I bring over them
the River's waters,
powerful and many.

Other passages in the prophetic books are structured similarly or in reverse order, sometimes without the formulaic word "therefore." The structure has impeccable logic: because A, therefore B. The difficulty is that Eliphaz's "because" section in verses 6–9 is sheer fiction.[15] It also reverses and denies the praise of Job's compassion for those in trouble with which Eliphaz began his first speech (4.3–4).

What are we to make of this prophet-like talk? It is surely climactic in Eliphaz's retributive structure of things. The oracular style, moreover, suggests a portentous moment of solemn, divinely authorized charge. If Claus Westermann is right that such prophetic judgment speeches stemmed from the practice of the law court,[16] Eliphaz adopts simultaneously the accusatory message of the prophet and the judge's guilty verdict.

He accuses Job of pushing the lowly and oppressed even further down (22.6–7, 9) and of raising the high even higher (v. 8).[17] The punishment by "snares" and "terror" (v. 10) reminds us of Bildad's list of traps (18.7–10), and the threat of darkness and the flood (22.11) reminds us of Job's expectations (see, respectively, 10.21–22; 9.23). But when Eliphaz says, "You will fail to see darkness" (22.11a), he seems to predict, perhaps with a hint of gloating, some personal devastation, which will fall suddenly and unexpectedly on Job.

At verse 12 Eliphaz starts on Job's theological sins with a figure of divine transcendence:

Is not Eloah the apex of the sky?
Look at how high is the topmost star.

Zophar used the idea in a slightly different form in 11.8: "Heights of the sky—what can you do?"[18] Eliphaz is sure that Job must grant that the god is high, and therefore Job is mistaken to deny his knowledge (vv. 13–14). As the purported quotation in these lines quotes nothing that Job actually said, Eliphaz adds to his accusations of deeds that Job has not done, accusations of thoughts he has not expressed: "Clouds conceal him, and he does not see" (v. 14a) is unconnected with any idea Job has stated. He has characteristically complained that the god "sees" all too much and too constantly.[19] Eliphaz cannot seriously suppose that Job believes the clouds hinder the god's activity. No doubt he wants a way to mark Job's supposition that the god might be ignorant as itself foolish ignorance. But he puts the idea in Job's mouth in laughably exaggerated terms, especially because they implicitly deny precisely the transcendence that Eliphaz assumed Job would agree to in verse 12a.

He returns to the divine transcendence by implication at verses 15–16. Job neither watches over nor guards (*šmr*) that "ancient path / that worthless men have trodden." The verb can mean both overseeing (JPS's "observed" seems to me weak) and guarding. Eliphaz is asking not merely whether Job sees that dishonorable path but whether he can be responsible for it. The implied answer is certainly negative, the implication, once again, that an exalted god is responsible for the fates of worthless men on that path (v. 16), whereas the lowly Job is both ignorant and incapable of determining them.

Concluding his descriptions of Job's theological sins in verses 17–20, Eliphaz verges on the irrational and inarticulate. Verse 17a is almost a quotation of 21.14a, where Job had referred to the happy wicked who succeed in telling the deity "Get away from us!" and who ask "What does Shaddai do about it?" Eliphaz does not accuse Job of talking this way, but he blurts out that Shaddai fills "their houses with good" (22.18a), an incautious acquiescence in Job's postulate in chap. 21 that the god showers good on the wicked. Eliphaz then quotes Job accurately: "The counsel of the wicked is far from me!" (22.18b) It is a very strange quatrain, for the logical connection between lines 18a and 18b is more than just difficult to see.[20]

Now Eliphaz moves strangely to the other side of the theological fence, to describe in verses 19–20 the response by the "righteous" (*ṣaddīqīm*) and "innocent" (*naqī*) to the destruction portrayed in verse 16. It is a remarkable echo of Job's claim in 17.8–9 that "good" folks are hardened in their attitudes by his plight. Eliphaz portrays, indeed, a savagely joyful cursing:

> If our adversary is not destroyed,
> what's left of them the fire does not eat— (22.20)

Surely Eliphaz includes Job as an "adversary," at one with "those who say to El, 'Get away from us!'" We should expect him to reject Job's argument that the god rewards the wicked (though he has just admitted it in 22.18a) and punishes the moral. But the rejection is much more heartfelt than headthought, and it degenerates into something at best difficult to follow.

All the more surprising, then, is the sudden solution (vv. 21–25) and vision of a happy outcome (vv. 26–30). Eliphaz's tone changes drastically at verse 21 from curse to warm concern, but his head is not completely together. He begins, "Then benefit [*hasken-na'*] him and regain your health [*šᵉlam*, or 'be at peace']," forgetting that he opened the speech by denying that a human *could* "benefit" (*yiskan*) the deity (v. 2). He then proceeds to conventional good advice: Job ought to take "instruction" (*tōrah*, perhaps a hint at accepting law or regulation), take what the god says to "heart" (*lēbab*, v. 22b), turn to the deity, put iniquity at a distance (v. 23). He closes with a briefly extended metaphor of the deity as Job's "treasure" (v. 25), in the interests of which he will throw away as refuse the crasser treasure of prized Ophirian gold (v. 24).[21]

The outcome will be a future filled with the greatest personal and religious success: pleasure in the deity (v. 26), prayer answered and vows paid (v. 27), the ability to decide something definitively (v. 28a), the presence of light on the way rather than the darkness predicted in verse 11, the rescue of lowly souls from their depths (vv. 29–30). He paints the portrait of an admirable, successful man, a man, one might think, "scrupulously moral, religious, one who avoids evil." And it sounds so easy to achieve. As Eliphaz prescribes the process in verses 21–25, Job has but to do it. He does not consider—or has failed to perceive—Job's bitter rage, his unfair trial, the divine attacks upon him, and his avenger. He has forgotten the depth of evil that he himself has ascribed to Job. One might wonder whether chap. 22 is the work of a rational mind. On the other hand, it deconstructs itself as the works of rational minds do.

Job (Chapters 23–24)

Job's problem in this speech differs from the one in chap. 21. There he argued that experience with the god shows that the conventional notion of the relation of moral status to circumstance is upside down; the wicked are rewarded and the good punished. It can be claimed that he obscures that point here. The focus of his discourse this time, however, is the god's absence.

Job begins with two allusions to what Eliphaz has said. He calls his "complaint" (*śīaḥ*) bitter, that "complaint" to the deity that Eliphaz had said, in 15.4, Job was restricting for others. And his "hand is heavy," that hand whose "pure palms," Eliphaz has just promised (22.30b), will help in the god's rescue operations. Such willing assistance is not among the capacities of Job's "heavy hand."[22]

Complaint finished, he jumps immediately into the theme of the god's absence, wishing he "knew, and could find him" (23.3). The expression is odd. "Knew" what? Most interpreters say "knew where or how to find him." Perhaps also "knew him, and could find him," or "knew [as in v. 5] what he would say." Job wants to lay out his arguments in the trial (vv. 3b–4). It is a strange shift, which he has made before. It seems not to occur to him that, after depicting the god as unjust in rewarding evil and punishing good, he suddenly switches to wish for a trial before this god.

More than that, he begins to talk about the trial in positive terms, suggesting a possible rapprochement with the god. He anticipates that the deity will say something that he will understand (v. 5), expects personal attention (v. 6), thinks that the case will be handled rationally and that he may win (v. 7). Job was not thinking of a trial in this way in 9.13–24 or 13.23–27. There the trial looked like something already decided—and lost. Here he is suddenly possessed by something like euphoria.

> Would he prosecute me by an attorney?
> No, he himself would attend to me. (23.6)

Amazing! Job uses the emphatic separate pronoun *hū'*, "he," in verse 6b: no agent but the god himself. And the pun between "prosecute" (*yarīb*) and "attorney" (*rab koaḥ*) calls attention to the latter person. It is another strange switch that Job is pleased that the deity will not deal with him through an agent, when he himself has postulated his own agent-advocates, the "witness" and the "avenger." We are reminded of the fact, which Job does not know, that the god did deal with Job at the beginning through an agent, the Prosecutor, who carried out the deeds against Job. But the "attorney," like Job's "arbiter" (9.33), is attached to a negative and is dismissed. Unlike the "arbiter," the "attorney" will not reappear.

Discouragement returns in force, as Job boxes the compass in search of the god in 23.8–9. The search in all directions is unsuccessful. The god is "not there" (v. 8a),[23] cannot be discerned (or "understood," *bīn*, v. 8b) or perceived ("grasped," *'ḥz*, v. 9a). He is simply not available, it seems, and when Job reaches the south (v. 9b), he understands why: "He *hides* in the south." The god deliberately avoids the petitioner.

And Job knows why: "Because [*kī*] he knows the way I'm on" (v. 10a). "Way" (*derek*) is a common biblical metaphor—possibly a dead one—for the conduct and quality of a person's life. The god knows not only where Job is but what kind of life he leads, what sort of person he is. Job puts the lie to Eliphaz's egregious supposition (22.13–14) that he thinks the god is ignorant. Quite the opposite. The god avoids the sufferer precisely because he knows that the trial will turn out in Job's favor. Job piles up the terms of his adherence to the god's wishes, sure that he will pass any test superbly well (23.10b), because he has stepped carefully in the god's very footprints ("track," *'ašūr*, v. 11a), has kept close to the life-style prescribed by the god ("way," *derek* again, v. 11b), has obeyed, nay, "treasured," his commands (v. 12). He protests almost too much how extraordinarily good and pious he has been. To be sure, a person facing a trial will wish the best possible public relations and will state the case as positively as can be. And perhaps Job does not exceed the claim of that emotional moment in 9.21: "I am perfect" (*tam 'anī*). The burden of this self-congratulatory stanza, moreover, is less to inflate the sufferer's excellence for its own sake than to underscore and explain a divine absence that seems out of character.

As Job ponders further the character of that absent god (23.13–17), he centers not on the absence or its injustice, nor on the inverted justice of chap. 21, but on the deity's arbitrariness. "His soul wishes something, and he does it" (23.13b). My translation is even a bit extensive; more nearly, "His soul wishes and he does [acts]" (*wᵉnapšō 'iwwᵉta wayya'aś*). There is no space between the god's desire and his deed, no thoughtful reflection, no canvasing of implications.[24]

The thinking comes later: "He will come to terms with my sentence" (v. 14a). The range of connotations in the verb *šlm* allows both "making peace" (in the Hiph'il) and "paying back, requiting." In the latter sense, the object of the verb, "my sentence" (*ḥuqqī*), has further connotational possibilities. In v. 12b, the same word meant approximately "limit, boundary," a sense derived from the legal connotation of *ḥōq*, "rule, statute." To "pay back a *ḥōq*" might suggest the god's getting even with Job for being so faithful to his own rules. The following line, "many like it are in his mind" (*'immō*, "with him"), moves on to the ironic idea that, if there is a conflict, the deity resolves it within himself.

And it explains why Job refers to "terror" (*bhl*, twice) and "dread" (*pḥd*). Job ruefully agrees with Eliphaz, who had combined the same two words in 22.10 to predict that "terror [will] suddenly panic you" (*wībahelka paḥad pit'ōm*). But the deity's terrorism does not "silence" Job (*niṣmattī*) with the prospect of overwhelming darkness (23.17). He refuses to be cowed. The more his divine opponent exerts absent and arbitrary force, the more Job presses his claims for justice and a hearing.

> Why are not proper times treasured by Shaddai,
> and those who know him don't see his days? (24.1)

"Proper times" is sometimes rendered "times of (or for) judgment."[25] Whether or not the point is Job's wish for a trial, he complains again about the irresponsible arbitrariness of the god's absence.

Yet Job makes no effort to bring the deity near. Unlike all his earlier speeches except that in chap. 19, throughout the rest of chap. 24 he does not address the deity, not even in an interjected line like 21.3b. Chapter 24 is complex in its images, ambiguous in its syntax, full of verbs with unspecified subjects and of pronouns with uncertain antecedents and referents. An indication of the difficulty may be found in the fact that, in verses 16–18 alone, the RSV renders as plural five different expressions that in Hebrew are singular, with never a footnote acknowledging the changes.[26] No wonder scholars have attempted to recover from the chapter traces of "lost" parts of Bildad's and Zophar's speeches. It is comforting to think that one can thus explain so intractable a text. I admit uncertainty about much in the following paragraphs that may seem confident.

The divine absence continues to be the key. The god fails to "treasure proper times" (24.1), and therefore humans bereft of his guidance can go wrong. They tyrannize over the weak, engaging in illegal land dealing (v. 2a), sheep and ass rustling (vv. 2b–3a), oppressive lending practices (v. 3b), and arrogant behavior toward the poor (v. 4a). Job compares them in an extended metaphor with the wild asses (vv. 5–8), who forage for their food, take their shelter where they can find it—or find none[27]—and live by their wits. Humans live in the same ways, whether they are the oppressive evil (v. 9) or the oppressed poor (vv. 10–11). The text swings back and forth from tyrannizers to tyrannized without clear signals. The analogy to the wild asses, whose search for food brings both success (v. 6) and hardship (vv. 7–8) in the battle for survival, suggests no moral criticism of either kind of person. The closing tercet underscores it:

> From the city the dying cry out,
> the throats of the wounded call,
> but Eloah thinks nothing amiss. (v. 12)

Because the god overlooks those who ought to be under his care, his absence results in human sufferings and misdeeds. They are the fault of neither doers nor sufferers but of the god. People behave like beasts if divine guidance is withheld from them.

That is an interesting switch on the theory of retribution. In chap. 21 Job argued that the god rewards human misbehavior. Here he argues that the god causes it. The god is precisely irresponsible: he neither takes responsibility to oversee, guide, and assist humans nor responds to them when, from their misery, they cry to him. Both translations of verse 12c point nicely to this conclusion. "Eloah thinks nothing amiss" accepts MT's *tiplah* and suggests unheeding irresponsibility. "Eloah pays no attention to prayer," repointing *tiplah* to *t^{e}pillah*, suggests nonresponse.

Next Job depicts an opposition between the god and the humans.

Verses 13–17 set out the evil humans do under the central image of the opposition of light and darkness, from the opening "rebellers against light" to the closing "familiar with darkness's terrors." The murderer kills in broad daylight (v. 14a–b) and expands his activities at night (v. 14c), the adulterer uses twilight (v. 15), and the thief depends on darkness (v. 16). The stanza has more darkness than light, more avoidance of light or rebellion against it than acceptance of it.[28] With the picture in verse 16 of the thief who digs through walls to get into houses, whether from the ancient fear of guardian spirits at doorways or from fear of being seen walking through a door, we come at verse 17 to an odd ambiguity. Verse 16 ends with a plural, "They do not know light," the antecedent of which may be the "houses" earlier in that verse or even "rebellers" back in verse 13. Verse 17 suddenly reverts to the singular ("Morning and deep darkness are the same to him"), and it is not clear whether we are reading about the thief in verse 16a or about the god, who likewise seems not to notice the difference between light and darkness.

The deity must be the subject at verse 18. The description of human evildoers opened in verse 13 with the emphatic plural pronoun "they," *hēmmah*. Verse 18 matches it with "Swift is he," *hū'*, an equally emphatic singular pronoun. As the implicit cause of the human wrongdoings defined by that earlier plural, the god is the obvious referent.

We now enter a difficult, complex account of the further effects of the deity's absence (vv. 18–20) and of his arbitrariness (vv. 21–24). The image of a god "swift across the waters" (*qal-hū' 'al-pᵉnē-mayim*) is reminiscent of the divine "wind" that blew at creation "across the waters" (*'al-pᵉnē hammayim*, Gen 1.2). That in its turn suggests that these "waters" are not lakes and streams but are the cosmic waters of chaos. This god is familiar not only with "darkness's terrors" (Job 24.17b—if that can refer to the deity) but with the pre-creation and anti-creation chaos, familiar with it, indeed, not as the enemy of chaos but as its perpetrator.

Job puns on a further chaos in nature, where the fertile land that ought to produce crops is "cursed" (*tᵉqullal*) because the "swift" (*qal*) deity "does not turn toward the vineyards" (v. 18), and where the forces of drought and heat work their will on life-giving water (v. 19). The chaos continues into society, where the god reverses life and death; the womb, the image of birth, "forgets" him, and the maggot, the image of death, is a delicacy to him (v. 20a). Viable social structure is turned upside down. The god curses the "plot of land," and the wood that ought to be its glory becomes the image of its wickedness (v. 20c). The pasturage that ought to allow prosperity stands for the god's oppression of the feminine weak: the barren, the childless, the widow. All of the images defining the god's dealings with people are made more perverse by the fact that insidiously they have become images not of absence but of presence. Not only the weak but also the strong become targets of his oppression, "the mighty" (*'abbīrīm*, v. 22a, "bulls") are temporarily made more mighty yet (vv. 23a, 24a) but are then thrown down in his renewed absence.

> They are exalted a little, and he is not there.
> They are brought down like . . . , are closed up,
> and like the ear of grain they wither. (v. 24)

"Exalted" (*rōmmū*) is a grim pun with *rimmah*, "maggot," in v. 20a, which exhibits just the reversal that is going on. "He is not there" (*'ēnennū*), reiterating absence, echoes Job's earlier complaint that the god would search for him, but he "would not be there" (*'ēnennī*, 7.21; cf. Bildad, 8.22). Because this absence, with its further images of agricultural failure, completes what began in 24.18, we now see that the god's "swiftness" was not mere description but characterization: he has departed swiftly from the scene, leaving behind disaster and chaos both for those who, in Job's terms, deserve it and for those who do not. This absence also completes the absence in 23.8–9, where Job vainly sought the god. When we get to *'ēnennū* in 24.24a, we wonder again why Job wants a trial with this judge. His accusations seem to undercut its justification. Delving deep into the ground of human corruption, Job finds there the actions or the absence of the god. Now we know why in chap. 23 he feared the outcome of the trial: a deity who is the source of human corruption is unlikely to acquit an uncorrupted human being.

The theme of the divine absence is modified by images of an arbitrary, whimsical, completely unjust presence. But Job returns decisively to absence and challenges the friends once more with a couplet about words:

> If it is not so, who will prove me a liar
> and bring my words to naught? (v.25)

The friends are not equal to the challenge. I do not think that Elihu (chaps. 32–37) meets the demand of 24.25, and Yahweh makes no effort to do so (chaps. 38–41). In a sense, Job has already won the argument.

Bildad (Chapter 25)

Where Eliphaz's final contribution combines the harshest accusations against the sufferer with ostensibly warm hopes for his future,

Bildad's last speech hardly has time for more than good-bye. His has been the tersest style among the friends, but this speech is short even for him. For that reason, many scholars have attempted to discover in Job's speeches on either side of chap. 25 remnants of an original longer intervention by Bildad and a speech by Zophar. Thinking such rewriting unnecessary, I will make no gestures toward it.[29]

In five couplets, Bildad makes only two points: the god is utterly powerful, and nothing in the creation can measure up to his standards. Neither point is remotely novel. The first one is linked interestingly to some things Job has said earlier.

> Dreaded rule is with him
> who imposes peace on his heights.
> Is there any counting his troops?
> On whom does his light not arise? (vv. 2–3)

Job opposed "dread" (*paḥad*) to "peace" (*šalōm*) in 21.9: "Their houses are safe [*šalōm*] from terror [*mippaḥad*]." Bildad combines them in the activity of the god's rule (*mašal*), which is fearful but also achieves peace "on his heights" (*bimᵉrōmayw*). But Job had placed his witness "on high" (*bammᵉrōmīm*) in 16.19. By allusion, Bildad counters both Job's account of the happiness of the wicked in chap. 21 and his claim that anyone independent of the god, let alone opposed to him, could stand in his lofty bailiwick. So much for Job's witness.

Verse 25.3, moreover, proposes that Job might have underestimated the deity's "troops" (*gᵉdūdīm*) in describing the attack in 19.12, for those troops are uncountable. Bildad presses the idea that the god cannot be resisted. His commonplace that the god's light shines on everyone (25.3b) may counter Job's rebellious statement in 23.16–17 that, though the deity has "weakened his mind [heart]" and "terrified" him, he, Job, is "not silenced before darkness."

Bildad's second point is familiar:

> How is any man righteous with El,
> how is one born of woman pure?
> Oh, even the moon is not bright,
> nor are stars pure in his sight,
> much less a man, that maggot,
> child of Adam, worm that he is. (25.4–6)

Verse 4 is exactly the idea that Eliphaz received in his vision:

> Is a man more righteous than Eloah,
> or a hero purer than his maker? (4.17)

Bildad adds to it in 25.5 what Eliphaz added in 15.15b: "and the sky is not pure in his eyes." But he comes back in 25.6 to a word Job used in a rather different way in 17.14b, where he spoke of death in the figure of calling the "maggot" his "mother, sister." Where Job evoked the horror of an unjust death, Bildad uses the figure to diminish all of Adam's children to the status of worms.

It is interesting that at the end of the dialogue, Bildad returns to the point with which Eliphaz virtually began the discussion. It seems that the friends have learned nothing. That is not to say that there is no movement among their speeches and thoughts. I argued that the second cycle is different in tone and effect from the first. The third is different from the second, I think, in three ways: Eliphaz both lambasts Job and promises him a future, which he did not do in the second cycle; Bildad comes finally to Eliphaz's cynical view of the human race, that it is impossible for a human being to be really good; and Zophar has nothing whatever to say. In 13.13 Job had urged the friends to be silent, and Zophar at last acquiesces.

At the same time, the friends are consistent in their idea of the world's moral structure. Eliphaz's view that human righteousness is impossible makes it easy for him to diagnose Job's condition as sinful. Any human will fall under the same disability, and on Eliphaz's reading, the god has reacted to Job in the predictable way. Eliphaz, more than the other two, sees the positive condition of humans as a matter of cooperation between the human and god. Bildad and Zophar, I believe, are less subtle than Eliphaz (though Eliphaz's subtlety abandons him in his last speech). They think straightforwardly that Job must be a sinner because his outward circumstances require that thought, and Zophar adds some mildly mystical talk about the divine transcendence. Eliphaz at least holds out the expectation that the god is willing to pay attention to humans, even while having contempt for them. But when Bildad comes around to the divine contempt in chap. 25, he does not mitigate it by any thought of an accompanying mercy.

There is still another point. In the third cycle, one might argue, the three friends react in the three classic ways that people respond to arguments they have lost.[30] Eliphaz leaps at Job with false accusations. Rather than admit, even to himself, that his retributive theory founders on the experience of the sufferer sitting before him, Eliphaz clasps it closer and talks more wildly than ever. Job had ironically predicted such a reaction:

> Moral people are astounded by this,
> the guiltless rouses up against the impious,
> the innocent holds tight to his way,
> and the clean of hands grows ever stronger. (17.8–9)

Bildad likewise cannot admit that his theory is devastated. He falls lamely back on the conceded point that the god is powerful, as if going again over the same ground might produce the right result. And Zophar—Zophar is reduced to silence. Unwilling, we can only speculate, to confess that he has no more arguments, he simply does not speak.

Perhaps there is a fourth classic way, namely to attack the winner of the argument for being just as bad as the losers. That is different from what Eliphaz did; he attacked Job for being worse than the losers. But the fourth way is not a bad characterization of Elihu's method (chaps. 32–37), which we will examine in Chapter 7.

Job (Chapters 26–27)

Against Bildad's Eliphazian argument that the god "imposes peace on his heights" (25.2), Job emphasizes his own weakness by piling up negatives: he is "powerless" (*lō'-kōaḥ*), his arm has "no strength" (*lō'-'ōz*), he possesses no "wisdom" (*lō' ḥokmah*) (26.2–3a). Yet his positive terms, "helpful, deliverance, advise, propound," are deeply sarcastic. And as his questions focus on associations, Job moves the issue to the sinister:

> By whose help do you declare these words?
> Whose breath comes out from you? (v. 4)

The implication is that the help is illicit,[31] the breath something one would be ashamed to admit.

But the mystery deepens as we observe that the second-person pronouns in verses 2–4 are singular. When Job used a singular second-person address before, it was to the god. In the second cycle, the scope of address to the god was greatly reduced, and in Job's previous speech, chaps. 23–24, he did none of it. Are verses 2–4 directed to the god, or are they directed to Bildad?

We can take them either way, though address to an immediately prior speaker in the singular does not otherwise happen in the dialogue.[32] Directed to Bildad, the opening tramples down whatever may be left of the friends' kindliness. Heaping scorn on their help to the helpless and their sagacity to the unwise, he suggests that they would do better to disavow the sources of their talk. Directed to the god, the vitriol is more extreme, for Job addresses a deity who is not only absent but who has said absolutely nothing to him.

> How you advise one lacking wisdom,
> effusively propound knowledge! (v. 3)

And in verse 4, Job suggests that the silent god must have help in all his speaking. But who could help him say so much without saying anything? Perhaps he is thinking of such an episode as the prophet Micaiah ben Imlah's vision of the heavenly court (1 Ki 22.19–23), where one of the "spirits" proposes to go and be a "lying spirit" in the mouths of the prophets in order to give King Ahab his comeuppance. Even more cynical is the nonspeaking that is carried by this nonbreath:

> Whose breath [*n*ᵉ*šamah*] comes out from you?

In Genesis 2.7, the god transforms the human (*'adam*) from dust to soul (*nepeš*) by blowing into the inert form the "breath of life" (*nišmat ḥayyīm*). Job's allusion, denying to the god his own independent breath, condemns his power as immoral and, in effect, collapses chaos and creation together.

Job expands on the character of divine power in creation. Following Bildad's speech and his own opening, this canvasing of the cosmic powers would appear on the surface to agree with the friends' assessment of the divine transcendence. Yet the tone, tinged by the sarcasm of verses 2–4, makes Job's cosmological outburst something quite other than a positive doctrinal statement. The cosmos is under the thumb of a cruel, harshly present tyrant, and perhaps Bildad spoke better than he knew in saying, "Dreaded rule is with him" (25.2a). The dead "writhe" (*ḥll*, 26.5a), and Sheol, the place of the dead, like the wild asses and the destitute (24.7, 10), is "naked," has "no covering."[33] The entire universe lies passive under his rule (vv. 7–10), and parts of it "tremble, stunned by his blast" (v. 11). Why would the god blow away "Sky's pillars"? They seem to be in the same category as the cosmic divine enemies, Sea (*yamm*), the "fleeing Dragon" (vv. 12a, 13b), of whom we know from Isaiah 27.1, or Rahab (v. 12b), whose status as divine enemy is mentioned elsewhere but of whose activities no story remains.[34] And Sky (v. 13a)? In no myth anywhere in the ancient world does any deity successfully displace a sky god in combat. The Sumerian An and Babylonian Anu, like the Greek Zeus and the Roman Jupiter, were very stable sky gods. Job turns Sky itself into an enemy of the hero-god in a combat myth.[35] He is wildly concocting new mythic themes. Depicting a universe no longer deserted by the god but closely and tyrannically supervised, he twists into new conformations the structures of power that his and other cultures devised mythically to explain the universe.[36]

The friends trivialized and domesticated the transcendence they so readily ascribed to the deity.

> Oh, these are but the edges of his way.
> What whispered word do we hear of him,
> and the thunder of his might who understands? (v. 14)

The divine power is beyond human reach, and only its "edges" (*q^eṣōt*), its "whispered word" (an allusion to Eliphaz's vision in chap. 4?) are accessible to humans. That whisper is but a ghost of the real "thunder." Those who are privy only to a tiny corner of the god's power cannot draw conclusions from what is beyond understanding. Job is sure that Bildad's and Eliphaz's certainties are misplaced, and we are at liberty to think that Zophar has lost his confidence. Bildad referred to the transcendence of the divine power, but he did not know the half of it, and his limping cosmology of moon and stars is blown apart by Job's depiction of cosmic tyranny.

Yet Job claims that he has been denied any divine word of explanation, unlike the friends, who claimed the wisdom of past generations, access to special knowledge, and private revelation from the god. He does not reveal where he obtained his knowledge, and it is by no means clear why we must believe his negative account of power in the universe.

Before Job turns to that subject, it seems that he waits for Zophar to take his opportunity to speak. At 27.1 for the first time, the formula introducing a character's speech is changed. Always before, except at the dialogue's very beginning in 3.1–2, it has been, "Job [Eliphaz, Bildad, Zophar] answered and he said," which I have translated "answered thus." At 27.1, it is, "Job again lifted his discourse [*mašal*], and he said." The same words recur in 29.1, again suggesting that Job pauses for Zophar to speak, if he will. Zophar does not, and the field is left to Job.

Chapter 27 is a most remarkable turning of the tables, perhaps more than once. On the one hand, Job opens this part of his argument by a solemn oath *upon the life of the god himself*! "As El lives . . . and Shaddai," he swears; more explicitly, "As El lives [*ḥay 'ēl*], who has turned away my case, / Shaddai, who has embittered my soul" (v. 2). The oath affirms of the deity what Job had affirmed in 19.25 about his "avenger," that he "lives." That seems surprising, but Job appears to notice no difficulty. Perhaps he has convinced himself about the god by the description of cosmic powers in chap. 26 more than the sarcasm in 26.2–4 predicted. Yet the oath describes El as the one "who has turned away my case," and Shaddai "who has embittered my soul." Job's legal and moral opposition to him remains intact. To take an oath upon an unjust god might seem a contradiction in terms. But Job will continue his course of honest speaking while he still has breath (*n^ešamah*; v. 3, cf. 26.4b). In the same sentence he speaks of the god's injustice and of the necessity for life of "Eloah's wind." With the familiar self-curse formula, Job calls down an unnamed catastrophe upon himself if he does not continue his truth-speaking opposition to the god (v. 4). The opening oath, then, presents a duality between Job's truthfulness and the deity's injustice that the rest of the chapter takes even further.

What is so fascinating about the remainder of this speech is the way it completely redefines the debate by, in effect, redefining its protagonists. In order to maintain his moral rightness, Job inverts the terms of the prior discussion, thus standing the entire moral universe upon its head. The only factor that remains stable throughout this redefinition is what Job, unknowingly following Yahweh's lead, calls his "integrity" (*tummah*; cf. 2.3). That, indeed, is the bedrock of Job's assertion of his identity.

> I'm damned if I'll say you [plur.] are right [*'aṣdīq*];
> until I perish, I'll not turn away my integrity.
> To my rightness [*ṣ*^{e}*daqah*] I hold fast, will not weaken it;
> my heart finds nothing from my days to taunt. (27.5–6)

He opposes his own "rightness" to his refusal to declare the friends "right." His "integrity" depends on their *not* being "right, innocent," and on his "holding fast" (*ḥzq*) to his own "righteousness, innocence." The language is like Yahweh's remark to the Prosecutor in 2.3: "He is still holding fast to his integrity" (*'ōdennū maḥ*^{a}*zīq b*^{e}*tummatō*). Job will "not turn away" (*lō'-'asīr*) his integrity, though the god has "turned away" (*hēsīr*) his case (*mišpaṭ*, 27.2a). In chap. 24 Job argued strenuously that the god is the source and cause of human corruption. Here he claims that he himself is the exception, for the god has failed to corrupt him.

Now Job proceeds to redefine the god. It is not that he says anything new, but he had always before said it more as an implication than as a straightforward statement.

> Let my enemy be considered wicked,
> the one who rises against me, vicious. (27.7)

This is no vague generality about possible enemies. Job has but one enemy. In 13.24 he wondered why the god thought of him as enemy (*'ōyēb*), in 16.9 he referred to the god as "my foe" (*ṣarī*), and in 19.11 he decided that the god "considers me like his foes" (*ṣarayw*). In 9.24, Job declared that insofar as the earth is in the divine hands, it "is given over to a wicked hand." At last he combines the two ideas. The god is not only

Job's enemy, who attacks him (chaps. 16, 19), but he is now dismissed as "wicked" (*raša'*) and "vicious" (*'iwwal*). Job seals his alienation from this silent god and condemns him out of hand, fulfilling the images of corrupting power. He is not the god's enemy but, even more, his moral superior. Job is righteous (27.6a), the deity wicked (v. 7a), Job the one who refuses to speak "viciousness" (*'awlah*, v. 4a), the deity the "vicious" one (*'iwwal*, v. 7b).

Therefore Job has no possible future. Given the god's bald power, which Job displayed for the friends in chap. 26, he can hope for nothing. He will be destroyed, as the friends have threatened. But more:

> For what hope has the godless when he is snipped off,
> when Eloah carries his life away? (27.8)

It is another redefinition. Job accepts the term the friends have implicitly applied to him all along: godless.[37] If Job persists in his "rightness," he must willingly be alienated from an inimical and vicious deity. Godlessness, pollution, and hopelessness are the price demanded for being who he is. He is distanced from the god and repugnant to him. The god will make no move to alleviate Job's misery, nor will Job ever again take any "pleasure" in the god (vv. 9–10). In order to maintain the integrity of his moral stance, Job has redefined the deity as wicked enemy and himself as alienated and godless. The meanings of words are radically reversed.

Job knows that the friends will be aghast at this reconstruction of reality, but he is willing (v. 11) to help them. Yet the friends must already realize the truth of what he says. No other interpretation of what has occurred right in front of them is possible.

> You, of course, have all seen it,
> and why, then, are you so utterly vapid? (v. 12)

"So why talk nonsense?" is the blunt, interpretive translation in JPS; *Hebel tehbalū*: "Why do you puff a wind-gust?" *Hebel* is the motto word in Qoheleth, there often rendered "vanity." I argue elsewhere that English "vanity" is inadequate.[38] The basic metaphor in *hebel* is a puff of wind. The friends have gone all vaporous, insubstantially ephemeral. The ironically strengthened expression in the use of the verb with its cognate as accusative emphasizes the weakness of which Job accuses them.

He reminds them of what they ought to have seen by quoting Zophar, who closed his last speech:

> This is the lot of evil humankind from Elohim,
> the heritage that El bespeaks him. (20.29)

Zophar's parting shot summed up his idea that evil people receive their just deserts from the deity. Job skews the quotation a bit, and adds something crucial to it, but the two passages are so similar that 27.13 must allude to 20.29:

> They receive this lot of evil humankind with El,
> this heritage of oppressors from Shaddai.

The verb in 27.13 ("receive") appears last in Hebrew, and I have brought it to the first line as English syntax requires. A preposition may make a great difference. Zophar's "lot of evil humankind" is received "*from* Elohim," and it is punishment. Job's "lot of evil humankind" is received "*with* El," in the presence, with the connivance, of the deity, and it is reward. The race receives its "lot" insofar as its character matches the deity's, insofar as it is *rašaʿ*, "evil," just as Job's divine enemy in verse 7a is *rašaʿ*, the source, as Job said before, of human corruption.

The plurals in verse 13b, the "oppressors" who "receive" (*yiqqaḥū*) the heritage, divide "evil humankind," who are on the god's side, from Job, the singular "godless" (*ḥanēp*, v. 8a). In verses 14–23 Job turns to that singular in describing the fate of the "godless." These verses, often analyzed as another topos of the suffering of the wicked like what we have seen from the friends, especially in the second cycle, are usually attributed to Zophar in the effort to give him a voice in the third cycle.[39] The attribution is superficially attractive, especially in view of the opposition of that singular to the "righteous" and the "pure" in verse 17. But giving the words to Zophar is inappropriate in the light of Job's redefinitions of terms and of the difference between the singular person of verses 8–10 and the plural of verse 13. Verses 14–23 return to that singular, and "he" is, in effect, Job himself.

The passage is indeed a parody upon the friends' conventional diatribes, using the terms about the horrible fate of the wicked we have learned from the friends. The best index to its success as parody is the way we moderns, with our sophisticated approaches to authorship and convention and the disarray of ancient texts, have been hoodwinked into thinking that the speech belongs to Zophar. At the same time, given Job's ironic reversals of the meanings of words in verses 7–8, these verses are in fact a topos on the fate of the "godless." Job describes his expectation of destruction at the hands of a wicked god exactly as the friends have described their expectation that he would be destroyed at the hands of a righteous god. That irony works at many depths.

At last Job can refer to the deaths of his children in more negative terms than he used in chap. 1 and to the tyranny that will not permit "widows" to weep (27.15b).[40] Then the "righteous" and the "innocent," who mop up the spoils from the "godless" when he is gone, demonstrate how ironically and completely Job has inverted the terms.[41] Though he looks for a hard fate in the end, he makes clear—as the friends never did—that the "godless" may have a good life temporarily (vv. 16, 19a) but must expect it to disintegrate:

> He lies down rich, but has no harvest,
> opens his eyes and is no more [*'ēnennū*]. (v. 19)

With the last word, Job even parodies himself (see 7.8, 21).

At verses 20–22, the natural agents of dissolution, "tempest" (*sūpah*) and "east wind" (*qadīm*), are no less pitiless (v. 22a). It is unclear whether the unstated masculine subject of the verbs in verse 23 is the storm or the god who "claps its hands over him, / whistles derisively at him from his own place." I do not know how one would decide between the two, and I willingly accept a double meaning. Surely we may expect no less in so formidable a parody as this.

I almost wish this were the conclusion of the third cycle. The depth of irony, the conceptual deconstruction that Job has laid over the entire dialogue by his redefinitions, the profundity of his alienation from the god, all would lead a modern author to stop here. But the speech as it stands has another part.

Job (Chapter 28)

Most scholars are certain that chap. 28 does not belong here, was not composed by the same mind that produced the rest of the book, and not only does not continue the prior discussion but was interpolated long after the book was completed.[42] I join them in doubting that the "Hymn to Wisdom" was here in the earlier stages of the book's composition. But here it is now, and it makes a contribution to its context.

Any way one looks at it, chap. 28 is a surprise. Immersed as we have been in issues of righteousness and punishment, of moral virtue and divine response, we suddenly find ourselves in a description of the technologies of mining and metalworking. The learning that lies behind the text of Job is formidable indeed, but nothing has prepared us for this particular leap.

The poem is a roundabout definition of wisdom, which passes through several definitions of what wisdom is not and rings changes on knowledge, skill, and ignorance before it comes down to the point in the closing punch line. Mining is the prime exhibition of human "wisdom" as the ancient world understood it, and I suspect that the primary sense of the Hebrew word *ḥokmah* is "skill." The first section of the poem (vv. 1–11) moves from the technological knowledge implied in mining through images of distance (vv. 3–4), surprising discovery (vv. 5–6), ignorance (vv. 7–8), and hard work yielding knowledge (vv. 9–11). It presents a kind of spiral from implied to explicit knowledge, running through ignorance.

At verses 12–14 we have the first question about wisdom and where she is to be found.[43] The responses reveal universal ignorance about wisdom. "No human knows her dwelling" (v. 13a); even the cosmic powers, "Abyss" (*t^ehōm*, cf. Gen 1.2) and "Sea" (*yamm*), are ignorant of her whereabouts. What is important in the central section of the poem (Job 28.15–19) is Wisdom's incommensurability with all ordinary values. The text lists many precious gems in a somewhat repetitious catalog of Wisdom's matchless qualities. We need not pause over the details, especially because they are unclear, several words denoting unknown jewels. Yet, in the light of verses 12–14, and again of verses 20–22, this comparison favoring Wisdom over jewels is somewhat hollow, for the jewels, however rare they may be, are at least available.

The refrain before the catalog of gems stated ignorance as to Wisdom's whereabouts. The second refrain-like question and answer (vv. 20–22) asks whence Wisdom comes and repeats the answer of ignorance in terrestrial and cosmic nature. Unlike rare jewels, Wisdom cannot be found. We are left to ponder the question of the real value of what is so rare as to be inaccessible. The birds do not know where Wisdom might be, and even the realms of death can say no more than "a rumor of her has reached our ears" (v. 22b). An interesting echo of Canaanite mythology appears here and in the other refrain (v. 14). In the first refrain, the Abyss (*t^ehōm*) and Sea (*yamm*) did not know about Wisdom. Here Abaddon (which seems to mean something like "perishing") and Death (*mōt*) do not. We have seen Sea and Death as personified forces before. In the Canaanite mythology, both Yamm and Mot were sons of El, the titular head of the pantheon, and both were opponents of Ba'al, the fertility deity.[44] The ignorance of precisely these two figures, then, points to the mythic theme that the deity's cosmic opponents are also his inferiors, which may remind us of 26.12–13 and the deity's assaults upon Sea and other foes.

At last knowledge appears (vv. 23–26). The god "understands" (*byn*, cf. vv. 12b, 20b) how to find her, as human and cosmic knowledge did not, "knows" that her "place" is different from the "place" (v. 1b) where humans know about working gold. The god's knowledge is complete, whereas human and even cosmic knowledge are not, for, as verses 24–26 make clear, the god is in charge of it all. Human skill and technological prowess discover only what the god has done long before them. Divine knowledge is original, human knowledge derivative, and even the "knowledge" ascribed to cosmic and mythic forces like Sea and Death is bounded. Whatever "concealed things" the human miner can "bring to light" (v. 11b), whatever "precious" things he can "see," are nothing compared to what the god "sees," for the god has seen Wisdom, even "dug her out" (*ḥqr*, v. 27), as the humans dig out the ore (*ḥqr*, v. 3b).

More than that: the god is willing to let humans know about wisdom by telling them:

> Now, the fear of Adonai, that is wisdom,
> and avoiding evil is understanding. (v. 28)

Wisdom, as the god defines and conveys it to humans, has nothing to do with knowledge as we habitually think about it. Our culture takes as an unambiguous good, our model of and precondition for wisdom, the scientific or technological knowledge exhibited by the first part of this poem. The culture that produced the Book of Job looked on that kind of knowledge with contempt. Our research universities and laboratories and government grants would have been unthinkable in that culture, where wisdom came not from the acquisition of knowledge but from religion and morality. To be wise was to fear the god and to avoid evil. We have seen that expression before. Job "feared Elohim and avoided evil" (1.1, 8; 2.3). In the opening tale Job was certified by Yahweh as possessing what the "Hymn to Wisdom" presents in 28.28 as the divine definition of wisdom.

Job, of course, does not know that Yahweh so defined him, and the "Hymn to Wisdom" is in Job's mouth. Its outcome is even a bit more surprising when we think of that. In chap. 27, Job redefined and reversed some terms, and those reversals still hold. "To fear" the god is conventionally to be religious. Here that religiosity is paired with "avoiding evil." But "wicked" has become the term for the god, and it is but a short step to understand that "avoiding evil" means avoiding the god. "Religious" becomes its opposite, a matter not of making contact with the god but of evading him. Perhaps we need even to see "fear" resuming its literal sense. Job surely knows how dangerously powerful the deity is, for he has described the god's power in 27.14–23.

The "Hymn to Wisdom," then, adds to Job's powerful assertion of unassailable moral righteousness (27.4–6) the claim to a divinely certified wisdom.[45] To be sure, it is ironic, especially because the terms of the definition of wisdom are perceived as meaning their opposites. Job does not claim to be the god's superior in wisdom, as he claims in chap. 27 to be his moral superior. Though the hymn may not belong in the original dialogue, whoever inserted it here was by no means stupidly insensitive to the rest of the text.

To read the third cycle in this way, letting the attributions of poems to speakers stand and not attempting to reconstruct a hypothetical original, dazzlingly clarifies Job's alienation from the god. That alienation is present no matter how we read or reconstruct the third cycle. But chaps. 24, 26, and 27 (precisely those passages in which scholars wish to find remnants of the friends' missing speeches) emphasize and extend Job's contentions about the divine absence, culpability for human corruption, overwhelming power over the cosmos, and cynical ruthlessness. Job's hope is completely gone, as his concluding redefinitions of terms make utterly clear. He enters his summation speech (chaps. 29–31) with no illusions about the outcome of the trial he demands. His experience has transvalued his values.

Dermot Cox misses, I think, the radicality of this final stance.[46] It is not simply the removal of the "signposts," the loss of earlier cherished norms. It is the *reversal* of them, the value system suddenly, absurdly, upside down.

6

"A Cliché, Like Dust and Ashes"

I hate
A tendency. The minute you get on one
It seems to start right off accelerating.
—Robert Frost,
"A Masque of Reason"

Job ends the dialogue in chaps. 29–31 with the final preparations for the trial that he sought in chap. 23. Then he was doubtful that it could turn out as he wished, and perhaps that is why he pauses here to sum up his story and his situation.

The summation speech divides neatly into three parts, corresponding to the chapter divisions. In chap. 29 Job describes the "good old days," when he got on well with life and the god and his fellows. In chap. 30 he vividly sketches the miserable present to which life and the god and his fellows have brought him. Chapter 31 proceeds to the fantasy (as we may take it) of the trial, in which Job takes a series of oaths—curses on himself, indeed—to clear himself of whatever cloud of accusations hangs over his head. He closes the dialogue as he began it in chap. 3: with curses. But that rhetorical observation does not by itself show that Job has come back to the same position he occupied in chap. 3.[1]

Chapters 29–30 are implicitly addressed to the friends, though almost exactly in the middle of the entire speech, in 30.20–23, Job addresses the deity in the second-person singular. The curses on himself are addressed to the universe out there.

Chapter 29

Verse 27.1 opens with a novel introductory formula: "And Job again took up his discourse and said." It was Zophar's turn to speak, but he did not. I suggested in Chapter 5 that it looked as if Job paused to allow Zophar to enter the discussion. He uses the same formula at 29.1, having spoken, with only that silence at 27.1, since 26.2. Again he seems to pause to let Zophar speak. Again Zophar passes up the opportunity; he will not have another.

What Job says in this chapter seems surprisingly uncomplicated, especially in light of its symmetrical structure:[2]

A. Past blessing (vv. 2–6)
B. Past honor and admiration (vv. 7–10)
C. Administration of justice (vv. 11–17)
A′. Expected blessing (vv. 18–20)
B′. Past honor and admiration (vv. 21–25)

The thematic repetition of verses 2–10 (A-B) in verses 18–25 (A′-B′) may remind the musical reader of the ABA form of many a song or slow movement of a sonata. An opening theme gives way to a contrasting middle section, followed by a repetition of the opening, often with interesting and elegant variation. Here the opening section has two parts, and the variation in the third section consists of a switch in the first part from past experience to expected future and a return to the past in the second part.

Beloved by the god, respected by the people, helper of the weak and scourge of the wicked, flourishing in prosperity, as influential as if he were royal, Job moves from one positive aspect of his life to another. One might almost believe that he has forgotten his pain and suffering. Chapter 30 will show that he has not, and closer examination of Job's words here suggests that what he says is not as simple as it seems.

> Would that I were as past months,
> the days when Eloah watched over me. (v. 2)

We have seen "watched" (*šmr*) before. In 10.12, "your care [*pᵉquddatka*] has guarded [*šamᵉrah*] my spirit" looked positive, but Job immediately used a negative sense of the verb:

> If I sin, you put a guard on me [*šᵉmartanī*]
> and don't acquit me of my fault. (10.14)

In 7.12, Job wondered if he were the god's cosmic enemy, "that you station a guard [*mišmar*] over me." He complained in 13.27 that the god "watch[es] [*tišmōr*] all the paths I walk." Such "watching" looks like the hostile supervision of a prison guard rather than the benevolent care of a hospital nurse. Job has complained throughout the dialogue that the god watches him too much. Has he now forgotten that complaint? Perhaps "the days when Eloah watched over me" (29.2) were not entirely happy.

Even verse 3, with its images of light against darkness, receives an odd darkening from the resonances of earlier uses:

> when his lamp [*nēr*] shone over my head,
> and I walked the dark by its light [*'ōr*].

Bildad used the same two words in close proximity to each other:

> Surely knaves' light [*'ōr*] is snuffed out,
> its fire's blaze doesn't shine,
> light [*'ōr*] goes dark in his tent,
> the beacon [*nēr*] above him is snuffed out. (18.5–6)

Bildad was sure that the wicked's "light" and "beacon" were "snuffed out." But Job responded in 21.17 with a rhetorical question whose implied answer is "not often":

> How often is the beacon [*nēr*] of the wicked snuffed out?

That question came in the context of Job's proposal that the god rewards bad people and punishes good ones. As we recall Job's redefinition in 27.7, "Let my enemy be considered wicked," we see that the connection between the "light" and the "beacon" of the wicked in 18.5–6 and 21.17 and the "lamp" and "light" of the god in 29.3 has suddenly become complex. Perhaps the amiable friendship is not as straightforward as it seems.

Two points in verses 4–5 continue the theme of past blessing. Job thinks of the past as his "autumn days" (*y^e^mē ḥorpī*). European and American cultures conventionally think of autumn as symbolizing an end, the year's downward movement from "summertime, when the livin' is easy," to winter, the season of death.[3] The natural time for the new year in Europe and North America is the passage from winter to spring in late February to May. In the Near East, especially in the rain culture of Palestine and Canaan, that meaning of the seasons is reversed. Summer is the season of death, drought, and desperate heat, through which animals and crops often barely make it. In winter come the rains that will grow the wheat, turn the grazing meadows green, and replenish the water sources. Autumn is the natural time for the new year, when people are victorious over summer's death and look forward eagerly to the coming of the rains and burgeoning life. Job's "autumn days" are days not of decline but of youth, what Shakespeare called "salad days."[4]

Second, verse 5b appears to be a somewhat rueful recollection of a father's pleasure at his now-dead children.[5] It is combined with verse 4b in what may seem an equally rueful memory of a very different relation between Job and the deity, a relation of "friendship" (*sōd*) and harmony, when the god was "still with me." That claim of close friendship (v. 4b) may also be an implicitly positive answer to Eliphaz's sarcastic question, "Do you listen in Eloah's council [*sōd*]?" (15.8a)

"Things are seldom what they seem," Little Buttercup insisted, and the value of her skepticism becomes clearer in the picture of idyllic prosperity in verse 6, the footsteps "washed [one might say bathed] with milk," the rock having some presumably positive relation to "streams of oil."[6] Multiple and surprising possibilities occur in these verses too. "Shaddai was still with me" (v. 5a) has that ambiguous preposition *'im*, in its usual poetic form with suffixes, *'immadī*. It does, to be sure, mean "with," but also quite frequently in Job it means "against." By now, readers understand that I reject the view that in any context a word has but one primary meaning, which allows conflicting meanings to be eliminated forthwith. Though the general tone of these verses makes acceptable the surface meaning of *b^e'ōd šaddai 'immadī*, "Shaddai was still with me," the underlying "Shaddai was still against me" is a meaning to be reckoned with.

Verse 6a presents a pleasantly positive image of a man in luxury: "My steps were washed with milk" (*birḥōṣ h^alīkay b^eḥēmah*). The image depends on the common scholarly proposal that *ḥēmah*, "milk," is a variant spelling of *ḥem'ah*.[7] *Ḥēmah* might mean anger or rage, and "steps washed with rage" proposes a metaphor very different from luxury and sinister in the absence of all indication of the rage's origin. Even more interesting is the other sense of *ḥēmah*: "poison." The picture is of something approaching assassination, all the more frightening in that the source of the insidious poison is completely unknown. The original readers were not ignorant of their own language. They knew that *ḥēmah* means "rage" or "poison." We cannot know whether they would have said to themselves, as we tend to: "No, Job could not possibly mean that. Some scribe misspelled *ḥem'ah*." Even the "corrected" spelling is not an unambiguous metaphor of luxury, for milk is a very slippery substance on which to walk.

Perhaps verse 5a on one level and verse 6a on two present images both positive and positively demonic. Only illusion is helped if we pretend but one meaning. At the very least, both lines cast shadows over verses 4–6, shadows very like the ones in verses 2–3. "Eloah's friendship over my tent" might have screened the coming calamity from Job's awareness. "Autumn" with its youthful expectations might have been a misleading hope. The god's friendship, seen now through the haze of pain, may have set Job up for the catastrophe to come as a false, deliberately misleading pretense.

Job's picture of his proud past as a civic leader (vv. 7–10) gives the impression of a nostalgic look into the long past, an impression strengthened by the stark contrast drawn in the next chapter between the past and the terrible present. In fact, when we think of it, the past is not very distant. The dialogue is completely devoid of time reference. Only seven days of silence (2.13) passed between the three friends' arrival and the opening of the debate, and, because no length of time between Job's affliction and their coming is hinted at in the text, we need not consider it as an issue. The book's leisurely pace balances its depth of intensity, and the reader forgets the passage of time altogether.

Powerful, rich, wise, and elderly men in Israelite cities were expected to be present in the city gate to act as intermediaries in disputes and to hear legal cases. The evidence for judicial office in the Hebrew Bible is slim, but it does not point toward a professional or elected judiciary.[8] We may imagine that any man who aspired to status and influence would hang around the open space in the city gate, where legal activities were carried on. He would gain standing and experience by being asked to assist in judgment.

Job claims not only that he went there but almost that he had a regular place (*mōšabī*, "my seat," 29.7b), which he always occupied, a very different seat from the one he now occupies outside the city in the ash heap (*yōšēb*, 2.8). In these verses, by the way, he is clearly a city dweller. From chaps. 1–2 we might have thought of a seminomadic sheikh, wealthy in herds and flocks. To be sure, 29.4 says that he lived in a tent, but perhaps "tent" was simply a conventional, perhaps half-deprecating, reference to one's home.[9]

The most interesting aspect of Job's self-portrait as a community leader is his description of other people's attitudes toward him:

> Young people saw me and hid,
> old ones stood in their places,
> princes restrained words
> and laid their hands on their mouths,
> the voices of leaders were hidden,
> and their tongues stuck to their palates. (vv. 8–10)

Job describes respect there, but also terror.[10] The young hide, not only from admiration; the "princes" (*śarīm*) are silent, and "leaders" (*n^{e}gīdīm*) are not only silent but are silenced, their voices refusing to work. Even the elderly, it seems, rise for other than respectful reasons. The phrase may mean something like "stood stock still," wishing, we might conjecture, not to be caught in motion. The "restraint" the princes impose on their words (v. 9a) is actually more like "constriction" (*'ṣr*), or even, in a cognate noun, "oppression" (*'ōṣer*, Ps 107.39; Isa 53.8). The root *'ṣr* gives the feeling of a disciplined restraint self-imposed with enormous energy. And if the prior use of the phrase "to lay the hand on the mouth" in 21.5 indicates its meaning here, the princes are silent out of terror.[11] The terms in 29.10 are equally overbearing. "Hidden voices" is an unusual phrase that makes one think either that no one deliberately undertakes audible speech, or that people are whispering unobtrusively together in order to escape notice. And "tongues stuck to their palates" is palpably a sign of fear.[12]

The attractive portrait of Job as an honored, respected leader of a happy, prosperous civic life disintegrates when we look closely at the words he uses to describe it. Those words are patent of positive understandings, especially taken together. Each of them, however, is also understandable in negative ways, and the total effect of these sardonic images is quite overwhelming. We hear Job's self-satisfaction at his well-deserved success in his community, and behind it we hear an arrogant man's testimony to the successful exercise of his arrogance.

At the center of this chapter is a symmetrically organized description of Job's administration of justice (vv. 11–17). Job refers in every other couplet to parts of the body, typically in pairs:[13] in verse 11 to "ear" and "eye"; in verse 13 to "heart" and perhaps to "knees" (*berek*) in a pun on "blessing" (*birkat*); in verse 15 to "eyes" and "feet"; and in verse 17 to "jaws" and "teeth." Between them, he intersperses descriptions of his action in achieving justice: in verse 12, rescuing the traditionally helpless, the "poor" (*'anī*) and the "orphan" (*yatōm*); in verse 14, metaphorically describing his personal attributes of righteousness (*ṣedeq*) and justice (*mišpaṭ*) as clothing; in verse 16, in a nicely alliterative line (*'ab 'anōkī le'ebyōnīm*), as being "father" to the "needy" and as selflessly investigating cases with which he is unacquainted.[14]

But Job's justice goes beyond administration. It is his very character, the priestly "robe and turban" that accompanies his dressing in "righteousness" (*ṣedeq*).[15] It is reinforced by the eye that sees him (v. 11b), which "testified" for him (*te'īdēnī*), in opposition to his earlier claim (16.8) that his own emaciation testified against him (a different verb, *'nh*). He is an activist jurist, one who engages in "rescue" (v. 12), in personally leading and assisting the handicapped (v. 15), and in wreaking terrible hurt on the hurtful (v. 17).

The earlier part of this description is put in terms of sound, of hearing (v. 11a), crying out (v. 12a),[16] and singing (v. 13b), in contrast to the enforced, terrified silence in verses 9–10. In verse 17, the "vicious" (*'awwal*, the sound echoes *'iwwēr*, "blind," v. 15a) are forcibly rendered silent by the breaking of their jaws, which recalls the silencing of mouths in verse 9. But the last time we heard about someone "vicious" in Job's mouth was where he defined the god in 27.7 as his "vicious" (*'awwal*) enemy in stringent contrast to his own "rightness" (27.6a: *ṣᵉdaqah*). The echo takes us back to the arrogance of the powerful man who instills fear in ordinary humans (29.7–10). But Job claims more: working justice for the weak of his own kind against the "vicious," he extends his triumph over his real enemy, the deity, whom he robs of his prey by the power of his "righteousness" (*ṣedeq*, v. 14a), which "clothes" him and to which in 27.6a he proudly claimed to "hold fast." Job is still claiming to be the surpassing exemplar of justice not only for human beings but also over and against the god. Even where it looks straightforward, this text still surprises us.

As Job goes on to the blessing he expected from his devotion to justice (29.18–20), the undercurrent of double meaning continues. Habel is right: "The language describing this blessing is replete with lavish images."[17] The relaxed satisfaction of dying with his "nest" (v. 18a; "with" is odd in Hebrew too), presumably with his family, goes in the opposite direction from "multiplying days like sand,"[18] for the former has to do with the end of life, the latter with its continuance. Even that logical disturbance seems not to confuse the basically positive tenor of the images.

What follows in verses 19–20 sounds very positive indeed. Water is as significantly related to the maintenance of life in that arid territory as the image of light (v. 3) is to happiness and truth. Job's plant-self is watered both at the root and at the twigs. That image of a burgeoning, well-fertilized, well-fed plant, which contains sexual overtones, goes on to a related image of a renewed "vigor" (*kabōd*, "weight, glory") and to a slightly more distant one of a "successful" bow; both terms suggest sexual and military prowess.[19]

Both of these couplets, moreover, echo Job's other comparison of himself to a plant, in 14.7–9. There he contrasted his hopeless destiny with the hope that a felled tree can have. Here he represents himself in the image of the apparently dead tree, which comes to fresh life with water below and dew above, and which is even "successful" (*ḥlp*—the same verb in 14.7b, "come new"). Job thought he might be like the tree that has hope for the future. It is all very pleasant.

Or is it? The "root opened out to water" is very like Bildad's image of the "well-watered" wicked person in 8.16–17, especially verse 17a: "His roots twine about the pool." But in 8.18, his "place" rejects and ignores him, and the image of the irrigated garden turns ironic. Job also echoes his own reversal in 14.7–9 of Bildad's image, and yet there is an odd difference between the "branches" (*qaṣīr*) that are grown in 14.9 and these "twigs" (also *qaṣīr*) on which dew lodges (*lyn*, 29.19). "Lodging" is usually a temporary stay, and dew notoriously vanishes with the first heat of day (e.g., Hos 6.4). Moreover, though the opposition of root at the bottom of the tree and twig at the top suggests the health of the whole tree, the "twigs" remind us of harvest (also *qaṣīr*), and that reminds us of the cognate verb(s) *qṣr*, having to do with reaping or harvesting on the one hand and more generally being short or shortened (cut off?) on the other. "Twigs," then, may be not only an image of health but precisely its opposite, something chopped off and perhaps wounded.

The same duality comes out in verse 20, not so much in the first line as in the second. In the first, the preposition "with" occurred before in verse 5a, where we saw that Shaddai's being "with" Job might actually mean being "against" him.[20] If Job's "vigor" (*kabōd*) is "new with" him in the same way that Shaddai is "with" him, the statement is at least ambiguous. But the picture of the "bow successful in his hand" is even more stinging, looked at in an alternative way. I noted above that "bow" might be a sexual image as well as a military one, perhaps a euphemism for the penis, perhaps more generally a reference to masculine sexuality. Or perhaps "in my hand" is the more specifically sexual term, as *yad* sometimes refers to the phallus (e.g., Isa 57.8, 10). "Success," moreover, echoes Job's hopeful tree in 14.7, where *ḥlp* described its power of resuscitation. Yet the verb has mainly to do with changing, as in Genesis 35.2, where it means to change an article of clothing, or to exchange something for something else, as in the ironic boast in Isaiah 9.9 (Eng. 10), that cedars will be exchanged for sycamores, or in the prohibition in Leviticus 27.10 of exchanging one animal for another in a sacrifice. Surely the meaning of "my bow changed (or exchanged for something else) in my hand" is not identical to "my bow successful in my hand." Sexually the latter would suggest undiminished virility, the former perhaps greatly diminished virility. If the military image (which forecasts 29.25) predominates, then the "changed" bow might portend an inability to fight or an inexplicable defeat.

The constant duality beneath the surface of Job's apparently positive reminiscence of the past can hardly be tossed aside as insignificant. It continues in verses 21–25 as Job repeats his motif of being honored and respected.

His description in verses 21–22 of the silence of others seems less harshly arrogant than verses 8–10, more expectant, as if the hearers anticipate the justice of verses 12–17 rather than the power of the earlier passage. Job quickly takes up language that points to royalty. Images of rain and dropping water (vv. 22–23) echo the expectation of irrigation in verse 19 and suggest the concept of kingship in its function as guarantor of natural fertility. Perhaps the clearest instance is the simile for the king in Psalm 72.6:

> May he come down like rain on mown grass,
> like showers sprinkling the earth.

The king's reign not only coincides with natural fertility but affects and causes it:

> May there be plenty [?] of grain in the earth,
> on top of the mountains may it shake.
> Like Lebanon his fruit,
> and may they blossom from the city
> like earth's grass. (Ps 72.16)

Job's words likewise have the causative quality of rain (the same word as in Ps 72.6a) on people's lives. He has not only improved life for people, as he boasted in verses 11–17; he has empowered it. They depend upon him as they depend on the giver of showers.

If this language of life-giving rain, which continues in verses 24–25, is not about the king, it is about the deity. We will see such language later in the mouths of Elihu and of Yahweh himself. Job describes himself, then, either as a king or as a god. We are faced once again by a man who is not exactly understating his own power. He can say of his "subjects," presumably with a straight face, that they did not (could not?) believe that he was smiling at them (v. 24a), that they, as it were, hoarded ("did not let fall") "the light of my face."[21] "The light of my face" (*'ōr pᵃnay*) is a phrase we expect to refer to a king (e.g., Prov 16.15) or to a god (Num 6.25; Ps 4.7 [Eng. 6]), and the expression of disbelief at the great man's amiability is not only of wonder but also of surprise. It was too good to be true—and was therefore to be doubted.

The summary tercet (v. 25) makes the royal language explicit. Job determined the "way" of his troops,[22] "sat at the head," language that reflects the military functions of king or deity (see Ps 29.10). Those same "troops" attacked Job at the behest of the god (Job 16.13; 19.12). But even when the way of the troops led to human disaster, Job retained his royal function, untouched personally by the hazard of battle ("like a happy man," indeed in the cognate verb in 29.11a, "commended" by all) and magnanimously playing the leader, "who consoles mourners." Job claims to exercise the sort of compassion with which Eliphaz began his first speech (4.3–4), the kind Job has needed from the friends and has not received (cf. 21.34).

This rehearsal of Job's departed happiness is a remarkable speech. But its details, with their multiple resonances, open up the many levels upon which the poem moves and the many directions in which it goes. It may leave us with vertigo.

Chapter 30

In chap. 29 Job used images of silence to describe the attitudes of lesser people toward his leadership, though his righteous dealing with the weak produced "singing for joy" (29.13). Other people "restrained words and laid their hands on their mouths" (v. 9), were terrified into silence (v. 10), listened silently for Job's plans (v. 21). When they opened their mouths, it was metaphorically to drink (v. 23b). Job might "smile" (*śḥq*, v. 24), but they would not.

Now they "laugh" at him in derision (again *śḥq*, 30.1), they "shout" (v. 5b) and "bray" (v. 7a). He is their (mocking) "song" and "word" (v. 9). At the end of the chapter, Job refers to his sounds: weeping (vv. 25, 31), crying for help (v. 28), disgusting noises in his bowels (v. 27). The oppositions of sound and silence in chap. 29 divided Job's power from his peers' weakness. In chap. 30 the standings are reversed: sounds and silences show Job as weak and his opponents as strong.

It shows even in the poetic structure. Three times (vv. 1, 9, and 16) Job starts a new thought with "and now" (*w*ᵉ*'attah*). In verses 1–8, he expresses contempt for his tormenters' worthlessness, in verses 9–15 describes their terrifying brutality, and in verses 16–19 ascribes the torment to the god. He complains directly to the god (vv. 20–23) about the mistreatment and states his expectation of death. Finally, in verses 24–31, he reverts to his own feelings of pain and hopelessness.

Job's contempt has dropped its mask of double meanings and appears on the surface:

And now they laugh at me,
those much younger than I,
whose fathers I disdained
to station among my sheepdogs. (v. 1)

The laughing is topsy-turvy. When Job was in power, he could "smile" (*śḥq*) and people could not believe it. Now they "laugh" (*śḥq*) at him in contempt, and his only rejoinder is in kind. But it is the sarcasm of weakness. Job does not enjoy occupying the place he once enjoyed keeping others in, but he can do no more than snap at the harassers, like one of his weary sheepdogs.

The remainder of the section is confusing in a way typical of Hebrew poetry—by mixing prepositions and singular and plural forms. Verse 2a surely refers to Job's tormenters with the plural possessive, "their hands," but a masculine singular pronoun in the next line has an uncertain referent: "Upon him [or it] perishes vigor" (*'alēmō 'abad kelaḥ*). I translated it as referring to Job, somewhat unusually in the third person, but the antecedent could be the masculine singular noun "strength" (*kōaḥ*):

What is their hands' strength to me,
the vigor of which is gone,
sterile by want and hunger. (vv. 2–3a)

In that case, verses 3–4 continue Job's sarcastic description of his tormenters.

To take verses 1–4 as referring to Job's upstart opposition makes a bit better sense of the plural verb in verse 5a, "From the community they cast [him] out." But that "him," which is explicit in *'alēmō* in verse 5b seems to refer to Job in an echo of *'alēmō* ("upon him") in verse 2b. Therefore the "vigor" in verse 2 is Job's, and verses 3–4 describe his desiccation. In order to make sense of both verse 2 and verse 5, it seems that we must take verses 2–4 to refer simultaneously to both Job and his persecutors.

With another plural verb, "they bray" in verse 7a, the hounded one ("him," v. 5b) has suddenly become a group, living a primitive, beast-like life in the wilderness, away from the comforts and harassments of civilization, braying and huddling together like those wild asses whose hard life Job described so vividly in 24.5–8. Why has the discommunicated single person—Job or the type of which Job is an exemplar—suddenly become many? And why is Job suddenly so contemptuous of him/them in verse 8? If "they" in verse 7a is the same "they" as in verse 5a, the pursuers have given up the chase and have fantastically become the pursued.

On one account, these verses portray not merely some poverty-stricken members of the society, living in misery on its fringes, but "a class of outcasts who lived like wild beasts in the desert scrub and wilderness caves."[23] Yet the analogy to 24.5–8, where the wild asses are compared to the poor, and Job's passionate feeling that he is hatefully persecuted seem enough to account for the vivid imagery. Not every detail in the text must reflect some ancient actuality. But one bit of detail is interesting. Job calls these outcasts *b^{e}nē-nabal*, which I translate "churls" (30.8a). "Sons of a fool" is more nearly literal, and one might connect it to Job's reply in 2.10 to his wife: "You're talking like a fool" (*'aḥat hanne^{e}balōt*, literally "one of the [female] fools"). The contempt in 30.8 lends a deeper tone to 2.10 than we saw there before.

It is not possible to arrive at a single meaning of verses 1–8. The text has gone kaleidoscopic again, opening up several possibilities, not all of which cohere logically with the others. If the reader, weary of contradictions and complexities, cries out in frustration, "Just tell me what it means!" I can say only that what the Book of Job means is often confusing and almost always multiple. If it were not so, Job would not be the exhilarating book it is. Yet exhilaration always verges on hyperventilation.

The second strophe (vv. 9–15) is not as confusing. Job's adversaries act as the god's agents to overwhelm him. "Song" used as a derisory expression against someone is familiar from passages like Psalm 69.13 (Eng. 12) and Lamentations 3.14, though "word" (*millah*) does not occur elsewhere in this negative sense.[24] The devastating hatred toward Job of these presumably healthy and respectable people leads him to a mixed image that says more about his state of mind than about theirs: they both "keep their distance" from him and "spit" in his face (30.10)—not easy to do at the same time. They hate because the god hates, disdainfully "loosening his bowstring" (*yitrō*, Ketib), casting the weapon aside to demonstrate the victim's complete helplessness and to humiliate him (v. 11a); or because the god "loosens my bowstring" (*yitrī*, Qere), disdainfully disarming the victim. So motivated, the god's human agents "put off the bridle" (v. 11b). The metaphor might signify the underlings' rejection of restraint and discipline or their becoming wild beasts, a fascinating echo of the donkey's bray in verse 7.

The metaphor turns military in verses 12–14, with roads built to besiege Job (as in 19.12b), the simultaneous destruction of his own path (vv. 12c–13a), and the comparison to a "breach" in a wall (v. 14a).[25] In any case, verse 15 reduces Job to besieged passivity (*hohpak*, "are dumped," and *tirdōp*, "is driven off").[26] The "terrors" are overturned upon him, and the panoply of social standing of which he was so arrogantly proud in chap. 29 is swept away. Bildad had referred to those terrors at the beginning and end of 18.11–14:

> Terrors all around make him shiver,
> chase after his feet.
> His strength is famine-ridden,
> and disaster is ready for his stumbling.
> Devours his skin-covered limbs,
> Death's first-born devours his limbs.[27]
> He's wrenched from the tent he trusted,
> marched off to the king of terrors.

One might see in "the king of terrors" a fearful king of the underworld, like the Mesopotamian Nergal, the Greek Pluto, the Roman Dis. In any case, the "terrors" Bildad portrayed extend further than fear contained inside someone's head. Whether these tormenters are human or more, Job imagines them as motivated by and under the control of the god and as bringing upon him terrors cosmic in scope.[28]

Job lays the blame not merely on unfriendly people but, in the short strophe in 30.16–19, directly on the god. No one else can be the subject of the singular verbs in verses 17 and 19. The surgical action described there is similar to descriptions of divine mayhem in 16.9, 12–13, and the contemptuous tossing of Job "to the muck" (30.19a) resembles what he was expecting in 9.31. What the unintelligible 30.18 might have said cannot be guessed, except that it might have a metaphor of clothing. But its opening phrase is interesting: "With great power" (*b^e^rob-kōaḥ*). In 23.6, Job wondered whether the god would prosecute him *b^e^rob-kōaḥ*, and there I saw reason to translate the phrase as "by an attorney," a plenipotentiary. In chap. 23 Job thought that the god would not deal with him through an agent. Now, having seen many agents, perhaps he thinks of one at work on him.

Concerned throughout the dialogue with the use and misuse of words, Job now finds himself reduced to a word: "I'm a cliché, like dust and ashes" (30.19). *Mšl* is a verb of comparison, stating the likeness of one thing to another or comparing something to something else. Its cognate noun, *mašal*, came to mean a proverb or wise saying—*mišlē š^e^lōmōh*, "Solomon's Proverbs," is the Hebrew title of the Book of Proverbs—perhaps because such sayings so often involved unexpected and instructive comparisons. I think that the Hithpa'el form of the verb may have the sense not of *being* like something (JPS: "I have become like dust and ashes"), but of the outcome of proverb mongering—"I have become a comparison, a proverb, a dead metaphor," such as those the pseudo-wise and "miserable comforters" bandy about. Job said earlier (v. 9) that he had become "song" and "word" (*millah*) to his persecutors. Now he has become a cliché to an entire culture. (Yes, indeed. Mention Job, and your interlocutor will almost invariably speak of patience, so much does the misreading of the book by the author of James 5.11 control our implicit reading.[29])

Once again, Job addresses the god (vv. 20–23). He will do so only twice more (40.4–5; 42.1–6). Fitting the rest of the speech, he begins with the images of sound and silence (30.20). No matter whether Job makes noise or stands quiet, the god responds to him inappropriately. If Job cries out (*šwʿ*—perhaps a pun with *yᵉšūʿah*, "safety," v. 15c), the god is silent; if Job is silent, the god volubly cross-examines him. Job makes another claim of superiority. When the poor person "cried out" (*mᵉšawwēaʿ*, 29.12a), Job rescued him. The god does not do as well.

It is blatantly overt tyranny, and Job complains (surprisingly, in the light of much that he has said before) that the god has "changed." To be sure, it is the opposite of the friendship that he described in 29.4, and the verb (*hpk*), echoing the terrors "dumped" upon him (*hohpak*, overturned, 30.15a), implies a complete change. It is almost as if he is saying "You have been dumped as cruelty upon me." The language echoes that of 16.9–14 in several ways, but especially with the verb *śṭm* (30.21b, cf. 16.9a), which seems to have a connotation of overt attack rather than inner animosity. Job's further description exhibits the arbitrary, unpredictable character of tyranny, its sudden inconsistency.

> You lift me to the wind, make me ride,
> you dissolve me, level me. (30.22)

"Riding the wind" reminds us of divine activity, riding the clouds (cf. Ps 68.5 [Eng. 4]) or the wings of the wind (Ps 18.11 [Eng. 10]). It looks like a claim that the deity acknowledges Job's pretensions to divinity and royalty (chap. 29).[30] Yet that same "wind," like his "standing," is driven off (30.15b). The line puts forth at the same time, then, the divine soaring above earthly limitations and the evanescent disappearance of human status. The following line reminds us of the same ephemerality and also, with "level,"[31] states another opposition to the positive sense of riding the wind. The deity both lifts Job up and casts him down, makes him comparable to the god and ruthlessly delimits him. He can be sure of nothing but death, indeed, of being "returned" (*tᵉšibenı*, v. 23—a pun on *tᵉšawweh*, v. 22b?) to Death's house, the great negative to which all positives revert. It is a curious couplet, stating in somewhat portentous terms ("For

I know"—the last thing Job knew was that his avenger was alive, 19.25a) the cliché that everyone dies. Yet perhaps in this context that is not quite such a cliché as we might think. Job is not just everyone, and his death carries a freight of reflected meaning that, in the argument about justice, goes beyond common death.

At verse 24 Job leaves off addressing the god and refers to him, nearly unintelligibly, in the third person.

> Surely he would not put out his hand to a ruin.

In verses 11b and 12b the verb "put out" (*šlḥ*) has to do with attacking, a sense it certainly carried in the mouth of the Prosecutor in 1.11 and 2.5, and in Yahweh's mouth in 1.12. In the light of those passages, Job here complains that the god is unfairly attacking a "ruin." But the expression *šlḥ yad*, "put out the hand," need not mean assault. In Genesis 3.22, the phrase seems a neutral description of taking fruit from a tree (though the act is to be prevented), and if the verb here does not mean an attack, Job seems to complain that the god does not assist the "ruin" that Job has become.[32]

In some ways, the series of self-curses in preparation for the trial that occupies chap. 31 begins at 30.25 with the "If I did not" form of the curse without a result clause that we have seen many times before. But chap. 31 multiplies the curse formulas, whereas here we have only one, followed by Job's dilation on his terrible situation. I analyze 30.25–31 as a unit, in part because of the occurrence in its first and last lines of forms of the verb *bkh*, "to weep." Such inclusive verbal repetitions are often clues to structure.

Job's smiling (29.24) is now completely reversed. He swears that he wept over days that were difficult for people, that he grieved for the poor (30.25). And he closes this part of his speech with the image of his weeping, mourning musical instruments—again a presumed reversal of the usual musical role of zither and flute.[33]

Between those two descriptions of weeping, Job describes his pitiful state in more images of reversal. His expectations of good were frustrated (v. 26), his body is ravaged by suffering (vv. 27a, 30). In contrast to the status that he described in chap. 29, his experience in political assembly is unsuccessful (v. 28b), and he consorts only with animals of the humanly uninhabitable desert (v. 29—an echo of the donkeys braying in the brush, v. 7). But the most interesting aspect of this lament of the sufferer over the details of his suffering is his inner reversal, a reversal that will be emphasized even more in chap. 31:

> But I hoped for good, and evil came,
> waited for light, and darkness came. (30.26)

It is an extraordinary statement. He has "hoped" (*qwh*) for good, not merely stood around waiting for it (though he has "waited for light"). It is the hope (*tiqwah*) that, in 14.7, he had ascribed to the cut tree, which can come new again, in contrast to a man's hope (*tiqwah*), which the god destroys (14.19). Job has not stated his hope so positively before, though he has argued that he does not deserve the punishment he has received. Indeed, "and evil came" directly contradicts what he said to his wife: "We receive good from Elohim and do not receive evil" (2.10). More than that, he begins to reverse the position to which he came in chap. 27, in which he drastically redefined the words in the controversy, such as "wicked," "godless," and the like. He has reverted to the retributive structure of things, which he had apparently denied earlier. Good is the reward for doing what the god and one's fellows approve of, and evil is punishment for its opposite.

In reversing his position from being "like a happy person who consoles mourners" (29.25) to being himself the mourning lyre (30.31), is Job weeping not only for his painful body but also for his failure of nerve? Has he seriously gone back on his hard-fought freedom from the god and all his regulations? We must see what happens in chap. 31.

Chapter 31

Job gets a good press for this part of his speech. Gordis calls it "the code of a man of honor" and emphasizes that Job declares his freedom from fourteen sins—twice seven, an important symbolic if not magical number.[34] The implied ethical system indeed seems impressive by our standards, involving not merely external actions but also inner attitudes and principles of ethical thinking. Several recent studies concentrate on the legal implications of the chapter, some referring to the disclaimers that the dead Egyptian king makes in the Book of the Dead in order to gain entrance to his full destiny, others discussing the analogy of Job's oaths to the oath of innocence that an accused person takes in court.[35]

We have seen before that Job wants a trial to establish his innocence, and the notion of an oath of clearance prior to the judge's appearance and the trial procedure would seem to make very good sense. His rehearsals of his own administration of justice in chap. 29 point in the same direction. Yet we had reason earlier to wonder whether he might have dropped the idea. Especially 27.7–23 suggested that Job had given up all hope of a trial that acknowledged his real character, and 30.20 almost proposed that a trial had already in effect taken place, in an atmosphere that was not conducive to justice.

> I cry out to you, and you don't answer me,
> I stand [silent], and you examine me.

In chap. 9, Job had already written off the trial as a waste of energy:

> If I'm innocent, my own mouth condemns me;
> if I'm perfect, he'll do me fraud. (v. 20)
>
> I'll be condemned—
> why do I struggle with the breeze?
> If I wash myself with snow water,
> purify my palms with lye,
> then you'll plunge me into the muck,
> and my clothes will make me disgusting. (vv. 29–31)

He had changed his mind in the interim:

> How long! I'll take my flesh in my teeth,
> grasp my throat with my hand.
> He's going to kill me; I cannot wait,
> but I must argue my ways to his face. (13.14–15)

He was ready to start the procedure right then, though he asked the god for some safeguards (vv. 20–21):

> Call, and I will answer,
> or I will speak, and you respond to me. (v. 22)

Later he advised the friends:

> Fear for your lives before the sword,
> for the sword is fury on wrongdoing,
> so that you may know that there is a trial. (19.29)

And in chap. 23 he reached the high point of his conviction that, if the trial could be fair and he could maintain his position, he would be vindicated in it.

> I would know the words of his answer,
> understand what he says to me.
> Would he prosecute me by an attorney?
> No, he himself would attend to me.
> There a moral person could argue with him,
> and I should bring forth my case successfully. (vv. 5–7)

But the redefinitions in chap. 27 seemed, like much of chaps. 29–30, to render the notion of a trial quite impossible. If the god had become Job's vicious enemy, then by definition the trial would be unjust, and Job could hope only for death (30.23), as he had done much earlier (6.8–10).

Yet now it seems that Job makes the final preparations for the trial, if indeed this series of curses upon himself is an oath of innocence, a response to a charge, implicit or explicit, that inaugurates the legal procedure he wishes. Four kinds of expressions are mixed up together in this chapter: questions, rhetorical and ordinary (e.g., vv. 2–4, 14–15); statements of fact or of expectation (e.g., vv. 11–12, 28, 30, 32); an exclamation (v. 35); and curses (e.g., vv. 5, 7–8, 9–10, 13). There are two kinds of curses: (1) eleven (or twelve, depending on how we read vv. 19–20) are the kind of "if (not)" curses without result clauses that we have seen again and again throughout the book; (2) unusually, four are "if (not)" curses with result clauses:

> If my step has strayed from the way,
> my heart has gone after my eyes,
> a stain has stuck to my palms,
> may I sow and another eat,
> and my descendants be uprooted. (vv. 7–8)
>
> If my heart has been fooled over a woman,
> and at my neighbor's door I have lain in wait,
> may my woman grind for another,
> others kneel over her. (vv. 9–10)
>
> If I have shaken my fist at the orphan
> because I saw my helpers in the gate,
> may my arm fall from my shoulder,
> my forearm be broken at the elbow. (vv. 21–22)
>
> If my ground cries against me,
> its furrows weep together,
> if I have eaten its strength without silver,
> made its Baals gasp,
> instead of wheat may thorns come up,
> instead of barley, stinkweed. (vv. 38–40)

It is structurally interesting that these four curses are spread out through the chapter: the first two are the second and third curses in the chapter, the third is the seventh (or eighth, if vv. 19–20 are two curses), and the last is the fifteenth and last curse. It is also structurally interesting that the curses with result clauses are always preceded by curses without result clauses, though a statement (v. 6) intervenes between the first pair

(vv. 7–10) and the preceding curse (v. 5). Other structurally interesting points about the chapter may be shown in this outline:

1. Questions: retribution (vv. 1–4; 8 lines)
2. Curses and statements (vv. 5–12; 17 lines)
   a. Curse without result: fraud (v. 5)
   b. Statement: integrity (v. 6)
   c. Curse with result: impurity (vv. 7–8)
   d. Curse with result: adultery (vv. 9–10)
   e. Statement with *kī*, "for": crimes (vv. 11–12)
3. Curses, questions, and statement (vv. 13–18; 13 lines)
   a. Curse without result: justice for slaves (v. 13)
   b. Questions: the god and common origin (vv. 14–15)
   c. Curse without result: aloofness (vv. 16–17)
   d. Statement with *kī*: care for the poor (v. 18)
4. Curses and statement (vv. 19–23; 10 lines)
   a. Curse without result: clothing for the poor (vv. 19–20)
   b. Curse with result: fairness (vv. 21–22)
   c. Statement with *kī*: fear of disaster (v. 23)
5. Curses and statement (vv. 24–28; 10 lines)
   a. Curse without result: wealth (v. 24)
   b. Curse without result: power (v. 25)
   c. Curse without result: idolatry (vv. 26–27)
   d. Statement with *kī*: crimes (v. 28)
6. Curses and statements (vv. 29–34; 13 lines)
   a. Curse without result: arrogance (v. 29)
   b. Statement: curse (v. 30)
   c. Curse without result: food (v. 31)
   d. Statement: hospitality (v. 32)
   e. Curse without result: hypocrisy (with *kī*; vv. 33–34)
7. Statement and curses (vv. 35–40; 13 lines)
   a. Statement (exclamation): challenge to trial (v. 35)
   b. Curse without result: pride (vv. 36–37)
   c. Curse with result: soil (vv. 38–40)[36]

The structure is not symmetrical, though sections 3–6 with their chiastic structure of thirteen, ten, ten, and thirteen lines almost are. The occurrence of the particle *kī* ("for, because") with the statements at the ends of sections 2–5 and in the oath that closes section 6 is the most compelling clue to the architecture of the speech for me. Nevertheless, the design is a way by which we may more efficiently see what Job is saying. It allows us to see, for example, how the poem moves from the steps in verse 4 to the walking and hurrying in verse 5, and how the steps in verse 4 are matched by numbering steps in verse 37. The threat of "disaster" in verse 3 is matched by the fear of "disaster" in verse 23. Such linkages between sections (see, e.g., "eyes," vv. 1, 7; "orphan," vv. 17, 21; "fist" [*yad*, "hand"], v. 21, and "hand," vv. 25, 27, "rejoice," vv. 25, 29) show that the speech is not mere words flung into the air or onto the page, but structured, carefully calculated thought.

Not surprisingly, the thought is complex and self-serving. Job is ill-inclined to take his pain in silence, and here he engages in the most forthright defense of his life and value system. He would surely accept Gordis's tag, "the code of a man of honor." From the cultic covenant of verse 1 to the covenant with his agricultural land in verses 38–40,[37] he ranges over the sins he has not committed and the attitudes he has had. I need not list the vices avoided and the virtues cultivated. The curses that Job calls down upon himself "if" he has done such crimes as fraud (v. 5), idolatry (vv. 26–27), adultery (vv. 9–10), overbearing arrogance in the presence of assistants (vv. 21–22), and senseless exploitation of the soil (vv. 38–40) are matched by statements of assurance that the god knows his integrity (the familiar *tummah*, v. 6), that certain crimes are notoriously actionable (vv. 11, 28), that he has refrained from loose cursing (v. 30), and that he has hospitably opened his doors (v. 32). He wishes disaster on himself not only for overt actions like withholding food from the starving (vv. 16–17) but also for inward attitudes: despising the justice due to the slave (v. 13), depending on wealth and power (vv. 24–25), being pleased ("stirred," *'rr*, "emotionally moved") at an enemy's misfortune (v. 29), and concealing himself because of fear of someone else's displeasure (vv. 33–34).

The claims fall for us on appreciative ears. These are sins we take seriously, attitudes we wish inwardly to avoid. Through its whole ethical history, our culture has taught us to avoid precisely these deeds and these thoughts. The principles Job espouses are those we are enjoined to have, those we accept as "right," even if viewed through eyes that a heart has followed into impurity (v. 7). Job depicts himself as the epitome of the ethical man, as he depicted himself in chap. 29 as the epitome of the successful leader. Both inwardly and outwardly, this speech lends credence to the first characterization of the man we saw: *tam w^{e}yašar*, "scrupulously moral" (1.1, 8; 2.3). The narrator said it, the god said it, Job himself has claimed it in passing before. Now he describes in detail just what it means, both in outward act and inward thought, to be *tam w^{e}yašar*.

The chapter has another side, however. The series of curses is, after all, designed to prepare the ground for Job's trial with the god. The litigant claims in this remarkable speech attention from his adversary. And he claims it in the strongest possible way. The frequent use of the term "oath of clearance" by scholars may mask that,[38] because scholars are prone, as I have complained before, to take the self-curse as more or less equivalent to a strong denial or affirmation and to deal with these statements as affirmations and denials, not as self-curses. Our culture does not know what to do with curses, because we do not believe in their magical efficacy. No such disability informed ancient Hebrew culture. A curse was not a casual expression, to be trifled with or tossed aside. It was the most powerful way people had of setting in train forces of action and reaction, and no one would take a curse lightly. I have argued that the curse is a way of forcing the god to respond, requiring his attention, because the curse cannot go unattended.[39] It will work ineluctably through to its end result, and the god himself is under its sway. Habel calls this series of oaths "a barbed provocation."[40] His only error is that the words are too weak.

I noted in Chapter 2 that the most common form of the curse is "If A (or not A)—" without specifying the result the curser calls down upon himself. That was the form of the Prosecutor's self-curse in 1.11: "If he does not curse you to your face—." The Prosecutor left unspoken the terrible result for himself in that event, and we saw no catastrophe, though we see nothing further of the Prosecutor after chap. 2. This kind of curse is present in eleven of the fifteen curses in chap. 31 (vv. 5, 13, 16–17, 19–20, 24, 25, 26–27, 29, 31, 33–34, 36–37). In each case Job implies some disaster for himself.

In four of the curses (vv. 7–8, 9–10, 21–22, and 38–40), Job specifies the disaster. The result in verse 22 exceeds the evil from which Job wishes to clear himself.

> If I have shaken my fist [*yad*, hand] at the orphan
> because I saw my helpers in the gate,
> may my arm fall from my shoulder,
> my forearm be broken at the elbow. (vv. 21–22)

For raising his hand, Job calls down the fracture of his arm. In each case, the result is correlated with the evil. In verses 38–40, the evil is exploitation of the soil, and the result is that the soil will grow inedible produce. But the other two curses with result clauses are very curious. In verses 7–8, the result of Job's hypothetical straying from the "way" or his having an impure stain on his palm is the producer's loss of consumption ("may I sow and another eat"), a penalty presumably upon himself, and the "uprooting" of his descendants, a penalty on those involved only by association. To be sure, the law allows the penalty for a person's crime to fall upon that person's descendants (Exod 20.5), but Job opposed that idea in 21.19–20.

Even more shocking is 31.9–10, where Job's possible adulterous behavior will issue in the bondage of his "woman," who becomes the slave of "another" (singular) and the sexual toy of "others" (plural). The retribution for his sexual misdeeds, if any, is to fall not upon himself but upon her! For a speech full of high-flown ethical principles, this one falls with a crash to earth. Significantly, I find no commentator who sees in verses 9–10 cause to criticize the ethical honor of the hero. Slaves are promised far better treatment than Job's "woman." Such oppressiveness is quite enough decisively to undercut the consistent picture of "honor" that interpreters see in chap. 31.

Pondering the Prosecutor's self-curses in chaps. 1–2, I found them crucial to the situation of Job's suffering. In fact, they brought that suffering about by putting the Prosecutor at hazard of disaster. Now, having begun the dialogue by cursing his birthday (3.3–10), Job ends it with this catalog of fifteen curses upon himself.[41] One might wonder whether one or two would have been enough to accomplish what Job wished. Perhaps the provocation of fifteen curses is a blunt rather than a barbed instrument. At any rate, Job puts the heat on the god in a way that matches the heat the Prosecutor applied in the first two chapters.

Not only does Job specifically call out for a trial:

> Oh that I had someone to hear me—
> here is my mark; let Shaddai answer me—
> and the inscription my accuser has written! (31.35)

The "hearer" is no doubt a "hearing officer" in the legal sense. Job puts his signature, his *taw* (we would say his X), on the claim for a trial, and the very word may echo *tummah*, his "integrity" (v. 6b). The accuser's "inscription" is somewhat confusing,[42] in that the sentence appears to imply that Job does not have the "inscription" and wishes he did have it. Carrying on a hypothetical cross-examination (13.23), he had demanded information about his faults but had no satisfaction of it.[43] Now he proceeds to another self-curse. Translators are at one in rendering 31.36–37 as strong statements, but they have the familiar "If I do not" form:

> If I do not carry it [*sc.*, the inscription] on my shoulder,
> tie it on me like a wreath,
> the number of my steps imprint upon him,
> like a prince approach him—

Job reverts to the same kind of royal language that he used at the end of chap. 29, though he used "leader" (*nagīd*) for his subordinates in 29.10a. But he emphasizes the word here by the nice wordplay in the verb "imprint," *'aggīdennū*. This curse calls attention to his determination to deal with the god as an equal. An element of comedy is also present. Job, "the disheveled victim arising from his ashes to parade with his 'paper crown,'"[44] is a parody of his arrogant parading to his seat of justice in 29.7–10, flaunting as a badge of honor or a crown of glory both the hypothetical document, which he does not possess, and his own self-assurance. Job will "inform" (*'aggīd*) the god of the count of his steps, which the god has long been not only tracking (cf. 13.27) but "numbering" (31.4).

The provocation is barbed, to be sure, but it is greater than that. It includes an element of sarcasm as well as of irony, of comic parody as well as of serious argument. And as an overwhelming series of curses upon himself, it puts Job's future (and, as vv. 7–10 show, the futures of others) absolutely on the line.

The remaining factor in this speech, most surprising of all, is perhaps most clearly seen at the very beginning:

> What is Eloah's portion from above,
> Shaddai's inheritance from on high?
> Is it not disaster for the vicious,
> calamity for evildoers?
> Does he not see my ways,
> number all my steps? (vv. 2–4)

Verse 4 denies that Job qualifies for the "inheritance" from Shaddai that verse 3 describes as applying to the "vicious." That "portion" and "inheritance" (*ḥēleq* and *naḥ^{a}lah*, respectively) are what Job described in 27.13 as the "portion" and "inheritance" from El and Shaddai for the wicked. There Job was redefining terms to mean their opposites, and "vicious" was his reversal word for the god himself in 27.7. Here, we have two simultaneous possibilities. If "vicious" in 31.3a has the same referent as the word has in 27.7 (it is singular in both places), Job now claims that the logical outcome of the god's own bequeathing is disaster for the god himself. There is a catastrophic inconsistency within the god's single front.

But 31.4 also seems to distinguish Job from the "vicious" and the "evildoers" of verse 3, and that seems consistent with the following series of self-curses, designed to assert the hero's high moral stature. On the other hand, if verse 3 is aimed at the destruction of the deity, the curses sound like a kind of self-immolation by the hero, who takes to flaunting his goodness before an evil and doomed god.

If, however, Job distinguishes himself from the malefactors of verse 3, he has returned to conventional reference. The series of curses demonstrates that he has been the very model of the ethical man, the assiduous follower of all the rules and the attitudes that the ancient Hebrew superego inculcated. In that case, Job has dropped back to the full retributionist position, has departed the depth of his despair about receiving a fair trial (chap. 23) and the savage redefinition of terms that in chap. 27 portrayed him as the god's moral superior. Now he trots out the standard terms of reward and punishment to which he so furiously objected when the friends enunciated them. The other meaning, consistent with chap. 27, is certainly present, but it stays beneath the surface, as an ominous subtext. Retributionism is now the heart on Job's sleeve.

His assurance about the trial rests on his certainty that he *deserves* reinstatement and acquittal, precisely because he is free of all of the actions and attitudes from which he so vigorously dissociates himself in this chapter. The man of honor (except for the lapse in vv. 9–10) demands his due, will wear the claim to the contrary as proudly as a prince wears a crown. It is an astounding reversion to a position it seemed Job had definitively left, especially as he first defined the objects of the god's favor as the wicked in chap. 21, then accounted for the god's avoidance of a trial for him by his own excellence in chap. 23, began in chap. 24 to show the divine power as arbitrarily whimsical, admitted its tremendous scope in chap. 26, and finally defined it as evil and vicious in chap. 27. Accounting for the sudden reversal here is difficult. Perhaps it is an effect of the nostalgic recollection in chap. 29 of his "autumn days," when everything was nice for him, if not for others. Perhaps Job has been so enraptured by his self-portrait in power and influence, in contrast to his present debility, as to want to recapture not only the circumstances of social authority but also what he recollects were their grounds and ground rules. He got where chap. 29 showed him to be by attention to the god's rules, and if he wishes to get there again, perhaps he must resume obedience to those rules.

Surely we can understand the wistful longing for those good days. Especially does it show up in the interlocking conclusions of the three parts of this summation speech. Job proudly remembered his royal authority and his function as "a happy person who consoles mourners" (*'ªbēlīm*, 29.25c). By contrast, his present hapless state is one where

> my lyre has become mourning [*'ēbel*],
> my flute a weeping [*bōkīm*] voice. (30.31)

Now his last self-curse in the interests of reinstatement denies that his actions have caused his "ground" (*'ªdamah*; cf. *'adam*, 31.33a) to cry out or its furrows to "weep" (*yibkayūn*, 31.38). He has moved from consoling mourners through mourning and weeping to denying weeping.

The narrator has the last word: "Job's words were spent" (*tammū*, v. 40c). They were finished (the verb's surface meaning), completed, used up; they were perfected, in a connotation corresponding to Job's own *tummah*, his integrity, his perfection (*tam*). But they are none of those. Job will have more to say, twice; he has not arrived at his final stance yet; and he has at least one, perhaps two, important changes yet to make.

A question remains to the reader: what will come next? No matter that we have already read the book and know. To read carefully is to read as if one did not know, to read along the book's own line, watching it unfold, letting it disclose or disguise itself. What now? Surely Job has come to the end of his rope, has said everything he has to say, has spent his entire psychic and intellectual capital. He has made as thorough and effective a challenge to the god as he could. The Prosecutor's curses upon himself brought an immediate response and activity with Job, and we must expect the same of Job's curses. There *must* be some divine response. Will it be a trial? A rational dialogue? A denunciation? A show of threatening force? A frontal attack? At one time or another in the discussion with the friends, Job has wished for or expected each of these. Informed by the background of the dialogue, the reader must think of some response. That the god would remain silent is surely impossible. That anything but his direct entry on the scene must come next seems highly unlikely.

7

"I Will Impart My Knowledge"

> The free use of words and phrases, rather than minute precision, is generally characteristic of a liberal education, and the opposite is pedantic; but sometimes precision is necessary.
>
> —Plato, *Theaetetus*

We completed the last chapter expecting to hear the voice of the god next. Turning to chap. 32, we are not surprised by an opening narrative statement matching the exhaustion of 31.40 and echoing conclusions familiar from earlier in the dialogue: "These three men stopped answering Job"—yes, they had stopped answering him a long time ago—"for he considered himself right" (32.1)—yes, he certainly did, and the friends certainly did not, however lamely they disputed him.

We are surprised by the next sentence: "Elihu, son of Barachel, the Buzite from the clan of Ram, was angry." Nothing has prepared us for the appearance of Elihu. Eliphaz, Bildad, and Zophar arrived in 2.13 and debated with Job from chap. 4 to chap. 25. There is never a hint that anyone else is present.[1] Suddenly here is Elihu with his panoply of genealogical credentials. We learn more about him than we do about the other three, of whom we are told only their territories of origin. We are even told more external facts about Elihu than we know about Job. Of Job, to be sure, we know his country, Uz, the makeup of his family, and the size of his fortune. Of Elihu we learn his father's name, Barachel, his father's descent as a Buzite, and the clan, Ram, within which that descent took place. Do the genealogical *bona fides* replace more substantial qualifications, such as age or wisdom?[2] Elihu emphasizes his youth in his first remark (v. 6), however sarcastic the contrast he draws with the aged others, and he goes on to claim vast wisdom.

Habel tells us that these facts about Elihu have no significance, though he, like others, points to the relationship between Elihu's name and Elijah's. Ancient readers of Hebrew would not have missed that connection, but it is not certain how seriously it ought to be drawn.[3] As for the other names, Barachel (*barak'ēl*) makes "El," the deity-name, either the subject or the object of that familiar verb *brk*, "bless, curse," that so confuses chaps. 1–2: "El blesses" or "he blesses El." In the light of chaps. 1–2, moreover, the verb calls attention to "curse" as well as blessing. Both Elihu's name and his father's, then, involve ambiguities.

Barachel is a "Buzite," a descendant, we may suppose, of Buz, according to Genesis 22.21 the son of Abraham's brother Nahor and the brother of Uz, in whose land Job is said to live.[4] Elihu and Job seem to be somewhat distant cousins. Elihu's clan name, Ram, occurs in Ruth 4.19 and 1 Chronicles 2.9, 25, as one of David's ancestors. This young fellow has good connections! These names too have meanings.[5] The noun *būz* occurs several times in Job (12.5, 21; 31.34), meaning "contempt." Is a "buzite" someone contemptuous or contemptible? "Ram" can be analyzed as a participle of the verb *rwm*, "to be high," both as "exalted" (see 2 Sam 22.47, of God) and as "haughty" (see Deut 8.14, of the human heart; Ps 18.28 [Eng. 27], of eyes).[6] Translated, the whole phrase comes out "My-god-he, son of Bless-El, the Contemptible, of the clan of Uppity."[7] That may be at least a subliminal message.

The brief prose introduction to Elihu's speeches (32.1–5) centers on two words. One is "answer" (the verb *'nh*, or the noun *ma'ᵃneh*). The friends "stopped answering Job" (v. 1), they "found no answer" (v. 3), and Elihu "saw that no answer was forthcoming from" them (v. 5). The friends' function, then, is at an end. Elihu will take up the function of "answering," as he will shortly tell us. The other word describes Elihu specifically: "anger" (in the phrase *ḥarah 'appō*, lit. "his nose burned"), an emphatic anger that is mentioned four times. Elihu is "angry" in general (vv. 2, 5), angry with Job (v. 2), angry with the friends (v. 3). If by the time we hear Elihu's voice we do not know either his emotion or the reason for it, it is not the narrative's fault.

Elihu is angry that the friends have failed to find an answer to Job, and have abandoned the debate because Job "considered himself right" (v. 1, Heb. *hū' ṣaddīq bᵉ'ēnaw*, "he was righteous in his [own] eyes," "he" being emphasized). He is angry with Job for a different reason: Job thinks himself "more right than Elohim" (v. 3, *ṣaddᵉqō napšō mē'ᵉlōhīm*, "his making his soul more righteous than Elohim"). The verb form implies that Job's declaring himself "rightcous" (*ṣaddīq*) is the claim of legal innocence.[8] Clearly Elihu will take up the image of the trial, and, indeed, that is the implication of his interest in "answering," a term full of legal implications, as we have seen.[9]

I noted in the Dispensable Introduction that most scholars think Elihu arrived late in the process of the book's compilation. The conclusion is not uncontroversial, and several of the best recent treatments of Job have argued that the reasons for denying Elihu's authenticity as a product of the major poet of the book are inadequate.[10] I do not deal with Elihu in as much detail as with the other persons in Job, not because the speeches may have been interpolated along the way, but because I think they are harder to understand than their substance warrants. I find Elihu a pompous, insensitive bore: an opaque thinker and an unattractively self-important character. His language is pretentious, often difficult, sometimes quite unintelligible.[11]

Elihu's significance lies in two points. First, he interprets suffering somewhat differently from the friends, though his proposal does not carry the debate forward any distance. Second, he heightens our anxiety about the deity's response to Job's curses, intervening at this monotonous length between our expectation that the god will appear and his actual appearance. The longer Elihu talks, the more nervous we get that the deity might not appear. That raising of emotional temperature justifies Elihu's presence structurally and provides him with a dramatic function.[12]

Elihu's First Speech (32.6–33.33)

All of Elihu's deference to the aged and the presumptively wise cannot mask the arrogance of his insistence that he, Elihu, he himself, is about to speak with an effectiveness denied to the others. "I myself" will speak, he says several times (vv. 10, 17a, 17b), in the idiomatic phrase *'ap-'anī*. But he has been described again and again in the introduction as "angry," and that word too is *'ap*.[13] Habel puts it well: "While *'ap-'anī* is a common emphatic idiom of self-assertion, the words themselves suggest a hidden rendering of 'I am anger.'"[14]

Like many a youngster after him, Elihu is given to long prefaces. A good half of this speech, 32.6–33.7, is a throat-clearing introduction; the substance comes in 33.8–33.[15] Yet we must allow Elihu a certain orderliness of mind (we will see reason later to doubt it). The preface falls into four stanzas alternating between twelve and fourteen lines in length: 32.6–10 (12 lines), 32.11–16 (14 lines), 32.17–22 (12 lines), and 33.1–7 (14 lines). In the first stanza, Elihu addresses the friends,[16] and verses 11–14 of the second are evidently spoken to the friends. At the end of that stanza, verses 15–16, Elihu discusses the friends in the third person, perhaps implicitly speaking to Job. In the third stanza, he declares to anyone who is listening how much he wants to speak and how good he will be at it. The fourth is spoken to Job by name (33.1), with singular verb forms in verses 1 and 5 and second-person masculine singular pronouns in verses 6–7. That is a stylistic peculiarity of Elihu. Of all the persons who speak in this book, only Yahweh, the Prosecutor, and Elihu refer to Job by name, and only Elihu directly addresses him by name.[17]

The preface urges that Elihu's youth is no hindrance to his wisdom, just as the other friends' age is no guarantee against incompetence. The first stanza both apologizes for youth and urges its abilities over against decrepitude.

> Young am I of days,
> and you are decrepit;
> therefore I have crawled about, afraid
> of imparting my knowledge to you. (v. 6)

Elihu's fear is gone by the end of the stanza, because he believes that wisdom is not a function of age. Perhaps he wishes to ally himself temporarily with Job. In 12.12, Job had quoted the proverb, "In age is wisdom, / length of days is understanding," in order to sweep quickly beyond it to claim that only the deity has wisdom—and power (v. 13).[18] Elihu may want to be in that camp even if Job is mistaken. At least he claims wisdom for himself. "The wind is that in a man, / and Shaddai's breath, that makes them understand" (v. 8), and that wind and breath do not inhabit only the elderly (v. 9). "Therefore I say," Elihu concludes, echoing his first quatrain,

> "Listen to me,
> I will impart my knowledge, I myself." (v. 10)[19]

The line exhibits the two points of Elihu's brashness: his "imparting" his "knowledge," vast as it is, and the telltale, hasty phrase, "I myself" (*'ap-'anī*), with its echo of "he was angry" (*ḥarah 'appō*, vv. 2, 3, 5).

The next stanza attacks the friends. Having waited futilely while they "were digging for words" (*taḥqᵉrūn*, v. 11),[20] Elihu denies them the title of "arbiter" (32.12), the legal functionary whose existence Job denied in 9.33. An arbiter (*mōkīaḥ*) "answers," as Elihu describes it (32.12), does what the friends had not done. They cannot "answer" (vv. 15, 16), nor are their words competent to refute Job (v. 14). Elihu is very much concerned with words, with the ways in which Job's words and the friends' words do not meet (vv. 12, 15), with the fact that there is no verbal collusion between Job and himself (v. 14), and with the friends' complete loss of words (v. 15):

> They are terrified, they answer no more,
> words move away from them.

Clearly, if Job had been thinking of the friends in 9.33, he was right to deny that there was an arbiter.

As the next stanza (32.17–22) begins, Elihu volunteers for the post.

> I, I myself, will answer for my part,
> I will impart my knowledge, I myself. (v. 17)

Elihu's Hebrew is as overloaded as my English with first-person verb forms, first-person pronouns, first-person suffixes, and the repetition in the successive lines of the emphatic *'ap-'anī*, "I myself." He is not merely earnest but excessively self-important as he accepts the arbiter's job of "answering," of "imparting knowledge." His enthusiasm for talk carries him to the gross image of a belly distended with gas, which must be permitted a belch in order to have relief:

> For I am full of words,
> the wind in my belly pushes on me.
> Ah! my belly is like unopened wine,
> like new wineskins, it will burst.
> Let me speak, and I will get relief,
> open my lips and answer. (vv. 18–20)[21]

Recalling the duty of a legal officer like an "arbiter" to be impartial, Elihu officiously exhibits his objectivity: "I do not know how to give honor" (v. 22).

At the end of his preface, Elihu addresses Job (33.1–7). But he can never resist bragging:

> My straightforward mind, my statements,
> my lips' knowledge talk plainly. (v. 3)

"Straightforward" (*yōšer*) echoes *yašar*, used of Job in 1.1, 8, and elsewhere, and Elihu goes on as if he knew that he was alluding to Job. He and Job are, after all, equals—a smile must come to the lips at that. They were made in the same way, by "El's wind" (*rūaḥ*) and "Shaddai's breath" (v. 4; cf. 32.8), pinched from the same sort of clay and molded into the same kind of jar (v. 6). He implicitly distinguishes himself from the friends, reassuring Job about his own good faith:

> After all, fright of me does not terrify you,
> and my pressure on you is not heavy. (v. 7)

"Terrify" is not the same as the friends' "terror" (32.15), but the subject is the same. The friends pressed Job, and Elihu disclaims that intent. Given their human equality, Elihu should not frighten Job in the slightest. The reader can see already that Elihu poses neither spiritual nor intellectual threat to Job, and the claim of equality is rather hollow. Though he has assured the friends that he will not use their speeches to refute Job (32.14), presumably because they have proved inadequate to the task, we can already see from his use of and interest in words that his speech is unlikely to be a better refutation than theirs.

At last Elihu takes up his "arbiter's" duty of answering: "Ah, but you are not right about this, I answer you" (33.12). He has come to his own point (33.8–33), which is new in its emphasis, though not more than a variant on the friends' retributionism. To the question of the meaning of suffering, Elihu replies that it is a message, a communication from the deity to the human. The god is the Great Educator.

> For El speaks once,
> and twice he does not regard it. (v. 14)

Job has complained about the deity just what Elihu complains about the friends: that he "does not answer" (v. 13). But Elihu purports to quote as the preamble to his idea a more extensive complaint from Job (vv. 9–11), namely that his perfection (v. 9) is greeted by enmity (v. 10) and by the punishment due the wicked (v. 11).[22] Elihu responds simultaneously to Job's certainty that the deity is wrongly punishing him and to the accusation that the deity does not answer. The god does answer, he says, both "once, / and twice" (v. 14), and Elihu expounds four different forms of divine answer: through dreams (vv. 15–18), through pain (vv. 19–22), through agents (vv. 23–24), and through his response to human entreaty (vv. 25–28). Advancing the numbers in verse 14 ("once, twice"), Elihu underscores the divine patience:

> Ah, El does all these things
> twice, thrice with a man. (v. 29)

In each stanza he carefully states the deity's purpose in this educating, namely to maintain humans alive, to keep them from the "Pit" (Heb. *šaḥat*, the place of the dead). "Pit" appears in the next-to-last line of each stanza (vv. 18a, 22a, 24b, 28a, 30a); in four of the five occurrences, it is the last word in the Hebrew line.[23]

The issue, then, is revelation and its methods. Elihu reiterates Eliphaz's claim of the authority of a dream (4.12–16), not as the special prerogative of people like Eliphaz but as a normal mode of divine communication: "he uncovers men's ears, / and seals up with chastisement" (33.16). The dream is castigation for a person's faults, a warning message. Likewise pain (vv. 19–22) is reproof (*hūkaḥ*, from *ykḥ*, to decide a case or to criticize) and trial (*rīb*, litigation, the Ketib). Elihu's description verges on the vivid (vv. 20–21) but never quite arrives there, just as pain sends the sick person to the edge of the Pit, nearly to death,[24] but no closer. Pain's message is intended to frighten people out of badness.

Where dreams and pain teach by castigation and fright, education by the god's agents (vv. 23–24) and by human entreaty (vv. 25–29) is more positive. Elihu refers to two kinds of agents, an "angel" (*mal'ak*, "messenger") and an "interpreter" (*mēlīṣ*). It is not clear that either must be superhuman; the "messengers" who told Job about the loss of his fortune and family in 1.14–19 were *mal'akīm*, and there is no reason to think them anything but humans. But Job's "interpreter" (16.20), apparently the same as his "witness," appears to be more than human. Does Elihu refer to Job's third parties? He has already spoken of, and implicitly claims to be, the "arbiter." He never refers to an "avenger" (19.25), and if the "interpreter" is an allusion to the witness, Elihu turns that person's function around. Job's "witness/interpreter" was his advocate against the deity, but Elihu's "interpreter" speaks to humans. Elihu understands that both of these agents instruct (*haggīd*) the human about morality (*yōšer*, 33.23), as a result of which favor and a "ransom" (v. 24) keep the person from the Pit. But whose morality and whose favor? The text says "his," which might be the human's (Heb. *'adam*), the "angel/interpreter's," or the deity's. The verbs in verse 24 have an unspecified masculine subject, which sounds like a reference to the god but could refer to the "interpreter": "He favors him [*yᵉḥunnannū*] and says." Does the "interpreter" instruct the human about the deity's morality as prelude to the deity's relenting from the punishment?[25] Does the "interpreter" instruct the human about the human's own morality as the necessary precondition for the deity's or the "interpreter's" favor?[26] Does the "interpreter" call the deity's attention to the human's morality to justify the deity's favor?[27] Or does the "interpreter" instruct the human about the interpreter's morality as background for the interpreter's favoring the human?[28] The sentences can be read in all four ways, and doubtless in some others, and the quotation in verse 24 could be either from the "interpreter" or from the deity. Somehow this "angel/interpreter" intervenes to keep the sinful person out of the Pit.

One other mode of education remains. It is not clear whether the sinner's "plump" flesh (v. 25) is the result of the restoration proclaimed in verses 23–24, or whether it is the misleading prosperity of wicked people. In any case, the person applies for spiritual restoration to the god (v. 26), and the god restores his "righteousness" (*ṣᵉdaqah*). Then the favored human sings a testimonial hymn (vv. 27–28), confessing to others his former wickedness and the deity's redemption. Surely Elihu wants Job to change his own tune. In 7.20, Job had admitted, hypothetically in the context, "I sin" (*ḥaṭṭa'tī*), and had gone on to the point, made also by Eliphaz, that his sinning had no effect on the god. Here Elihu quotes the restored sinner's hymn as beginning, "I sinned [*ḥaṭṭa'tī*], perverted morality" (33.27). Job did say the former, but his denial of the latter was too emphatic for Elihu to succeed any more than did Eliphaz in getting him to admit crimes of any consequence.[29] But Elihu is patient, as he claims the deity is.

> El does all these things
> twice, thrice with a man,
> to turn his soul back from the Pit,
> to shine with the light of life. (vv. 29–30)

The long Western tradition of Hell as punishment of the wicked dead makes it easy for us to assume that sense of the Pit. Here it seems to signify only death itself, not postmortem punishment. But death is to be avoided as long as possible.

Elihu's concluding invitation to Job is nicely confused.[30] He asks Job to keep listening to him (v. 31) and to speak in reply (v. 32). One might expect the latter first, but once Elihu has mixed them, he has to resort to the awkward "if not" (v. 33) in order to get back to his evident wish to go on talking. The confusion may partly explain his insufferably pompous final clause: "I'll familiarize you with wisdom."

The revelational aspect of Elihu's speech is not unrelated to Eliphaz's first speech, which adumbrated the notion that the god brings on suffering in order to give people the discipline needed for restoration (see 5.17–18). Elihu wishes to claim authority for his idea, and he would prefer divine authority to that of the incompetent friends. But the educational, disciplinary idea of suffering is not completely new. And the insistence on divine revelation almost makes Elihu the caricature not merely of the wise man, but also of the prophet, the purveyor of the divine word in castigation and promise.[31]

Elihu's Second Speech (34.2–37)

In this speech, Elihu speaks mostly to "wise people" (*ḥakamīm*, v. 2) and "intelligent men" (*'anšē lēbab*, "men of heart," v. 10).[32] Only at the end (v. 33) does he speak briefly to Job, and he moves on immediately (v. 34) to report what wise, intelligent listeners would say about him. The speech is, to be sure, a defense of the deity against Job's slurs, but it is also an offense against Job. I pointed out in the annotations that verses 5–6, which purport to quote Job directly, are a tissue of skewed allusion. All the more ironic, then, is Elihu's brash assurance to his gathered hearers,

> Justice we will decide for ourselves;
> we know among us what is good. (v. 4)[33]

After that dogmatic certainty and the following unjust malattribution, Elihu's sarcasm about Job

> He drinks derision like water,
> wanders in company with evildoers,
> walks with wicked men. (vv. 7–8)

is not an attractive advertisement of Elihu's knowledge of "what is good." The portrait of Job as moving about among bad folks is especially unfair, glued as he is by his boils to the garbage dump outside Uz.

Elihu does not dispose us to take his exposition of his theology (vv. 10–32) terribly seriously, no matter how earnestly he addresses himself to the "intelligent men" of his audience. Yet that theology is in many respects unexceptionable and indistinguishable from those of the friends. Elihu thinks that the deity is perfectly good (34.10–12):

> Of course, El does not cause wickedness,
> Shaddai does not bend justice. (v. 12)

Job had argued that the god does cause human wickedness (chap. 24), but Bildad had asserted the latter (8.3). The deity is perfectly powerful (34.13–15), governing the world by no permission but his own (v. 13), keeping it alive by his own decision (v. 14). Arguing that the deity controls powerful humans, Elihu comes very close to Job's arguments at 24.22–24, but without accusing the god of maltreatment of high and low, as Job did.

> Suddenly they die when it's midnight,
> he touches nobles, and they pass on,
> and they remove a mighty one without a hand. (34.20)

In contrast to Job's problems with the deity who watches him too closely, Elihu likes the fact that the god sees all and knows all:

> There is no dark, no deep gloom,
> where evildoers can hide. (v. 22)

But though the god sees into every hiding place, no one can peer into his mystery:

> Unscrutinized, he breaks the powerful
> and sets successors in their stead. (v. 24)

Elihu is still refuting Job as he goes on with the deity's opposition to the wicked, "crushing" them (v. 25; cf. the same verb in 6.9), "jeering" at them (34.26). In effect (and the effect seems unintended) the god turns those people away from him (v. 27) and very nearly, as Job argued in chap. 24, causes their wickedness by his own action. At the same time, Elihu argues that Job was wrong about the deity's positive actions toward humans. Those who turn away from him fail "to bring to him the outcry of the poor" (that outcry that, Job claimed, the god ignores, 24.12), but he hears it nevertheless (34.28). Elihu seems to perceive more compassion in the deity than either Job or the friends do. "He gives content—and who finds that bad?" (v. 29) But his language becomes garbled and his thought unclear in verses 29–32. He wants to be sure that Job's kind of folks do not come into power, as the line "the godless [*ḥanēp*] from ruling the race" (v. 30) suggests. *Ḥanēp* was the word Job used for himself in 27.8.

Finally Elihu addresses Job (34.33), castigating him for choosing to be where he is ("For you choose, not I") and for not knowing what to say. But, though the rest of the speech purports to report to Job what the audience will say, it is surely a devastatingly cruel put-down by the "intelligent men" and the "wise men" who denigrate Job's knowledge (v. 35) and wish his badness might be more thoroughly exposed (vv. 36–37).[34]

The whole speech is a tangent, it seems, intended to criticize Job and to display Elihu's theological prowess rather than to advance the argument. But the maladroit misquotations and the often unintelligible language make the speech a complete misfire.

Elihu's Third Speech (35.2–16)

One has a feeling of unreality about Elihu, as if he were not in touch with the same world as ordinary people. His opening address to Job in this speech is like that.

> Is this what you consider justice,
> that you say, "I am more righteous [*ṣedeq*] than El"? (v. 2)

Job had said the opposite of that in 9.2: "How can a man be innocent [*yiṣdaq*] with El?" Nowhere has he said what Elihu here imputes to him. To be sure, in 27.6–7 he implied his moral superiority to the god, and perhaps we should give Elihu credit for recognizing it. Yet he goes on to compound the error:

> For you say, "How is he of use to you?
> How do I profit from my sin?" (35.3)

The language is confusing. Only Eliphaz has used the verb *skn*, first denying that a human can "benefit" the god (22.2) and then urging Job to be of use to him (v. 21). Job has never asked any such thing as this, and it is garbled even as an allusion to Eliphaz. As for the other line, Job himself used the verb *y'l* only twice, in 30.13 to describe the actions of his tormentors ("promote my destruction") and in 21.15 to describe the attitude of those bad people who remain aloof from the deity ("What is Shaddai that we should serve him? / What the profit [*mah-nō'īl*] that we should beg of him?"). He has never asked whether sin (*ḥaṭṭa't*) might profit him.[35] Is Elihu thinking of Eliphaz, who used the verb about Job's unprofitable words in 15.3? It is hard to reconstruct the thought that produced these words. Perhaps it is distant from commonsense reality. It almost seems that Elihu has a unique mental structure that does not correspond to ordinary reason, especially when he goes on to say,

> I will refute your words,
> and your companions with you. (v. 4)

If he has no grasp on Job's words, how can he begin to refute them?

I think that Elihu takes Eliphaz as his model. Bildad's ideas have come up more than once and Elihu has yet to allude to Zophar, but his language and ideas are much more like Eliphaz's than anyone else's. He parrots both Eliphaz (22.2–3) and Job (7.20) on the divine impassibility (35.5–8), the idea that the god is not affected by human acts and feelings:

> If you sin, what have you done [*p'l*] to him?
> Multiply transgression, what do you accomplish with him?
> If you are innocent [*ṣdq*], what have you given him? (vv. 6–7)

Job, too, had raised the former thought in addressing the deity: "I sin. What have I done [*p'l*] to you, / you watcher of men?" (7.20) Without saying so, 35.6 comes closer to quoting Job than Elihu usually does when he claims to quote.

The other side of the same idea (v. 7a) refers more directly to Eliphaz's question, "Is Shaddai pleased that you are innocent [*ṣdq*]?" (22.3) But the pair of terms, "innocent" or "righteous" (*ṣdq*) and "sin" (*ḥṭ'*), both referring to Job, echo the same pair in 35.2–3.[36] It seems that Elihu wants to cut Job down, deny him too much stature:

> Your wickedness is confined to a man like yourself,
> your innocence to a human being. (v. 8)

Job is not so important. Yet Job himself had accepted the same limitation with the metaphor of straying: "Have I truly strayed? / My straying stays at home with me" (19.4). He does not claim the overweening power and influence that the friends and Elihu ascribe to him, even as they deny it. People often overestimate the efficacy of those who differ drastically from them. Americans worry about Russian world empires, and Russians worry about American imperialism, fundamentalists worry that secular humanists are taking over the country, and atheists worry that fundamentalists may become the majority they claim they are. For the same reason, Elihu, denying Job's influence, in effect asserts it.

And he worries about humans who fail to pay attention to the god (35.9–12), who "cry out" (*z'q*) about oppression (v. 9), but do not apply to the deity for help (vv. 10–11). Elihu implies the availability of help in the "songs in the night" (v. 10) and the instruction that animals and birds can give (v. 11). So when they "cry out" again (*ṣ'q* this time, probably a variant or dialectic form of *z'q*, v. 9), the god does not answer. But it seems that Elihu summarily deflects that outcry, as if the god will answer only if the petitioner is properly prepared, has the right attitude or the right connections. The divine apathy, which met Job's morality or its opposite in verses 6–8, here meets the outcry of those who are not certified answerable. What has happened to Elihu's assurance that the god "hears the outcry [*ṣaʿ*^{a}*qah*] of the oppressed" (34.28)? Elihu offers no assistance to Job if he should wish to apply for inclusion in that group.

Yet it is as if he has heard the objection:

> Surely it's false that El does not hear,
> that Shaddai does not look at it. (35.13)

As in 34.28, Elihu seems to be saying that he hears, he looks; it's merely that he does not answer. To be sure, Elihu has taken it upon himself to do the answering. Job's behavior is not acceptable: he grumbles about the god's handling of the case (35.14 allows us to see that much, though it is strange and difficult in detail), he spews his anger out without proper reserve or resistance (v. 15), and he spouts the windy verbiage to which the friends objected in the earlier dialogue (v. 16). The last claim has a certain irony, as Elihu has been speaking so constantly and with so many words that Job has no chance to break in between syllables. At the end, Elihu returns to his opening salvo about what Job says:

> Job opens his mouth with vapor,
> without knowledge increases words. (v. 16)

Someone else will say that later with considerably more authority.

Elihu's Fourth Speech (36.2–37.24)

Elihu's third speech was his shortest. The fourth is the longest.[37] Claiming that "Eloah still has words" (36.2), perhaps Elihu really means that he himself still has words. He comes closer here than before to a vision of a divinely ordered universe. But as he has done before, Elihu almost spoils it—perhaps in fact spoils it—by his braggadocio:

> I'll display my knowledge afar,
> show my maker's righteousness.
> For certainly my words are not lies,
> faultless knowledge is in your presence. (vv. 3–4)

One tends to roll one's eyes toward heaven.[38]

Elihu's intellectual confusion has not abated. "Now, El is mighty, does not despise," he says (v. 5), forgetting that he described his "jeering" at the wicked (34.26). He insists on overstating his case for retributive justice: "He does not give the wicked life" (36.6). Even if that means that the god does not maintain the wicked alive (a frequent sense of the Piʿel of the verb *ḥyh*), it is the kind of statement that must always be taken back and modified: he keeps them alive long enough to make life miserable for them. "And he grants justice to the wretched" (v. 6), yet Elihu described in 35.9–12 those wretched who were granted neither justice nor a hearing.

> And as for kings on their thrones,
> he seats them permanently, and they are exalted. (36.7)

To be sure, it is hard to recall every word one has said, even in the last few hours, but Elihu's memory seems very shaky for a young person with "faultless knowledge." We might remind him of 34.20:

> Suddenly they die when it's midnight,
> he touches nobles, and they pass on,
> and they remove a mighty one without a hand.

That at least suggested that rulers were not so permanent (*laneṣaḥ*) as Elihu states in 36.7.

What do you do with a debater who constantly reverses his position? For one thing, you do not ascribe to him "faultless knowledge," nor do you pay him much heed if he claims it for himself. For another, you take his succeeding arguments with some skepticism, even if his eloquence exceeds its earlier standard.

In verses 8–25, Elihu amplifies the theory that he expounded in chap. 33, namely that suffering is educational.

> If they are bound in fetters,
> trapped in cords of misery,
> he is telling them their deed
> and their transgressions, that they have outdone themselves.
> He opens their ear to discipline,
> says they must turn back from evil. (vv. 8–10)

The "misery," as evidence of the "deed," provides instruction by which a new "discipline" (*mūsar*, v. 10) can relieve the person's being "bound" (*'asūr*, v. 8). But Elihu recognizes that there are two possible responses to the message. One is to hear it (*šm'*, v. 11), with the result of good (*ṭōb*) days and pleasant years. The other is not to hear it (v. 12), with the result of death. It sounds very like the prophetic construction on obedience, as in Isaiah 1.19–20:

> If, then, you agree and give heed [*šm'*],
> you will eat the good things [*ṭūb*] of the earth;
> but if you refuse and disobey,
> you will be devoured [by] the sword. (JPS)

Elihu even uses some of Isaiah's language. But he introduces a pun that matches the *'asūr–mūsar* one in verses 8–10, with the opposition between "hear and serve" (*ya'abōdū*, v. 11a) and "do not hear, cross" (*ya'abōrū*, v. 12b) the channel.[39] One hardly expects such subtle wordplay from Elihu; perhaps he is improving as he goes along.

In any case, the message is given, whether it is heard and heeded or not. The "binding" is there (v. 13; cf. v. 8a), even if the "godless of mind" (*ḥanēp*—Job's word for himself in 27.8) ignore it and send themselves to death. The solution to the problem of suffering is to be found *in* the suffering:

> He rescues the miserable in their misery,
> opens their ears in their torment. (36.15)

The preposition would even permit "He rescues the miserable *by* their misery, / opens their ears *by* their torment." Suffering is something more than education and has become the rescuing experience itself, the means by which and the situation in which restoration takes place. That is surely an advance on Elihu's earlier discussion of suffering as educative in 33.25–28, where the restoration seems to follow the request for it.

But Job is in danger of failing to take advantage of this restorative situation (36.17–21). Elihu warns him against being obsessed with a bad case (v. 17) that might lead to a bribe with all of its unhappy consequences (v. 18).[40] He advises against the kind of death wish with which Job began the debate (chap. 3):

> Don't pant for the night
> when peoples disappear from their place. (36.20)

And he seems to warn him away from accepting the notion that, on the deity's terms, he is wicked:

> Be careful, don't turn toward evil [*'awen*],
> because this you have preferred to misery. (36.21)

"Misery," we have seen (vv. 8–9, 15), is the very possibility of restoration. One in Job's position ought to seek it in preference to anything else.

Before moving on to the cosmic deity, Elihu recalls Job to the power, exaltation, and praiseworthiness of the god.

> Remember to extol his deed,
> of which men sing. (v. 24)

He had described singing as the response to restoration in 33.27–28 and had criticized those who did not accept the god's "songs in the night"

(35.10). Elihu even uses the word that for him best defines the deity's function with sufferers: "Who is a teacher [*mōrah*] like him?" (36.22)

In the rest of the speech (36.26–37.24), Elihu proposes a mode of revelation different from that he has proposed before. The god's activities in nature are also a message to those willing to hear it.[41] Nature has not been an important part of Elihu's thinking. He acknowledged that he and Job had been created similarly ("I too was pinched from clay," 33.6), and in 35.5 he called Job's attention to sky and dust clouds as an analogue to the deity's distance from and transcendence over Job. He criticized people who ignore the deity and fail to recognize that he "teaches us by the beasts of the earth, / makes us wise by the birds of the air" (35.11), a point Job had urged on the friends (12.7–8).

Now Elihu goes into the storm in detail (36.26–33), beginning from the unsearchable age of the deity (v. 26—a nice counterpart to his own plea of youth, 32.6, etc.) and going on to the rain (36.27–28) and the clouds and lightning (vv. 29–30). Then he gives the interpretation (vv. 31–33): the storm is simultaneously a judgment (*dīn*) upon peoples and the provision of food (v. 31), a force "commanded" by the deity (v. 32), and a message to the sinner about the sinner's failings:

> He tells him of his wickedness,
> extending anger against iniquity. (v. 33)

He elaborates the detail of his description in 37.1–6. There is no moral to this description, as there was to the last, though Elihu expresses his fright at the power of the deity's thunderstorm (v. 1). This description seems addressed to the friends ("Listen," v. 2, is a plural imperative), but it is not clear why. The sound and light effects are rather good here, especially "rumble" (*rōgez*) and "growl" (*hegeh*) in v. 2, followed by "roar" (*ś'g*) in v. 4a. Elihu lets repetitiousness get away from him in verses 4–5, with the word "voice" in four successive lines and "thunders" twice in alternating lines. "Voice" (*qōl*) frequently connotes thunder, though it is also a general word meaning "noise," but the repetition of words for thunder seems more than would be needed to suggest even a violent thunderstorm.

Elihu uses the storm again as a means of education, presuming that the juxtaposition of storm and the "seal" on "every human hand" (v. 7) means that the storm is a sign from the deity, "so all the men he has made may know." The couplet is difficult, and the next one ("And the beast enters its lair, / lies down in its den," v. 8) follows by logic less than inexorable.[42] Perhaps the idea is that, though animals have natural knowledge (dare one say "instinct" these days?), humans need divine education for knowledge. It is not always easy to trace Elihu's mind through its workings.

Storm continues to be the focus of his vision, now apparently in reference to winter storms, "cold," "frost," and the narrowing, perhaps by ice, of "the wide water" (vv. 9–10). In verse 11 as in 36.27–28, the clouds are the source of moisture, and, as in 36.29–30, lightning affects the cloud cover. It is as if Elihu's repertoire of observations on storms begins to reach its limits, and he must turn at verse 12 from things moist to things dry. Those lines too are confusing. Rather than name cyclones or dust devils, he speaks only of "things that whirl" (*m*^e^*sibbōt*). It is as if he assumes that the more abstract one's vocabulary, the deeper the thought. The rest of verses 12 and 13 makes one shake one's head over how obscurely Elihu can say that the deity controls such natural forces as those "that whirl." At least I *think* that is what the idea is.

He now turns to Job with a series of questions so similar to Yahweh's speeches in the next chapters that sometimes direct imitation is proposed. Yet Elihu's questions lack Yahweh's mordance, and Elihu confines his questions to Job's knowledge of and activity with clouds. The weather remains the subject, but the character of these clouds is not quite clear, except that verse 17 implies that they are hot-weather clouds, "south wind" clouds that probably afford no relief from heat. Elihu wonders about Job's knowledge:

> Do you know when Eloah considers them,
> makes light shine in his cloud?
> Do you know about the cloud rolls,
> the marvels of perfect knowledge,
> you whose clothes are hot
> when the land lies still from the south wind? (vv. 15–17)

And he wonders about Job's ability to act:

> Can you hammer out the clouds with him,
> strong as a cast-metal mirror? (v. 18)

The simile of the clouds as a mirror is an unusual one, and some interpreters read *š*^e^*ḥaqīm* as "sky" rather than "clouds."[43] To compare the clouds' strength to that of the metal mirror is, to say the least, unusual, though Elihu may emphasize the "hard" side of *ḥazaq*. Perhaps Habel is right, that Elihu wants Job to affect the weather, to cause the clouds to spread over the sky in order to give relief from the heat.[44] It causes more trouble with Elihu's language than I can solve. Elihu uses an interesting image that he cannot quite control.

He now challenges Job to be not only the god's coworker but also his co-educator:

Make known to us what we say to him;
we are drawn up before darkness.
Is it said to him, "I'll speak"?
Does a man say he will be swallowed up? (vv. 19–20)

There *is* an analogy with what Yahweh will say to Job. After describing divine activity in chaps. 38–39, Yahweh will invite Job to occupy the divine function in chap. 40. Here Elihu, having described the deity's power in sending his forces to humans as messages, invites Job to give the message that will allow humans to address the god. "We are drawn up before darkness." The image is of a military formation that cannot see its object. Speaking to the god is a fearful matter, as the Israelites could remember from their preference to leave it to Moses in Exod 20.18–21. And with "swallowed up" (*bl'*), Elihu may refer to the frightful episode of Korah, Dathan, and Abiram, whose eagerness to have priestly access to the deity led to their being "swallowed up" (*bl'*) by the earth (Num 16.30–34). Elihu seems to enjoin upon Job a decent reticence in his speech to the deity.

Yet he hardly obeys his own strictures. At the end, he is still certain that he knows whatever is worth knowing about the deity. Ordinary people do not see the god's brightness in the clouds (Job 37.21), but Elihu does:

From the north gold comes forth,
over Eloah is fearful splendor. (v. 22)

Just in time, he withdraws from claiming too much, and reverts to the god's own ability to see:

Shaddai—we cannot find him;
exalted in just power,
greatly righteous, he does not oppress.
Therefore men are afraid of him,
he does not see any who are wise of heart. (vv. 23–24)

It is a curious pastiche of humility and forgetfulness. The deity is beyond human discovery. Job was wrong in looking so hard and far as he claimed in chap. 23. But Elihu is sure he knows about the right combination of justice and power—just the combination that Job denied. And he turns around his own contention (e.g., 34.25–26) that this God is so powerful that he can oppress. "He does not oppress," Elihu says confidently.

He then adds the fascinating connective "therefore" to it: "Therefore men are afraid of him" (v. 24). They are afraid of him *because* he does not oppress. It is a thought that could repay a great deal of pondering, if one wished to pursue the implications of a fearful deity who is, for no discernible reason, graciously disposed to humans. One might take the thought as comfort—if one had received the grace—or as further evidence of arbitrariness.

Elihu falls again into forgetfulness: "he does not see any who are wise of heart." "See" surely has to do with the positive, supportive sight that the god withdraws from those who are "wise of heart." Elihu undercuts his own claims and pretensions to the right to speak. His wisdom justified his entrance into the discussion in the first place ("Not the great are wise, / or the elderly understand justice," 32.9), and he adduced it as justification for continuing to speak ("For certainly my words are not lies, / faultless knowledge is in your presence," 36.4). But the deity pays no attention to wisdom. Elihu, making the powerful point in relation to his theology of grace that the deity's attention is not based on the human's status or qualifications, forgets his own concern about his status and qualifications.

That fault of inconsistency is not confined to the young.

The general effect of Elihu's intervention is an odd one. The familiar device of delaying an expected event or resolution can be effective. In this instance, however, it is overdone. The delay is too long, the content of the speeches not impressive or interesting enough to justify the intervention, a requirement if the delay is to be effective.[43]

Not that Elihu gives us nothing. He expounds in more detail than we have seen before the theory of suffering as educative, the human condition as both revealing the deity's intentions and restoring the human's integrity. He spends many lines recognizing—though not more deeply than Job or even Zophar—the god's power and its dual direction to the maintenance of life and to its destruction.

But his theology is depressingly conventional, adding nothing except detail to what the friends have given us in quite sufficient detail. His style is more than depressingly opaque, uttering sentence after sentence in which the words make sense one by one but defy comprehension in combination. It is wordy, convoluted, often scarcely intelligible. The speeches contain some nuggets of semiprecious metal, but embedded in such thick clods of ordinary dirt as to weary the miner beyond reason. Dealing with good poetry is hard and exhilarating. Dealing with Elihu is just hard.

8

"A Road for the Thunderclap"

Be thou that wintry sound
As of the great wind howling,
By which sorrow is released,
Dismissed, absolved
In a starry placating.

—Wallace Stevens,
"Mozart, 1935"

Turning the page from Elihu's efforts with some relief, we are confronted by the god himself in an outpouring of poetry unlike that of the earlier dialogue.[1] Yahweh's appearance has produced more than ordinary disagreement among the book's interpreters, even given the more than ordinary contentiousness that the entire book brings into play.

In form, verses 38.2–42.6 are a dialogue, in which each participant has two speeches: Yahweh speaks "from the whirlwind" in 38.2–40.2, and Job replies, 40.4–5; Yahweh speaks again, 40.7–41.26,[2] and Job answers in 42.2–6. The disproportion in verbiage between the two speakers is obvious. Never has Job been so terse, whereas Yahweh compensates for his long silence with a verbal flood.

What do we expect Yahweh to do? Will he meet Job's expectations in 23.5–7 that he will answer Job's questions clearly, attentively, and instructively with some assured, divinely attested truth? Will he meet Job's expectations in 9.13–16 and 27–31 that he will ask difficult, condemning questions of his own to which Job has no answers? Will he sit as judge over a trial, inviting witnesses to testify and rendering the verdict? Will he attack and destroy the querulous hero? These questions about the reader's expectations rest upon what we have seen in the book to this point, as well as upon ways our traditions have conveyed the book to us and have taught us to ask questions of it.

As assistance to thinking about these questions, it is worth noting some diverse responses to these speeches. Apart from scholars who would excise all or parts of them as not original to the book,[3] some readers find the Yahweh speeches a meaningful conclusion to the book, whereas others find them irritating and irrelevant. Each category of appreciation, moreover, contains vast differences of opinion. Some see Yahweh's speeches as meaningful because Yahweh overwhelms Job with the divine power, some because the speeches bring Job to a proper humility, others because they show Job how to have significant faith, and still others because they imply that the universe has an aesthetic and moral beauty beyond human comprehension.[4] Some readers, however, think that the speeches avoid Job's issue. They strike some interpreters as a "sublime irrelevance," others as not merely a failure to heal Job's wound but a cynical show of force to smash him to mindless submission, another as evidence of a deity so lofty as to be completely removed from contact with real human beings having real problems, still another as "inadequate and empty . . . a three-hour lecture on natural science."[5] On the other hand, some argue that the content of the speeches is completely insignificant; the important thing is that Yahweh made them.[6]

The Whirlwind

We may have expected the divine voice, and we may even have expected a sight of the god (though the strictures in the Hebrew Bible against seeing the deity ought to warn us off the latter). I doubt that we expect the whirlwind (Heb. *s^e'arah*), though perhaps we ought to.[7] Job has said he expects one, has already experienced it:

> he who tramples me down with a whirlwind,[8]
> enlarges my wounds for no reason. (9.17)

Job has loudly proclaimed his wish to meet the god face-to-face and has looked forward to it with trepidation. In chap. 23, he waxed ironic about the god's inaccessibility, and in the next to last of his curses on himself (31.36–37), he set himself to approach the god with the "inscription" tied on him "like a wreath, / the number of my steps imprint upon him, / like a prince approach him." There Job claimed royal status, wreathed with honor and heroic in stature.[9]

Indeed, this event justifies that certainty. The whirlwind is evidence of the deity's visible arrival. It is not like Eliphaz's dream, to which he alone was privy (4.12–21), or the educative dreams to which Elihu referred (33.15–18). This is more like the fearsome torch passing between butchered animal parts when Yahweh covenants with Abram (Gen 15.17), the thunder, cloud-shrouded lightning, and supernatural trumpet blasts at Mt. Sinai (Exod 19.16), and the mountain-shattering wind, earthquake, and fire at Elijah's visit to Horeb (1 Ki 19.11–12). This is top-of-the-line theophany, the sort of thing that happens at crucial junctures of the culture's experience and to people not like Eliphaz and Elihu but like Abram and Moses.[10]

Yahweh, moreover, answers. We may have become drowsy over that word. It has occurred before every speech in the book: "And Job [Eliphaz, Bildad, etc.] answered thus" (*wayya'an 'îyyōb ['ᵉlîpaz, bildad] wayyō'mer*). Job desired an "answer" from his trial (9.16; 13.22; 14.15; 19.7; 23.5). The narrative introducing Elihu insistently noticed how no one had "answered" Job (32.1, 3, 5), and Elihu himself repetitiously defined his function as answering (32.12, 17, 20; etc.), though it seemed less than adequate. When at last Yahweh appears so impressively, and the text says "Yahweh *answered* Job from the whirlwind," we may have two simultaneous reactions: "At last, a real answer!" or "At last, a real answer?" We cannot yet know whether to exclaim or to query.

Yahweh's First Speech (38.2–40.2)

> Who is this who darkens counsel
> with ignorant words? (38.2)

"This" (*zeh*) is singular, as is the participle ("darkener"), and we assume that Yahweh refers to one person. The introductory formula implies that it is Job, but Elihu's words were the last thing we heard. Job's later admission of ignorance (42.3) shows only that he accepted the stricture's application to himself. It can also apply to Elihu, however, whom we may imagine scuttling off into the thickets along with his pretensions to knowledge. His intervention, like Job's arguments, is disavowed as "ignorant words" (*millîn bᵉlî-da'at*).

Such a dismissal must strike us as strange. Appearing on the scene with all the panoply of his appearances to the culture's heroes Abraham, Moses, and Elijah, Yahweh treats Job as the opposite of a hero, dismissing him as if he were a mere Elihu. It might seem an odd use of the theophany, not presenting revelation but beginning, at least, by giving notice that the entire structure of argument and pain, recantation and avowal, was nothing worth. Or perhaps the god tacitly approves what the friends said, and his reference to Job as *geber*, "real man," is sarcastic.[11]

Gird your loins like a real man.
I will ask questions, and you instruct me. (v. 3)

The two lines are oddly disproportionate, apart from the possible sarcasm of *geber* and the invitation to "instruct" Yahweh (*hōdīa'*, "cause to know"), another reminder of Elihu's educational pretensions and of the words just characterized as "ignorant." To "gird the loins" is often to prepare for battle (e.g., 1 Sam 2.4) or for some other physically strenuous undertaking, such as hard running (1 Ki 18.46) or escaping from Egypt (Exod 12.11). Exhorting Jeremiah to gird his loins (Jer 1.17) in preparation for prophesying, Yahweh implies that people will reject him. Though girding the loins does not always imply a hopeless situation, it surely poses a stark opposition between Job and the deity.[12] To ask someone "without knowledge" (*bᵉlī-da'at*) to "give knowledge" (*hōdīa'*) is either illogical or stacking the deck. This is a deity whose cosmic wisdom Job has already described more than once (Job 26.5–14; 28.23–27). In so adversarial an encounter as this one, the god's invitation must have some sarcasm in its tone.

This *geber*, bidden to "instruct" the deity while the whirlwind roars around him, is the one whom the god has just described as "darkening counsel" (*'ēṣah*). The word *'ēṣah* may have several different meanings. There is "advice," perhaps of a personal or political sort, such as Ahithophel's "counsel" described in 2 Samuel 16.23 or the various pieces of advice for which Rehoboam asked on assuming the throne (1 Ki 12). Those passages portray a process of debate that leads to a conclusion. In Job, the debate concluded in Job's silencing the friends.

'ēṣah also suggests "plan," a considered, structured intention that leads to action (e.g., Judg 20.7), such as for battle (2 Ki 18.20) or for human destiny that is alleged and sometimes disbelieved of the deity (Isa 5.19).[13] If the "plan" be human, it is hard to perceive any intended action on Job's part, unless the deity accuses him of concealing his plan. One might think, on the strength of Job 1–2, that the god had a "plan" that informed what he caused or allowed to happen to Job, though no information about it is clear in those chapters. On the other hand, there is also in *'ēṣah* the idea of a plan more grandiose than either of the others, something like the "design" of a universe that has not just structure but order.[14] We will see that Yahweh's view of cosmic order is rather different from the one Job earlier proposed.

Interpreters tend to assume that the "counsel" is Yahweh's, not someone else's. That may be why many prefer the senses of "plan" or "design" to "advice" or "debate." But Yahweh does not say "Who darkens *my* counsel?" All "counsel" has been darkened, Job's, the friends', the god's, perhaps even Elihu's. The debated conclusions, plans of action, and designs of cosmic order—and *'ēṣah* must point to all three—have been "darkened" by ignorance, Yahweh says. The metaphor in "darkens" is both active and declarative.[15] Job has surely obscured the debate of the friends, by constantly changing his mind about its subject and scope, and in that sense he may also have obscured his own debate, his own "counsel" as conclusion. He has cast darkness over the intentions of the deity by his ignorance, even though his ignorance is as nothing compared to that of the friends. And, unless his vision of the universe (for example, in chap. 26) is more accurate than what we will now receive from Yahweh, Job has confused the picture of the universe's order, again by ignorance. Or like the friends, he has declared that the debate, the intentions and plans of the god, the order of the world, all are unclear. All those are contained in the deity's perception that Job "darkens counsel by ignorant words."

Yet that very "darkness" recalls Job's most passionate talk about darkness, namely his opening curses in chap. 3.

> That day, let there be darkness [*ḥōšek*],
> may Eloah not seek it from above
> or daylight beam over it.
> May darkness [*ḥōšek*] and thick gloom avenge it,
> clouds settle down upon it,
> blackness of day terrify it.
> That night, may dusk take it,
> may it not rejoice among the year's days,
> not arrive among the months' number.
> . . .
> May its evening stars be dark [*yeḥšᵉkū*],
> wait for light and see nothing,
> no sight of dawn's eyelids. (3.4–6, 9)

Among several "darkness" words, the one used in 38.2 stands out. Job wished that the world and its ways become darkness, and in that sense he cast darkness over the deity's *'ēṣah*. Still another connection among several wants notice:[16] Yahweh invites Job to gird his loins "like a *geber*" in verse 3. Job had begun his curse on his birthday:

> Perish the day on which I was born,
> the night that said, "A man [*geber*] is conceived!" (3.2)

"Make good on your boast," Yahweh is saying. "You claimed to be a *geber*. Now act like one."

Yet the questions he wishes Job to answer are not the sorts of things a human, even a *geber*, is accustomed to deal with.

> Where were you when I laid earth's foundations?
> Tell me, if you know so much.
> Who set its measurements—surely you know!—
> or who stretched the line out on it?
> Upon what were its pedestals sunk,
> or who laid its cornerstone
> when the morning stars sang together,
> and all the sons of Elohim shouted? (38.4–7)

Those questions inquire not whether Job is properly human but whether he has the knowledge and experience of a god. Yet before embarking on this line of questions, Yahweh called Job ignorant and ordered him to comport himself like a man. As the speech goes along, Yahweh asks after Job's possession of divine, not human, knowledge, knowledge of Sea, Death, and earth (vv. 16–18),[17] of light (vv. 19–21), of snow, wind, and storm (vv. 22–27). In each case, the question is whether Job knows (vv. 18, 21; see also v. 33), whether he has seen (vv. 17, 22), whether he has been present at such events (vv. 16, 20, 22).

In a couple of instances, Yahweh asks questions that imply that Job has knowledge:

> Who cut a channel for the flood
> and a road for the thunderclap . . . ? (v. 25)

> Who counts clouds with wisdom,
> and the jars of the sky, who tilts them
> when the dust is molded in a cast,
> and clods are stuck together? (vv. 37–38)

If Job can answer such questions as these, he displays the kind of knowledge that other queries request directly.

Yahweh asks another kind of question too:

> During your days have you commanded morning,
> instructed dawn of its place,
> snatched the skirts of earth,
> when the wicked are shaken out of it? (vv. 12–13)

> Can you tie up the Herd with fetters
> or loose the Fool's chain?

Can you bring out Mazzarot at its time
or lead the Lioness with her cubs? (vv. 31–32)[18]

Can you raise your voice to the cloud
so that a flood of waters covers you?
Can you send off lightnings, and they go,
and say to you, "Here we are"? (vv. 34–35)

Here Yahweh demands not knowledge but action to control day and light and darkness (vv. 12–14, 19–20), stars and floods and lightning (vv. 31–32, 34–35). It is action proper to the deity, not to a human.

Nothing changes when, from 38.39 to the end of chap. 39, Yahweh leaves the cosmic elements of sea, earth, sky, weather, stars, and the like to ask about a series of animals. Sometimes he asks about Job's knowledge of them:

Do you know the birth season of rock goats,
watch the fallow deer calve? (39.1)

Who sets the wild ass free?
Who opens the onager's bonds,
whose home I have put in the desert,
his dwellings the salt barrens? (vv. 5–6)

Sometimes he asks about Job's power of activity with them:

Can you hunt prey for the lioness,
fill the bellies of young lions? (38.39)

Can you hold the wild ox in the furrow with a rope?
Will he harrow the valleys after you? (39.10)

Do you give the horse his strength,
clothe his neck with thunder? (v. 19)

Does the peregrine soar by your wisdom,
spread his wings to the south?
Does the eagle soar at your command,
the vulture build his nest up high . . . ? (vv. 26–27)

In both parts of the first speech, Yahweh's questions, whether about knowledge or about action, are postulated on Job's divinity, not on his humanity. And they are interlarded with the lofty sarcasm of such interjections as "Tell me, if you know so much" (38.4) or "surely you know!" (v. 5), "Tell it, if you know all this" (v. 18) or "You know, for you were born then, / the number of your days is many" (v. 21). Such a tone makes clear how ironic is this address to the ignorant human. Yahweh is not merely exhibiting objectively what is there in the cosmos or showing Job the majesty and glory of the god in contrast to human frailty. The sarcasm proposes that Job is not only limited and out of his depth in trying to joust with the deity but also off limits, out of order. Nor are these questions merely rhetorical, aimed at instructing Job about things. Yahweh's own introduction forbids that:

> I will ask questions, and you instruct me. (38.2)

He has declared that he wants a recitation, not that he is engaging in a Socratic method of teaching.

In that sense, we must see that some at least of Job's earlier words were not so "ignorant" as they might seem but predicted the themes of the theophany with remarkable accuracy:

> What strength have I that I should wait?
> What end, that I extend my life?
> Is my strength the strength of rock
> or my flesh bronze? (6.11–12)

Job aired his human limitation in comparison not to the deity but to the natural and technological worlds. He described himself with the metaphor of the wind in exposing his frailty:

> Consider that my life's a wind [*rūaḥ*],
> my eye will not again see good.
> No eye that looks will spy me;
> your eyes will be on me, but I'll not be there. (7.7–8)

He used similes of a withering blossom and of a shadow:

> Worn out like something rotten,
> like a garment that moths eat,
> humankind, born of woman,
> few of days and sated with turmoil,
> comes out like a blossom and withers,
> flees like a shadow and does not stay. (13.28–14.2)

He contrasted the deity's power to his own powerlessness:

> Ah, he seizes, who can turn him back?
> Who can say to him, "What are you doing?" (9.12)

> For he's not a man like me whom I could answer,
> come together with him to trial. (9.32)

> You [singular] hunt me down, repeat your wonders on me,
> bring new witnesses before me,

increase your fury against me,
fresh squadrons against me. (10.16–17)

Job's only question about the deity's strength is whether it includes any care or compassion.

With him is wisdom—and power—
his are counsel [*'ēṣah*] and understanding.
Oh, he tears something down, it's not rebuilt,
shuts a man up, he's not opened;
he restrains the water, it's dry,
sends it out and it tosses the land about. (12.13–15)

If [a human's] days are determined,
the number of his months with you,
you've set him limits he cannot exceed. (14.5)

If Yahweh expects Job to deny his power, he has paid no attention to what Job said in the dialogue. And if Job's debate with the friends "darkens counsel / with ignorant words," it is not clear that Yahweh's questions, aimed at establishing divine power and human limitation, shed any light upon the counsel that Job has not shed before. At the least, we now hear about—indeed, in the vivid language of these speeches, we *see*—the divine power from the point of view of the one who owns it, rather than from the side of the powerless.

We cannot tell from this outpouring of divine power whether Yahweh is infuriated with a human's pretensions to enter upon alien territory or is amused that anyone would wish to try. Sarcasm is a very hazardous way to say things, because it can signify either profound contempt for the one to whom it is directed or lighthearted wit that intends no wound—but frequently inflicts one nevertheless.

Yet these speeches portray something about Yahweh by reference to the world, cosmic and animate. Perhaps one clue lies in the ways in which Yahweh refers to the world as ordered. The earth (*'ereṣ*) is like a building, "measured" (38.5), sitting on "foundations" (v. 4) or "pedestals" (v. 6), with a cornerstone (v. 6). Death and cosmic darkness have "gates" (v. 17), and Sea is contained within doors and bars (vv. 8, 10) like a city with barred gates. Sea also has "limits" (*ḥōq*, v. 10), a metaphor of law when it refers to the "statutes" of the sky (*ḥuqqōt šamayim*, v. 33), which, with the implication of government in the parallel phrase, "its rule [*mišṭarō*] on earth," no doubt implies astrological control. Other images point in the same direction: the "roads" and "ways" by which light, darkness, and storm travel (vv. 19–20, 24–25), the parentage of rain, dew, and ice (vv. 28–29), and the "counting" of the clouds (v. 37) and of the months in the fertility cycle of wild goats and deer (39.2). Such metaphors suggest a universe with regularity and something analogous to the rule of law.

But this world also has less ordered facets. Sea, mythologically an enemy to the ordering deity, represents a disorderly, though contained, element. It "burst out of the womb" (38.8) and had to be restrained, "blocked" (Heb. *skk*; cf. 1.10; 3.23), clothed (*lbš*) and swaddled (*ḥtl*, v. 9), shut up inside barred gates and ordered to stay there (vv. 10–11). It is like Job's reluctant emergence from the womb (chap. 3) to find himself likewise clothed and swaddled as an infant and "hedged" (*skk*) inside limited ways (3.23).[19] Wondering whether Job has "commanded morning" (38.12), Yahweh asks whether he violently snatched at earth's skirts, shaking the wicked out of it (v. 13), keeping dawn's light from them, and attacking the rebellious (v. 15). Other disorderly elements must be attended to. Job is asked about taking light "to its territory" (*g*ᵉ*būl*), as if one might discover it playing truant beyond its boundaries and have to conduct it back home (v. 20). Yahweh describes the treasuries (*'ōṣ*ᵉ*rōt*) of snow and hail as hoards "which I store up for a troubled time, / a day of attack and battle" (v. 23). The universe may be regulated, but the order is by no means placid. Cosmic enemies must be constrained, trouble and battle must be anticipated, storms travel known roads but sometimes water uninhabited desert—which may be an excess of divine exuberance or a disorderly waste of the most valuable commodity.

With the animals, the impression of natural order, which has so obsessed European minds in late centuries, very nearly evaporates. On the one hand, the deity provides for the needs of all of these animals—food for the raven (38.41) and prey for the lioness (v. 39), freedom for the wild ass (39.5–8), indomitable strength for the wild ox (vv. 9–12), overwhelming speed and also uncaring stupidity for the ostrich (vv. 13–18), courage in battle for the war horse (vv. 19–25), and sharp eyesight for the carrion birds (vv. 26–30). On the other, there is a bursting, uncontainable vitality in them that outruns any kind of control. "Nature for the Job poet is not a Newtonian clock operating with automatic mechanisms."[20] Yahweh himself gives the wild ass his freedom, so that

> He laughs at the city's uproar,
> does not hear the driver's shouts,
> roams the hills for his pasture,
> seeks after any patch of green. (vv. 7–8)

The god himself "deprived" the ostrich of wisdom, "apportioned her no understanding" (v. 17), made the horse courageously foolish in battle, so that, however admirably he "laughs at fear" (v. 22), he also "does not heed the trumpet call" (v. 24), refuses to retreat even when his human masters are in panic (v. 25). No "living to fight another day" for him, and perhaps the picture of carrion birds in verses 26–30 is a sideways comment on the brave charger's destiny.

Yahweh's apparently single-minded self-glorification portrays an ambiguous world, whose order contains disorder, whose disorder undermines the order.[21] Both stem from the mind that scoffs at the limitations on the mere human who "darkens counsel" by "ignorant words." Insofar as the "counsel" signifies cosmic design, the ambiguity of simultaneous order and disorder seems to darken itself in the deity's own words. We come to Yahweh's last question to Job with a quite double sense of the foregoing portrait of the universe.

> Will an accuser of Shaddai yield,
> Eloah's arbiter answer it? (40.2)

Suddenly Yahweh closes down on the special, legal sense of "counsel" (*'ēṣah*), as debate leading to a conclusion. Job wanted a trial, and now Yahweh uses legal language. The "accuser" and the "arbiter" are both legal terms,[22] and we have seen the latter before. In 9.33 Job denied that there was an "arbiter" (*mōkīaḥ*). Elihu, boldly taking up the function of arbiter in 32.12–22, in effect redefined the term. For Job, the arbiter would have been someone who would "lay his hand on" his shoulder and the god's, with authority to make a decision between the disputants. For Elihu, the *mōkīaḥ* spoke for the deity in the dispute, "answering [Job's] statements" (32.12).

Yahweh uses the crucial verb "answer" (*'nh*), as Elihu had used it, as the function of the "arbiter." Yet Elihu's arbiter would answer Job's accusations, while Yahweh's arbiter is invited to answer—what? The text says "answer *it*," feminine singular, one of the wonderfully protean pronouns in which Hebrew style abounds. Perhaps it is a general pronominal reference to "all of the above."[23] If Job is still sure, as he was back in chap. 9, that he is unable to answer the deity's questions, perhaps his advocate, his "witness" (16.19) or his "avenger" (19.25), can take his place on the stand and respond to the long series of questions that Yahweh has asked.

Job was summoned in 38.3 to answer for himself: "I will ask questions, and you instruct me." There was no hint of the third parties to whom Job referred in the debate. Yet when Yahweh unexpectedly mentions one of them, it is strangely the *mōkīaḥ*, whose existence Job denied in 9.33. It would be fairer if he invited Job to ask assistance from one of whom he was certain, the "witness" (16.19) or the "avenger" (19.25). If Yahweh refers to the *mōkīaḥ* in order to demolish the idea of a powerful third party, it is ineffectual of him to take up one whom Job rejected. If he does not cast doubt upon the third party, he has no reason to refer to the *mōkīaḥ* at all. Moreover, Yahweh uses the *mōkīaḥ* surprisingly as Elihu used him, as one who would "answer it." Perhaps he does not after all think that Elihu "darkened counsel."

Job could indignantly respond that he is not the one who adduced a *mōkīaḥ* and that he has already put himself on record as being incompetent to answer such questions as that. Though Yahweh's question in 40.2 does, indeed, revert to the motif of the trial through its legal language,[24] the reason the "arbiter" is in it is quite obscure.

Job's First Reply (40.3–5)

Job last spoke in a final self-curse, centering on his relationship to the land (31.38–40), and just after he had declared his wish to encounter the deity:

> Oh that I had someone to hear me—
> Here is my mark; let Shaddai answer me—
> and the inscription my accuser has written!
> If I do not carry it on my shoulder,
> tie it on me like a wreath,
> the number of my steps imprint upon him,
> like a prince approach him— (vv. 35–37)

Not all of that demand has come to pass. Shaddai has answered and, presumably, has heard him. Job has no written inscription from his accuser (Heb. *'īš rīb*) to flaunt on his shoulder. Nor has he assumed the posture of "prince," though Yahweh ordered him to stand up like a *geber*.

Job's response is much less assertive than we might expect:

> Oh, I am small, what could I reply to you?
> I put my hand to my mouth.
> I spoke once, and I will not answer,
> twice, and I will add nothing. (40.4–5)

One important interpretation of this response is that Job is overwhelmed by the scope and virtuosity of the divine cosmology. "He sets forth his weakness and insignificance and his determination to remain silent."[25] Thus Gordis, who does not explain why Job is determined to be silent. Weakness could conceivably produce a voluble complaint that the cosmology is an excessive demonstration of the weakness. Habel goes further in thinking that "smallness" is Job's being "humbled." The silence, therefore, is both refusal to engage in the pretense of "instruction" to which Yahweh challenged him and his "reluctant admission that Yahweh is the greater power and that he will press his case no further against such a formidable opponent."[26]

Another important interpretation is that Job is approaching a perception of his guilt. "He thus dimly becomes aware of the folly of his previous judgment of God and realizes that his presumption has been criminal. . . . The way is being cleared for the inception of his sense of sin." This interpretation rings a change on insignificance, though Terrien finds a possible "evil connotation" in "I am small" (Heb. *qallōtī*).[27] Here the notion of human frailty collapses into the notion of sin. Job's very humanity is his fault, and to be human and therefore weak is of itself to be sinful. Those who argue this point of view, however, point to Job's arrogance as the sign of guilt.[28] Yet Job pleads not that he was arrogant but that he is small.

Dhorme translates the word as "thoughtless,"[29] suggesting that Job rejects his argument with the friends as worth nothing, because it proceeds from the ignorance of which Yahweh accused him in 38.2. Such a response seems premature, and it removes the motivation from Yahweh's following question (40.8). A somewhat similar way is one that I suggested somewhat diffidently in an earlier book: "I have been trifling."[30] It proposes that Job would have brought forth a more powerful argument if he had been better aware of the force with which the god would come after him. Now it seems too late, and he will not try.

Whedbee seems to require that we already know Yahweh's second speech and Job's reply.[31] He argues that Yahweh's presentation of the cosmos gives Job a new double view of himself and the world, combining the divine perspective with his own view informed by the divine one, neither of which he could have had before the theophany. "The mystery and incongruity remain—they are now accepted but not resolved." From that vantage point, Job's silence in 40.4–5 is "a profoundly authentic response of one who has become wise," and Whedbee quotes Terrien that now there must be a second divine speech and a continuation of the encounter. But Terrien is thinking of a process of "conversion," and I am not certain that Whedbee is. Moreover, Whedbee does not spell out why this silence is authentic, where another might not be. Job's reticence makes it hard to extend his meaning with confidence.

In addition to the views that this reply is (1) Job's realization of his human insignificance, (2) the awareness, perhaps incipiently, of his guilt, (3) regret that he had failed to take the matter seriously enough, or (4) his acquisition of a newly universal wisdom, there is another, distinctly minority view. David Robertson implies that Job's silence conceals his real response.[32] Yahweh comes across not as impressively powerful but as a tyrannical, blustery windbag, somewhat like a cosmically inflated Elihu. Robertson argues cogently that Job has anticipated earlier in the dialogue much of what Yahweh attempts, and that, being overwhelmed, Job must now either submit to the power or expose it as the despotism it is by making a show of submission. He thinks that Job does the latter, pretending submission while maintaining his integrity. This view must be taken very seriously, and we will return to it with respect to Job's second reply.[33]

The possibilities of meaning in this brief quatrain of Job's first response are multiple, and I have not wished to reject any. Indeed, if anything, I want to confuse the issue still further with yet another possibility that I have seen mentioned only in passing.[34] The verb "I am small" (*qallōtī*) is a form of *qll*, which, as various scholars note, also has the sense of being "light, swift" (see 7.6; 9.25, where it describes the rapidity with which Job's life passes). Two other uses of the verb in Job, however, are even more interesting. The narration opening the dialogue, 3.1, says: "After that, Job started to speak and cursed (*y^eqallēl*) his day." This form, unlike the one in 40.4, is a Pi'el, which always has to do with cursing;[35] a cognate noun, *q^elalah*, "curse," is often an antithesis to *b^erakah*, "blessing."[36] Another rather curious use of *qll* is in Job 24.18, which describes the god, in what seem uncomplimentary terms, as being "swift [*qal*] across the waters." All four of those occurrences may be simultaneously echoed in our word. Confronted by the vast scope of the divine vision, Job feels more keenly than before how swiftly his life passes. There may be a certain irony in the echo of 24.18, where Job fulminated against the deity's swift, irresponsible departure across the waters, while Job now likewise departs quickly. There can also be an echo from 3.1 in Job's seemingly subdued reply here, in the sense that Job sees no reason to insist on continuing a life that is so painful to him. But the allusion to 3.1 is submerged, like a shoal.

The rest of the reply may be looked at more quickly. The second half of the first line has at least a double sense: "Oh, I am small, what could I reply to you?" The Hiph'il of the verb *šwb*, "to turn," has a transitive sense of turning, and "reply" suggests turning back an answer. But "turning back" has a pronominal object, "you" (singular): "How can I turn you back?" That might signify something like "How could I change your mind?" or "How could I change your direction?" Job may add to the resignation of one who thinks that no reply can be made to this power the resignation of one who thinks that the power would pay no attention to a reply in any case. The god is not about to alter his viewpoint in response to one so "small" and "swift," if not "cursed," as Job.

He throws in a little dig at the friends: "I put my hand to my mouth." In 21.5, he enjoined the gesture on the friends as the proper response to his appalling condition and in anticipation of proposing that the deity's moral governance honors the wicked and punishes the good. In 29.9, he attributed the same gesture to "princes," who used it to "restrain words" in honor and in terror of himself. Putting his hand to his mouth, then, he does what the friends ought to have done, and perhaps for the same reason: he is appalled at what he has just been given to see. He does not, of course, say that the vision appalls him, and only David Robertson of all the scholars I have read suggests that it does.[37] But his self-silencing gesture hints at it.

He also takes a mild dig at the deity.

> I spoke once, and I will not answer,
> twice, and I will add nothing. (40.5)

The rhetorical convention of reference to a number and the next number higher ($x, x + 1$) is frequent in the Hebrew Bible.[38] Here it is not a statement of numerical fact but a way of saying "I spoke several times." Still, it has that rigidly formulaic manner: "I spoke once, and A, / twice, and B," where A and B are in effect the same. Yet Yahweh (40.2) did not invite Job to answer; he asked about the *mōkīaḥ*: "Will . . . Eloah's arbiter answer it?" Job long ago denied the existence of the sort of arbiter he might want, and the only arbiter who wanted to answer was Elihu. He will not substitute Elihu for the nonexistent arbiter, and he will not answer if he is not required to. There is a feisty undertone to that flat refusal.

Job has said what he intends to say. His reaction to Yahweh's first speech remains—for all the prose I and others have spilled over it—ambiguous and unclear.

Yahweh's Second Speech (40.6–41.26)

Yahweh is not satisfied.

Gird your loins like a real man.
I will ask you questions, and you instruct me. (40.7)

He made exactly the same demand in 38.3. It is as if Job had not spoken, almost as if Yahweh had not said anything since 38.3. But what has intervened makes 40.7 different from the same words in 38.3. Having asked many questions and received no answers, Yahweh rejects Job's silence, either with the impatience of a humorless tyrant who will brook no playing of games or with a patient, insistent resumption of the discussion. Job's refusal to respond is ignored, his intent to stay where he is denied. We cannot be sure of Yahweh's tone of voice in 40.7, but one observation may suggest its peremptory quality: in 38.2–3, Yahweh asked his question first ("Who is this?" etc.) and made his demand second. In 40.7–8, the order is reversed: he makes the demand first and asks the question second.

Yahweh's question is new, and I have argued that it decisively shifts the issue.[39] It is, indeed, the pivot on which the whole book turns:

Would you even annul my order,
treat me as guilty so you may be innocent? (v. 8)

The couplet nicely exhibits the impossibility of translation, as I pointed out in the "Indispensable Introduction." I render *mišpaṭ* as "order" in the interests of a readable text.[40] Though the connotations of *mišpaṭ* include social and natural order, the word is much more complex than that. "Custom" as a habitual way of acting is another ingredient. "Justice" as a principled way of acting is still a third, and the supposition that that is the word's "meaning" has determined many an interpretation: "Would you impugn My justice?" (JPS); "Would you pervert my justice?" (Habel); "Will you deny my justice?" (Gordis).[41] A fourth is "judgment," meaning not the deity's ability to make decisions but the legal verdict that he hands down: "break (or render ineffectual) my judgment" (Rowley); "Would you annul my judgment?" (Pope); "Do you dare to deny my judgment?" (Mitchell); "Do you really wish to cancel my just verdict?" (Fohrer)[42]

The verb *prr*, used with *mišpaṭ*, may have a basic meaning of "breaking up" or "invalidating," and it occurs most often with command and covenant words like *bᵉrīt* and *miṣwōt*.[43] All the more reason, some may think, to insist on the covenantal meaning of *mišpaṭ*, "justice" or "judgment." On the contrary, all the more reason to insist on additional complications of meaning. Adding together the varying notions of breaking up the "social order," "cosmic order," "customary action," "justice," "legal verdict" and who knows how many other connotations, what we have is much more interesting than lifting out only one, like Little Jack Horner's plum, and congratulating ourselves on being right.[44]

Yahweh inquires of Job, then, whether he intends to nullify or break down the ways the deity has made the world to work, in its natural and social order, its necessary rules, the consistent concept lying behind and within it. That is the generality, and the second line comes down to cases:

> treat me as guilty so you can be innocent?

Yahweh uses a standard antithetic pair, *ršʿ* and *ṣdq*. If he is talking morality, the words oppose "wickedness" (*ršʿ*) to "righteousness" (*ṣdq*). If he is talking in terms of legal process, *ršʿ* is "guilt" and *ṣdq* is "innocence." The connotational field of these two terms is narrower than with *mišpaṭ*, perhaps in part because they came to be used conventionally as an antithetical pair.

The absence of grammatical parallelism between the two terms is interesting. "Treat me as guilty" is the Hiphʿil ("causative") form of *ršʿ*, which, used of morality, means to deal with someone in terms of that person's intrinsic immorality or wickedness. Yahweh's question recalls Job's reversals of values and terms in chap. 27, and especially Job's characterization of himself as "godless" (27.8) and the deity as "wicked" (*rašaʿ*, 27.7). In legal procedure, the verb has to do with declaring a guilty verdict on someone. In those terms, we have returned to the language of a trial, and Yahweh's question almost suggests a response to Job's wish (which he has not stated) to act as judge. But the "righteous/innocent" half of the line is not in the Hiphʿil but in the simple Qal stem. It denotes not treating someone as innocent or declaring the person innocent but the person's being innocent. Yahweh proposes an imbalance in Job's hypothetical judgment between a characterization of "wicked" or a verdict of "guilty" for Yahweh and the quality of innocence for Job, Yahweh as "dealt with" in terms of wickedness, Job as *being* righteous. It almost sounds, moreover, as if the one determination will automatically entail the other: if Yahweh should be declared guilty in the trial, the declaration will confer innocence on Job or give evidence of it.

No doubt the question also works in reverse: if Job were declared guilty, Yahweh is made innocent. It presents an ironic symbiosis between guilt and innocence, in which there can be no innocence without guilt, no guilt without innocence, a world teetering on the knife-edge balance, with righteousness and wickedness in equal supply. If so, blame could not attach to guilt or praise to innocence. Either would be a matter of mere happenstance, and it would imply a moral fatalism that allows no weight of moral decision.

Even if Yahweh's question does not imply such a generality about the balance of guilt and innocence in the world, it perceives Job's insistence that the situation contains one right and one wrong. Quite apart from general rights and wrongs, the antithesis between Job and Yahweh must hold to the end. The goodness of one entails the badness of the other. That antithesis has been the center of Job's argument to the friends and the underlying structure of their arguments to him. Of course, the friends could not conceive that the deity could be guilty, and therefore to them Job was the only possible candidate. Job began somewhere near there, but he came to think that perhaps the god is wicked ("Earth is given over to a wicked hand," 9.24), then to think that the god's structure of favor and blame was the opposite of that of humans (chap. 21), and later to think decisively that he, Job, was innocent and the god was guilty (chap. 27). In chap. 31 he pulled back, asserting only that he himself was innocent without detailing what the god was.

Now Yahweh asks the question in such a way that he sweeps away the fabric of the dialogue between Job and the friends.

> Would you even annul my order,
> treat me as guilty so you may be innocent? (40.8)

The world does not balance upon sin and righteousness, on guilt and innocence. In order to survive lions must have prey, which is sometimes the wild ass. Wild asses must have freedom, including the freedom to become the lion's prey. Ostriches are praiseworthy for their magnificent speed but blameworthy for their ineptitude in rearing young. The world's order entails both regularity and irregularity, both law and lawlessness, both order and disorder. Job has wanted to have it only one way, supposing that unless his goodness is rewarded with prosperity, goodness is meaningless and the world unjust. Now Yahweh asks whether Job is willing to pay that price, whether he really thinks that the world spins that way.

The form of Yahweh's question indicates that requiring the antithesis and balance of guilt and innocence shatters divine order and breaches justice. Why must everything come out even? It is not the case that all that happens is a function of human morality. Events in the world cannot be explicated simply as reactions to Job's and his friends' moral actions. The moral retributionism that Job and the friends alike have put forth at such length is simply not the way the world goes. Yahweh's question in 40.8 indicates that the debate around the ash heap at Uz was a tangent, perhaps an interesting thought experiment, but not the production of truth.

This divine speech is not so irrelevant to the issues of the dialogue as some interpreters have thought. Responding directly to those issues, it rejects them. Yahweh has decisively shifted the issue from the question of morality, its rewards, its punishments, and its cosmic reverberations. Indeed, it seems that morality has no cosmic reverberations at all. At the same time, curiously, Yahweh makes his point so indirectly, so subtly, that it is not at all difficult to miss it.

Before Job has a chance to reply, Yahweh sets off some further poetic fireworks. After challenging Job to exert authority in the human world and to mete out punishments (40.9–14), he resumes the bestiary from chap. 39 in a decisively new mode. He now refers not to animals familiar from normal experience like war horses, lions, and ostriches, but to two creatures quite beyond ordinary nature: Behemoth (40.15–24) and Leviathan (40.25–41.26).

Yahweh begins by challenging Job to be an authority:

> If you have an arm like El's,
> and with a voice like his you thunder,
> deck yourself with pride and puissance,
> with glory and grandeur clothe yourself. (40.9–10)

The challenge asks about Job's divine attributes of strength ("arm") and voice and suitable costume. The garb is metaphorical and alliterative, "pride and puissance" (*ga'ōn wagōbah*) and "glory and grandeur" (*hōd wᵉhadar*).[45] The danger of such two-headed literary devices is that they may be clichés, as *hōd wᵉhadar* is,[46] or they may carry unhelpful connotations, as *ga'ōn wagōbah* does. This phrase frequently refers not to genuine height (the basic metaphor in both words) but to illicit height or to haughty, prideful eminence. One should avoid superciliousness, *gōbah 'ap*, "height of nose," a wonderful phrase (Ps 10.4); King Hezekiah almost lost his position because of a "haughty heart," *gōbah lēb* (2 Chron 32.25–26); and the deity promises to "put a stop to the pride of arrogant people" (*ga'ōn zēdīm*, Isa 13.11). Proverbs 16.18 joins the two in a warning:

lipnē šeber ga'ōn
w^e lipnē kiššalōn gōbah rūaḥ

Before a break is pride,
and before a stumble is a haughty spirit.[47]

While inviting Job to imitate him,[48] Yahweh threatens him with the effects of overweening arrogance. The terms of the power Yahweh enjoins upon Job (Job 40.11–13) emphasize a double bind in this challenge to be godlike; Job is to exercise not only indignation against wickedness but an excess of anger (*'ebrōt 'appeka*, v. 11a), not simply a redress of imbalance in bringing the haughty proud low (*hašpīl*, v. 11b) but the excess of humiliating them (*haknia'*, v. 12a). He is to deal with the guilty not by just punishment but by "trampling" them (*hdk*, v. 12b), burying them in the ground and "binding their faces" in the grave.[49] Though the precise meaning of each expression is difficult to ascertain, the lines convey a power used beyond the limits of necessity.

Yahweh proposes that Job deal with these contemptible humans in the way Job has claimed the god dealt with him.[50] He wished to be a "concealed abortion" instead of alive (*nēpel ṭamūn*, 3.16), to be "concealed" among the dead until the god should come around to deal properly with him (14.13, though he did not use the root *ṭmn* there). He felt himself the recipient of divine anger (16.9; 19.11), and he complained that the deity "tramples me down with a whirlwind" (9.17, with *šwp* rather than *hdk*). Not every expression here has a corresponding expression elsewhere, but the connections are suggestive. Ironically, if Job were to handle humans as Yahweh invites him to, the recipients of Job's treatment could justly complain of exactly the tyranny of which he has complained. The implication in 40.8 that order does not entail strict retributive justice ought to make a quid pro quo at least surprising, but Yahweh's challenge in verses 9–14 looks very much like just that. If the challenge that Yahweh flings is ironic, it must be so deeply so that he can hardly mean it. If he does mean it, one might think that he implicitly admits Job's denunciations of his moral failures.

If so, the shifting of the issue from the problem of guilt and innocence that we saw in verse 8 turns out to be hollow, and the challenge to exert authority masks the crucial question about the world's order. But then we must ask about the force of his promise to praise Job's victory (v. 14).

Even I, I will praise you,
for your right hand won you victory.

The victorious "right hand" is attached to "an arm like El's" (v. 9a) in a nice bracketing construction. "Praise" (*'ōd*) puns on "glory" (*hōd*, v. 10b), and "victory" (*tōšīa'*) is the outcome of Yahweh's demand at the beginning of both of his speeches that the hero "gird [his] loins" for battle. Job is to battle against Yahweh, and in the process is to humiliate and trample proud, wicked humans. It seems an admission that Job was right in chap. 27, when he transvalued morality so that it meant its opposite. It is as if Yahweh sends Job out to do battle not only against the proud and the arrogant but against their proud, arrogant deity. "Beat down my troops, and I will surrender." Job despairingly complained of those troops back in chaps. 16 and 19. Nothing has changed. The deity is still wrapping Job in double binds.

Perhaps the crucial word in 40.9–14 is the first one, "If," and it necessitates a series of questions. If Job denies that he has "an arm like El's" or can thunder "with a voice like his," is he relieved of this battle? If he tries to humiliate the wicked and fails, will Yahweh gloat over his defeat instead of praising his victory? Does Yahweh really mean that if Job succeeds, he will elevate him to divine rank? Or is this the last irony in the profoundly impossible task that he sets before the hero? Whether the tone of voice contains genuine challenge or ironic goading, it is hard to think that this invitation is seriously meant. It is pure hypothesis. "If you have an arm like El's" finally looks very much like "Suppose you had an arm like El's." But Job does not.

Perhaps the issue did not really change at verse 8. Or perhaps Yahweh does what Job did in chap. 31; namely, having decisively changed the issue earlier, he drops back into the prior construction. In that case, the vivid portrayals of Behemoth and Leviathan would be mere audiovisual aids to the hero's fantasy life. We must turn now to them.

Is Behemoth a hippopotamus? That impressive animal does eat grass, though it does not crop it like cattle (40.15), and it is very strong (v. 16). But hippopotami do not have stiff or large tails (v. 17),[51] nor are their thigh sinews intertwined. The major argument in favor of the hippo is the description not of the animal but of its habitat. A beast that lies under river plants (thorn-lotus, wadi-poplar) and among reeds and in the marsh with the river flowing past him (vv. 21–24) might easily be thought to be a hippopotamus.[52] But the description of the beast is reason for grave skepticism on the point.

Does Leviathan make sense as a crocodile? Certain aspects of the description could be taken from the crocodile. In favor of the identification are his mouth "ringed with terrifying teeth" (41.6) and

his rows of shields,
closed with a flinty seal,
one touching another,
and wind can't come between them.
Each clings to its brother,
clasping inseparably. (vv. 7–9)

That sounds like the scaly hide of the crocodile, as does the wonderfully metaphoric verse 22:

His underbelly is sharpened shards,
he stretches out, a threshing-sledge on the mud.

But crocodiles do not go to sea, and I do not think that "deep" (*m^eṣūlah*) and "sea" (*yam*) in verse 23 can be taken to mean merely water.[53] Apprehension about fighting with Leviathan (40.25–32) and the creature's contempt of normal human weapons (41.18–21) is understandable of the crocodile or of any powerful, frightening animal, say the elephant.

There are, moreover, other bits of information to consider. In 12.7–8, Job invited the friends to consult Behemoth for instruction along with three other groups of natural beings: "the birds of the sky," "the plants of the earth," and the "fish of the sea." The affinities of that language with characteristic phrases in the creation myth in Genesis 1 are clear.[54] Leviathan turns up in several passages in the Hebrew Bible as a cosmic enemy of the god. In Psalm 74.14, the deity "crushed the heads of Leviathan" (JPS), and in Isaiah 27.1 he is expected "in that day" to visit punishment

upon Leviathan, the fleeing Dragon [*naḥaš*],
upon Leviathan, the twisting Dragon.[55]

"Dragon" might be "serpent," but the same phrase (*naḥaš barīaḥ*) also occurs in the context of a cosmic battle with a monstrous enemy in Job 26.13, which we could take as another allusion to Leviathan. In Psalm 104.25–26, Leviathan seems to have been tamed by the deity:

Here is Sea, great and broad,
there innumerable creatures,
animals both small and great.
There ships travel,
Leviathan, the one you formed
to play with him.

Job 40.27–30 suggests the opposite for a human. The god may "play with him" (*śaḥeq bō*, Ps 104.26), but Yahweh's question, "Can you play with him (*t^e śaḥeq bō*) like a bird?" (Job 40.29) demands the answer "Not on your life!" This hugely powerful creature has a double meaning, in that the deity's order involves both a certain sportiveness with Leviathan (Ps 104) and also rigid control of him by combat (Isa 27).

Yahweh boasts about his implicitly playful handling of Leviathan: "None is fierce enough to rouse him" (Job 41.2). Let sleeping monsters lie. Yet Job's opening curse on his birthday called for support, not in order to play games but to undo the creation:

> May those who put spells on Sea curse it [the day],
> those skilled at rousing Leviathan. (3.8)

Perhaps all this is not enough to overcome the sometimes unexamined consensus that Behemoth is a hippo and Leviathan a croc. Keel, having concluded for the consensus opinion, supports with a great deal of iconographic detail from Egyptian sources the argument that hunting and killing hippopotami and crocodiles was the business only of Horus, the deity who occupied the person of the Egyptian king.[56] Only the king is protrayed as killing these animals, and often specifically in his identity as Horus. That is most interesting, following upon Yahweh's challenge to Job in 40.9–14 to take up divine powers over the human world.

I remain unpersuaded. For one thing, the context and the language of the reference to Behemoth in Job 12.7 showed clear affinity with the Israelite creation myth in Genesis 1, and Leviathan is a Canaanite-Hebrew term about an identifiable Canaanite-Hebrew combat myth, not about anything Egyptian. For another, I see no clear reason why, for the only time in the Book of Job, we are suddenly transported to Egypt for the last and crucial point about Job's possession of divine powers.[57] There is no reason why Job would be asked whether he is Horus. Surely the plagues and the escape and the crossing of the Sea at the Exodus demonstrated once and for all to Israelites that Horus is no match for Yahweh. If Behemoth and Leviathan point to Horus, Yahweh is stacking the deck, inviting Job to take on the powers of an already defeated god, and we have once again a contest that is not remotely fair. Job is intelligent enough to see that it would be unwise to apply to Horus for assistance.

The location of the myth seems to me determinative against the hippopotamus and the crocodile. Perhaps those beasts were mythically worrisome to Egyptians, and I do not object to the notion that Israelite thinkers might have conflated myths from divergent ethnic sources. But I think that we gain nothing we must have for this divine speech from thinking of those animals, and we lose some freedom of purchase on it by the thought.

Not that other identifications of these beings with known animals are more helpful. Milton's thought of Leviathan as a whale took him not to Egypt but to Norwegian waters:

> that sea-beast
> Leviathan, which God of all his works
> Created hugest that swim the ocean-stream.
> Him, haply slumbering on the Norway foam,
> The pilot of some small night-foundered skiff,
> Deeming some island, oft, as seamen tell,
> With fixèd anchor in his scaly rind,
> Moors by his side under the lee, while night
> Invests the sea, and wishèd morn delays.
> (*Paradise Lost*, I, 200–208)

Some passages in the description, e.g., 41.23–24, might make the whale believable, but for others it will not do, such as the description of the creature's exterior as "rows of shields, / closed with a flinty seal" (41.7).

There is simply no plausible natural counterpart to Leviathan. If it be argued that the poet describes a crocodile or a whale without ever having seen one, then the beast has been constructed in the imagination. An imaginary creature is not identical with any known one. I agree, then, with those who find Behemoth and Leviathan to be not actual animals but mythic ones, creatures whose very excesses are the point—whatever the point may be.

To that question we must now turn. There are several important interpretations of Yahweh's invitation to Job to ponder Behemoth and Leviathan. One group of interpretations poses variants on the basic idea that the descriptions convey nothing but the divine power. Another proposal, not unrelated to the first group, is that the descriptions of Behemoth and Leviathan are a way of maintaining the divine and cosmic inscrutability. A third argument is that Yahweh's entire second speech challenges Job to be divine. We may not be forced to choose one to the exclusion of others.

Yahweh does not actually invite Job to control Behemoth. He merely calls him to Job's attention with that exclamatory *hinnēh-na'*, "Hey, there!"[58] which so many interpreters take to mean "behold." Yahweh describes the beast as superhuman. Power words in verse 16, "strength" (*kōaḥ*) and "potence" (*'ōn*), give way to the comparison of the tail to a cedar's stiffness (v. 17) and to the metaphors of bronze tubes for bones and iron rods for limbs (v. 18), as Yahweh runs through the catalogue of

Behemoth's body parts, from loins and belly muscles through tail and sinews of the thigh to bones and legs. This group of interpretations emphasizes the origin of this strength in the divine creation: "He is first of El's ways" (v. 19a).[59]

It is the second reference to the divine creation of Behemoth. Yahweh began in verse 15 with the idea:

> Ah, then! Behemoth,
> whom I made with you,
> eats grass like cattle.

"Made" is the creation verb *'śh*, and the question is what "with you" means. Most commentators argue, on analogy with Genesis 1.24–31, that the reference is temporal, "at the same time as you," referring to the sixth day of creation, when land animals (including, in vv. 24–25, *b^ehēmah*, a collective usually translated "cattle") and humans were both created.[60] That would emphasize Job's common origin with Behemoth, but Behemoth's power shows how much greater he has become. There may even be a snide allusion back to Yahweh's sarcasm in 38.4–5, 12, and 21 about Job's firsthand knowledge of the creation.

Ending the stanza with the same idea, Yahweh uses a somewhat odd term for creation, the "first of El's *ways*" (*rēšīt darkē 'ēl*). "First" (*rēšīt*) indicates "primary, pre-eminent" as well as "primal," as the creation begins with the "beginning" (*b^erēšīt*, Gen 1.1). But what is a "way" as an element of creation? In Proverbs 8.22, something similar is said by the personified Wisdom:

> Yahweh created me first of his way [*rēšīt darkō*],[61]
> ahead of his works from of old.

The central metaphorical use of "way" in the Hebrew Bible is as the conduct of one's life, and Proverbs 8.22 and Job 40.19 almost suggest that Wisdom and Behemoth are both primary and primal in Yahweh's own life-style. But the strange image of the creator ("maker," *'ōśeh*) drawing the sword (v. 19b) might suggest that Yahweh's conduct of life from the beginning has involved keeping his monsters in control. It seems strange that the creatures make difficulties for the creator. Was the maker of the world unable to take charge of it? When you set "his maker" (*ha'ōśō*)[62] next to "made" in verse 15 ("whom I made with you": *'^ašer 'aśītī 'immak*), the apparently placid Behemoth becomes a source of trouble for Yahweh. What is more, the pairing of Behemoth and Job ("you," v. 13) might indicate that Yahweh must keep Job similarly under control.

Perhaps Behemoth is an inadequate evidence of the divine power. If

Yahweh has trouble controlling Behemoth and with him Job, as verses 15 and 19a suggest, he will surely be unable to manage Leviathan. Yet the second stanza, verses 20–24, seems to have nothing to do with divine control of the monster.[63]

That is also a problem with Leviathan, who is more fearsome than Behemoth. Very little in the Leviathan section emphasizes divine control over this monster. The first stanza, 40.25–32, shows how Job and his like could not hope to control and capture Leviathan. Verse 41.1 asks, "Is El himself thrown down at sight of him?"[64] The assumed negative answer is continued by what I take as a parenthetical remark in verses 2b–3a, which answers the assertion that no one dares to rouse Leviathan with rhetorical questions boasting against those who think of standing up against Yahweh. And Yahweh claims to possess and control Leviathan, indeed, to be the only one remotely capable of doing so: "Under the whole sky, he is mine" (v. 3b).[65]

If verses 2b–3a are not parenthetical, verse 2b implicitly compares opposing Yahweh to opposing Leviathan. If "none is fierce enough to rouse" Leviathan—though Job called for those "skilled in rousing Leviathan" in 3.8b, as if someone were capable of it—Yahweh is more frightful. If the "fight" with the irresistible Leviathan (40.32) is to be avoided at all costs, taking a military position ("take a stand," *yityaṣṣēb*, v. 2b) before Yahweh is to be avoided even more. But this reading of verse 2 leads to grave troubles with verse 3, which impresses Pope as "a lofty thought entirely out of keeping with the context."[66] It is difficult to combine Yahweh's promise in verse 3a of punitive repayment (*šlm*) to anyone who "confronts" (*qdm*) him with the statement in verse 3b that he possesses the confronter. Verse 3 gives the reader more trouble if verse 2b is taken as the parallel to verse 2a. Yahweh portrays himself in verse 3 as vengeful and tyrannical, not an unprecedented portrait, but the object of his vengeance is obscure.

Elsewhere the claim to power over Leviathan is implied only in the polytheistic statement of verse 17:

> Gods are frightened at his rising,
> at his crashing down, they shrink away.

This jibe at "gods" implies that Yahweh alone of all the gods is immune from such fright. The scene is reminiscent of the gods' terror at the great flood in Tablet XI of the Gilgamesh Epic.

> The gods were frightened by the deluge,
> And, shrinking back, they ascended to the heaven of Anu.

The gods cowered like dogs
  Crouched against the outer wall.[67]

Or is Job 41.17 an admission that Yahweh, like the other gods, has his moments of terror before his astounding monster? The text does not say "the gods" (*ha'ēlīm*), which might be taken distributively, or "other gods" (*'ēlīm 'ᵃḥērīm*), but just, in the abstract generality, "gods" (*'ēlīm*). Surely no claim is implied that Yahweh is not a "god."

There is no other explicit reference to the divine power in the Leviathan passage. Yahweh owns Leviathan and, by implication, controls him (41.1–3), but the rest of the description of Leviathan focuses either on the impossibility of Job's controlling him or on the creature's terrible power. The rhetoric itself calls more attention to Leviathan's power than to Yahweh's.

The chief proponent of the view that these portraits of Behemoth and Leviathan are ways of extending the notion of the divine mystery and inscrutability is Gordis.[68] Where the animals in Yahweh's first speech were variously admirable and fascinating, even, as with the ostrich, criticizable, Gordis thinks that Behemoth and Leviathan "are not only dangerous to man, but positively repulsive from man's perspective." What is to be admired is not any moral justification for their presence in the universe but the breadth of the divine creativity: "Yet for God, these monstrous creatures are beautiful, for they, too, reveal the creative power of God and elicit His joy and pride."

The universe, then, is not focused upon the human problem or the human moral construction of life. Behemoth and Leviathan are presented as utterly independent of human influence and control, in Gordis's view, in order to show that the universe is patterned and meaningful precisely as it transcends the limited patterns and meanings that mere humans can perceive. What from our perspective looks stupendously ugly and evil has a more fundamental beauty from the spacious standpoint of the divine. "The harmony and beauty of the natural order support the faith that there is a similar pattern of meaning in the moral sphere, since both emanate from the One God." Gordis does not characterize the pattern, perhaps because it transcends human comprehension. It is a matter of faith, of a hypothesized analogy from a natural pattern to a moral one, that ultimately everything is good.

It is a moving vision of the universe. Gordis does not make clear its relation to the apparent rejection of the "guilt-innocence" opposition in 40.8. There are those who think that the poetry of these two descriptions is inferior,[69] but I find it stylistically intensified over chaps. 38–39. The beauty in the terrible is attested by poets and others from all times and places.[70] Gordis takes these descriptions to show that beauty is precisely the point about the divine mystery.

The idea is perhaps more persuasive in the proposing than in the application to the text. No conclusion about the meaning of Behemoth is presented in 40.15–24, nor, as we have noted above, is any action respecting him demanded of Job. The action advised to Job about Leviathan is inaction, avoidance of any contact with or skirmish against him. Observation, it seems, is either objective ("His sneezes flash with light, / his eyes are like dawn's eyelids, / from his mouth come flares, / fiery sparks fly out," 41.10–11) or mightily impressed ("He considers iron as straw, / bronze as rooted wood. / Bow's child cannot put him to flight, / sling stones are turned by him to stubble. / A cudgel seems to him like stubble, / he laughs at the battle sword's clatter," vv. 19–21). Our culture trains us to find that poetically beautiful.

I am willing to think that the monsters' inaccessibility points to the inaccessibility of indubitable truth, to a deity who stands outside of humanly definable comprehension and truth. I am unwilling to think that the portrayals of Behemoth and Leviathan do more than imply that, and even the implication lies beyond any statement in the text itself. It is the sort of implication that one may wish to draw, having looked closely at the text and said, "This poetry does not come out and tell me what it thinks about its subject. I shall have to speculate without certainty."

Another interpretation of the Behemoth-Leviathan passage is intriguingly different, taking into account facets of the text ignored in other interpretations. J. V. Kinnier Wilson proposed that the point of these passages is not what they tell us about the deity or the natural universe but what they tell us about Job.[71] Job is pretending to be three different kinds of deity: the god who governs human life, the creator god, and the hero god.

Kinnier Wilson points out that the Behemoth and Leviathan passages follow directly from Yahweh's demand upon Job in 40.9–14 to take up the divine power. "Deck yourself with pride and puissance, / with glory and grandeur clothe yourself" (v. 10) recalls the god's majesty. If Job takes over the universe's throne and succeeds in ruling it, then even Yahweh will "confess thee (to be a god)," as Kinnier Wilson translates Job 40.14a—an interpretive expansion on "I will praise you" (*'ōdekka*), the kind of praise proper to a deity.

Kinnier Wilson thinks of verses 9–14 as Job's imaginative acting out of the god's invitation to occupy the divine function of ruling the universe. One might want to specify that this challenge has to do with ruling the human realm of the universe, though Kinnier Wilson does not narrow it down that far. He is most interested in the deity's invitation to Job to play governing god and promises to render him divine honors if he succeeds (v. 14).[72]

The Behemoth passage, Kinnier Wilson argues, presents Job's effort to be a creator god and the Leviathan passage his attempt at being the hero god. Job botches both enterprises. The portrayal of Behemoth (vv. 15–24) is a laughable depiction of an impossible animal who is an embarrassment to other animals and a shame to its maker. He has a "tail stiff like a cedar" (v. 17a), completely incapable of the function of any decent tail, to be flexible enough to swish flies and other insects away from the beast's hide. "The sinews of his thighs are intertwined" (v. 17b), which is no way to design thighs, for it renders the beast immobile. The ribs are copper tubes, and copper is a soft, easily crushed metal, quite unsuitable in strength,[73] whereas the backbone is "as a bar of iron," stiff and unbending as no backbone ought ever to be (v. 18).[74] Whether or not Kinnier Wilson has the specific bones right—and it is questionable—the skeleton is depicted as not suiting its function.

Verse 19 ("He is first of El's ways" in my translation) begins with the emphatic "he" (*hū'*), which can also be the demonstrative pronoun, "this." It suggests to Kinnier Wilson a scornful pointed finger: "Shall *this* be the first of the works of a 'God'?" He goes on to interpret the difficult *būl* in verse 20 ("wood," I said, with some trepidation) as cognate to Akkadian *būlu*, "cattle," with G. R. Driver,[75] and the ambiguous *śḥq* ("play" in my translation) as "laugh," which it can certainly be, for the following very interesting reading:

> Why, the cattle of the mountains would howl[76] at him
> And every beast of the field laugh (in scorn).[77]

Behemoth's own kind recognize how bizarre he is, and Kinnier Wilson suggests that verses 22–23 portray a "shame-faced" Behemoth hiding abjectly under cover, refusing to emerge even if the Jordan were to flood.[78]

This proposal makes the best sense of the difficult verse 15:

> Ah, then, Behemoth,
> whom I made with you,
> eats grass like cattle.

Other readings must turn "with you" into "at the same time as you" or "in the same manner as you." No, says Kinnier Wilson: "with you" equals with your assistance. You and I cooperated in the creation of this beast, and look what a mess you made of it! As a creator god, Job, you are a flop. Your help made this poor thing an impossible animal who cannot face being seen in public, all his strength concentrated in his belly (v. 16), a stiff, unusable tail, a sinew system in his legs that does not permit proper movement (v. 17), a skeleton both weak and rigid (v. 18). No self-respecting god would admit having made this animal. It is good for nothing but to be slaughtered on the spot (v. 19b).[79]

The Leviathan passage depicts Job's effort to be the youthful hero god battling the cosmic chaos monster: the Sumerian Ninurta against Asag, the Babylonian Marduk against the frightful Tiamat, the Canaanite Baal against Sea (Yamm), St. George and the dragon. If Leviathan is a mythic beast, Yahweh's questions to Job about doing battle against him are already challenges to be the hero god, and the questions promised in 40.7 intensify those Yahweh asked about the animals in chaps. 38–39:

> Can you drag out Leviathan with a fishhook,
> press down his tongue with a rope,
> put a line in his nose,
> pierce his jaw with a barb?
> Will he beg you abjectly for mercy,
> speak weakly to you?
> Will he make a covenant with you,
> and you take him as a perpetual slave?
> Can you play with him like a bird,
> put him on a leash for your little girls? (vv. 25–29)

It is no doubt unfair for Yahweh to remind Job of his dead children, but the purport of the questions is quite clear. Job must face up not merely to pondering Leviathan, as he was bidden to ponder Behemoth, but rather to *catching* him. And for that "Job finds that he has neither the qualities nor even the equipment."[80] His career as hero god is over before it begins.

Yahweh must, to be sure, rub in the failure by extending his description of this frightening animal beyond necessity. The questions of 40.25–31 are sufficient, and the warning of verse 32 is terse and complete:

> Put your hand upon him—
> think of the fight; don't do it again.

The divine boast in 41.1–4 brings us to what we might think is a good point of closure. But Yahweh has 22 more couplets of poetry to get through, and he begins with a different form of questions. It is no longer "can you?" or "will he?" but "who would?" (vv. 5–6). The implied answer is plain enough.

The questions end there, and from verse 7 on we have the portrait of a monster of whom even gods—presumably including fledgling hero gods—are terrified. In contrast to Behemoth, who is the object of other animals' laughter (40.20b), Leviathan "laughs at the battle sword's clatter" (41.21b), the very sword that Behemoth's maker ought to take to that unfortunate beast (40.19b). Far from skulking under thorn-lotuses and wadi-poplars in the rivers, Leviathan's domain is Tehom, the abyss, the waters that reach all the way to the bottom of the universe, those waters that, welling up in fountains, brought on the great flood (Gen 7.11). Nothing can stand against him, and certainly no "proud beasts" can do so (Job 41.26).[81]

Kinnier Wilson concludes from this reading of the Behemoth-Leviathan passage that, indeed, Job receives a trial, but not the trial he expected. Rather it is an ordeal, the requirement that he be god three times over, once as world governor, once as creator, once as hero. Failing the ordeal, Job's "whole argument comes crashing to the ground, and, with it, the fullness of his former pride and presumption."[82]

It is interesting that many interpreters of the Yahweh speeches find it necessary to conclude that Job is defeated. We are, it seems, so attuned to the power of the deity that we do not find overexertions of that power offensive. The humiliation of a human being strikes both Jewish and Christian interpreters as quite acceptable. He had it coming to him, Kinnier Wilson, among many others, implies.

Yet the divine speeches are full of a lordly rhetorical sarcasm that brutally puts Job down, and interpreters seem eager to assist in that process. Are we afraid of the daring example of the person who stands up and argues human importance and dignity? Do we, like the friends, feel that Job's suffering indicates that he deserved what he got and that his feistiness against the god compounds a felony whose basis we never know? It seems like people's quick tendency to suppose that a woman who was raped must somehow have invited it.

Yahweh's speeches both do and do not respond to Job's problem. Job does not need to be reminded of the divine power, but Yahweh parades that power with every word. Job does not need to be reminded of human limitations of strength and wisdom, but Yahweh calls them emphatically to his attention. In both of those senses, Job's expectations are both met and not met. He expected early in the debate (chap. 9) that the deity would overwhelm him with unanswerable questions. The deity has done that. The vision in chap. 38 of a cosmic order completely outside of human control, the observable but not dominatable animal world that is the focus of chap. 39, and the challenges to deal with realms of mythic power in chaps. 40–41 do not suggest that Yahweh aims to increase Job's comfort in the universe. From beginning to end, Yahweh's rhetoric insistently calls on Job to do the divine work, to take up the mantle of divine power, to embark on divine responsibilities. Even if the Behemoth passage describes a failed effort, it points to Job's occupying the deity's place.

By posing the legal question in 40.8, Yahweh responds to Job's concern, yet he puts the question in such a way as to shift the issue. Job wanted a trial between equals, even if that equality were a legal fiction. He demanded a choice between his moral and legal innocence and the deity's, contrasting his own goodness to the deity's wickedness. Yahweh's speech, especially 40.8, comes near to suggesting that Job misplaced the question. Such "order" (*mišpaṭ*) as the universe has is not necessarily moral. There is no hint of a moral order in chaps. 38–39, and the only hint of one in chap. 40 is Yahweh's invitation to Job in verses 9–14 to impose a somewhat brutal one. However we read Behemoth and Leviathan, we cannot call them exemplars or signs of a moral order.[83] Whether Behemoth be an impressive instance of divine creative power or a ludicrous evidence of Job's creative impotence, there is no taint of morality in him. Leviathan as crocodile or as chaos monster indicates nothing except invincible might.

Perhaps that is why it is so easy to read Yahweh's speeches as an exercise in power. They start and end with power, and in the middle there is more power. They taunt Job's lack of power and invite him to exert power he does not have. That is one way to shift the issue. Job has demanded a legal solution to what he has come to see as the problem of the morality of the divine power: the god is punishing him for something he did not do. Yahweh's case for the divine power has no necessary ingredient of the moral in it, and, indeed, the question in 40.8 points precisely away from structuring the universe in moral terms, of righteousness and wickedness, innocence or guilt, and toward power, annulling "order" or its obverse.

If the problem is purely one of power and Yahweh completely lacks morality of any sort, asking about his morality raises a question that cannot be answered. When Eliphaz brought up the issue of the efficacy of morality to alter one's circumstances, he set the discussion off on the tangent from which Yahweh rescues it in 40.8. For Yahweh's question moves the issue away from the retributive supposition that both Job and the friends held, that led Job through his third-party hypotheses in the second cycle and his reversals of the moral nature of the divine rule in the third, though he resumed it in the series of curses in chap. 31.

If Yahweh has shifted the issue to that of divine power, we must wonder about its effect on Job. In 40.4–5, Job remained noncommittal, making a laconic remark that could be taken variously as standing pat on what he had said before, as a submission to power, as a subversive but ambiguous apparent acquiescence in power. Having been now through Behemoth and Leviathan, we must wonder what is left for Job except unalloyed submission. The claim that the content of Yahweh's speeches is insignificant, that all that matters is that he made them,[84] strikes me as a way to avoid thinking about the problem. As we come down to Job's final speech, we must, I believe, have in mind what we think Job may now say. Job must at least respond to the questions of the divine power and, if he heard the question of 40.8, to the relation to it of the divine morality.

Job's Second Reply (42.1–6)

Clearly Job heard Yahweh's demand in 40.7, as well as the question and demand in 38.2–3. He quotes both, in 42.3 and 4, though not quite exactly. What is more, he begins with the question of Yahweh's power:

> I know that you can do everything,
> no plan is inaccessible to you. (42.2)

Something very strange is there. The first singular form, "I know," is the Qere. The Hebrew has *yd't*, with no *yod* at the end of the word, not *yd'ty*. The Ketib is presumably second-person masculine singular, *yada'ta*, "you know."[85]

Those two statements propose two very different meanings. "I know that you can do everything" admits the divine power and perhaps submits to it. Indeed, it constitutes an unusually sweeping claim of Yahweh's omnipotence. "You know that you can do everything" repeats what Yahweh has been claiming throughout his speeches, with very ambiguous effect. We could read it as submission to power, as noncommittal nonsubmission, or as more. We could hear several tones of voice in it. It could be straightforwardly submissive: "You know everything, and I shall have to change my ways." It could be indignant: "Why are you hassling me like this? You know that you can do anything you want." It could be sarcastic: "You are a pretentious know-it-all." It could be obsequious: "You are so big and strong, and you know *everything*!"[86]

The last possibility requires David Robertson's view that Job is faking submission. That would also depend on Yahweh's unconsciousness of a human pretension, and it would entail that the second line, "no plan is inaccessible to you," is a flattering untruth. If Yahweh cannot see through insincerity, he hardly has access to every scheme.

Job's quotation (or misquotation) of and response to 38.3 is compatible with either meaning of verse 2. Moreover, it plays especially with the opening motif of knowledge. Where in 38.3, Yahweh referred to "darkening counsel with ignorant words" (*maḥšīk ʿēṣah bᵉmillīn bᵉlī daʿat*), Job speaks in 42.3 of "obscuring [hiding] counsel ignorantly" (*maʿᵃlīm ʿēṣah bᵉlī daʿat*). If verse 2 states what Job knows now, the quotation and response in verse 3 emphasize what he did not know then:

> Therefore I told, and didn't understand,
> wonders beyond me, and I didn't know.

Job has apparently accepted Yahweh's evaluation of his arguments throughout the dialogue, reversing his stand in 40.4–5. He thought he knew as he spoke to the friends, but he now sees that he did not know. Now—Socrates would be proud of him—he knows that he does not know.[87] Job admits that in ignorance he understated Yahweh's power, but he does not necessarily submit to it as something admirable.

If we take "you know" as the reading in verse 2, Job applies the divine knowledge newly to the situation. Yahweh had accused him of ignorance in 38.3, and he now agrees. Whether what he did not know before was the extent of the divine power or how impressively convincing it was is not clear from what he says. "Wonders" (*nipla'ōt*) might suggest that he is convinced now. But it might also be an ironic exaggeration of impressive but not convincing power. Job had talked about the god's power and had described it as immense (e.g., in chap. 26). He now knows far better how immense it is, but he sees that it is brute, uncaring power, "marvelous" in objective scope, less than "marvelous" in its moral effect on weak human beings. So verse 3 is compatible not only with both readings in verse 2 but with alternative understandings of those readings.

Now Job quotes—in part—again. "Hear, and I will speak" (*šᵉmaʿ-na' wᵉ'anōkī 'ᵃdabbēr*) is nothing Yahweh has said before. Indeed, it is much more like something Elihu said:

> Pay attention, Job, listen [*šᵉmaʿ*] to me,
> be silent, and I will speak [*wᵉ'anōkī 'ᵃdabbēr*]. (33.31)

It is less like some things Job said to the friends in chap. 13, when he was girding himself for the trial. "Be silent a while," he urged the friends, "and I will speak" (*wa'ᵃdabbᵉrah-'anī*, v. 13). Later, urging the deity to refrain from terror tactics in the trial (13.21), he said:

> Call, and I will answer,
> or I will speak ['ᵃ*dabbēr*], and you respond to me. (v. 22)

The line is not unlike the opening of Job's speech in chap. 21:

> Now listen carefully [*šim'ū šamōa'*] to my word;
> you may get some consolation from this.
> Lift me up so I can speak [*wᵉ'anōkī 'ᵃdabbēr*]. (vv. 2–3a)

If 42.4a is not a quotation of Yahweh but is Job speaking in his own right, he may be seizing the opportunity to take the initiative in the trial, as he had wished to do in chap. 13, or he may be correcting what he has said before. He spoke without knowledge, and now he will speak with the knowledge that he was ignorant. The second line would flow from that point quite nicely as a quotation from Yahweh:

> I will ask you questions, and you instruct me.

Yahweh had said precisely that in 38.3 and 40.7. As quotation, the statement serves as a reminder of why Job must now speak. But the language remains noncommittal and purely formal, and it gives no indication whether Job will speak out of his newfound awareness of ignorance, whether he will be cooperative or combative.

On the other hand, if Job speaks the first line, he might also speak the second, adapting Yahweh's demand to his own need. He might, in his newly found humility, sincerely request instruction. Or perhaps he turns the divine sarcasm back on its originator, suggesting that the tutelage in chaps. 38–41 was inadequate and indirect, especially if verse 2a was "You know that you can do everything." An omnicompetent deity could surely give a clear lecture, but the pupil needs further clarification.

When you think of it, "Hear, and I will speak" is a strange thing to put into Yahweh's mouth. Such an opening gambit is used most often by an inferior speaking to a superior, though there are instances of similar remarks in the deity's mouth (e.g., Ps 50.7; Ezek 2.8). Still, one thinks of statements all through the Psalms, in which the supplicant asks the god to "hear my voice" (e.g., 27.7; 64.2 [Eng. 1]) or "hear my prayer" (54.4 [Eng. 2]; 84.9 [Eng. 8]; 143.1), using the same singular imperative. But it puzzles me that Job would quote Yahweh as saying that, when Yahweh had not laid the demand on Job. And, of course, the Hebrew text has no quotation marks to show us how to identify the speaker.

Still, we must allow the possibility that "Hear, and I will speak," followed by the promise of questions, is an implied quotation of Yahweh. It may equally well be not a nonquotation masquerading briefly as a quotation but Job's own statement about his own activity. Job does, in fact, speak.

He refers, not surprisingly, to hearing and speaking:

> With ears' hearing I hear you. (42.5a)

If we could be sure of the time references of the Hebrew tenses, we might insist that "I hear" be in the past. It is in the "perfect" tense, the tense that presents action as grasped entire. And if the "and now" opening the next line is a time contrast, the past tense would be acceptable. I do not find satisfactory the notion, proposed by several scholars,[88] that Job is speaking of his past experience of hearing at secondhand. "I had heard of you," say several translators, and "I had heard by hearsay," say others. Some point to 28.22, where Abaddon and Death say "A rumor [*šim'ah*] of [Wisdom] has reached our ears" (*b^{e}oznēnū šama'nū*, "with our ears we have heard a hearing of her"). The expression in 42.5a is different from that, and the argument of hearsay is not convincing.

Job has, after all, just spent a considerable time "hearing" Yahweh's extremely long, complex, difficult speech. "I had heard You with my ears," says JPS, and I object only to the past perfect tense. At the first challenge he determined not to reply (40.4–5), but now he must. This line adds plausibility to the idea that 42.4a is Job's demand of Yahweh, not a recollection of Yahweh's demand of him. "You listen now, Yahweh. . . . I have been listening to you for quite a while."

And we expect, no doubt, some feisty fireworks of argument. But no:

> And now my eye sees you.

It is a new activity. Job has referred to knowing and speaking, to hearing, asking, and instructing. Suddenly he speaks of seeing, and it is most surprising. Yahweh has spoken "from the whirlwind" (38.1), with no indication that he is visible, and perhaps the whirlwind is intended to mask sight of him. He calls Job's attention to other sights, the sky and the earth and the weather, animals both normal and abnormal. He does not suggest that Job look at him, though he insists that Job speak to him.

Humans, of course, are not supposed to see the deity at all. "You are unable to see my face," Yahweh told Moses, "for the human being does not see me and live" (Exod 33.20). There are, to be sure, exceptions. Moses himself was permitted to see Yahweh's back (33.23). "In the year of King Uzziah's death," Isaiah reports, "I saw the Lord, sitting upon a throne" (Isa 6.1). But Ezekiel is careful to place the sight of the deity behind several layers of opacity: "That was the appearance of the semblance of the radiance of Yahweh" (Ezek 1.28). Daniel's vision of the "Ancient of Days" on the throne reports only similes of peripheral sights: "His garment was like white snow, / and the hair of his head was like lamb's wool" (Dan 7.9). But there is that astonishing mass vision after the covenant ratification at Mt. Sinai:

> Moses and Aaron, Nadab and Abihu, and seventy of the elders of Israel went up [to the top of Mt. Sinai], and they saw [*yir'ū*] Israel's god. Under his feet was something like a sapphire terrace, like the sky itself in clarity. Upon the leaders (?) of the Israelites he did not lay his hand. They looked at [*yeḥᵉzū*] the god, and they ate and drank. (Exod 24.9–11)

The tone of amazement in "he did not lay his hand" is evident, and the use in the passage of two different verbs for seeing has to be emphasis.

When people see the god, they are very specially placed, or are placed at very special times. The ratification of the covenant at Mt. Sinai was utterly central in the religious structure of ancient Israel, and the inaugural visions of prophets like Isaiah and Ezekiel are profoundly significant. Job's claim that his eye sees Yahweh is startling, to say the least. Given the strictures against seeing the divine, many scholars argue that his seeing must be metaphorical: Job is now convinced (Pope); he has direct experience in contrast to secondhand (Driver and Gray, Dhorme); his consciousness of the god comes directly from the god and not from his own musing upon experience (Terrien). There are, however, enough instances in the Hebrew Bible of people who see the god that I do not feel the compulsion of metaphor.

And it is not evident that "seeing" is to be contrasted with "hearing." Though many translators read the conjunction at verse 5b as "but," nothing in the context requires that it be anything except the usual "and." "Now" might be taken as an opposition to an implied "then," but no "then" accompanies "hearing," and "hear" and "see" in Hebrew have the same tense. We cannot argue that "I heard" must be past, and "My eye sees" must be present. Both could be present perfect: "I have heard," "My eye has seen." The distinction is entirely a matter of interpretation.

Of course, it is possible to contrast seeing with hearing. I do not believe that "at the hearing of an ear" (*l*^{e}*šēma‘ ’ōzen*) can mean only "by hearsay," but it can mean that among other things. Take the connotation "hearsay," add to it "now" as a contrast between hearing and seeing, and it works. So does the parallel, noncontrastive reading, "I have heard you with my ears, / and now my eye has seen you," or "I hear you with my ears, / and now my eye sees you." Nothing in the text elevates the one above the other. The lines simultaneously present contrast and parallel.

At the least Job is saying that he has come to a new experience of the divine presence, which stems from both hearing and seeing the god. Yahweh has asked questions and has demanded instruction, sarcastically. It is not clear that Job is being sarcastic, though some points allow the possibility. He can now "instruct, inform" (*hōdīa‘*) Yahweh that the words from the whirlwind have changed his orientation to the world and the god. That is one way of reading "now."

The question is, how has he changed? That we discover in verse 6:

> Therefore I despise and repent
> of dust and ashes.

I discussed this translation and something of its meaning in the "Indispensable Introduction," and I indicated both there and in the annotation to the verse my reasons for translating the couplet so and for rejecting what some other people say.

It is the punch line of the Book of Job. Job himself says nothing further. We shall have to see in the next chapter what his silence in the closing narrative might mean. Here he is terse but not silent. What has happened? Has Job been smashed into the earth by the vision of the divine grandeur as contrasted with his own smallness? That idea troubles me about the JPS version of this couplet: "Therefore I recant and relent, / being but dust and ashes." He submits because he is tiny. Mitchell moves the idea over by seeing the verb *nḥm* as meaning "comforted," rather than "changed the mind."[89] Job submits in the calm security of comfort that he is small and insignificant. So "cognitive dissonance" achieves consonance, the acceptance of the brute power that Job so furiously attacked in the dialogue. Some such reading of verse 6 must lie behind Robertson's ironic vision that Job recognizes Yahweh's tyrannical intention to unman him and responds with outward submission but rebellious inward rejection. This view necessitates, I think, one attitude or the other—acceptance of the tyranny as too overpowering to oppose or the pretense of accepting it as the only way of undermining it. Coming from the same perception but with a different conclusion is Briggs's thought that Job simply rejects the deity outright: "Therefore I feel loathing contempt and revulsion [toward you, O God]; and I am sorry for frail man."[90] The divine tyranny and distance from human concerns calls up Job's refusal.

We need not canvass the entire range of alternatives, but we must at least notice the RSV's

> Therefore I despise myself,
> and repent in dust and ashes.

It will not do as a representation of the language, as I argued in the Introduction. It is, moreover, a very Christian notion. Terrien lands hard in the idea: "Like a prophet, who sees a holy God, he is thrown into the grip of self-abhorrence and the awe of self-destruction. . . . At last Job, the proud sheik, is conscious of his sinfulness and is able to confess it."[91] Job has been so distant from God that only massive contrition and awareness of prior sin can return him to the divine sphere of influence. But those who find in these lines "self-abhorrence" and abject repentance do not take seriously that just this is what the friends urged on Job all along.[92] This kind of repentance will do for this passage only if it can be shown to be utterly different from what the friends advised. If the outcome of Job's confrontation with Yahweh is that he slips back into taking the counsel of the friends, it is very disappointing. More than that, it is entirely contrary to Yahweh's own view of the friends, as we will see in 42.7–9.

The text does not encourage that view. The syntax and grammar are, I think, very clear. "I despise" must have an object, and the nearest one is "dust and ashes."[93] The preposition *'al* ("upon") following upon the verb *nḥm*, "I repent" or "I am comforted," introduces the object of the repentance or the subject of the comfort. "Dust and ashes," then, does double duty as the accusative of both "I despise" (*'em'as*) and "I repent" (*nḥmty*).

Then what is the connotation of "dust and ashes"? "Dust" often refers to mortality (e.g., 10.9; 17.16) and in 2.12 may even be used in a mourning rite; "ashes" are associated with ritual acts of mourning or lament at situations of pain or guilt (2 Sam 13.19; Jon 3.6; not to mention Job 2.8), and "dust and ashes" (*'apar wa'ēper*) occurs as a kind of self-abasement (Job 30.19; Gen 18.27). A sense of lowliness, mourning, perhaps even sin, is attached to the words, and therefore the notion of an abject repentance lies attractively at the surface.

Just that lowliness and mourning Job says he "despises" and "repents." As usual, there are several possibilities of meaning. For Dale Patrick, who showed the basis for the construction I have put on the couplet,[94] the "forswearing" of dust and ashes, as he translates it, entails Job's abandonment of his insistence on being declared innocent, his acceptance of being a creature, like Leviathan, and his change from anger and opposition to the praise of the god. Job does not resignedly submit to being sinful or to being small but joyfully embraces a world more powerfully under the control of a gracious god than he had realized.

Habel, however, sees the dust and ashes as symbolizing Job's role "as isolated sufferer and humiliated litigant."[95] To "repent" of dust and ashes is to abandon that role, to drop his idea of proceeding with a trial, and to resort once more to normal life. His innocence, Habel thinks, has been established, and Yahweh's appearance has definitively dismissed the law of retribution.

Both of these interesting proposals are vitiated by the apparent efforts to prove them the only right ones. Patrick goes too far in claiming that Job gives himself up to joy and praise of the god; nothing in the text hints at any such thing. Habel's interpretation comes out to something very like an anticlimax. "Well, I guess we needn't have a trial after all. Thank you very much." That the retributive dogma has been effectively shattered is clear enough. That Job's innocence in the eyes of Yahweh is established seems to me much less clear.

There is another possibility in the words. "Dust and ashes" has to do with lowliness and mourning, with death and with sin. By metonymy, it also refers to activities associated with those attitudes and attributes. Insofar as the "ashes" stand for the isolation of the city dump, in which Job sits in his pain (2.8), Habel rightly points to the outcome of this departure from "dust and ashes" as resumption of normal life. Insofar as "dust and ashes" stands for the abjection of rituals of repentance for sin and of mourning for the dead, to "repent of dust and ashes" is to give up the religious structure that construes the world in terms of guilt and innocence. It is to repent of repentance. The world's events are not responses to human moral activity and inward disposition. Job has indeed heard that crucial question of 40.8, and has come to realize not merely that he need not proceed with his trial but positively that the issue of repentance and the admission of sin, with its concomitant restoration of the former sinner to favor with the deity, is the wrong issue. That structure of guilt and innocence was the focus of the friends' arguments. But the world spins on its own kind of order, of which Job had very little sense.

I would argue, then, that Job's innocence is established, but not by anything Yahweh says. Job himself re-establishes it, having spent the entire discussion with his friends twisting about to assert his innocence in terms that were unsatisfactory because Job could think about guilt and suffering only in terms of deserving. But as we saw in thinking about 40.8, those terms skew the universal order into disorder.

I will grant this to those who think Job repents of some sin.[96] If wilfully misconstruing the world is a sin, Job repents of it. If thinking that the issue of sin is important in construing the world is a sin, Job repents of it. If the essence of religion is that it solves the problem of sin, Job repents of religion.

9

"Consoled and Comforted"

I quarreled and devised a while
  but went on
having sensed a nice dominion in the air,
the black so round and deep.
—A. R. Ammons, "Consignee"

Where the opening tale centered on deprivation, the closing one luxuriates in restoration. Job is restored from the ash heap (2.8) to his "house" (42.11). His relationship with acquaintances and relatives is resumed (v. 11) after the desperate alienation he described earlier (19.13–19). His fortune in flocks and herds comes back to him twofold in the same numbers of good omen, the sevens and threes adding up to tens (42.10, 12). A new family of sons and daughters matches the numbers of animals (v. 13).[1] Finally the long, satisfactory life, with four generations of "progeny established," "offspring in [his] sight," of the lack of which he complained in 21.8, ends as it should (42.16–17). The friends, too, are restored, on performance of duties and with Job's acquiescence (42.7–9).

A pair of discourses such as Yahweh's and Job's second ones would be hard to match in any case. The cosmic breadth in Yahweh's images of Behemoth and Leviathan and the understated but unexpected interior and concluding dialogue in the mouth of Job might make any further statement seem bland and tame. Yet the conclusion avoids banality by being both short and unexpected. It is a bit surprising to return suddenly to prose. We have been immersed in poetry ever since the beginning of chap. 3, and the absence of that rhythmic, dense medium is unexpected enough to keep our attention. Moreover, the narrative of 42.7–17 contains one surprise after another, which keep us thinking and pondering long after the words themselves have ended. "Did it really say that?" we have to wonder. Yes, it really did, and as we read it again, we find that it seems to mean something other than and additional to what we had seen the first time.

The narrative is brief: 195 Hebrew words in 42.7–17 (my translation takes about 300 English ones), shorter than the Leviathan speech in Hebrew (40.25–41.26), slightly shorter than the Hymn to Wisdom (chap. 28). And because the concluding tale is prose, its pace seems quicker than those pieces of densely packed poetry.

The surprises are the crucial elements in understanding this ending, and they require that we ask what kind of ending it is. Many people are troubled by what they sometimes call the "Hollywood" ending,[2] perhaps because our sensibilities may be upset by a mixture of genres. We so habitually think of Job as tragic that the reversion to a comic ending may seem by itself banalization.[3] We are not used to combining tragedy and comedy, though there are dramas labeled "tragi-comedy." Perhaps we are mistaken to think of Job as tragedy at all.[4]

Rather than resolve that question by recourse to theory, whereby the category determines the approach to the instance, I prefer to resolve it, if at all, by examining the text. To decide from the outset that the Book of Job is or is not tragedy or comedy or something else, including a scapegoat story, and then to look at the work is to imprison the open text under the lid of a box.

Yahweh, Job, and the Friends (42.7–9)

The concluding tale begins where the beginning tale left off, with the friends. Eliphaz, Bildad, and Zophar arrived in the last episode of the first narrative (2.11). They make their final appearance in the first episode of the last narrative (42.7–9).[5]

It is even more interesting that this episode begins by referring to Yahweh's speech, not to Job's final remarks. "After Yahweh had spoken these words to Job," it says (v. 7), ignoring Job's meditation in 42.2–6, with its studied but enormous conclusion. Perhaps Yahweh was not listening carefully while Job spoke, but was thinking about what he would say to the friends.[6] Perhaps his remark to Eliphaz, "You have not spoken truth of me, as has my servant Job," implies that Job's renunciation of religion did not register on the divine consciousness.

Yet most remarkable in Yahweh's statement to Eliphaz is the way in which the god dismisses the theologies of all three friends as quickly and thoroughly as he dismissed Job in 38.2. Yahweh is "very angry" with them, or, as the Hebrew has it, his "anger burns in" (*ḥarah 'ap b^{e}*) them, exactly the words used for the emotion Elihu felt toward the friends in 32.2–3. One might shrug one's shoulders at Elihu's burning anger, but one probably would not at Yahweh's.

Elihu was equally angry at the friends and at Job (36.2), whereas Yahweh is not angry at Job at all. They have not spoken "truth" of him, and Job has (42.7). "Truth," *n^{e}kōnah*, is an unusual word to convey the thought, used for a number of other ideas in the book. Job used *nakōn* in 12.5 for the "ready" torch that illuminates unsteady feet and in 21.8 for the "establishment" of the wicked's progeny. Eliphaz described the knave's knowledge that "a dark day is ready in his hand" (15.23; cf. Bildad's remark at 18.12). Bildad used the Polel imperative, *kōnēn*, in 8.8, for "adhering" to the ideas of the past, and Job expressed the notion of a common "establishment" of all humans by the deity with another Polel form in 31.15. The Hiph'il, with its suggestion that one is "preparing" something, occurs in Zophar's mouth in 11.13 in the sense of preparing the heart to encounter the deity, in Job's ironic discussion of "piling up" (preparing) clothing for the "righteous" to wear (27.16–17), in Eliphaz's image of the womb that "fosters" deceit (15.35), and in Yahweh's question about who "provides" (or prepares) food for the raven (38.41). At the end of the poem on wisdom, the god has established Wisdom, "made her fast" (28.27). Job also uses the word for his occupying his judicial seat (29.7), and a cognate noun, *t^{e}kūnah*, refers to Yahweh's "throne room" (23.3), where the trial would take place if only Job could find it.

Such a galaxy of differing meanings shows that the word does not signify "truth" in the merely intellectual sense but bears on the satisfaction of what has been established. The basic connotation of "establishment," "preparation," "readiness," suggests that Yahweh criticizes the friends and praises Job because they have not, and he has, said something "established," properly prepared. Moreover, the relationship of the word's root, *kwn*, to creation[7] connects Yahweh's praise of Job to his perception of the cosmic order about which Yahweh asked in 40.8. The friends, for all of their certainty about traditional dogma, have failed to speak satisfactorily of the deity, whereas Job has done so.

Of course, Yahweh does not say when and how the friends have misspoken. Most interpreters assume either that Yahweh's statement indicates approval of Job's arguments throughout the dialogue and disapproval of the friends' contentions,[8] or that he condemns the friends for their specific mistake about the relation of the human to the divine and commends Job's coming around to the correct view.[9] I suggested that in

38.2 Yahweh effectually dismissed what the friends said. But his question there, "Who is this who darkens counsel / with ignorant words?" throws a shadow over the assumption that the deity approves of everything that Job said. The second assumption takes care of that problem with Job, allowing the thought that at last, in 42.2–6, he has spoken "truth," but it does not explain why the narrative does not refer to Job's final speech or why the friends never get the chance to change their minds.

The presence of verses 2–6 means that in verse 7 Yahweh in effect approves Job's renunciation of religion. We cannot be sure whether Job's speaking "truth" refers exclusively to that last speech or to something else too. After all, in verses 2–6, I argued above, Job accepted a changed ground for the entire discussion. He took advantage of the opportunity Yahweh's speeches afforded him to change his mind—and not for the first time.

Perhaps the friends change theirs too. Eliphaz is bidden to gather his friends (why are they not all addressed?) [10] to sacrifice bulls and rams and get Job to intercede to the deity (Job 42.8). The sacrifice is a "burnt offering" (Heb. *'ōlah*), in which the entire animal is consumed in fire, and its function is to restore an attenuated connection between the human and the deity.[11] The sacrifices by themselves are not enough to restore the friends, though seven bulls and seven rams constitute a very expensive, weighty offering of a magical number.[12]

Beyond the sacrifice of bulls and rams goes Job's interceding prayer. Job becomes for the friends the interceding "witness," even Elihu's "angel" (33.23). It is ironic that he must now act as intercessor for the friends, though no intercessor was available to him. It is, if anything, more ironic that Yahweh's prescription of the intercessory action ranks Job well below the implicit superior of whom Job dreamed in the "arbiter," the "witness," and the "avenger." "My servant Job" is Yahweh's expression, as it was to the Prosecutor in chaps. 1–2, but here it suggests the restoration of a subjection that Yahweh very nearly lost. Notice how Yahweh insists on it: four times in verses 7–8 he mentions "my servant Job." In all of chaps. 1–2 he used the phrase only twice. The words are more than a message to Eliphaz. It was not an expression Job would have been happy to hear during the dialogue at the height of his paranoia. We never learn Job's response to the phrase, nor can we know whether he knew it was used of him.

The friends did what they were told, and "Yahweh accepted Job" (42.9), as he had said he would (v. 8). The idiomatic phrase is "Yahweh lifted Job's face" (*yiśśa' YHWH 'et-pᵉnē 'īyyōb*), an idiom that answers to another, more difficult, one that Yahweh uses of himself (v. 8): "without doing anything foolish to you" (*l^e biltī ʿ^a śōt ʿimmakem n^e balah*). It is an odd echo of Job's reply to his wife in 2.10, when he accuses her of "talking like a fool" (*k^e dabbēr ʾaḥat hann^e balōt*). Yahweh has to restrain himself, it seems, from what he feels he would like to do, because doing it would be somehow foolish.

It is a strange episode. By his speeches defining cosmic order, Yahweh gave Job the opportunity to change his mind, to fill his words with knowledge instead of ignorance. Refusing the opportunity in 40.4–5, Job took it in 42.2–6, renouncing the entire religious structure of guilt and innocence, together with the paraphernalia of repentance and forgiveness implied by them. Now Yahweh does two things: first, he accepts Job's conclusion as "truth"; second, he bids the friends and Job, as a condition of restoring the friends, to engage in precisely the kinds of religious activities that Job's concluding renunciation appeared to reject.

The question arises again: Has Yahweh heeded what Job said in verse 6? Perhaps Robertson is right that Job's submission was tongue-in-cheek and, what is more, that Yahweh had no clue.[13] If so, this intercession can hardly be sincere, and Job has pulled the wool over Yahweh's eyes twice: first by getting a faked repentance accepted as the real thing and then by getting Yahweh to let the friends off on the impression of a genuine intercession.

The penitential sacrifices and Job's intercession seem to function for the friends as Job's rejection of repentance does for him: they permit some sort of rapprochement with the deity, but we are not told what sort. If, as Gordis proposed (see note 10 to this chapter), Job's intercession turns the tables on Eliphaz's assurance (22.26–30) that repentance will enable Job to intercede for other sinners, the justice is poetic indeed. Eliphaz becomes the very sinner who requires Job's intercession for his own restoration.[14]

Yet there remains the puzzlingly partial statement about restoration: "Yahweh accepted [lifted the face of] *Job*." The text never says that he lifted the faces of the friends, nor did he promise in verse 8 to do so. He promised only that he would not do anything foolish to them. Perhaps we may infer that Job's praying "over" (*ʿal*) the friends means that Yahweh's acceptance of him includes fulfilling his intercessory request.[15] And perhaps Eliphaz and the others are just glad to escape further attention.

It is a most interesting turn from Job's speculations about his own intercessors and advocates. He thought he needed assistance against the deity. Yahweh chided him with the ineffectuality of accuser and arbiter

(40.2), yet he now sets Job up as intercessor. It seems that the friends were right when they proposed that Job simply change his stance over against the god and return to his favor (e.g., Zophar, 11.13–14; Eliphaz, 22.21–23). Ironically, Job has succeeded in doing so when, in 42.2–6, he renounces the religion that on his own account (chap. 31) had informed his every action. On the other hand, it seems that Job was right in thinking that the means to the divine approval was in some sort of coercion by a third party, for he himself has now become a third party in praying over the friends. Perhaps the prayer is not coercion, so that Job's shrill certainties in 16.19 and 19.25 were misplaced in that respect. It seems that there is more than one route to the divine approbation. The friends get there by something like the way Job, in his deepest certainty of the god's injustice, had postulated for himself. Job gets there by the means that the friends, in their moments of greatest theological blandness, had set forth. But they have been castigated for not speaking "truth," and he has been praised for speaking it.

Yahweh, Job, and the Family (42.10–17)

The reversal of Job's circumstances that follows is complete. His lost fortune is doubled (v. 10), with twice the numbers of animals as before (v. 12), in what is described as a greater divine "blessing" than ever before. His lost family is replaced (v. 13). Some scholars have even argued that the number of his sons is doubled, and the somewhat odd numerical form *šibʿanah* (v. 13) of the sons is a dual, meaning not seven but fourteen.[16] Like most of my colleagues, I am not persuaded by the linguistics of the argument.[17] It is enough that a new family of seven sons and three daughters is given Job. Perhaps we should not be surprised that that sexist society did not wonder whether for Job's wife bearing ten more children was more than enough.

Job's restoration goes beyond the return of the same number of children and the doubling of his wealth. He returns from his isolated place in the ash heap (2.8) to his "house" (42.11), where he is visited by his brothers, sisters, and acquaintances—those whose alienation from him was the subject of a bitter complaint in 19.13–19.[18] The visit, indeed, is not mere formality. They eat with him, they "console and comfort him," and they give him money (42.11).

All of these restorations are remarkable, not merely for their scope but also for how they are and are not stated. First, Job's restoration and the doubling of his fortune by the deity's manipulation are explicitly related to Job's intercessory prayer (v. 10): "Yahweh reversed Job's fortune when he prayed for his friends." Once again, as in the foregoing part of the story, one must wonder whether (1) Yahweh has missed Job's renunciation of the religious construction of the world, or (2) he has misinterpreted it as a positive declaration, or (3) Job thinks the intercession is meaningless but does it because he was asked to, or (4) Job does it in full knowledge that Yahweh will respond retributively to what looks like a sincere religious deed. We can do no more than wonder about that. The text merely narrates. The circumstances around the narrated events are by no means uncomplicated, and the deity's doubling of Job's fortunes *as a result* of his praying for the friends certainly seems to confirm the friends' theory of the relation between religious excellence and personal well-being. After 42.6, the intercession is either a religious act of a sort that Job has apparently renounced, or it is a purely magical act whose efficacy has nothing to do with Job's religious feelings or ideas.

In an earlier book, I argued that 42.6 was the quietus on magic.[19] I am not nearly so sure of that now. Job's intercession for the friends in verse 10 is the occasion for his acceptance by the god, the doubling of his fortune, and the restoration of his social standing. We are not told whether it is also the occasion for the friends' return to good standing with the god, but such favor would be less surprising than the god's persisting in being grumpy with them. I do not think that we must have some objective statement of causation to think of that structure as a magical one. If it is not magic, it works exactly like magic. If it does not reflect the friends' retributive theology, it works exactly as they said their retributive theology would work. This book keeps doubling back on itself.

The "brothers and sisters and acquaintances" whom we meet in verse 11 were nowhere in evidence in the opening story, though I noted Job's feeling of alienation from them during the dialogue. They eat with Job in his house, an activity that in the ancient culture was no mere casual snack. For one thing, this meal reflects back on the feasts that Job's children used to have (1.4–5). For another, to offer a meal in that culture was an act of hospitality that cemented relationships among people, and to accept one was to take on a web of obligations and rights with the host. Job is not merely back in his house, inhabiting a building; he has returned to social acceptability, the pleasures of which he described in chap. 29 and the loss of which he lamented in chap. 30. He is once again somebody in his community, both among blood relatives ("brothers and sisters") and among "acquaintances"(*yōdeʿayw*, "those who know him"). But we saw in chap. 29 that Job's pleasures in his former status in the community included more than a hint of arrogance, even tyranny, about his place and his sense of it. We cannot say whether that too has returned, but the necessary harking back to his description of his "autumn days" in chap. 29 must at least remind us of it. In any case, the meal with brothers, sisters, and acquaintances reminds us both of the dead children and of the former community of which Job was a leader.

The brothers, sisters, and acquaintances also remind us of Job's three friends. "They consoled and comforted him about all the evil that Yahweh had brought upon him" (v. 11). That is a remarkable statement. Now that it is all over, the relatives and acquaintances succeed in doing what Eliphaz, Bildad, and Zophar had come to do (2.11 has infinitives of the same verbs, *nwd* and *nḥm*). They failed, as Job told them several times, but the brothers, sisters, and acquaintances do not.

Even more: they comfort him "about all the evil that Yahweh had brought upon him." The three friends came to visit Job because they heard about "all the evil that had come upon him" (2.11). But the end is even more devastating. It was "evil"; there is no pretense that Job has had pleasure. But here the story specifies that Yahweh brought about the evil, with no mention of the Prosecutor. To be sure, the Prosecutor is gone, and we have heard nothing of him.

The closing tale lays responsibility for Job's suffering squarely on Yahweh, and it shows that the solution to it was provided by Job's brothers, sisters, and acquaintances. The three friends had no solution. Though they intended to console and comfort him and had every opportunity in their long speeches, they did not succeed. Comfort about the meaning of suffering is not found in debates and truths about the theology or theory of the matter, nor in divine descriptions of the working of the cosmos. Comfort comes to Job in the presence of family and friends, who acknowledge the source of the trouble and console the sufferer by their presence. The Book of Job, then, solves the problem of suffering by this almost passing reference to the visits of Job's brothers, sisters, and acquaintances. It is an existential, personal solution to the problem of suffering as it affected Job, not an intellectual solution to the general question about the meaning of suffering.

These people have one other, seemingly strange action: they give Job money—a great deal of money, it seems. A *qeśiṭa* is a sizable amount, and a gold ring, given the value of gold in the ancient world, is a princely gift. We do not know how many brothers, sisters, and acquaintances thus heaped wealth on Job, but the impression is that he received a great deal of money.[20] This element in the story seems to embarrass the commentators. Most remark on the value of the *qeśiṭa*, but they do not go beyond such an offhand remark as Terrien's: "Such gifts were symbols of courtesy and friendship."[21] Clearly the value of these gifts makes them something more than that. There is no indication in any period that Israelites used elaborate or rich gifts as a customary way to honor someone or to express friendship. This outpouring re-establishes Job's wealth and is necessary to his resumption of his former status in the community. Without wealth, Job could not take his place at the head of the community, and in order that he do so, it is necessary to extract the wealth even from lesser folks. It is more like chap. 29 than we might have thought.

Yet an additional ground for Job's restored wealth is given in the divine intervention. The echo of Job's nostalgia for his "autumn days" (29.4) in 42.12, "Yahweh blessed Job's later life more than his earlier life," takes Job's final status well beyond what he regretted having lost. The echo, furthermore, is not only of Job's rueful recollection of an earlier happiness but of an implied definition of happiness. For Yahweh to "bless" (*brk*) someone's life surely brings the apex of happiness. In that respect, Job resumes his earlier life as described in chap. 1, in kind but in greater degree. The implicit definition of happiness here, moreover, matches the implicit definition there in the mouth of the Prosecutor: "Haven't you yourself hedged around him and his family and all he has, blessed [*bērakta*] anything his hands do, so that his possessions burst out over the earth?" (1.10) It is one of the places in that opening narrative where the ambiguous *brk* must mean something close to the dictionary definition.

Indeed, the Prosecutor's definition of the "blessing," that Job's "possessions burst out over the earth," precisely coincides with what the tale proceeds to tell us, namely that Job's flocks and herds (the measure of a great sheikh's wealth in those days) came to twice their former number. If a mere seven thousand sheep, three thousand camels, five hundred span of oxen, and five hundred female asses "burst out over the earth," we would expect more startling ecological effects from twice those numbers. In one respect, however, Job's riches in chap. 1 are not restored, even as far as the equivalent of earlier holdings. In 1.3, Job had not only thousands of animals but also "a great many slaves"; 42.7–17 makes no mention of slaves. Are we to conclude that Job gave up the practice? If so, he was unique in the ancient—and not only the ancient—world.[22]

The Prosecutor implicitly used Job's wealth to explain his religious and moral excellence. "Is Job religious for nothing?" (1.9) He went on to argue that the religion proceeded from the blessing, which produced the wealth. Therefore the special favor that Yahweh showed to Job in making him wealthy accounted in the Prosecutor's mind for the excessive piety Job showed to Yahweh. The one, it seems, caused the other.

Job resumes his wealth by the deity's implied intervention.[23] We have seen that Yahweh used to Eliphaz the same phrase describing Job that he had used to the Prosecutor: "my servant Job" (*'abdī 'īyyōb*, 42.7–8; cf. 1.8; 2.3). Evidently, along with his wealth, Job has resumed the standing with the deity to which the Prosecutor objected at the beginning. Indeed, the reference in 42.12 to Yahweh's "blessing" makes us realize that we might have passed too quickly over an earlier sentence: "Yahweh reversed Job's fortune [*šab 'et-šᵉbūt 'īyyōb*] when he prayed for his friends, and he increased Job's holdings twofold" (v. 10). There *was* cause and effect between Job's act of religious compassion or of magical intercession and Yahweh's restoration of wealth to him. The reversal of fortune accompanied, or immediately followed, Job's prayer, and it consisted in the doubling of Job's wealth. The Prosecutor may have had good reason to think that Job was religious because of divine interference, and that makes equally plausible the thought that the deity responds to piety with evidences of special favor.

Because Job is never quoted as saying anything, we have no indication of what he thought about it. We do not know whether he considered his intercession on the friends' behalf a means to get rich again. We know only that Yahweh used the occasion to heap riches on him again. Perhaps it is a direct refutation of Job's reversal of the doctrine of retribution in chap. 21, or perhaps the deity is eager to be appreciated instead of being vilified as "wicked" and "vicious," as in 27.7.

It is interesting that Job never says anything in this final tale. He has been tending toward the taciturn ever since his last long speech in chaps. 26–31. Granted, his second reply to Yahweh (42.2–6) was longer than the first (40.4–5), but it cannot be called voluble. Perhaps the exhaustion of 31.40, "Job's words were spent," is still in force, or perhaps his silence stems from his exposure to the dreary discourses of Elihu and the expansive rhetorical display of Yahweh's two speeches. There has been quite enough talk. The tale refers to only two kinds of speech on Job's part: prayer for the three friends (42.10) and naming of daughters (v. 14). It is not that those occasions of speech are unimportant, though the story does not care what Job actually said on any of the occasions. Job seems not to occupy his days any longer with words.

With the restored family, we probably must simply recognize cultural and psychic differences between ourselves and the ancients. Commentator after commentator notes that you cannot "restore" or "replace" lost children.[24] You can purchase and breed new flocks and herds, and the difference between the earlier and later animals is nothing more than the numbers. You can have other children, of course, but our culture thinks that they in no sense replace the earlier ones. No person is exactly like any other person, and therefore when a person is lost, something irretrievable, uniquely itself, is gone.

It is not at all certain that Job and his culture shared our emphasis on the unique, irreplaceable, eternal value of the individual as the definitive understanding of human beings. Of course, the ancients, Israelite or other, considered human life precious and individual human life important. At the same time, our story did not find it important to show the individual identity of the ten daughters and sons in chap. 1. It was enough to notice that there was an eldest among them, that some were male and some female, and they got along very well together. Yet only the first of those qualities is the characteristic of an individual in a group and that by logical definition: in any group of people of varying ages, one will be the eldest. In 42.13–15, the only pointers to individuality are to the daughters, who are named (as none of the children in chap. 1 were), who are beautiful (but none is more beautiful than the others), and who inherit. What we might call individuality can be derived from nothing except the names, and the sons remain as anonymous as those in chap. 1. We do not observe in this tale a culture that thinks of individual identity as the prime, fundamental quality of human beings.

I mean to suggest that perhaps the story, by repeating the satisfyingly round and symbolic numbers from chap. 1, proposes precisely what we would reject, that Job's lost children were replaced. The new family of sons and daughters is implicitly a more satisfactory one, and the respect in which they are described as more satisfactory is another factor whose importance we would reject: the beauty of the daughters. Our culture impresses upon us as an eternal truth that female beauty is an ephemeral quality without permanence or significance in the scheme of things. Yet the daughters' beauty is the one respect in which Job's second family differs from the first.[25] It is an element of the fact that "Yahweh blessed Job's later life more than his earlier life." The entire depiction of Job's doubled wealth and his new family proclaims that it was a greater blessing than the lost wealth and family. And one of the aspects of its greater blessedness is that the three new daughters are the most beautiful women "in the whole country."

Let it be noted that Job's life is blessed, but there is no mention of any blessing to his wife, without whom the second family could hardly have come into being. The story understands the children as profoundly Job's children and, in common with most of the ancient world, ascribes to their mother no significance other than as their carrier. The sexism of that understanding and whatever feminism may be in the daughters' inheriting mutually mitigate and deconstruct each other.

That inheritance to the daughters as well as to the sons presents something revolutionary in the difference between the two families. We were given no information about the financial arrangements among the first ten. We knew about them only that they got together for regular parties, to which the brothers invited their sisters as social equals (1.4), which was revolutionary enough. Daughters inherited wealth in Israel only if their father had no sons to inherit it (see Num 27). In one sense the two modes of social equality balance each other. The social equality implied in the sisters' being invited to their brothers' feasts in chap. 1 is not the same as the social equality of inheritance in chap. 42,[26] but each equality defines the relations of sisters to brothers in its part of the tale. And each is ground only for speculation or midrash. We have no further detail about the inheritance to allow us to perceive its meaning to Job himself or to those who received or observed it. And in the beginning tale, we know only that one feast given by the oldest brother ended in the death of the entire group.

The inheritance might more clearly define the daughters' relation to their father. At least it suggests that Job is not now concerned about his children's piety as he was before (1.5). Perhaps he trusts that they will outlive him, will not be destroyed by a deity vengeful against their religious shortcomings, or that they can take care of their own shortcomings with the god. But there is also a conjunction in the middle of 42.15 that joins the clause about the beauty of Job's daughters and the clause about his settling inheritances upon them. In one sense, a conjunction is to be expected between almost any two clauses in Hebrew narrative, and this one is not at all unusual. Hebrew style, as I noted in the "Indispensable Introduction," typically uses "and" at the beginning of clauses and sentences—sometimes even at the beginnings of books.[27] We must wonder why that constant parade of conjunctions is so typical. There is presumably a reason for joining clauses together without subordination, as in "A took place, and B took place, and C happened," rather than subordinating one or two to the others, as in "After A and B had taken place, C happened," or "A and B having taken place, C happened." When no subordination among the clauses is indicated, the significance of A, B, and C is presumably approximately equal, and only some specific statement in the text will show that one is emphasized over the others. With the subordination of "after," C is called to our attention as, apparently, the goal and climax of a series of events. The subordination of "having taken place," on the other hand, suggests not merely a series in time or in importance but that A and B were necessary predecessors of C, that C could not have happened unless A and B had happened first.

We have the rather uncommunicative conjunction: the daughters were most beautiful, *and* Job gave them an inheritance. Neither clause is emphasized, neither can be elevated in importance above the other, neither is evidently the implied motivation or cause of the other. We must do the best we can with no more than the juxtaposition. Perhaps Job gave his daughters inheritances because they were extremely beautiful. Perhaps because he gave them inheritances and made them wealthy, they were considered by those thinking of marriage for themselves or for their sons to be the most beautiful women in the land. Perhaps he gave them inheritances in spite of their beauty, or perhaps the two facts had no connection in Job's mind. We cannot speak for Job's mind, except to note that it told him to give his daughters inheritances. Nor can we decide what the narrator had in mind; the narrator gave us nothing more than an "and" between the two statements. Let the matter remain undecided and undecidable. It is not necessary that every question be answered.

It remains now to see Job through the rest of his life. One surprising thing about this book is how it deals with time. I noticed earlier that we have no indication how long the tale in chaps. 1–2 took in the living or of any passage of time during the dialogue. We saw the formula "It was the day when" several times in chap. 1 and again in 2.1. The occasion in 2.1 seemed the same as or similar to that in 1.6, but we saw nothing that suggested any specific interval of time between 1.6 and 2.1. Verse 42.7 says only that Yahweh's speaking to Eliphaz happened "after" (*'aḥar*) he had spoken to Job, with no indication how long "after."

Now, in verse 16, there is another "after," and a real time designation: "Job lived after this [*'aḥ^a^rē-zōt*] one hundred forty years." Suddenly, at the very end of 42 chapters that have taken a long time to read and that cover an indeterminate amount of time, is one seven-word clause that covers 140 years. Nothing could be more revealing of the relative indifference of this book to details of time.

Yet the 140 years surely matter, even in the inflated form that the LXX gives.[28] For one thing, if the tale knew Psalm 90.10 ("The days of our years among them are seventy years, / and if in strength, eighty years, / their storming about [?] is trouble and woe"), we may think of 140 as twice 70, and thus Job's life mirrors his newly granted fortune in being double its normal expectation. But that counts only his life after the disturbances. The LXX wanted to see his life before them as already the allotted 70 years, but turned the years after them into a seemingly meaningless number. If the 140 is supposed to be double the standard 70-year life, the expression "after this," which is somewhat strange,[29] emphasizes that Job had a life before "this," a life full of wealth and begetting. And however much better the latter one was (and v. 12 was sure it was), it was not all.

Still, one is reminded of the ancient patriarchs, who also lived long lives: Abraham 175 years (Gen 25.7), Isaac 180 (Gen 35.28), Jacob 147 (Gen 47.28). Some earlier ones lived even longer than that, as the fabulous numbers of Genesis 5 and 11.10–32 show. The 140 years of Job 42.16 allows us to compare Job's life span to those of the great patriarchs without the precision of number that gives him a rank in longevity. Long life signified excellence in those days, and Job lived long enough to see four generations after him. A fitting length of time, the story thinks, for so great a character, and, like Ezekiel, it implicitly ranks Job with the most worthy ancients.[30]

Even the phrase that we might take as a kind of sigh of relief that all of that time had come to an end points to the patriarchal tradition. "Then Job died, old and sated with days" (*śᵉbaʿ yamīm*, 42.17). The same phrase is used of Isaac's death (Gen 35.29), and something very like it is said at Abraham's death: "And Abraham expired and died at a good, gray age, and sated" (*śabēaʿ*, Gen 25.8). Some Hebrew manuscripts and some ancient translations have the same expression as in Job 42.17: "sated with days."[31]

It also points back, however, to some other places in the Book of Job itself. The notion in "sated" is sometimes "satisfied,"[32] as in 31.31, where Job quotes his retainers as saying:

> Would that we were not well fed [*niśbaʿ*];

and also in 19.22, where he asks why the friends

> pursue me like El,
> not satisfied [*tiśbaʿū*] with my flesh?[33]

The word also means "full beyond comfort." I used "gorged" for it in 9.18:

> He won't even let me catch my breath
> but gorges me [*yaśbiʿanī*] with bitter things.

Job uses the same metaphor for his sleepless nights:

> I'm gorged [*śaba'tī*] with tossing till dark. (7.4)

He describes the god with the word: "Gorged with dishonor" (10.15), and the human race as "sated with turmoil" (14.1). There is at least as much of "gorged" in the book as there is of "contentedly full," and we cannot, I think, take "sated" in 42.17 as unambiguous pleasure.

The word might also point back to the last time we had a sentence concluding a major section. In 31.40, the dialogue was brought to an end with:

> Job's words were spent [*tammū*].

It is by no means the same, but 42.17 reminds me of it. "Spent" is partly "perfected, completed," almost "fulfilled," though that might imply a closer connection between 31.40 and 42.17 than is present. I suggested in Chapter 6 that *tammū* in 31.40 had a tone of exhaustion in it, and that Job's words were, in effect, used up. We have noticed his terseness and his silence since then. If the rigors of the debate with the friends emptied Job of words, his long years have perhaps filled him fuller than he might wish of life, and he would gladly die, not with a pleasantly full contrast to his prior emptiness but with a fullness that makes him yearn for emptiness.

"Sated with days," then, may indicate not only an impressive life comparable to the great patriarchs but also a life eagerly departed, more life than one would really want. Is the price of excellence and veneration that one lives too long? Or is "days" not merely a metonymy for passing time but also an echo? We have had days before too. There was a time when Job complained bitterly at how rapidly his days passed, "faster than a shuttle" (7.6);

> faster than a runner,
> they flee, see nothing good,
> sweep by on skiffs of reed
> like a vulture swooping on a meal. (9.25–26)

There were also the days that structured the beginning story, the feast days of his first children (1.4), the day of assembly when the Prosecutor and Yahweh first fell to discussing Job (1.6), the ill-omened day of the last feast of those sons and daughters (1.13), the second assembly day that ended in Job's isolation on the ash heap (2.1), the seven silent days after Eliphaz, Bildad, and Zophar arrived to console and comfort him (2.13). And there was the day and the night that Job cursed as the debate about justice and truth began (3.1–6). We have known for a long time that Job was, as it were, "sated" with those days. Only at the end, when the rest of his days are added to them, does the story itself tell us so. In death, whose arrival has been prolonged almost beyond reason, Job can get rid of that earlier series of days that so thoroughly changed his life. The effect of this part of the meaning of "sated with days" is that those days have by no means been overcome by the latter-day "blessings" with which Yahweh has showered Job (42.12). The end, like the rest of the process, is open.

The Turns of the Tempest

If I were making the case for a particular, unitary meaning of the Book of Job, it would be time for a concluding chapter, in which my position would be argued, the data telling in its favor would be exhibited, the major alternative interpretations would be expounded, and the reasons why they are inadequate would be presented. Because I come to the end of my reading of Job with the conviction that the book remains open and multiple, its "meaning" indeterminate and undecidable, I can conclude more simply.

Most interesting is the way in which the Book of Job turns back on itself, weaves from side to side in search of never-found certainty, and ends at a more ambiguous place than it began. There are two invariant points in the book: first, Job never loses his sense of his own high moral quality, but insists on it throughout; second, the friends never change their certainty that high moral quality is the key to positive relations with the deity. The question of moral worth, then, is constant, but the friends' sense of what it must signify leads them to deny it to Job, whereas he firmly asserts it.

More important, the friends' certainty about the importance of moral worth results in Yahweh's denunciation of them and Job's intercession, which restores their positive relations with him. Job's sense of his high moral quality is at last irrelevant to his conclusions about the world, and he abandons the issue of moral guilt and innocence as the means of getting along in Yahweh's world. Thus the two constant positions on moral worth in the book, identical in their structure but in their applications quite different, are both shown at the end to be wrong.

Job runs through a remarkable intellectual movement as he wrestles with his pain—pain whose origin and motivation he does not know, though at times he is sure he does know it. Beginning by accepting it as compatible with Yahweh's governance of the world (chaps. 1–2), he shortly finds it running beyond his capacity to withstand, and he wishes to get off the world (chaps. 3, 6–7). Pondering Eliphaz's notion that suffering demonstrates that Yahweh governs the world by punishing those who depart from the right moral stance, he begins to conclude that the administration has missed a signal. Job suffers but does not deserve to do so, and the deity ought either simply pardon (7.21) the minor sins he may have committed (he knows of a certainty that he has committed nothing worse) or allow a trial to prove Job's innocence of the implicit charges the friends have brought (chaps. 9–10).

There is a problem about the trial, Job thinks, because if he is right about himself and if the deity is wrong in punishing him, perhaps something is wrong with the deity (9.19–24). As Job becomes more and more distant from the god and more and more sure that his punishment is unwarranted, he becomes less and less comforted. He begins to think not only of a trial but of a superhuman advocate on his side (16.19–21), then of a powerful avenger (19.25) who might remedy the wrong that pain has brought Job. As the pain continues to wring him with its pressure, he realizes that he has been mistaken in thinking that the deity takes the same moral construction on the world that he does. Clearly his suffering is not a wrongful punishment for being wicked but his just deserts for being good. This deity rewards bad people (chap. 21), refuses trial to good people (chap. 23), runs a world that is not merely skewed morally but is upside down (chap. 24). The very cosmic structures show that the deity works in the same immoral way upon them (chap. 26), and Job finally decides that he himself is the god's moral superior (chap. 27).

He has followed a winding road to get there, but we can observe his moving around each bend. Job still thinks there may be a way to bring the deity to confront him, and he ponders his past happiness (chap. 29), his present personal and social misery (chap. 30), and his moral excellence (chap. 31). In the last is his solution: the long series of curses upon himself, referring to all the good things he has done and the bad things he has not, will force acknowledgment from the god. But it dawns on us as we follow him through his nostalgia about his "autumn days," his wretched present state, and his self-defensive curses that Job has given up all the ground he had previously occupied. The curses will work because the universe must recognize and reward the objective demonstration that Job has been moral. It is not that Job flings curses into the air to have them come out whatever way they may; they must come out in the "right" way, his way, with his reinstatement. At the end of the dialogue with the three friends, he has rejoined them on the bulwarks of divine retribution behind which they have been resisting attack ever since chap. 4.

When the theophanic tempest has come and Yahweh has finished his first speech, Job's noncommittal response (40.4–5) gives us no indication of where his mind is now. The divine portrayal of cosmic power and its challenge to Job to exert it could have smashed him down, or it could have amazed and moved him. After Yahweh's second speech, inviting him to act as the creative hero-god, has proposed (40.8) that the moral qualities of the world are not the key to understanding it, Job turns through some very ambiguous phrases and for a second time gives up his assumption that moral quality determines his or the world's circumstance (42.6).

He seems to have returned to where he was in the opening tale, though we do not hear the language of blessing in Job's mouth in chap. 42, as we did in chap. 1. Yet suddenly we see that all of the blessings that have been supposed to accrue to piety are showered on Job. He is rewarded with more wealth than he had before and more happiness for deciding that religion does not pay in precisely that way. Indeed, this concluding situation, following upon the discussion between Job and his friends and the confrontation between Job and the deity, seems to reverse the implicit tone of chaps. 1–2, where Job did not consider misery and loss of fortune a disturbance to his religion. Here, having renounced religion, but using it on behalf of the friends, Job loses his misery and regains his fortune.

That makes no unitary sense. The friends, who have just been told by no less an authority than Yahweh that they are wrong, are really right. Job, whose renunciation of religion has just been declared by no less an authority than Yahweh to be right, is wrong. Yahweh, who proposed to Job that the ethical construction of the world is mistaken, constructs the world on ethical grounds. Yet Job dies "old and sated with days" (42.17), and we saw reason to think that that "sated" is more complex than "contented."

Those who would like to sever the book from itself, break it into assumed component and "originally" separate parts, will have no difficulty with this conclusion. The problem, they will argue, is not that the book is inconsistent. That is the fault not of the book, but its history. Others than the "original" author have interfered with its "original" consistency, and discovery of the original requires that we analyze the layers and seal the various consistencies away from the other consistencies with which they are inconsistent. Then we decide which one we like best, show that that one is the "genuine" Book of Job, and rest content that we have found the truth.

The cop-out is in thinking that we have found the truth. The marvel of the Book of Job is that it constantly outruns our certainties that we know how to find the truth about it. It steadfastly refuses to reveal any unitary truth to us. How, then, did it come to be in the Bible? I do not know the answer to that question, either historically or theologically, nor will I waste energy trying to find an answer. For one thing, its presence in the Bible has ceased, in the modern world, to guarantee that its truth is religiously unavoidable. Even more, its presence in the Bible has ceased to guarantee for many readers that it has religious truth at all.

I am sure of only one thing. If we are to find truth in Job, it must come from the whole book, it must be ringed around with doubt and uncertainty, and it must be something other than the truth with which we came to the book. But we may find truth best if we do not try to find it. The world is full of jokes. Religion is only one of them.

Reference Matter

Notes

For complete authors' names, titles, and publication data, see the Bibliography, pp. 445–65. For complete forms of abbreviations used here, see the List of Abbreviations, pp. xiii–xiv.

Dispensable Introduction

1. Wimsatt and Beardsley's classic essay "The Intentional Fallacy" remains persuasive to me, and Hirsch's relatively subtle proposal of authorial intention as the only sure route to "valid" interpretation (*Validity in Interpretation*) does not sway me. See also Fox, esp. pp. 53–55. To me, "validity" is too constrictive a goal for interpretation. For my views on the intentional fallacy with respect to Joḅ, see "Job and the Literary Task."

2. See Tur-Sinai, pp. viii–xl; Guillaume, "Arabic Background," and *Studies*, pp. 1–7; and Foster.

3. The case was most influentially proposed by Humbert, *Recherches*, not solely on the basis of the animals in chaps. 40–41, though that was part of it.

4. See Chap. 8.

5. Ezek 14.14–20. See Chap. 2.

6. Babylonian Talmud, Baba Batra 15b.

7. Pope (*Job*, p. xxxii) gives a convenient summary of these Rabbinic opinions.

8. See esp. Terrien, "Quelques remarques."

9. The process by which the Torah achieved its present form is an extremely complex scholarly puzzle. Common opinion finds two creation stories in the first two chapters of Genesis, one in 1.1–2.4a, which carries out the seven-

day scheme and puts the creation of humans last, and a quite different one in 2.4b–25, which has no time framework and has the man created first and the woman last. The consensus of scholars is that the story in Gen 1 originated later than the one in Gen 2.

10. Richard Elliott Friedman's popular *Who Wrote the Bible?* (New York, 1987), like its predecessors, is insufficiently rigorous in distinguishing guess from knowledge. I object not to the guessing games but to the pretense that guesses added to other guesses produce knowledge.

11. Medieval and earlier Jewish interpretations of Job often proposed that Elihu, in fact, gave the correct answer to the problem of the book and the problem of suffering. See Glatzer, "Book of Job"; and Carstensen, *Persistence*.

12. Some scholars (e.g., Gordis, *Book of God*, pp. 73–75) argue that the three friends did not originally belong to the folktale. Others think that the original form of the folktale included a discussion among Job and the friends, which the poetic dialogue has displaced (Pope, *Job*, p. xxvi, with a careful "perhaps"). Still others think that all of 42.7–17 was a later addition in order to give the book the happy ending necessary to gain it admission to the biblical canon (e.g., Fullerton, "Original Conclusion"). And there is a fascinating argument that the poetry came first and the tale later. See *n*18 below.

13. The assumption, on the whole, is that at this stage the third cycle was complete, with a normal-length speech by Bildad and a speech by Zophar. Some scholars still hold to an older critical view that the Yahweh speeches entered later, and the "original" poet wrote only the dialogue of Job and the friends (see Girard, pp. 142–45). Some of those who conclude that Yahweh's speeches were a later interpolation think that Yahweh originally had one speech, excluding the sections on Behemoth and Leviathan (40.15–41.26). The current consensus, however, is that 38.1–42.6 was the work of the poet of the dialogue. The consensus also holds that the poet did not disturb the tale, unless the poetic dialogue was substituted for a conversation originally in the tale.

14. Analyses of displacements in parts of Job's speeches vary somewhat. Most scholars add 26.5–14 to Bildad's speech in 25.2–6. Pope's reconstruction of Zophar's speech (*Job*, pp. 187–96) as 27.8–23 followed by 24.18–20, 22–25 may stand for a good many similar ones. Pope also thinks that remaining parts of chap. 24 have been considerably rearranged.

15. Freedman ("The Elihu Speeches") suggests from allusions and references to the main dialogue in Elihu's four speeches that their author intended to interpolate them at the ends of the cycles of the dialogue. There is some difficulty in identifying which speech belongs with which cycle, and Freedman collapses Elihu's second and third speeches into one, which would have belonged to both the second and third cycles. The proposal is hypothetical, as Freedman himself says, and I am intrigued but not persuaded.

16. This presupposition has often been informed by a religious view of the divinely guaranteed coherence of the biblical text, whether under a "fundamentalist" doctrine of divine inspiration and inerrancy or not. Even those who reject

that theological assumption about the Bible may continue to hold to the centrality of coherence. It is also characteristic of many modern critical assumptions about the mind of any "author."

17. For a careful distinction of text-oriented and source-oriented reading, see Sternberg, pp. 7–23.

18. Hurwitz argues that the tale has the linguistic marks of post-exilic Hebrew and cannot be earlier than the sixth century B.C.E. Some scholars (e.g., D. A. Robertson; Freedman, "Orthographic Peculiarities") date the poetry early, Freedman to the seventh or early sixth century B.C.E., Robertson as early as the eleventh or tenth century. If we set Hurwitz's argument next to Freedman's or Robertson's, we would conclude that the prose tale was added to the poetry, not the other way around. I continue to doubt the idea, both because I think the poetry betrays knowledge of the tale and because there are some points at which the tale may know the poetry. To be sure, once the two were joined together, if they were, any further modifications were based on the conjunction.

19. See the very different arguments of Frye (*Anatomy of Criticism*), for whom every literary work exhibits various strands from the entire literary tradition, and of Bloom (*Map of Misreading*), who holds that each work in a poetic tradition betrays its ancestry by *mis*understanding something important in that tradition.

20. See Fuente; John Gray, "Book of Job in the Context of Near Eastern Literature"; Humbert, *L'Ancien Testament*; Kramer; Krieger; Kuschke; Müller, *Das Hiobproblem* and "Keilschriftliche Parallelen"; Nougayrol; Preuss; Stamm; van Dijk, *La sagesse suméro-accadienne*; and R. J. Williams, "Theodicy."

21. That form, among other things, led Kallen to his revolutionary thesis that Job is a tragic drama on the Greek model, influenced by the tragedies of Euripides. That the formal contention is dubious did not prevent Kallen from some extremely perceptive interpretations of Job.

22. For translations, see *ANET*, pp. 438–40, 601–4, 437–38, 600–601, 405–7; Lambert, pp. 70–89, 144–49; Lichtheim, 1: 163–69; and Simpson, pp. 201–9.

23. *ANET*, pp. 410–11, 592–93.

24. Lambert (p. 1) assumes the legitimacy of the term "wisdom literature" for the Bible but expresses dissatisfaction with it for the Babylonian material he presents. Gordis (*Book of God*, chap. 4) accepts the idea and the structures of thought it implies quite enthusiastically. Crenshaw (*Old Testament Wisdom*, pp. 11–25), however, finds the term doubtful even for the Hebrew Bible as he catalogs the many views of what constitutes wisdom literature.

25. See my chapter on Qoheleth in *Irony*.

26. Westermann (*Structure*, pp. 1–15) spends his first chapter doubting that "wisdom" is an adequate genre designation for Job (for a listing of earlier scholars who agree, see his *n* 1).

27. For example, 11.12; 12.12; 17.5; 28.28b–c.

28. Westermann (*Structure*, pp. 1–2) notes that many interpreters have ar-

gued that Job is wisdom literature because it deals with and expounds a "problem," variously identified. He thinks rightly that too many scholars have not examined the jump from classifying the book as wisdom literature to assuming that therefore it deals with a "problem." I think that Westermann in turn collapses too many diverse generic types into his own choice of "lament" as the genre of the poem.

29. Some of these works are Aiura; Bic; Brueggemann; Bruston; Causse; Crenshaw, "Shift"; Duesberg; Gese; Gordis, "Wisdom Literature"; Humbert, *Recherches*; Müller, "Das weisheitliche Lehrerzählung"; Murphy; Priest; Rankin; Ranston; Heinz Richter, "Die Naturweisheit"; Schmid, *Gerechtigkeit* and *Wesen und Geschichte*; Schmitt; Scott; Steinmann, *La souffrance humaine*; Thomas, "Types of Wisdom"; von Rad, "Job 38" and *Wisdom in Israel*; Wevers; Whybray.

Indispensable Introduction

1. There are, of course, a great many details with which I am dissatisfied.

2. I distinguish between prose and poetry in full awareness of doubts recently expressed about the distinction and the means of making it, most cogently by Kugel (*Idea of Biblical Poetry*, esp. chap. 2). Kugel does not deny that there is in the Hebrew Bible a densely textured, basically parallelistic kind of writing that the rest of us call poetry, and his definition of parallelism, which I will use below, is the most elegant, parsimonious account of that well-gnawed bone of contention that I know. He decides that "poetry" is simply a style at one end of the continuum from relatively casual, loose, conversational talk to densely allusive, parallelistic talk. In my view, he emphasizes stylistic analogies between prose and poetry because he has given up on analyzing the rhythmic patterns of poetry (see esp. pp. 70–76, 287–304); I am unwilling to do so. I have more to say about Kugel in the section below on poetry.

3. Some analysts think that chap. 3 is introductory to and outside the structure of the cycles, and that Job's summation, chaps. 29–31, is also beyond the cycles. In that case, the cycles begin with Eliphaz and end with Job, respectively chaps. 4–14, 15–21, 22–27 (28?). There is a certain amount of arbitrariness in such structural analysis, and I will not be dogmatic about it.

4. Or, in Derrida's fine phrase, "impoverishment by univocality" (p. 90).

5. I am again indebted to Derrida (p. 102) for this point: "Totally translatable, it disappears as a text, as writing, as a body of language [*langue*]. Totally untranslatable, even within what is believed to be one language, it dies immediately."

6. Interestingly, though the Hebrew text refers to plural "children," it refers to a singular "heart." The usage is not unknown, as in 2 Sam 15.6 or Isa 51.7, and the plural is relatively rare. At the same time, it might suggest that the "hearts" of Job's children are a single unit.

7. See the engaging account of reception theory in Eagleton (chap. 2) and such exemplars of the theory as Fish and Iser.

8. Chamberlain's article "Gender and the Metaphorics of Translation"

showed me some of these metaphors. The words various languages use for the enterprise are very interesting indeed. I referred to "version." "Translate" itself is interesting, coming from a Latin participle, *translatus*, which became attached to *transferre*, "to carry across," as from one bank of a river to another. The translator, then, becomes the ferry operator. The French *traduction* is from Latin *transducere*, "to lead across," which is more like the Boy Scout helping the old folks across the street. German is more brusque: *übersetzen*, "to set over," make something sit down on the other side, or, in almost an effort to co-opt *transferre* into itself, *übertragen*, "carry across." In all these words, the metaphor puts the translator in command, even where it proposes assistance. Such metaphors reveal cultural bias, whether or not we think of the etymologies.

9. And in Job 41.26, Leviathan is "king over all proud beasts."

10. Blank's important article, "Curse," covers the ground well. I pointed out in "Job and the Literary Task," p. 475, that the Prosecutor's sentence in 1.11 is a curse formula.

11. The word comes from Greek, *hēn dia dys*, "one through two."

12. Perhaps I should apologize to the translators and publishers of the RSV and JPS versions for constantly holding them up as the counterexamples. They are, of course, the two most commonly used English translations, their familiarity alone makes them easy targets, and readers are likely to have one or the other at hand. In my opinion, the JPS version is now the best English translation of the Hebrew Bible available.

13. Patrick, "Translation." The verb *niḥamtı* can, in addition, mean to be comforted, and Stephen Mitchell, among others, translates it so here.

14. See *n*2 for Kugel's doubt of the existence of poetry in the Hebrew Bible. For a recent general book on Hebrew poetry, see Alter, *Poetry*. See also Watson, *Classical Hebrew Poetry*; and Schökel, *Estudios de Poética hebrea*. Much is still to be learned from such older works as Condamin; G. B. Gray; and Robinson, *Poetry*.

15. The names of the meters derive from Greek meters, but English uses them differently from Greek.

16. Act V, scene i, lines 1–3. Prospero is speaking. In order to make the meter of the second line work, we must slide over "spirits" as if the word had but one syllable. Of course, a good actor will speak those lines not in exaggerated, sing-songy rhythm but with an interesting counterpoint of the spoken rhythm to the underlying regular meter. The actor will probably say not "Now dóes my próject" but "Nów does my próject," etc. As in music, this cross-rhythm plays around and against the regular and basic "beat" of the poetry.

17. Any complex poetic tradition, of course, knows important poems that break the "rules." Gerard Manley Hopkins wrote poems that he and others called sonnets, which had lines longer than pentameter and more than fourteen lines, some of which cannot be scanned in the iambic meter. Poetic "rules" are not laws but conventions.

18. For a clear account of various of these efforts, see Alter, *Poetry*, chap.

1. The major alternative to counting accents is to count syllables, as, for instance, Stuart does. I find syllable counting by itself inadequate.

19. Those who know Hebrew will recognize these as instances of segholate nouns. The vowel changes correspond to some assumptions about how those types of nouns came to have their present forms.

20. The vowels in the text were added to the consonants in the Middle Ages. They show us, I believe, medieval synagogue pronunciation, but we may be skeptical of them as guides to pronunciation in the biblical period.

21. The asterisk shows that the form is conjecturally reconstructed. The Hebrew text reads *ḥōšek*.

22. Kugel (*Idea of Biblical Poetry*, p. 154) translates Jerome's "Preface to Job," in which Jerome describes poetic meter: "From the beginning of the book to the words of Job, the Hebrew version is in prose. But from the words of Job where he says, 'May the day perish . . .' [Jerome quotes all of 3.3] to the place before the end of the book where it says '. . . dust and ashes' [again he quotes all of 42.6], there are hexameter verses made of dactyls and spondees [*hexametri versus sunt, dactylo spondeoque currentes*] and, owing to the special character of the language, frequently containing as well other [sorts of] feet [*alios pedes*], which have not the same number of syllables, but the same qualities [*temporum*]. Sometimes also a sweet and pleasing rhythm is obtained by the lines being set free from the laws of meter." Jerome translated into Latin, of which he was a master, from Hebrew, which he apparently knew fairly well, and I am fascinated that he recognized mixed meters.

23. *De sacra poesi hebraeorum praelectiones*, 1753, rev. 1763, translated into English only in 1815.

24. Some recent studies, apart from the general books on poetry I refer to in *n*14, are Gevirtz; Geller; O'Connor, *Hebrew Verse Structure*; and Berlin, *Dynamics*.

25. Kugel, *Idea of Biblical Poetry*, p. 8.

26. See especially O'Connor, *Hebrew Verse Structure*, pp. 122–29.

27. It seemed for a time as if the search for "fixed" word pairs would be the only game in town, for word pairs looked like a Hebrew analogue to the regnant formulaic analyses of the Homeric epithets, especially associated with the names of Milman Parry and Albert Lord. See Avishur; Cassuto; Craigie, "Note" and "Problem"; Dahood, "Ugaritic-Hebrew Parallel Pairs"; Gevirtz, p. 101; Watson, "Fixed Pairs" and *Classical Hebrew Poetry*, pp. 128–44; Watters; and Yoder. Whallon proposed a subtler analogue between the function of the epithets in Greek poetry and the function of parallelism in Hebrew. With such studies as Kugel's and Berlin's, we may be returning from a seeming sidetrack to a broader sense of how parallelism works.

28. See esp. Kugel, *Idea of Biblical Poetry*, pp. 1–95. At the end of *Dynamics* (pp. 127–41), Berlin discusses some questions of style and effect.

29. Kugel, *Idea of Biblical Poetry*, p. 272.

30. A useful general book on Canaanite culture is John Gray, *Canaanites*. For an accessible version of the main mythic texts from Ras Shamra, see Coogan. The texts are also translated in *ANET*.

31. See esp. Blommerde, *Northwest Semitic Grammar*; and Ceresko, *Job 29–31*. Mention ought also to be made of Michel, *Job in the Light of Northwest Semitic*, vol. 1. Michel was not a student of Dahood, but he worked with him, and his book is dedicated to him. Pope's important commentary made considerable and judicious use of Blommerde (Ceresko's book was not yet published). Another work rather independent of Dahood is Grabbe. Other significant studies of the relation of the Hebrew Bible and Northwest Semitic texts are Cohen; Craigie, "Job and Ugaritic Studies"; Ginsberg, "Ugaritic Texts and Textual Criticism"; Greenfield, "Hebrew Bible"; Held; Hillers; Watson, "Verse-Patterns"; and Whitley.

32. Freedman, "Orthographic Peculiarities." Most recent scholars date Job to during or shortly after the Babylonian Exile of the sixth century B.C.E., some as late as the fourth century. Freedman argues a date in the late seventh or early sixth century, in what he calls the "North Israelite diaspora."

33. In looking through the first edition of *Irony* for misprints needing correction for the second edition, I was shocked to see how many times I had emended the text. I say more about emendation in Chap. 1.

34. Even Sarna does that in his article "Some Instances."

35. This is a theological paradox, I know. Still, the medieval Jewish view of the holiness of the text of the Bible is abundantly attested, and at the same time the Ketib-Qere pairs stand as evidence that some words in that holy text had been mistakenly written.

36. As do, for example, S. R. Driver and Gray, Pt. I, p. 184; Guillaume, *Studies*, p. 44; Mitchell, p. 52; Stevenson, *Notes*, p. 97; and the NEB version.

37. See, e.g., Gard; and Ziegler. Orlinsky's series of articles sought to reinstate the worth of the Septuagint.

38. For example, the first word of 17.16 in Hebrew is *baddē*, which some translators take as "bars" or "gates" (the consonants are *bdy*). The Septuagint has *ē met' emou*, an interrogative "with me." Many scholars have liked that meaning better than what they can make of the Hebrew and have emended the text on the basis of it. But what Hebrew did the Greek translators read? I find among the scholars five different proposals: *hᵃbaʿᵃdī* (Graetz, *Monatsschrift für Geschichte und Wissenschaft des Judentums* 36 [1887]: 247), *habᵉyadī* (Dhorme, p. 255), *ha'ittī* (Ehrlich, cited by Stevenson, *Notes*, p. 76), *haʿimmadī* (S. R. Driver and Gray, Pt. II, p. 115), and *haʿimmī* ("others" cited by Stevenson, *Notes*, p. 76; I have been unable to identify them). Except for the first two, no one explains how the proposed form became corrupted into *baddē*. My own solution is to repoint *baddē* to *bīday*, "at my hand, beside me."

39. Modern Hebrew has turned these two tenses and the participle into the past, future, and present tenses.

Chapter 1

1. See both chap. 7 of *Irony* and my article, "Job and the Literary Task."

2. See esp. Eco; and Barthes.

3. It is possible to think that a unitary text was produced by two or more minds, but the idea is difficult to grasp. It is easier if we think of "joint authorship," two or more authors working together to produce the text. With successive authorship, in which a second, a third, a fourth, etc., author laid layers of text over the work of an earlier author, it is more difficult for us to think that the text is unitary. Indeed, unless the work gives evidence of incoherence, it is nearly impossible to discern the presence of those layers and to distinguish the later from the earlier. But we become confused if a text that we know was written by a single author contains incoherences. Coherence for us tends to be the definitive quality of an acceptable text.

4. But Culler's remarkable paragraph on literary criticism in a paternalistic culture (*On Deconstruction*, pp. 60–61, in the chapter "On Reading as a Woman") makes clear that this is less parodistic than one might think.

5. Eco, p. 4.

6. We are not accustomed to thinking this way of literary texts, though the thought is not surprising when we think of musical texts. The music does not consist only of notes in a score but in one sense comes into being only when performed. Similarly, though a drama can be read as if it were a literary text, it needs performance, and that inserts something else between text and receiver. Riffaterre alludes to the musical analogy (p. 4) and goes on to argue that the "literary phenomenon" lies "between text and reader, and not between text and author, or text and reality" (p. 25). Music and drama are complicatedly more interesting, with the involvement of performer along with text and hearer. I will not enter on the problem of electronic music.

7. Aspiring to be a feminist, I read as a man because I cannot read as anything else. But I wish my reading to transcend the constrictions of what has been properly criticized as "phallocentrism" or, more complicatedly, "phallogocentrism." I am encouraged by such examples as Culler (see *n*4 above).

8. I find the clearest exposition of deconstruction to be Culler, *On Deconstruction*. See also Bloom et al.; Johnson; and Leitch. The only other deconstructive reading of Job that I know is Clines's unpublished paper, "Job: A Deconstruction" (1987). Clines is preparing a larger commentary, and I wish it had been available for this book. Patriquin's brief essay is more programmatic than interpretive with respect to Job, and Jacobson's is partly deconstructive.

9. Those who know their deconstructionists will recognize that I am not what Hartman calls a "boa-deconstructor" (in the Preface, p. ix, to Bloom et al.).

10. "Synchronic" (Greek *syn*, "with," + *chronos*, "time") refers to study that interprets a text or other phenomenon as a whole system and ignores changes over time. The antonym is "diachronic" (Greek *dia*, "through," + *chronos*, "time"), which studies changes over time. "Historical criticism" for the most part

has followed a diachronic method, though that is not the only way to do historical criticism.

11. This is the counterpart in reading of the simultaneous translatability and untranslatability of texts to which I referred in the "Indispensable Introduction."

12. One sees the assumption in the very structure of most commentaries on biblical books. They typically begin with introductions that present the answers to just such questions as the ones I have mentioned, and only after completing the exposition of those matters do they proceed to draw out the meanings of the text itself. My modest protest against that structure of assumptions is contained in the title of my first introduction.

13. Alt's view, that the original tale was chaps. 1 and 42.11–17 and that chap. 2 and 42.7–10 were a later stratum, was influential. Batten, on the other hand, argued that the Satan passages, 1.6–12 and 2.1–7, were interpolated into the book.

14. A stark instance in our own day is the murderous condemnation by Muslims of a novel that fictionalizes fantasies about Muhammad and his wives or the less violent but no less horrified protests by Christian fundamentalists against a film based on Nikos Kazantzakis's novel *The Last Temptation of Christ*. When all you can think of is truth, there is no such thing as fiction.

15. Perhaps the most important dissenter from this view is Dhorme (p. xcvii).

16. A few, especially Gordis (*Book of God*, pp. 100–103; and *Book of Job*, "Special Note 23," pp. 536–38), believe it was written by the same author who wrote the rest of the poetic debate. Habel (*Book of Job*, pp. 391–93) shows its place in the design of the whole and speaks of "the poet" as intending that structure.

17. My lack of interest in these subjects for purposes of this book does not prevent my having opinions about them. See the "Dispensable Introduction." But I remain convinced that historiographic criticism asks external questions not essential to reading the work. To read, we do not need to know who authored the text, when that author wrote, or whether there were several authors instead of one.

18. The chapter on Isaiah in *Irony* is the prime exhibit of my sins in this regard. I am now shocked at how freely I rewrote the text in that chapter.

19. Eight of Fohrer's most important articles are collected in *Studien zum Buche Hiob (1956–1979)*, 2nd ed. The first edition (1963) had six essays.

20. Fohrer, *Das Buch Hiob*, pp. 108–11.

21. I did so in print about Mitchell's *Book of Job* in "Stephen Mitchell's *Job*."

22. I do not fall into Kallen's trap of literalizing the dramatic analogy. His book was an undergraduate paper reconstructing Job as a tragedy on the model of Euripides. He had some very interesting insights into Job, however doubtful his historiography was.

23. See, e.g., Habel, *Book of Job*; Pope, *Job*; Gordis, *Book of Job*; Rowley, *Job*; and Fohrer, *Das Buch Hiob.*

Chapter 2

1. For a detailed account of the tale (including 42.7–17) using Propp's formalist terms (*Morphology of the Folktale*), see Fontaine.

2. Ezekiel spells the name in that way, *dan'ēl*, rather than *danīyyē'l* as in Daniel. Scholars agree that Ezekiel's "Dan'el" has nothing to do with the Book of Daniel, whose hero is contemporary with Ezekiel and hardly comparable to Noah and Job. The Canaanite Dan'el story (the title is usually given as *Aqhat*, the name of Dan'el's son) is translated in Coogan, *Stories from Ancient Canaan*, and in *ANET*.

3. Spiegel (p. 319) and Müller (*Hiob und seine Freunde*, p. 27) emphasize how Ezekiel's description does not cohere with the story in Job.

4. Sarna, "Epic Substratum."

5. I do not believe that the speeches in chaps. 1–2 are in poetry, disagreeing with Pope (*Job*, pp. lv–lvi), who notes, though he does not expand the point, that he has set the speeches as poetry.

6. Though Alter (*Narrative*, p. 17) calls this tale a "deliberately schematic folktale frame," he knows too much about narrative to think it naive. Day (pp. 77–79) argues cogently that the folktale would be received immediately by its audience as fictional.

7. See Alter, *Narrative*, chap. 4, on the ways in which narration in the Hebrew Bible frequently rides upon dialogue.

8. The qualification "did not sin *with his lips*" in 2.10 may be important. It could imply that he did sin otherwise, but nothing in the text suggests it. Yahweh himself says twice that "there's certainly no one like him on the earth" (1.8; 2.3). At the same time, 2.10 follows 2.3, and perhaps something has happened in the interim (see below).

9. Pedersen (*Israel*, 1: 102, 104, etc.) refers to the heart as the operative soul, the person in action, and he believes that thinking and deciding too narrowly describe the heart's functions. But "thought" seems most accurate if we do not confine it to its narrowest logical sense.

10. Weiss (pp. 30–31) emphasizes the heart as a place "where man has no control." That would point precisely to inadvertent, unintended sin.

11. In my chapter on Job in *Irony* (see esp. p. 197), I did criticize magic, as Gordis properly saw (*Book of God*, p. 337, *n*23). On the other hand, I also described it, I think accurately, and Fingarette (pp. 1602–3, *n*59) failed to distinguish between the description and the criticism. Correspondence with him persuaded him that some of his criticisms ought to be modified.

12. The implicit polytheism may trouble some readers. I cannot in all conscience claim that the Book of Job is monotheistic.

13. Though the last sentence is one with which he would agree, I cannot

accept Jung's understanding of Satan (*Answer to Job*), which collapses the whole history of the myth of the Devil back on a Hebrew Bible that is not heir to that history. It would be absurd for an Israelite to say, for example, that Satan is a "doubting thought" (p. 38). Weiss's account of the Prosecutor (pp. 34–42) gives me some of the same difficulties. See Day's comments on the motif of the divine council in Job 1–2 (pp. 79–80).

14. Berlin, *Poetics and Interpretation*, p. 42.

15. Dhorme (p. 8) and Weiss (p. 46) see that the formula is a curse, but both ignore the fact that a curse formula is not only a formula but a *curse*. Dhorme points out, however, that St. Thomas Aquinas said (*Expositio in libro Sancti Iob*) that the words *malum mihi accidat*, "let evil happen to me," ought to be inserted into the sentence. From a great distance, I bow to the Angelic Doctor.

16. The alternative is to retain the notion of Yahweh's omnipotence and to think that the Prosecutor has caught him unawares (which raises some problems about omniscience) or that he loftily permits this unjust disturbance of Job's bona fides (which raises some moral problems about Yahweh). The curse poses a problem, of course, and it is the problem of the book. But in the book's own world, it is not a moral problem about Yahweh.

17. See esp. Day, pp. 80–81.

18. The best treatment of curse forms is Blank, "Curse." Blank did not, however, notice that this statement is a curse. See also Horst, "Der Eid"; Pedersen, *Der Eid*; Schottrof, *Der altisraelitische Fluchspruch*; and Wehmeier, *Der Segen*. David Robertson (*The Old Testament*, p. 35) and Fingarette (p. 1586) have accepted my argument, made originally in "Job and the Literary Task." Fontaine (p. 211) refers ambiguously to "self-curse/wager," and calls (p. 213) "the Satan's wager with Yahweh" "an implicit self-curse." Day (p. 81, *n*30) wishing to make the challenge a legal one, is also ambiguous about the curse, though she denies the notion of a wager and agrees that the sentence can be a curse-formula. I have never seen the quotation of an actual wager from the ancient Near East.

19. This account of the fourth messenger closely agrees with Weiss's reading (pp. 56–57).

20. It may be that Job's compliant acceptance of a rude fate, ascribing all events to the deity, is the stuff of the most profound faith. I find the quatrain *poetically* banal, however theologically profound it may be. Job's reference to Yahweh, by the way, suggests that Weiss's emphasis (pp. 21–24) on the fact that Job is a Gentile, which he derives from Uz in 1.1, is not really in the story. Weiss's account of 1.21 (p. 60) is rather lame on that issue.

21. I use this somewhat odd term to jolt the reader a bit by something unfamiliar where one might expect something familiar. When in American and European cultures we say "God," we have a fairly good idea of what we mean, part of which is that there is only one member of the category, who is eternal, omnipotent, omniscient, male, loving, just, etc. Capital-G "God" carries a heavy freight with it, and we tend to assume that set of meanings both when we use the term and wherever we see it. We usually use the lower-case "god" to refer to a deity in

a polytheistic system, often somewhat patronizingly. A "god" is considerably inferior to "God" in our minds. I add the definite article to the uncapitalized word, "the god," to identify the divine character who is identified by several terms (El, Eloah, Elohim, Shaddai, and Yahweh). I think that all of those terms point to the same character in the story, and I wish to distinguish that character from the divine being upon whom our religious traditions have loaded all the baggage I mentioned above. I will use "the god" and "the deity" interchangeably.

22. Gordis (*Book of Job*, p. 20): "Skin in exchange for skin"; Pope (*Job*, p. 20): "Value for value"; Davidson and Lanchester (p. 15): "Like for like." Others prefer the idea of giving one thing for another, e.g., trading one animal hide for another (Fohrer, *Das Buch Hiob*, pp. 96–97; Weiss, p. 65), or giving up one bodily member to save another (S. R. Driver and Gray, Pt. I, p. 21, an idea also found in the Targum). Others argue that *b*^{e}*ʿad* means "behind," i.e., when one layer of skin has been peeled off, another remains beneath it, which the person takes as comfort and protection (Rowley, *Job*, p. 35, among others). These are the best of a great many interpretations of the proverb.

23. Gordis (*Book of Job*, p. 6) rightly has "preserve," and Fohrer (*Das Buch Hiob*, p. 95), "Schone sein Leben."

24. Habel (*Book of Job*, p. 95) suggests that in ignorance of the Prosecutor Job later accuses the deity of playing the Prosecutor's spying role.

25. Fontaine (p. 214) takes this as the necessary movement by the Hero in a folktale, "setting out from home," before the expected restoration to home can take place.

26. Several non-exegetical interpreters of Job have portrayed Job's wife more sympathetically than the text seems to imply. In William Blake's engravings, she is present throughout in active sympathy with Job. Archibald MacLeish's drama *J. B.*, in its published version (the Broadway production script is quite different), gives her some of the central themes and images of the work. In Robert Frost's "Mask of Reason," though she is the butt of some rather gentle humor, she comes across as having more than ordinary intellectual perspicuity and persistence. And Margrethe, the companion of the protagonist in Robert Heinlein's *Job, A Comedy of Justice*, is a powerful, magnetic woman.

27. Weiss's reading of Job's wife (p. 70) is the source of this last possibility. Job misunderstands her pity, Weiss thinks, by taking her literally.

28. It is less clear that Job's words are "hostile," as Fontaine (p. 215) maintains. Her formalist structure, involving tests of the Hero, requires that this response be a negation.

29. To turn the sentence into a question, many scholars play sleight of hand with *gam*. Not one points to good evidence that *gam* can be used interrogatively.

30. "Good and evil" is a serious step beyond "giving and taking," the issue in 1.21, not because "good" means more than "pleasant" and "evil" more than "unpleasant," but because they are what lands immediately on one's own person. The notion that "good" and "evil" are cosmic and abstract in scope seems to me not present here.

31. The Talmud (Baba Batra 16b) alleges that "Job did not sin with his lips, but in his heart he did," and Weiss (pp. 71–74) accepts the conclusion.

32. Some suggest that the friends take over the Prosecutor's function and receive their judgment in 42.7–9; others that Elihu does; still others that, in effect, Yahweh does in chaps. 38–41. It is even suggested that we find the Prosecutor again in Behemoth and Leviathan in chaps. 40–41. Day (pp. 88–101) suggests that the Prosecutor moves over to Job's side in the third parties to whom Job refers in the dialogue: the "arbiter" (9.33), the "witness" (16.19), and the "avenger" (19.25). None of these substitutes is really satisfactory, though one may perfectly well be reminded of the Prosecutor by any or all of them.

33. Esp. Gordis, *Book of God*, p. 73.

34. Buttenwieser, pp. 43–46. The argument depends partly on Pedersen's evidence about curses in *Der Eid*, partly on gestures described in Acts 22.22–23 and in Mishna Sanhedrin 7.5. The presence of one who has been cursed is itself cursed, and these ritual gestures preserve the friends from the contamination. Weiss (p. 76) confines his explanation of the magic to the dust thrown "toward the sky" and compares the language to Exod 9.8 and the plague of boils. Buttenwieser goes on to argue that the silence that follows is in contrast to the friends' first intention to "console and comfort." Habel (*Book of Job*, pp. 97–98), on the other hand, sees the entire gesture as one of total empathy with Job. See also Pope, *Job*, p. 25.

35. See Lohfink. 1 Sam 31.13 may show that seven days was a conventional period of mourning.

Chapter 3

1. Cox, p. 38.

2. I shall make constant appreciative reference to the eloquent, compelling analysis of this chapter by Alter, *Poetry*, pp. 76–84.

3. See Ps 91.5, the only example I can find. In Ps 30.6 [Eng. 5] *'ereb*, "evening," precedes *bōqer*, "morning," as, of course, they do in the daily formulas of Gen 1.

4. Alter, *Poetry*, p. 78.

5. Alter (*Poetry*, p. 79) fails to notice that the movement from *'ōr^{e}rē*, "put spells on" Sea (or "day," *yōm*), in v. 8a to *'ōrēr*, "rouse" Leviathan, in v. 8b intensifies the consonantal sound from *'aleph*, a light glottal stop, to *'ayin*, a very heavy one. This combination of words, especially *'ōr* and *yir'eh*, "light" and "see," makes one think again about reading MT's "day" (*yōm*) as "Sea" (*yam*). But Dhorme's argument for retaining *yōm* (p. 29) does not take into account that Job is calling up chaos against order. Sea represents that chaos, whereas "day" stands among these images for order. Still, perhaps now we need not reject one in favor of the other.

6. We come across Sea a number of other times in the dialogue, especially in 7.12. Yamm is one of Baal's two principal enemies in the Canaanite Baal texts.

Leviathan, of course, is the subject of 40.25–41.26, where he is not in my judgment a crocodile, but rather an inimical sea monster, as in Isa 27.1. He appears in the Baal texts as Lotan. See Chap. 8.

7. Translated by Robert H. Pfeiffer in *ANET*, pp. 437–38; for a new translation, by Robert D. Biggs, see *ANET*, Supplement, p. 601; see also Lambert, pp. 139–49.

8. In v. 14, translating *bnh*, the usual word for building, as "rebuild" (see, e.g., Gordis, *Book of Job*, pp. 28, 37) is unnecessary. The expression is economically and ironically elliptical: "built ruins" compresses construction and decay into a single stage. See also Alter, *Poetry*, p. 81.

9. See, e.g., the text titled by Simpson "The Man Who Was Tired of Life." A series of poignant stanzas, each beginning "Death is in my sight today," ends: "Death is in my sight today / As when a man desires to see home / When he has spent many years in captivity" (Simpson, p. 208).

10. Alter, *Poetry*, p. 78. *Geber* also refers back to the opening of the poem: "The night that said, 'A man [*geber*] is conceived'" (v. 3).

11. *Kī paḥad paḥadtī*, more literally "For I was terrified of a terror." Intensification of a verb by its cognate noun as an accusative is frequent in Hebrew.

12. See von Rad, *Wisdom in Israel*, p. 209.

13. Müller (*Das Hiobproblem*, pp. 76–95) canvasses the contributions to the debate about the genre of the dialogue.

14. Heinz Richter tries in *Studien zu Hiob* to cram the entire book of Job into the forms of legal language. Von Rad (*Wisdom in Israel*, p. 209) denies that the speeches are "contentious debates." Yet parts of them are precisely that. The genre question has been debated mainly in the terms of form-criticism, which searches for typical speech patterns, and some form-critics become confused if they find more than one kind of speech pattern. The world is supposed to be neat!

15. Clines ("Arguments," p. 205) refutes von Rad's contention (*Old Testament Theology*, 1: 410) that the speech "does not in any sense consist of a fairly unified sequence of thought." To be sure, there are points of doubtful logic even beyond those pointed out by Clines: e.g., the deity's apparent responsibility for the troubles of lions (4.10–11) as indication of his retributive dealing with bad people (vv. 8–9). No necessary logic connects the two subjects, and only juxtaposition suggests that a connection is being made. Likewise, the switch from what looks in 5.6 like the idea that human beings are responsible for their own behavior to the denial of that idea in v. 7 transgresses logic in any system. I doubt that Clines has his finger on the best points of coherence, however.

16. Clines, "Arguments," pp. 201–2.

17. Like most others, Clines implicitly changes the text, omitting the conjunction on *tōm*: "Is not your piety your source of confidence? / Does not your blameless life give you hope?"

18. Fullerton, "Double Entendre."

19. See ibid., p. 336.

20. The meaning of "stolen" (y^{e}*gunnab*) might be the privacy of visionary experience, the allegation that someone is "leaking" divine secrets, or the god's bypassing normal communication channels. The first of those seems to me clearly present in the passage, but "stolen" does not point unmistakably to it. I suspect that Eliphaz implicitly claims special access to divine knowledge, yet the passive verb form throws that interpretation into doubt.

21. See Chap. 5.

22. Notice how much like a prophetic oracle, e.g., Isa 2.6–22, is Eliphaz's depiction of justice in 5.9–16. The promise of retribution, both in punishment and in restoration, is a constant theme in the prophets. Roberts ("Israelite Religious Tradition") argues that we do not need Israel's retributive doctrine to explain the idea in Job, because it was an idea common to the ancient world and the friends' version of it is more individualistic than that of the prophets: "Neither party in the debate sounds anything like the classical prophets" (p. 112). I refer to Isa 2 precisely to disagree with that statement, though Eliphaz says something quite different from Isaiah, even while "sounding" like him. The notion of divine retribution was indeed common to the ancient Near Eastern world, and later retributionism transferred the idea simplistically to individual experience, with devastating effects on moral perception. Still, the fact that both Deuteronomy and Job were written in Hebrew justifies our thinking that Deuteronomy lies closer to Job than, say, Babylonian wisdom literature does.

23. Irwin ("Examination") argued that the issue of retributive justice has been overdone in the discussion of Job, and his article on chap. 8, "First Speech of Bildad," written at about the same time, rewrote that speech by means of textual criticism so as greatly to reduce the retributionism.

24. See Terrien, *Job*, p. 80, *n*4 (his reference there to 4.17 is a typo for 5.17).

25. Some accounts of the structure of Job's argument (e.g., Cox, p. 53; Thompson, pp. 54–55; Terrien, *IB*, p. 892, and *Job*, p. 79) analyze this speech as continuing chap. 3 without reference to Eliphaz, proposing a leapfrogging structure between statement and reply, in which Job answers Eliphaz in chaps. 9–10, Bildad in chaps. 12–14, Zophar in chaps. 16–17, and so on. Granted that the participants in the dialogue do a great deal of talking past each other, I think that the cross-references among the speeches are more complicated than the simple leapfrog pattern would suggest.

26. Macdonald (*Hebrew Literary Genius*, chap. 3, esp. p. 25) thinks that the entire dialogue presents the thoughts of the poet, and we must therefore identify the poet with Job. Would that it were so easy to approach the truth. I do not wish to disparage Macdonald. With Richard Moulton, he was the earliest in this century to attempt a genuinely literary examination of the Hebrew Bible. He was, moreover, better equipped than Moulton for the task, being a Hebraist and an Arabist of the first rank.

27. *Ṣedeq* is often translated "righteousness." I translate it "innocence"

most of the time because it frequently signifies a legal decree acquitting an accused person of a charge, and I think that in Job it more often denotes the legal claim than the moral one.

28. See JPS; Pope, *Job*, p. 49; S. R. Driver and Gray, Pt. I, p. 67.

29. So Skehan, "Strophic Patterns," p. 103; and Fohrer, *Das Buch Hiob*, p. 175. Others (e.g., Pope, *Job*, p. 60; S. R. Driver and Gray, Pt. I, p. 69; and Habel, *Book of Job*, pp. 159–60) find the beginning of the address to the god only in v. 7. The singular imperative there makes it certain.

30. In its reference to time, 7.1–6 is more like 6.8–13, with its wish for an end and the impossibility of extending life, than like any other part of chap. 6. Because 7.1–6 corresponds in theme to the first stanza of the poem proper, the case could be made that 7.7 begins the address to the deity. I remain uncertain about this matter. The verb *qwh* ("counts on," 7.2b) and its cognate noun *tiqwah* ("hope," 7.6b), together with *baśar* ("flesh," 7.5a), also connect this stanza verbally with 6.8–13 (see vv. 8b, 12b), and the "hardened" skin (7.5c) reminds us of the "bronze" flesh (6.12b).

31. The comparison to Enoch is Habel's (*Book of Job*, p. 161).

32. Pope (*Job*, p. 59) refers to that mythology, found in the Babylonian creation myth. See *ANET*, p. 68.

33. Clines, "Arguments," p. 206.

34. The friends differ among themselves, not only in personality but also in viewpoint, and I now think I understated the differences in *Irony*. Clines ("Arguments," p. 209) justly says, "If they all have the same point to make, the book is indeed long-winded and flabby."

35. See Chap. 2.

36. See the annotation to the translation of 8.4.

37. The omnipresent *yašar*. But Bildad is not nearly so certain as Yahweh was (1.8; 2.3) that Job *is* moral.

38. Habel (*Book of Job*, pp. 167, 175) points out that *šḥr* is often used cultically of an eager, diligent search for the deity.

39. Verse 6b has a fine alliteration of *'ayin*: *kī-'attah ya'īr 'aleyka*. "Repay" (*šillam*) suggests the return of health (*šalōm*) to the dwelling (*nawah*), a word that Eliphaz used in a different sense (5.3b, 24b), and "innocence" (*ṣedeq*) is "righteousness," which Bildad used of the deity in 8.3b.

40. Irwin ("Examination," p. 155) proposed that the latter point was the central intent of the friends, but this ignores the movement of thought through which the friends go. Clines's more subtle account of the friends' intentions shows both how the friends differ from each other and how each is coherent with himself, but he too thinks there is no "development in the position, theology, or argument of Job's friends" ("Arguments," p. 213). My readings of later speeches will demonstrate wherein I think Clines is mistaken on that count.

41. The larger structure of the speech, which is unusually symmetrical, can be exhibited as follows:

A (vv. 2–10)
1. vv. 2–4 (6 lines in couplets)
2. vv. 5–7 (7 lines, couplet-tercet-couplet)
3. vv. 8–10 (6 lines in couplets)
B (vv. 11–22)
1. vv. 11–13 (6 lines in couplets)
2. vv. 14–15 (4 lines in couplets)
3. vv. 16–17 (4 lines in couplets)
4. vv. 18–19 (4 lines in couplets)
5. vv. 20–22 (6 lines in couplets)

The first four stanzas of the second part, moreover, present an intricate, partly chiastic set of images:

A plants (vv. 11–12)
B paths (v. 13)
C house (v. 14b)
C house (v. 15a)
A′ plants (vv. 16–17a)
C house (v. 17b)
C′ place (v. 18a)
B′ way (v. 19a)
A plants ("sprout," v. 19b)

This ties the first four stanzas nicely together, but it leaves out the fifth, unless one rings in the rather different image of the "tent" (v. 22b). My structure differs from Skehan's seven strophes ("Strophic Patterns," pp. 99, 103). His analysis of vv. 14–19 misses the connection between vv. 16 and 17. Skehan would disagree that this speech is *unusually* symmetrical. He finds astonishingly regular formal structures everywhere, but as I attempt to follow them through the text, I find them trampling across lines of distinction that I wish to preserve. My structure also differs from Habel's (*Book of Job*, p. 170), which centers on a *topos* of "appeal to ancient tradition" in vv. 8–20.

42. My student Jacqueline Bocian noted a parallel with the quickly growing and dying plant over which Jonah becomes "angry enough to die" (Jon 4.9). The tone of the irony seems different, but the comparison is suggestive.

43. Pope (*Job*, pp. 66–67) justifies an emendation that comes out to "gossamer." One would like the word to mean just that, but I refuse to emend to get it.

44. See *n*25 above.

45. See Westermann, *Structure*, pp. 73–74. The actions are expressed in Hebrew participles, the verbal noun of the actor (hence "[the one] who" does the action).

46. My point of similarity requires no conclusion on the question whether the Second Isaiah influenced the Book of Job or vice versa. See the discussion in the "Dispensable Introduction."

47. Two slight differences of diction between the two passages do not damage the perception that 9.10 quotes 5.9.

48. No extant texts narrate a myth about Rahab, but allusions in Isa 51.9; Ps 89.11 (Eng. 10); and Job 26.12 to creation by combat, like that of Marduk against Tiamat in the Babylonian creation text, indicate that there was such a myth. Isaiah sarcastically identifies Egypt as a kind of anti-Rahab, "Rahab who sits still" (Isa 30.7). See Gordis, *Book of Job*, p. 105.

49. Pope (*Job*, p. 72), like several others, thinks that the verb *swp* is not suitable for a windstorm (*śeʿarah*), and repoints the storm to a "hair" (*śaʿarah*), which he finds a closer parallel to *ḥinnam*, "for no reason," in v. 17b. The chimera of "synonymity" in parallelism is to be opposed at every turn. I do not see why "trampling down," the sense of the verb in Gen 3.15, is metaphorically inappropriate to a storm. As a boy in Ohio, I often saw wheatfields that wind or a rainsquall had "trampled down." Moreover, we ought not give up the connection to be made to this storm by the one referred to, with the same word, spelled with *samek* instead of *śin*, in 38.1.

50. The lower-case "p" does not refer to the character titled *haśśaṭan* in chaps. 1–2.

51. Pope (*Job*, p. 75) shows the connotation, without referring to *Inferno*, Canto 6. In Elihu's speeches (especially 33.18–30), the same word seems to refer to the place of the dead, though Elihu does not think of the Pit as a place of punishment, as Dante does.

52. A human being may complain bitterly to the deity, as Job does, argue with the deity as Abraham (Gen 18) and Moses (Exod 3) do, or accuse the deity of wrongs, as Habakkuk does (Hab 1). Such interchange does not alter the difference between divine and human. The thought that a deity might beget a child with a human mother, as with Achilles in Homer or Gilgamesh in Mesopotamia, would be abhorrent to ancient Israel. That might have some bearing on the strange tale in Gen 6.1–4 (on which see Ronald S. Hendel, "Of Demigods and the Deluge: Toward an Interpretation of Genesis 6:1–4," *JBL* 106 [1987]: 13–26). There is, of course, the difficult statement about humans created "in the image of God" in Gen 1.26–27, but that phrase does not propose equality of power or substance.

53. See the annotation to 9.33 on whether "there is no" (*lōʾ*) might be read "would that there were" (*lū*).

54. Cf. Job 39.11, 16, and the cognate verb in 2 Sam 23.10; Isa 40.28, 30; etc.

55. So NEB; Clines, "Arguments," pp. 206–7; Gordis, *Book of Job*, p. 121; Habel, *Book of Job*, p. 203.

56. Clines, "Arguments," p. 206.

57. I wish the Hebrew expression in 11.8a were not *gobhe šamayim*, "heights of the sky," but, with Vulgate, *excelsior Caelo*, assumed by Fohrer (*Das Buch Hiob*, p. 221), Gordis (*Book of Job*, p. 122), Guillaume (*Studies*, pp. 89–90), and others to represent *gebōhah miššamayim*, "higher than the sky." It is not my duty to repair Zophar's stylistic failings for him.

58. Clines ("Arguments," pp. 201–3) properly calls these promises a topos.

Chapter 4

1. See the annotation to 12.8 for "plants."

2. See the annotation to 13.4. JPS's "quacks" is the gist of it.

3. The expression *nś' panīm*, "to lift the face," has to do with showing partiality in a trial. The expression may derive from the idea of noticing the identity of litigants; the image of blindfolded Justice implies the same idea.

4. See the annotation to 13.8 for the pun involving "weight" (*śᵉ'ēt*). "Final decision" (v. 10a) is another form of *ykḥ*.

5. *Zikkarōn* is strange. "Memories" seems wrong, "memorials" (cf. the commemorative monument of stones in the Jordan, Josh 4.7, and the commemorative altar covering, Num 17.4–5 [Eng. 16.39–40]), makes no sense. JPS translates "your briefs," a legal term, which might suggest something approaching "memoranda," but I find no parallel to the usage. Because *zikkarōn* can apparently refer also to "mentioning" something, it may continue the speech-silence dichotomy.

6. The annotation justifies this translation of 13.15, which differs from others.

7. Verse 21b, *wᵉ'ēmatka 'al-tᵉba'ᵃtannī*, is nearly identical to what Job wished of the "arbiter" in 9.34b, put, however, in the third person, with "terror" as the nominative: *wᵒ'ēmatō 'al-tᵒba'ᵃtannī*. I take the verb here as second-person masculine singular.

8. I do not understand why Gordis (*Book of Job*, p. 146) thinks that "bitter things" is "manifestly inappropriate" for *mᵉrōrōt*.

9. "Stocks" may not be the meaning of the word *sad*, which occurs elsewhere only in Elihu's quotation of this passage, 33.11. I have been unable to satisfy myself that punishment in stocks was used in the ancient Near East.

10. Most interpreters take "open your eyes" to mean a careful look, "fix the gaze" (JPS), and the demonstrative *zeh* in the expression *'ap-'al-zeh* to refer to Job ("Is it upon this person?"). I take *'ap-'al-zeh* to mean "Is it for this reason?" referring to the human ephemerality that the prior images propose. To be sure, *'ap* can also mean "anger," and "anger over this?" adds a dimension of incredulity to the statement.

11. Arguments that *rṣh* means "to complete" (e.g., Gordis, *Book of Job*, p. 148; see also Dhorme, p. 198; Hölscher, p. 37) rest primarily on a perceived inappropriateness of "enjoy," which I do not share.

12. Job uses the verb in 7.11 and 13, and the noun *śīaḥ* in 9.27; 10.1; 21.4; and 23.2.

13. In 1 Ki 18.27, Elijah suggests sarcastically that the silent Baal, for whom Jezebel's prophets are shouting, is off "meditating" in an outhouse.

14. Cf., e.g., Jer 23.18, 22; 1 Ki 22.19–23.

15. The verb, *tigra'*, is the same as the one I translated "constraining" in v. 4b. Tur-Sinai (p. 246) interprets it as "stolen" in both places, though he gives it a quite different connotation in 36.7. The basic sense of the verb seems to be to "diminish," and the twin notions of constraint and constriction carry it a bit further. But the image of theft—a Promethean motif—would suggest that Job cannot claim legitimately to be in the divine council.

16. Dhorme, p. 212.

17. I agree with most scholars in taking *qᵉdōšīm* here and in 5.1 as superhuman, something like what will later be called angels. If the word were *qᵉdēšīm*, "sacred male prostitutes," however, the picture would be somewhat different. One might almost wish that Eliphaz had mispronounced the word—or perhaps *qᵉdōšīm* is the mispronunciation.

18. One might twist the passage into what seems conceptual unity by taking *kī* in vv. 25 and 27 not as the emphatic conjunctive particle "for" that I have used, but as a relative particle, "because." In that case (see, e.g., Dhorme, pp. 219–22), v. 29 is the result of the opening conditional clauses. To paraphrase: "Because he fought against the god, because he is so wickedly prosperous, his prosperity will be temporary." The unity of the concept is illusory, however. The images of prosperity and of battling against the god remain very different from the preceding images.

19. I disagree with Clines ("Arguments," p. 202) that in this speech Eliphaz "is clearly maintaining that Job is *not* one of the truly wicked." He is right that the topos on the fate of the wicked (topoi, if my perception of the shift at v. 25 is right) does not by itself prove that Eliphaz applies the picture to Job. The language around it, and especially, but not solely, v. 16, persuades me that Eliphaz does refer the subject to Job, or, if he is trying not to do so, he fails. The absence of encouragement in the speech also suggests that Clines's concluding comment (p. 213), that "the author of Job does not portray any development in the position, theology, or argument of Job's friends," needs modification. Certainly the theology does not change. But I think that on the basis of his consistent, rigid theology, Eliphaz does change his argument to and about Job. He has changed (and confused) it here, and he will do it again in chap. 22.

20. I do not mean that the later addresses to the god in chaps. 30, 40, and 42 are unimportant. What interests me is the structural fact that beginning here Job drastically reduces the scope of his direct talk to the deity.

21. Any explanation of that remarkable metaphor would be lame. The commentators with one accord turn the metaphor into its tenor, interpreting it as "glare" or something similar.

22. Cf. Num 23.22; Deut 33.17; Jer 48.25; etc.

23. *Za'ᵃqah* may be cognate to *ṣō'ᵃqīm*, "crying out," in Gen 4.10.

24. There was once an interpretive consensus that in this "witness" the deity split himself in two, as it were, in order both to maintain the legal order and to stand compassionately on Job's side. Some scholars still hold that view, but I find

it quite opposed to the context, and it seems an effort only to preserve Job's positive relationship to the deity. The text, especially of v. 20, is difficult, to be sure, but the difficulty does not, in my view, encourage claims for a divine schizophrenia. Its main feature is the difficult preposition *'el*, "to," which I attach to the nouns describing the witness. Others take *'el 'ᵉloah*, "to Eloah," with the following verb, usually taking *dlp* as in Eccl 10.18 to mean "drip," therefore "weep." I take *dlp* as "to be sleepless" as in Ps 119.28.

25. See Boecker, *Redeformen*, pp. 45–47 on *ykḥ* in these senses. Following Horst, *Hiob*, p. 253, he translates: "Er bring' des Menschen Streit mit Gott zurecht" (He sets the human's quarrel with God to rights).

26. The use of the preposition *lᵉ* after *bēn* ("between") to define the second term of the pair is unusual but not incorrect. Thus the seeming parallel in the two lines between *lᵉgeber* and *lᵉrē'ēhū* is not there.

27. So Horst, *Hiob*, p. 253. This reading of the word throws two opposed legal senses of *rēa'* at us in a very short space. Clearly *rē'ī* in v. 20a is as much the advocate in the trial as *rē'ēhū* in v. 21b is the opponent. That opposition is confusing, but it cannot be ruled out.

28. I retain MT's *'orbēnī*, the Qal infinitive, rather than repointing to the noun, either *'erbōnī* or *'erᵉbōnī*. Not that it makes any difference.

29. Several scholars (e.g., Gordis, *Book of Job*, pp. 181–82; Dhorme, pp. 245–46) think that *yaggīd* is "invite" and find an idea of inviting friends to share goods; others (e.g., Habel, *Book of Job*, p. 266; Pope, *Job*, p. 129; S. R. Driver and Gray, pp. 151–52) find a basic idea of "informing on" in the word, as does RSV. *Yaggīd* is "inform, tell," but I do not think it means "inform on, give evidence against." The counterinstance sometimes adduced in Jer 20.10 is shown by William L. Holladay (*Jeremiah 1: A Commentary on the Book of the Prophet Jeremiah Chapters 1–25*, Hermeneia series [Philadelphia, 1986], pp. 555–56) to mean not "denounce" but "announce," not underhanded toadying but open declaration. Terrien (*IB*, pp. 1029–31) gives up on all readings and thinks the text corrupt.

30. Gordis (*Book of Job*, Special Note 14, pp. 524–25) thinks that in vv. 8–9 Job suddenly realizes that suffering is not necessarily a punishment for sin, nor is the sight of a good person's suffering a block to genuine virtue. Though genuinely righteous people will be shocked at Job's calamity, they will nevertheless persist with their righteousness. I am impressed with the doctrine, but I think Gordis too quickly moves some details of the text in the direction of his view, especially the preposition *'al* in v. 8b, which JPS has rendered "against." And I see v. 10 as related more closely to vv. 8–9 than to v. 11. But better Gordis's reading than those that simply drop vv. 8–10 from the text (cf. Mitchell's failure of nerve, p. 112, in referring to "the wreckage of this chapter").

31. See *Irony*, p. 219.

32. The LXX reads singular verbs in vv. 2–3, and S. R. Driver and Gray (Pt. II, p. 116) apparently adopted the singular on the basis of the Greek. Pope

(*Job*, p. 133) changes the forms but is ambiguous as to the reason. Gordis (*Book of Job*, p. 190) speculates about a convention of plural address, as in Song of S 5.1, but seems unconvinced. Guillaume (*Studies*, p. 99) takes the plural as "a mark of politeness" but does not wonder why it appears only here.

33. Weiser (p. 136) proposes that Bildad addresses Job together with what he calls "a larger fictive audience" (*eine grössere fiktive Hörerschaft*), which Job has called into play in 17.6, 8–9. Because I disagree with him about those verses in Job's previous speech, I agree with Fohrer's response to his fiction: "improbable" (*Das Buch Hiob*, p. 300, *n*3).

34. Though the friends speak directly to Job and he to them, they never address each other by name. Only Elihu both refers to and calls Job by name.

35. Pope, *Job*, p. 134.

36. This seems an allusion to the birth of Jacob, given the similarity of language between Bildad's *yōʾḥēz bᵉʿaqēb* and *ʾōḥezet bᵉʿaqēb* in Gen 25.26. The snare "snatches" at the wicked person as Jacob's hand "snatched" at Esau's heel.

37. See the annotation to v. 20.

38. Ten was a round, relatively large number in many cultures, Israel's included, and the expression "ten times" (*ʿeśer pᵉʿamīm*) occurs several times as an inexact round number. Cf. Gen 31.7, 41; Neh 4.6 (Eng. 4.12); and perhaps Num 14.22.

39. See the annotation to 19.3.

40. Cf. "troops," *rabbīm*, 16.13; "gangs" in 19.12, *gᵉdūdaw*, often refers to raiding parties and the like.

41. Gordis (*Book of Job*, p. 201) points out the military connection but misses the disparity between the scope of the operation and its objective.

42. If I could find another passage where I thought the sense "to trick" was apt for *ʿwt*, I would use that meaning here. This is the verb with which Bildad denied that the deity "bends" justice or right (8.3).

43. The word sometimes has a connotation of perjury, as in Exod 23.1; Deut 19.16; Ps 35.11; and Hab 1.3.

44. Lambert, p. 35. For other translations, see *ANET*, pp. 434–37, 596–600.

45. E.g., Ps 31.12–14 (Eng. 11–13); 38.12–13 (Eng. 11–12); etc. See Weiser, p. 146.

46. Interpreters who take as their task understanding the poet, as distinct from the poem, argue that, because the poet knows that the children are dead (see 8.4), the rather odd expression here (*bᵉnē biṭnī*, "sons of my belly or womb") means "sons of my [mother's] womb," hence "my brothers." Then they must show that "my brothers" (*ʾaḥay*) in 19.13a means something else. See, e.g., Terrien, *IB*, pp. 1046–47. The problem stems from the principle of consistency, which I discussed in Chap. 1.

47. That verb refers to the unity of wife and husband, "cleaving to each other," in Gen 2.24.

48. This verb appears in the Prosecutor's proposal that Yahweh "touch"

Job's possessions (1.11) and his person (2.5), and in the messenger's narration about the wind that "touched" the house where Job's children were (1.19).

49. See the annotation to 19.23 on "inscription." I envision an inscribed tablet of wood or stone.

50. Already in the Middle Ages, Rashi, the great Jewish commentator, proposed that this was what "with an iron stylus and lead" meant. Some scholars (e.g., Dhorme, p. 282) have argued that no such technology was known, but Pope (*Job*, p. 144) refers to the technique in part of the Behistun inscription. *'ēṭ* is the usual word for "pen," but iron was not the usual material for pens.

51. I agree with the basic views of Terrien (*IB*, pp. 1051–53) and Pope (*Job*, p. 146), though I would put the matter rather differently from them. Gordis's trenchant counterargument (*Book of Job*, pp. 204–6, 526–28) shows that he has seriously considered the alternative I propose and has rejected it for reasons compelling to him. He finds a radical reversal on Job's part comprehensible and religiously moving. I do not. If Job makes here the move to profound faith that Gordis attributes to him, his return in the rest of the dialogue to angry opposition to the god is incredible. If this line expresses his "assurance of future vindication" (p. 205), the later anger sounds like adolescent stridence, and I wonder that Yahweh wastes a whirlwind on it.

52. Translated by H. L. Ginsberg in *ANET*, 3rd ed., p. 140. The reference is the tablet referred to there as I AB, col. iii, ll. 8–9 (G. R. Driver, *Canaanite Myths and Legends*, gives it as Tablet III). With respect to Job, see Terrien, *IB*, p. 1053; Gordis, *Book of Job*, p. 205. Given the problem with tenses in Hebrew and Ugaritic, it is difficult to know whether these two passages are comparable. The word order is different, the Ugaritic has no emphatic pronoun, and its verb "to know" is in the prefixed, or "imperfect," tense, whereas the Hebrew has the suffixed, or "perfect," tense. Coogan (p. 112) translates the line, "Then I will know that Baal the Conqueror lives."

53. Those who use the Canaanite texts to interpret the Book of Job have concentrated on linguistic detail, and I know of none who has pondered the parallel between Job's fall and rise and that of Baal and other dying and rising gods. I want to do no more than point to the pattern common to both, for there are other structures of fall and rise than that of the fertility god, e.g., the common structure of comedy from Aristophanes to the present (cf. Whedbee; and my article, "Apocalyptic as Comedy: The Book of Daniel," *Sem* 32 [1984]: 41–70). Still, I wish anyone well who wants to pursue the thought of Job as Baal-Adonis-Tammuz.

54. Day, pp. 100–101.

55. Day (p. 99) argues that uses of *'apar*, "dust," in 17.16; 20.11; and 21.26 point to its meaning the grave. She assumes that "stand up" (or "rise," *qūm*) means that the Avenger will rescue Job from the grave. I find v. 25b too obscure to interpret with confidence.

56. Day applies the same point to the "witness" in 16.19, and I saved it for here because I find the implied irony more interesting here.

57. Pope (*Job*, p. 153) refers to Dahood's interpretation of the same phrase,

qešet n^e^ḥūšah, in Ps 18.35 (Eng. 34) (= 2 Sam 22.35), as the "miraculous bow." Dahood takes *n^e^ḥūšah* from the root *nḥš* meaning "to practice divination," and refers to Aqhat's wonderful bow made by Kothar the artisan-god in the Canaanite Aqhat story. Without explaining why, Dahood (*Psalms I*, p. 115) distinguishes the phrase in Ps 18 from this one and does not venture to explain this bow. The bow in the Aqhat story has no function as a weapon, being but an object for whose acquisition its owner, Aqhat, is killed. If Zophar alludes to the Aqhat tale (and I would not deny that he might), it is a flawed allusion. Perhaps that is why Dahood saw no "miraculous bow" in Job 20.24.

58. See Terrien, *IB*, pp. 1063–64, among others.

59. See the phrase *yōm 'ap YHWH*, Zeph 2.2.

Chapter 5

1. I owe this idea to a suggestion of Chaplain (Major) Janet Y. Horton, USA, made when she was a graduate student at Stanford. Day's reading (pp. 88–101), that the audience would ironically contrast the "witness" and the "avenger," along with the "arbiter" (9.33), with the Prosecutor, does not change the notion.

2. Terrien, *IB*, p. 1065; Dhorme, p. 308; Gordis, *Book of Job*, p. 228; Pope, *Job*, p. 157; Habel, *Book of Job*, p. 326; S. R. Driver and Gray, Pt. I, p. 182; Kissane, p. 135; Rowley, *Job*, p. 146; Weiser, p. 164.

3. Interpreters have differed on this important point. Job and the friends agree on the basic structure of divine retribution (see Reventlow, p. 283, among others), and that very agreement sharpens the disagreement between Job and the friends about what is happening to Job. Without the retributive assumption, Job's development of thought and the depth of his anger make no sense.

4. The interrogative sense is possible in the absence of an interrogative particle, a possibility that introduced the interesting complexity into 2.10.

5. Dhorme, p. 314; Terrien, *IB*, p. 1068; Tur-Sinai, p. 328. Rowley (*Job*, p. 149) thinks rightly that "this reduces the line to a platitude," but we need not be aggressive toward all platitudes. Blommerde (*Northwest Semitic Grammar*, p. 92) does not need LXX to justify taking the suffix on *mennī* as the third person; his own method is sufficient.

6. I set v. 19a as a question, as does Pope, *Job*, p. 156, making it an attribution to the friends. RSV, Gordis (*Book of Job*, p. 224), and Habel (*Book of Job*, p. 321) interpolate "You say" (Habel, "You may say"), in order to make the attribution clear.

7. One is reminded of the Greek myths of the Fates, one of whom snips the thread of a person's life, or draws it off the spindle, at the moment of death. There are some uncertainties whether the image in *ḥṣṣ*, "cut off," is of cutting.

8. Terrien, *IB*, p. 1070: "The fact of death reveals less the equality of all men than the injustice of their destiny, and consequently the irresponsibility of God."

9. The echo in the two occurrences of *ybl* with the earlier picture of wicked

people's "wearing out" (y^e*ballū*, from the root *bll*) their lives (v. 13a) is another reason for adopting that reading there.

10. *Hebel* is the word usually translated "vanity" in Qoheleth (Ecclesiastes). See *Irony*, pp. 176–83. Its sound makes it another echo of the y^e*ballū-yūbal-yūbalū* group of words.

11. The verb is *tmm*, cognate to *tam*, "perfection," of which we have heard so much. It is possible that v. 3b refers to "profit" not for the god but for Job, in parallel to v. 2b, referring to a wise person's benefit to himself.

12. The annotation to v. 4b refers to an alternative rendering: "[Does he] enter trial against you?" In that case, "justice" (*mišpaṭ*) in the second line is not syntactically parallel to "religiousness" in the first, but the whole second line expresses a parallel to "charge," the legal term. My version of the line is simply somewhat more biting.

13. Gordis, *Book of Job*, p. 238.

14. See Westermann, *Basic Forms*, esp. pp. 129–94.

15. There is, of course, nothing wrong with a fiction within a fiction. But Eliphaz's concoction is more troublesome than Hamlet's play "wherein I'll catch the conscience of the king," because, though Eliphaz too thinks of catching Job's conscience, he seems not to be aware that he is perpetrating a secondary fiction. That upsets the balance of the book's world.

16. Westermann, *Basic Forms*, p. 146. Westermann also refers to Boecker, *Redeformen*. Fohrer (*Das Buch Hiob*, p. 353) gives the two sections the technical, form-critical names as prophetic speeches: vv. 6–9 are a *Scheltwort* against an individual, vv. 10–11 (he extends this section to v. 14) the expected *Drohwort*. See also Murphy, p. 34.

17. The presence of that metaphoric opposition leads me to reject Skehan's contention ("Strophic Patterns," p. 111), that v. 8 does not belong where it is. It is precisely not, as Skehan says, "out of harmony with the otherwise complete stanza in which we find it."

18. Eliphaz's *gōbah šamayim* is singular, Zophar's *gobhē šamayim* plural. It seems inaccurate to render 22.12a with JPS, "Eloah is in the heavenly heights," because the line is a question and lacks a preposition corresponding to "in." The statement may indicate more astral religion among the ancient Israelites than we have perceived.

19. Cf. 7.19–20; 13.27; 14.3, 6; 16.9.

20. Gordis (*Book of Job*, p. 248) takes v. 18b as a ritual formula disavowing these sinful ideas, and therefore he need not find a logical connection that may not be there.

21. I am not sure whether the metaphor of the deity as treasure was a cliché in those days or whether it strikes me as one from hearing too many preachers use it too often. So does intertextuality interfere with interpretive certainty.

22. The emendation of *yadī*, "my hand," to *yadō*, "his [the god's] hand," opposes the subsequent motif of the divine absence.

23. *'ēnennū*; Job used the same word of himself in 7.8, 21.

24. The idea is not unlike Jung's portrait in *Answer to Job* (esp. pp. 34–55) of the pre-Joban Yahweh, a god whose mind and emotions are completely separated from each other.

25. So, among others, RSV; JPS; Gordis, *Book of Job*, p. 263; and Mitchell, p. 60. Pope (*Job*, p. 175) does not fill out the translation, but he refers to the "days of decision" in the opening narrative (1.6; 2.1). The point about *'ēt* is, I believe, the regularity of the time, its expectability if not predictability. The parallel "days" reminds us of the shifting "days" in chaps. 1–2 and the "day" that Job cursed in chap. 3.

26. They are (1) in v. 16a, "In the dark they dig," the verb, *ḥatar*, is singular; (2) in v. 16b, "they shut themselves up," the phrase *ḥittᵉmū-lamō* is difficult, but the suffix on *lamō* is singular and does not permit "themselves"; (3) in v. 17a, "deep darkness is morning to all of them," again *lamō* requires "to him"; (4) in v. 17b, "they are friends," the verb *yakkīr* is singular; and, most remarkable of all, (5) in v. 18a: "they are swiftly carried away," the Hebrew has *qal-hū'*, "swift is he," and the presence of *hū'* makes "he" emphatic. These five are by no means the only instances of such rewriting, nor is the RSV the sole offender. JPS agrees with all of these plurals, though the translators note at the beginning of v. 18 that their translation to the end of the chapter is "largely conjectural."

27. The line "Naked they lodge, without clothing" (v. 7a) rings oddly in a stanza about wild asses. I think that the line prepares for v. 10a, which describes the poor in the same terms, and the repetition emphasizes Job's behavioral analogy between the wild beasts and humans outside of divine care and presence.

28. Some scholars change *la'ōr*, "at light" (v. 14a), to *lō' 'ōr*, "not [yet] light," i.e., "before light" (so S. R. Driver and Gray, Pt. II, p. 169, followed by Mitchell, p. 118), and others think that *'ōr* must have a later Mishnaic meaning, "nightfall" (Gordis, *Book of Job*, p. 268). Pope (*Job*, p. 178) appeals to a Ugaritic separative sense of *lᵉ*, which allows "at light" to mean "from light," i.e., "at twilight."

29. I explained in the introduction why I would not reconstruct Zophar's speech. The text is readable as it stands, and if it were not, we should simply have to leave it unread. Were I to cobble together Zophar's speech, it would be a fiction of my invention.

30. I am indebted for this perception too to Chaplain Horton (see *n*1 above).

31. The expression for "help" is "with whom" (*'et-mī*).

32. I expressed doubt above that 21.3b is addressed to the prior speaker.

33. The repetition of words from 24.7, 10 suggests the connection between the two thoughts: *'arōm*, "naked," appears in all three passages, and *'ēn kᵉsūt*, "no covering," in both 24.7 and 26.6b. Sheol and Abaddon, places of the dead, are weak and oppressed like the wild asses and the unguided humans of chap. 24.

34. See Job 9.13; Ps 89.10; Isa 30.7; 51.9–10.

35. Some doubt must remain about this point, given the uncertainty of *šiprah* in v. 13a. The stilling of Sea, the smashing of Rahab, and the piercing of the Dragon in the immediate context all suggest allusion to a myth of cosmic combat.

36. Perhaps it is not the first time. Diewert argues that in 7.12 Job skews the combat myth with a "guarding" that changes its meaning. Janzen's reply ("Another Look") casts doubt on that point but suggests that the deity proposes a new myth of the birth of Sea in 38.8–11.

37. "Godless" is not a good translation of *ḥanēp*, which carries no connotation of a lack of something. See the annotation to 27.8. Job is not talking anything like theoretical atheism.

38. *Irony*, chap. 6.

39. See, among others, Terrien, *IB*, p. 888; Pope, *Job*, p. 191; Gordis, *Book of Job*, pp. 291–96, 536; Dhorme, pp. xlix–li; S. R. Driver and Gray, pp. xxxix–xl, Pt. I, pp. 227–32; Rowley, *Job*, pp. 175–76; Westermann, *Structure*, pp. 93–94*n*, 133.

40. The noun is plural, with a singular possessive, "his widows," though we have heard of no more than one wife.

41. Weiser (pp. 19, 195–96) argues that Job turns the friends' own weapons upon themselves here. He does not explain how vv. 14–23 apply to the friends, nor do I see how it can.

42. Terrien (*IB*, pp. 1099–1100) cogently argues the contrary in terms largely of style and vocabulary, and Habel (*Book of Job*, p. 38) argues it in terms of structure. Both arguments assume the validity of the search for an author as the key to a work.

43. The annotation to 28.12 explains why I personify Wisdom.

44. Greenfield, "Hebrew Bible," p. 556.

45. Habel (*Book of Job*, p. 393) takes the opposite direction, thinking that the framing function of this chapter with 1.1 points away from the thought that wisdom is part of the point. To be sure, Habel is trying to divine the poet's intent. I should like to have it both ways, to say that Wisdom both is and is not Job's claim, but I do not see how to do so.

46. Cox, p. 99: "The world man knows is *radically* absurd. In his [Job's] own experience this is manifested. He is the type of the innocent man of God, who always walked in God's ways; a friend of God—yet he is unable to understand his ways or even to come to him. Man cannot understand the puzzle of the world he experiences. He cannot rely on any absolute norm, for there are no norms. God remains silent, so man is lost in a world without signposts."

Chapter 6

1. This *inclusio* around the dialogue, chaps. 3–31, seems to me structurally significant. Habel (*Book of Job*, p. 393) proposes another between 1.1 and 28.28, resting on the description of Job. He finds the dialogue with the friends through chap. 27 to be a "pre-trial" and thinks that chaps. 29–31 are spoken before "an assumed court" (p. 30), in effect, a trial.

2. Cohering mostly with that proposed by Habel (*Book of Job*, pp. 406–7).

3. Cf. Frye, *Anatomy of Criticism*, pp. 206–22, where tragedy is "the mythos of autumn."

4. *Antony and Cleopatra*, I, 5, l. 73. Even JPS's "When I was in my prime" proposes the wrong image. The literal is often much more interesting than our conventionalities for it.

5. Job's word is *na'ar*, which, as in 1.19, I have translated "youngsters," though in 1.15, 16, and 17, I translated the same word "servants." It has both senses, and perhaps, as in 29.8 in explicit contrast with *y*[e]*šīšīm*, the basic meaning of "youth." Habel (*Book of Job*, p. 409) uniformly translates "servants." I think the presence of 1.19 in the background forces the wider meaning.

6. "Presumably" because, as the annotation to this verse shows, the verb is not intelligible. But *ṣūr yaṣūq* presents a nice alliteration and assonance.

7. The proposal is so common that Habel (*Book of Job*, pp. 402, 409) does not even refer to the presumed re-spelling: "Cream was so plentiful that his feet bathed in it." But Job may not refer to "feet" at all. *H*[a]*līkay* is a hapax legomenon, clearly cognate to *hlk*, "to go, walk," and I have translated it as "steps" to suggest walking rather than the feet that walk.

8. Boecker (*Law*, pp. 31–36) confirms this opinion and notes (pp. 32–33) that Ruth 4.1–2 fictionally pictures legal procedure in the city gate. The officers called "judges" in Judges and 1 Samuel combine military, priestly, and judicial roles. On the other hand, the deity is frequently referred to as *šōpēṭ*, "judge."

9. Some scholars have taken the evidence that Job lived in the city as showing the separate authorships of the "frame tale" in chaps. 1–2 and the poetry. But a sharp distinction between urban and rural life, between city dwellers and people living on farms or ranches or nomadically in the "country" may not have been made in ancient Israel. Farmers, herders, and such folks may well have lived in town and gone out to the country for their daily labor. The familiar phrase, "your going out and your coming in" (Ps 121.8), may refer to just such a daily rhythm of work and home.

10. See also van Praag, p. 176.

11. In 21.5, "lay the hand on the mouth" is a gesture of terrified horror. For another meaning, see 40.4.

12. The uses of the same phrase in Ezek 3.26 and Ps 137.6 appear to mean only being struck dumb. The cumulative effect of the lines in our passage leads to my conclusion that the phrase signifies fear here.

13. Habel, *Book of Job*, p. 407.

14. See the annotation to v. 16. Notice the implicit claim to divinely given wisdom in "investigate" (*ḥqr*), used for mining ore (28.3b) and for the deity's "digging out" Wisdom (28.27b).

15. The "robe" (*m*[e]*'īl*) and "turban" (*miṣnepet*—cognate to *ṣanīp* here) are listed among the high priest's garments in Lev 8.7, 9.

16. *Mešawwēa'*, "crying out," is a not entirely satisfying pun with *šam*[e]*'ah*, "heard," in v. 11a. The "crying out" of the poor calls up Job's hearing and responding in rescue, whereas his own activity correspondingly calls up "hearing" by other ears. In vv. 11–12 is another set of wordplays, in chiastic order: *'ōzen*, "ear," v. 11a, is matched by *'ōz*[e]*r*, "helper," v. 12b, and *'ayin*, "eye," v. 11b, corresponds to *'anī*, "poor," v. 12a.

17. Habel, *Book of Job*, p. 411.

18. See the annotation to v. 18 on the proposal that *ḥōl* means "phoenix." I do not object to the idea that Job might apply a mythic theme to himself—he has done so several times—but I am not persuaded that he uses a phoenix myth that is attested only in Greece, being found in Hesiod and Herodotus.

19. See the use of *kabōd* in Hos 9.11, where it is clearly related to sexual activity. The bow likewise appears in contexts suggesting virility, e.g., Gen 49.24; 1 Sam 2.4 (?).

20. The expression in v. 20a is "new with me" (*'immadī*), which I turned in the translation into "ever new."

21. It is a constant temptation to take Job completely at his own face value. Indeed, one must steel oneself to hear the dissonant overtones. Such shrewd readers of and listeners to Job as Pope and Habel let him suck them in in v. 24. "Those who enjoyed the kindness of Job's lifegiving favor could hardly believe their good fortune" (Habel, *Book of Job*, p. 412); "A smile from Job was regarded by his loyal retainers as such an unmerited and unexpected favor that they could hardly believe their good fortune" (Pope, *Job*, p. 211).

22. Habel is even willing (*Book of Job*, p. 412), inconsistently, I think, to identify "way" (*derek*) as "destiny," and to let Job say that, like (or as?) a deity Job determines the destinies of his underlings—"loyal retainers," if you like Pope's language better.

23. Habel, *Book of Job*, p. 419.

24. Gordis, *Book of Job*, p. 332.

25. It cannot be certain whether the breach is a comparison to the enemies themselves, as I have translated, or whether "like a breach" (*k*^{e}*pereṣ*) means "as [through] a breach," referring to their action.

26. See the annotation to 30.15 on the fact that the first verb, *hohpak*, is singular and its subject, "terrors" (*ballahōt*), is plural.

27. See the annotation to 18.13 for the unusual syntax of this sentence.

28. Habel (*Book of Job*, p. 420) cannot quite decide whether these forces are real or exist only in Job's mind. Perhaps that duality can never be resolved.

29. Bloom (*Anxiety of Influence* and *Map of Misreading*) thinks that such misreading is the way in which the poetic tradition makes its way. I take it that we have neither means nor need to undo the misprision that one writer works on another. Indeed, reading is by definition misreading, so we are always extending the tradition.

30. The phrase "rider of the clouds" is used of Baal in the Ugaritic texts (e.g., *ANET*, p. 130, where the artisan-god Kothar wa-Khasis addresses Baal as "Rider of the Clouds" and promises him victory).

31. See the annotation to 30.22. There may be a sound play in *t*^{e}*šawweh* with *'*^{a}*šawwa'*, v. 20a—leveling and an unsuccessful outcry being related to each other.

32. Habel (*Book of Job*, p. 416) following Dhorme, p. 445, uses the LXX to justify turning the verb into a first-person singular, meaning "I did not attack a

ruin" (Habel emends *'ī*, "ruin," to *'anī*, "poor"). The second line of this couplet is mostly opaque to me.

33. For zither, see the annotation to 30.31.

34. Gordis, *Book of Job*, p. 339. I count not fourteen but fifteen curses, and I think that vv. 19–20 have one curse rather than two. The matter can be argued.

35. See, e.g., Dick, "Oath" and "Legal Metaphor"; and Roberts, "Job's Summons." For a different view of this matter, see Holbert, "Rehabilitation."

36. By far the most sensible account of the structure of this chapter is Habel's (*Book of Job*, pp. 427–31). I disagree with him in detail only, but some of the detail forces a quite different perception of structure. For example, in the interest of a most intriguing, symmetrical outer frame (A: covenant and curse, vv. 1–3; B: challenge, vv. 4–6; C: catalog of crimes, vv. 7–34; B1: challenge, vv. 35–37; A1: covenant witness and curse, vv. 38–40), Habel associates v. 4 not with the questions of vv. 1–3 but with vv. 5–6, partly because the word *ṣa'ad* ("step") occurs both in v. 4b and in v. 37a. I do not think that balance is enough to justify the pursuit of so rigid a symmetry as Habel finds. I see structural uses of the particle *kī*, "for, because," that suggest a division of the whole that is almost too close to symmetry, especially in the light of an often-noticed tendency in Hebrew poetry to skew structures that threaten to become symmetrical.

37. Habel, *Book of Job*, pp. 427–28, 440.

38. See works cited in *n*35; Fohrer, "Righteous Man"; and Janzen, *Job*, pp. 210–13.

39. See my "Job and the Literary Task."

40. Habel, *Book of Job*, p. 431. Janzen's similar but milder metaphor of the "prick of conscience" (*Job*, pp. 210–12) strikes me as even weaker, especially because it seems to find in this chapter nothing more than Job's reflection on himself. Janzen specifically objects to the language of coercion I used in "Job and the Literary Task."

41. Gordis (*Book of Job*, pp. 542–43) claims not that there are fourteen curses, but that Job affirms freedom from fourteen separate sins. I am as interested in the structure of curse combined with statement and question as I am in the ethical content, and I suspect that the structure of fifteen curses combined with eight statements and two groups of questions (totaling, if I count them correctly, six questions) efficiently masks the fourteen sins for readers. I would also quibble with Gordis over reading vv. 1–2 as having to do with lust (I think that the "virgin" refers to the goddess Anat, hence that the sin is false worship, the same sin as in vv. 26–27) and over combining vv. 24–25 into a single sin, where I read "trusting" in gold (v. 24) and "rejoicing" over power (v. 25) as two different bad attitudes.

42. See Gehman, "*Sēper*." *Sēper* is often translated "book," which is anachronistic. Perhaps "document" is our closest equivalent.

43. Habel (*Book of Job*, pp. 231, 438) reads 13.23 as demanding a "bill of particulars," implying a written indictment.

44. Ibid., p. 439.

Chapter 7

1. Gordis (*Book of Job*, p. 358) thinks that Elihu is "probably one of several witnesses to the debate," but no others are ever mentioned. Elihu is familiar with the arguments, and we can accept the fiction that he was present, though only when he appears is there any reason to think of spectators. Schökel ("Dramatic Reading") suggests that Elihu is a spectator at the drama who leaps spontaneously to the stage to become a participant.

2. Gordis, *Book of Job*, p. 366.

3. Habel, *Book of Job*, p. 448. See also the annotation to 32.2. Without emphasizing the relation between the names, Janzen (*Job*, pp. 217–25) discusses Elihu as a caricature of a prophet and the prophetic movement (see *n*31 below). The connection with Elijah's name would strengthen but not establish that point. I disagree with Habel that the associations discussed below have no significance.

4. There are some inconsistencies with respect to this not very central point. In Gen 22.21, Uz is Nahor's son, Buz's brother, and Aram's uncle, but in Gen 10.22–23 he is Aram's son, and Shem's grandson. Gen 36.28 lists Uz as a Horite descendant of Dishan, son of Seir, one of the pre-Edomite clans (and cf. Lam 4.21). Both Uz and Buz (the two words do not rhyme in Hebrew, having different closing consonants: *tsadhe* in Uz and *zayin* in Buz) occur in Jeremiah's message of destruction to many lands (Jer 25), Uz just before the Philistines (v. 20) and Buz among some Edomite names, "Dedan, Tema, . . . and all who cut the corners of their hair" (v. 23). Perhaps we should think of Elihu as having a crew cut. The prophet Ezekiel is also a "son of Buzi" (Ezek 1.3), an uncertain connection with Elihu.

5. Van Selms (p. 119) assures us that they do not: "We should not attempt to interpret his [Elihu's] name—which means 'my God is he' symbolically, for then we would also have to find symbolic explanations for the names Barakel, Buz, and Ram, which, concerning the last two, we cannot do." Perhaps van Selms does not like what he finds when he does.

6. The verb occurs in various forms in Job: 17.4; 22.12; 38.34; 39.27; in the participle in 21.22; 38.15; and perhaps 24.24 (unless that verb is *rmm*).

7. Alternatively: "My-god-he, son of Curse-El, the Contemptuous, of the clan of Exalted." Not much more inviting.

8. Gordis (*Book of Job*, p. 366) points out the declarative force of the form *ṣaddᵉqō*. Job claims innocence (*ṣᵉdaqah*) in 27.6, and Eliphaz (4.17; 15.14) denies that any human can be "righteous" (*ṣdq* in both passages) with respect to the god.

9. Habel (*Book of Job*, pp. 445–46) stresses this.

10. See Habel, *Book of Job*, pp. 36–37; Janzen, *Job*, p. 218; Gordis, *Book of Job*, pp. xxxi–xxxii, 546–52; and Freedman, "The Elihu Speeches," pp. 51–59. Different scholars give rather different reasons for thinking that Elihu belongs integrally to the book (Janzen, for instance, says only that he sees no reason against it and cites Gordis and Freedman on the linguistic problem).

11. Dhorme, p. 485: "It has pleased the author to depict the new speaker

as interminably prosy." See also Whedbee, pp. 18–20, and his characterization of Elihu as an *alazon*, as in Greek Old Comedy, with a twist: "Though there may be 'no fool like an old fool,' Elihu, as a young fool, comes close" (p. 20).

12. Interesting as Schökel's dramatic idea is (see *n* 1 above), it requires almost a literal notion of performance. To those steeped in the European literary tradition, that is a nearly irresistible idea in the presence of a book made up of nothing but speeches. But it remains a European import—fun to drive but perhaps more expensive than we can afford.

13. The primal meaning of *'ap* is "nose" or "nostril." Perhaps because the emotion of anger frequently causes a flaring of the nostrils or heavy breathing through them, the organ itself came to be a metonymy for the feeling.

14. Habel (*Book of Job*, p. 443) wishes to know the author's "intention" that the pun alludes to Elihu's true character. The text's cumulative evidence about Elihu's character is enough.

15. Very close indeed to half: 32.6–33.7 is 52 lines of poetry, 33.8–33 is 57 lines. If we take vv. 31–33 as a kind of coda, the substantive argument of the speech in vv. 8–30 is just 51 lines. Some scholars end the preface at 32.22 (e.g., Habel, Terrien).

16. "You" in v. 6 is plural, though the imperative "Listen" in v. 10 is singular, doubtless aimed at Job.

17. Pope (*Job*, p. 247) explains this phenomenon lamely as Elihu's, or the author's, temperament. Gordis (*Book of Job*, p. 548; cf. p. 371) attributes it to Elihu's youth: "He is worried as to whether he will gain and hold Job's attention and, therefore, addresses him by name." Neither points to anything in the text that connects Elihu's psychological insecurity or his temperament to his calling Job by name. And we certainly cannot read the author's "temperament" from Elihu's speeches. Tur-Sinai (p. 464, 1957 ed.), noting that "there is no real need" for Elihu to address Job by name, simply points to the stylistic difference. I think we can say no more. It is a mere fact in the text.

18. Greenfield ("Hebrew Bible") notes the connection of 32.7, 9 with 12.12.

19. The verb "impart" (*ḥwh*) is used only by Elihu (32.6, 10, 17; 36.2) and Eliphaz (15.17), besides its occurrence in Ps 19.3. Job uses a somewhat unusual noun formation from the root in 13.17.

20. Job's verb for mining rocks and wisdom in 28.3, 27, and for investigating cases in 29.16.

21. Habel (*Book of Job*, pp. 453–54) delightfully points out that Elihu had argued in v. 8 that the "wind" (*rūaḥ*) gives people understanding, but when he describes his own *rūaḥ*, he comes out as a "windbag." "He acts," says Habel, referring to Eliphaz's terms in 15.2, "as no wise man would ever act."

22. Elihu carefully marks this quotation as accurate (v. 8: "But you have said in my ears / [I heard the sound of the words]"), and the last three of the six lines are quite good quotations, as Freedman ("The Elihu Speeches," p. 331) notes. The first three lines (vv. 9–10a) are considerably less like anything Job says than Freedman implies. See the annotations to vv. 9–11.

23. Symmetry is broken in v. 22a, where the word is the second of three words in the line. Broken symmetry has often been noticed in Hebrew poetry, but I have no explanation for it.

24. The verb is *qrb*, "to be near, approach," used, in a few contexts, even for sexual purposes (e.g., Gen 20.4; Lev 18.6).

25. So Weiser, pp. 223–34, proceeding from the Christian certainty that only divine grace can provide a "ransom" from sin.

26. Dhorme (pp. 499–500) translates "to tell a human his morality" as "to reveal to man his duty." Ross (p. 40, *n*13) agrees with Dhorme.

27. Gordis, *Book of Job*, pp. 377–78.

28. Habel, *Book of Job*, p. 470; cf. van Selms, p. 125.

29. See also Habel, *Book of Job*, p. 471.

30. In reconstructing Elihu's speeches, Westermann (*Structure*, p. 141) rests a good bit of weight on the insistence that rhetorically vv. 31–33 must be the introduction to a speech rather than the conclusion. Why should we shield Elihu, the inexperienced rhetorician, against confusing his proemic and perorational styles?

31. Janzen (*Job*, pp. 217–25) makes this point persuasively, though perhaps he misses some additional dimensions in the irony with which Elihu is presented. He adds to the notion of Elihu as prophetic caricature the suggestion that the speeches embody a wider critique of the prophetic tradition. The thought wants a larger development than Janzen has space to give.

32. Westermann (*Structure*, p. 140) identifies the speech as "a lecture by a teacher of wisdom in a circle of the wise" and argues that this removes it entirely from the dramatic fiction of the book as a commentary on Job's speeches. Form-critics seem almost unable to deal with parody or imitation. See Keel's nicely nuanced reference to Procrustes' bed (pp. 27–28) regarding some interpretations of Yahweh's speeches.

33. No one agrees with me in reading these sentences as declarative. Everyone takes the verbs as cohortatives, e.g., JPS: "Let us decide for ourselves what is just; / Let us know among ourselves what is good." The "lengthened" verb forms, *nibḥ*^{a}*rah* and *nēd'ah*, give some justification for that, but the cohortative can also mean a determination to do something (cf. *GK*, pp. 319–20). The hortatory construction would follow from v. 3, which describes the wisdom debate as the testing of words, and it does not damage the ironic relationship between v. 4 and the botched quotations of vv. 5–6. The declarative reading points forward as a contrast to Job's presumed wickedness, demonstrated by his bad companions (v. 8).

34. The order of "intelligent" and "wise" here reverses that in vv. 2 and 10.

35. Verse 3b is difficult. JPS seems to take the preposition "from" as the equivalent of a negative: "What have I gained from not sinning?" RSV: "How am I better off than if I had sinned?" (so also Rowley, *Job*, p. 224). Gordis (*Book of Job*, p. 400) and Habel (*Book of Job*, p. 487) read the preposition as the *mem* of separation: "What is my gain [so Habel] if I avoid sin?" Fohrer (*Das Buch Hiob*,

p. 472) makes the preposition comparative and gets from "more than my sin" to "without my sin." I am not sure how that trick works. Pope (*Job*, p. 263) reads the line as I do, though he does not make clear whether he thinks Elihu is distorting Job.

36. In chiastic order again: *ṣedeq*, v. 2b, *ḥṭ'*, v. 3b; *ḥṭ'*, v. 6a, *ṣdq*, v. 7a.

37. But not by very much. This speech has 112 lines, the first speech (32.6–33.33), 109. Readers interested in statistics may wish to know that the second speech (chap. 34) has 78 lines, and the third (chap. 35) has 30 lines.

38. "Faultless" is, ironically, *tamīm*, that word for perfection whose cognates *tam* and *tōm* we have seen frequently ascribed to Job, both by himself and by others.

39. Dhorme (p. 542), Pope (*Job*, p. 250), and Habel (*Book of Job*, pp. 468–69) agree that *šelaḥ*, which is sometimes taken as a weapon (e.g., JPS's "sword"), means "channel" (or Channel) here.

40. That might be the sense of vv. 17–18, but it is very difficult to say. The connectives are not clear, and one cannot be sure that v. 18 is presented as a consequence of v. 17.

41. The Hebrew Bible does not have a concept corresponding to our culture's notion of "nature" or the "natural" world. With that demurrer, I think our idea is usable nevertheless.

42. Some commentators separate between vv. 7 and 8; Habel (*Book of Job*, p. 496), for example, takes v. 7 as continuing a sentence beginning in v. 6b, and v. 8 as beginning a sentence that continues through v. 9.

43. Gordis (*Book of Job*, pp. 430–31) sees the image as that of a cloudless sky, and Pope (*Job*, p. 286) points out that the sky was conceived as a solid dome above the earth. Nevertheless both Gordis and Pope translate *š^eḥaqīm* as "clouds" in 36.28.

44. Habel, *Book of Job*, p. 515. That assumes that "hammer out," *harqīa'* (related to *raqīa'*, the bowl-shaped "firmament" of the sky in Gen 1.6–7), means "cause to spread out" in a more general sense than its usual "beat down, flatten" (e.g., 2 Sam 22.41; Ezek 6.11). I take the verb as describing the metalsmith who hammers out the cast-bronze mirror.

45. This "delay" is called by various names. Kermode (p. 18) calls it "peripeteia" and discusses it in terms of both confidence in how the story will end and a disconfirmation or upsetting of the confidence along the way. "The interest of having our expectations falsified is obviously related to our wish to reach the discovery or recognition by an unexpected and instructive route." It is, as he says in the same place, a mixture of credulity and skepticism that wishes to find in the peripeteia that the fiction is discovering (precisely—*un*covering) something real we might otherwise have overlooked.

Chapter 8

1. Alter (*Poetry*, p. 87) makes a similar comment. The Yahweh speeches are written in a difficult but fluently idiomatic, powerful Hebrew that makes them

a pleasure to work with. Compared with Elihu's crabbed obscurity, the Yahweh speeches are easy—which is to say that their difficulty lies on a plane different from that of Elihu's.

2. Hebrew chapter and verse numbering. Christian versions begin chap. 41 at Hebrew 40.25.

3. See the Dispensable Introduction on this matter and on my response to it.

4. Respectively, Scott, pp. 159–62; Fingarette, pp. 1611–12; *Irony*, esp. pp. 238–39, and Terrien, *IB*, p. 902; and Gordis, *Book of Job*, pp. 435, 558. This time, I will not propose a good Protestant doctrine of faith. Gordis (*Book of God*, p. 337, *n*23) rightly identified my theological ground. In "Job and the Literary Task," I stepped away from "faith" as the point, and I step even farther away below.

5. Respectively, Carstensen, *Job*, p. 91 (see also MacKenzie, "Purpose," p. 436: "like waving a rattle before a crying infant, to distract him from his hunger"—not exactly "sublime," but certainly "irrelevant"), and Pope, *Job*, p. lxxxi: "seemingly magnificent irrelevance"; Volz, p. 85, and David Robertson, "Book of Job," and, somewhat more subtly, *Old Testament*, pp. 48–49; Briggs, "Job's Response," p. 511; and L. Steiger, "Die Wirklichkeit Gottes in unserer Verkündigung," in *Festschrift H. Diem zum 65. Geburtstag* (Munich, 1965), p. 160, as quoted by Keel, p. 11: "dürftig und leer . . . drei Stunden Naturkunde für Hiob."

6. Ruprecht, "Das Nilpferd," p. 231: "The content of this answer is not important. The only essential thing is that he [God] encountered Job in a theophany and turned toward him as one who also hears the individual person and responds to him" ("Der Inhalt dieser Antwort ist nicht wichtig. Wesentlich ist nur, dass er Hiob in einer Theophanie begegnet und sich ihm zuwendet als einer, der auch den einzelnen Menschen hört und auf ihn eingeht"). Steiger (*n*5), quoted by Keel, p. 14: "*That* God speaks is *everything*. Nothing more is necessary" ("*Dass* Gott redet is *alles*. Mehr bedarf es nicht").

7. Storms are frequent settings for divine appearances in the Hebrew Bible (e.g., Judg 5.4–5; Ps 18.8–16), and *s*[e]*'arah* (whirlwind) is used so in Ezek 1.4 and Zech 9.14. The word also accompanies other divine activities, most often of a destructive sort (e.g., Ezek 13.11, 13; Isa 29.6; Jer 23.19; 30.23) but also less destructive (e.g., Elijah is carried to the sky in a *s*[e]*'arah*, 2 Ki 2.1, 11; cf. Ps 107.25, 29, where the whirlwind is under the deity's control).

8. The word is *ś*[e]*'arah* (as in Nah 1.3), spelled differently from the *s*[e]*'arah* in 38.1, but clearly the same word.

9. The "wreath," *'*[a]*ṭarah*, was a sign of honor for aged, powerful, successful people in Israel; see, e.g., Job 19.9; Lam 5.16; Prov 16.31; Jer 13.18.

10. *Theophany* (Greek *theos*, "god," + *phaneia*, "appearance") is a technical term for any perceptible appearance of a god to humans. See also Habel, *Book of Job*, p. 535.

11. In the annotation to 38.3, I note my dislike of this rendering of *geber*.

12. Some scholars see girding the loins as an allusion to belt-wrestling. See Gordon, "Belt-Wrestling"; Keel, pp. 27 *n*76, 54.

13. So S. R. Driver and Gray, p. 326; Weiser, p. 244 ("Weltregierung"); Gordis, *Book of Job*, p. 442; Rowley, *Job*, p. 241.

14. Dhorme (pp. 574–75) calls this overarching vision of the universe "Providence," which Pope (see *Job*, p. 291) accepted in his first edition and abandoned in the second, and von Rad (*Wisdom*, p. 224) adopts without reference to Dhorme. See also Keel, pp. 53–54 ("Who, then, explains the [world]-plan as dark?" ["Wer erklärt da den (Welt)Plan für dunkel?"]); Habel, *Book of Job*, pp. 536–37 ("Who is this who clouds my design in darkness?"); Janzen, *Job*, p. 231; Mitchell, p. 79 ("Who is this whose ignorant words / smear my design with darkness?").

15. Mitchell's phrase "smear my design with darkness" (see *n*14) points to Yahweh as the artist whose work Job has defaced by making clear lines and outlines unclear or by blotching dark spatters over it. Habel's "clouds my design in darkness" suggests veiling the picture or hiding it. Gordis (*Book of Job*, p. 442) thinks "darkens" (*maḥšīk*) is declarative, as does Keel (see *n*14).

16. For an excellently nuanced account of the connections between the cosmological part of chap. 38 and Job's speech in chap. 3, see Alter, *Poetry*, pp. 96–102.

17. Sea (Yamm) and Death (Mot) are nearly always to be understood as personified forces, not inanimate events. Verses 8–11 make clear that Sea is a personal force. See also Habel, *Book of Job*, p. 538.

18. These are constellations, which I decline to identify with any that we see.

19. Habel (*Book of Job*, p. 539) argues that the "hedging" in 38.10 "counters Job's contention that the limits of God are unfair limitations." "From Job's vantage point such limits are unfair; from God's perspective limits are fundamental to the ordering of things." The unanswered question is whether the limits present in the divine order are right, simply because they are in the divine order. Job complains that the god guards him as if he were Sea (7.12), though he is not Sea but is only Job. If the god actually limits Job in that way and for that reason, the limit is unfair.

20. Alter, *Poetry*, p. 103.

21. Lacocque (pp. 36–37), however, finds Yahweh's universe nearly Newtonian, operating by fixed laws with no personal element in them, though he calls it "demythologized." I am unpersuaded of the near-Deism in "once-for-all set laws" (p. 37), given Yahweh's sarcasm. But Lacocque is certainly right that "ethics is absent from the picture" (p. 36).

22. See the annotation to 40.2. I repoint MT *rōb*, "accusation," to *rab*, "accuser," and *yissōr*, "faultfinder," to *yasūr*, "yield."

23. Dhorme (p. 615), Gordis (*Book of Job*, p. 465), and S. R. Driver and Gray (p. 325) refer to GK, par. 135p, for parallel instances; cf. Fohrer, *Das Buch Hiob*, p. 494. Habel (*Book of Job*, p. 520) comes to the same thing, translating "answer me," an interpretive translation (at least he mentions no emendation in the textual notes).

24. Habel (*Book of Job*, pp. 548–59) is one of very few interpreters who perceive that Yahweh responds to Job's legal challenge. He argues that 40.2 calls on Job to change his view of the divine order and refuses to recognize him as "an equal in court" until he understands the truth about the divine governance. Habel fails to attend to the crucial word *mōkīaḥ*, which brings into high relief the ambiguity of the entire first speech. The "truth" about the world's governance is less evident in chaps. 38–39 than Habel wants to think.

25. Gordis, *Book of Job*, p. 466.

26. Habel, *Book of Job*, p. 549.

27. Terrien, *IB*, p. 1183. See also Rowley, *Job*, p. 253: "The verb means 'be swift,' 'be light,' and then 'be contemptible,'" citing Gen 16.4–5; 1 Sam 2.30; Nah 1.14. Habel (*Book of Job*, p. 549) thinks those texts do not bear on this one. KJV translates v. 4a, "Behold, I am vile," and Terrien's "evil connotation" can perhaps be connected to that rendering.

28. I did it myself, arguing (*Irony*, p. 239) that his fault is "elevating himself to deity's rank." I am not now convinced that he is guilty of that.

29. The one sentence Dhorme devotes to the phrase (p. 615) does not show how he derives "thoughtless": "The verb *qll* in its basic sense of 'to be light,' from which is derived that of 'to be swift' (7:6; 9:25)." It is hard to see "thoughtless" on the other side of "swift" without turning some unspecified mental corner.

30. *Irony*, pp. 236–37.

31. Whedbee, pp. 25–26. Seeing the necessary distinction between the two speeches and between Job's two replies, he nevertheless collapses the two into one in order to unpack meanings.

32. David Robertson, *Old Testament*, p. 52, in an essay somewhat abbreviated from his earlier "Book of Job: A Literary Study." Robertson understands Job's reaction to Yahweh's speeches as feigned submission, but he does not specify the meaning of the silence in 40.4–5. I infer what I think he would say.

33. I rejected it in "Job and the Literary Task," my response to Robertson. I do not now reject things quite so confidently.

34. By Habel (*Book of Job*, p. 549).

35. I am not satisfied with the explanation in K-B, s.v. *qll*, of the move from "light" or "insignificant" to "curse," i.e., "to declare [too trifling, of no account] cursed." In the ancient world, one did not curse persons or things because they were unimportant, but for precisely the opposite reason. On the other hand, I can imagine the Pi'el meaning to declare something "swiftly gone," suddenly destroyed, thus defining not the character or status of the thing cursed but the manner of the curse's operation. We need a more thorough investigation of ancient curses than we have. Even Blank's article leaves some fuzzy edges.

36. See, e.g., Deut 11.26–29; 27.12–13; Zech 8.13; Ps 109.17.

37. One might read Jung (p. 25) as suggesting it: "the only possible answer for a witness who is still trembling in every limb with the terror of almost total annihilation. What else could a half-crushed human worm, grovelling in the dust,

reasonably answer in the circumstances?" There is more terror in Jung's reading than in Robertson's.

38. E.g., Amos 1–2 *passim*; Prov 30.15–16, 18–22, 29–31. See Roth, "Numerical Sequence x/x + 1."

39. *Irony*, p. 238; "Job and the Literary Task," pp. 480–81.

40. See the "Indispensable Introduction" and the annotation to 40.8.

41. A few interpreters specify the idea of justice as the idea of "right," as in "Wilt thou even disallow my right" (S. R. Driver and Gray, who go on to interpret "right" as "that which is my due . . . my claim that I rule the world justly," p. 349), or "Willst wirklich du mein Recht zerbrechen" (Weiser, who later makes *Recht* the equivalent of *Gerechtigkeit*, "justice," p. 258).

42. Fohrer's original is "Willst du wirklich meinen Rechtsanspruch aufheben?" *Aufheben* is interestingly complex in meaning, as in Hegel's central use of it. Fohrer's interpretive comment (*Das Buch Hiob*, p. 519) points toward something close to "break up." Mitchell's "Do you dare" is boldly interpretive, setting a tone of voice and therefore a definitive interpretation.

43. See Eliphaz's complaint in 15.4a: "But you are breaking up religion" (*'ap-'attah tapēr yir'ah*—an interesting verbal parallel to 40.8a: *ha'ap tapēr mišpaṭī*).

44. Recall Derrida's phrase (p. 90): "impoverishment by univocality."

45. In Ps 104.1, the deity is said to be "clothed [*lbš*] with glory and grandeur [*hōd wᵉhadar*]."

46. The phrase occurs in Ps 21.6; 45.4; 96.6; 104.1; 111.3; 1 Chron 16.27.

47. *Lipnē* can mean either spatial presence ("at the face of, facing") or temporal precedence ("in front of, ahead of").

48. Habel (*Book of Job*, p. 563) thinks in Job 40.9–10 of the "storm god in action." It is at least that.

49. Gordis (*Book of Job*, p. 475) argues against the meaning "bind" for *ḥbš*, seeing the action as an indignity against the dead. Exactly what act is contemplated is not clear. Guillaume (*Studies*, p. 135) points to an Arabic cognate meaning both "bind" and "veil," but does not explain why veiling dead faces is a sign of power or of contempt.

50. Terrien (*Job*, pp. 246, 261–67) proposes the interesting possibility that "guilty" in v. 12 refers not to humans at all but to Behemoth and Leviathan. That understanding might mitigate the excesses of Job's action in vv. 9–14, but it entails a moral evaluation of the monsters that I do not see in the text.

51. Many scholars think that "tail" is a euphemism for penis. See, e.g., Pope, *Job*, p. 324; Pope, however, gives no evidence that *zanab* was used euphemistically in Hebrew but refers only to analogies in English and other languages.

52. The feminine plural form of the word Behemoth is belied by the fact that the verbs and the pronominal suffixes are all masculines, and v. 19 describes Behemoth with the emphatic pronoun *hu'*, "he." *Bᵉhēmōt* is either a feminine plural abstract noun, of which there are some instances (see GK, pp. 397–98), or a proper name. The masculine forms point to the latter.

53. Keel (p. 143) thinks it "obvious" (*unverkennbar*) that v. 23 describes

the way the animal goes from land to water. That strikes me as banalizing a vivid description of a monster's treating cosmic waters as a swimming pool.

54. Nor is this Job's only allusion to Gen 1. I pointed out the parody on Gen 1.3, "Let there be light" (*y^{e}hī 'ōr*), in Job 3.4: "That day, let there be darkness" (*hayyōm hahū' y^{e}hī ḥōšek*). Several scholars, e.g., Terrien (*Job*, pp. 111–12) and Horst (*Hiob*, pp. 184, 190–91), argue that 12.7–12 is a later interpolation. It is true, however, that Behemoth's verb in 12.7 is feminine singular (*tōrekka*), which could suggest that the noun is collective "cattle" or "beasts."

55. The words are found almost verbatim in a Ugaritic tablet in the Baal-Anat mythic cycle, which describes a beast called in that language *ltn*, conventionally vocalized Lotan (Tablet I*, AB, col. i; see *ANET*, p. 138). The step from *ltn* to Hebrew *lwytn* is a short one.

56. Keel, pp. 126–56. Both hippopotamus and crocodile were to be found in Egypt, and, so far as I can discover, only there were they then (and are now) to be found together.

57. Gordis (*Book of Job*, p. 480) notes that crocodiles are also known from streams in Palestine. No doubt, but hippopotami are not.

58. Likewise Habel, *Book of Job*, p. 558: "Job is not called on to do anything except look, listen, and learn." I see no "learning" inculcated, differing from Gammie's suggestion (p. 222) that the Behemoth passage is didactic and consoling, a kind of object lesson in how to cope with adversity. Gammie lays no weight on the absence of a command for Job to do something.

59. See esp. Habel, *Book of Job*, p. 558; his account of the divine power seems to me more subtle than some others.

60. The Apocalypse of Baruch 29.4, a Jewish work of the late first century C.E., says that Leviathan and Behemoth were created on the fifth day, as *tannīnīm*, "sea monsters" (cf. Gen 1.21). On the question of temporality, see Habel, *Book of Job*, p. 565.

61. The parallel would be nicer if *darkō*, "his way," were plural, as it is in Job 40.19, but cf. 26.14a, where *darkō* in the phrase "edges (or ends) of his way" is the Ketib. JPS renders the Proverbs line "at the beginning of His course," taking *rēšīt* ("beginning") as primarily temporal, "primal" as distinguished from "preeminent."

62. The form of the word is strange. It is against the rules, we are told (see GK, p. 358, *n*1), to prefix the definite article to a construct form of a noun. Gordis (*Book of Job*, p. 477) reads *he'aśu*, a passive participle of a root *'śh*[*y*] meaning "to cover," and understands it as a well-protected, thoroughly armored warrior.

63. The idea (see, e.g., Gammie, p. 219) that the deity is the subject of the verbs in v. 24 is possible but doubtful. It is odd for the god to refer to himself in the third person.

64. See the annotation to this line.

65. Habel (*Book of Job*, p. 551), like JPS, turns this line into the divine claim to possess everything: "For everything under the heavens is mine." But the first phrase of *taḥat kol-haššamayim lī-hū'* is not "all under the sky" but "under

all the sky." Gordis (*Book of Job*, p. 483) emends *lī* to *lō'*: "Under all the heavens—no one!" (see p. 470). Pope (*Job*, pp. 337–38) emends *lī* to *mī*, "who," making this line parallel to the prior one. The emphatic pronoun *hū'* with the possessive *lī* leads me to pair vv. 2b and 3a in a parenthetic statement, so that v. 3b is poetically parallel to v. 2a.

66. Pope, *Job*, p. 337. Habel (*Book of Job*, p. 555) contradicts the idea.

67. Gilgamesh Epic, Tab. XI, ll. 113–15, *ANET*, p. 94. I claim no connection between the Akkadian word translated "shrinking back" and Heb. *ḥṭ'*, in the Hithpa'el, which I have translated "shrink away." I wish I could.

68. See Gordis, *Book of Job*, Special Note 35, pp. 565–67. Gordis adds to the notion of mystery a quality of aesthetic joy.

69. E.g., Rowley, *Job*, p. 255; S. R. Driver and Gray, p. 352.

70. See also Alter, *Poetry*, p. 109: "The poet's figurative language dares to situate rare beauty in the midst of power and terror and strangeness."

71. Kinnier Wilson, "A Return to the Problems of Behemoth and Leviathan."

72. Kinnier Wilson damages his own point by translating the opening of v. 9 not "If you have an arm like El's," which sets up a neutral attitude to the claim and awaits its outcome, but "Even if thou hadst an arm as strong as God's." The scorn in that clause already tells us the outcome: Job is incompetent as a god.

73. *N^eḥūšah* can mean either copper or bronze. I translated "bronze," but Kinnier Wilson prefers copper. Bronze is hard and strong, copper soft and crushable. Still, tubular ribs, even of bronze, might be less than sufficiently strong.

74. Kinnier Wilson takes the rare *gerem* as "backbone" because of LXX's *rachis*, "spine," but *gerem* is never certainly anything but "bone" in general (Gen 49.14; Prov 17.22; 25.15).

75. G. R. Driver, "Mythical Monsters," p. 237, *n*3.

76. Taking *nś'*, "lift" ("bear" in my translation) as elliptical for "lift the voice, sing" (*nś' qōl*), as in 21.12. Cf. also Tur-Sinai, p. xxx; and Gordis, *Book of Job*, p. 478.

77. I translated *śḥq* as "play," referring to games and to sexual activity, but "laugh" is just as good. Kinnier Wilson makes no connection to the rather strange LXX reading of v. 19b, which he quotes in another context (p. 8, *n*1): "A thing made to be laughed at by His angels." This reading may have been influenced by "play/laugh" in v. 20b, where LXX has *charmonē*, "joy."

78. Kinnier Wilson, p. 9.

79. Kinnier Wilson does not see the possibilities in the present text of v. 19b for his own case, and this interpretation is my effort to improve on his. He changes *ḥarbō*, "his sword," to *ḥ^abēraw*, "his companions," with the very doubtful reading, "Will his 'Maker' then bring near companions for him?"

80. Kinnier Wilson, p. 12.

81. It is tempting to compare v. 25a, "Upon the dust is not his ruler" (*'ēn-'al-'apar mošlō*) to 19.25b, where Job's "avenger" (*gō'ēl*) may "rise upon dust" (*'al-'apar yaqūm*). I am uncertain enough of the meaning of that line to leave it blank, and I refuse to base interpretations on unintelligible lines.

82. Kinnier Wilson, p. 14.

83. Tsevat, *Book of Job*, pp. 31–37, arrives at this point without reference to Behemoth and Leviathan, whom he apparently excises.

84. See *n*6 above.

85. So Elliger and Rudolph. Fohrer (*Das Buch Hiob*, p. 532) and Gordis (*Book of Job*, p. 492) accept GK's plausible explanation (p. 121, par. 44i), that this and similar occurrences in 1 Ki 8.48; Ezek 16.59; and Ps 140.13 are remains of an earlier spelling, omitting vowel letters at the ends of words. Hölscher (p. 98) emends to first-person singular, apparently without noticing the Qere. Other commentators ignore the problem.

86. David Robertson could have made good use of this reading in his argument that Job pretends to submit to Yahweh. See "Book of Job"; and *Old Testament*, p. 52.

87. In Plato's *Meno*, Socrates, leading a slave boy through a problem in geometry, brings him to realize that his answers have been wrong. He turns to Meno with the comment, "Now he does think himself at a loss, and as he does not know, neither does he think he knows," which puts him "in a better position with regard to the matter he does not know" (84a–b, Grube translation).

88. E.g., Terrien, *IB*, p. 1192; Gordis, *Book of Job*, p. 492; Pope, *Job*, p. 345; S. R. Driver and Gray, Pt. I, p. 372; Fohrer, *Das Buch Hiob*, p. 531; Dhorme, p. 646; Mitchell, p. 88; Weiser, p. 254; Hölscher, p. 98; Habel, *Book of Job*, p. 575.

89. Mitchell, pp. 88, 129.

90. Briggs, "Job's Response," pp. 510–11. "Loathing contempt and revulsion" is Briggs's reading of *'em'as*, and the deity is the unstated accusative. "Dust and ashes" is a metaphor for human frailty (see ibid., p. 501).

91. Terrien, *IB*, p. 1193. See also my use of "faith" in *Irony*, pp. 239–40, as the touchstone of what happens here.

92. I tried to squirm around the point in *Irony*, unsuccessfully, as I now think.

93. Habel (*Book of Job*, p. 576) finds an implicit object of *'m's* in Job's claim in 31.13 that he did not "dismiss the case" (*'im-'em'as mišpaṭ*) of his servant, and here he "dismisses/retracts" his own legal case against God. I think that *m's* has more feeling in it, both here and in 31.13, than "dismiss." Habel's dependence on an implicit accusative from another passage makes his explanation less attractive than it otherwise might be.

94. See Patrick, "Translation." Patrick's more extended interpretation in *Arguing with God* (pp. 97–98) is marred in my opinion by an excessive use of Christian terminology, such as "salvation," for what happens to Job. It has been pointed out several times that in Pt. II, chap. 23, of *The Guide to the Perplexed*, Maimonides anticipated this understanding of *niḥam 'al-'apar wa'ēper*. Laks (p. 362) reads Maimonides to mean that Job "abhorred his earlier values which had led him to mourn his earthly losses and to give vent to sensations of loss by covering himself with 'dust and ashes.'" Maimonides did not have the benefit of Patrick's demonstration about *m's*.

95. Habel, *Book of Job*, pp. 582–83.
96. I myself thought so in *Irony*.

Chapter 9

1. On the number of sons, see the annotation to 42.13 and *n*16 below.
2. See Girard, p. 144: "The epilogue drowns the scapegoat in the puerile acts of revenge of a Hollywood success story." Girard approves only of 42.8 (and ought to approve of v. 7), because it refers to Job's speaking the truth about God, which he believes took place in the dialogue with the friends.
3. See Sewall, chap. 2, on Job as a tragedy.
4. Whedbee's "Comedy of Job" persuasively broke the ground, and even so formidable a reader as Frye (*The Great Code*, p. 196) calls Job "technically a comedy by virtue of its 'happy ending.'" In his earlier *Anatomy of Criticism*, Frye had discussed Job in terms of "tragic irony," though he denied the book the status of "Promethean tragedy" (p. 42).
5. This chiastic correspondence made Gordis (*Book of God*, p. 73) think of both episodes as patches between the original story of Job and the poetry.
6. It is no good dismissing this statement as a remnant from an earlier form of the tale or of the book, which one might speculate went directly from something Yahweh said to Job to this remark to the friends. We cannot explain a statement from the silence of a text that does not exist, but we can deal with it only as part of one that does exist.
7. E.g., Isa 45.18; Ps 24.2; 119.90; Prov 3.19.
8. E.g., Habel, *Book of Job*, p. 583; S. R. Driver and Gray, p. 374; Pope, *Job*, p. 350, with some uncertainty; van Selms, p. 157; Weiser, pp. 267–68.
9. E.g., Gordis, *Book of Job*, p. 494: "Job's courageous and honorable challenge to God is more acceptable to Him than conventional defenses of God's justice that rest upon distortions of reality"; Fohrer, *Das Buch Hiob*, p. 539.
10. Gordis (*Book of Job*, p. 494) says that it is "not only because he is the oldest and intellectually the most distinguished of the Friends, but because it is he who has presumed to 'promise' Job the power of intercession for sinners if he repents," referring to 22.26–30. I doubt that we can know that Eliphaz is older and more distinguished, but the reference to intercession is very neat. One might add that Eliphaz is the only friend who claims immediate contact with the divine, in his account of the vision in 4.12–21. Perhaps singling him out for address is also a reminder of that claim.
11. See Pedersen, *Israel*, 2: 299–375.
12. Cf. Num 23.1–2, 14, 29–30; Ezek 45.22–25.
13. See David Robertson, *Old Testament*, pp. 53–54.
14. Habel (*Book of Job*, p. 584) refers to Job's taking up the function of priest and of patriarchal mediator (on the analogy of Abraham in Gen 18.23–33), a view that misses some of the irony of this episode.
15. In v. 10, Job prays not "over" but "for" (*b*ᵉ*'ad*) the friends. It is an

echo of the Prosecutor's difficult, proverb-like "Skin up to [*b^e'ad*] skin!" in 2.4, but I have no neat way to tie the two together.

16. Dhorme, pp. 651–52. Gordis (*Book of Job*, p. 498) quotes that notorious misogynist Ben Sira (Ecclus 26.10–12; 43.9–11) as representing the "true Semitic spirit," in which sons are a blessing and daughters but a source of worry. Therefore Job ought to rejoice in fourteen sons and be satisfied that, as to daughters, "enough is enough." Ancient Israel was sexist enough without having to be identified altogether with Ben Sira, who was worse than most.

17. See the annotation to 42.13; and Sarna, "Epic Substratum," p. 18; cf. Habel, *Book of Job*, p. 577.

18. Another connection between the poem and the tale.

19. *Irony*, pp. 239–40.

20. Jacob paid 100 *qeśiṭas*, apparently a large unit of weight, for a piece of land near Shechem (Gen 33.19; cf. Josh 24.32), on which he built an altar. "Money," of course, does not mean coinage. The earliest mention of a coin in the Hebrew Bible is a reference to Persian "darics" (Ezra 2.69). Unless the *qeśiṭa* in Job 42.11 is a deliberate archaism (and it may well be), the use of weighed metal rather than of coinage for exchange might suggest a date for the tale not later than the sixth or early fifth century.

21. *IB*, p. 1196.

22. I find no scholar who comments on the absence of slaves from Job's restored wealth.

23. The text does not explicitly say that Yahweh provided the animals, but the juxtaposition of "blessed" in one clause with "he had fourteen thousand," etc., in the next makes causation the most believable reading.

24. No one, indeed, suggests that you can.

25. The daughters' names do not demonstrate this point. We may assume that the first three daughters and the sons had names too, just as all children in the ancient world had them. The difference in chap. 42 is that we learn the names.

26. I think that is social equality. The phrase *naḥ^alah b^etōk '^aḥēhem* (with an odd masculine plural pronominal possessive), "inheritance in the midst of their brothers," allows the meaning of something equal rather than spatial. Still, *b^etōk* does mainly mean "in the middle," and *naḥ^alah* often refers not to money or goods inherited but to land. That meaning would not damage the perception of social equality.

27. Lev 1.1: "And he called [*wayyiqra'*] to Moses"; Josh 1.1: "And it happened [*way^ehī*] after Moses' death"; Ezek 1.1: "And it happened [*way^ehī*] in the thirtieth year."

28. LXX adds thirty to the number and assumes that Job was already seventy when the calamity struck: "Job lived after the affliction one hundred seventy years, and all the years he lived were two hundred and forty" (in a few manuscripts, "two hundred forty-eight").

29. Gordis (*Book of Job*, p. 499) notes that it appears elsewhere only in Ezra 9.10.

30. See Habel, *Book of Job*, p. 586.

31. Habel (ibid., p. 585) gives the variant in Gen 25.8, "sated with days," as if that were the MT reading.

32. JPS translates "sated" in Gen 25.8 as "contented."

33. See also 27.14; 38.27.

Bibliography

For complete forms of abbreviations used here, see the List of Abbreviations, pp. xiii–xiv.

Aiura, T. "Wisdom Motifs in the Joban Poem." *Kwansei Gakuin University Annual Studies* 15 (1966): 1–20.

Albertz, Rainer. "Der sozialgeschichtliche Hintergrund des Hiobbuches und der 'Babylonische Theodizee.'" In Jörg Jeremias and Lothar Perlitt, eds., *Die Botschaft und die Boten: Festschrift für Hans Walter Wolff zum 70. Geburtstag* (Neukirchen-Vluyn, 1981), pp. 349–72.

Alt, Albrecht. "Zur Vorgeschichte des Buches Hiob." *ZAW* 55 [n.s. 14] (1937): 265–68.

Alter, Robert. *The Art of Biblical Narrative*. New York, 1981.

———. *The Art of Biblical Poetry*. New York, 1985.

———. "The Characteristics of Ancient Hebrew Poetry." In Alter and Kermode, pp. 611–24.

Alter, Robert, and Frank Kermode, eds. *The Literary Guide to the Bible*. Cambridge, Mass., 1987.

Andersen, Francis I. *Job: An Introduction and Commentary*. Tyndale Old Testament Commentaries. Downers Grove, Ill., 1976.

Aufrecht, Walter E., ed. *Studies in the Book of Job*. Canadian Corporation for Studies in Religion/Corporation Canadienne des Sciences Religieuses, Supplements 16. Waterloo, Ont., 1985.

Avishur, Y. "Word-Pairs Common to Phoenician and Biblical Hebrew." *UF* 7 (1975): 13–47.

Baab, Otto. "The Book of Job." *Interpretation* 5 (1951): 329–43.

Barr, James. "The Book of Job and Its Modern Interpreters." *Bulletin of the John Rylands Library* 54 (1971): 28–46.

———. *Comparative Philology and the Text of the Old Testament*. Oxford, 1968.

Barthes, Roland. "The Death of the Author." In *Image Music Text*, comp. and tr. Stephen Heath (New York, 1977), pp. 142–48.

Batten, Loring W. "The Epilogue to the Book of Job." *Anglican Theological Review* 15 (1933): 125–28.

Baumgärtel, Friedrich. *Der Hiobdialog: Aufriss und Deutung*. Stuttgart, 1933.

Baumgartner, Walter. "The Wisdom Literature." In H. H. Rowley, ed., *The Old Testament and Modern Study* (Oxford, 1951), pp. 210–37.

Berlin, Adele. *The Dynamics of Biblical Parallelism*. Bloomington, Ind., 1985.

———. *Poetics and Interpretation of Biblical Narrative*. Bible and Literature Series. Sheffield, Eng., 1983.

Berry, D. L. "Scripture and Imaginative Literature: Focus on Job." *Journal of General Education* 19 (1967): 119–31.

Bic, M. "Le juste et l'impie dans le livre de Job." *VT* 15 (1965): 33–43.

Blank, Sheldon H. "The Curse, Blasphemy, the Spell and the Oath." *HUCA* 23 (1950/51): 73–95.

———. "An Effective Literary Device in Job XXXI." *Journal of Jewish Studies* 2 (1951): 105–7.

Blenkinsopp, Joseph. *Wisdom and Law in the Old Testament: The Ordering of Life in Israel and Early Judaism*. Oxford Bible Series. New York, 1983.

Blommerde, Anton C. M. "The Broken Construct Chain, Further Examples." *Bib* 55 (1974): 549–52.

———. *Northwest Semitic Grammar and Job*. Biblica et Orientalia 22. Rome, 1969.

Bloom, Harold. *The Anxiety of Influence*. London, 1975.

———. *A Map of Misreading*. Oxford, 1975.

Bloom, Harold, Paul de Man, Jacques Derrida, Geoffrey Hartman, and J. Hillis Miller. *Deconstruction & Criticism*. New York, 1979.

Boadt, L. "A Re-examination of the Third-Yod Suffix in Job." *UF* 7 (1975): 59–72.

Boecker, Hans Jochen. *Law and the Administration of Justice in the Old Testament and Ancient East*. Tr. Jeremy Moiser. Minneapolis, 1980.

———. *Redeformen des Rechtslebens im Alten Testament*. Wissenschaftliche Monographien zum Alten und Neuen Testament 14. Neukirchen-Vluyn, 1959.

Brenner, A. "God's Answer to Job." *VT* 31 (1981): 277–81.

Brichto, Herbert Chanan. *The Problem of "Curse" in the Hebrew Bible*. *JBL* Monograph Series 13. Corrected repr. of 1963 ed. Philadelphia, 1968.

Briggs, John Curtis. "On Job's Response to Yahweh." *JBL* 98 (1979): 497–511.

———. "On Job's Witness in Heaven." *JBL* 102 (1983): 549–62.

Brown, Francis, S. R. Driver, and Charles A. Briggs. *A Hebrew and English Lexicon of the Old Testament.* Corrected imprint. Oxford, 1952.

Brueggemann, Walter. "A Neglected Sapiential Word Pair." *ZAW* 89 (1977): 234–58.

Bruston, E. "La littérature sapientiale dans le livre de Job." *Etudes Theologiques et Religieuses* (1928): 297–305.

Buttenwieser, Moses. *The Book of Job.* New York, 1925.

Buttrick, G. A., et al., eds. *The Interpreter's Bible*, vol. 3. New York and Nashville, Tenn., 1954.

Caquot, André. "Israelite Perceptions of Wisdom and Strength in the Light of the Ras Shamra Texts." In Gammie et al., pp. 25–33.

———. "Traits royaux dans le personnage de Job." In *Maqqél shāqédh: Hommage à Wilhelm Vischer* (Montpellier, France, 1960), pp. 32–45.

Carstensen, R. N. *Job, Defense of Honor.* Nashville, Tenn., 1963.

———. "The Persistence of the 'Elihu' Point of View in Later Jewish Literature." Microfilm. Ann Arbor, Mich., 1981.

Cassuto, Umberto. "Parallel Words in Hebrew and Ugaritic." Repr. in Cassuto, *Biblical and Oriental Studies II: Bible and Ancient Oriental Texts* (Jerusalem, 1975), pp. 60–68.

Causse, Antonin. "Sagesse égyptienne et sagesse juive." *Revue d'Histoire et de Philosophie Religieuses* (1929): 149–69.

Ceresko, Anthony R. "The A:B::B:A Word Pattern in Hebrew and Northwest Semitic with Special Reference to the Book of Job." *UF* 7 (1975): 73–88.

———. "The Chiastic Word Pattern in Hebrew." *CBQ* 38 (1976): 303–11.

———. *Job 29–31 in the Light of Northwest Semitic: A Translation and Philological Commentary.* Biblica et Orientalia 36. Rome, 1980.

Chamberlain, Lori. "Gender and the Metaphorics of Translation." *Signs* 13 (1988): 454–72.

Claudel, Paul. *Le livre de Job.* Paris, 1946.

Clines, David J. A. "The Arguments of Job's Three Friends." In D. J. A. Clines, D. M. Gunn, and A. J. Hauser, eds., *Art and Meaning: Rhetoric in Biblical Literature*, *JSOT* Supplements 19 (Sheffield, Eng., 1982), pp. 199–214.

———. "Job: A Deconstruction." Unpublished paper, 1987.

———. "Verb Modality and the Interpretation of Job iv 20–21." *VT* 30 (1980): 354–57.

Cohen, Harold R. *Biblical Hapax Legomena in the Light of Akkadian and Ugaritic.* Society of Biblical Literature Dissertation Series 37. Missoula, Mont., 1978.

Condamin, Albert, S.J. *Poèmes de la Bible: avec une introduction sur la strophique hébraïque.* 2nd ed. Paris, 1933.

Coogan, Michael David. *Stories from Ancient Canaan.* Philadelphia, 1978.

Cook, Albert. *The Root of the Thing: A Study of Job and the Song of Songs.* Bloomington, Ind., 1968.

Cox, Dermot, O.F.M. *The Triumph of Impotence: Job and the Tradition of the Absurd*. Analecta Gregoriana 212. Rome, 1978.

Craigie, Peter C. "Job and Ugaritic Studies." In Aufrecht, pp. 28–35.

———. "A Note on 'Fixed Pairs' in Ugaritic and Early Hebrew Poetry." *Journal of Theological Studies* 22 (1971): 140–43.

———. "The Problem of Parallel Word Pairs in Ugaritic and Hebrew Poetry." *Semitics* 5 (1979): 48–58.

Crenshaw, James L. "Impossible Questions, Sayings, and Tasks." *Sem* 17 (1980): 19–34.

———. *Old Testament Wisdom: An Introduction*. Atlanta, 1981.

———. "Popular Questioning of the Justice of God in Ancient Israel." *ZAW* 82 (1970): 380–95.

———. "The Shift from Theodicy to Anthropodicy." In Crenshaw, *Theodicy*, pp. 1–16.

———. "The Twofold Search: A Response to Luis Alonso Schökel." *Sem* 7 (1977): 63–69.

———, ed. *Theodicy in the Old Testament*. Issues in Religion and Theology 4. Philadelphia and London, 1983.

Crook, Margaret Brackenbury. *The Cruel God: Job's Search for the Meaning of Suffering*. Boston, 1959.

Cross, Frank Moore. *Canaanite Myth and Hebrew Epic: Essays in the History of the Religion of Israel*. Cambridge, Mass., and London, 1973.

———. "Ugaritic *DB'AT* and Hebrew Cognates." *VT* 2 (1952): 162–64.

Crüsemann, Frank. "Hiob und Kohelet." In Rainer Albertz, Hans-Peter Müller, Hans Walter Wolff, and Walter Zimmerli, eds., *Werden und Wirken des Alten Testaments: Festschrift für Claus Westermann zum 70. Geburtstag* (Göttingen and Neukirchen-Vluyn, 1980), pp. 373–93.

Culler, Jonathan. *On Deconstruction: Theory and Criticism After Structuralism*. Ithaca, N.Y., 1982.

Dahood, Mitchell. "Chiasmus in Job: A Text-Critical and Philological Criterion." In H. N. Bream et al., eds., *A Light unto My Path: Old Testament Studies in Honor of Jacob M. Myers* (Philadelphia, 1974), pp. 119–30.

———. "Congruity of Metaphors." In B. Hartmann et al., eds., *Hebräische Wortforschung: Festschrift Walter Baumgartner, VT* Supplements 16 (Leiden, 1967), pp. 40–49.

———. "Hebrew-Ugaritic Lexicography, I." *Bib* 44 (1963): 289–303.

———. "*Ḥōl* 'Phoenix' in Job 29,18 and Ugaritic." *CBQ* 36 (1974): 85–88.

———. "*Mišmar* 'Muzzle' in Job 7,12." *JBL* 80 (1961): 270–71.

———. "Nest and Phoenix in Job 29,18." *Bib* 48 (1967): 542–44.

———. "Northwest Semitic Philology and Job." In J. L. McKenzie, ed., *The Bible in Current Catholic Thought: Gruenthaner Memorial Volume*, St. Mary's Theology Series 1 (New York, 1962), pp. 55–74.

———. *Psalms I*. The Anchor Bible 16. Garden City, N.Y., 1966.

———. "Some Northwest-Semitic Words in Job." *Bib* 38 (1957): 306–20.

———. "*Ś'RT* 'Storm' in Job 4,15." *Bib* 48 (1967): 544–45.

———. "Ugaritic-Hebrew Parallel Pairs." In *Ras Shamra Parallels*, vol. 1, ed. Loren Fisher, Analecta Orientalia 49 (Rome, 1972), pp. 71–382; vol. 2, ed. Loren Fisher, Analecta Orientalia 50 (Rome, 1975), pp. 1–39; vol. 3, ed. Stan Rummel, Analecta Orientalia 51 (Rome, 1981), pp. 1–206.

Davidson, A. B., and H. C. O. Lanchester. *The Book of Job*. Cambridge Bible for Schools and Colleges. Cambridge, Eng., 1918.

Day, Peggy L. *An Adversary in Heaven: Satan in the Hebrew Bible*. Harvard Semitic Museum, Harvard Semitic Monographs 43. Decatur, Ga., 1988.

DeBoer, P. A. H. "*Wmrḥwq yryḥ mlḥmh*—Job 39:25." In P. R. Ackroyd and B. Lindars, eds., *Words and Meanings: Essays Presented to David Winton Thomas* (Cambridge, Eng., 1968), pp. 29–38.

Derrida, Jacques. "Living On / Border Lines." Tr. James Hulbert. In Bloom et al., pp. 75–176.

De Wilde, A. *Das Buch Hiob: Eingeleitet, übersetzt und erläutert*. Oudtestamentische Studiën 22. Leiden, 1981.

Dhorme, Edouard. *A Commentary on the Book of Job*. Tr. Harold Knight. London, 1967.

Dick, Michael Brennan. "Job 31, the Oath of Innocence, and the Sage." *ZAW* 95 (1983): 31–53.

———. "The Legal Metaphor in Job 31." *CBQ* 41 (1979): 37–50.

Diewert, David A. "Job 7:12: *Yam, Tannin* and the Surveillance of Job." *JBL* 106 (1987): 203–15.

Dressler, Harold H. P. "Is the Bow of Aqhat a Symbol of Virility?" *UF* 7 (1975): 217–20.

Driver, G. R. *Canaanite Myths and Legends*. 1st ed. Leiden, 1956.

———. "Mythical Monsters in the Old Testament." In *Studi Orientalistici in onore di Giorgio Levi della Vida*, vol. 1 (Rome, 1956), pp. 234–49.

———. "Problems in Job." *American Journal of Semitic Languages and Literatures* 52 (1935/36): 160–70.

———. "Problems in the Hebrew Text of Job." In Noth and Thomas, pp. 72–93.

———. "Two Astronomical Passages in the Old Testament." *Journal of Theological Studies*, n.s. 7 (1956): 1–11.

Driver, Samuel Rolles, and George Buchanan Gray. *A Critical and Exegetical Commentary on the Book of Job*. International Critical Commentary. Edinburgh, 1921.

Duesberg, Hilaire. *Job, l'Ecclésiaste, l'Ecclésiastique et la Sagesse*. Paris, 1939.

Dunn, Robert Paul. "Speech and Silence in Job." *Sem* 19 (1981): 99–103.

Duquoc, Christian, and Casiano Floristán, eds. *Job and the Silence of God*. Marcus Lefébure, English-language ed. Concilium: Religion in the Eighties. Edinburgh and New York, 1983.

Eagleton, Terry. *Literary Theory: An Introduction*. Minneapolis, 1983.

Eco, Umberto. *The Role of the Reader: Explorations in the Semiotics of Texts*. Bloomington, Ind., 1979.

Eerdmans, B. D. *Studies in Job*. Leiden, 1939.

Eitan, I. "Biblical Studies IV: Notes on Job." *HUCA* 14 (1938): 9–13.

Elliger, K., and W. Rudolph, eds. *Biblia Hebraica Stuttgartensis*. 2nd ed. Stuttgart, 1983.

Fensham, F. C. "Widow, Orphan, and the Poor in Ancient Near Eastern Legal and Wisdom Literature." *Journal of Near Eastern Studies* 21 (1962): 129–39.

Fine, Hillel A. "The Tradition of a Patient Job." *JBL* 74 (1955): 28–32.

Fingarette, Herbert. "The Meaning of Law in the Book of Job." *The Hastings Law Journal* 29 (1978): 1581–617.

Fish, Stanley. *Is There a Text in This Class? The Authority of Interpretive Communities*. Cambridge, Mass., and London, 1980.

Fishbane, Michael. "Jeremiah IV 23–26 and Job III 3–13: A Recovered Use of the Creation Pattern." *VT* 21 (1971): 151–67.

Fisher, L. R. "ŠDYN in Job 19,29." *VT* 11 (1961): 342–44.

Fohrer, Georg. *Das Buch Hiob*. Kommentar zum Alten Testament 16. Gütersloh, 1963.

———. "Form und Funktion in der Hiobdichtung." *Zeitschrift des deutschen morgenländische Gesellschaft* 109 [n.s. 34] (1959): 31–49. Repr., with some alterations, in Fohrer, *Studien zum Buche Hiob (1956–1979)*, 2nd ed. (1983), pp. 60–77.

———. "Gottes Antwort aus dem Sturmwind, Hi 38–41." *Theologische Zeitschrift* (1962): 1–24. Repr., with some alterations, in Fohrer, *Studien zum Buche Hiob (1956–1979)*, 2nd ed. (1983), pp. 114–34.

———. "Nun aber hat mein Auge dich geschaut: Der innere Aufbau des Buches Hiob." *Theologische Zeitschrift* (1959): 1–21. Repr., with some alterations, as "Der innere Aufbau des Buches Hiob," in Fohrer, *Studien zum Buche Hiob (1956–1979)*, 2nd ed. (1983), pp. 1–18.

———. "The Righteous Man in Job 31." In J. L. Crenshaw and J. T. Willis, eds., *Essays in Old Testament Ethics* (New York, 1974), pp. 1–22. Repr. in Fohrer, *Studien zum Buche Hiob (1956–1979)*, 2nd ed. (1983), pp. 78–93.

———. *Studien zum Buche Hiob (1956–1979)*. 2nd ed. Beihefte zur *ZAW* 159. Berlin and New York, 1983.

———. "Überlieferung und Wandlung der Hioblegende." In Johannes Herrmann, ed., *Festschrift Friedrich Baumgärtel zum 70. Geburtstag, 14. Januar 1958, gewidmet von den Mitarbeitern am Kommentar zum Alten Testament (KAT)* (Erlangen, 1959), pp. 41–62. Repr., with some alterations, in Fohrer, *Studien zum Buche Hiob (1956–1979)*, 2nd ed. (1983), pp. 37–59.

———. "Die Weisheit des Elihu (Hi 32–37)." *Archiv für Orientforschung* 19 (1959/60): 83–94. Repr., with some alterations, in Fohrer, *Studien zum Buche Hiob (1956–1979)*, 2nd ed. (1983), pp. 94–113.

———. "Zur Vorgeschichte und Komposition des Buches Hiob." *VT* 6 (1956): 249–67. Repr., with some alterations, in Fohrer, *Studien zum Buche Hiob (1956–1979)*, 2nd ed. (1983), pp. 19–36.

Fontaine, Carole. "Folktale Structure in the Book of Job: A Formalist Reading." In Elaine R. Follis, ed., *Directions in Biblical Hebrew Poetry*, *JSOT* Supplement Series 40 (Sheffield, Eng., 1987), pp. 205–32.
Foster, Frank Hugh. "Is the Book of Job a Translation from an Arabic Original?" *American Journal of Semitic Languages and Literatures* 49 (1932–33): 21–45.
Fox, Michael V. "Job 38 and God's Rhetoric." *Sem* 19 (1981): 53–61.
Freedman, D. N. "The Broken Construct Chain." *Bib* 53 (1972): 534–36.
———. "The Elihu Speeches in the Book of Job: A Hypothetical Episode in the Literary History of the Work." *Harvard Theological Review* 61 (1968): 51–59. Repr. in Freedman, *Pottery, Poetry, and Prophecy: Studies in Early Hebrew Poetry* (Winona Lake, Ind., 1979), pp. 329–37.
———. "Orthographic Peculiarities in the Book of Job." *Eretz-Israel* 9 (William Foxwell Albright Vol., 1969): non-Hebrew section, 35–44.
———. "The Structure of Job 3." *Bib* 49 (1968): 503–8. Repr. in Freedman, *Pottery, Poetry, and Prophecy: Studies in Early Hebrew Poetry* (Winona Lake, Ind., 1979), pp. 323–28.
Frye, Northrop. *Anatomy of Criticism: Four Essays*. Princeton, N.J., 1957.
———. *The Great Code: The Bible and Literature*. New York, 1982.
Fuente, Olegario García de la. "La prosperidad del malvado en el libro de Job y en los poemas babulónicos del 'Justo paciente.'" *Estudios Eclesiasticos* 34 (1960): 603–19.
Fullerton, Kemper. "Double Entendre in the First Speech of Eliphaz." *JBL* 49 (1930): 320–74.
———. "On Job 9 and 10." *JBL* 53 (1934): 321–49.
———. "On the Text and Significance of Job 40.2." *American Journal of Semitic Languages and Literatures* 49 (1932–33): 197–211.
———. "The Original Conclusion to the Book of Job." *ZAW* 42 (1924): 116–36.
Gammie, John G. "Behemoth and Leviathan: On the Didactic and Theological Significance of Job 40:15–41:26." In Gammie et al., pp. 217–31.
Gammie, John G., W. A. Brueggemann, W. L. Humphreys, and J. M. Ward, eds. *Israelite Wisdom: Theological and Literary Essays in Honor of Samuel Terrien*. Missoula, Mont., 1978.
Gard, Donald H. *The Exegetical Method of the Greek Translator of the Book of Job*. *JBL* Monograph Series 8. Philadelphia, 1952.
Gehman, Henry Snyder. "*Sēper*, an Inscription, in the Book of Job." *JBL* 63 (1944): 303–7.
———. "The Theological Approach of the Greek Translator of Job 1–15." *JBL* 68 (1949): 231–40.
Geller, Stephen A. *Parallelism in Early Biblical Poetry*. Harvard Semitic Museum, Harvard Semitic Monographs 20. Missoula, Mont., 1979.
Gerleman, Gillis. "Der Nicht-Mensch, Erwägungen zur hebräische Wurzel *NBL*." *VT* 24 (1974): 147–58.
———. *Studies in the Septuagint I: Book of Job*. Lund, Sweden, 1946.

Gese, Hartmut. *Lehre und Wirklichkeit in der alten Weisheit: Studien zu den Sprüchen Salomos und zu dem Buche Hiob*. Tübingen, 1958.

Gevirtz, Stanley. *Patterns in the Early Poetry of Israel*. The Oriental Institute of the University of Chicago Studies in Ancient Oriental Civilization 32. Chicago, 1963.

Gibson, J. C. L. "Eliphaz the Temanite: Portrait of a Hebrew Philosopher." *Scottish Journal of Theology* 28 (1975): 259–72.

Ginsberg, H. L. "Job the Patient and Job the Impatient." In *Congress Volume Rome, 1968*, *VT* Supplements 17 (1969), pp. 88–111.

———. "The Ugaritic Texts and Textual Criticism." *JBL* 62 (1943): 109–15.

Girard, René. *Job: The Victim of His People*. Tr. Yvonne Freccero. Stanford, Calif., 1987.

Glatzer, Nahum M. "The Book of Job and Its Interpreters." In Alexander Altmann, ed., *Biblical Motifs: Origins and Transformations*, Philip W. Lown Institute of Advanced Judaic Studies, Studies and Texts 3 (Cambridge, Mass., 1966), pp. 197–220.

———, ed. *The Dimensions of Job: A Study and Selected Readings*. New York, 1969.

Good, Edwin M. *Irony in the Old Testament*. 2nd ed. Bible and Literature Series. Sheffield, Eng., 1981.

———. "Job." In James L. Mays, gen. ed., *Harper's Bible Commentary* (San Francisco, 1988), pp. 407–32.

———. "Job and the Literary Task: A Response." *Soundings* 56 (1973): 470–84.

———. "Stephen Mitchell's *Job*: A Critique." *The World & I* 12, no. 2 (Dec. 1987): 368–74.

Gordis, Robert. *The Book of God and Man: A Study of Job*. Chicago, 1965.

———. *The Book of Job: Commentary, New Translation, and Special Studies*. Moreshet, Studies in Jewish History, Literature and Thought 2. New York, 5738/1978.

———. "Elihu the Intruder." In Alexander Altmann, ed., *Biblical and Other Studies* (Cambridge, Mass., 1963), pp. 60–78.

———. "Job 40:29—An Additional Note." *VT* 14 (1964): 492–94. Repr. in Gordis, *The Word and the Book: Studies in Biblical Language and Literature* (New York, 1976), pp. 355–57.

———. "The Lord out of the Whirlwind: The Climax and Meaning of 'Job.'" *Judaism* 13 (1964): 48–63.

———. *Poets, Prophets, and Sages: Essays in Biblical Interpretation*. Bloomington, Ind., 1971.

———. "Quotations in Biblical, Oriental and Rabbinic Literature." *HUCA* 22 (1949): 157–219. Repr. in Gordis, *Poets*, pp. 104–59.

———. "The Social Background of Wisdom Literature." *HUCA* 18 (1943): 77–118. Repr. in Gordis, *Poets*, pp. 160–97.

———. "The Temptation of Job— Tradition Versus Experience in Religion." *Judaism* 4 (1955): 195–208. Repr. in Glatzer, *Dimensions*, pp. 74–85. Also repr. as "The Temptation of Job," in Gordis, *Poets*, pp. 305–24.

———. "Wisdom Literature and Job." In S. Sandmel, ed., *Old Testament Issues* (London, 1969), pp. 213–41.
Gordon, Cyrus W. "Belt-Wrestling in the Ancient World." *HUCA* 23 (1950/51): 131–36.
———. "Leviathan: Symbol of Evil." In Alexander Altmann, ed., *Biblical Motifs: Origins and Transformations*, Philip W. Lown Institute of Advanced Judaic Studies, Studies and Texts 3 (Cambridge, Mass., 1966), pp. 1–9.
———. *Ugaritic Textbook*. 3 vols. Rome, 1965.
Grabbe, Lester L. *Comparative Philology and the Text of Job: A Study in Methodology*. Society of Biblical Literature Dissertation Series 34. Missoula, Mont., 1977.
Gray, George Buchanan. *The Forms of Hebrew Poetry: Considered with Special Reference to the Criticism and Interpretation of the Old Testament*. Prolegomenon by David Noel Freedman. Library of Biblical Studies. New York, 1972 [1915].
Gray, John. "The Book of Job in the Context of Near Eastern Literature." *ZAW* 82 (1970): 251–69.
———. *The Canaanites*. Ancient People and Places Series. London, 1965.
———. "The Massoretic Text of the Book of Job, the Targum and the Septuagint Version in the Light of the Qumran Targum (11 Qtarg Job)." *ZAW* 86 (1974): 331–50.
Greenberg, Moshe. "Job." In Alter and Kermode, pp. 283–304.
———. "Reflections on Job's Theology." In *Sepher 'Iyyob: The Book of Job*, pp. xvii–xxiii.
Greenfield, Jonas C. "The Hebrew Bible and Canaanite Literature." In Alter and Kermode, pp. 545–60.
———. "The Language of the Book." In *Sepher 'Iyyob: The Book of Job*, pp. xiv–xvi.
———. "Some Glosses on the Keret Epic." *Eretz-Israel* 9 (William Foxwell Albright Memorial Vol., 1969): non-Hebrew section, pp. 60–65.
Griesen, Georg. *Die Wurzel [sb'] "Schwören": Eine semasiologische Studie zum Eid im Alten Testament*. Bonn, 1981.
Gros Louis, Kenneth R. R. "The Book of Job." In K. R. R. Gros Louis, J. S. Ackerman, and T. S. Warshaw, eds., *Literary Interpretations of Biblical Narratives* (Nashville, Tenn., 1974), pp. 226–66.
Guillaume, A. "The Arabic Background of the Book of Job." In F. F. Bruce, ed., *Promise and Fulfilment: Essays Presented to S. H. Hooke* (Edinburgh, 1963), pp. 106–27.
———. *Studies in the Book of Job*. Leiden, 1968.
———. "The Unity of the Book of Job." *Annual of the Leeds University Oriental Society* 4 (1962–63): 26–46.
Habel, Norman C. *The Book of Job*. Cambridge Bible Commentary on the New English Bible. London and New York, 1975.
———. *The Book of Job: A Commentary*. The Old Testament Library. Philadelphia, 1985.

———. "'Naked I Came . . .': Humanness in the Book of Job." In Jörg Jeremias and Lothar Perlitt, eds., *Die Botschaft und die Boten: Festschrift für Hans Walter Wolff zum 70. Geburtstag* (Neukirchen-Vluyn, 1981), pp. 373–92.

———. "The Narrative Art of Job: Applying the Principles of Robert Alter." *JSOT* 27 (1983): 101–11.

Held, Moshe. "Rhetorical Questions in Ugaritic and Biblical Hebrew." *Eretz-Israel* 9 (William Foxwell Albright Memorial Vol., 1969): non-Hebrew section, pp. 71–79.

Hermisson, Hans-Jürgen. "Observations on the Creation Theology in Wisdom." In Gammie et al., pp. 43–57.

Hertzberg, H. W. "Der Aufbau des Buches Hiob." In Walter Baumgartner et al., eds., *Festschrift Alfred Bertholet zum 80. Geburtstag* (Tübingen, 1950), pp. 233–58.

———. *Das Buch Hiob*. Stuttgart, 1949.

Hillers, Delbert R. "The Bow of Aqhat: The Meaning of a Mythological Theme." In H. A. Hoffner, Jr., ed., *Orient and Occident* (Neukirchen, 1973), pp. 71–80.

Hirsch, E. D., Jr. *Validity in Interpretation*. New Haven, Conn., 1967.

Hoffman, Y. "The Relation Between the Prologue and the Speech Cycles in Job." *VT* 31 (1981): 160–70.

Hoffmann, H. W. "Form—Funktion—Intention." *ZAW* 82 (1970): 341–46.

Hölscher, Gustav. *Das Buch Hiob*. Handbuch zum Alten Testament I/17. Rev. ed. Tübingen, 1952.

Holbert, John C. "The Function and Significance of the Klage in the Book of Job with Special Reference to the Incidence of Formal and Verbal Irony." Ph.D. dissertation, Southern Methodist University, 1975.

———. "The Rehabilitation of the Sinner: The Function of Job 29–31." *ZAW* 95 (1983): 229–37.

———. "'The Skies Will Uncover His Iniquity': Satire in the Second Speech of Zophar (Job XX)." *VT* 31 (1981): 171–79.

Holladay, William L. *A Concise Hebrew and Aramaic Lexicon of the Old Testament, Based upon the Lexical Work of Ludwig Koehler and Walter Baumgartner*. Grand Rapids, Mich., 1971.

Hone, Ralph E., ed. *The Voice out of the Whirlwind: The Book of Job*. Materials for Analysis. San Francisco, 1960.

Horst, Friedrich. "Der Eid im Alten Testament." *Evangelische Theologie* 17 (1957): 366–84. Repr. in Horst, *Gottes Recht: Gesammelte Studien zum Recht im Alten Testament*, ed. Hans Walter Wolff, Theologische Bücherei 12 (Munich, 1961), pp. 292–314.

———. *Hiob*. Vol. 1 (chs. 1–19). Biblischer Kommentar, Altes Testament 16/1. Neukirchen-Vluyn, 1968.

Humbert, Paul. *L'Ancien Testament et le problème de la souffrance*. Neuchâtel, 1917.

———. "A propos du livre de Job." In Humbert, *Opuscules d'un Hébraisant*. Mémoires de l'Université de Neuchâtel 26. Neuchâtel, 1958.

———. "Le modernisme de Job." In Noth and Thomas, pp. 150–61.

———. *Recherches sur les sources égyptiennes de la littérature sapientiale d'Israël.* Mémoires de l'Université de Neuchâtel 7. Neuchâtel, 1929.

Humphreys, W. Lee. *The Tragic Vision and the Hebrew Tradition.* Overtures to Biblical Theology 18. Philadelphia, 1985.

Hurwitz, A. "The Date of the Prose-Tale of Job, Linguistically Reconsidered." *Harvard Theological Review* 67 (1974): 17–34.

Irwin, William A. "The Elihu Speeches in the Criticism of the Book of Job." *Journal of Religion* 17 (1937): 37–47.

———. "An Examination of the Progress of Thought in the Dialogue of Job." *Journal of Religion* 13 (1933): 150–64.

———. "The First Speech of Bildad." *ZAW* 51 [n.s. 10] (1933): 205–16.

———. "Job and Prometheus." *Journal of Religion* 30 (1950): 90–108.

———. "Job's Redeemer." *JBL* 81 (1962): 217–29.

Iser, Wolfgang. *The Act of Reading.* London, 1978.

Jacob, B. "Erklärung einiger Hiob-Stellen." *ZAW* 32 (1912): 278–87.

Jacobson, Richard. "Satanic Semiotics, Jobian Jurisprudence." *Sem* 19 (1981): 63–71.

Janzen, J. Gerald. "Another Look at God's Watch over Job (7:12)." *JBL* 108 (1989): 109–14.

———. *Job.* Interpretation: A Bible Commentary for Teaching and Preaching. Atlanta, 1985.

Jastrow, Morris. *The Book of Job: Its Origin, Growth, and Interpretation.* Philadelphia, 1920.

Jeshurun, George. "A Note on Job XXX:1 [error for XXXI:1]." *Journal of the Society of Oriental Research* 12 (1928): 153–54.

Johnson, Barbara. *The Critical Difference: Essays in the Contemporary Rhetoric of Reading.* Baltimore, 1980.

Jongeling, B. "L'expression MY YTN dans l'Ancien Testament." *VT* 24 (1974): 32–40.

Jung, Carl Gustav. *Answer to Job.* Tr. R. F. C. Hull. New York, 1960.

Junker, Hubert. *Job.* Echter-Bibel. Würzburg, 1951.

Kallen, Horace G. *The Book of Job as a Greek Tragedy.* New York, 1959 [1918].

Kapelrud, Arvid S. *The Violent Goddess: Anat in the Ras Shamra Texts.* Oslo, 1969.

Kautzsch, E. *Gesenius' Hebrew Grammar.* 2nd English edition, ed. by A. E. Cowley. Oxford, 1910.

Keel, Othmar. *Jahwes Entgegnung an Ijob: Eine Deutung von Ijob 38–41 vor dem Hintergrund der zeitgenössischen Bildkunst.* Forschungen zur Religion und Literatur des Alten und Neuen Testaments 121. Göttingen, 1978.

Kennedy, James M. "The Root *G'R* in the Light of Semantic Analysis." *JBL* 106 (1987): 47–64.

Kermode, Frank. *The Sense of an Ending: Studies in the Theory of Fiction.* The Mary Flexner Lectureship at Bryn Mawr College, 1965. New York, 1967.

Kinnier Wilson, J. V. "A Return to the Problem of Behemoth and Leviathan." *VT* 25 (1975): 1–14.

Kissane, Edward J. *The Book of Job*. Dublin, 1946.

Koch, Karl. "Is There a Doctrine of Retribution in the Old Testament?" Tr. Thomas H. Trapp from *Zeitschrift für Theologie und Kirche* 52 (1955): 1–42. In Crenshaw, ed., *Theodicy*, pp. 57–87.

Koehler, L., and W. Baumgartner. *Lexicon in Veteris Testamenti Libros*. Leiden, 1958.

Kraeling, Emil G. *The Book of the Ways of God*. London and New York, 1939.

Kramer, S. N. "Man and His God: A Sumerian Variation on the 'Job' Motif." In Noth and Thomas, pp. 170–82.

Krieger, Paul. *Weltbild und Idee des Buches Hiob, verglichen mit dem altorientalischer Pessimismus*. Inaugural-dissertation, Erlangen. Leipzig, 1930.

Kroeze, Jan Hendrik. "Die Elihureden im Buche Hiob." *Oudtestamentische Studiën* 2 (1943): 156–70.

Kubina, Veronika. *Die Gottesreden im Buche Hiob: Eine Beitrag zur Diskussion um die Einheit von Hiob 38,1–42,6*. Freiburg im Breisgau, Basel, and Vienna, 1979.

Kugel, James L. *The Idea of Biblical Poetry: Parallelism and Its History*. New Haven, Conn., 1981.

———. "On the Bible and Literary Criticism." *Prooftexts* 1 (1981): 217–36.

Kuhl, C. "Neuere Literarkritik des Buches Hiob." *Theologische Rundschau* 21 (1953): 163–205, 257–317.

———. "Von Hiobbuche und seinen Problemen." *Theologische Rundschau* 22 (1954): 261–316.

Kuschke, A. "Altbabylonische Texte zum Thema 'Der leidende Gerechte.'" *Theologische Literaturzeitung* 81 (1956): 69–76.

Kuyper, L. J. "The Repentance of Job." *VT* 9 (1959): 90–94.

Lacocque, André. "Job or the Impotence of Religion and Philosophy." *Sem* 19 (1981): 33–52.

Laks, H. Joel. "The Enigma of Job: Maimonides and the Moderns." *JBL* 83 (1964): 345–64.

Lambert, W. G. *Babylonian Wisdom Literature*. Oxford, 1960.

Larcher, Chrysostome. *Le livre de Job*. 2nd ed. La Sainte Bible. Paris, 1957.

Laurin, Robert. "The Theological Structure of Job." *ZAW* 84 (1972): 86–89.

Leitch, Vincent B. *Deconstructive Criticism: An Advanced Introduction*. New York, 1983.

Levenson, Jon Douglas. *The Book of Job in Its Time and in the Twentieth Century*. Cambridge, Mass., 1972.

Lévêque, Jean. *Job et son Dieu: Essai d'exégèse et de théologie biblique*. 2 vols. Etudes Bibliques. Paris, 1970.

Lichtheim, Miriam. *Ancient Egyptian Literature: A Book of Readings*. 3 vols. Berkeley, Calif., 1973–80.

Lindblom, Johannes. *Boken om Job och hans lidande*. 2nd ed. Lund, Sweden, 1966.

———. *La composition du livre de Job*. Humanistiska vetenskapssamfundet i Lund. Lund, Sweden, 1945.

———. "Joblegenden traditionshistorisk undersökt." *Svensk exegetisk Årsbok* (1940): 29–42.

Loewe, Raphael. "Divine Frustration Exegetically Frustrated—Numbers 14:34, *tnw'ty*." In P. R. Ackroyd and B. Lindars, eds., *Words and Meanings: Essays Presented to David Winton Thomas* (Cambridge, Eng., 1968), pp. 137–58.

Lohfink, Norbert. "Enthielten die im Alten Testament bezeugten Klageriten eine Phase des Schweigens?" *VT* 12 (1962): 260–77.

Loretz, Oswald. "Der Gott *šlḥ*, he. *šlḥ* I und *šlḥ* II." *UF* 7 (1975): 584–85.

———. "Ugaritisch-Hebräisch im Job 3,3–26." *UF* 8 (1976): 123–27.

Maag, Victor. *Hiob: Wandlung und Verarbeitung des Problems in Novelle, Dialogdichtung und Spätfassungen*. Forschungen zur Religion und Literatur des Alten und Neuen Testaments 128. Göttingen, 1982.

Macdonald, Duncan B. *The Hebrew Literary Genius*. Princeton, N.J., 1933.

———. "Some External Evidence on the Original Form of the Legend of Job." *American Journal of Semitic Languages and Literatures* 14 (1898): 137–64.

MacKenzie, Roderick A. F. "The Cultural and Religious Background of the Book of Job." In Duquoc and Floristán, pp. 3–7.

———. "The Purpose of the Yahweh Speeches in the Book of Job." *Bib* 40 (1959): 435–45.

Many, Gaspard. *Der Rechtstreit mit Gott (rīb) im Hiobbuch*. Ph.D. dissertation, Munich, 1971.

Marcus, Ralph. "Job and God." *Review of Religion* (1949): 5–29.

May, Herbert G. "Prometheus and Job: The Problem of the God of Power and the Man of Wrath." *Anglican Theological Review* 34 (1952): 240–46.

Michel, Walter L. *Job in the Light of Northwest Semitic*, vol. 1, *Prologue and First Cycle of Speeches, Job 1:1–14:22*. Biblica et Orientalia (Sacra Scriptura Antiquitatibus Orientalibus Illustrata) 42. Rome, 1987.

———. "The Ugaritic Texts and the Mythological Expression in the Book of Job (Including a New Translation of and Philological Notes on the Book of Job)." Ph.D. Dissertation, University of Wisconsin, 1970.

Miles, John A., Jr. "Gagging on Job, or The Comedy of Religious Exhaustion." *Sem* 7 (1977): 71–126.

Minn, Herbert R. *The Book of Job: A Translation with Introduction and Short Notes*. Auckland, 1965.

Miscall, Peter D. *The Workings of Old Testament Narrative*. *Sem* Studies. Philadelphia and Chico, Calif., 1983.

Mitchell, Stephen. *The Book of Job*. Tr. and with an intro. by Stephen Mitchell. Rev. version of *Into the Whirlwind* (1979). San Francisco, 1987.

Möller, Hans. *Sinn und Aufbau des Buches Hiob*. Berlin, 1955.

Morrow, William. "Consolation, Rejection, and Repentance in Job 42:6." *JBL* 105 (1986): 211–25.

Moulton, Richard G. *The Book of Job*. The Reader's Bible. New York and London, 1910.

Mowinckel, Sigmund. "Hiobs *gō'ēl* und Zeuge im Himmel." In *Vom Alten Testament: Festschrift Karl Marti*, Beihefte zur *ZAW* 41 (Berlin, 1925), pp. 207–22.

Müller, Hans-Peter. "Altes und neues zum Buche Hiob." *Evangelische Theologie* 37 (1977): 284–304.

———. *Das Hiobproblem: Seine Stellung und Entstehung im alten Orient und im Alten Testament*. Erträge der Forschung 84. Darmstadt, 1978.

———. *Hiob und seine Freunde: Traditionsgeschichtliches zum Verständnis des Hiobbuches*. Theologische Studien 103. Zurich, 1970.

———. "Keilschriftliche Parallelen zum Hiobbuch: Möglichkeit und Grenze des Vergleichs." *Orientalia*, n.s. 47 (1978): 360–75.

———. "Das weisheitliche Lehrerzählung im Alten Testament und seiner Umwelt." *Die Welt des Orients* 9, no. 1 (1977): 77–98.

Murphy, Roland E., O. Carm. *Wisdom Literature: Job, Proverbs, Ruth, Canticles, Ecclesiastes, and Esther*. The Forms of Old Testament Literature 13. Grand Rapids, Mich., 1981.

The New English Bible. Oxford and Cambridge, Eng., 1970.

Noth, Martin. "Noah, Daniel und Hiob in Ez xiv." *VT* 1 (1950): 251–60.

Noth, Martin, and D. W. Thomas, eds., *Wisdom in Israel and the Ancient Near East*. *VT* Supplements 3. Leiden, 1955.

Nougayrol, J. "Une version ancienne du 'juste souffrant.'" *Revue Biblique* 59 (1952): 239–50.

O'Connor, Michael Patrick. *Hebrew Verse Structure*. Winona Lake, Ind., 1980.

———. "The Pseudosorites: A Type of Paradox in Hebrew Verse." In Elaine R. Follis, ed., *Directions in Biblical Hebrew Poetry*, *JSOT* Supplement Series 40 (Sheffield, Eng., 1987), pp. 161–72.

———. "The Pseudo-Sorites in Hebrew Verse." In E. W. Conrad and E. G. Newing, eds., *Perspectives on Language and Text: Essays and Poems in Honor of F. I. Andersen's Sixtieth Birthday* (Winona Lake, Ind., 1987), pp. 239–53.

Olson, Alan M. "The Silence of Job as the Key to the Text." *Sem* 19 (1981): 113–19.

Orlinsky, Harry M. "Studies in the Septuagint of the Book of Job." *HUCA* 28 (1957): 53–74; 29 (1958): 229–71; 30 (1959): 153–67; 32 (1961): 239–68; 33 (1962): 119–52; 35 (1964): 57–78; 36 (1965): 34–47.

Parunak, H. Van Dyke. "A Semantic Survey of NḤM." *Bib* 56 (1975): 519–21.

———. "Transitional Techniques in the Bible." *JBL* 102 (1983): 525–48.

Patrick, Dale. *Arguing with God: The Angry Prayers of Job*. St. Louis, 1977.

———. "Job's Address of God." *ZAW* 91 (1979): 268–82.

———. "The Translation of Job XLII 6." *VT* 26 (1976): 369–71.

Patriquin, Allan. "Deconstruction, Plurivocity, and Silence." *Sem* 19 (1981): 121–23.

Paul, Shalom M. "Job 4.15—A Hair-Raising Encounter." *ZAW* 95 (1983): 119–21.

Peake, Arthur S. *Job*. The Century Bible. Edinburgh [1905].
———. *The Problem of Suffering in the Old Testament*. Hartley Lecture, 1904. London, 1904.
Pedersen, Johannes. *Der Eid bei den Semiten*. Strasbourg, 1914.
———. *Israel, Its Life and Culture*. 2 vols. London and Copenhagen, 1926, 1940.
Pfeiffer, Robert H. "Edomite Wisdom." *ZAW* 24 (1926): 13–25.
Polzin, Robert. *Biblical Structuralism: Method and Subjectivity in the Study of Ancient Texts*. *Sem* Supplements. Philadelphia, 1977.
———. "The Framework of the Book of Job." *Interpretation* 28 (1974): 182–200.
Pope, Marvin H. *Job: Introduction, Translation, and Notes*. 3rd ed. The Anchor Bible 15. Garden City, N.Y., 1973.
———. "The Word *šaḥat* in Job 9.31." *JBL* 83 (1964): 269–78.
Power, J. A. "A Study of Irony in the Book of Job." Ph.D. dissertation, University of Toronto, 1961.
Preuss, H. D. "Jahwes Antwort an Hiob und die sogenannte Hiobliteratur des alten Vorderen Orients." In Herbert Donner, Robert Hanhart, and Rudolf Smend, eds., *Beiträge zur alttestamentlichen Theologie: Festschrift W. Zimmerli* (Göttingen, 1977), pp. 323–43.
Priest, John F. "Humanism, Scepticism, and Pessimism in Israel." *Journal of the American Academy of Religion* 36 (1968): 311–26.
Pritchard, James B., ed. *Ancient Near Eastern Texts Relating to the Old Testament*. 3rd ed. Princeton, N.J., 1969.
Propp, Vladimir. *Morphology of the Folktale*. 2nd ed. Austin, Tex., 1968.
Pury, R. de. *Job ou l'homme révolté*. Geneva, 1955.
Rankin, O. S. *Israel's Wisdom Literature*. Edinburgh, 1954.
Ranston, Harry. *The Old Testament Wisdom Books and Their Teaching*. London, 1930.
Reichert, Victor Emanuel. *Job: With Hebrew Text and English Translation, Commentary*. Soncino Books of the Bible. Bournemouth, Eng., 1946.
Reventlow, Henning Graf. "Tradition und Redaktion in Hiob 27 im Rahmen der Hiobreden des Abschnittes Hi 24–27: A. H. J. Gunneweg zum 60. Geburtstag am 17.5.1982." *ZAW* 94 (1982): 279–92.
Rhodokanakis, Nicolaus. "Das Buch Hiob." *Wiener Zeitschrift für die Kunde des Morgenlandes* 45 (1938): 169–90.
Richter, Heinz. "Erwägungen zum Hiobproblem." *Evangelische Theologie* 18 (1958): 202–24.
———. "Die Naturweisheit des Alten Testaments im Buche Hiob." *ZAW* 70 (1958): 1–19.
———. *Studien zu Hiob: Der Aufbau des Hiobbuches dargestellt an den Gattungen des Rechtslebens*. Theologische Abhandlungen 11. Berlin, 1959.
Richter, Wolfgang. *Exegese als Literaturwissenschaft: Entwurf einer alttestamentlicher Literaturtheorie und Methodologie*. Göttingen, 1971.
Ricoeur, Paul. *The Symbolism of Evil*. Tr. E. Buchanan. Boston, 1967.

Riffaterre, Michael. *Text Production*. Tr. Terese Lyons. New York, 1983.

Roberts, J. J. M. "Job and the Israelite Religious Tradition." *ZAW* 89 (1977): 107–14.

———. "Job's Summons to Yahweh: The Exploitation of a Legal Metaphor." *Restoration Quarterly* 16 (1973): 159–65.

Robertson, D. A. *Linguistic Evidence in Dating Early Hebrew Poetry*. Missoula, Mont., 1972.

Robertson, David. "The Book of Job: A Literary Study." *Soundings* 56 (1973): 446–69.

———. "The Comedy of Job: A Response." *Sem* 7 (1977): 41–44.

———. *The Old Testament and the Literary Critic*. Philadelphia, 1977.

Robinson, Theodore H. *Job and His Friends*. London, 1954.

———. *The Poetry of the Old Testament*. London, 1947.

Rosenberg, David. *Job Speaks: Interpreted from the Original Hebrew of the Book of Job*. A Poet's Bible. New York, 1977.

Ross, James F. "Job 33:14–30: The Phenomenology of Lament." *JBL* 94 (1975): 38–46.

Roth, Wolfgang. "NBL." *VT* 10 (1960): 394–409.

———. "The Numerical Sequence x / x + 1 in the Old Testament." *VT* 12 (1962): 302–7.

Rowley, H. H. "The Book of Job and Its Meaning." *Bulletin of the John Rylands Library* 41 (1958): 167–207. Repr. in Rowley, *From Moses to Qumran: Studies in the Old Testament* (New York, 1963), pp. 141–86.

———. *Job*. Rev. ed. The New Century Bible Commentary. Grand Rapids, Mich., and London, 1976.

Rowold, Henry. "*Mi hu'? Li hu'*! Leviathan and Job in Job 41:2–3." *JBL* 105 (1986): 104–9.

Ruprecht, E. "Leiden und Gerechtigkeit bei Hiob." *Zeitschrift für Theologie und Kirche* 73 (1976): 424–45.

———. "Das Nilpferd im Hiobbuch." *VT* 21 (1971): 209–31.

Sanders, James A. *Suffering as Divine Discipline in the Old Testament and Post-biblical Judaism. Colgate-Rochester Divinity School Bulletin* 38 (Rochester, N.Y., 1955).

Sanders, Paul S., ed. *Twentieth-Century Interpretations of the Book of Job: A Collection of Critical Essays*. Englewood Cliffs, N.J., 1968.

Sarna, Nahum M. "The Book of Job: General Introduction." In *Sepher 'Iyyob: The Book of Job*, pp. ix–xiii.

———. "A *Crux Interpretum* in Job 22:30." *Journal of Near Eastern Studies* 15 (1956): 118–19.

———. "Epic Substratum in the Prose of Job." *JBL* 76 (1957): 13–25.

———. "The Mythological Background of Job 18." *JBL* 82 (1963): 315–18.

———. "Some Instances of the Enclitic M in Job." *Journal of Jewish Studies* 6 (1955): 108–10.

———. "*'ytnym*, Job 12.19." *JBL* 74 (1955): 272–73.

Schmid, Hans Heinrich. *Gerechtigkeit als Weltordnung: Hintergrund und Geschichte der alttestamentliche Gerechtigkeitsbegriffes*. Beiträge historische Theologie 40. Tübingen, 1968.

———. *Wesen und Geschichte der Weisheit: Eine Untersuchung zur altorientalischen und israelitischen Weisheitsliteratur*. Beihefte zur *ZAW* 101. Berlin, 1966.

Schmidt, Ludwig. *De Deo: Studien zur Literarkritik und Theologie des Buches Jona, des Gesprächs zwischen Abraham und Jahwe in Gen 18,22ff. und von Hi 1*. Beihefte zur *ZAW* 143. Berlin and New York, 1976.

Schmitt, Ernst. *Leben in den Weisheitsbüchern Job, Sprüche und Jesus Sirach*. Freiburg im Breisgau, 1954.

Schökel, Luis Alonso. *Estudios de poética hebrea*. Barcelona, 1963.

———. "God's Answer to Job." In Duquoc and Floristán, pp. 45–51.

———. "Toward a Dramatic Reading of the Book of Job." *Sem* 7 (1977): 45–61.

Schökel, Luis Alonso, and J. L. Sicre Diaz. *Job: Comentario teológico y literario*. Nueva Biblia Española. Madrid, 1983.

Schoental, R. "Mycotoxins and the Bible." *Perspectives in Biology and Medicine* 28, no. 1 (Autumn 1984): 117–20.

Scholnick, Sylvia Huberman. "The Meaning of *Mišpaṭ* in the Book of Job." *JBL* 104 (1982): 521–29.

———. "Poetry in the Courtroom: Job 38–41." In Elaine R. Follis, ed., *Directions in Biblical Hebrew Poetry*, *JSOT* Supplement Series 40 (Sheffield, Eng., 1987), pp. 184–204.

Schottrof, Willy. *Der altisraelitische Fluchspruch*. Wissenschaftliche Monographien zum Alten und Neuen Testament 30. Neukirchen-Vluyn, 1969.

Scott, R. B. Y. *The Way of Wisdom in the Old Testament*. New York, 1971.

Sekine, Masao. "Schopfung und Erlösung im Buche Hiob." In J. Hempel and L. Rost, eds., *Von Ugarit nach Qumran: Beiträge zur alttestamentlichen und altorientalischen Forschung*, Eissfeldt Festschrift: Beihefte zur *ZAW* 77 (Berlin, 1958), pp. 213–23.

Semeia 7 (1977): *Studies in the Book of Job*.

Semeia 19 (1981): *The Book of Job and Ricoeur's Hermeneutics*.

Sepher 'Iyyob: The Book of Job. A New Translation According to the Traditional Hebrew Text. With introductions by Moshe Greenberg, Jonas C. Greenfield, and Nahum M. Sarna. Philadelphia, 5740/1980.

Sewall, Richard B. *The Vision of Tragedy*. New Haven, Conn., 1959.

Silberman, Lou H. "Questing for Justice: Reflection on Deuteronomy and Job." In *Founders Day Addresses, 1986* (Cincinnati, Ohio, 1986), pp. 18–27.

Simpson, William Kelly, ed. *The Literature of Ancient Egypt: An Anthology of Stories, Instructions, and Poetry*. New ed. New Haven, Conn., 1973.

Singer, Richard. *Job's Encounter*. New York, 1963.

Skehan, Patrick W. "Strophic Patterns in the Book of Job." *CBQ* 23 (1961): 129–43. Repr. in Skehan, *Studies in Israelite Poetry and Wisdom*, *CBQ* Monograph Series 1 (Washington, D.C., 1971), pp. 96–113.

Snaith, Norman H. *The Book of Job*. London, 1945.
———. *The Book of Job: Its Origin and Purpose*. Studies in Biblical Theology, 2nd series 11. Naperville, Ill., 1968.
———. *Notes to the Hebrew Text of Job i–vi*. New York, 1945.
Sokoloff, Michael. *The Targum to Job from Qumran Cave XI*. Jerusalem, 1974.
Spiegel, Shalom. "Noah, Danel and Job." In *Louis Ginzberg Jubilee Volume* (New York, 1945), pp. 305–55.
Stähli, Hans Peter. *Knabe, Jüngling, Knecht: Untersuchung zum Begriff [*na'ar*] im Alten Testament*. Frankfurt am Main, Bern, and Las Vegas, Nev., 1978.
Stamm, Johann Jakob. *Das Leiden der Unschuldigen in Babylon und Israel*. Abhandlungen zur Theologie des Alten und Neuen Testaments 10. Zurich, 1946.
Staples, William Ewart. *The Speeches of Elihu: A Study of Job xxxii–xxxvii*. University of Toronto Studies, Philological Series. Toronto, 1924.
Steinmann, Jean. *Job*. Témoins de Dieu 8. Paris, 1946.
———. *Job, témoin de la souffrance humaine*. Foi vivante 120. Paris, 1969.
———. *Job: Text française, introduction et commentaire*. Connaître la Bible. Bruges, 1961.
———. *Le livre de Job*. Lectio Divina 16. Paris, 1955.
Sternberg, Meir. *The Poetics of Biblical Narrative: The Drama of Ideological Reading*. Bloomington, Ind., 1985.
Stevenson, William B. *Critical Notes on the Hebrew Text of the Poem of Job*. Aberdeen, Scot., 1951.
———. "Job 13,9–11: A New Interpretation." *Expository Times* 62 (1950/51): 93.
———. *The Poem of Job: A Literary Study, with a New Translation*. Schweich Lectures, 1943. London, 1947.
Stier, Fridolin. *Das Buch Ijjob: Hebräisch und Deutsch*. Munich, 1954.
Strolz, Walter. *Hiobs Auflehnung gegen Gott*. Opuscula aus Wissenschaft und Dichtung 36. Pfullingen, 1967.
Stuart, Douglas K. *Studies in Early Hebrew Meter*. Harvard Semitic Museum, Harvard Semitic Monographs 13. Missoula, Mont., 1976.
Sutcliffe, E. F. *Providence and Suffering in the Old and New Testaments*. London, 1953.
Tanakh: A New Translation of the Holy Scriptures According to the Traditional Hebrew Text. Philadelphia, 1982.
Terrien, Samuel L. "The Book of Job: Introduction and Exegesis." In *IB* 877–1198.
———. *Job*. Commentaire de l'Ancien Testament 13. Neuchâtel, 1963.
———. *Job, Poet of Existence*. New York and Indianapolis, 1957.
———. "Le poème de Job: Drame para-rituel du Nouvel-An?" In *Congress Volume, Rome, 1968, VT* Supplements 17 (Leiden, 1969), pp. 220–35.
———. "Quelques remarques sur les affinités de Job avec le Deutéro-Isaïe." In *Volume du Congrés, Genève, 1965, VT* Supplements 15 (Leiden, 1966), pp. 295–310.

Thomas, D. Winton. "The Interpretation of *besōd* in Job 29,4." *JBL* 65 (1946): 63–66.

———. "*ŠLMWT* in the Old Testament." *Journal of Semitic Studies* 7 (1962): 191–200.

———. "Types of Wisdom in the Book of Job." *Indian Journal of Theology* 20 (1962): 157–65.

Thompson, K. T., Jr. "Out of the Whirlwind: The Sense of Alienation in the Book of Job." *Interpretation* 14 (1960): 51–63.

Torczyner, N. Harry (Tur-Sinai, Naphtali Herz). *Das Buch Hiob: Eine kritische Analyse des überlieferten Hiobtextes*. Vienna, 1920.

———. "Hiobdichtung und Hiobsage." *Monatsschrift für Geschichte und Wissenschaft des Judentums* (1925): 234–48.

Tromp, Nicholas J. *Primitive Conceptions of Death and the Nether World in the Old Testament*. Biblica et Orientalia 21. Rome, 1969.

Tsevat, Matitiahu. "The Canaanite God Šälaḥ." *VT* 4 (1954): 41–49.

———. *The Meaning of the Book of Job and Other Biblical Studies: Essays on the Literature and Religion of the Hebrew Bible*. New York and Dallas, 1980.

Tur-Sinai, N. H. (Torczyner, N. Harry). *The Book of Job: A New Commentary*. Rev. ed. Jerusalem, 1967.

Urbrock, William J. "Evidences of Oral-Formulaic Composition in the Poetry of Job." Ph.D. dissertation, Harvard University, 1975.

———. "Oral Antecedents to Job: A Survey of Formulas and Formulaic Systems." *Sem* 5 (1975): 111–37.

———. "Reconciliation of Opposites in the Dramatic Ordeal of Job." *Sem* 7 (1977): 147–54.

Usmiani, Renate. "A New Look at the Drama of Job." *Modern Drama* 13 (1970): 191–200.

van der Ploeg, J. P. M., and A. S. van der Woude. *Le Targum de Job de la Grotte XI de Qumrân*. Leiden, 1971.

van Dijk, J. J. A. "Note sur la sagesse suméro-accadienne." *Sumer* (1954): 139–42.

———. *La sagesse suméro-accadienne*. Leiden, 1953.

van Praag, Herman M. "Job's Agony: A Biblical Evocation of Bereavement and Grief." *Judaism* 37 (1988): 173–87.

van Selms, A. *Job: A Practical Commentary*. Tr. John Vriend. Text and Interpretation Series. Grand Rapids, Mich., 1985.

Vermeylen, J. *Job, ses amis et son dieu: La légende de Job et ses relectures postexiliques*. Studia Biblica 2. Leiden, 1986.

Volz, Paul. *Hiob und Weisheit*. Die Schriften des Alten Testaments in Auswahl, ed. H. Gunkel, 3, no. 2. Göttingen, 1921.

von Rad, Gerhard. "Job 38 and Ancient Egyptian Wisdom." In von Rad, *The Problem of the Hexateuch and Other Essays* (Edinburgh and London, 1965), pp. 281–91.

———. *Old Testament Theology*. 2 vols. Tr. D. M. G. Stalker. New York and Evanston, Ill., 1962, 1965.

———. *Wisdom in Israel*. Nashville, Tenn., and New York, 1972.

Watson, Wilfred G. E. *Classical Hebrew Poetry: A Guide to Its Techniques*. *JSOT* Supplement Series 26. Sheffield, Eng., 1984.

———. "Fixed Pairs in Ugaritic and Isaiah." *VT* 22 (1972): 460–68.

———. "Verse-Patterns in Ugaritic, Akkadian and Hebrew Poetry." *UF* 7 (1975): 483–92.

Watters, William R. *Formula Criticism and the Poetry of the Old Testament*. Beihefte zur *ZAW* 138. Berlin and New York, 1976.

Wehmeier, Gerhard. *Der Segen im Alten Testament: Eine semasiologische Untersuchung der Wurzel* brk. Basel, 1970.

Weiser, Artur. *Das Buch Hiob*. 5th ed. Das Alte Testament Deutsch 13. Göttingen, 1968.

Weiss, Meir. *The Story of Job's Beginning: Job 1–2. A Literary Analysis*. Jerusalem, 1983.

Wernberg-Møller, P. "A Note on *zwr* 'to Stink.'" *VT* 4 (1954): 322–25.

Westermann, Claus. *Basic Forms of Prophetic Speech*. Tr. Hugh Clayton White. Philadelphia, 1967.

———. *The Structure of the Book of Job: A Form-Critical Analysis*. Tr. Charles A. Muenchow. Philadelphia, 1981.

Wevers, John W. *The Way of the Righteous: Psalms and the Books of Wisdom*. Westminster Guides to the Bible. Philadelphia, 1961.

Whallon, William. *Formula, Character, and Context: Studies in Homeric, Old English, and Old Testament Poetry*. Cambridge, Mass., 1969.

Wharton, James A. "The Unanswerable Answer: An Interpretation of Job." In W. E. March, ed., *Texts and Testaments: Critical Essays on the Bible and Early Church Fathers* (San Antonio, Tex., 1980), pp. 37–70.

Whedbee, J. William. "The Comedy of Job." *Sem* 7 (1977): 1–39.

Whitley, C. F. "Some Aspects of Hebrew Poetic Diction." *UF* 7 (1975): 493–502.

Whybray, R. N. *The Intellectual Tradition in the Old Testament*. Beihefte zur *ZAW* 115. Berlin, 1974.

Williams, James G. "Comedy, Irony, Intercession: A Few Notes in Response." *Sem* 7 (1977): 135–45.

———. "Deciphering the Unspoken: The Theophany of Job." *HUCA* 49 (1978): 59–72.

———. "Job's Vision: The Dialectic of Person and Presence." *Hebrew Annual Review* 8 (1984): 259–72.

———. "'You Have Not Spoken Truth of Me': Mystery and Irony in Job." *ZAW* 83 (1971): 231–55.

Williams, Ronald J. "Current Trends in the Study of the Book of Job." In Aufrecht, pp. 1–27.

———. "Theodicy in the Ancient Near East." *Canadian Journal of Theology* 2 (1956): 14–26. Repr. in Crenshaw, *Theodicy*, pp. 42–56.

Wimsatt, W. K., Jr., and Monroe C. Beardsley. "The Intentional Fallacy." In W. K. Wimsatt, Jr., *The Verbal Icon: Studies in the Meaning of Poetry* (Lexington, Ky., 1954), pp. 3–18.

Yoder, Perry. "Fixed Word Pairs and the Composition of Hebrew Poetry." Ph.D. dissertation, University of Pennsylvania, 1970.

Zerafa, Peter Paul, O.P. *The Wisdom of God in the Book of Job*. Studia Universitatis S. Thomae in Urbe 8. Rome, 1978.

Ziegler, Joseph. "Der textkritische Wert der Septuaginta des Buches Hiob." *Miscellanea Biblica* 2 (1934): 277–96. Repr. in Ziegler, *Sylloge: Gesammelte Aufsätze zur Septuaginta* (Göttingen, 1971), pp. 9–28.

Zink, J. "Impatient Job." *JBL* 84 (1965): 147–52.

Index of Biblical and Other Text Citations

Entries refer to Hebrew Bible verse numbers; variant English Bible numbers are not listed. References to larger spans of books or verses precede references to smaller spans or to individual verses. In this index an "f" after a number indicates a separate reference on the next page, and an "ff" indicates separate references on the next two pages. A continuous discussion over two or more pages is indicated by a span of page numbers, e.g., "57–59." *Passim* is used for a cluster of references in close but not consecutive sequence.

Index of Subjects

In this index an "f" after a number indicates a separate reference on the next page, and an "ff" indicates separate references on the next two pages. A continuous discussion over two or more pages is indicated by a span of page numbers, e.g., "57–59." *Passim* is used for a cluster of references in close but not consecutive sequence.

199–201, 205, 412; in non-exegetical versions of Book of Job, 412
Wimsatt, W. K., Jr., and Monroe C. Beardsley, 401
Wind, 120, 210, 224, 244, 307, 322ff, 340–44 *passim*, 432; east, 122, 242, 290; as image of ephemerality, 215, 217, 288, 307, 345. *See also* Storm; Whirlwind
Winter, 296
Wisdom, 10, 58, 164, 234ff, 243, 245, 290–93, 319–22 *passim*, 348, 427; personified, 122, 362, 381, 427; debate, 208, 220, 433; divine, 222, 230f, 292, 341, 350–51, 428; possessors of, 327, 337; acquisition of, 432; teachers of, 433. *See also under* Hymns
Wisdom literature, 10–11, 403–4, 415. *See also under* Genre
Witness, 229, 242–48 *passim*, 382; Job's, 245–50 *passim*, 282, 325, 413, 420–23 *passim*; and Job's other third parties, 258–59, 264, 277, 348–49, 382, 424
Woman, women, 132, 192
Womb, 207, 229, 381
Word plays, 134, 202, 211, 316, 358, 419, 432. *See also* Puns
Words, 218–19, 257, 306–9 *passim*, 316, 318, 323f, 331, 388
World, *see* Universe
Worship, 430
Wrestling, 435
Writing, 257, 423

Yahweh, 18, 50, 80, 189–203 *passim*, 248, 302, 322, 340; speeches of, 7f, 13f, 335–49 *passim*, 353–73 *passim*, 379f, 388, 396, 402, 433–37 *passim*; and Prosecutor, 22–23, 211, 228, 243, 413; approval of Job, 224–25, 287, 380–83, 396, 443; poetry of, 338, 356, 364, 434–35; and animals, 347–48; tyranny of, 351, 357, 363, 375–76; character of, 354–55; seen by humans, 374; view of Job's friends, 376, 380; fooled, 383; as bringer of evil, 386; and whirlwind, 423; mind and emotions of, 426; as artist, 436; response to Job's question, 437
Yamm (Canaanite deity), *see* Sea
Youth, 319–22, 428, 432

Zeus (Greek deity), 285
Zither, 130, 308, 430
Zophar, 76–78, 102–4, 229–34 *passim*, 240–46 *passim*, 260–65 *passim*, 288–89, 330, 415, 424; and other friends, 7f, 14, 202–3, 252, 380, 386; on divine power, 274, 337; absent from third cycle, 279, 283–89 *passim*, 294–95, 402, 426; on being ready for deity, 381–84 *passim*; style of, 418, 425

Library of Congress Cataloging-in-Publication Data

Good, Edwin M. (Edwin Marshall), 1928–
In turns of tempest: a reading of Job, with a translation / Edwin M. Good.
p. cm.
Includes bibliographical references.
ISBN 0-8047-1785-0 (cl.) : ISBN 0-8047-3338-4 (pbk.)
1. Bible. O.T. Job—Criticism, interpretation, etc. I. Bible. O.T. Job. English. Good. 1990. II. Title.
BS1415.2.G59 1990
223'.106—dc20 90-30350
CIP

♾ This book is printed on acid-free, recycled paper.

Original printing 1990
Last figure below indicates year of this printing:
07 06 05 04 03 02 01 00 99 98